IMPORTANT

HERE IS YOUR REGISTRATION CODE TO ACCESS MCGRAW-HILL PREMIUM CONTENT AND MCGRAW-HILL ONLINE RESOURCES

For key premium online resources you need THIS CODE to gain access. Once the code is entered, you will be able to use the web resources for the length of your course.

Access is provided only if you have purchased a new book.

If the registration code is missing from this book, the registration screen on our website, and within your WebCT or Blackboard course will tell you how to obtain your new code. Your registration code can be used only once to establish access. It is not transferable

To gain access to these online resources

1. USE your web browser to go to: **www.mhhe.com/brydon5**

2. CLICK on "First Time User"

3. ENTER the Registration Code printed on the tear-off bookmark on the right

4. After you have entered your registration code, click on "Register"

5. FOLLOW the instructions to setup your personal UserID and Password

6. WRITE your UserID and Password down for future reference. Keep it in a safe place.

If your course is using WebCT or Blackboard, you'll be able to use this code to access the McGraw-Hill content within your instructor's online course.

To gain access to the McGraw-Hill content in your instructor's WebCT or Blackboard course simply log into the course with the user ID and Password provided by your instructor. Enter the registration code exactly as it appears to the right when prompted by the system. You will only need to use this code the first time you click on McGraw-Hill content.

These instructions are specifically for student access. Instructors are not required to register via the above instructions.

The McGraw·Hill Companies

Higher Education

Thank you, and welcome to your McGraw-Hill Online Resources.

978-0-07-319155-3
0-07-319155-8 t/a
Brydon
Between One and Many, 5/e

Between One and Many

The Art and Science of Public Speaking

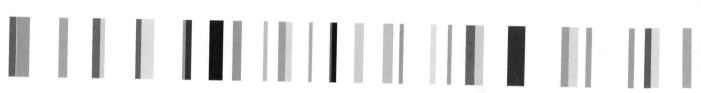

Steven R. Brydon & Michael D. Scott

California State University, Chico

Mc
Graw
Hill

Boston   Burr Ridge, IL   Dubuque, IA   Madison, WI   New York   San Francisco   St. Louis
Bangkok   Bogotá   Caracas   Kuala Lumpur   Lisbon   London   Madrid   Mexico City
Milan   Montreal   New Delhi   Santiago   Seoul   Singapore   Sydney   Taipei   Toronto

Higher Education

This book is printed on acid-free paper.

2 3 4 5 6 7 8 9 0 CTP/CTP 0 9 8 7 6

ISBN-13: 978-0-07-295976-5
ISBN-10: 0-07-295976-2

Editor in Chief: *Emily Barrosse*
Publisher: *Phillip Butcher*
Executive Editor: *Nanette Giles*
Marketing Manager: *Leslie Oberhuber*
Developmental Editor: *Joshua Hawkins*
Managing Editor: *Melissa Williams*
Project Manager: *Holly Paulsen*
Manuscript Editor: *Kay Mikel*
Art Director: *Jeanne Schreiber*

Design Manager: *Laurie Entringer*
Text Designer: *Kiera Pohl*
Cover Designer: *Laurie Entringer*
Art Editor: *Ayelet Arbel*
Photo Research: *Natalia Peschiera*
Print Supplement Producer: *Louis Swaim*
Production Supervisor: *Tandra Jorgensen*
Media Producer: *Nancy Garcia*

Composition: 10/12 Baskerville by Thompson Type
Printing: CTPS

Cover (left to right): © Bettmann/Corbis, © Robert Shafer/Brand X Pictures/Getty Images, © Photodisc, © Martin Moos/Lonely Planet Images/Getty Images

Credits: The credits section for this book begins on page 436 and is considered an extension of the copyright page.

Library of Congress Cataloging-in-Publication Data has been applied for.

The Internet addresses listed in the text were accurate at the time of publication. The inclusion of a Web site does not indicate an endorsement by the authors or McGraw-Hill, and McGraw-Hill does not guarantee the accuracy of the information presented at these sites.

To the memory of Tom Young—
gifted teacher, colleague, and trusted friend.

Brief Contents

Contents

v

Chapter 3　Managing Speech Anxiety　51

Chapter 8 Supporting Your Message 183

Chapter 9 Organizing Messages 201

Chapter 10 Language: Making Verbal Sense of the Message 235

Chapter 11   Delivery: Engaging Your Audience   259

Chapter 12   Using Media in Your Speech   289

Chapter 15   Thinking and Speaking Critically   371

Chapter 16   Speaking Across the Life Span   397

Appendix A   Guide to Source Citations   419

Appendix B   Public Speeches   424

Preface

Public speaking is a dynamic transaction "between one and many"—between the one who is speaking and the many who are listening. The meaning of the message emerges from the relationship between speaker and audience. Speakers cannot succeed without knowing their audience, and no audience member can benefit by just passively receiving a message. Both speaker and audience—and the transaction between them—are essential to the process. As teachers and as authors, we focus on the transactional nature of successful public speaking.

Public speaking is also an art, a science, and a skill—one that can be learned, improved, and polished. We encourage our students to think of public speaking as a learning experience—they don't have to be perfect at the outset! We also encourage them to think of their speech transactions as a refined extension of their everyday conversations, and we offer them the tools to become the speakers they want to be. Public speakers can draw on a vast body of information, ranging from classical rhetorical theories to empirical communication research. In this book we include traditional topics, such as logos, ethos, and pathos as the roots of persuasive speaking, and current ones, such as research on cultural diversity, the role of nonverbal communication in delivery, and the *appropriate* uses of technology in public speaking.

Today's students of public speaking will face many different speech situations in their lives, and they will face audiences of increasing cultural, demographic, and individual diversity. Throughout this book, we focus on ways to adapt to audiences to have the best chance of being heard and understood. We stress the responsibilities and ethical issues involved in being a good public speaker. And we discuss how to be a good audience member: one who knows how to listen, to behave ethically, and to critically evaluate the message being presented. In sum, we attempt to provide students with a broad understanding of the nature of public speaking as well as the specific skills they need to become successful, effective public speakers, both as college students and throughout their lives.

Features of the Book

Bringing Visual Life to the Text   This edition of *Between One and Many* continues the tradition we pioneered with our very first edition—bringing visual life to the art and science of public speaking. We provide students with an integrated package of text and CD-ROM. In addition to the usual videos of sample speeches found with most texts, the innovative Speech Coach CD-ROM provides video segments on the role of public speaking in the lives of people with whom students can identify, concrete techniques for mastering speech anxiety, examples of delivery techniques, and concrete advice on the proper role of visual aids, including the frequently misused Microsoft PowerPoint. Text and CD are coordinated, and each of the nine sample student speeches outlined or transcribed in the text is *presented in full* on the CD. Sample speeches range from a speech of introduction and a storytelling presentation, to informative and persuasive speeches, to a speech fully supported with PowerPoint slides. The Speech Coach CD also provides a wide range of learning tools, such as Audio Tips and Tactics and Key Terms Flashcards, and supporting software, such as Outline Tutor and PowerPoint Tutorial.

Speech Coach is not an afterthought but rather an integral part of the learning package provided by *Between One and Many*. All of the video segments on the Speech Coach CD are also available to instructors in VHS or DVD format for classroom viewing.

Integrated Pedagogy   Throughout the text, boxes are used to focus attention on subjects of special interest. Four different types of boxes appear. In Their Own Words boxes provide examples of speeches by students and public figures, including several student speeches in outline form with annotations. Self-Assessment boxes allow students to evaluate their own skills and attributes (such as speech anxiety and overall communication apprehension). Considering Diversity boxes show how the topic of a chapter applies to today's multicultural, multiracial, and multiethnic audiences. More than an afterthought, these boxes not only add to the discussion of diversity throughout the book but also challenge students to think about diversity as it specifically applies to the topics covered in a given chapter. Speaking of . . . boxes contain current, topical information that relates to the text discussion.

Throughout the book, speechmaking skills are highlighted in special lists labeled Tips and Tactics. A popular feature with students, Tips and Tactics make it easy to apply practical suggestions to speeches. Finally, Speech Coach icons in the margins call attention to corresponding video segments and other CD features.

Help for Speech Anxiety   We recognize that many students come to a public speaking class with some trepidation. As we have done in every edition, we devote a full chapter early in the text to speech anxiety. The text offers many specific, concrete techniques students can use to productively manage and channel their anxiety, and several of these are visualized on the Speech Coach CD-ROM. In keeping with the most recent research on speech anxiety and communication apprehension, we distinguish between generalized anxiety about communication and fears that are specific to public speaking and thus are responsive to the techniques we offer to students.

Emphasis on Adapting to Audience Diversity   We give significant attention to audience diversity based, in part, on Geert Hofstede's work on understanding cultural diversity. Using Hofstede's dimensions of collectivism and individualism, power distance, uncertainty avoidance, masculinity and femininity, and long-term versus short-term orientation, we offer ideas on how to analyze and adapt to audience diversity across cultures. Diversity encompasses more than culture. Thus we also offer specific Tips and Tactics students can use to analyze and adapt to the demographic and individual diversity in their audience.

Full Chapter on Ethics   We feature a full chapter on ethics. Working from classical and contemporary notions about what constitutes ethical behavior, we provide and reinforce ethical guidelines for both public speakers and audience members. We pay particular attention to the growing problem of plagiarism from the Internet and offer concrete advice on how students can ethically use and cite such sources.

Emphasis on Critical Thinking   Central to effective and ethical communication are the abilities to critically evaluate evidence, to present sound reasoning in speeches, and to detect fallacious reasoning in the speeches of others. *Between One and Many* continues to provide a strong critical thinking component based on Toulmin's model of argument. Our discussion of critical thinking encompasses listening as well as speaking and is integrated into our discussion of supporting a speech with valid reasoning and reliable evidence.

Using Technology in Speaking   Two major technological innovations have had a great impact on public speaking in the last few years. Presentational software, especially Microsoft's PowerPoint, is a regular feature of presentations in corporations, military briefings, classroom presentations, and professional meetings. We wish we could say that this has been a completely positive development in the history of speechmaking, yet we cannot. For every presentation that uses Power-Point to good effect, we see many more that punish audience members with too much information, superfluous graphics, and overkill. As a result, we have focused in our text and the Speech Coach CD not so much on the mechanics of creating slides (although there is a tutorial to guide students unfamiliar with PowerPoint through the process) but on the dangers of overreliance and the potential benefits of the technology when used properly.

The other major technology, which also has a dark side, is the use of electronic resources for researching a speech. We have devoted a full chapter to research and have put the emphasis on finding high-quality resources rather than simply typing the speech topic into a search engine. A five-point test of the quality of supporting materials has been added to this edition, along with fresh examples of how the Internet can be used to spread misleading information. We know students will turn to electronic sources for their research, so our goal is to teach them the difference between reliable and unreliable information wherever it is found.

Highlights of the Fifth Edition

Based on feedback from many instructors, we have incorporated a number of changes into this edition to strengthen the book.

Improved Organization   At the suggestion of users, we have reorganized chapters to flow more logically throughout the semester and divided one long chapter (Researching and Supporting Your Message) into two. This allows us to discuss the qualitative aspects of research in more depth and to introduce reasoning as well as evidence to students as part of the process of supporting their messages. We also have moved the guide to source citations from Chapter 7 to Appendix A, as suggested by many reviewers. This will enable students to readily consult it for assistance in using APA or MLA citation styles. We have updated our treatment of proper citation of online sources for both styles. We have moved Maslow's hierarchy of needs to the chapter on audience analysis. We offer two examples of beginning speeches in Chapter 2, one a storytelling speech and the other a speech of self-introduction. More complex speech topics are saved for later chapters.

Balance of Theory and Practice   This edition returns to a focus on understanding and applying theories of communication and rhetoric—a hallmark of the first three editions. However, we have been sure to emphasize the link between theory and practice, so that students will readily see these theories as relevant and useful to the development and delivery of their speeches.

Improved Treatment of Listening   We have made significant changes in the listening chapter, with greater emphasis on critical listening and on the importance of speakers listening to their audience. To facilitate critical listening, we now introduce Toulmin's model of reasoning and fallacies in the same chapter, so that students realize these are important not only to the construction of their own speeches but also to their role as members of an audience.

Expanded Treatment of Organizational Patterns   Organic methods of organization have been fully integrated into the chapter. A new chart lists all of the recommended patterns of organization and describes how each is typically used according to differing speech purposes.

Improved Treatment of Persuasion   The persuasive speaking chapter is significantly rewritten, and students now are shown how to analyze their own values as well as those of their audience (VALS). As a means to contextualize the discussion of persuasion in practice, we now cover the elaboration likelihood model early in the persuasion chapter.

New Sample Speeches   New storytelling, informative, and persuasive speeches are included in the text and Speech Coach CD. Appendix B now includes the eulogies delivered by Presidents Ronald Reagan and George W. Bush on the loss of the space shuttles, with suggested questions for students to consider in comparing the two.

Organization of the Text

The basic chapter structure of the fifth edition has been modified to allow students to move more smoothly through the text. However, as with earlier editions, the chapters are designed so that instructors may assign them in any order they find appropriate.

Part One deals with the foundations of the art and science of public speaking. Chapter 1, Practical Speaking, focuses on the personal, professional, and public reasons for becoming a good public speaker, with specific examples of people with whom students can identify who use public speaking in their daily lives. We also introduce a model of public speaking and preview the remainder of the book. Chapter 2 provides an overview of the skills needed by public speakers and allows instructors to assign speeches early without having to assign chapters out of order. Topic selection and writing purpose statements have been incorporated into this chapter to provide an early foundation for students in preparing their first speeches. Chapter 3 provides students with the tools they need to cope with the nearly universal experience of speech anxiety. Chapter 4 deals with ethical speaking and listening with a special emphasis on avoiding plagiarism.

Part Two makes explicit that focusing on the transaction between speaker and audience is key to success in public speaking. Chapter 5 presents a thorough treatment of listening, with a focus on listening to public speeches, including the importance of speakers listening to their audiences when taking questions. The box on handling the Q&A has been moved to this chapter. Chapter 6 provides the tools for analyzing the cultural, demographic, and individual diversity of audience members. In addition, we offer practical suggestions for adapting speeches to audiences once the analysis has been completed.

Part Three is about putting theory into practice. Chapter 7 covers researching the speech. In recognition of the fact that most students already use the Internet, but often without applying critical standards to the information they find, we have focused on the skills needed to distinguish reliable from unreliable Internet sources. Chapter 8 is a new chapter devoted to supporting speeches with reasoning as well as evidence. Chapter 9 treats organization from an audience-focused perspective. We include a variety of traditional organizational patterns, such as alphabetical, categorical, causal, time, spatial, Monroe's motivated-sequence, extended narrative, problem–solution, and stock issues. We also discuss organic patterns such as the star, wave, and spiral. Material related to transitional statements is also located in this chapter. Chapter 10 addresses language use, with particular attention to adapting language to diverse audiences. We suggest ways to choose language that is inclusive rather than exclusive, nonsexist rather than sexist, and thoughtful rather than stereotypic. We also offer techniques for enhancing the effective use of language. Chapter 11 deals with delivery skills, again focusing on audience adaptation. This chapter provides both a strong theoretical foundation based in nonverbal communication research and solid, practical advice for the public speaker. Chapter 12 presents a comprehensive discussion of visual, audio, and audiovisual media that can be adapted to the audience and occasion to enhance most public speeches. Our discussion of PowerPoint has been updated for this edition, with an emphasis on using it to enhance, rather than take the place of, public speaking. The Speech Coach CD has a PowerPoint tutorial that will enable students to learn the best practices in an interactive fashion.

Part Four addresses the most common contexts for public speaking that students are likely to face in the classroom and in their lives after college. Chapter 13 on informative speaking stresses audience adaptation, particularly in terms of diverse learning styles. Practical applications of learning theories are discussed in relation to speeches that explain, instruct, demonstrate, and describe. Chapter 14 on persuasive speaking has been significantly revised. The elaboration likelihood model is made more central to the discussion, and a method of analyzing audience values has been added. Chapter 15 builds on the information we introduce early in the book on critical listening. A detailed treatment of critical thinking, with a special focus on recognizing and responding to fallacies of reasoning is presented. A side-by-side comparison of arguments taken from student speeches helps students develop their own critical thinking skills as well. Finally, Chapter 16 provides a discussion of speaking throughout the student's lifetime. It includes guidelines for impromptu speaking; speeches of acceptance, introduction, recognition, and commemoration; speeches to entertain; speaking on television; and speaking in small groups. A box on writing humor by Emmy Award winner Russ Woody has been relocated to this chapter.

Teaching Support Package

The textbook is part of a comprehensive package designed to help you solve teaching problems in your public speaking course.

Instructor's Resource CD-ROM (IRCD)   Written by the authors, the Instructor's Manual includes a variety of excellent resources for new and experienced teachers. These include strategies for managing multisection courses, a primer for graduate assistants and first-time teachers, and quick references to the speechmaking skills highlighted in each chapter. The IRCD offers a number of in-class activities, sample syllabi for semester- and quarter-length terms, sample evaluation forms, and transparency masters. The contents of the IRCD are based on the authors' decades of teaching experience; many of the activities and materials have been class tested with the thousands of students enrolled in the basic public speaking course at California State University, Chico.

Computerized Test Items   Approximately 1,800 test items, including multiple-choice, true-false, and essay, are included on the Instructor's Resource CD-ROM. As with other materials in the instructor's package, many of these test items have been class tested. The complete test bank is offered in MS Word and in the EZ Test computerized format, allowing you to edit the existing test items and incorporate your own questions. The test bank can be used with both Windows and Macintosh systems.

Online Learning Center (OLC) Web Site   Instructors will have password-protected access to the Instructor Center at <www.mhhe.com/brydon5>, where they will find a fine selection of supportive materials. Included are a number of useful pedagogical aids for the instructor, such as PowerPoint slides, the Instructor's Manual, and activities.

Students will have access to the Student Center, which features multiple-choice and true-false practice quizzes, flashcards and crossword puzzles using chapter key terms, and a number of useful links to other Web sites that can assist in developing speeches. OLC icons in the text direct students to the site for further review.

Speech Coach CD   This fully integrated CD is packaged with new copies of the text. In addition to its many video segments, Speech Coach contains a number of interactive learning features for students. Chapter quizzes, key terms flashcards, outlining software, a PowerPoint tutorial, and other materials are either on the CD itself or on the Online Learning Center, which is linked to the CD.

The Speech Coach CD allows us to show what most texts only talk about. It also frees up valuable class time for the instructor and students to use in other ways. Each video segment can be viewed independently of the others and is coordinated with a specific chapter in the text. Speech Coach icons in the margins of the book indicate where a particular video segment would be appropriate. Speech Coach not only reinforces the text but also previews material to be covered later in more depth. In addition to the CD, the video segments are available to instructors in VHS and DVD for classroom viewing.

Acknowledgments

We gratefully acknowledge the support and assistance of many people at McGraw-Hill who played a role in this book, including Nanette Giles, executive editor; Josh Hawkins, developmental editor; Jessica Bodie, Nancy Garcia, and Erin Flasher, media producers; Holly Paulsen, project manager; Laurie Entringer, design manager; Ayelet Arbel, art editor; Natalia Peschiera, photo researcher; and Tandra Jorgensen, production supervisor. We also thank Kay Mikel, manuscript editor, for her attention to detail.

We are especially grateful to Dr. George Rogers, Professor Emeritus at Chico State, who supplied many of the photos for the text and produced the video segments of the Speech Coach CD that accompanies this text, and to the numerous students who consented to be videotaped for this project. Special thanks go to the speakers who shared their talents in providing sample speeches: Jonathan Studebaker, Montana Kellmer, Karen Shirk, Shelly Lee, Evan Mironov, Kelsey Kinnard, Mary Schoenthaler, Miranda Welsh, and David A. Sanders. We would also like to thank these individuals for generously consenting to contribute to our effort: Enrique "Rick" Rigsby, Tomoko Mukawa, and Russ Woody. They are friends, colleagues, former students, and role models; they have all enriched our book and our lives. We also thank Dr. Nichola Gutgold of Penn State Berks-Lehigh Valley College, Lehigh Valley Campus, for sharing her research on Elizabeth Dole.

A grateful thank-you for the reviews and counsel of our peers in the classroom who graciously prepared careful critiques of our manuscript and videotape in various stages of development:

Marcia Berry, Azusa Pacific University

Isaac E. Catt, Millersville University

Susan Childress, Santa Rosa Junior College

Arlie V. Daniel, East Central University

Cynthia De Riemer, J. Sargent Reynolds Community College

Beth Eschenfelder, Florida Southern College

Jill Henke, Millersville University

Robert L. Strain Jr., Florida Memorial College

James Spurrier, Vincennes University.

We also would like to extend our gratitude to those instructors who took the time to respond to a rather extensive survey concerning our text:

Eileen Berens, Villanova University

Carol Bledsoe, University of Central Florida

Arlie V. Daniel, East Central University

Cynthia De Riemer, J. Sargent Reynolds Community College

Edie S. Gaythwaite, University of Central Florida

Nichola Gutgold, Penn State Lehigh Valley

Christine Hanlon, University of Central Florida

Bret Jones, East Central University

Lois P. McGuire, Central State University

Nicole Phanstiel, University of Central Florida

Ken Robol, Halifax Community College

Tara J. Schuwerk, University of Central Florida

Matthew Thompson, University of Central Florida

MJ Wagner, University of Central Florida

We appreciate the help of all these individuals in preparing this book, but we are, of course, ultimately responsible for its content. Any errors or omissions are solely our own.

And last, but certainly not least, we wish to thank our families, Pamela, Robert, Julie, Randi, and Colin, who not only showed great patience as we worked on this project but often provided assistance in more ways than we can possibly list.

A Visual Preview of Between One and Many
Fifth Edition

Between One and Many presents public speaking as a living and dynamic transaction in which the meaning of the message emerges from the relationship between speaker and audience. From this perspective, students are encouraged to think critically about their communication and recognize the centrality of the audience in speech preparation. The Fifth Edition was revised to emphasize the classical and contemporary theories of communication that support the art and science of public speaking and which create a foundation for effective, everyday "one to many" speaking.

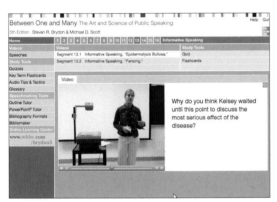

Speech Coach CD-ROM 2.0 is fully integrated with the text. Thirteen video segments, nine of them full student speeches, illustrate the various presentation techniques and elements of a speech. CD icons in the text margins guide students to the CD resources (e.g., speech videos, interactive quizzes, and outlining software), which extend the pedagogical methods of the text to enhance comprehension and to help build confidence in public speaking.

The Online Learning Center, also fully integrated with the text through margin icons, offers students and instructors a focused selection of resources, all designed to contribute to a successful public speaking course. These include practice quizzes, key term crosswords, and PowerPoint slides for the lecture component. The Online Learning Center also provides a gateway to Public Speaking PowerWeb, a unique site that offers the transcripts of select speeches from recent Vital Speeches of the Day, news and journal articles on topics that are relevant to public speaking, and articles on topics that students may use as source material for their speeches.

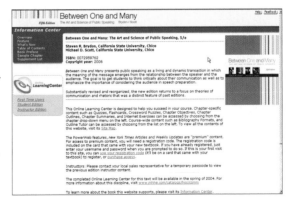

This Visual Preview provides a guide to the special features of the text, CD, and Web site.

The Art and Science of Public Speaking Is Demonstrated Through Strong, Consistent Coverage of Classical and Contemporary Theories

Canons of Rhetoric

The five canons of rhetoric are presented in Chapter 2, "Your First Speech," and discussed in more detail in Chapters 7 through 12. Since ancient times, these classical arts have been considered the basis for successful speeches.

Toulmin Model of Argument

The Toulmin Model of Argument and its explanation of claims, grounds, and warrants is introduced as a model for sound arguments in Chapter 5, "Listening," and integrated throughout the book, notably in Chapter 8, "Supporting Your Message," and Chapter 15, "Thinking and Speaking Critically."

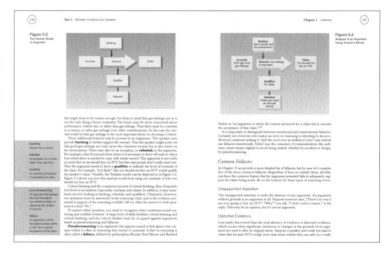

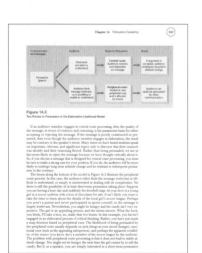

Elaboration Likelihood Model

Chapter 14, "Persuasive Speaking," has been substantially revised to make the Elaboration Likelihood Model more central to the discussion of persuasion and audience reaction to persuasive communication.

Research-Based Content Emphasizes the Importance of Ethics and Critical Thinking in Both Speaking and Listening

Ethical Speaking

Chapter 4, "Ethical Speaking," offers practical information for ethical speaking, ethical listening, and cultural understanding, and includes new information on Internet plagiarism, inducing fear in speeches, and civility in listening.

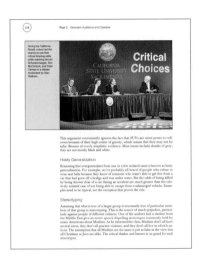

Critical Listening

Chapter 5, "Listening," features expanded coverage of critical listening and introduces the Toulmin Model as a means to effective listening.

Critical Thinking and Speaking

A full chapter on critical thinking, Chapter 15, "Thinking and Speaking Critically," provides information on sound reasoning, fallacies, and the use of critical thinking skills to avoid stereotyping.

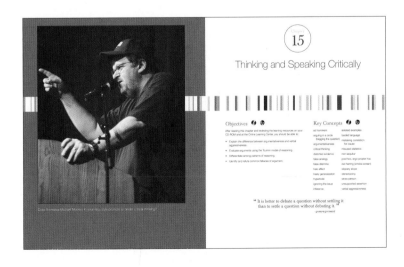

Theories Are Balanced in Each Chapter With Multiple Opportunities to Learn Skills and Practice the Steps of Speechmaking

Sample Speeches

"In Their Own Words" boxes provide sample outlines and speech excerpts, in addition to full student speeches. Many of these boxes provide commentary to focus students on speaking techniques and critical thinking.

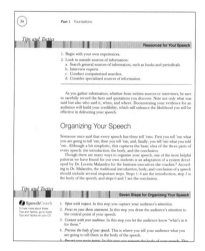

Tips and Tactics

These highly-regarded sections offer practical strategies for speakers on a variety of topics such as improving listening skills, avoiding plagiarism, and evaluating sources. Tips and Tactics are highlighted to make it easy for students to apply these suggestions to their own speeches.

Self-Assessment

These boxes provide research-based measurement tools, which allow students to assess their own attributes, experience key insights, and practice skills to become stronger communicators.

Presentational Media and Technology

Chapter 12, "Using Media in Your Speech," highlights the appropriate use of all types of visual media during speeches and offers tips and current research for avoiding common mistakes, including the misuse of Power-Point.

Appendix A
Guide to Source Citations

AMERICAN PSYCHOLOGICAL ASSOCIATION (APA) STYLE

www.mhhe.com
/brydon5
For more information on citing sources in APA or MLA style, go to the Online Learning Center.

The following information is based on the *Publication Manual of the American Psychological Association*, Fifth Edition, 2001, and on their Web site, www.apastyle.org. Please note that there are several changes in APA style from the fourth edition. Hanging indents (not tabs) are to be used in the references list, titles should be *italicized* rather than underlined, and the citation of online sources has changed. It is important that you fully document the sources of information you use in preparing a speech outline. Cite the source in parentheses in the actual body of the outline by name and date. Include page numbers for quotations or specific facts, for example, (Jones, 2005, p. 1).

Include a list of "References" at the end of your outline. Always include the author, date, title, and facts of publication. Personal communications, such as letters, phone calls, e-mail, and interviews, are cited only in the text, not the reference list; for example, J. Q. Jones (personal communication, April 1, 2005). The format varies depending on the type of work referenced.

Here are some of the most common types of works you may use in a speech. Notice that APA style does not place quotation marks around the titles of articles or book chapters. Also, titles of books and articles are not capitalized, except for the first word, the first word following a colon, and proper names. Periodical titles are capitalized. Authors are listed by last name first, followed by first and sometimes middle initials.

Books

Single Author
Freeley, A. J. (1990). *Argumentation and debate: Critical thinking for reasoned decision making* (7th ed.). Belmont, CA: Wadsworth.

Multiple Authors
Germond, J. W., & Witcover, J. (1989). *Whose broad stripes and bright stars?* New York: Warner Books.

Corporate Author
American Psychological Association. (2001). *Publication manual of the American Psychological Association* (5th ed.). Washington, DC: Author.

Government Document
Department of Health and Human Services. (1989). *Smoking tobacco and health: A fact book.* (DHHS Publication No. CDC 87-8397). Washington, DC: U.S. Government Printing Office.

419

New "Guide to Source Citations" Appendix

This appendix offers students a handy reference for both APA and MLA guidelines for source citation. Sample works cited include both print and online materials.

Examples and Visuals Treat Diversity as an Essential Aspect of Listening, Audience Analysis, and the Overall Speaking Process

Valuing Culture

This book emphasizes understanding and valuing cultural diversity. Textual and visual representations of speakers and listeners from a variety of cultures and ethnic groups are included.

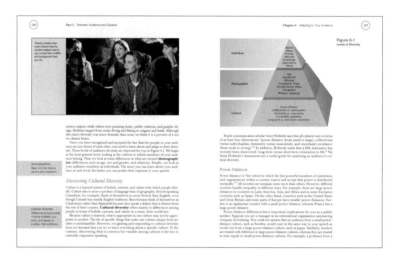

Analyzing Audiences

Chapter 6, "Adapting to Your Audience," offers guidelines for audience analysis that include cultural, demographic, and individual levels of diversity.

Considering Diversity

These boxes encourage students to understand and explore the effects of all aspects of diversity in order to help them become more competent speakers and listeners.

Comprehensive Guidance on Research, Support, and Organization Places Value on Sound Speech Preparation

Evaluating Sources

Chapter 7, "Researching Your Message," provides strategies for speech research, including the use and misuse of the Internet, as well as for evaluating sources using the CRAAP test (Currency, Relevance, Authority, Accuracy, Purpose). Research is now in its own chapter, as is support, Chapter 8, "Supporting Your Message."

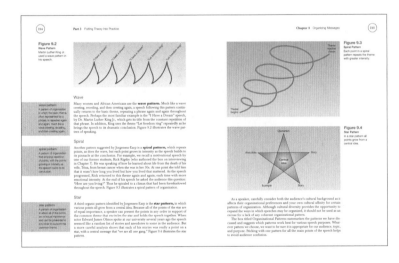

Organizing Speeches

Patterns of organization, including alphabetical, wave, spiral, and star patterns, are included in Chapter 9, "Organizing Messages."

Speaking Of . . .

These boxes contain current, topical information related to the text discussion and provide tips for speech preparation, including opportunities for research and critical thinking.

Speaking of . . .

Codes of Conduct for Public Speaking

Although it is not a full-fledged ethical code, such as those found in law and medicine, the National Communication Association's Credo for Free and Responsible Communication in a Democratic Society forms an important touchstone for the ethical public speaker. Other guidelines that may be of help to the public speaker are found in the American Advertising Association's Code of Ethics, the Code of Ethics of the International Association of Business Communicators, and the Public Relations Society of America's Code of Professional Standards for the Practice of Public Relations.[1]

Credo for Free and Responsible Communication in a Democratic Society[2]

Recognizing the essential place of free and responsible communication in a democratic society, and recognizing the distinction between the freedoms our legal system should respect and the responsibilities our education system should cultivate, we the members of the National Communication Association endorse the following statement of principles:

We believe that freedom of speech and assembly must hold a central position among American constitutional principles, and we express our determined support for the right of peaceful expression by any communicative means available.

We support the proposition that a free society can absorb with equanimity speech which exceeds the boundaries of generally accepted beliefs and mores; that much good and little harm can ensue if we err on the side of freedom, whereas much harm and little good may follow if we err on the side of suppression.

We criticize as misguided those who believe that the justice of their cause confers license to interfere physically and coercively with the speech of others, and we condemn intimidation, whether by powerful majorities or strident minorities, which attempts to restrict free expression.

We accept the responsibility of cultivating by precept and example, in our classrooms and in our communities, enlightened uses of communication; of developing in our students a respect for precision and accuracy in communication, and for reasoning based upon evidence and a judicious discrimination among values.

We encourage our students to accept the role of well-informed and articulate citizens, to defend the communication rights of those with whom they may disagree, and to expose abuses of the communication process.

We dedicate ourselves fully to these principles, confident in the belief that reason will ultimately prevail in a free marketplace of ideas.

[1]Richard L. Johannesen, *Ethics in Human Communication*, 4th ed. (Prospect Heights, Ill.: Waveland Press, 1996), chap. 10.
[2]Used by permission of the National Communication Association.

Speech Coach CD-ROM Makes Public Speaking Accessible to a Variety of Learning Styles

Speech Coach 2.0 is an easy-to-use CD-ROM packaged free with every new textbook. It provides a variety of learning tools to help students prepare, organize, and deliver speeches. It also offers a range of engaging study tools for exam preparation and research. Speech Coach brings to life the theories and skills discussed in the text. Icons within the text prompt students to use the features on the CD.

Speech Preparation

Thirteen video segments, nine of them full student speeches, illustrate the various presentation techniques and elements of a speech. Student speeches feature optional commentary boxes to highlight organization, signposts, and techniques. Students can view and study these speeches and delivery styles during their own time, at their own pace, and in their own space.

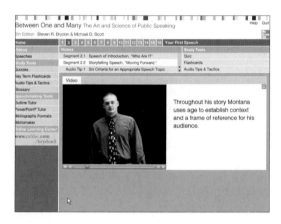

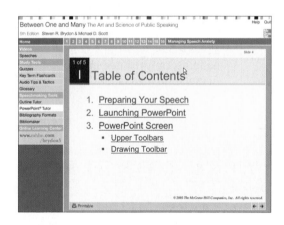

Basic steps in creating and effectively using PowerPoint in a presentation are explained in this vivid tutorial.

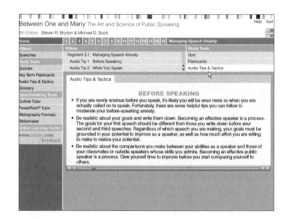

Eleven Audio Tips and Tactics are based on the text versions. This useful advice, recorded by the authors, provides students with an opportunity to see and hear some of the most popular Tips and Tactics from the text.

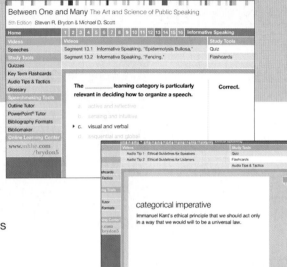

Exam Preparation

Multiple-choice quizzes with immediate feedback reinforce chapter objectives and aid in preparation for exams.

Key Terms Flashcards reinforce the terms and concepts from the text and are ideal for learning and studying vocabulary.

Speech Coach 2.0 also is a gateway to www.mhhe.com/brydon5 and to Public Speaking PowerWeb.

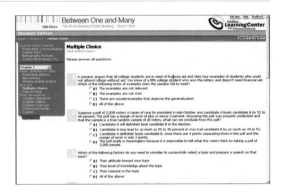

To support and extend the content of the text, the Brydon/Scott Online Learning Center, a text-specific Web site, offers students and instructors an array of resources, including chapter quizzes, vocabulary-enhancing crossword puzzles, outlines, summaries, and other helpful resources (www.mhhe.com/brydon5).

PowerWeb: Table of Contents

Public Speaking PowerWeb is designed to support you with examples of public speaking in action, including a series of speech transcripts of public interest from *Vital Speeches of the Day* and news and journal articles on topics such as rhetoric, speech anxiety, and visual aids.

Unit 1. Our Rhetorical World

Part A. Perspectives on Rhetoric

Article: 1. Stories and the Rhetoric of Contrariety: Subtexts of Organizing (Change), Martha S. Feldman and Kaj Sköldberg, *Culture & Organization*, Volume 8, Number 4, 2002
View in: Acrobat | HTML | Test Your Knowledge Form | Quiz Question

This article used the enthymeme, a concept from *classical rhetoric*, to reveal the underlying *logic* contained in stories. The authors go on to discuss the importance of stories and their meaning in our *culture*.

Article: 2. Narratives and Culture: The Role of Stories in Self-Creation, Arran Gare, *Telos*, Winter 2002
View in: Acrobat | HTML | Test Your Knowledge Form | Quiz Question

Author Arran Gare examines the connection between *narratives* and *culture*. Structural *semiotics* is used to understand narrative.

Article: 3. Ancient Egyptian Rhetoric in the Old and Middle Kingdoms, David Hutto, *Rhetorica*, Summer 2002
View in: Acrobat | HTML | Test Your Knowledge Form | Quiz Question

In this study, David Hutto presents classical Egyptian views on *rhetoric* and *communication*. He contrasts Egyptian views with prevailing Western views of rhetoric.

Article: 4. Reconceptualizing Communication and Rhetoric From a Feminist Perspective, Jessica Lee Shumake, *Guidance & Counseling*, Summer 2002
View in: Acrobat | HTML | Test Your Knowledge Form | Quiz Question

In this essay, Jessica Shumake provides a *feminist* view of rhetoric. She first puts forth the view that communication is an act of co-creating meaning and then provides a contrast between feminist views of *rhetoric* and more traditional views.

New Public Speaking PowerWeb

The Online Learning Center provides links to Public Speaking PowerWeb, a password-protected Web site that is offered free with new copies of the text. It provides instructors and students with the following resources: recent speeches from Vital Speeches of the Day; news and journal articles on topics that are relevant to public speaking, such as speech anxiety, visual aids, and persuasion; and articles on a variety of topics that students may use as source material for their speeches.

Also on Speech Coach
- Glossary
- Outline Tutor
- Bibliography Formats and BiblioMaker

About the Authors

Steven R. Brydon
California State University, Chico

Steve Brydon received his Ph.D. from the University of Southern California. He has been a professor at Chico State for more than 3 decades, where he teaches courses such as public speaking, argumentation, advanced presentational speaking, and political communication. He coached speech and debate for 12 years and served as department chair for 10 years over two separate terms. He has co-authored three books and has also published in the areas of political communication and argumentation and debate.

Michael D. Scott
California State University, Chico

After receiving his Ph.D. from the University of Southern California, Mike received a joint appointment in the departments of Communication and Educational Psychology at West Virginia University. In 1981 he joined the Center for Communication and Information Studies at CSU, Chico as a professor and Director of Graduate Studies. Mike is a recipient of two outstanding teaching awards and is the co-author of several books on topics ranging from the role of communication in the classroom to interpersonal communication. Currently he co-directs the basic course in public speaking at Chico alongside Steve Brydon.

Foundations

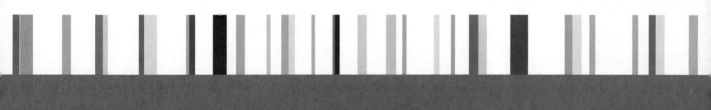

Actor and activist Edward James Olmos speaks frequently to high school and college students about issues of diversity and gang violence, as he is shown doing here at California State University, Chico.

Practical Speaking

Objectives

After reading this chapter and reviewing the learning resources on your CD-ROM and at the Online Learning Center, you should be able to:

- Describe the relationship between personal needs and the ability to speak publicly.
- Explain the role speaking plays in the professional promotion of self.
- Describe how speaking skills can make people better citizens.
- Demonstrate an understanding of the transactional and symbolic nature of the process of public speaking.

Key Concepts

In each chapter we will introduce you to some key terms you need to know. We place these at the beginning of each chapter to alert you to important terms you will encounter. In this chapter look for the following terms:

channel

content (of messages)

decoding

encoding

feedback

interdependence

message

needs

perception

relational component
  (of messages)

symbol

system

transaction

> " If all my talents and powers were to be taken from me . . .
> and I had my choice of keeping but one, I would unhesitatingly ask
> to be allowed to keep the Power of Speaking, for through it,
> I would quickly recover all the rest. "
>
> —DANIEL WEBSTER

At the start of each new term we ask students two straightforward questions. First, how many of you resent having to take a class in public speaking because you believe you could better spend the time with your major? Second, how many of you fail to see the connection between a class in public speaking and your personal and professional goals?

We ask these questions because we know they are ones students are asking themselves. After all, wouldn't your time be put to better use in a class in your major? And is there truly a connection between a class in public speaking and becoming a computer scientist, information manager, chemist, Web designer, graphic artist, biologist, nurse, exercise physiologist, or writer?

Much as we understand these questions, we try that first day of class to demonstrate to our students that these questions are misplaced and based on too little experience in the so-called real world. Simply put, time spent in this class can have more bearing on your success than some of the courses in your major. The reason is simple. People who are good at what they do get promoted to positions that have less to do with their initial job title and more to do with managing people both inside and outside their profession. With this kind of promotion comes increased responsibility for communicating both interpersonally and in public. Communication skills, including public speaking, top the list of qualities that companies that recruit on your campus and throughout the world seek in a prospective employee.[1] Knowledge and skill in public speaking are *that* important. Further, this is true whether we're talking about science and medicine, the law and public service, education and the social sciences, and even the fine arts.

But don't just take our word for it. Consider the stories of the three people shown in the photos on this page. Although Keith Hawkins always wanted to work with people and actually enjoyed speaking in public, he was never certain he could use these two interests to carve out a career. Keith learned in his speech class that some of the highest paid people in the United States are professional public speakers. Whether Keith now counts himself in the highest paid group of professional speakers we can't say. But we do know that Keith, who has been featured in articles

Professional speaker Keith Hawkins

School principal Sandi Young

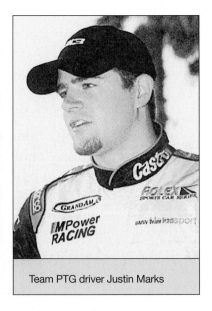

Team PTG driver Justin Marks

in *Time* and the *New York Times,* is a paid professional speaker who has even spoken before the General Assembly of the United Nations.

Sandi Young's story is different from Keith's. As a then single mom of two small children, Sandi began her professional life as an elementary school teacher, thinking that would always be her heart's desire. Before too long, however, she found herself back in school as a part-time graduate student. She completed a master's degree and credential in special education and took on a new job and title as a resource specialist for children with special needs. Soon thereafter Sandi was being called on to lead training workshops for other teachers, school administrators, and even parents. "I was doing the very thing I dreaded most as a college student," Sandi says, "making presentations in public to audiences ranging from a few teachers to as many as 1,200 parents, teachers, and administrators." Sandi has since moved on and now is the principal of an elementary school with a staff and student body of more than 300, speaking to groups two or three times a week.

Finally, there is Justin Marks. He is trying to balance his schedule between being a college student and pursuing his goal of becoming a full-time race car driver. Majoring in Motor Sports Administration, Justin is occasionally required to make presentations in class. As a factory sponsored driver for BMW, though, Justin is almost constantly required to speak before media, company groups in partnership with BMW, and BMW sports car clubs across North America. "Being fast no longer cuts it if you want to be a successful race car driver these days," Justin tells us. "You also have to be able to represent your employer. For me that means being able to stand up in public and articulate a positive image of both myself and BMW cars."

Public speaking is an essential communication skill in today's world. Public speaking also is an extension and refinement of many of the skills you already practice in your one-on-one and group communication encounters. Our goal in this initial chapter is threefold. First, we demonstrate how common it is for people to use their speaking skills to satisfy their personal and professional needs, and to help empower others to satisfy theirs. Second, we make clear the connection between public speaking and the other forms of communicating you routinely practice, and we discuss public speaking as a specific kind of system of communication. Finally, we preview the chapters that follow this one.

SpeechCoach

Segment one of Speech Coach shows you the role public speaking can play in people's lives. See segment 1.1 on your CD.

Personal Reasons for Developing Speaking Skills

Although we may not consciously realize it, human communication is a need as basic to our well-being as the food we eat, water we drink, and air we breathe. Both clinical and case studies compellingly show that when we are deprived of this need, we are affected both physically and psychologically.

Understanding Needs

Many of our most important needs are satisfied through communication. Examples range from our need for clean water to drink to our need to know which chapters in our book to read in preparation for a test. **Needs** can be physical or psychological. Physical needs are straightforward. They involve our biological survival and

needs
Physical and mental states that motivate us to behave in ways that lead to the needs' satisfaction; for example, eating when we are hungry.

include food, shelter, water to drink, and clean air to breathe. Psychological needs are more complex and concern our mental health.

Both types of needs can be potent sources of motivation in our lives. And, as Professor Alan Monroe points out in his motivated-sequence model of public speaking (see Chapter 9), these needs also play a frequent and important role in prompting us to speak up in public about matters that affect us and others.[2]

Satisfying Our Needs

Many of the most impassioned speakers and speeches have been motivated at least in part by individually felt needs the speakers believed were either (1) not being satisfied or (2) whose satisfaction was in jeopardy. Randy Larson, for example, was once our student and is now a syndicated talk show host and environmental activist. He is also an excellent speaker who has presented literally hundreds of speeches on the environment to groups both sympathetic and hostile to his beliefs. By his own admission, his initial motivation to become such a visible activist and public speaker was related to his fear that his individual health was being jeopardized by "people polluting water, fouling the air, and poisoning our food with harmful pesticides."

Meeting the Personal Needs of Others

Public speaking skills also can empower others to satisfy their needs. Often people need someone who can bring their needs into better focus and enable them to act to meet those needs. Some of the best speeches presented by some of the best speakers are motivated by needs that they regard as important to both themselves and the public at large. Examples range from Dr. Martin Luther King Jr. to people you may not recognize but whose efforts have influenced the satisfaction of your most important needs as well. The list includes people such as Mary Fisher (see Chapter 6), a prominent Republican who contracted the HIV virus from her husband and who now speaks out on the importance of *everyone* learning about and protecting themselves against HIV.

Actor/activist Edward James Olmos, star of *Stand and Deliver* and *American Me,* spoke at the authors' campus on the topic "We Are All the Same Gang."[3] Having succeeded in meeting his personal and professional needs as a critically acclaimed actor, Olmos is now using his talents to speak out for the needs of others. He targets his message to those who are tempted to join gangs. His speeches promote peace, racial harmony, and the need for children to be vaccinated against violence. As he points out, "No child comes out of his mother's womb with a pistol."[4]

Professional Reasons for Developing Speaking Skills

Besides satisfying needs, there are many professional reasons for honing your public speaking skills. One major reason is to become an agent of influence in your career. As an agent of influence, you will be in a position to (1) promote your professional self, (2) better present your ideas to decision makers, (3) create positive change in the workplace, (4) become a functioning force in meetings, and (5) develop critical thinking and listening skills.

Promoting Your Professional Self

The chance to speak in public frequently presents us with an ideal opportunity to enhance our professional credibility. Some time ago the authors of this text were treated to a presentation by Dr. Bonnie Johnson. She spoke about work she had done for Intel, the world's largest manufacturer of silicon chips. As someone trained in organizational communication, Dr. Johnson was given permission by Intel to study how well personnel were adapting to technological change in the workplace–for example, electronic workstations. When she had concluded her study, Intel offered her a position with the corporation.

Following her presentation, Dr. Johnson welcomed questions from the audience. One undergraduate asked her why she thought Intel had hired her. "Do you want to know candidly?" she asked. "Because initially they were more impressed with the public presentation I made to top management on the results of my study than with the study itself. They hired me because I not only knew my subject but could effectively speak about it and its implications for Intel."

As shown by Dr. Johnson's evaluation of her experience with Intel, communication skills in general and public speaking skills specifically are both desired and rewarded in the workplace. Surveys of personnel managers at top companies consistently demonstrate that they look for college graduates who not only can communicate interpersonally and in writing but also can deliver a speech well. Ask just about anyone who has climbed the corporate ladder, and you will learn that public speaking skills helped tremendously along the way.

Presenting Ideas to Decision Makers

Another reason organizations put such high value on speaking skills concerns the effective communication of ideas. Your success depends not only on your ideas but also on how well you can present those ideas to people whose decisions will affect your career. When you think about it, every occupation and profession involves selling ideas to other people. For example, the life insurance salesperson who must persuade a client to increase coverage is unlikely to close the deal simply by dropping a brochure in the mail. On a larger scale, most corporations require managers to present reports or briefings describing their accomplishments and future plans and goals. Those individuals who seek to move beyond entry-level positions need to be able to convince others of the wisdom of their ideas. Thus, being able to speak to decision makers with confidence and authority is an indispensable tool for corporate success.

Dave Davies's experience at 3M is a good case in point. Although scientists by training, Davies and the people in his department have to justify resources they believe are necessary to their research. Thus, when Davies needed $20 million to advance his work on laser disks, he was required to publicly present his case to 3M's executive operations council, which included 3M's CEO. This was no sit-down presentation at a conference table. As is usually required in such cases, Davies made a stand-up presentation using both a lectern and visual media.[5] The fact that Davies was successful in procuring the money reflected not only the promise of the product but also the skill with which Davies presented its promise to 3M's executive council.

Creating Change in the Workplace

One of the most important tasks for any supervisor or manager is to be able to convince subordinates that proposed changes are desirable. To remain competitive, companies must implement new technologies and procedures. Yet many employees fear change. Often the best way to introduce change is to sell employees on new ideas rather than to tell them to simply get used to those ideas. A willing and enthusiastic workforce is far more likely to accept change in the workplace than is a reluctant and suspicious one.

In addition, change need not always be initiated from the top. Many of the best ideas in industry come from employees who convince their managers that change is necessary. Consider the example of America's most successful retail store, Wal-Mart. Founder Sam Walton believed, "Our best ideas come from clerks and stock boys."[6] To prove the point, Walton once rode 100 miles in a Wal-Mart truck just to listen and talk to the driver.

Companies as diverse as Delta Airlines and Hewlett-Packard also listen to their employees. For example, "Delta spends a lot of time and money . . . checking out the employee's side of the story. Often the result is a substantial policy change," according to management consultants Tom Peters and Robert Waterman.[7] They report that senior management at Delta meet in an "open forum" at least once a year. Those in the lowest ranks of the organization have the opportunity to speak directly with those at the highest levels. And Hewlett-Packard has an "open lab stock" policy that allows workers to take equipment home for their personal use, in the hope that they might come up with an innovation.[8] Successful organizations don't just talk to their employees, they listen to them as well.

Becoming a Functioning Force in Meetings

Although small-group communication is not the main focus of this book, many of the skills we discuss—ranging from active listening to critical thinking to making impromptu presentations—are directly applicable to functioning in group meetings. As communication professor Ronald Adler reports, the average business executive spends about 45 minutes out of every hour communicating, much of this time in meetings.[9] Further, surveys show that executives spend as many as 700 hours per year in meetings.[10] Your ability to speak effectively in meetings will be indispensable to your success in the workplace.

Developing Critical Thinking and Listening Skills

It is not enough to know how to present your ideas to others. You also need to listen to the needs of others and to what they say in response to your ideas. On average we spend up to 55 percent of our day in situations that involve the potential to listen.[11] Seldom, however, do we take full advantage of this opportunity. Active listening, which we discuss at length in Chapter 5, is essential to your development as a speaker. First, you won't have anything important to say unless you have listened actively to those around you. Second, listening will make you more effective in working with people. Study after study demonstrates that people who actually hear what is being communicated to them are much more responsive to others than those who listen with "only one ear." Responsiveness to one's audience, moreover, is one of the distinguishing characteristics of some of our nation's best public speakers.

Public speaking skills will help your development as a listener in several ways. For example, learning to give an effective speech requires the ability to analyze your audience, including what they think about you as a speaker and about the topic you plan to address. As part of their audience analysis, the best speakers listen to what audience members say well in advance of speaking. These speakers know that what they hear contains clues about what an audience is thinking. These speakers then use these clues in both the preparation and delivery of their speeches.

Learning to speak requires skill in organizing your thoughts and highlighting key points for listeners. As you learn to do this for your speeches, you will also learn how to organize the information you receive from speakers, separating the important ideas from the unimportant. Finally, speakers have to learn how to research and support their ideas. As a listener, you will need to evaluate the research and support other speakers provide to you. In fact, almost every public speaking skill we will discuss has a parallel skill for the listener.

Public Reasons for Developing Speaking Skills

Skilled public speakers serve as agents of change not only in the workplace but in the larger world as well. Were it not for those who spoke out publicly, the voting age would still be 21 and only White male property owners would be able to vote. All the progress of the past century has resulted from people coming up with new and sometimes controversial ideas and speaking out to persuade others of the wisdom of adopting them.

Becoming a Critical Thinker

As we first discuss in Chapter 5, the ability to think critically about your own messages and those of others is essential to reaching sound conclusions about the issues of the day. Not only should speakers strive to base their persuasive efforts on sound reasoning, listeners need to take responsibility to detect unsound reasoning. Some arguments that seem valid actually contain flaws that render them invalid. Becoming a critical thinker will make you less susceptible to phony arguments and less prone to engage in them yourself.

Functioning as an Informed Citizen

Our nation is a democratic republic based on the premise that for our country to thrive there must be a free exchange of ideas. Thus, it is no accident that the First Amendment to the Constitution guarantees freedom of speech, as well as freedom of the press, religion, and peaceable assembly. The fundamental premise of our Constitution is that the people must have the information necessary to make informed decisions. Even if you don't have an immediate need to speak out on an issue of public policy, you will be the consumer of countless speeches on every issue imaginable—from atmospheric warming to zero-tolerance policies in college dorms for drug possession. The ability to forcefully and publicly present your thoughts to others—whether as a speaker or as an audience member questioning a speaker—is more than a desirable skill. It is also a responsibility you owe to others and yourself.

Preserving Freedom of Speech

For some people, the way to deal with unpopular ideas is to invoke a quick fix: censorship. One of our goals in this book is to give you an appreciation for the importance of free speech in a democratic society. The empowerment of more and more citizens to express their views publicly should lead to vigorous debate about those ideas. Those who have confidence in the truth of their own views should welcome the opportunity to debate, rather than suppress, opposing views. Yet hardly a day goes by when we are not treated to an account of some person or some organization trying to suppress another's right to speak freely.

Raising the Level of Public Discourse

Regrettably, much of the public discourse of recent years in response to controversial issues has degenerated into name-calling and emotional appeals. Daytime TV is overrun with programming on which people verbally assault each other with messages that bear little to no semblance of reason. Geraldo Rivera quit his enormously profitable daytime talk show, for example, because he believed it was contributing to the erosion of reasoned speech in the United States. Even so-called current events shows such as *The O'Reilly Factor* on FOX News frequently break down into name-calling and emotional screeching.

We believe almost any topic—from abortion to religious zealotry—can be debated without the debaters personally attacking each other's pedigrees. Learning to focus one's public speaking skills on the substance of a controversy rather than the personality of an opponent is an important step in raising the level of public discourse. As more Americans learn how to make their views known rationally, and learn the critical thinking skills necessary to evaluate public discourse, the overall level of debate about issues in contemporary society is likely to improve.

Promoting Ethics

People have studied and written about public speaking for more than 2,000 years. One of the constants we find in what people have said about the topic, moreover, is the central role of ethics in the development and presentation of public speeches. Although we may live in a time where some people believe that the ends justify any means, all public speakers have an obligation to embody the practice of ethics in both their message and its presentation. In doing so, public speakers have a unique opportunity to encourage the practice of ethics in the audience members with whom they share their message.

The Public Speaking Transaction

Although this book deals with public speaking specifically, we recognize that public speaking is but one of many modes of human communication. We communicate one on one, in small groups, and through the mass media, as well as in public. Although each context in which we communicate has its own distinguishing features, certain principles of communication apply to all of them. Whether the focus is an intimate conversation between lovers, an informative speech before your class, or a speech at a political rally, the process of communication is best viewed as a transactional system.

A **transaction** involves an exchange of messages between two or more people. A **system** is a collection of interdependent parts, parts arranged so that a change in one produces corresponding changes in the remaining parts. Consider a mechanical system such as a car. Its parts show varying degrees of interdependence. **Interdependence** exists when things have a reciprocal influence on one another. Changes in some of a car's parts will produce subtle changes in others. For example, even minor tire tread wear will affect a car's handling. The change is so subtle, though, that most drivers don't notice it. In contrast, changes in other parts of the car can produce changes drivers cannot help noticing. Engine failure, for example, produces obvious changes throughout the hydraulic system of the car, including failure of the car's power steering and power brakes.

Perhaps this is why the public speaking transaction seems such a significant departure from the more familiar contexts of communication in which we engage. Whereas the changes that occur to the communication system when moving from an interpersonal to a small-group exchange are subtle, the changes that occur to the system when moving to an exchange between one and many can seem rather pronounced. Consider something as simple as the number of people communicating in a system and the number of lines of communication between or among them. As illustrated in Figure 1.1, the lines of communication increase geometrically as the number of communicators increases. Whereas this change isn't especially dramatic as you move from two communicators to three or four, the change is staggering by the time you get to a group of even seven.

transaction
An exchange of verbal and nonverbal messages between two or more people.

system
A collection of interdependent parts arranged so that a change in one produces corresponding changes in the remaining parts.

interdependence
A relationship in which things have a reciprocal influence on each other.

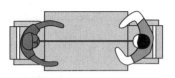
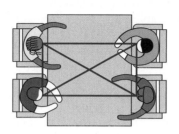
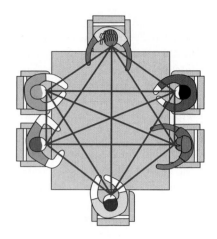

Dyad
(1 line of communication)

Group of 4
(6 lines of communication)

Group of 6
(15 lines of communication)

Figure 1.1

Lines of Communication.

The lines of communication increase with the number of people. This may be one reason people are fond of the saying "Too many cooks spoil the broth."

Figure 1.2 models the interdependent parts of the public speaking transaction as a system. Consider (1) the situation (context) in which the public speaking transaction takes place, (2) the speaker and the audience, (3) the messages they exchange, (4) the process of constructing and interpreting the symbols they use to convey their messages, (5) the channels through which the messages are sent, and (6) the role perception plays in the process.

The Situation

The situation (or context) in which any communication transaction takes place affects the nature of the transaction. This is especially true of public speaking. The situation includes the physical environment in which the speech is shared between speaker and listener. For example, is the speech shared in a classroom? An assembly hall? An outdoor amphitheater? It makes a critical difference.

Usually the situation also defines the purpose of the speech transaction. Are the people gathered to hear a speech eulogizing a beloved family member? To learn about a new policy that affects the amount of tuition charged students? Or to listen to a politician announcing her decision to seek higher office? Does the speaker want simply to pass on information to the audience? To motivate the audience to take some action? To persuade the audience to abandon old beliefs in favor of new ones? The purpose of the speech, too, makes a critical difference in the overall transaction.

The Speaker and the Audience Members

In contrast to early models of speaking, which implied the speaker first talks and the audience then responds, the transactional model tells us speaker and audience exchange verbal and nonverbal messages. Even as speakers share their messages

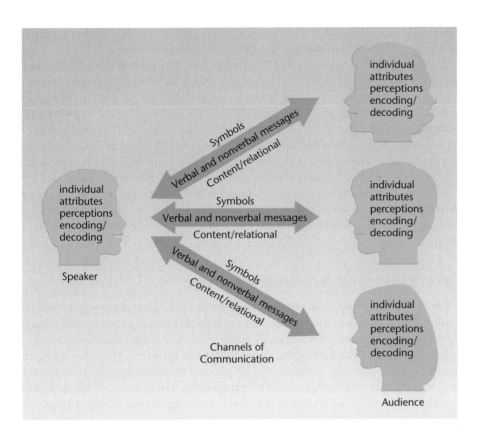

Figure 1.2
Public Speaking as a Transaction.
In this model of the speech transaction, messages are simultaneously conveyed between speakers and listeners, with both parties functioning simultaneously as sources and receivers of messages. Communication is bound by the situation, and each person's perceptions are significant in interpreting the content and relational components of messages.

with audience members, for example, individual members of the audience are sharing messages right back. Generally this **feedback** is nonverbal in nature and includes such things as eye contact, facial expressions, and body orientation. In some situations, these audience-initiated messages may be verbal, as is the case when members of parliament in the United Kingdom vocalize their approval or disapproval of what the prime minister shares with them. In either case, the audience is not passive during a public speech, and the speaker should note these messages and adapt to them.

The sheer number of people in an audience also affects the overall speech transaction. It's one thing to speak with 25 other students in a traditional college classroom. It's quite another to speak to an assembly of the entire graduating class at commencement as people shift restlessly in their seats. Thus, you can no more afford to ignore the size of your audience than you can afford to ignore their feedback, the environment in which the transaction takes place, or the purpose for which you have gathered.

feedback
Audience member responses, both verbal and nonverbal, to a speaker.

Messages: Content and Relational Components

The **message** is the meaning produced by the speaker and the audience members. In the transactional system modeled here, the message and the medium through which it travels are intentionally blurred. This is because the two are *interdependent*–not independent. What we would like to say to our audience is significantly affected by the manner in which we say it, and the way we convey the

message
The meaning produced by communicators.

message is affected by what we want to say. This reciprocal process has a tremendous impact on how our message is perceived by our audience.

All messages are composed of two parts. The first part of the message is its **content,** the essential meaning, the gist or substance, of what a speaker wants to convey. For example, you might wish to convey your affection for another with the three words "I love you." The second part of a message, called its **relational component,** involves the combined impact of the verbal and nonverbal parts of that message as it is conveyed. Consider how you might use your voice, face, and eyes to alter the impact of the words "I love you." You could make these three words an expression of sincere endearment, a plea, or even a statement of wanton desire.

Meaning is derived from both the content and the relational parts of a message. Moreover, neither part is more important than the other in its contribution to meaning. What you say and how you say it, in other words, are roughly equal in this regard.

Constructing and Interpreting Symbols

When we try to convey our thinking to other people, there is no way to directly communicate our ideas. Our thoughts must be converted into words and gestures whose meaning can be interpreted by those receiving the message. These words and gestures are really **symbols,** things that stand for or suggest other things by reason of relationship or association. This process of converting our thoughts and ideas into meaningful symbols is called **encoding.** These symbols are then interpreted when received by audience members, a process known as **decoding.** This is simpler said than done. Whether an audience decodes a speaker's message as encoded depends on many factors, including but not limited to:

- Language
- Culture
- Age
- Gender

On occasion, for example, some of our male students have referred to female audience members as "girls." When they used this label, we doubt these men meant adolescent and immature members of the opposite sex. Yet that's exactly how most women in our classes decode the word. Thus, those males who have used the word *girl* in reference to women have "turned off" many, if not most, of the women in their audience.

Channels

A **channel** is the physical medium through which communication occurs. The transmission of the light and sound waves that make up the picture you see on your TV set requires a channel through which they can be signaled and received. Picture and audio are encoded into electronic impulses, which must be decoded by your television receiver. In human communication, we primarily use our senses as channels for the messages we send and receive. We use our voice, eyes, and body, for example, to channel our speeches, conversations, and group discussions. On occasion, we also use our sense of touch, sense of smell, and even our sense of taste as channels of communication.

---

content (of messages)
The essential meaning of what a speaker wants to convey.

relational component (of messages)
The combined impact of the verbal and nonverbal components of a message as it is conveyed.

symbol
Something that stands for or suggests something else by reason of relationship or association.

encoding
The process by which ideas are translated into a code that can be understood by the receiver.

decoding
The process by which a code is translated back into ideas.

channel
The physical medium through which communication occurs.

In the case of public speaking, we can also use supplementary channels of communication to augment the five senses. We can electronically amplify our voice so that it can be better heard or use visual media such as poster boards, overhead transparencies, and PowerPoint slides.

Perceptions

The transactional system we've been describing demands that we both understand and appreciate the role of perception in public speaking. **Perception** is the process by which we give meaning to our experiences. This process begins when we decide to attend to some stimulus that our senses have picked up on: for example, the driver of the oncoming car whose bright lights are blinding you to the road ahead. Based on your past experiences you instantly organize a message—you flash your bright lights, signaling the other driver to dim his.

Communication unfolds in much the same way. Our senses pick up a smiling face as we walk from one class to the next. When we hear the words, "What's up," also coming from the smiling face, this is what usually happens. First, we organize the facial expression and audible sound into a whole. Second, we give meaning to this whole. Third, we organize a response, smiling back and saying, "Nothing much." Such transactions not only take place in microseconds but also require little to no conscious thought.

On one hand, the instantaneous way we make sense of and respond to the messages we attend to is essential to our survival. On the other, it also can make us overconfident and prone to making mistakes about what we sense, how we perceive what we sense, and how we respond to it.

Take a close look at the lithograph by M. C. Escher on the next page. Though it appears at first glance that the water is running downhill, a more careful examination tells you that this is impossible because the water is flowing continuously. Escher was able to create "impossible illusions" by taking advantage of our perceptual predispositions. We assume that the perspective in this print is an accurate representation of reality, when, of course, it cannot be so. When people look at an ambiguous stimulus such as this picture, they automatically look for something familiar . . . something for which they have a preexisting meaning. This helps fool the eye, in this case, into seeing something that cannot exist.

Again, this tendency to perceive the familiar is both good and bad from the standpoint of public speaking. It is good because it enables us to quickly establish a reference point from which we can plan our own speaking behavior as well as interpret that of others. It's bad because it can blind us to other data that may be even more important to how we behave and interpret the messages of others.

Consider a cross-cultural example. Direct eye contact is perceived as a sign of attention and respect in most of North America. Thus, when we give a speech, we use this knowledge to gauge how our audience is reacting to our message and delivery. This North American norm, however, is not universal. Direct eye contact in some cultures, such as certain Asian societies, is perceived as an aggressive sign of disdain and disrespect.

It's common, then, for unaware North Americans who speak in one of these cultures to walk away from the experience with their confidence severely shaken. They mistakenly perceive their audience's lack of eye contact with them as a sign of disapproval. This mistaken perception, in turn, usually has a negative influence on their entire speaking performance.

> **perception**
> The process by which we give meaning to our experiences.

This lithograph, *Waterfall* (1961), by M. C. Escher, creates an "impossible illusion" by taking advantage of our perceptual predispositions.

As a public speaker, you can never assume that your perceptions of such things as the context, your audience, or the messages your audience feeds back to you are foolproof. Just because some person, some place, or some circumstance strikes you as familiar, that doesn't necessarily make it so.

Words and Things

Finally, public speaking, like other forms of communication, is symbolic.[12] Words are verbal symbols that we use to describe persons, places, and things. Gestures, too, can be symbols, as is the case when we wave our hand to signal good-bye or shake our fist at someone to signal that we are angry. But they are nonverbal.

Although we deal with the symbolic nature of public speaking at length in Chapters 10 and 11, we mention it here because you need to understand that the meaning you attach to the verbal and nonverbal symbols you use to express your-self may not correspond to the meaning others attach to them. What's more, this may be the case even when you think you share a common language. Native speak-ers of English, for instance, both use and understand what we call idioms, expres-sions unique to our culture or sometimes to the circle of friends with whom we most identify. Although you may have no trouble making sense of an expression such as "Dude's ride is sweet," imagine how much trouble an international student recently arrived on campus would have in "getting" what the words used in the expression actually mean.

As you prepare for your first speeches, think about the degree to which you and your audience share meaning for symbols you commonly use to express your-self. This means, at a minimum, checking out the degree to which you and your audience share a common language, come from a similar culture, and share a similar socioeconomic background.

Preview

The preceding discussion is a framework for the entire book. In the chapters to follow we flesh out this framework. The concepts just introduced will be refined and expanded to fit the primary topic of a specific chapter.

Because public speaking classes typically are taught in a limited period of time, you can expect to be up on your feet and speaking long before you have learned everything you need to know about the subject. We wrote Chapter 2—which pro-vides an overview of the process of developing, organizing, and delivering your first speech—with this fact clearly in mind.

If you are the least bit anxious about your first speech, then you can look for-ward to reading Chapter 3. This chapter clears up confusion about the common fear of speaking in public, explains the origins and consequences of this fear on speech performance, and provides you with easily understood and practiced skills to help you manage your fear. What's more, you will learn from reading Chapter 3 that these same skills can help to improve your performance even if you are completely confident about your speaking ability.

Chapter 4 zeroes in on a topic of real significance to today's world: ethics. You will learn about varying ethical perspectives and their relationship to the speech transaction. You also will be called on to make a commitment to the ethical prac-tices described there in your own speeches.

To repeat, a major reason for learning about public speaking is the develop-ment of listening skills. Much as we need to listen, most of us are not as skilled at it as we need to be. Research shows that most of us would benefit from listening training. Chapter 5 discusses the relationship between good listening habits and effective public speaking. In the process, it details for you the types of listening in-volved and suggests practices for improving each of these types.

The best prepared and delivered speeches are those that are developed with the audience in mind. Competent public speakers try to learn as much about their audience and the speaking situation as they possibly can. What they learn assists them in predicting what kind of speech will succeed with their audience. Chapter 6 details the process of analyzing your audience and speaking situation, and the ne-cessity of adapting your speech to both.

One of the toughest tasks for many beginning students is getting started. Aristotle called this process of getting started invention. In Chapters 7 and 8 you will learn not only about developing your speech but also about avenues for research you can travel to prepare your speech, including the Internet.

Just as there is more than one way to putt a golf ball, there is more than one way to organize a speech. This is especially true in light of the fact that today's multicultural audience may decode your message using different patterns of organization. You will learn about organizing your message using alternative patterns of speech organization in Chapter 9.

As noted earlier, public speaking is a symbolic transaction. We elaborate on this fact in Chapter 10's treatment of the language of public speaking. You will learn that language is both complex and central to one's cultural heritage. You also will learn how to use this knowledge to your and your audience's advantage in your speeches.

Chapter 11 throws a realistic light on a subject fraught with misinformation: the delivery of your message. How nonverbal communication functions in the delivery of your speech is explained and examples are provided. Common misconceptions about this type of communication also are dispelled.

Using media to enhance your speeches seems such a simple thing. Yet, as you will read in Chapter 12, nothing could be further from the truth. Media such as overheads or media projected from a laptop computer in combination with a projection machine require precise care in both their construction and execution. Public speakers routinely abuse these presentational media in the classroom, in business, and in government.

Informative speaking is far and away the most common type of public speaking you are likely to encounter. Informative speeches are an essential component of most college classes, whether or not they are labeled as such. A lecture essentially is an informative speech. So too is a book report or an oral presentation based on a term paper. Chapter 13 outlines and discusses the types of informative speeches common in everyday life and details the elements that combine to make an effective informative speech.

Chapter 14 builds on the discussion about informative speaking. You will learn about the process of persuasion as well as the process of persuasive speaking. You also will be shown the perceptual characteristics that influence judgments about your credibility and will read about message variables that can enhance the persuasive effect of your speeches.

Chapter 15 extends what you learn about persuasion to thinking and speaking critically. You will be treated to information on deceptive communication practices that are commonly used by unscrupulous communicators, and you'll learn how to recognize the fallacies that frequently characterize their messages. In the process, you also will learn how to avoid using such fallacies in your own reasoning and speaking.

Finally, Chapter 16 introduces life circumstances in which you can expect to be called on to speak. Some of these circumstances, such as a wedding toast, are social. Others, such as being asked without warning at school or at work to make a progress report on a project, are task oriented.

All in all, we think these chapters combine to provide you with the introductory knowledge and skills necessary to see you through not only the speeches you will share in your class but also the lifetime of public speaking all college graduates can expect. Good luck as you proceed.

Summary

There are many good reasons to study and practice public speaking. Among them are these:

- Public speaking is an essential skill in the professional world.

- Communication in general and public speaking specifically help you satisfy your own needs and the needs of others.

- Public speaking helps you with your other classes, including those in your major.

- Public speaking skills help to make you a more effective force for change.

- Public speaking helps you become a better listener.

- Public speaking is a key to becoming an informed and active citizen.

- Public speaking helps you think more critically about the issues of the day.

As you move on to the next chapter, remember these important elements:

- Public speaking is a transaction between speaker and audience.

- This transaction is comprised of interdependent rather than independent parts.

- These parts include (1) the situation, (2) the speaker and the audience, (3) the message, (4) verbal and nonverbal symbols, (5) the channels used, and (6) perceptions.

Check Your Understanding: Exercises and Activities

1. This chapter suggests that public speaking can help you satisfy needs. How can public speaking skills help you satisfy your most pressing personal and professional needs? Write a short paper or give a brief speech explaining your answer and giving examples.

2. How important are public speaking skills in the profession for which you are preparing? If possible, interview either a practitioner of the profession or a professor in the appropriate department about the ways public speaking might be applicable in your field. Give a brief (1- to 2-minute) presentation to your classmates, or write a short paper about your findings.

3. Attend a meeting of a local government agency, such as a city council, planning commission, or board of supervisors, or attend a student government meeting on your campus. Chances are you will see several speakers present their views in a public forum. Write a short paper about one of the speakers. What impressed you most about the speaker, and what impressed you least? How did the ability to speak help this person achieve his or her goals?

Notes

1. National Association of Colleges and Employers, "New College Grads With Communication, Interpersonal, Teamwork Skills Have the Edge Say Employers," 30 March 2001. [Retrieved from http://www.naceweb.org/press/display.cfm/2001/pr033001.htm, 3 September 2001.]

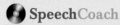

SpeechCoach

To evaluate your understanding of this chapter, see the Quizzes on your CD.

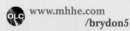

www.mhhe.com
/brydon5

Visit the Online Learning Center for helpful study resources, including practice tests, key term crossword puzzles, and PowerWeb articles for research and review.

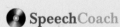

SpeechCoach

For a review of key terms in this chapter, see the Key Terms Flashcards on your CD.

2. Alan Monroe, *Principles and Types of Speech* (New York: Scott, Foresman, 1935).

3. Elaine Gray, "Actor/Activist Brings His Message of Peace to a Packed Laxson," *Chico Enterprise Record,* 16 September 1995, A1.

4. Gray, "Actor/Activist Brings His Message," A8.

5. *In Search of Excellence* [video recording]. (Boston: Nathan/Tyler Productions, 1985.)

6. Thomas J. Peters and Robert H. Waterman, Jr., *In Search of Excellence: Lessons From America's Best Run Corporations* (New York: Harper & Row, 1982), 247.

7. Peters and Waterman, *In Search of Excellence,* 253.

8. Peters and Waterman, *In Search of Excellence,* 245.

9. Ronald B. Adler, *Communicating at Work: Principles and Practices for Business and the Professions,* 3rd ed. (New York: Random House, 1989), 4.

10. Adler, *Communicating at Work,* 216.

11. Anthony P. Carnevale, Leila J. Gainer, and Ann S. Meltzer, *Workplace Basics: The Skills Employers Want* (Washington, D.C.: U.S. Government Printing Office, 1988), 11.

12. W. Barnett Pearce and Vernon E. Cronen, *Communication, Action and Meaning: The Creation of Social Realities* (New York: Praeger, 1980).

Your first speeches to your classmates will help you gain experience and confidence, as you can see in the face of our student Satinder Gill.

Your First Speech

Objectives

After reading this chapter and reviewing the learning resources on your CD-ROM and at the Online Learning Center, you should be able to:

- Analyze the basic features of the speech situation as it applies to your first speech.

- Identify the general purposes associated with public speaking.

- Select an appropriate topic for your first speech.

- Construct a specific purpose for your first speech.

- Develop a clear thesis statement for your first speech.

- Prepare your first speech, utilizing appropriate sources for information.

- Organize your speech to (1) open with impact, (2) focus on your thesis statement, (3) connect with your audience, (4) preview your main points, (5) organize your ideas with three to five main points, (6) summarize your main points, and (7) close with impact.

- Present your speech in a conversational, extemporaneous manner.

Key Concepts

audience

brainstorming

canons of rhetoric

credibility

extemporaneous delivery

general purpose

impromptu delivery

invention

main points

manuscript delivery

memorized delivery

preview

signposts

specific purpose

thesis statement

" A journey of a thousand miles begins with a first step. "

–CHINESE PROVERB

The wisdom of the proverb "A journey of a thousand miles begins with a first step" rings true for anyone who has ever given a speech. Often the toughest part of a speaking assignment is deciding where to begin. For example, you may have a general idea of what you'd like to speak about but have no clue about where to begin your research. Or you may be like many of our students, uncertain about a topic that you find interesting. Will your audience also find it interesting? Is it appropriate for the classroom?

This chapter takes a general look at the individual steps you need to master in the process of developing and delivering your first speech. This is not a substitute for the content to follow in later chapters but a detailed preview of it. It's designed to assist you in developing an overall sense of what effective public speaking involves, starting with choosing the right topic and ending with identifying a style of delivery that best suits the situation. The steps we discuss are (1) analyzing the situation with which you are faced, including your audience; (2) deciding on a purpose; (3) choosing a topic that is suitable to both the situation and chosen purpose; (4) constructing a specific purpose and developing a clear thesis statement for your speech; (5) preparing the substance of your speech; (6) organizing your speech; and (7) presenting your speech effectively.

First Things First

Analyzing the Situation and the Audience

One of your first speech assignments may be to introduce a classmate or yourself, to share a brief story with the class, to prove a controversial point, or to illustrate your pet peeve. Whatever the assignment, you need to understand completely the situation in which you find yourself and the expectations that come with the situation. This is essential to effectively develop a speech that fits the situation and addresses those expectations.

For starters, you need to know who your audience is. **Audience** refers to the individuals who listen to a public speech. Typically, you will be speaking to your classmates, some of whom you may already have come to know in the first few days of class. But even if you have not, you can make certain assumptions about them based on their attendance at your university or college. Do you attend a small, rural, liberal arts college or a large, urban university? What are the common majors emphasized at your institution? Beyond knowing these general facts, you can also observe your classmates in the effort to discover things about them. Are most of them the same age as you, older, or younger? People of the same age tend to share many of the same experiences. For example, the authors of this text grew up in the '50s and '60s. For us, the assassination of President John F. Kennedy was a defining experience. Yet for most of today's younger college students, Kennedy is but a distant historical figure. Although Kennedy's death is still important in a historical sense, the deaths at the World Trade Center, in Pennsylvania, and at the Pentagon on September 11, 2001, probably seem like a defining experience for you and your classmates.

Knowing the common experiences you share with your audience allows you to predict what topics are likely to elicit a favorable response. Factors such as the age, sex, and social status of the people with whom you speak may also help you predict audience response. Depending on who they are and what experiences they share,

audience
The individuals who listen to a public speech.

Today's public speakers need to adapt to multicultural, multiethnic, and multiracial audiences, such as this group of students on our campus.

audience members come to any speech situation with a variety of expectations. For example, your classmates probably expect you to speak to them as a peer. If you violate that expectation, taking on an air of superiority, for example, you may not get the response you desire. Only after you thoroughly understand your speech situation, your audience, and their expectations should you begin to consider the purpose for your speech.

Choosing a Topic

Once you've analyzed your audience and the situation you face, one of the hardest things for many beginning speakers is the selection of a topic. Sometimes your instructor will do this for you, but it's just as likely you'll have to decide on a topic yourself.

In many classes, the first speech you give may not require choosing a complex topic. For example, we sometimes ask our students to introduce themselves or a classmate. We often ask our students to tell a story about something that has happened to them or to someone they have known. Thus, many of the suggestions in the pages that follow will not become relevant until later in the class. However, even if you are simply introducing yourself or telling a story, you still need to choose what you will say about yourself or what experience you will relate. Many of the same criteria that govern topic choice for research-based topics also apply to these early speeches. They should be interesting, appropriate, and worthwhile, as should any speech topic.

An obvious place to begin is with your own interests, experiences, and knowledge. Remember to look for topics as you go through your day. For example, you may see a television program, such as *20/20* or *60 Minutes,* that deals with a topic that interests you. Or a magazine or a newspaper may suggest a topic. For example, an article in *Newsweek* titled "Overexposed" was the source of an excellent speech on skin cancer prevention.[1] Moreover, because the article pointed out that skin cancer is the leading cancer for people ages 25 to 29, the topic proved to be of interest to other students.

Television, newspapers, and magazines are but a few of the places where you might find a topic. Other sources include campus publications, instructors, and fellow students. Computer users who surf the Internet may find ideas there. The number of places to find a good topic, in fact, is limited only by how aware you are of what's going on around you. The following list summarizes a few good places to look for a topic.

Tips and Tactics

Suggestions for Finding a Topic

- *Make a personal inventory.* What hobbies, interests, jobs, or experiences have you had that would interest others?
- *Talk to friends and classmates.* Perhaps they have ideas to share with you, including topics they would like to know more about.
- *Read.* Newspapers, newsmagazines, and books are filled with ideas. You should commit to reading at least one newspaper a day and one newsmagazine a week while enrolled in this course.
- *Check the Internet.* Many subject areas are discussed on the Internet, and there is a wide range of interest-based chat groups. If you enjoy "surfing the Net," you may well find speech ideas there for the taking.
- *Brainstorm.* **Brainstorming** in a group is a creative process used for generating a large number of ideas. (The activity in the box "Brainstorming for Topics" explains the process in more detail.)

brainstorming
A creative process used for generating a large number of ideas.

In addition to knowing *where* to look for a topic, it is important to know *what* to look for. First, the topic should be interesting to you. If you don't care about the topic, how can you expect your audience to care? Second, select a topic that will be interesting to your audience—or at least one that can be made interesting to them. This is why it is crucial to know as much as possible about your audience. Third, your topic should be appropriate to the situation. If your instructor has asked you to speak on your pet peeve, she or he probably is thinking of topics like dorm food, roommates, or people who blow smoke in your face, not the destruction of the rain forests. Fourth, make sure your topic is appropriate to the time available. One limitation facing all speakers, not just those in a public speaking class, is time. Know what your instructor expects and stick to it. Further, consider the time you have available to prepare. If the speech is due next week, you won't be able to send off for information from your state's senator. Pick a topic that you can research in the time available. Fifth, make sure your topic is manageable. Don't pick a topic that is beyond your abilities or resources. One of your greatest assets in speaking is your own **credibility,** which is the degree to which your audience trusts and believes in you. Nothing will undermine your credibility faster than speaking on a topic with which you are unfamiliar. Know more than your audience. Why else would you speak to them? Finally, it is crucial that your topic be worthwhile. We treat time in our society as a commodity. We bank time, spend time, and buy time. You are angered if someone wastes your time, so don't waste your audience's time.

credibility
The degree to which an audience trusts and believes in a speaker.

Speaking of . . .

Brainstorming for Topics

In a group of about three to five people, brainstorm different possible speech topics. During brainstorming the following rules apply:

- The goal is quantity of ideas; even silly ideas should be listed.

- No criticism or evaluation is allowed during the brainstorming process.

- One person is designated to write down every idea. Ideally, write ideas on a chalkboard or an easel so that everyone can see them.

- "Hitchhiking" ideas is encouraged. If you can add to or improve on someone else's idea, do it.

- When you think everyone is out of ideas, try to get at least one more from each group member.

- After all the ideas are listed, go through the list and select the best ones. Look for ideas that fit the assignment, are feasible given the time limits, and would be appropriate for this class. Cross off ideas that don't seem to apply.

- Now rank the remaining ideas in order of value. You may want to modify or combine ideas in this process. Which ones are most promising? How well do these possible topics fit the assignment? Will they be interesting and worthwhile for the members of the class?

Pick a topic that will inform, persuade, or entertain the audience by presenting them with ideas or information they haven't already heard. Just as we hate to hear an old joke told over again, we don't like to hear for the umpteenth time that we ought to recycle our aluminum cans, unless the speaker tells us something new and insightful about why we should do just that. If you pick a well-worn topic, then you must give it a different "spin" or focus.

Tips and Tactics

Six Criteria for an Appropriate Speech Topic

1. The topic should be interesting to you.
2. It should be interesting to your audience—or at least be capable of being made interesting to them.
3. It should be appropriate to the situation.
4. It should be appropriate to the time available.
5. It should be manageable.
6. It should be worthwhile.

SpeechCoach

To hear more about these Tips and Tactics, go to Audio Tips and Tactics on your CD.

Choosing a General Speech Purpose

One of the first decisions a speaker faces is to decide on the **general purpose**—the primary function—of the speech. The three commonly agreed upon general purposes are to inform, to persuade, and to entertain. The most common types of speeches seek to *inform* others about things they do not already know or to *persuade* others to believe or behave in certain ways. Persuasive speeches not only seek change, they also may seek to reinforce social values, as when someone gives a Fourth of July speech or a sermon. Other speeches seek to *entertain* by sharing an enjoyable experience. Obviously, these general purposes are not mutually exclusive. A persuasive speech will also inform the audience, and an informative speech should be interesting enough that it encourages the audience to listen.

> **general purpose**
> The primary function of a speech. The three commonly agreed upon general purposes are to inform, to persuade, and to entertain.

Nevertheless, the general purpose you either have been assigned or have decided on yourself should tell you something about the topic you ultimately choose. Simply put, some topics may be inappropriate or only marginally appropriate to your purpose. Though controversial topics, for example, lend themselves to a persuasive speech, they are less well suited to an informative speech.

Writing Your Specific Purpose Statement

specific purpose
The goal or objective a speaker hopes to achieve in speaking to a particular audience.

You may be assigned a general purpose—to inform, to persuade, or to entertain—for your early speeches. But you will not be assigned a specific purpose. The **specific purpose** is the goal or objective you hope to achieve in speaking to a particular audience. What you want to accomplish specifically with your audience rests with you. For example, assume you are asked to introduce yourself to the rest of the class. What do you want your classmates to think and feel about you? As the speech in the box "Speech of Introduction" shows, one of our former students, Jonathan Studebaker, used the opportunity of a speech of self-introduction to inform his audience about his disability. More than that, however, he sought to educate them to understand that persons with a disability are really just like everybody else. Even in early speech assignments, you should try to articulate a specific purpose for your speech.

SpeechCoach
To view Jonathan Studebaker's Speech of Introduction, see segment 2.1 on your CD.

The specific purpose of a speech is typically expressed in terms of an infinitive phrase that begins with "to." Specific purposes usually fall under one of the general purposes: to inform, to persuade, or to entertain. If you were giving an informative speech on computer viruses, for example, you might express your specific purpose as "to inform my audience about the methods of transmission of computer viruses." This purpose, however, is somewhat vague. More specifically, you might express it as "to enable my audience to explain in their own words the ways a computer virus can be transmitted." Because this specific purpose includes a way of measuring your results—the audience should be able to describe how the virus is transmitted—it will point you toward a specified goal. The level of audience understanding should be realistic: One speech cannot make them computer experts, but they should know how to protect themselves against viruses.

On the same topic, you might have as a persuasive specific purpose "to convince my audience to purchase a virus-detection program for their personal computer." Thus, a successful speech given this goal would lead to a number of audience members eventually purchasing such a program. Of course, there is a difference in content as well as purpose between a speech to inform the audience on computer virus transmission and one designed to persuade them to purchase a particular virus-detection software product. The persuasive speech would probably require the speaker to compare products, prices, and ease of use. The informative speech would not. Both speeches, however, would need to explain the nature of the threat to computer data from viruses. The persuasive presentation might do more to raise the level of concern among audience members so as to motivate them to purchase software to combat the threat.

Speeches to entertain have the advantage of instantaneous feedback. Speakers know by the audience's laughter or applause whether they have succeeded. So, a speaker might express a specific entertainment purpose as "to entertain my audience with the story of my worst computer nightmares." It is not necessary to state how you will measure whether this goal has been met because success or failure is immediately evident.

In Their Own Words

Speech of Introduction

In the 35 short years of his life, Jonathan Studebaker had an impressive list of accomplishments: honorary football coach for the East-West Shrine game (pictured here), kicking coach for the Chico State Wildcat football team, college graduate, television sports commentator, member of the Chico city planning commission, writer, motivational speaker, and founder of "Project Speak Out." Speaking was Jonathan's passion. When we interviewed him for the first edition of this book, he put it this way, "Speaking isn't broccoli; it's fun!" In the speech transcribed here, Jonathan introduces himself and explains that he is far more than a person with a disability. Compare the experience of reading this speech with that of viewing it on your Speech Coach CD.

Our former student, Jonathan Studebaker, is pictured here as honorary coach at the Shrine East-West game.

WHO AM I?
by Jonathan Studebaker

Good morning!

Who am I? Why am I here? Seems like I've heard that before. For myself, I've been asked these and other questions. Two of them I'd like to answer for you today.

I've been asked: "Are you a midget?" "What do you have?" "What's your disability?" "Why are you small?" But I'd really like people to ask me: "What do you like to do?" "What's your favorite color?" So what I'll try to do is answer both of these today.

I'm a nice guy. Don't worry, I won't bite. I like to do many things, except water ski. I've gone to school. I've gone to elementary school, high school, and I graduated from Cal State Chico.

A lot of people ask, "So why are you here?" Well, I'm here because I want to educate others. I've coached football at Chico State University. I was the kicking coach for three years. And out of those three years I had two kickers make first team all-conference. So how do you coach football? You do it by simply telling people what to do. Well, how do you do that? You do it by doing a lot of the things that we all do—by studying, by reading, by listening to others. And that's what I've done throughout my life, and that is what made me who I am.

Like I said, I'm a nice person. I'm cheerful, I'm energetic. Okay, so I have a disability. I was born with osteogenesis imperfecta, a disease which causes my bones to be fragile. Have you ever accidentally dropped a glass on the floor? What happens? It breaks. Well, my bones kind of break like glass, which is why I tell people, when you carry me, treat me like your best crystal.

I'm happy about being who I am. I wouldn't change a thing. I've done a lot of things in my life. Like I said, I've coached football, I graduated from college, things that people wouldn't think a person with my condition would do.

So who am I? Well, I'm Jonathan Studebaker, Jonathan Peter Charles Studebaker. Why such a long name? Well, my middle name is Charles, which came later. And Charles is kind of a symbol of a lot of things. My dad used to call me chicken when I was younger. And then it evolved to chicken Charles, and now Charles. Now, some of you might be offended by being called chicken. But, you know what, it doesn't matter to me. I like being who I am. I've been put here to educate others, not by teaching others, but by just being myself.

Thank you.

As you continue to give speeches in your class, work on developing specific purposes that are realistic, that are worthwhile for the audience, and that fulfill your goals as a speaker. Realistic specific purposes are those that can be accomplished in the brief time you have to present your speech considering the views of the audience you are addressing. For example, you might well motivate your audience to drink alcohol responsibly—something that is noncontroversial for most people. But to convince an audience that disagrees with your point of view to change its opinion on a topic like gun control or abortion is unrealistic. On such topics your specific purpose should be more modest—perhaps to have the audience become more open to your point of view.

Thus, examples of realistic specific purposes for persuasive speeches would include:

- To persuade audience members to avoid binge drinking.
- To persuade audience members to consider that a prison sentence is not always the best punishment for youthful offenders.
- To persuade the audience that privatization of Social Security is or isn't a good idea.

For informative speeches, examples of specific purposes would include:

- To teach my audience the basic principles involved in the Heimlich maneuver.
- To have my audience learn the basic steps of swing dancing.
- To have my audience learn about the earliest contributors to hip-hop culture.

Again, your specific purpose must be realistic. It is one thing to explain the basics of the Heimlich maneuver, and quite another to successfully instruct people in using the maneuver in a brief time without any hands-on practice. You can explain the basic steps of swing dancing in a few minutes, but teaching someone to really "swing" takes much longer.

In addition to ensuring that your specific purposes are realistic, make sure they are worthwhile. For example, the Heimlich maneuver can save a life. But unless your audience has some interest in swing or hip-hop, why would audience members be motivated to listen to your speech?

Finally, you need to assess your specific purpose carefully in terms of your own goals. What, exactly, do you want to achieve (other than a passing grade on your speech)? For example, what is your reason for teaching the steps of swing? Do you go swing dancing every Saturday night? Do you want to encourage others to join you? Or are you just a fan of the style, but not a participant? Understanding your own goals can help you write a clear and useful specific purpose.

As you develop your specific purpose, keep in mind these factors and the four guidelines listed in Tips and Tactics.

Tips and Tactics

Guidelines for Refining the Specific Purpose of a Speech

- Describe the results you seek.
- Be as specific as possible.
- Express your goal in measurable terms.
- Set a realistic goal.

Whatever speech topic you select, therefore, you need to clarify in your own mind and for your instructor what specific purpose you intend to achieve through the speech. Make sure the specific purpose is realistic, is worthwhile for your audience, and helps you achieve your own goals as a speaker. It will make what comes next much easier.

Writing Your Thesis Statement

Every speech should have a central idea or point. If you want people to save for their retirement at the earliest age possible, your point might be that doing so can make an early retirement possible. You should be able to express this point in a single declarative sentence. We call this a **thesis statement,** a sentence that focuses your audience's attention on the central point of your speech. A thesis statement should make your central point clear; express your point of view on that point; and, if accepted, fulfill your specific purpose.

Your thesis statement should help the audience understand what response you seek from them. As a case in point, you might be opposed to further restrictions on what you can do in dorm rooms. Assuming you are speaking to a group of student colleagues, you may wish to focus your speech on what they can do to fight the restrictions. Thus, your thesis statement might be, "We need to lobby the board of trustees of the university to stop this unjustified and harmful plan." Notice that the thesis statement here is directly related to the specific purpose of your speech. In this instance, your specific purpose is "to convince other students to lobby the board of trustees to stop the proposed restrictions." The thesis statement, if accepted and acted upon by the audience, will fulfill your specific purpose. While the specific purpose expresses your goal for the audience's response to the speech, the thesis statement expresses the essential message that is designed to fulfill that purpose.

Although the specific purpose is not normally stated explicitly to the audience, the thesis statement should be sufficiently related to that purpose to allow the audience to know what you want to accomplish. As an example, consider a speech on binge drinking. If your specific purpose was to persuade audience members to drink responsibly, your thesis statement might be, "Binge drinking can destroy lives." Or if you wanted to inform your audience of the basic principles of the Heimlich maneuver, your thesis statement might be, "The Heimlich maneuver involves applying pressure to the victim's diaphragm to expel air from the lungs and thus dislodge what is caught in the throat."

The thesis statement is usually stated in the introduction to the speech. There are some exceptions to this guideline, which will be discussed in later chapters. But as a general rule, letting your audience know your central point is important if you are to fulfill your goals as a speaker.

Even a speech to entertain should have a clear thesis. Obviously, there's no easier way to turn off an audience than to say, "Today I'm going to make you laugh." But it would be logical to say, "First dates are often a disaster, and mine was no different." Unlike a David Letterman monologue, which is often just a string of jokes, a speech to entertain should have a clear purpose, thesis, and structure.

Preparing Your Speech

Ancient speakers in Greece and Rome knew that public speaking involved several arts, which were sometimes called the **canons of rhetoric.** First, the orator

thesis statement
A single declarative sentence that focuses the audience's attention on the central point of a speech.

canons of rhetoric
The classical arts of invention, organization, style, memory, and delivery.

invention
The creative process by
which the substance of a
speech is generated.

or speaker had to create the substance of a speech, a process known as **invention.** The material used in the speech had to be arranged to have an effective *organization.* The orator had to choose the best words to convey the message, which was known as the *style* of the speech. Once prepared, the speech had to be learned. Ancient speakers did not use notes or other aids and devoted considerable attention to improving their *memory.* Finally, the speech had to be presented orally to an audience. The *delivery* of the speech to an audience involved using both voice and body effectively. Four of these five canons are taught today in virtually every public speaking class or effective speaking seminar. Although speakers today rarely memorize their speeches, they do need to invent them, organize the content, use an appropriate style, and deliver the speech to an audience. These topics are discussed in more detail in Chapters 7 through 12.

It may seem odd, at first, to think of a speech as an invention. However, just as it was not enough for Thomas Edison simply to have the idea for the lightbulb, it is not enough for you just to have an idea for a speech. You need to invest time and effort in inventing the substance of what you plan to say. Where do you go for the substance of your speech? Here are some general suggestions, which we develop in more detail in Chapter 7.

Personal Experience

Begin with your own experiences. Each of us has had experiences that make us unique. Many early speech assignments require you to look no further than to the things that have happened in your own life. For example, you may be asked to introduce yourself or tell a story about a personally significant experience. You may be able to rely on hobbies or past job experiences for an early informative speech. Even if you cannot rely solely on personal experience, it is the logical place to begin searching for information.

Speaking about matters with which you have firsthand experience connects you to your message. What's more, this personal connection may also tell you how to connect your message to the personal and professional needs of your audience. For example, a successful actress, who was enrolled in one of the author's classes at the University of Southern California, gave a speech on how to break into "show biz." Unfortunately, she failed to mention her own experience, which included a role in a Clint Eastwood movie and a recurring role on the sitcom *The Odd Couple.* Had she done so, her speech would have connected more effectively to the audience, in effect saying, "If I can do this, so can you!"

Even though your personal experience and knowledge are good sources with which to start, don't stop there. No matter how intense your experience or extensive your knowledge, there is always more to learn. In the effort to augment personal experience and knowledge, consult other sources as well.

Outside Sources

Look to general sources of information. Books, reference books, general-circulation periodicals (*Time, Newsweek, U.S. News & World Report,* etc.), and even public affairs programs such as *60 Minutes, Dateline,* or *20/20* are good places to look for information on topics of general interest. Keep in mind that books may have a long lead time before they are published. Thus, on topics that require up-to-date information, you need to rely on more recent sources, such as periodicals, rather than books. A speech on why the United States got involved in the Vietnam War, for example, might well rely on books and encyclopedias, whereas a speech on the current situation in Iraq would require the most recent sources available.

Sometimes you can interview an expert on the topic of your speech. You may not have to look any further than the other classes you are taking. An interview with an environmental science instructor, for example, could provide a wealth of information for a unique speech about global warming. Further, experts often provide leads to other sources of information the speaker can obtain. Be sure to prepare thoroughly for your interview so that you know what questions to ask. Chapter 7 contains specific guidelines for conducting interviews, which you should consult before interviewing sources for any speech.

Conduct computerized searches, including the Internet. At one time the beginning public speaker relied primarily on print indexes, such as the *Readers' Guide to Periodical Literature*. In some libraries, these may still be the best means of access. However, libraries now provide computerized databases, such as Academic Search. In addition, most students now have access to the Internet either through their universities or through private Internet service providers (ISPs). Although you must be cautious about the reliability of many Web sites on the Internet, there is a wealth of information available to the average citizen. You can learn everything from the latest sports scores to up-to-the-minute political news. However, the Internet is also rife with misinformation and outright fraud. Imagine that you are surfing the Web and end up at http://malepregnancy.com/. The site includes the latest reports on reproductive research, including the first male pregnancy! Woe to the student who bases a speech on this bogus site. It is just one of many realistic looking, but phony, Web sites. In Chapter 7 we discuss how to tell legitimate sites from bogus ones. For now, be sure to apply the test of common sense. Just because something outrageous is found on the Internet, that is not proof that it is true.

Your school library may also provide access to a number of Internet-based databases that have the advantage of being reviewed by experts for the quality of their information. For example, if you are interested in topics in the humanities, general science, education, or the social sciences, Academic Search provides full text articles from more than 1,200 different periodicals. ABI/Inform has articles from scholarly journals, trade journals, magazines, and newspapers that cover business topics, such as advertising, economics, and marketing. In Chapter 7 we discuss these resources in more detail. The point we want to emphasize here is that there are two Internets—the open Internet, which has no quality controls on the information, and the Internet gateway provided by academic libraries, which has sources that are every bit as high quality as the books on its shelves.

Finally, consider specialized sources of information. Every discipline has specialized journals and books, as well as indexes to provide access to them. Chapter 7 discusses some of the more commonly used indexes. If you are dealing with a specialized topic early in the class, you probably should skip ahead to that chapter or meet with a reference librarian to help familiarize yourself with the resources available at your school. You might also consider other types of specialized sources, such as trade publications and government publications, if they are appropriate to your topic. For your early speeches, such specialization probably will not be necessary, but you should be aware that there is more to researching a speech than simply consulting the general books and periodicals found in most libraries.

Tips and Tactics

1. Begin with your own experiences.
2. Look to outside sources of information:
   a. Search general sources of information, such as books and periodicals.
   b. Interview experts.
   c. Conduct computerized searches.
   d. Consider specialized sources of information.

As you gather information, whether from written sources or interviews, be sure to carefully record the facts and quotations you discover. Note not only what was said but also who said it, when, and where. Documenting your evidence for an audience will build your credibility, which will enhance the likelihood you will be effective in delivering your speech.

Organizing Your Speech

Someone once said that every speech has three tell 'ems. First you tell 'em what you are going to tell 'em; then you tell 'em; and, finally, you tell 'em what you told 'em. Although a bit simplistic, this captures the basic idea of the three parts of every speech: the introduction, the body, and the conclusion.

Though there are many ways to organize your speech, one of the most helpful patterns we have found for our own students is an adaptation of a system developed by Dr. Loretta Malandro for the business executives she coaches.[2] According to Dr. Malandro, the traditional introduction, body, and conclusion of a speech should include several important steps. Steps 1–4 are the introduction, step 5 is the body of the speech, and steps 6 and 7 are the conclusion.

Tips and Tactics

 **Speech**Coach

To hear more about these Tips and Tactics, go to Audio Tips and Tactics on your CD.

1. *Open with impact.* In this step you capture your audience's attention.
2. *Focus on your thesis statement.* In this step you draw the audience's attention to the central point of your speech.
3. *Connect with your audience.* In this step you let the audience know "what's in it for them."
4. *Preview the body of your speech.* This is where you tell your audience what you are going to tell them in the body of the speech.
5. *Present your main points.* In this step you present the body of your speech. This step constitutes the bulk of your presentation.
6. *Summarize your main points.* In this step you tell the audience what you've told them.
7. *Close with impact.* In this step you leave your audience with a lasting impression.

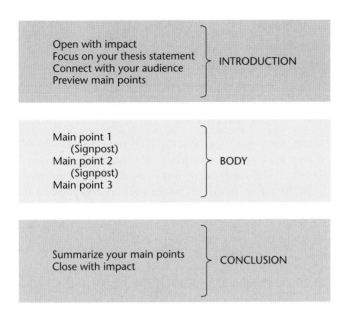

Figure 2.1
Organizing Your Speech.
This seven-step organizational pattern relates closely to the traditional introduction–body–conclusion pattern.

Let's briefly examine each of these steps and how they relate to the traditional introduction–body–conclusion format of a speech. This relationship is illustrated in Figure 2.1.

SpeechCoach
To help you prepare your speech outline, see the Outline Tutor on your CD.

Introduction

Although you will present the introduction first, in actually writing your speech you normally begin with the body or main points. It is difficult to know how to best introduce a speech before you write it. What follows, therefore, is the order of presentation, not the order of preparation of your speech. To present an effective introduction, you should follow four steps.

Open With Impact

Introduce your presentation dramatically or humorously. There's no surer turn-off than beginning a speech, "Uh, um, well, I guess I'll talk about dorm food today." Begin the speech with something that captures your audience's attention, such as an appropriate joke, a startling statistic, an anecdote, or a reference to current affairs.

Tips and Tactics

Ways to Open Your Speech With Impact

1. Tell a brief story.
2. Use a quotation.
3. Make a startling statement.
4. Refer to the audience, the occasion, or a current event.

SpeechCoach
To learn more about these Tips and Tactics, see Audio Tips and Tactics on your CD.

5. Use appropriate humor.

6. Relate a personal experience.

7. Ask a thought-provoking question.

Focus on Your Thesis Statement

As we noted earlier, the thesis statement captures the central point of your speech. For example, if you are opposed to a planned tuition hike on your campus, you should state clearly, "The students of this campus should not be forced to pay more for less." On the other hand, you might want to inform your audience about the types of financial assistance available to them: "With effort and persistence, you can obtain a student loan or scholarship to help meet your college expenses."

Connect With Your Audience

Answer the questions "What's in this for my audience?" and "Why is it in their personal or professional interest to listen to me?" For example, will the proposed tuition hike keep some in your audience from completing their degrees? Make the connection to your specific audience clear in the introduction to the speech. This is also a good place to build your credibility as a speaker. Let the audience know you understand their concerns and have their best interests at heart. If you have expertise on the topic, let your audience know this now so that they can appreciate what is to come.

Preview

preview
A forecast of the main points of a speech.

main points
The key ideas that support the thesis statement of a speech.

Generally, people like a map of the territory they're entering. The **preview** provides your audience with a map to where you are taking them. It forecasts the **main points** of a speech. You should mention all your main points briefly before treating each one in detail. This is the "tell 'em what you're going to tell 'em" part of the speech. It may be as simple as saying, "I'm going to present three ways to save money on your groceries: clipping coupons, watching for store ads, and buying generic brands." On the other hand, a preview may specifically enumerate the three main points of the speech: "You can save money on your groceries, first, by clipping coupons; second, by watching for store ads; and third, by buying generic brands." The preview helps reduce the audience's uncertainty about what is to follow, and it helps them see the relationship among your various points.

Body

The majority of your speech should develop the thesis you are trying to convey. Usually, the body of the speech is divided into three to five main points that in aggregate develop the thesis of your speech.

Organize Your Main Points

A speech that wanders off the topic or whose main points don't follow a logical pattern of development is likely to lose the audience. The same is true of an overly complex speech. Here are some basic patterns for organizing your main points:

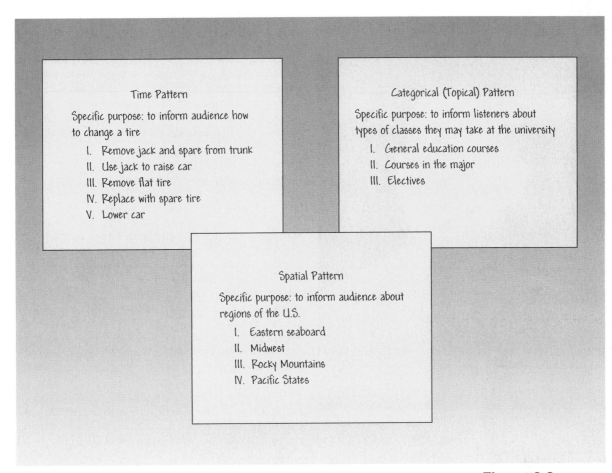

Time Pattern

Specific purpose: to inform audience how to change a tire
 I. Remove jack and spare from trunk
 II. Use jack to raise car
 III. Remove flat tire
 IV. Replace with spare tire
 V. Lower car

Categorical (Topical) Pattern

Specific purpose: to inform listeners about types of classes they may take at the university
 I. General education courses
 II. Courses in the major
 III. Electives

Spatial Pattern

Specific purpose: to inform audience about regions of the U.S.
 I. Eastern seaboard
 II. Midwest
 III. Rocky Mountains
 IV. Pacific States

Figure 2.2
Common Patterns for Organizing the Main Points of a Speech

- *Time pattern.* Most stories are arranged chronologically. The use of a narrative or time pattern is one of the most basic forms of speech making. In fact, one of our former professors, Walter R. Fisher, has argued that humans are storytelling animals. In the box "Storytelling Speech," you will see how one of our students, Montana Kellmer, used time in an unusual way to tell his story. Rather than beginning at the beginning, he began part-way through his story, and then used a flashback to tell the audience how he got to that point. He then took us forward from that point to the story's conclusion and its implications for how all of us lead our own lives. You can read his speech on pages 38–39 and view it on your Speech Coach CD.

- *Spatial pattern.* Some topics are best dealt with spatially. A speech on the solar system might begin with the sun and work out to the most distant planets.

- *Categorical pattern.* Many topics fall into obvious categories. A teacher explaining the federal government to a civics class, for example, is likely to talk about the legislative, judicial, and executive branches. This is sometimes called a topical pattern of organization. If a topic lends itself to natural divisions, this is an excellent way to arrange your speech.

These three ways to organize a speech are summarized in Figure 2.2. Other ways to organize a speech are discussed at length in Chapter 9. For now, this will give

 **Speech**Coach

To view Montana Kellmer's storytelling speech, see segment 2.2 on your CD

In Their Own Words

Storytelling Speech

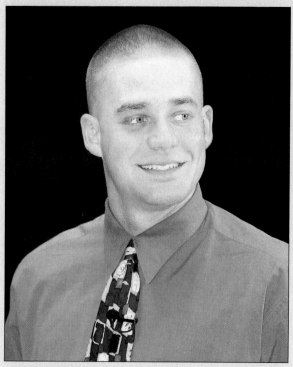

Montana Kellmer

The best speeches tell a story with a purpose in mind. As you read this speech, ask yourself what the speaker's purposes were. How did his story impact you in terms of your own life experiences? This transcript was prepared from a video of Montana's speech. Compare the experience of reading this speech with that of viewing it on your Speech Coach CD.

MOVING FORWARD
by Montana Kellmer

"Fourth and goal, six seconds left, let's do this guys, it's our last shot. [Inaudible] 24 crossbow pass, on one, it's coming to you, ready, break!" I walk up to the line, put my hands under the center, check to see if everyone's set, call off the cadence: "Down, six, hut!" I take the snap, drop back to pass; the whole world fades to black.

Let's back up 14 years. "Where you going dad?" "Son, I gotta go." "Where you going dad?" "Son, I have to leave." My parents split up when I was 3 years old. While most kids were worrying about what time Cookie Monster was coming on, when mommy was bringing home cookies, all I wanted to know was when my father was coming back.

My family had three custody battles. Each cost them $30,000 apiece. That's a total of $90,000. Money wasn't the biggest issue, though. It was the head games. I'm 9 years old, my father comes to me and tells me he's not going to talk to me if I live with my mother. My mom comes to me and asks me to pick. I'm 9 years old, how am I supposed to choose which parent I want to live with? I love them both equally.

you a start. The key thing to remember in this regard is to pick a simple pattern and stick with it for the entire speech.

Provide Signposts

We also want to emphasize the importance of using **signposts,** transitional statements that bridge your main points. For example, you might say something as simple as, "My second point is . . ." or "Now that you understand the problem, let's examine some possible solutions." The goal in using signposts is to provide your audience with guides along the path of your speech so that they will know where you have been, where you are, and where you are going next.

Conclusion

All too often, speakers invest so much energy in developing the introduction and body of their speeches that they run out of gas at the end. The impact with

Some time passes and a sad little boy grows into an angry young man. Adolescence comes. I'm hurt, lonely, and confused, and now it has all led to rage. I turn to baseball and football to deal with my anger. I'm doing pretty well. Pretty proud of myself—I'm starting on both teams. It's pretty fun, but there's some problems. I started drinking when I was 13; started drinking pretty heavily; and now I'm 17. Grades have gone down; I'm getting in a lot of fights. I actually recall this one time I was walking down the hall, someone said something about my mother, I didn't let it slip for 2 seconds out of their mouth. I slammed his head into a pole. He began to slide down. Worst thing about it was that I started laughing at him. He was unconscious. I had an apathetic attitude; I didn't care. I was tired of the hurt, tired of the pain, and tired of the confusion. I didn't feel anything anymore.

Back to where we started. What had happened was, junior year, I was playing in a football game and dropped back to pass and I had a heart attack. They're loading me into the ambulance and all I could hear was, "Stay with me kid," slap me in the face, "stay with me kid," slap me in the face. And they brought out those paddles. Clear, boom, nothing. Clear, boom, the whole world was fading to white. What was happening was I was dying. For the first time I felt at home with myself, at peace, this mess was over. I could move on.

This turned my life around. Coming out of the hospital, I looked in the mirror and realized what I was doing to myself. Told myself, Montana, you can no longer hold this against yourself. Get over it, move past it, and move on. And I did.

If one good thing came out of all this, it's my independence. Growing up, I grew up by myself and I learned to be an independent young man. I set goals and I attained them. If I see something I want, I usually get it. I walked through fire twice, once when I was 3 years old and once when I was 17. What hasn't killed me has only made me stronger.

Forgiving is easy, forgetting is harder. But I feel I have. Abe Lincoln once said, "People are just as happy as they want to be." I firmly believe that. Don't let the emotions get the best of you. Just remember when you wake up and you're having a rough day, and you look in that mirror, and you feel like the whole world has let you down, you feel like you can't go on any longer. Just realize it's never too late to turn yourself around. Get back on that horse and keep riding. Thank you.

which you conclude a speech is just as important as the impact with which you began.

Summarize Your Main Points

Tell 'em what you've told 'em. That is the first and most important function of a conclusion. Remind the listeners of what they've heard.

Close With Impact

Just as a salesperson doesn't like the customer to walk out the door without buying something, you don't want your audience to leave without at least thinking about doing what you've asked them to do. So, find a way to reinforce your specific purpose. It's also your last chance to leave a favorable impression. Just as listeners are turned off by an introduction that begins "Today I want to tell you about . . . ," you can undermine the effectiveness of an excellent speech with a poor conclusion, such as "Well, I guess that's about it." Finish with a flourish that is as powerful as your opening.

Tips and Tactics

SpeechCoach
To hear more about these Tips and Tactics, go to Audio Tips and Tactics on your CD.

Ways to Close Your Speech Effectively

- Present a short, memorable *quotation.*
- Use an *anecdote* or a brief *story* that illustrates your point and leaves a lasting impression on your audience.
- Make a *direct appeal* or "call to action."
- *Return to your opening.* This is one of the best ways to end a speech because it brings the listeners full circle.

So, conclude your speech by *summarizing* your main points and *closing with impact.*

Presenting Your Speech

There's a story told about the great speaker of ancient Greece, Demosthenes, who said that the first, second, and third most important things in rhetoric were—delivery, delivery, and delivery.[3] Although the story is probably apocryphal, it does illustrate the importance of effective delivery. No matter how well thought out your speech, or how many hours you put in at the library, or how elegant your outline, unless the speech is effectively presented, your message will not have its desired impact. In Chapter 11 we deal at length with the nature of delivery, including the important functions nonverbal communication serves for a speaker. In the meantime, the following guidelines will help you present your beginning speeches.

Keep in mind that you have three tools as a public speaker: your *voice,* your *face and eyes,* and your *body.* If you manage these effectively, you will be able to get your message across to your audience.

Use Your Voice Effectively

How you use your voice is critical to effective communication. Some basic guidelines will enable you to speak most effectively.

Breathe Properly

Breathe deeply, from your diaphragm. Give your voice enough support to be heard, but avoid straining your voice or shouting.

Speak Conversationally

Think of public speaking as heightened conversation. Don't attempt to emulate political orators: Most audiences are put off by their techniques. Speak as you do in conversation, but enlarge your voice sufficiently to be heard by all in the room.

It is certainly appropriate and even advisable to ask those in the back of the room if they can hear you, should there be any doubt.

Vary Your Voice

Nothing is more deadly to a speech than a monotone voice. Vary the rate at which you speak, the pitch (high or low) at which you speak, and the volume (loudness). The goal is to present your speech enthusiastically, sincerely, and energetically. Let the audience know you care about your topic.

Use Your Face and Eyes Effectively

The face is one of the most complex and expressive parts of our anatomy, capable of communicating thousands of messages. Use your facial expression to reinforce your verbal message. The eyes, in particular, convey a great deal. Consider a person who gazes at you without pause. This will tend to make you uncomfortable. On the other hand, in our North American culture, a person who refuses to look at us communicates a negative message. (In some other cultures, such as certain Asian societies, no such negative message is communicated by avoiding eye contact.) As a speaker communicating to an American audience, therefore, maintain eye contact with your audience. This does not mean staring at just one portion of the room or shifting your eyes randomly. Rather, look at one member of your audience, then shift your gaze to another member, and so on. Be alert for audience responses to what you are saying. Are they restless, interested, puzzled? Such feedback can help you adapt to the audience as you speak.

Use Your Body Effectively

Your body is the third tool you use to communicate your message. Your body communicates to your audience through *posture, movement, gestures,* and *dress.*

Posture

How do you want to stand during your speech? Some speakers are comfortable behind a lectern, whereas others prefer to move away from it or dispense with it entirely. Choosing not to use a lectern can be an effective way of lessening the physical and psychological distance between yourself and the audience. If your preference is to use a lectern, do not use it as a crutch or bass drum. Avoid leaning on or clutching the stand, as well as beating on it with your open palm. Instead, find a comfortable, erect posture and stand slightly behind the lectern. Keep in mind that to breathe effectively you need to have good body posture.

Movement

Movement should be spontaneous and meaningful. Though good speakers avoid pacing and random movements, it is perfectly appropriate—in fact, desirable—to move to emphasize an important idea or a transition between points. There is no reason a speaker's feet have to be nailed to the floor. Use your body to communicate your message whenever possible and practical.

Delores Huerta, once a farm worker herself, uses gestures and an expressive face as she speaks in honor of Cesar Chavez before a group of young Latino/Latina students.

Gestures

It is common in everyday conversation to gesture with your hands. In fact, try this experiment: Give someone directions from your school to your home *without* moving your hands. You will find it virtually impossible. The key to effective use of gestures in a public speech is that they should be appropriate to the point you are making and clearly visible to your audience. The larger the room, the larger the gesture needs to be for your audience to see it. On the other hand, too many gestures, especially if they appear to be the result of nervousness, such as fidgeting, can be distracting to an audience. Finally, your gestures should be natural extensions of what you do in everyday conversation. They should never be or appear to be forced.

Dress

Your dress as a speaker should be *appropriate* to the situation and the audience. A good rule of thumb is to dress as you might for a job interview. People make instant judgments about other people and, as one shampoo ad proclaims, "You never get a second chance to make a first impression." In no case should your dress detract from the message you want to convey.

Methods of Delivery

There are four common ways to deliver a speech:

- Write out a *manuscript* and read it to your audience.
- *Memorize* your speech and recite it from memory.
- Present a spontaneous, unrehearsed *impromptu* presentation.
- Combine preparation and spontaneity in an *extemporaneous* presentation.

We discuss each type of delivery in turn, along with its advantages and limitations.

Manuscript Delivery

manuscript delivery
A mode of presentation that involves writing out a speech completely and reading it to the audience.

When a speaker uses **manuscript delivery,** the speech is written out completely and read to the audience. Few speakers are very good at reading a speech. In fact, except for politicians and other officials who rely on ghostwriters to prepare their speeches, most of us will not have occasion to give a manuscript speech.

Though it might seem easy to write out your speech in advance and read it to the audience, this is easier said than done. One disadvantage of written speeches is that most people don't write as they speak. Speeches delivered from a manuscript can have an artificial quality. Sentences are often too long and complex. The audience often loses track of the point being made. "Oral essays" tend not to be an effective way to communicate with an audience.

This speaker is so tied to reading his speech that he has lost eye contact with his audience.

If the manuscript pages get out of order or some are missing, you may be forced to improvise or stop your speech altogether. Most teachers have had the painful experience of watching a speaker fumble for words as he or she looks frantically for the next page of the speech. Overreliance on a manuscript can lead to such embarrassing moments.

Another disadvantage of manuscript delivery is that you lose eye contact with your audience. Not only does this inhibit feedback, it reduces your contact with the audience, which, as we will see later, is a major factor in establishing your credibility as a speaker.

The principal situation in which you will want to deliver a speech from a manuscript is if it is critical that you be quoted accurately. For example, public officials usually speak from a manuscript to ensure that they are accurately quoted in the media, to which copies are usually provided. For your first speeches, however, you should avoid the manuscript speech.

Memorized Delivery

An alternative to reading a speech is to memorize it. **Memorized delivery** is a mode of presentation in which the speech is written out and committed to memory before being presented to the audience without the use of notes. This method of delivery does eliminate the problems associated with maintaining eye contact. And, presumably, an able speaker can quickly drop a section of a memorized speech should time run short. But, on the whole, memorized speeches today are confined to the theater and speech tournaments. The reason is simple: Memorization requires an enormous investment of time for even a brief speech. Further, if you forget the speech, you are faced with either a very noticeable silence or

memorized delivery
A mode of presentation in which a speech is written out and committed to memory before being presented to the audience without the use of notes.

"winging it." Finally, memorized speeches usually sound memorized. They are simply oral essays without the physical manuscript.

Impromptu Delivery

impromptu delivery
A spontaneous, unrehearsed mode of presenting a speech.

A spontaneous, unrehearsed mode of presenting a speech is termed **impromptu delivery.** We are frequently called on to give impromptu speeches, although we usually don't think of them as speeches. For example, when your instructor calls on you to explain the day's reading assignment—or when you explain to your bank why you really aren't overdrawn—you are making an impromptu speech. In fact, most of our everyday conversations are spontaneous.

Nevertheless, for most speaking situations, the impromptu method of speaking is of limited usefulness. Even experienced public speakers usually have "canned" or set pieces on which they rely when they are called on to make impromptu presentations. For example, candidates for public office prepare for their debates and press conferences for days beforehand. Every conceivable question is asked in rehearsal, and possible answers are practiced. The unprepared candidate is often caught off guard, as when in 1999 Texas Governor George W. Bush was unable as a candidate to name the leaders of several of our allies, such as Pakistan and India.

For beginning speakers, impromptu speeches should be approached as a learning tool to enhance the principles that apply to other speeches. To rely on impromptu speeches for all of your assignments is not wise.

Impromptu speaking is discussed in more detail in Chapter 16 but here are a few pointers to keep in mind if you are called on to give an impromptu presentation early in the semester.

Tips and Tactics

Making an Impromptu Presentation

- Think about what basic point you want to make about the topic. Are you for or against it? If you don't know, you might list the pros and cons of the issue and let the audience reach its own conclusion. If you are not informed on the topic, try linking it to something on which you do have information.
- Think of one or more points that support your position.
- If you have time, think of an attention-getter as an introduction.
- State your topic in the introduction: It buys you time and then you are sure the audience knows what you are saying.
- As a conclusion, summarize what you've said.

extemporaneous delivery
A mode of presentation that combines careful preparation with spontaneous speaking. The speaker generally uses brief notes rather than a full manuscript or an outline.

If you do not have time to organize your thoughts, at least take a moment to think of your thesis and two or three main points. Believe it or not, in a few seconds you can organize a fairly decent impromptu speech. We engage in spontaneous conversations all the time. Thinking and speaking are not mutually exclusive.

Extemporaneous Delivery

The best mode of presentation for most beginning speakers is **extemporaneous delivery,** which combines careful preparation with spontaneous speaking.

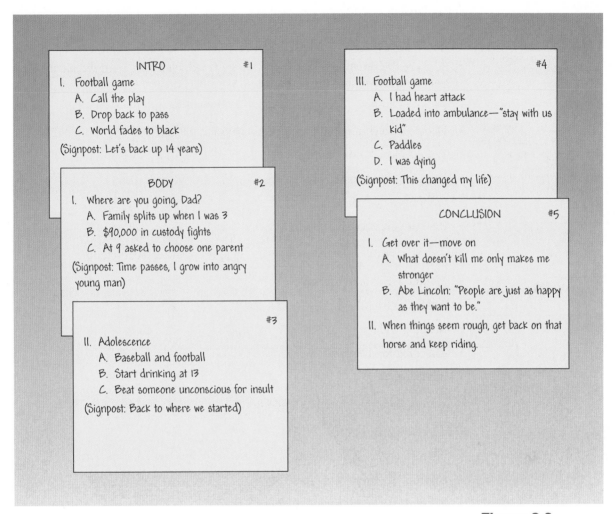

Figure 2.3
Speaker's Note Cards
These notes correspond to Montana Kellmer's speech found on pages 38–39.

The speaker generally uses brief notes rather than a manuscript or an outline. Some instructors require students to first outline their speech in a formal way, in which case the outline should serve as a preparatory tool, not an abbreviated speech manuscript. Other instructors require only that students prepare note cards to help them recall their main and supporting points. (For an example of a speaker's note cards, see Figure 2.3.) Practicing the speech in advance allows you to fix the ideas in your head without memorizing the exact wording.

The extemporaneous method allows you to be prepared yet flexible. If you see from the audience feedback that people are disagreeing with you, you can reexplain a point or add another example. If the audience seems bored, you might skip ahead to your most interesting example. Most teachers employ an extemporaneous method when lecturing to their classes. Students are invited to interact with their instructor, ask questions, and perhaps challenge a point. An extemporaneous speech should be a true transaction between speaker and listener.

Summary

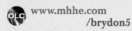
The essential steps in developing an effective speech are to:

- Analyze the situation with which you are faced, including both the nature of your assignment and the audience.
- Choose a topic that is suitable to both the situation and the audience.
- Decide on a general and a specific purpose.
- Write a clear thesis statement.
- Prepare the substance of your speech.
- Organize your speech.
- Present your speech effectively.

There are many ways to come up with an appropriate topic, including:

- Making a personal inventory
- Talking to friends
- Reading widely
- Checking the Internet
- Brainstorming

An appropriate speech topic should be:

- Interesting to you
- Interesting to your audience
- Appropriate to the situation
- Appropriate to the time available
- Manageable
- Worthwhile

The primary function of a speech is expressed as a general purpose:

- To inform
- To persuade
- To entertain

A specific purpose describes your goal or objective in speaking to a particular audience.

The thesis statement focuses your audience's attention on the central point you wish to make in your speech.

Resources for preparing your speech include:

- Your own experiences
- General sources of information

- Interviews with experts
- Computerized searches
- Specialized sources of information

A clearly organized speech:

- Opens with impact
- Focuses on your thesis statement
- Connects with your audience
- Previews your main points
- Organizes your ideas with three to five main points
- Summarizes your main points
- Closes with impact

Common organizational patterns include:

- Time
- Spatial
- Categorical

Transitional statements are called signposts.

In presenting your speech use your voice, face, and body.

Of the four methods of speech delivery, we recommend the extemporaneous method.

Check Your Understanding: Exercises and Activities

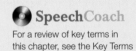

SpeechCoach

For a review of key terms in this chapter, see the Key Terms Flashcards on your CD.

1. Write a one- or two-page analysis of the audience for your first speech. What characteristics do your classmates seem to have in common? Are they similar to or dissimilar from you in age, social status, and background? What assumptions can you make about them based on their attendance at your university or college? How will what you know about your classmates affect your choice of speech topic and specific purpose?

2. Come up with three possible topics for your first speech. For each topic, consider whether it is (a) interesting to you, (b) interesting to your audience, (c) appropriate to the situation, (d) appropriate to the time available, (e) manageable, and (f) worthwhile. Based on this analysis, which topic do you believe is best for your first speech?

3. Once you have selected the best topic, determine what general purpose it would fulfill and phrase a specific purpose that you would hope to achieve in presenting the speech.

4. Make a list of appropriate sources for information about the topic you have chosen for your first speech.

5. Using the format discussed in this chapter, prepare an outline that organizes your speech so that it (a) opens with impact, (b) focuses on your thesis statement, (c) connects with your audience, (d) previews your main points, (e) organizes

your ideas with three to five main points, (f) summarizes your main points, and (g) closes with impact.

6. View a speech on video and then read a transcript of the speech. Both of the speeches transcribed in this chapter are on your SpeechCoach CD. After both reading and viewing the speech, write a short paper that answers the following questions: (a) What seemed to be the greatest strength of this speech? (b) What seemed to be the greatest weakness of this speech? (c) What differences did you note between reading a transcript of the speech and actually seeing the speech delivered?

Notes

1. Claudia Kalb, "Overexposed," *Newsweek*, 20 August 2001, 34–39.
2. The formula was originally developed by Dr. Loretta Malandro and is taught in her program "Speak With Impact," offered by Malandro Communication Inc., Scottsdale, Arizona. We have modified it to add a preview to the introduction.
3. George Kennedy, *The Art of Persuasion in Greece* (Princeton, N.J.: Princeton University Press, 1963), 283.

Although it may look funny, practicing in front of a mirror is a good way to begin managing speech anxiety.

Chapter

3

Managing Speech Anxiety

Objectives

After reading this chapter and reviewing the learning resources on your CD-ROM and at the Online Learning Center, you should be able to:

- Explain the relationship between arousal and anxiety.

- Distinguish speech anxiety from communication apprehension.

- Define anxiety and distinguish it from speech anxiety.

- Identify common sources of speech anxiety.

- Understand and use skills that have proved effective in controlling arousal and speech anxiety.

Key Concepts

communication apprehension

constructive self-talk

coping skills

negative self-talk

physical arousal

self-talk

speech anxiety

visual imagery

> " If your stomach disputes you—lie down and pacify it with cool thoughts. "
>
> –SATCHEL PAIGE

It often begins with butterflies in the pit of your stomach. Then your heart begins to palpitate. Your head starts to swim, making it difficult for you to concentrate, and a veil of perspiration begins to form on the palms of your hands. It may result from being asked to pinch-hit during a game of summer softball, from anticipating an important test you need to pass for your major, or from thinking about an interview for a needed internship. As pointed out in an episode of ABC television's *20/20,* however, for more than 40 percent of the adult population, these feelings are the result of people's anxiety about public speaking.[1]

Emotional and physical discomfort with public speaking has been called everything from stage fright and speech anxiety to shyness and communication apprehension. For our purpose, we'll call it speech anxiety. We define **speech anxiety** as the unpleasant thoughts and feelings aroused by the anticipation of a real or imagined speech in public.[2] It is different from stage fright because it concerns public speaking rather than acting. It is different from shyness because it is not the result of general discomfort with social situations. Further, it is different from communication apprehension because it affects at least twice as many people, and because highly communication apprehensive people are fearful about communicating interpersonally and in groups, not just in public.[3]

There is another important distinction between speech anxiety and communication apprehension. **Communication apprehension,** which is the fear of real or anticipated communication with others regardless of the situation, is difficult to change with skills training. In contrast, research shows that speech anxiety can be managed with mental and behavioral skills you can learn both inside and outside of your class.[4]

Seventy-five years of solid research have taught us much about the nature, effects, and constructive management of speech anxiety. In this chapter, we pass some of the most relevant research along to you, as well as the aforementioned skills. Topics discussed include (1) the physical and mental origins of speech anxiety, (2) how speech anxiety most commonly expresses itself in the speech process, and (3) the specific skills we can begin using to make our emotions work for us rather than against us before, during, and after our speeches. To assess your own level of communication apprehension and speech anxiety, fill out the scales in the box "How Anxious Are You About Public Speaking?" and follow the scoring guide when you are finished.

Physical Arousal and Speech Anxiety

The relationship between physical arousal and speech anxiety is paradoxical. When we speak of **physical arousal,** we mean the physical changes that occur when a person is aroused, such as an increased pulse rate, greater alertness, and more energy. Moderate arousal is necessary for everything from spiking volleyballs and kicking field goals to writing a good essay and delivering a powerful speech. The adrenaline charge from moderate arousal makes you more motivated and alert, energized, and ready to perform the activity at hand. A little arousal helps you to perform physical behaviors especially, but too much arousal can produce undesirable side effects (see Figure 3.1).[5] Too much arousal causes excessive adrenaline in the body, which can cause constricted muscles and vocal cords, rapid and shallow breathing, and light-headedness. Too much arousal also can make us feel weak

---

speech anxiety

The unpleasant thoughts and feelings aroused by the anticipation of a real or imagined speech in public.

communication apprehension

Fear about communicating interpersonally and in groups, not just in public.

physical arousal

The physical changes that occur when a person is aroused, such as increased pulse, greater alertness, and more energy.

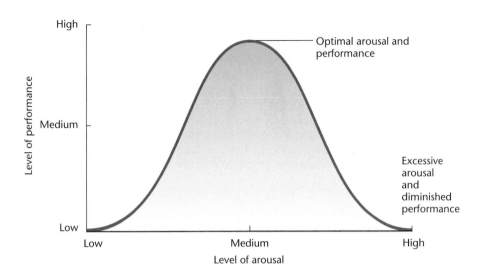

Figure 3.1
Arousal and
Performance

in the knees, make our hands tremble, and make it difficult to concentrate on the task at hand. Too much arousal, in other words, produces many of the signs that we commonly associate with being tense, nervous, and uncomfortable with the situation in which we find ourselves. As we approach the task of giving a public speech, the trick is not to make feelings of arousal disappear but to keep these feelings in check so that they do not unnecessarily interfere with the ability to speak effectively.

The Psychology of Arousal and Performance

The body does what the brain tells it to do. The body, moreover, does not distinguish what the brain communicates as real or imagined, exciting or terrifying. People sometimes cry out during a bad dream or jump in their seat during a scary movie because their imagination produces a physical response, even though they are not really in harm's way.

Such physical reactions to stimuli help us when we are actually threatened. For example, they help us get out of the way of an out-of-control car that jumps the curb onto the sidewalk where we stand. Our physical reactions also can help us fake out a would-be tackler as we break into the secondary while carrying the ball in a game of football. They can hinder us, however, when the threat is more psychological than real. For many people, the anticipation of and act of speaking are perceived quite negatively. Even though their physical well-being isn't truly threatened by the task of speaking, their highly negative view of the task causes their bodies to react as if it were. As a result, they may tremble, blush, and perspire. Such a reaction would be justified if they were running away from a knife-wielding attacker. But that is not the case. They are standing in front of a group of people who actually want them to succeed.

The key to overcoming this undesirable and illogical reaction is to find a way for people to alter their interpretation of the situation and their physical response to it. That may not be easy, but it can be done. In fact, thousands of people each year are able to go out in a crowd or give a speech because they have learned **coping skills** that help them control their fear of large groups or fear of speaking.

coping skills
Mental and physical techniques used to control arousal and anxiety in the course of speaking in public.

Roots: Why Some People Are More Anxious Than Others

As you can tell from the comments made by our own students in Table 3.1, not all people have the same reason for being anxious about speaking in public. The underlying sources of speech anxiety are varied. Still, research over the past three

_____ 17. While conversing with a new acquaintance, I feel very relaxed.

_____ 18. I'm afraid to speak up in conversations.

_____ 19. I have no fear of giving a speech.

_____ 20. Certain parts of my body feel very tense and rigid while giving a speech.

_____ 21. I feel relaxed while giving a speech.

_____ 22. My thoughts become confused and jumbled when I am giving a speech.

_____ 23. I face the prospect of giving a speech with confidence.

_____ 24. While giving a speech I get so nervous, I forget facts I really know.

Scoring

To determine your anxiety level, compute the following formulas. The higher your score, the more significant your level of anxiety. (The numbers in parentheses in the formulas refer to the numbered questions above.)

Group = 18 − (1) + (2) − (3) + (4) − (5) + (6)

Meeting = 18 − (7) + (8) + (9) − (10) − (11) + (12)

Dyadic = 18 − (13) + (14) − (15) + (16) + (17) − (18)

Public = 18 + (19) − (20) + (21) − (22) + (23) − (24)

Overall CA = Group + Meeting + Dyadic + Public

Making Sense of Your Score

Your combined score for all 24 items should fall somewhere between 24 and 120. If your score is lower than 24 or higher than 120, you need to recalculate it. A score above 83 indicates high communication apprehension; a score between 55 and 83 indicates moderate apprehension, which is the norm for most people. Low apprehension is anything less than 55. Your subscores indicate the degree to which you are anxious when speaking in public, talking in a group, or engaging in conversation with another person. These scores can range between 6 and 30. The higher your score is, the more anxiety you feel. A score above 18 on the public speaking subset suggests you feel a manageable level of speech anxiety. Regardless of your score on this subset, you can significantly benefit from the skills and techniques presented in this chapter. A score of 18 or above on the other two subsets also suggests you feel some anxiety about interpersonal and group communication.

Source: James C. McCroskey, _An Introduction to Rhetorical Communication,_ 7th ed. (Needham Heights, Mass.: Allyn & Bacon, 1997).

decades has given a good picture of the most common sources of anxieties about speaking in public. Further, recent studies reveal that the picture laypeople give for speech anxiety roughly corresponds to that uncovered in scholarly research.[6] College students much like you, for example, report that lack of preparation, the fear of making mistakes, appearance concerns, projections about audience interest, and lack of previous experience can feed speech anxiety. In a sense, these "reasons" reflect three stages in the process of becoming anxious. Stage one reflects concerns

Table 3.1
What Our
Students Say

> "In situations where the weight of the communication relies more and more on me, I become more nervous about speaking. When the discussion is dependent on more input from others, I feel less anxious about talking."
>
> "The situation doesn't matter. I think everyone is a little scared of public speaking."
>
> "I am involved in many group settings where I often enjoy sharing my opinion. I actually have a tendency to dominate conversations. However, when it comes to speaking in front of a large group of people, I tend to rush through the presentation and leave some information out."
>
> "In cheerleading I am able to perform with ease in amphitheaters filled with people while being on television. I see [speechmaking] as very different. In cheerleading we are able to practice the same routine over and over until it is so drilled in our heads we can do it without thought. Speaking in front of your peers as well as other people is different."
>
> "There are moments where I will be so nervous I sweat bullets and others where I do really well. I would say I am about normal."
>
> "I do get nervous and show a few nervous habits like moving my hands a lot or saying 'um' and 'and' too often. It greatly depends on the topic and the audience, naturally. If the topic is something I know about and understand well (especially if it is something I'm passionate about), I won't be nearly as nervous as if it were a topic I didn't feel completely knowledgeable on."

before speaking. Stage two reflects concerns that come up immediately before and during a speech. And stage three concerns what happens after speaking.

Stage One: Managing Anxiety Before We Speak

Many factors can preoccupy your mind and influence your behavior before you speak. Major ones include a pessimistic attitude, inadequate preparation and practice, negative or insufficient experience, unrealistic goals, negative self-talk, and misdirected concerns about what a speaker should focus on in preparing to speak. First we will discuss each of these sources of anxiety in turn. Then we will discuss two useful skills, visual imagery and relaxation techniques, that can help you manage your level of arousal.

Pessimistic Attitude

Though actual physical arousal is neither positive nor negative in itself, your perception of it can be either positive or negative. The box Thumbs Up, Thumbs Down shows that if you perceive and react to a situation positively, the arousal you feel will be perceived as a pleasant rather than an aversive sensation. What's more, it is not likely to exceed its optimal level. Conversely, if you perceive a situation negatively, you will perceive the arousal you feel as an unpleasant, even worrisome sensation. This increases the chances of arousal exceeding the optimal level for performance.

Research shows that the difference between being positively excited or negatively threatened by a situation such as public speaking is not a matter of arousal per se. It is a matter of how the arousal is initially interpreted. Consider riding a roller coaster. Some people love it; others hate it. If you were to measure arousal while people actually rode a roller coaster, however, you would find, in the beginning, very little difference in their level of physical arousal. But as the ride progressed and their positive or negative interpretation of the experience began to kick in, differences in arousal would begin to appear. So it is with public speaking. If we perceive it as an opportunity to become a more skilled communicator, chances are we will be able to maintain an optimal level of arousal before, during, and following our speeches. Of course, the reverse is also true. If we perceive public speaking as a task we prefer to avoid, or as an imagined threat to our well-being, we may begin to experience mental and physical signs of anxiety well in advance of speaking.

Inadequate Preparation and Practice

One reason for developing a pessimistic attitude about speaking is inadequate preparation and practice. Whereas most students would never dream of entering an athletic competition or taking a test crucial to their success in their major without preparation and practice, many seem to think that public speaking is different in this regard. So they put off preparing and practicing their speech until the last moment. Then they wonder why the act of speaking itself makes them nervous, prone to making mistakes, and negative about the overall experience.

Minimizing the importance of preparation and practice to the speaking experience only increases the amount of uncertainty surrounding the upcoming speech. Further, this uncertainty is a chief cause of the excessive arousal and anxiety that students begin to feel in the course of preparing to speak. Frequently, then, the real source of their discomfort when they actually do speak is a result of their own shortsightedness.

57

The difference between a "thrill ride" and a "chill ride" is a matter of perception, as is speech anxiety.

Sometimes students recognize the importance of preparation and practice but simply cannot confront the public speaking assignment. Much like writer's block, this aversion to preparing and practicing a speech occurs because students are afraid of what they'll feel when getting started. Perhaps they fear failure, or they just don't know where to begin. Whatever the reason, procrastination only postpones genuine speech anxiety. Procrastination also gives you less time to prepare. To avoid this vicious circle, we make the following two suggestions. First, choose the right topic. You should already know something about it, and you should be excited about it. This will help motivate you and keep you in a positive frame of mind. Second, overprepare. Always give yourself plenty of time to work on your speech. Make a commitment to become an expert on your topic. Then carry out the commitment with research that informs you. Don't be satisfied with knowing only enough about your topic to "just get by."

Practice delivering your speech well in advance of presenting it. Athletes practice much more than they formally compete. They realize there is a crucial connection between practice and performance on game day.

Negative or Insufficient Experience

Our prior experiences with any task influence how we approach and complete our present task. If our past experiences with public speaking proved both successful and personally rewarding, chances are we look forward to our speaking assignments in this class. But if our prior experiences with public speaking were unpleasant, we may harbor some doubt about our ability to succeed. Finally, if we have had little or no opportunity to speak in public, we may be mildly or even considerably anxious about speaking before a teacher and peers.

Our students report that their initial feelings of nervousness lessen once they start speaking.

The fact that your past efforts as a speaker were unrewarding, or even unpleasant, need not mean that your efforts in this class will prove likewise. The past need not dictate your future, assuming you are serious about becoming an effective speaker. Be realistic about your previous experience. You didn't learn to read and write overnight. Chances are you received a few psychological bumps and bruises in the process. You cannot expect to be an overnight speaking sensation either. It takes commitment and effort. Thus, the fact that your previous experience with speaking was unpleasant does not mean that you cannot become an effective speaker by the end of this class.

By the same token, the fact that you think you have had little experience with the skills necessary for effective public speaking shouldn't make you overly anxious. Just as running is an extension of walking, public speaking is an extension and refinement of the communication skills you put to use daily. Through your class and this book, you can learn to successfully extend your everyday communication skills to the task of speaking in public.

Unrealistic Goals

Another common source of anxiety for beginning speakers involves the goals they set for themselves. Though it is important to set high goals, they should also be realistic. Unrealistic goals can lead to irrational fears about the speaking situation. Research shows that people who set realistic goals for themselves are less anxious and more successful than their counterparts with unrealistic goals.[7] This finding has also been reported in studies of elite athletes, businesspeople, and students enrolled in public speaking courses.

Speech-anxious students often hurt themselves by establishing goals that are not only unrealistic but also well beyond their reach or commitment. They tell themselves that despite their inexperience and unwillingness to make their speech class a priority, they must be the best in their class or get A's exclusively. Such illogical and unrealistic goals, the research shows, harm much more than help students in coping with their speech anxiety.

Negative Self-Talk

Closely aligned with the problem of unrealistic personal goals is the more widespread problem of self-defeating patterns of self-talk before the speech transaction. **Self-talk,** or communicating silently to yourself, is natural before you speak, while you speak, and even after you speak. However, it is neither natural nor helpful to beat up on yourself verbally in this process. **Negative self-talk,** a self-defeating pattern of intrapersonal communication, is common among people who report that they experience speech anxiety.[8] Negative self-talk can result from several causes, including the following:

- Worrying about factors beyond your control, including how other students are preparing for their speeches
- Dwelling excessively on negative past experiences with public speaking
- Spending too much time thinking about the alternative approaches you might take in preparing your speech
- Becoming preoccupied with feelings of mental and physical anxiety, such as the inability to concentrate as you try to prepare for your speech
- Thinking about the worst and usually most unlikely consequences of your speech—people laughing at you or ridiculing your speech
- Having thoughts about or feelings of inadequacy as a public speaker

Such negative thinking usually leads to three specific types of negative self-talk: self-criticizing, self-pressuring, and catastrophizing. Let's look at each.

Self-Criticizing

Though realistic self-evaluation is important in self-improvement, it is well documented that many of us verbally question our self-worth or communication skills without sufficient cause. Without much evidence at all, we say negative things about ourselves, including that we're stupid and hopeless when it comes to speaking.

Not only students but people in all walks of life tell themselves they are poor speakers. Many of them do so despite the fact that they have never received any training in public speaking and have had few if any opportunities to speak in public. Their lack of skill doesn't justify their self-criticism.

Self-Pressuring

We also bring undue and added pressure on ourselves through our self-talk, never once thinking about whether such added pressure will help us to perform better. We tell ourselves, for example, that we must be "the best speaker in the class" without first considering why. As it is, all students invariably experience moderate pressure and arousal when speaking publicly. Moderate pressure can help them reach the optimal level of arousal needed to deliver their speeches effectively. If they feel no pressure at all, they will lack the motivation to properly prepare and prac-

self-talk
Communicating silently with oneself (sometimes referred to as intrapersonal communication).

negative self-talk
A self-defeating pattern of intrapersonal communication, including self-criticizing, self-pressuring, and catastrophizing statements.

tice. However, telling themselves that they must be the best speaker in class, or that their speech has to be perfect, can add unnecessary and harmful pressure with which they will be unable to cope. Such added pressure, in fact, is like throwing fuel on a raging fire!

Catastrophizing

We often blow things out of proportion when talking to ourselves. We project that the consequences of our actions are likely to be far more drastic than is realistic. Anxious public speakers can be guilty of the same thing. For example, they may tell themselves that an upcoming speech is the worst assignment they have ever had. Or they may convince themselves that the low grade they are bound to receive will keep them out of graduate school.

As is the case with unrealistic goals, this kind of self-talk increases arousal and speech anxiety. The more negative our self-talk about the ultimate outcome of our speeches, the more probable it is that we will exceed our optimal levels of arousal.

Misdirected Concerns

Finally, some research suggests that students who are highly anxious about speaking express very different concerns about an upcoming speech than do those who are only moderately anxious. For example, researchers found that highly anxious students were most concerned with how they would be evaluated, how long they should speak, what specific topic they should choose, whether they could use notes, and how much time they had to prepare.[9] In short, these students were concerned primarily with immediate factors that affect how they will be evaluated in the classroom situation. These concerns are classic signs of mental anxiety. Moreover, they suggest that truly anxious students may be so preoccupied with their misdirected concerns that they may neglect the preparation of their actual speech.

These researchers also found that students who reported little anxiety about speaking were most concerned with factors that would enable them to successfully attain their goals as speakers. In fact, these are the kinds of issues that even professional and highly paid speakers want to know about—for instance, the arrangement of the room, the availability of a microphone, and whether the audience would ask questions. To get a clearer idea of the concerns that make you most anxious, see the box "What Are the Sources of Your Speech Anxiety?"

Tips and Tactics

Before Speaking

If you are overly anxious before you speak, it's likely you will be even more so when you are actually called on to speak. Fortunately, there are some helpful tips you can follow to moderate your before-speaking anxiety.

 **Speech**Coach
To hear more about these Tips and Tactics, go to Audio Tips and Tactics on your CD.

• Be realistic about your goals and write them down. Becoming an effective speaker is a process. The goals for your first speech should be different from those you write down before your second and third speeches. Regardless of which speech you are making, your goals must be grounded in your potential to improve as a speaker, as well as how much effort you are willing to make to realize your potential.

Self-Assessment

What Are the Sources of Your Speech Anxiety?

Listed below are common sources of speech anxiety. As you read each item, consider how much it contributes to the anxiety you experience about public speaking. Rate each item on a scale of 1 to 10, from least important to most important.

SOURCES OF SPEECH ANXIETY	LEAST IMPORTANT/MOST IMPORTANT									
	1	2	3	4	5	6	7	8	9	10
Your attitude toward speaking	__	__	__	__	__	__	__	__	__	__
Lack of preparation and practice	__	__	__	__	__	__	__	__	__	__
Previous experiences with speaking —lack of or bad experiences	__	__	__	__	__	__	__	__	__	__
Unrealistic goals	__	__	__	__	__	__	__	__	__	__
Perception of your audience as hostile or unsympathetic	__	__	__	__	__	__	__	__	__	__
Negative self-talk	__	__	__	__	__	__	__	__	__	__
Misdirected concerns with how you will be evaluated	__	__	__	__	__	__	__	__	__	__

Rearrange the items in order of importance. Use this hierarchy to better understand the sources of your speech anxiety. What steps can you take to address and change your patterns of thought and behavior?

1. _____
2. _____
3. _____
4. _____
5. _____
6. _____
7. _____

- Be realistic about the comparisons you make between your abilities as a speaker and those of your classmates or outside speakers whose skills you admire. Becoming an effective public speaker is a process. Give yourself time to improve before you start comparing yourself to others.
- Inventory your routine self-talk as you prepare to speak. Note what kinds of things you routinely say to yourself and ask yourself: Do these statements make me more or less anxious about my speech? Substitute negative statements you routinely make with **constructive self-talk** modeled after the examples in Table 3.2.
- Consult with your instructor about your concerns and the degree to which they are valid. Don't assume your instructor shares your beliefs about what is and isn't essential to your success. Finally, do not fall victim to the misguided idea that you will appear stupid if you seek your instructor's counsel.

constructive self-talk
The use of positive coping statements instead of negative self-talk.

Table 3.2 Constructive Self-Talk Before You Speak

Prior to Practice	Actual Practice	During Behavioral Rehearsal
Get off to a good start: Prepare early . . . don't put it off.	Time for some imagery.	Use my coping statements.
This will be good for me.	Let's run through this in my mind's eye.	Speak slowly and clearly.
I like this topic.	Visualize the opening and hear myself sharing the thesis statement.	First work on knowing content.
Rough outline first . . . there's time to polish later.	Visualize connecting with the audience and previewing main points.	Okay, now I know it.
I have plenty of information.	Okay, hear and see myself make each point.	Make eye contact with people.
I bet my information will be pretty new to my classmates.	Try to see myself from the audience's point of view.	Speak conversationally.
I've uncovered a lot of interesting facts.	Visualize the summary and close.	Have fun with it.
Lay it out logically.	Try it again, but this time use relaxation imagery too.	Be myself but under control.
Time to rewrite.		

There are at least two other skills you can use in advance of speaking: (1) visual imagery and (2) relaxation techniques. These skills are excellent complements to the preceding tips and deserve additional comment.

Visual Imagery

Visual imagery is another way to rehearse your speech. It is the process of mentally seeing (imagining) yourself performing an action or a series of actions. Instead of practicing your speech out loud, you visually imagine yourself confidently and successfully giving the speech. Visual imagery is widely practiced in archery, baseball, basketball, football, golf, gymnastics, hockey, kayaking, skiing, and snow boarding. Athletes who use visual imagery include golfer Tiger Woods, quarterback Peyton Manning, and professional ice skater Kristi Yamaguchi. Visual imagery is part of the practice routines of whole teams as well. During the 2004 NCAA Baseball World Series, for example, the TV commentators repeatedly talked about how California State University, Fullerton's team had been taught to use both positive self-talk and visual imagery. Despite their lackluster 18–19 season start, moreover, they won the Collegiate World Series, sweeping number one seeded Texas in three straight games.

More to the point of this book, however, is the case of Dr. Loretta Malandro. The founder of a successful communication-consulting firm, Dr. Malandro travels worldwide as a professional speaker. One of the things she tries to do before each speaking engagement is to visually imagine herself giving the speech. Even if it means getting up before dawn, for example, she tries to run five miles and visualize her upcoming presentation as she runs. Because Dr. Malandro does this routinely,

visual imagery
The process of mentally seeing (imagining) oneself confidently and successfully performing an action or a series of actions.

she sees not only herself as she shares her message but also the positive feedback she is receiving from her audience.

Because it is yet another way to reduce your uncertainty about an upcoming speech, visual imagery can also assist you in controlling your level of anxiety and arousal. This technique works best when you are in a relaxed state and familiar with the content of your speech. It involves controlled visualization of your actual speaking situation, which will require practice on your part. The idea is to see yourself during all phases of your speech. For example, you might first visualize yourself seated at your desk, relaxed but appropriately aroused as you wait your turn to speak. Next, you might visualize yourself leaving your desk, moving to the front of the room, confidently facing your audience, and introducing your speech. From here on, you would visualize yourself speaking—moving, gesturing, and making eye contact with individual members of your audience right up to your conclusion. Finally, you would see your audience and teacher enthusiastically responding to your presentation. Once you become adept at visualizing, you can even add sound to the picture in your mind's eye. Hearing yourself take command of an audience as you turn a phrase or smoothly make a transition from one point to another will enhance the impact of visual imagining.

Visual imagery works best as a complement to actual practice. Study after study shows that visual imagery actually enhances behavioral rehearsal.[10] As a result, you will want to include it as part of your preparation and practice routine.

Making Effective Use of Relaxation Techniques

As discussed earlier, butterflies, a racing heart, trembling hands, and weak knees are the result of the excessive adrenaline that is pumped into our systems when we are overly aroused. One of the best ways to prevent these symptoms is to condition our bodies to relax in situations that are, characteristically, overly arousing. You can accomplish this in one of several ways.

Exercising before you speak is a great way to manage the stress and anxiety you feel in anticipation of speaking.

Exercise

The first way to help your body relax is to engage in some form of intense exercise one to two hours before you speak. The effects of physical exercise on physical and mental well-being are well known. Intense exercise assists us in decreasing signs of stress and has been linked to improved thinking and performance, regardless of the task.

Relaxation Imagery

If exercise is either inconvenient or impractical, another way to induce relaxation before speaking is to use relaxation imagery. Imagery is not the same as merely thinking. Imagery involves pictures, whereas thinking is a verbal process. Relaxation imagery involves visualizing pleasant and calming situations. Lying in a hammock or on the beach during a warm summer day are two examples of such pleasant and calming situations. If you were to visually linger on such situations, you would find your body becoming increasingly relaxed. As a result, you would significantly lower the level of arousal customarily felt as a result of the day's activities.

This latter point is important. As a busy college student, you may find your upcoming speech to be the most significant but not the sole source of arousal you experience during the day. By practicing relaxation imagery before you speak, you can reduce the arousal that began to climb with the start of your day.

Muscular Relaxation

This technique involves systematically tensing and relaxing the various muscle groups, as is visually demonstrated on your CD. It usually begins with the muscles in your face and neck, then gradually moves to your middle and lower torso. The idea behind this technique is to teach your body the difference between tension and relaxation. By first tensing and then relaxing your muscles systematically, you can also condition your muscles to relax even under the most stressful circumstances.

There's a good reason for practicing muscular relaxation. When we tense up, the range of movement in our muscles is restricted. They don't work as they are intended. In a game of basketball, this is seen when a free-throw shooter hits the front of the rim, loses "touch," or puts up an air ball. With a speaker, this is evident either in the absence of movement or gesturing or in movement and gesturing that are awkward and unnecessary.

SpeechCoach

For an example of relaxation techniques, see segment 3.1 on your CD.

Combining Techniques

By combining relaxation with visual imagery, you can enhance the effectiveness of both techniques. You will come to associate the speaking situation with relaxing images rather than anxiety-producing ones.

These techniques also work best when they become a habitual routine that you practice as you prepare to speak. Elite athletes don't use them only before they are about to compete; speakers shouldn't put off using them until the night before they speak. The research is clear. These techniques will serve you well only if you commit to their systematic use.

Stage Two: Managing Anxiety During Your Speech

Some of the same factors that give rise to pessimism before a speech also undermine the speech transaction itself. Negative self-talk frequently plagues speakers as they speak. But there are other factors we haven't discussed, for example, inaccurate perceptions of the audience and unjustified concerns about appearance.

The Audience

A recent study confirms that many beginning speakers view their audience as hostile toward them.[11] They convince themselves that the members of their audience are just waiting for them to trip over their feet, lose their train of thought, blow a quotation, or mumble through a sentence. Along the same lines, it is not uncommon for beginning speakers to read into the nonverbal feedback they receive from their audience such false conclusions as "they're bored to tears" or "they think I'm terrible." This is anything but the case, of course. Audiences, with rare exception, want speakers to succeed and are silently rooting for them to do so. Plus, research shows that audiences actually underestimate the level of anxiety experienced by speakers.[12]

In recognition of this fact, consider the case of the late Mary Martin, a well-known and highly praised stage actress who first popularized the Broadway productions of *Peter Pan* and *Annie Get Your Gun*. She used to do something before a performance that you may wish to try. Just before going on stage, she would close her eyes, take a deep breath, and say 100 times to herself, "I love my audience." Next she would repeat the process, but this time tell herself, "My audience loves me."

Beginning speakers also may convince themselves that their audience expects more from them than they can deliver. Such expectations about an audience can easily become a self-fulfilling prophecy. The students you face are in the same boat with you and want you to succeed as much as you do. If you still need convincing, consider how you feel when you are a member of an audience gathered to watch a public performance. Do you silently root for the performer to fail miserably? Do you take perverse joy in seeing the performer make an obvious mistake? Do you expect more from the person than he or she could ever deliver? We didn't think so!

As our student Katie Reid shows, appropriate dress can enhance a speaker's confidence and credibility.

Appearance

This is an appearance-obsessed culture. We are not so naïve as to recommend that you try to convince yourself that appearance is unimportant. However, we do recommend that you try to be reasonable in this regard. Although you cannot transform your body type or radically alter your appearance for your speech class, you can dress appropriately for the occasion. All too often we see students in our own classes whose inappropriate dress detracts unnecessarily from what they hope to say. They become self-conscious in the process, increasing their chances of becoming overly anxious.

Appropriate dress enhances your credibility. It also can help you feel more confident. Both are positive outcomes, ones that should reduce rather than increase feelings of speech anxiety. Thus, the easiest way to overcome concerns about your physical appearance is to dress for the occasion. But you may be asking yourself, "What constitutes appropriate dress in my public speaking class?" We asked our generally younger and unquestionably hipper teaching associates to answer

Do's	Don'ts*
Pants Skirts	Shorts Minis Low-riding jeans
Collared shirt Full-length blouse Sweater	T-shirt Tank-top Tube top or strapless top Midriff-baring top Sweats
Business shoes	Athletic shoes flip flops
Groomed hair	Ball caps or hats
Tasteful jewelry or accessories	Bling-Bling

Table 3.3
Fashion Do's and
Don'ts for Classroom
Speeches

*Exceptions where the apparel is part of the presentation

this question for us. They came up with what we perceive to be a reasonable and realistic set of guidelines, summarized for you in Table 3.3.

Self-Talk

Just as we use self-talk before a speech, we may also talk to ourselves as we actually deliver a speech. Again, we want to avoid negative self-talk in this regard. It's important to note that your audience will not be nearly as critical of you as you will be of yourself. Your audience is also less likely to pick up on mistakes than you are, because they don't know your speech like you know it. When you make mistakes, which even the most polished speakers do, avoid criticizing yourself. Refrain from saying such things as, "Way to go, stupid," or, "Why am I screwing up?"

Instead, as you speak, try to use statements such as those suggested in Table 3.4. These *process statements* will help to keep you in the moment and on track. They will also help to keep your mind from wandering or dwelling on minor mistakes your audience probably did not catch.

Tips and Tactics

While You Speak

- Take time to get comfortable before you start to speak. Take a couple of deep breaths, make eye contact with a friendly face, and smile. Also take a shoulders-width stance and try to stand tall.

- Don't obsess on your audience. Important as the audience is to your success, you need to keep their importance in perspective. Remember that your audience wants you to succeed and that the audience is uncomfortable when you are uncomfortable.

- Dress appropriately for the occasion. Not only will it help make you feel more confident, but it will also increase your credibility with your audience.

- If you engage in self-talk, follow the advice in Table 3.4. Talk to yourself about what's going well. Tell yourself that you are okay and that your audience is with you.

SpeechCoach
To hear more about these
Tips and Tactics, go to Audio
Tips and Tactics on your CD.

Table 3.4
Constructive Self-Talk
During Your Speech

Get comfortable.
Speak slowly.
I know my speech.
I was nervous to start, but I've calmed down.
It's okay if I'm not perfect.
The audience is interested in what I have to say.
This is easier than I thought.
Make eye contact.
Just like I practiced.
So far so good.
Don't rush it.
Time to summarize.
Take your time.
Not bad . . . not bad at all.

- Avoid reading "too much" into the feedback you receive while speaking. Not every cough or squint or wrinkled-up nose or furrowed brow is meant to "tell you" how you are doing. Also, the whispering between the two discourteous people at the back of the room is not about your appearance or your speech.

- Avoid overreacting to what you *perceive* to be negative feedback. Not only are we predisposed to notice it more than positive feedback, but we also tend to overcompensate by paying more attention than they deserve to the one or two people we *think* are negative.

- Remember, even if you are a little nervous, the research tells us your audience won't notice it as much as you will.

Stage Three: After Your Speech

Even experienced speakers can find themselves in a mental fog following their speech. They may find it hard to concentrate or stay focused on the comments directed toward them.

FOXTROT © 1995 Bill Amend. Reprinted with permission of Universal Press Syndicate. All rights reserved.

That wasn't half-bad.	**Table 3.5**
Find my seat.	Constructive Self-Talk
Smile, take some deep breaths.	After You Speak
Don't forget to take notes from the feedback I get.	
Talk with my instructor.	
Don't forget the "did well" and "room to improve" list.	
Go back over the speech tonight in my mind's eye.	
Write down goals for next time.	

What takes place after a speech will affect the way you approach and deliver your next speech. Comments directed to you by peers and your instructor can help you prepare your next speech, including: (1) the goals you set, (2) preparation and practice, and (3) your level of confidence as you take on these tasks. Constructive comments cannot help you, however, if you fail to hear and process them in the first place.

To get the most out of immediate feedback following a speech, we offer the following tips.

Tips and Tactics

After Speaking

- Take several deep breaths when you go back to your seat. This will help to bring down your heart rate.
- Minimize self-talk. You can mentally review your presentation later.
- Look for your instructor's eye contact and tell yourself to relax as you listen to your instructor and classmates.
- Write down what is said. You can check with your instructor later to determine the accuracy of the feedback you recorded.
- Within 24 hours review the entire process, and make a list with two columns: (1) things I did well and (2) areas where I realistically can improve. Refer to this list as you prepare for your next assignment.
- Practice self-talk patterned after the statements you see in Table 3.5.

 SpeechCoach

To hear more about these Tips and Tactics, go to Audio Tips and Tactics on your CD.

Summary

Speech anxiety is a result of our subjective interpretation of the arousal we experience when called on to speak publicly. Although some degree of arousal is necessary to prepare and deliver an effective speech, too much of it can lead to psychological side effects, such as excessive worry, and physical side effects, such as trembling hands. Too much arousal can lead to a debilitating level of speech anxiety. Managing speech anxiety involves the following:

 SpeechCoach

To evaluate your understanding of this chapter, see the Quizzes on your CD.

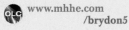

www.mhhe.com /brydon5

Visit the Online Learning Center for helpful study resources, including practice tests, key term crossword puzzles, and PowerWeb articles for research and review.

- Developing a positive attitude toward speaking

- Committing to practice and preparation and avoiding procrastination

- Replacing negative self-talk before, during, and following a speech with constructive self-talk

- Establishing realistic goals given your commitment to your class

- Recognizing and accepting the fact that your audience wants you to succeed

- Focusing on what you and your instructor agree are important considerations in the development and delivery of your speech

- Combining visual imagery with behavioral rehearsal

- Combining imagery with relaxation techniques

- Making the preceding skills and techniques part of your routine before, during, and after a speech

Check Your Understanding: Exercises and Activities

SpeechCoach

For a review of key terms in this chapter, see the Key Terms Flashcards on your CD.

1. In a short paper, describe the relationship between physical arousal and speech anxiety and give examples of both physical and mental symptoms of anxiety. Be sure to define anxiety and distinguish it from speech anxiety.

2. The chapter lists six common sources of speech anxiety and steps for controlling them. For your next speaking assignment, identify at least one such source of anxiety that concerns you and make an effort to remedy it. For example, if you have a tendency to procrastinate, make sure you start your speech sooner than usual. After the speech, assess how the remedy worked in alleviating at least one source of public speaking anxiety.

3. Before your next speech, make a list of the negative self-talk you have engaged in regarding speech assignments. Then come up with a series of constructive self-talk statements you will use in preparing for and while giving your next speech. Your instructor may ask you to turn in your list before you speak.

4. Two of the most convenient relaxation techniques you can use are relaxation imagery and muscular relaxation. Both initially require a quiet place and time where you will not be interrupted. This exercise allows you to practice relaxation on your own or with a friend. It is sometimes useful to have someone read the steps to you so that you can completely relax.

   a. Find a reclining chair or couch where you can make yourself comfortable.
   b. Lower or turn off bright lights.
   c. With your eyes closed, tense and then relax your muscles in this order: face, neck and shoulders, biceps and triceps, forearms, wrists and hands, chest, solar plexus, buttocks/hamstrings, quadriceps, calves, ankles and feet.
   d. Once you are completely relaxed, imagine a peaceful setting in which you feel calm. Learn to hold this image for as long as you can. After a minute or two, move on to the next step.
   e. Imagine your speech class. If you feel any sign of anxiety, return to the preceding image.

f. Continue to imagine your speech class and add yourself to the picture. See yourself calmly seated, enjoying others as they speak.

g. See yourself writing down the requirements of an assigned speech. See yourself involved with the various stages of preparation, including seeing yourself practice.

h. See yourself waiting to be called on, aroused but not anxious.

i. See yourself walking to the front of the room, turning to face your audience, smiling, and opening your presentation with impact.

j. See yourself speaking energetically, gesturing, and using your eyes, face, and voice.

k. See students and your instructor listening attentively.

l. See yourself concluding and your audience responding with genuine applause.

Practice this series of steps at least twice a week for 15 to 25 minutes each time. Remember, any time you begin to feel anxious during this exercise, replace whatever image you're holding with a pleasant and relaxing one.

Notes

1. *20/20*. ABC Television, 20 June 1990. Bruskin Associates, "What Are Americans Afraid Of?" The Bruskin Report 53 (July 1973).

2. J. A. Daly and J. C. McCroskey, eds., *Avoiding Communication: Shyness, Reticence and Communication Apprehension* (Beverly Hills, Calif.: Sage, 1984).

3. Karen K. Dwyer, "The Multidimensional Model: Teaching Students to Self-Manage High Communication Apprehension by Self-Selecting Treatments," *Communication Education,* 49 (2000): 72–81; Lynne Kelly and James A. Keaton, "Treating Communication Apprehension Anxiety: Implications of the Communibiological Paradigm," *Communication Education,* 49 (2000): 45–57. Research on this chapter's topic is ongoing; as a result, we have used multiple sources to support our claims. Some of these sources represent very early research, but others alert you to more contemporary research.

4. Michael J. Beatty and Kristen Marie Valencic, "Context-Based Apprehension Versus Planning Demands: A Communibiological Analysis of Anticipatory Public Speaking Anxiety," *Communication Education,* 49 (2000): 58–71. Ralph R. Behnke and Chris R. Sawyer, "Milestones of Anticipatory Public Speaking Anxiety," *Communication Education,* 48 (1999): 165–71.

5. R. M. Yerkes and J. D. Dodson, "The Relation of Strength Stimulus to Rapidity of Habit Formation," *Journal of Comparative Neurology and Psychology,* 18 (1908): 459–82.

6. Amy M. Bippus and John A. Daly, "What Do People Think Causes Stage Fright? Naïve Attributions About the Reasons for Public Speaking Anxiety," *Communication Education,* 48 (1999): 63–72.

7. William J. Fremouw and Michael D. Scott, "Cognitive Restructuring: An Alternative Method for the Treatment of Communication Apprehension," *Communication Education,* 28 (1979): 129–33; William J. Fremouw and M. G. Harmatz, "A Helper Model for Behavioral Treatment of Speech Anxiety," *Journal of Consulting and Clinical Psychology,* 43 (1975): 652–60.

8. Albert Ellis and Robert A. Harper, *A New Guide to Rational Living* (Hollywood, Calif.: Wilshire Book Company, 1975).

9. J. A. Daly, A. L. Vangelisti, H. L. Neel, and P. D. Cavanaugh, "Pre-Performance Concerns Associated With Public Speaking Anxiety," *Communication Quarterly,* 37 (1989): 39–53; J. A. Daly, A. L. Vangelisti, and D. J. Weber, "Speech Anxiety Affects How People Prepare Speeches: A Protocol Analysis of the Preparation Process of Speakers," *Communication Monographs,* 62 (1995): 383–97.

10. Fremouw and Scott, "Cognitive Restructuring"; Fremouw and Harmatz, "A Helper Model for Behavioral Treatment of Speech Anxiety."

11. T. Freeman, C. R. Sawyer, and R. R. Behnke, "Behavioral Inhibition and Attribution of Public Speaking State Anxiety," *Communication Education,* 46 (1997): 175–87.

12. C. R. Sawyer and R. R. Behnke, "Behavioral Inhibition and the Communication of Public Speaking State Anxiety," *Western Journal of Communication,* 66 (2002): 412–22.

On September 11, 2001, police, firefighters, and rescue workers risked their own lives to save others in a display of the highest ethical principles.

Ethical Speaking

Objectives

After reading this chapter and reviewing the learning resources on your CD-ROM and at the Online Learning Center, you should be able to:

- Demonstrate an understanding of the differences among ethical relativism, universalism, utilitarianism, and situational ethics.

- Apply ethical principles to a variety of different public speaking situations.

- Explain plagiarism and the role of attribution in avoiding plagiarism.

- Explain and apply the basic ethical obligations of both speakers and listeners.

Key Concepts

categorical imperative

cultural relativism

ethical relativism

ethics

goodwill

good reasons

plagiarism

situational ethics

trustworthiness

universalism

utilitarianism

❝ The time is always right to do what is right. ❞

–MARTIN LUTHER KING JR.[1]

Tom Burnett and other passengers on Flight 93 sacrificed their own lives to save countless others from terrorists, who intended to use the plane as a weapon.

On September 11, 2001, Thomas Burnett Jr., was onboard United Airlines flight 93. He was heading home from the East Coast to San Ramon, California, where he was chief operating officer of Thoratec Corp., a medical research and development company. He'd been scheduled to depart from Newark Airport on a later flight but was able to change his booking to get home to his wife, Deena, and three daughters sooner by taking United Airlines Flight 93. Of course, as we all know, Flight 93 never made it to California. It was hijacked by terrorists bent on destroying an American landmark. Unlike the three other planes hijacked that day, however, Flight 93 never reached its intended target. Rather, it crashed in rural Pennsylvania. As Burnett told his wife in the last of four cell phone calls made from the plane, he and other passengers had decided to retake the plane from the hijackers, knowing that they would undoubtedly lose their own lives but would prevent an attack on another American landmark, killing many more innocent citizens. Although his wife told him to "sit down and not draw attention to himself," he said, "no."[2]

How Burnett and other passengers resisted the hijackers, resulting in the plane plummeting to its destruction and killing all aboard, will forever remain a mystery. But what we do know is that they sacrificed their own lives for the greater good—to save the lives of countless others. In acting decisively, they embodied the highest of ethical principles, sacrificing their own good for the greater good.

Their sacrifices were the first of many spawned by the tragedies of September 11, 2001. Hundreds of police, firefighters, and rescue workers in New York City risked and even lost their lives trying to rescue victims in the World Trade Center. They entered the buildings at great risk to their own lives, and many were lost when the buildings collapsed around them.

These courageous acts not only represented heroism but also exemplified the highest principles of ethical conduct, the topic we focus on in this chapter.

Reading this chapter won't make you a hero, but it can further your understanding of what it means "to do the right thing" in general, and in the public speaking transaction specifically. Clearly *unethical behavior* is reported daily in our media, and it is easy to become confused about the principles that underscore ethics and the practice of these principles in daily life. As a result, we begin our discussion with some basic questions that repeatedly come up when discussing ethics. In the process of exploring these questions, we also introduce some of the thinking that has been advanced on the topic of ethics by history's best minds. Following this initial discussion, we then show how ethics can guide us in the development as well as delivery of our speeches and in our role as consumers of the information shared in the speeches of others.

Basic Ethical Questions

Ethics is a system of principles of right and wrong that govern human conduct. Ethical standards and practices should not be viewed as all-or-nothing propositions. In fact, there are degrees of ethical behavior, ranging from highly ethical to totally unethical.[3] To get a better grip on this latter fact, let's look at a number of important questions philosophers have been pondering for at least 2,000 years, beginning with the relevance of such an "old" subject to modern life.

Why Care About Ethics?

We live in a world where many people take to heart mottos such as "win at all costs" or " I'm spending my children's inheritance." So why should we look out for anyone's interests but our own? For example, why should we think or care about the fact that the shoes we wear were constructed by illiterate kids in another country for less than 50 cents a day or that the campaign commercial we just watched for a candidate contained half-truths at best?

For starters, we should care about ethics because, in the long run, ethical practices are in our own self-interest. We benefit from physicians being trained to "first do no harm," police informing us of our constitutional rights before interrogating us, and laws protecting against discrimination because of our gender or the color of our skin.

On the flip side, we owe those who behave ethically toward us the same in return. This kind of reciprocity, in fact, is a major ingredient in the social glue necessary to build relationships and communities of people bound by a common purpose: for example, the public speaking class in which you're currently enrolled. Can you imagine the consequences if everyone in your class lived by a different set of rules for developing and presenting speeches? Do you think you would be comfortable speaking in your class if there were no ethical guidelines for the audience about cell phones, talking during speeches, or blurting out opinions about what you say even as you say it?

Ethical practices, then, are to everyone's benefit. When we are treated ethically it increases the chances that we will treat others in kind. The payoff is a more cohesive, caring, and civil society in which to live and learn.

But there is yet another reason for us to look at the nature of ethical conduct as it relates to public speaking. Ethical behavior gives rise to trust. Perceptions of trustworthiness, moreover, influence the degree to which people actually believe what we have to say to them and vice versa. In a very real sense, then, the chances of our public speeches actually informing or influencing our audience depend on whether we are perceived as ethical *and* trustworthy.

Is Everything Relative?

Ethical relativism is a philosophy based on the belief that there are no universal ethical principles. This theory goes back at least as far as the Sophists, who believed that truth was relative and depended on circumstances.[4]

ethics
A system of principles of right and wrong that govern human conduct.

ethical relativism
A philosophy based on the belief that there are no universal ethical principles.

Even within cultures, expectations about dress and appearance can vary, as can be seen in this photo of a Palestinian couple where the woman does not cover her head.

The most radical version of relativism asserts that any one person's ethical standards are as good as the next person's. Although this philosophy has the advantage of simplicity, it makes a civilized society impossible. Life would be, essentially, a free-for-all. When a group of people holds such a radical view, the consequences for society are potentially disastrous. After all, the Nazis believed they were entitled to enslave and kill Jews and other "undesirables."

Yet, many people endorse, or, say they believe in, **cultural relativism,** the notion that the criteria for ethical behavior in one culture should not necessarily be applied to other cultures. This was the position of the Sophist Protagoras, who argued that moral laws are based on the conventions of a given society. Examples of such differences among cultures are easy to find. (See the box "Culture and Credit" for one.) So, too, is controversy. Consider polygamy, which usually involves a man having more than one wife. In the United States, polygamy is not only seen as immoral by most people, it is also against the law. Yet polygamy is practiced openly in parts of Arizona and Utah by a small number of people who believe it is consistent with their religious beliefs.

cultural relativism
The notion that the criteria for ethical behavior in one culture should not necessarily be applied to other cultures.

Similarly, there are cultural differences in ethical standards governing communication. One such difference involves the extent to which people should be "brutally honest" in certain situations. In collectivist cultures, "saving face" is important to the good of all society, so people are often indirect and may stretch the bounds of truthfulness in certain situations. To do either in an individualistic culture such as that of the United States could be regarded as unethical communication. Can either culture claim superiority over the routine communication practices of the other? Not really.

At the same time, there are limits to what most people will accept as culturally relative ethics. Even within a society, customs change over time as people reexam-

Considering Diversity

Culture and Credit

It is sometimes surprising to speakers who come from a traditional Euro-American background that practices they take for granted as being acceptable are held to be morally wrong in other cultures. For example, taking out a loan for college expenses, a car, or a new wardrobe is routine for most Americans. However, those who practice the religion of Islam may find such practices morally unacceptable. As reporter Fahizah Alim explains in an article about a Sacramento, California, restaurant owner, Khaled Umbashi, many Muslims view the interest charged today by banks as *riba* (usury), which is forbidden by the Quran. Umbashi refuses to borrow money to improve or advertise his restaurant because "his Islamic religion forbids him from borrowing the funds and paying interest on that loan. . . . 'Our Islamic religion prohibits paying or charging compounded interest,' says Umbashi, a native of Libya."

Not all Muslims agree with this interpretation of the Quran. For example, Asghar Aboobaker, a Muslim who has written on the topic, holds that "this is a very complicated issue, and there are many, many camps." On the other hand, Irfan Ul Haq, a Muslim businessman, economist, and author, believes, "Much of the world's financial crisis has to do with the interest based system."

Thus, although most of those raised in a Western culture find nothing wrong with borrowing money, some Muslims consider such a practice not just unwise but morally objectionable.

We mention this story because we have heard countless speeches on topics that involve credit or paying interest on a loan. We actually heard a student boast in a speech how he capitalized on the "bull market" by using money from student loans to purchase stock. This student emphasized that with a rate of return of 22 percent on one stock pick, he was making 14 percent on the $5,000 student loan on which he was being charged 8 percent interest.

Clever as our stock-wise student was, his ethics might be questioned by students in general. Certainly the Muslim students in his audience were given pause by his speech.

Knowing and respecting culturally diverse moral principles is often essential to your success in a culturally diverse society.

Source: Fahizah Alim, "No Credit: For Muslims, Asking for a Loan Is a Question of Religion," *Sacramento Bee,* 29 August 1998, Scene, 1, 3.

---

ine their ethical values. Human sacrifice was once a routine part of some religions, yet no one today would consider such behavior ethical. Less than a century and a half ago, a significant number of Americans believed that slavery was ethical and gave their lives to defend the institution. About 65 years ago, during World War II, American citizens of Japanese ancestry were interned in "relocation" camps. What makes one culture or one time period ethically superior or inferior to other cultures or other times? Or is it all relative?

We need to be careful not to exaggerate cultural differences, however. Philosophy professor James Rachels, for example, points out that different cultures often agree on underlying principles but disagree on how they are to be applied. For example, he notes that even apparently inhumane practices, such as that of the early Inuit, who once left the elderly to die in the snow, are grounded in the need of the family to survive in a harsh environment. Rachels argues that "the Eskimos' values are not all that different from our values. It is only that life forces upon them choices that we do not have to make."[5]

Are There Rules for Every Situation?

An alternative to ethical relativism is **universalism,** the philosophy that there are ethical standards that apply to all situations regardless of the individual, group, or culture. Immanuel Kant, an 18th-century philosopher, developed such a philosophy. He proposed the **categorical imperative:** *"Act only on that maxim through which you can at the same time will that it should become a universal law."*[6] To will the

universalism
The philosophy that there are ethical standards that apply to all situations regardless of the individual, group, or culture.

categorical imperative
Immanuel Kant's ethical principle that we should act only in a way that we would will to be a universal law.

maxim be universally applicable means that you would want everyone to obey the same rule as you are proposing.

Suppose, for example, that you think it's acceptable for anybody to lie at any time, so you propose, as a universal rule, that lying is permissible for any reason. What would the result be? Lies would deceive no one because lying had become the rule. Thus, a universal law that lying is permissible would in fact make lies ineffective. Consider voting as another example. You might think you don't need to vote because your own vote doesn't make a difference. But imagine that as a universal rule: "Since individual votes don't matter, voting is unnecessary." If not voting were a universal rule, democracy would collapse. So Kant gives us a test for specific ethical rules. To be an ethical principle, a rule or maxim must be capable of being applied universally.

One of the most important ethical rules that Kant proposed relates directly to the public speaker. Kant proposed the maxim _"Act in such a way that you always treat humanity whether in your own person or in the person of any other, never simply as a means, but always at the same time as an end."_[7] One practical implication of this maxim is that speakers should treat audience members with respect, not simply as a means of achieving their goals. Conversely, audience members should respect and treat speakers as fellow human beings, not as objects of derision. Obviously, then, tactics that deceive or demean either an audience or a speaker would be unacceptable.

Kant's categorical imperative is not without drawbacks. Consider truth telling. If lying is unacceptable in any circumstance, innocent people may suffer as a consequence. Miep Gies, for example, lied to authorities throughout World War II to protect the Jews she was hiding from the Nazis, including a young girl named Anne Frank. And this isn't an isolated example. History is replete with cases demonstrating that it's sometimes better to bend the truth to fit the situation.

Of course, one can reformulate Kant's rule and say people shouldn't lie except under certain circumstances, such as when necessary to save lives. But that creates another problem: How do we know which actions fall under these conditions? Rachels points out a key problem with Kant's universalism: "For any action a person might contemplate, it is possible to specify more than one rule that he or she would be following; some of these rules will be 'universalizable' and some will not. . . . For we can always get around any such rule by describing our action in such a way that it does not fall under that rule but instead comes under a different one."[8] To examine your own principles, see the box "When Is It Acceptable to Lie?"

Does the Good of the Many Outweigh the Good of the Few?

Another ethical standard, utilitarianism, was proposed by English philosophers Jeremy Bentham, John Stuart Mill, and Henry Sidgwick. **Utilitarianism** is based on the principle that the aim of any action should be to provide the greatest amount of happiness for the greatest number of people. These philosophers sought the greatest good for the greatest number. And they specifically defined the good as that which creates happiness—"not the agent's own greatest happiness, but the greatest amount of happiness altogether."[9]

> **utilitarianism**
> The philosophy based on the principle that the aim of any action should be to provide the greatest amount of happiness for the greatest number of people.

This certainly is a useful standard for the public speaker. Most topics on which you will speak are about choices and trade-offs. If we trim social spending to fund a tax cut, some people will suffer while others will benefit. If we crack down on crime and build more prisons, there will be less money for schools and colleges. What constitutes the greatest good for the greatest number? As a speaker, you have an obligation to your audience to thoroughly research your subject to determine what position will ensure the greatest good and to put that greatest good ahead of mere personal gain. If you fail to fully inform your audience of the facts, if you lie to or deceive them, how can *they* rationally decide what will promote the general good?

Utilitarianism, of course, has its critics. Many would say it promotes ethical relativism. After all, if the greatest good for the greatest number means that some minority of people are oppressed, would not utilitarianism justify that oppression? Could not a Hitler rationalize his extermination of the Jews in the name of the greater good for all of Germany? Certainly that is not what the utilitarians contemplated. But critics of utilitarianism have a point. Seeking the greatest happiness for all does not guarantee that particular individuals will not suffer unjustly.

If you think these issues are mere philosophical musings, think about the controversy surrounding the use of embryonic stem cells in basic research. A growing body of scientific data suggests that stem cell research could very well lead to effective treatments for Parkinson's disease, multiple sclerosis, and paralysis resulting from injury to the spinal cord. Because this research involves the use of embryonic cells from fertilized human eggs, however, many people consider it immoral and therefore unethical. Should the convictions of people who count themselves in this latter group be ignored because they are in a minority? Not only is this a very real dilemma, but it is one that is politically charged as well.

How Do Specific Situations Affect Ethical Principles?

Another approach to ethics is known as **situational ethics.** According to this philosophy, there are overriding ethical maxims, but sometimes it is necessary to set them aside in particular situations to fulfill a higher law or principle, such as love.

> **situational ethics**
> The philosophy that there are overriding ethical maxims, but that sometimes it is necessary to set them aside in particular situations to fulfill a higher law or principle.

As one writer put it, "What acts are right may depend on circumstances . . . but there is an absolute obligation to will whatever may on each occasion be right."[10]

Situational ethics is particularly useful in explaining how what appears to be the same kind of act can be ethical in one case and unethical in another. For example, most people agree that giving a classroom speech written by someone else is unethical. The principle that a student should do his or her own work is embedded in American education. At the same time, no one expects Jay Leno to write all of his own jokes or the president of the United States to write all of his own speeches. In those situations, everybody knows that Leno has comedy writers and the president has ghostwriters.

Critics of situational ethics argue that this is just relativism in another guise and thus provides no criteria for ethical judgment.[11] However, situationists do not contend we should abandon all ethical principles. As ethicist Joseph Fletcher writes: "The situationist enters into every decision-making situation fully armed with the ethical maxims of his community and its heritage, and he treats them with respect as illuminators of his problems. Just the same he is prepared in any situation to compromise them or set them aside *in the situation* if love seems better served by doing so."[12]

One problem with situational ethics, however, is that it would allow the use of unethical means to achieve ethical goals.[13] That brings us to our final question.

Do the Ends Justify the Means?

You may have heard the old saying "The ends don't justify the means." This means that it is not acceptable to do something wrong just because it will produce a good result. Of course, some people will use a good result as the justification for behavior normally considered immoral. But to do so raises serious ethical concerns. As a speaker you need to concern yourself with ends (goals) as well as the means you use to achieve them.

In terms of ends, many of your topics are likely to be about issues of right and wrong, morality and immorality, the weighing of the good of the many against the good of the few. Understanding how people make ethical decisions is important to your choice of topic and the goals you seek. Obviously, the first and foremost ethical obligation of any speaker is to seek ethical ends: that is, to make sure you are striving to achieve a goal that is ethical and just. So, as you choose your topics, adapt to your audience, and seek to fulfill your goals as a speaker, you should always focus on accomplishing ethical ends.

Not only should your goals be ethically sound, but how you seek to reach those goals should also be ethical. Good ends should never, for example, justify withholding the true purpose of a speech from our audience. Suppose we want to raise money to improve the medical care received by impoverished children in a third world country. Suppose, too, that the missionary arm of a controversial religious group would administer the money we raised. Should we reveal this in our speech, knowing that we have atheists and agnostics in the audience who would be less favorably disposed to donate if made aware of who would administer the money?

Consider our earlier example regarding stem cell research. Would a speaker raising money for the Muscular Dystrophy Society be justified in not telling the audience that some of the money could be used to fund stem cell research? It's not an easy question to answer, is it? But it is exactly the kind of question we need to ask ourselves when weighing the ends we seek with a public speech.

Speaking of . . .

Codes of Conduct for Public Speaking

Although it is not a full-fledged ethical code, such as those found in law and medicine, the National Communication Association's Credo for Free and Responsible Communication in a Democratic Society forms an important touchstone for the ethical public speaker. Other guidelines that may be of help to the public speaker are found in the American Advertising Association's Code of Ethics, the Code of Ethics of the International Association of Business Communicators, and the Public Relations Society of America's Code of Professional Standards for the Practice of Public Relations.[1]

Credo for Free and Responsible Communication in a Democratic Society[2]

Recognizing the essential place of free and responsible communication in a democratic society, and recognizing the distinction between the freedoms our legal system should respect and the responsibilities our education system should cultivate, we the members of the National Communication Association endorse the following statement of principles:

We believe that freedom of speech and assembly must hold a central position among American constitutional principles, and we express our determined support for the right of peaceful expression by any communicative means available.

We support the proposition that a free society can absorb with equanimity speech which exceeds the boundaries of generally accepted beliefs and mores; that much good and little harm can ensue if we err on the side of freedom, whereas much harm and little good may follow if we err on the side of suppression.

We criticize as misguided those who believe that the justice of their cause confers license to interfere physically and coercively with the speech of others, and we condemn intimidation, whether by powerful majorities or strident minorities, which attempts to restrict free expression.

We accept the responsibility of cultivating by precept and example, in our classrooms and in our communities, enlightened uses of communication; of developing in our students a respect for precision and accuracy in communication, and for reasoning based upon evidence and a judicious discrimination among values.

We encourage our students to accept the role of well-informed and articulate citizens, to defend the communication rights of those with whom they may disagree, and to expose abuses of the communication process.

We dedicate ourselves fully to these principles, confident in the belief that reason will ultimately prevail in a free marketplace of ideas.

[1]Richard L. Johannesen, *Ethics in Human Communication,* 4th ed. (Prospect Heights, Ill.: Waveland Press, 1996), chap. 10.

[2]Used by permission of the National Communication Association.

Ethical Norms for Public Speakers

Developing standards for ethical public speaking is not an easy task. Probably the closest thing to a code of conduct for public speakers is the National Communication Association's Credo for Free and Responsible Communication in a Democratic Society, reprinted in the box "Codes of Conduct for Public Speaking." More than by any specific code of conduct, however, ethical public speakers are guided by the traditional standards of rhetoric that date back more than 2,000 years. Sophists were known for their philosophical relativism. Some Sophists carried this philosophy to its logical extreme, arguing that virtually any rhetorical deception was justified if it furthered their cause.[14]

Such philosophical relativism ran counter to the philosophy of Socrates, who taught that absolute truth was knowable through a question-and-answer technique known as dialectic. Socrates' student Plato wrote two dialogues, the *Gorgias* and the *Phaedrus,* that promoted this Socratic view of rhetoric. To Plato, rhetoric, as practiced by the Sophists, was a sham, with no truth to it, designed to deceive listeners. In the *Phaedrus,* Plato proposes an ideal rhetoric, one based on philosophical truths. The basic function of this rhetoric is to take the truth discovered through dialectic and energize it for the masses.

The best-known response to Plato came from his student Aristotle, whose *Rhetoric* is probably the most influential book on communication to this day. To Aristotle, rhetoric was not the opposite of dialectic but rather its counterpart. Aristotle did not view rhetoric as either moral or immoral. Rather, it was an art that could be put to both good and bad uses. The moral purpose of the speaker was the determining factor. Aristotle believed that "things that are true and things that are just have a natural tendency to prevail over their opposites."[15] Therefore, he stressed the importance of training in rhetoric. Even arguing both sides of a question was not immoral; rather, it was a way of learning how to refute someone who misstates the facts on the other side of an issue. For Aristotle, in sum, rhetoric was an art, not a sham.

In the 1st century A.D., the Roman orator and rhetorician Quintilian provided an ethical standard that many emulate to this day. To Quintilian, the ideal citizen-orator is a good person, speaking well. As he put it, "Oratory is the science of speaking well."[16] Further, because no one "can speak well who is not good,"[17] the moral quality of the speaker is not irrelevant. Rather, it is central to the ideal orator.

Today, the issue of ethical standards for public speaking has once again become a central concern for communication educators. What constitutes ethical communication? Most of us would agree that speakers should not lie or distort the truth. Beyond that, however, what are the moral obligations of speaker to audience and audience to speaker? Based on the work of the philosophers discussed, as well as several communication scholars, we suggest the following norms or guidelines for the public speaker: (1) Be truthful. (2) Show respect for the power of words. (3) Invoke participatory democracy. (4) Demonstrate tolerance for cultural diversity. (5) Treat people as ends, not means. (6) Provide good reasons. Let's look at each of these more closely.

Be Truthful

James Jaksa and Michael Pritchard of Western Michigan University have developed a set of ethical norms for speakers. Three of these seem particularly relevant to us. The first is the norm of truthfulness, which is fundamental to all communication.[18] The speaker caught in a lie loses his or her credibility and the goodwill of the audience, which are essential to belief. As domestic diva Martha Stewart learned, sometimes the lie can be worse than the initial offense. Ironically, Martha Stewart was convicted not of insider trading, a crime for which she was never charged, but for lying to investigators about her well-timed sale of ImClone stock. Had she simply told the truth, no matter how painful, she would never have been charged with a crime.[19]

Of course one does not have to tell an outright lie to deceive listeners. As we discuss in more detail in Chapter 15, distortions and omissions can sometimes be as harmful to the truth as outright lies. If you doubt that, we invite you to check out the "facts" in many political ads. Although most are based on a kernel of truth, often what's left out changes the whole meaning of the ad. We recall one political challenger who showed a video clip of the incumbent saying, "I'll do anything to get reelected." What the ad failed to mention was that the incumbent was playing the part of the challenger! The video clip was edited to reflect the exact opposite of the meaning intended by the incumbent. Of course the ad didn't lie outright—the words were actually said—but because the context was omitted, the result was the same as a lie.

All too often inflammatory words incite unethical behavior.

A speaker who is unsure of the facts must learn the truth before speaking. Even a speaker who is simply misinformed, not consciously lying, must be held accountable. History is full of examples of people who were given the chance to speak and pass on information they believed to be factual but later was proven wrong. The most recent involved the claim by politicians that Saddam Hussein could launch weapons of mass destruction within 45 minutes and that he was in league with Osama bin Laden and al Qaeda. Both claims turned out to be questionable, although each was repeatedly stated in public as if it were irrefutable. This is not to say that the removal of Hussein wasn't positive, but not all of the reasons given as justification for his removal turned out to be true.

Show Respect for the Power of Words

Another norm cited by Jaksa and Pritchard is respect for the word.[20] The power of words is undeniable. Sometimes this power runs head-on into the First Amendment. At college campuses across the nation, student body governments and faculty senates have been forced to wrestle with the concept of "hate speech." Where does freedom of speech on a college campus end and hate speech begin? Like many of the questions raised in this chapter, this one is not easily answered. Do hurtful words constitute hate speech? Do words that marginalize groups of people or derogate their character constitute hate speech? Is hate speech similar to obscenity in the sense that "it's difficult to define, but you know it when you see or hear it?"

Although freedom of speech is central to our democracy, the courts have recognized that there are limits. As Chief Justice of the Supreme Court Oliver Wendell Holmes Jr. once said, freedom of speech does not give you the right to shout "fire!" in a crowded theater. Although Justice Holmes was speaking metaphorically, the principle he was expressing is as relevant to the current debate about speech codes as it was nearly a century ago. The fact that you can say almost anything that comes to mind in this country doesn't make the content of what you say either ethical or wise. The old saying "Sticks and stones can break my bones, but words can never hurt me" is rubbish. In fact, words are very powerful and can cause great harm as well as great good. The ethical speaker recognizes that words have consequences.

Invoke Participatory Democracy

Jaksa and Pritchard discuss the importance of participatory democracy, which rests on a foundation of choice and respect for people.[21] Citizens must have accurate and ample information to make informed choices. Further, the golden rule of treating others as we would have them treat us applies to public speaking as well as to interpersonal communication. Speakers should put themselves in the shoes of listeners and ask if they are treating them as they would like to be treated. The ethical speaker recognizes the audience as an equal participant in the communication transaction. Similarly, listeners need to show respect and tolerance for speakers, even if the speakers' views are different from their own. Shouting down a speaker, for example, infringes on the speaker's freedom of speech and the public's right to hear a full spectrum of viewpoints.

In other words, ethics in communication is a joint responsibility. For example, there have been many complaints in recent years about negative and deceptive political advertising. Yet political consultants say they are only giving the public what it wants. Although that is no ethical defense for their behavior, we must also realize that deceptive advertising succeeds only because voters fail to protest against it and continue to vote for candidates who engage in such practices.

Demonstrate Tolerance for Cultural Diversity

Clearly, what people regard as ethical or unethical depends a great deal on their culture and corresponding set of beliefs. It is difficult for people to avoid using their own culture's ethical standards when judging the behavior of people in another culture. In North America, for example, we generally like people to be "up front" with us: that is, to communicate honestly and directly, even if we don't like the message. We generally don't want people to beat around the bush on matters we personally perceive as significant.

But what we call beating around the bush is the norm in many cultures around the world. Physicians, businesspeople, and even family members may be less than direct or forthright in their transactions with each other. In Japan, physicians and family members commonly hide the truth from a terminally ill patient. They believe that telling the truth in this case will undermine the power of the person's mind to intervene and perhaps divert the disease's course.

Some cultures, groups, and individuals are more tolerant of diversity than others. Ethical speakers recognize that the customary criteria they use in making ethical judgments may be inappropriate in judging the behavior of people from other cultures. This tolerance guides ethical speakers in both interpreting and responding to the communication behaviors of those who are culturally dissimilar to them. Tolerance is not synonymous with unconditional approval, however. Ethical speakers may tolerate ethical norms with which they disagree, but they may also engage in constructive dialogue with the individuals who follow those norms.

Treat People as Ends, Not Means

To these principles we wish to add one taken from Kant: namely, that people should never be treated as mere means to an end. Their best interests should be the ends sought by the speaker. Using people as objects, manipulating them even to achieve desirable ends, is never justified. Consider the case of the now defunct *Jenny Jones Show,* a TV talk show. In 1994 Jones invited people to go on the air and meet their secret admirers. What the producers didn't tell these people, however, was that these secret admirers could be heterosexual, gay, or lesbian. You may recall the tragic results of this attempt to "entertain" the viewing audience. One guest discovered that his secret admirer was gay and later stalked and murdered the admirer.

Of course the guest's tragic overreaction was also unethical and far out of proportion to the deception perpetrated by Jones. Nevertheless, the television show was widely criticized as having gone too far. Embarrassing people on national TV as a means of simply building program ratings is clearly unethical.

Provide Good Reasons

Another principle of ethical speaking has been articulated by Karl Wallace, scholar and former president of the Speech Communication Association (now known as the National Communication Association). Wallace believes that the public speaker must offer his or her audience "good reasons" for believing, valuing, and acting.[22] **Good reasons** are statements, based on moral principles, offered in support of propositions concerning what people should believe or how people should act. Wallace believes that ethical and moral values, as well as relevant information, are the basic materials of rhetoric. Speakers who rely on "good reasons" value all people and the ethical principles to which they adhere. Not only does the use of good reasons help ensure that the speaker uses ethical means, it is also far more likely to be successful in accomplishing the ethical ends sought by the speaker.

good reasons
Statements, based on moral principles, offered in support of propositions concerning what we should believe or how we should act.

Special Issues for Speakers

As a public speaker, you face some special issues that might not be as relevant in other communication situations. A speech is a uniquely personal event. Unlike a written essay, for example, in which the author may be unknown to the reader, a speaker stands as one with his or her words. In fact, Aristotle said that character "may almost be called the most effective means of persuasion" possessed by a speaker.[23] Five important issues need to be addressed, therefore, because of their special significance for public speakers: (1) plagiarism and source attribution, (2) building goodwill and trustworthiness, (3) revealing or concealing true intentions, (4) discussing both sides of a controversial issue, and (5) inducing fear.

Plagiarism and Source Attribution

Plagiarism—stealing the ideas of others and presenting them as your own—is highly unethical. What makes it a particular sin for speakers is that they are jeopardizing their most important asset—their character. Few students begin their speech assignment intending to plagiarize. But other pressing assignments, poor time management, sloppy note-taking, or just plain laziness often intervene.

plagiarism
Stealing the ideas of others and presenting them as your own.

Students are tempted to use someone else's words or ideas without credit, assuming that no one will be the wiser. The consequences of such behavior can be severe. An example from the authors' own experience illustrates what can happen.

One of our teaching associates (we'll call him Jack) was ill and asked another TA (Jane) to cover his class. It happened that one of the students in Jack's class was the roommate of a student in Jane's. When Jane heard the same speech in Jack's class that she had heard earlier in the week in her own section, bells went off. Of course, it turned out that one roommate had appropriated the other student's speech. The plagiarizer was caught red-handed, but it didn't end there. The original speech writer was guilty of aiding and abetting the roommate. Both students had to face disciplinary action from the university as well as failure in the class.

Although it's true, of course, that this act might have gone undetected had Jack not become ill, this is not the only way plagiarism is discovered. At our university, and we suspect this is true at others as well, professors often talk about speeches they have heard in class. In fact, every speech at our university is recorded on videotape. Over the years, we have discovered several instances of plagiarism. Each time the students have been shocked and repentant. They have come to realize that they have put their college careers at risk for a few extra points on a speech. The negative consequences of plagiarism are not confined to students. Plagiarism can also destroy a reputation or even a career.

How can you avoid plagiarism? First, you need to recognize that there are varying degrees of the offense. Because plagiarism is a form of theft, we call these variations "the total rip-off," "the partial rip-off," and "the accidental rip-off."

The Total Rip-Off

The case of the roommates who used the same speech is an example of a total rip-off. Here a student simply gives someone else's speech. Usually it is not a speech from a published source, because such speeches don't often fulfill the assignment. Further, if the speech is well known, it is likely to be spotted instantly as a phony. More common is the use of a speech from a classmate who took the class in a previous term or who is in another section. This is clearly academic dishonesty equivalent to cheating on an exam or turning in someone else's term paper. Most universities and colleges suspend or even expel students caught in this sort of dishonesty. If the speech was knowingly given to the plagiarist, the original author can face the same penalties.

Avoiding this type of plagiarism is easy: Don't offer a speech or accept the speech of another person to present as your own. Most students who use other students' speeches do so out of desperation. Our advice is not to put off writing your speech until the last minute. Give yourself as much time to research and prepare as you would to write a paper for an English class. Realize also that giving a speech you don't really know is likely to be a disaster. You will stumble over words and be unable to answer questions. Even if you escape detection, you'll do yourself little good. If you simply cannot get a speech ready to deliver on time, talk to your instructor. Policies will vary, but your own speech, given late, even with a penalty, is far superior to a ripped-off speech given on time.

The Partial Rip-Off

More common than the total rip-off is the partial rip-off. Here a student creates a speech by patching together material from different sources. Rather than quoting the sources, the speaker presents the ideas as if they were original. The irony is that the speaker has done a lot of work. The problem was not that time ran out. Rather, the speaker wanted to be credited with the ideas.

The way to avoid this type of plagiarism is to give credit to your sources orally and to make sure that you use material from these sources only to enhance your own speech. Rather than simply using the words of another, tell the audience who made the statement or where the idea originated. Interestingly, research has shown that under many circumstances, citing sources in your speech enhances your persuasiveness.[24] Audiences are impressed that you have done your homework. It is important to cite sources as you speak, not just in the bibliography of your written outline. Only by citing sources orally can you inform your audience of where the words, phrases, and ideas came from, which is what you need to do to build your credibility as a speaker.

Citing sources is important for direct quotations as well as for specific facts, statistics, and ideas derived from the work of others. Thus, you might not quote Martin Luther King Jr. directly, but you would still refer to him as the author of the idea that people should be judged by their character, not their skin color.

The Accidental Rip-Off

Perhaps the most frustrating thing for an instructor who discovers a student's plagiarism is when the student simply doesn't understand what he or she has done wrong. For example, a student may take significant ideas or even quotes from sources listed in a bibliography accompanying the speech, without saying so in the speech. The student sees no problem, responding, "I did cite my sources—they are right there in the bibliography." For the listener, however, there is no way to know which ideas came from outside sources and which are the speaker's own, as mentioned in the previous section. A common variant of this is that the speaker attributes ideas to a source but actually uses a word-for-word quotation without making that clear to the audience. The written version of the speech outline should include quotation marks to distinguish between paraphrased ideas and direct quotations. Further, you should use "oral" quotation marks. Either state that you are quoting someone, or make it clear from your tone of voice that you are in fact quoting someone else's words. Use such phrases as "To quote Martin Luther King Jr. . . . ." or "As Martin Luther King Jr. said . . . ."

Try not to let ideas become disassociated from their source. We've all had the experience of remembering an idea or a quote but forgetting where we heard it. Unfortunately, the tendency in a speech is just to use the words. By taking careful notes as you research your speech, you are less likely to accidentally borrow an idea from another source without attribution.

The Internet

Although we deal at length with the use and abuse of the Internet in Chapter 7, we feel duty bound to caution you about the temptations of the Internet. Cyberspace is not only the preferred source of information among students as they prepare their speeches, it also is the source of most of the plagiarism we find in student speeches. Given the sheer amount of information available, it might seem to some that it's nearly impossible for an instructor to find out where a student's ideas and language originated. Think again: It is not only possible, it gets easier by the day.

Whether a full-scale rip-off, an incremental theft, or an accidental violation, plagiarism is a serious ethical offense for the public speaker. Our best advice is to resist the temptation, cite the sources of your ideas for your audience, and take pride in those ideas that are your own. In Chapter 7 we discuss how to record and cite sources in a speech. But the general principle is to let your audience know exactly where your ideas are coming from.

Building Goodwill and Trustworthiness

A speaker's credibility has several components. Two of the most important are goodwill and trustworthiness, which we introduced earlier. **Goodwill** is the perception by the audience that a speaker cares about their needs and concerns. A speaker who truly cares about his or her audience's needs, and who can communicate that to the audience, not only is more likely to be effective but also is much more likely to behave ethically. There is a huge difference, for example, between the speaker who is trying to put one over on the audience and the speaker who really cares about the well-being of the audience. If speakers apply the principle developed by Kant of treating people as ends and not means to ends, then that is a mark of goodwill.

goodwill
The perception by the audience that a speaker cares about their needs and concerns.

Trustworthiness is the perception by the audience that they can rely on a speaker's word. A promise made is as good as done. The effect on a speaker's trustworthiness of a broken promise or a revealed lie is devastating. In recent years, there has perhaps been no clearer example of the importance of telling the truth than President Clinton's problems following his categorical denial in January 1998 of having had "sexual relations with that woman, Monica Lewinsky." His subsequent televised admission of an improper relationship following his Grand Jury testimony fell short of an admission that he had lied, and it was followed by numerous attempts at public contrition. Clinton ultimately became only the second president ever impeached in the history of the United States. The allegations of perjury and obstruction of justice were not proven, however, and Clinton was not removed from office by the Senate. One reason politicians in general are held in such low regard by the public is that so many of them have broken their promises and become untrustworthy in people's eyes.

trustworthiness
The perception by the audience that they can rely on a speaker's word.

As a speaker, you need to realize that you rarely can accomplish your purpose in one speech or even in a short series of speeches. Often your goals will require a long-term commitment. And your relationship to your audience needs to be one of trustworthiness. If you violate their trust, not only have you behaved unethically, you have jeopardized your chances of achieving your goals as well. The solution to this problem is twofold. First, don't make promises you cannot or do not intend to keep. And second, if circumstances might require you to deviate from prior promises, make it clear what limits there are on your promise.

Revealing or Concealing Intentions

One of the thorniest issues you face as a speaker is whether or not to reveal your intentions to your audience. Sometimes, to begin your speech by announcing a position that you know your audience drastically opposes is to deny yourself the opportunity to be heard. On the other hand, to conceal your true intentions can be unethical, particularly if those intentions violate what the audience perceives as its best interests. In some ways, this decision requires the application of "situational ethics." Consider a couple of examples.

You are speaking to a potentially hostile audience about a controversial issue. Let's say you want to convince a group like the Moral Majority that we should not have state-sanctioned prayer in school. Should you begin by announcing your position? What is the likelihood that your argument would be heard? On the other hand, suppose you begin by describing a scenario in which the state requires everybody in school to study the Quran and pray to Allah. "How would you react?" you ask them. "Well, now reverse the situation," you continue. "What if Muslim students are required to study the Bible and say the Lord's Prayer?" The idea would be to work from a common ground–that Christians should not be forced to pray to a Muslim God–to the logical application of that principle to the issue of state-sanctioned school prayer.

Certainly this approach is no guarantee of persuading the audience of your viewpoint. But it is hard to argue that it is ethically wrong to begin with points of agreement before moving to areas of disagreement. The intentions of your speech are revealed to the audience. When and how those intentions are revealed is a strategic rather than an ethical issue.

On the other hand, consider the case of the person who telephones and asks you if you would be willing to participate in a survey about energy conservation. Sure, you reply, always happy to help out. After going through a series of questions, you realize that the "pollster" is actually a salesperson for a replacement window company. Your time has been wasted, and now you have to figure out how to get off the phone. The clear misrepresentation of intent–pollster as opposed to salesperson–is ethically wrong. And you have been harmed, if for no other reason than the salesperson stole your time. And, as many sellers know, once they get your ear, the likelihood of closing the sale increases.

What makes these two cases different? Both people begin by concealing their intentions, and both eventually do reveal their goals. But in the first case, the speaker does not misrepresent his or her intentions; rather, they are deferred until after some common ground is established. In the second case, a direct misrepresentation is made–there is no poll. While the two cases seem on the surface to be similar, we would argue that the situations are far different and that that difference is ethically relevant.

These types of cases are not always easy or clear-cut. A universal rule–always state your purpose up front–cannot be applied. Speakers must sincerely ask themselves in what ways their interests and those of their audience intersect. They must then decide the best approach to take in any given case, at the same time striving to maintain goodwill and trustworthiness.

Discussing Both Sides of a Controversial Issue

One question with both ethical and practical implications is whether you should provide an audience with only your side of an issue or mention arguments on the other side of the issue as well. For a number of years, speech experts answered this question pragmatically: It depends on the makeup of your audience. If the general level of education in your audience is high school or less, stick to your side only. If the level of education in your audience is beyond high school, introduce the other side as well. Of course this raises some real ethical concerns. It smacks of using the audience as a means rather than treating them as ends. Basically, it says if you can fool enough of the people, no need to worry about fooling all of them.

The authors have never thought much of the recommendation to present only one side of an issue. What's more, we now have research on our side. This research, which combined the findings of more than 25 studies done over the past four decades, suggests that speakers should use a two-sided persuasive message regardless of the audience's level of education. Specifically, the most effective persuasive strategy is to present both sides of a controversial issue along with a refutation of the opposing point of view.[25] If you think about it, this makes good sense. In general, your audience will have heard or will eventually hear the other side of the story. What does it do to the audience's perception of your credibility if they believe they've not been told the whole truth? Two-sided presentations are not only more ethical, they are also more effective. We discuss the issue of "message sidedness" in more detail in Chapter 14.

Inducing Fear

Speakers have used fear as a motivational tool throughout history. When used in moderation by a credible source, contemporary research tells us that fear appeals can influence what people think and how they behave. Used ethically, fear appeals are simply another rhetorical device speakers can build into their messages.

The research also shows, however, that when people are fearful they do not always think clearly or reason critically. Thus they are more susceptible to believing false claims and half-truths spoken by speakers who know they are vulnerable in this regard. Such behavior is clearly unethical, but the practice of inducing fear to make people compliant is also quite common.

As a remarkable book, *The Culture of Fear: Why Americans Are Afraid of the Wrong Things,* by Professor Barry Glassner documents, we are being made unnecessarily fearful for our personal safety by two primary sources: news media and politicians.[26] Local TV news media devote far more coverage to violent crimes and accidents than to any other topic. This trend gives rise to the impression that our local communities pose a greater threat to our personal safety than they actually do. During election cycles, politicians exploit this false impression by emphasizing the promise to be "tough on crime."

We think speakers should use fear appeals only when the personal safety of their audience is genuinely at risk. What constitutes a genuine risk may be debatable, but speakers should build fear appeals into their messages only after a legitimate, evidence-based debate has been held. To do otherwise is unethical at best.

Tips and Tactics

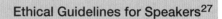

Ethical Guidelines for Speakers[27]

 **Speech**Coach
To hear more about these Tips and Tactics, go to Audio Tips and Tactics on your CD.

- Provide truthful, relevant, and sufficient information to allow audience members to make informed choices.

- Present "good reasons," not just those that may work. Appeal to the best, not the worst, in people.

- Reinforce and be consistent with democratic processes. Recognize the importance of free speech in a democratic society and the right of others to disagree.

- Demonstrate goodwill and trustworthiness toward the audience.
- Put yourself in the position of the listeners and treat them with the same respect you would expect were the roles reversed.
- Recognize that both the means and the ends of a speech should be ethical. Be concerned with the possible consequences of accepting the message as well as with its truthfulness and accuracy.
- Take responsibility for your own work. Plagiarism is the ultimate in intellectual dishonesty.

Ethical Norms for Listeners

People who find themselves in the primary role of listeners also need to think about their ethical obligations. Remember, audience members are very much a party to the public speaking transaction. When you are a listener, you too bear some responsibility for the consequences of the speech. Thus we suggest these norms for ethical listening: (1) Be civil. (2) Take responsibility for the choices you make. (3) Stay informed on the issues of the day. (4) Speak out when you are convinced that a speaker is misinforming or misleading people. (5) Be aware of your own biases.

Be Civil

When we go to the movies at our local Cineplex, we are usually treated to a set of rules that appear on the screen prior to the featured film. These rules basically tell us not to talk to our companions during the film, make sure our cell phones and pagers are turned off, and if in the company of a child who becomes a behavior problem, to retreat to the lobby out of respect for other audience members. Maybe we need to post a similar set of rules in our classrooms. Every new term it seems as if we have to single out audience members for one or more of the preceding infractions. It is as embarrassing for us as it is embarrassing for them. Moreover, it should never have to happen. The first ethical responsibility of audience members is to be civil to the speaker and other audience members. It is tough enough for people learning to become more effective speakers to manage their presentations without the added distraction of people talking or a cell phone "accidentally" ringing.

Take Responsibility for Choices

The second guideline for listeners is to recognize that unless coerced, they are responsible for the choices they make during and following a communication transaction. This means listeners cannot blame a speaker for the decision to riot following a speech or for violating human rights because they were persuaded to do so by a charismatic communicator. Just as the judges at the Nuremberg trials following World War II concluded that "following orders" was not an excuse for war crimes, audience members cannot excuse their unethical behavior on the grounds that they were complying with a speaker's request.

Advertisers frequently use men and women as sex symbols to promote smoking, even though the practice is both exploitive and unethical.

Stay Informed

A third guideline, which logically follows from the first two, is that listeners are responsible for keeping themselves informed on issues of the day. People who are uninformed about important topics and vital issues are easy prey for propagandists. History is replete with examples of people who have tried to attribute unethical behavior to ignorance, real or imagined. They range from the people who said they didn't know the Nazis were sending millions of Jews to their death during World War II to the tobacco company executives who claimed tobacco was not addictive. Simply put, ignorance is no excuse for unethical behavior. As a result, we ask our own students to at least think about making a commitment to do the following:

- Read a newspaper daily, preferably one published in a major metropolitan area.
- Read a weekly newsmagazine.
- Read a publication at least once a month that holds a political view contrary to their own.

Speak Out

The fourth guideline for listeners is related to the first three. It involves the audience members' ethical obligation to speak up after a speech when convinced that a speaker is misinforming or misleading people. Most of us have been in situations where we knew someone was bending the truth, leaving out pertinent details, or

Is it ethical to stand up in silent protest or to shout another speaker down, as shown here?

passing off another's ideas as original. Under some unique set of circumstances, keeping this knowledge to ourselves may be justified. In most circumstances, however, listeners owe it to themselves and others to speak up. Speaking up can take the form of a question for the speaker following a presentation, asking the appropriate agency for equal time to speak, writing a letter to the editor of a newspaper or magazine, or confronting the speaker one on one. Whatever the appropriate medium, constructive objections are generally preferable to silence.

Be Aware of Biases

The final guideline for listeners concerns our subjective view and the manner in which it biases how we receive and process a speaker's message. Perception is colored by our experiences, both real and vicarious. Rather than denying the fact, it's much healthier and realistic for us to admit this to ourselves. Only then can we determine how much of our reaction to a speech is based on its content and relational dynamic and how much is attributable to our individual biases.

Tips and Tactics

Ethical Guidelines for Listeners[28]

SpeechCoach

To hear more about these Tips and Tactics, see Audio Tips and Tactics on your CD.

- Be civil.
- Be aware that all communication is potentially influential and that there are consequences to accepting any message. Ask what influence the speaker is seeking to exert.
- Stay informed on important topics so that you can judge the accuracy of the communication provided by others. Be willing to independently confirm information that appears questionable.
- Be aware of your personal biases to reduce your susceptibility to appeals to prejudices. Be willing to listen to opposing views with an open mind.
- Be aware of deceptive communication ploys and work to expose those guilty of fallacious reasoning, propaganda ploys, and outright deception. Be willing to speak out in response to deceptive speech.
- Put yourself in the position of the speaker and treat him or her with the same respect you would expect were the roles reversed.
- Provide constructive feedback to the speaker if the opportunity is given.

Summary

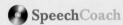

SpeechCoach

To evaluate your understanding of this chapter, see the Quizzes on your CD.

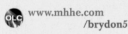

www.mhhe.com
/brydon5

Visit the Online Learning Center for helpful study resources, including practice tests, key term crossword puzzles, and PowerWeb articles for research and review.

Several basic ethical questions are of concern to speakers:

- Why care about ethics? Most people fundamentally want to do what is right.
- Is everything relative? Ethical relativists believe there are no universal ethical principles.
- Are there rules for every situation? Universalists believe there are ethical standards that apply to all situations regardless of the individual, group, or culture.
- Does the good of the many outweigh the good of the few? Utilitarianism is based on this principle.
- How do specific situations affect ethics? Situational ethicists believe it is sometimes necessary to set aside one ethical principle to fulfill a higher law or principle.
- Do the ends justify the means? Speakers should seek ethical ends utilizing ethical means, such as those found in the National Communication Association's Credo for Free and Responsible Communication in a Democratic Society.

Ethical norms for public speaking are:

- Be truthful.
- Show respect for the power of words.
- Invoke participatory democracy.
- Demonstrate tolerance for cultural diversity where consistent with ethical principles.
- Treat people as ends, not means.
- Provide good reasons.

Public speakers face special issues:

- Plagiarism—the stealing of words or ideas of another—is considered a serious ethical violation.
- Building goodwill and trustworthiness is essential to successful and ethical public speech.
- Whether to reveal or conceal one's intentions can present an ethical as well as a practical dilemma for speakers.
- Giving a two-sided presentation is both ethically sound and pragmatically more effective.
- Inducing fear can be ethically suspect if done to excess.

Listeners should adhere to the following ethical norms:

- Be civil.
- Take responsibility for the choices they make.
- Stay informed on the issues of the day.
- Speak out when they are convinced that a speaker is misinforming or misleading people.
- Be aware of their own biases.

Check Your Understanding: Exercises and Activities

1. In a brief speech or short paper, explain the reason you believe the best ethical standard for the public speaker is (a) relativism, (b) universalism, (c) utilitarianism, or (d) situational ethics. Define the version of ethics you endorse, and explain why you feel it is the best alternative for public speakers.

2. Read the following cases and answer the questions about each one. Depending on your instructor's directions, either write a short paper responding to one or more of the scenarios or discuss one or more of them in a small group.

   Case A: A student in your public speaking class presents a speech that contains glaring factual errors. As an audience member who is familiar with the topic, you realize that the speaker has not done research and has "made up" certain "facts." What should you do? What do you think the instructor should do?

   Case B: You are preparing a speech arguing against a tuition increase at your college. In your research, you discover strong arguments against your

SpeechCoach

For a review of key terms in this chapter, see the Key Terms Flashcards on your CD.

position. Nevertheless, you still believe the tuition increase is a bad idea. Should you share the arguments against your position with your audience, or present only your side of the story?

Case C: You are required by your instructor to attend a speech outside of class time. You discover on arriving at the lecture hall that the speaker holds views precisely the opposite of your own. What should you do?

Case D: You are assigned by your teacher to speak for a position you fundamentally oppose on a question about which you hold strong moral beliefs, such as abortion. What should you do?

3. In a short paper, discuss the differences and similarities between the ethical obligations of speakers and listeners. As a speaker, how would you deal with listeners who are unwilling to meet their basic ethical obligations? As a listener, how would you respond to a speaker you felt was unethical?

4. In a short paper, discuss whether you agree with Quintilian that "no one can speak well who is not good." Cite some contemporary or historical examples to support your position.

5. In a short paper, consider the question of whether there can be any situation in which it is ethical to "shock people into action" through the use of especially horrifying or unpleasant images. Give examples to support your position.

6. In your view, what modern politician is most successful at eliciting feelings of goodwill and trustworthiness? Why do you think this person is successful in doing so? Be prepared to discuss your example in class.

7. Administrators, faculty, and students on campuses across the United States are trying to come up with speech codes that strike a balance between First Amendment rights and the right of people in the college community to be protected from hateful and demoralizing language. Working either on your own or in an instructor-assigned group, find out if your school has a speech code that prohibits the use of certain types of words and language. If it does, how would you amend it to fit your or your group's thinking? If it doesn't, what would you include in such a code? Write a short paper on your findings or thoughts, or be prepared to discuss them in class.

Notes

1. "Quotations About Integrity, Ethics, Behavior, Character" [http://www.geocities.com/quotegarden/integrty.html, 2 October 2001].
2. Michelle Locke (AP), "Passengers Had a Plan," *Chico Enterprise-Record,* 13 September 2001, 1A, 9A.
3. J. Vernon Jensen, "Ethical Tension Points in Whistleblowing," in *Ethics in Human Communication,* 3rd ed., ed. Richard L. Johannesen (Prospect Heights, Ill.: Waveland Press, 1990), 281.
4. Samuel Enoch Stumpf, *Socrates to Sartre: A History of Philosophy* (New York: McGraw-Hill, 1966), 35.
5. James Rachels, *The Elements of Moral Philosophy* (New York: Random House, 1986), 21.
6. Immanuel Kant, *Groundwork of the Metaphysics of Morals,* trans. H. J. Paton (New York: Harper & Row, 1964), 88.
7. Kant, *Groundwork of the Metaphysics of Morals,* 96.
8. Rachels, *Elements of Moral Philosophy,* 108–109.
9. John Stuart Mill, *Utilitarianism,* in *Essential Works of John Stuart Mill,* ed. Max Lerner (New York: Bantam Books, 1961), 198–199.
10. William Temple, *Nature, Man and God* (New York: Macmillan, 1934), 405, as cited in Joseph Fletcher, *Situation Ethics: The New Morality* (Philadelphia: Westminster Press, 1966), 27.
11. James A. Jaksa and Michael S. Pritchard, *Communication Ethics: Methods of Analysis,* 2nd ed. (Belmont, Calif.: Wadsworth, 1994), 21.

12. Fletcher, *Situation Ethics,* 26.
13. Fletcher, *Situation Ethics,* 121.
14. Stumpf, *Socrates to Sartre,* 36.
15. Aristotle, *Rhetoric,* trans. W. Rhys Roberts (New York: Modern Library, 1954), 22.
16. Quintilian, *Institutio Oratoria,* trans. H. E. Butler (Cambridge, Mass.: Harvard University Press, 1920), 317.
17. Quintilian, *Institutio Oratoria,* 315.
18. Jaksa and Pritchard, *Communication Ethics,* 65.
19. Greg Farrell, "Martha Stewart Convicted of Four Felonies," USA Today.Com, 5 March 2004. [Retrieved 21 August 2004, from http://www.usatoday.com/money/media/2004-03-05-stewart_x.htm].
20. Jaksa and Pritchard, *Communication Ethics,* 64.
21. Jaksa and Pritchard, *Communication Ethics,* 74.
22. Karl R. Wallace, "The Substance of Rhetoric: Good Reasons," *Quarterly Journal of Speech* 49 (1963): 239–249.
23. Aristotle, *Rhetoric,* 25.
24. James C. McCroskey, "A Summary of Experimental Research on the Effects of Evidence in Persuasive Communication," *Quarterly Journal of Speech* 55 (1969): 169–176.
25. Mike Allen, "Meta-Analysis Comparing the Persuasiveness of One-Sided and Two-Sided Messages," *Western Journal of Communication* 55 (1991): 390–404.
26. Barry Glassner, *The Culture of Fear: Why Americans Are Afraid of the Wrong Things* (New York: Basic Books, 1999).
27. Several of these speaker responsibilities are derived from Sarah Trenholm, *Persuasion and Social Influence* (Englewood Cliffs, N.J.: Prentice Hall, 1989), 18–20.
28. Several of these listener responsibilities are also derived from Sarah Trenholm, *Persuasion and Social Influence.*

2

Between Audience and Speaker

To be a good speaker, you have to be a good listener.

Listening

Objectives

After reading this chapter and reviewing the learning resources on your CD-ROM and at the Online Learning Center, you should be able to:

- Explain what listening involves.
- Describe the significant role that listening plays for both speakers and audience members.
- Recognize and demonstrate the difference between hearing and listening.
- Identify common misconceptions about listening.
- Exhibit behaviors consistent with those of an active listener.
- Demonstrate understanding, appreciative, and critical listening skills.
- Identify and overcome obstacles to listening.
- Recognize common fallacies of reasoning.
- Provide and accept constructive feedback from classmates and your instructor about public speaking.
- Listen to audience questions and provide responsive answers.

Key Concepts

active listening

active mindfulness

appreciative listening

backing

claim

comprehension

connotation

context

critical listening

cross cue–checking

culture

denotation

fallacy

grounds

listening

metacommunication

pinpoint concentration

pseudoreasoning

qualifier

rebuttal

retention

selective attention

sensory involvement

warrant

wide-band concentration

❝ To listen is an effort, and just to hear has no merit. A duck hears also. ❞

–IGOR STRAVINSKY

Imagine that it is the 10th week in your term and you have heard approximately 60 speeches from your classroom colleagues. Topics have ranged from how a Vegan diet can save native grasslands to the amount of energy people waste while running the engines of their autos in the fast food drive-through. You've also heard speeches about saving the rain forests, impact-free backpacking, and the joys of using a bicycle to commute. Although you consider yourself a responsible citizen who cares about the environment, you now find yourself listening to another speech on the topic, this time about the evils of SUVs. Having grown up on a farm, you drive a full-size pickup, as does your dad. Because you come from a large family, there's also a Ford Excursion in the family motor pool. And now this student speaking in front of the class is arguing that people who drive these "fossil fueled monstrosities" are partly responsible for the war in Iraq. Having heard enough, you flip open your cell phone and begin sending text messages to your roommate about how bored you are and that you can't wait for the weekend.

Now put yourself in the speaker's shoes. You've waited all semester long for the opportunity to talk about your belief that our country's entanglements in the Middle East are partly a result of our wasteful consumption of fuels such as oil and gas. Your sister is in Iraq right now; her reserve unit was called up six months ago. You feel passionately about the need to reduce America's addiction to foreign oil, you've marshaled your facts, and you've rehearsed your speech for days. Yet you now find yourself losing your focus and fumbling over your words because you can't keep your eyes off this "yahoo" who is more interested in chatting it up on his cell phone than listening to what you have to say. How rude!

Although this example is intentionally over the top, it illustrates a point we make with our own students at the beginning of each semester. With roughly 25 students in a class, for every speech students give they will listen to 24. This means they will spend about 96 percent of their time listening to other speakers and only 4 percent actually giving speeches. Added to the time spent listening to their teachers, we half joke that the class really ought to be called "Public Listening."

We engage in listening much more than any other communication behavior. As Figure 5.1 shows, over the course of our lives listening easily eclipses all other communication activities.[1] Unfortunately, research reveals that most of us are not very good at listening. The average listener remembers only about half of what was said immediately after hearing a message, and only about half of that—a mere quarter of the original message—48 hours later.[2]

The ability to truly listen distinguishes the competent communicator from those less so. Good listening habits enable us to understand what other people think and feel; listening helps us learn how and why others see the world as they do. In turn, we have the opportunity to appropriately use what we discover about others in our everyday conversations *and* in our public speeches.

This chapter is designed to assist you in becoming a better public speaker and audience member by first becoming a better listener. We discuss (1) the importance of listening; (2) the nature of listening; (3) common misconceptions about listening; (4) obstacles to effective listening, including bad habits; (5) the three primary goals of listening, with an em-

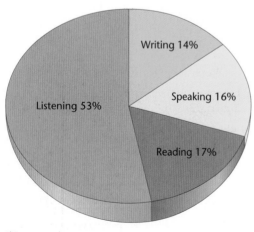

Figure 5.1

Listening Relative to Other Types of Communication

phasis on critical listening; (6) some practical techniques to improve your listening skills; (7) and the importance of listening to provide feedback to a speaker.

Everyday Importance of Listening

Specifically, the ability to listen effectively is important to succeeding in school, at work, in relationships with friends and family, and in situations where we need to share information with others. First, as a college student, you are exposed to hundreds of hours of lectures, group discussions, and mediated communication. The ability to process and absorb information is the essence of learning. Not every professor is a brilliant speaker, holding your attention with ease. You need to listen especially well if you are to obtain the maximum benefit from your college career.

Second, effective listening is essential to success in the workforce. One of the key complaints of many employers is that employees do not listen effectively, costing millions of dollars each year in mistakes and inefficiencies. Among the skills employers value in listeners are "listening for content; listening to conversations; listening for long-term contexts; listening for emotional meaning; and listening to follow directions."[3]

Third, listening is essential to interpersonal communication, especially in families. How many times have you heard children or parents complain that no one listens to what they say? In interpersonal contexts, listening must go well beyond content, focusing on the emotional and relational components of the communication transaction.

Fourth, listening is essential to effectively communicate information to others. You need to adapt your own messages to the feedback you receive from others. Understanding what others need is essential to successfully influencing their beliefs, attitudes, and actions through the speeches you share.

Research tells us that because we are accustomed to receiving information in the form of a story, storytelling is an excellent way to communicate information. In our public speaking classes, we usually begin the semester with a speech of introduction and a storytelling speech, which allows students to relate a personal experience to their classmates. Both of these speeches are excellent listening opportunities for the rest of the class to learn about their classmates' backgrounds and interests. The information gleaned from listening to such early speeches can be used later in analyzing the audience to which you will be speaking throughout the semester.

The Nature of Listening

There is no universally accepted definition of listening. For our purposes, though, **listening** is the process of receiving, attending to, and assigning meaning to aural as well as visual and tactile stimuli.[4] Important to this comprehensive definition is the idea of **active listening,** which involves conscious and responsive participation in the communication transaction.[5] Such active and complete participation encompasses the following:

- Active mindfulness
- Selective attention

listening
The process of receiving, attending to, and assigning meaning to aural as well as visual and tactile stimuli.

active listening
Listening that involves conscious and responsive participation in the communication transaction

- Sensory involvement
- Comprehension
- Retention

Active Mindfulness

Active mindfulness involves the degree to which speakers and audiences are consciously aware of the transactions between them. For example, the fact that someone responds to your message with a look of puzzlement doesn't automatically mean the person is hard of hearing. Yet many people automatically speak louder when their message is greeted with such a look rather than considering the alternatives. Before raising their voice, such people should at least consider the possibility that they were unclear or that the other person speaks another language. This kind of consideration demands complex thinking.

Active mindfulness also requires open-mindedness to ideas contrary or unfamiliar to the way you customarily think. This doesn't mean that you have to accept such ideas uncritically. Instead, it means that you do not automatically reject these ideas.

Selective Attention

As the discussion of mindfulness suggests, people are most likely to seek out and pay attention to speakers and messages that they perceive to be reinforcing. A person whose speech reflects your viewpoint, therefore, is more likely to get your undivided attention than one whose speech presents a diametrically opposed viewpoint. Similarly, lectures that involve your major are more likely to "have your ear" than those on topics you perceive to be less important to your future.

Understanding **selective attention** is important to your development as an audience-focused speaker and as an attentive and responsive audience member. You cannot learn to effectively communicate to your audience, for example, unless you first selectively choose to pay attention to the thoughts and concerns of the people in it. You can't be a responsive audience member unless you make the conscious choice to pay attention to what a speaker shares.

Listening to others speak, moreover, is one of the best ways to improve your own speaking ability. For instance, listening for such things as the developmental pattern a speaker follows, changes in pitch and rate, and the sources a speaker cites can assist you tremendously in preparing and delivering your own speeches. In a sense, listening facilitates the "modeling" of effective speakers and their speeches. However, you first must decide to consciously pay attention–selectively attend–to these models of effective public speaking.

Sensory Involvement

Once you've chosen to pay close attention to the speech transaction, you then need to practice **sensory involvement,** which means listening using all of your senses, not just the sense of hearing. As noted in Chapter 1, every message has two dimensions: a content and a relational dimension. Reading the text of a speech is not the same as physically participating in the transaction. Simply reading text limits you to the *content* of the message and its compositional elements. Although

what a speaker says is important, *how* a speaker says it is equally important. Gestures, movements, facial expressions, and eye contact serve to visually punctuate the content of a speech and suggest nuances of meaning, including what a speaker is saying "between the lines." The reaction of people to a speaker's message and the physical setting in which it's shared also affect the meaning of the message.

To truly appreciate the speech transaction, therefore, you need to involve as many of your senses as you can. Not only must you try to hear what is being said, but you also must try to see and feel what is being said. Only then will you be in a position to measure the totality of the message that has been communicated.

Comprehension

Comprehension is the act of understanding what has been communicated. Careful listeners make sure that they truly understand what a speaker means and do not hesitate to ask for clarification if the speaker's message is unclear. It is also important to make sure that understanding includes not just the explicit content of a message but the relational component as well. And speakers need to make sure that their choice of words is appropriate for their audience. Speaking in technical language to a nontechnical audience, for example, is a sure way to guarantee poor listening and little understanding of your message.

comprehension
The act of understanding what has been communicated.

Retention

Retention is the act of storing what has been communicated in either short- or long-term memory. What is viewed as a failure to remember is often actually a failure to comprehend or attend to the original message. But assuming a listener fully attends to and comprehends a speaker's message, there is still the important issue of retaining that message. The use of careful note-taking can help a listener to

retention
The act of storing what was communicated in either short- or long-term memory.

retain messages that would otherwise be forgotten. And a good speaker will repeat and reinforce the key concepts of a message to help the audience remember it.

Misconceptions About Listening

There are a number of common misconceptions about effective listening. These include but are not limited to the idea that listening (1) is easy, (2) is correlated with intelligence, (3) does not need to be planned, and (4) is related to skill in reading.[6]

"It's Easy to Listen"

Some people think that listening is like breathing, that we are born competent listeners. Of course, that is just as fallacious as assuming that because we breathe, we all breathe well enough to become professional singers. Just because someone can carry a tune and sing in the shower doesn't mean the person is ready for the New York Metropolitan Opera. Similarly, just because we've heard others talk to us all of our lives does not mean we are effective listeners. Quite the contrary, our complacency about listening is one of the very things that makes us susceptible to poor listening habits. Have you ever had the experience of hearing a song on the radio and thinking the lyrics said one thing and, when you later read the lyrics, found out they were quite different? Most of us have either misheard lyrics or know someone who has. One of our kids thought Iron Butterfly's heavy-metal classic "In-A-Gadda-Da-Vida" was "In the Garden of Eden." A friend thought the Beatles' "Lucy in the Sky with Diamonds" was "Lucy in Disguise with Diamonds." Gavin Edwards actually wrote two books of such "misheard lyrics." The title of his first book, *'Scuse Me While I Kiss This Guy and Other Misheard Lyrics,* comes from a mishearing of the Jimi Hendrix lyric, "'Scuse me while I kiss the sky."[7] Edwards's second book title, *He's Got the Whole World in His Pants and More Misheard Lyrics,* is based on a mishearing of the old gospel song, "He's Got the Whole World in His Hands."[8]

"I'm Smart, So I'm a Good Listener"

Even highly intelligent people can fail to listen. For example, submarine crew members are among the most intelligent, tested, and trained members of the Navy. But failure to listen caused the submarine USS *Stickleback* to collide with a destroyer escort and sink off Hawaii in May 1958. Although no personnel were lost, tragedy was narrowly avoided. And it all happened because an electrician's mate thought he heard the order "Come on" when the actual order was "Come off." Instead of turning his rheostat *down,* as he was ordered, therefore, he turned it *up,* tripping circuit breakers, cutting off power, and causing the sub to lose control, plunging it directly into the path of its destroyer escort.[9]

Intelligence far from guarantees effective listening. Although some highly intelligent people have been trained to use effective listening skills, equal numbers have not. As the USS *Stickleback* incident illustrates so well, some people may fail to listen carefully in spite of their intelligence.

"There's No Need to Plan Ahead"

A third common misconception is that listening just happens–that there's no need to plan for it. Of course, sometimes you will end up listening to an unexpected conversation. But if you know in advance that you will be in a listening situation such as the one you face in your speech class, you should plan ahead. For example, in most introductory speech courses, students provide each other with both oral and written feedback. Who do you think will do a better job: the student who prepares in advance, including a review of criteria for the speech, checklists for speech evaluation, and a clear understanding of the speech assignment, or the one who shows up to class only to be surprised by the fact that he or she will be responsible for providing classmates with feedback about their speeches? Finally, when the tables are turned, whose speeches do you think most likely will benefit from critical evaluation by classmates?

"I Can Read, So I Can Listen"

Although reading and listening skills might seem to be correlated, that is not the case. In fact, the skills required are quite different. The reader controls the pace of communication, whereas a listener is at the mercy of the person speaking. A reader can reread a confusing passage, whereas a listener may have only one chance to get the point. Reading is typically a solitary activity; listening most often takes place in groups, where it might be hard to hear the speaker or there might be distractions. Listening skills, as you can begin to see, require development in their own right.

Obstacles to Listening

Several factors can intervene to prevent effective listening. Seven of the most important obstacles to listening are physical conditions, cultural differences, personal problems, bias, connotative meanings, anxiety, and poor listening habits.[10] Most of these obstacles are directly influenced by our perceptions. Thus the discussion of perception and communication in Chapter 1 directly relates to problems in listening.

Physical Conditions

The physical environment clearly affects our ability to listen. Among the factors that can inhibit listening are noise, an unpleasant room temperature, poor lighting, physical obstacles, and uncomfortable chairs. A noisy, hot, poorly lit room, with uncomfortable chairs and a post blocking your view, is hardly an ideal listening environment. On the other hand, a quiet, well-lit room with a clear line of sight, comfortable (but not too comfortable) chairs, and a pleasant temperature allows you to concentrate on the speaker. Although there is usually not much the listener can do about the physical environment, being aware of its impact on listening helps you know how much you need to focus. In addition, you can often choose your location to listen. Students who sit in the back of the classroom, where their

Not only is it difficult to speak during a luncheon, it's also difficult to listen as a result of clinking spoons and dishes and the arrangement of the room.

view is limited, often are tempted to let their attention drift. Those who move front and center clearly are interested in listening to what is said.

The best speakers try to minimize the effects of a troublesome physical environment on audience listening. If the acoustics are bad, they may raise or amplify their voice so that it is more audible. If their line of sight is blocked from some audience members, they may move toward audience members in the back of a room. If some loud activity is occurring within earshot of the audience, they may make light of the situation rather than show that the noise bothers them. No matter what a speaker does to overcome a problem environment, however, audience members also bear some responsibility in this regard.

Cultural Differences

culture

A learned system of beliefs, customs, and values with which people identify.

context

Information that surrounds an event and contributes to the meaning of that event.

Communication patterns vary from culture to culture. **Culture** is a learned system of beliefs, customs, and values with which specific people identify. The relative importance of the context in which listening takes place differs from one culture to another. Anthropologists Edward T. Hall and Mildred Reed Hall define **context** as the information that surrounds an event and contributes to the meaning of that event.[11] For example, suppose you receive a message on your answering machine from a relative you almost never hear from except in an emergency. The message simply says, "Call me right away." Needless to say, you would be alarmed because you know this person never calls you unless there is a serious problem. On the other hand, if you received the same message from a friend with whom you often get together, you might assume he or she just wants to set up a meeting. The same message has a very different meaning because of the context in which it occurs.

Some cultures rely more than others on unspoken information contained in the context to determine the meaning of a message. In high-context (HC) cultures, such

When high- and low-context cultures meet, listening may become more difficult.

as Japan, the Arab states, and the Mediterranean countries, the context of statements can be extremely important. Much of the meaning in such cultures is carried not only by the words that are spoken but also by the situation in which they are uttered. In low-context (LC) cultures, such as the United States, Germany, and most northern European countries, people rely less on the overall communication situation and more on the words spoken to convey meaning.

When low- and high-context people communicate with each other, the results can be frustrating. Hall and Hall note that HC people are apt to become impatient and irritated when LC people insist on giving them information they don't need. Conversely, low-context people are at a loss when high-context people do not provide *enough* information. Too much information frequently leads people to feel they are being talked down to; too little information can mystify them or make them feel left out.[12]

Although we cannot give you any simple rule of thumb for dealing with cultural differences in listening, our best advice is to be aware of the culture of the person(s) to whom you are listening or with whom you are speaking. Then, take differences from your own culture into account and try to adjust your behavior accordingly. Finally, if you expect to be listening or speaking to someone from a different culture, which is increasingly likely on a college campus, learn as much as you can in advance about the person's culture.

Personal Problems

Most people have had the experience of being so preoccupied with a personal problem they couldn't pay attention to what someone was saying. Personal problems can easily detract from listening to what is being said. The best advice for overcoming this obstacle is to recognize the situation and to focus on what is being said, as difficult as that may be. For example, if you were plagued by a personal problem

Considering Diversity

Listening in High- and Low-Context Cultures

As discussed in this chapter, some cultures place greater emphasis on the context in which communication occurs than on what is actually said. In such high-context cultures, as they are called, people realize that what one hears while listening must be deciphered only after thoroughly considering the context in which it is heard. Yes may mean no and vice versa, for example, depending on where and under what circumstances they are uttered. The opposite is true in low-context cultures, where the greatest emphasis is given to the spoken word. People trust what they think they hear without giving undue attention to the context in which it is heard.

One of the major stumbling blocks to the Paris Peace Conference, which laid the foundation for ending the war in Vietnam, was the shape of the conference table. Why? Because the North Vietnamese were concerned about the "message it would send" to those observing the negotiations. Vietnam is a high-context culture.

What kinds of problems do you see occurring when people from high- and low-context cultures listen to each other's speeches? Which of the listening skills discussed in this chapter do you think would most help in overcoming these problems? Be specific!

Source: Edward T. Hall and Mildred R. Hall, *Hidden Differences: Doing Business With the Japanese* (Garden City, N.Y.: Anchor/Doubleday, 1987).

prior to an important job interview, chances are you would tell yourself to "get your act together." You need to do exactly the same thing before listening to (or giving) a speech.

Bias

As you might suspect, bias gets in the way of active mindfulness. It predisposes us to hear only what we want to hear. All people are biased, though not to an equal degree. Bias reflects an opinion formed without evidence, usually about a person or group of people. Racial, religious, sexual, and other such biases, although forbidden by law, often exist in the reality of people's opinions. Recognizing bias is an important step to overcoming it.

Bias isn't always based exclusively on false generalizations about groups of people. Prior, but incomplete, knowledge can cause people to form hasty judgments. Such was the case with the man who shot and killed a Sikh gas station owner in Arizona shortly after the September 11, 2001, terrorist attacks on the World Trade Center and Pentagon.[13] Not only is it wrong to assume all Arabs and Muslims are terrorists or support terrorists' goals, Sikhs are neither Arab nor Muslim, but actually are a different religious group originating in India.

Regardless of its source, bias is a serious impediment to listening. To overcome bias, listeners need to first recognize its existence, mentally set it aside, and recognize its irrationality. Although this may seem easier said than done, the ability to put bias in its rightful place is one of the keys to critical thinking and decision making.

denotation
The generally agreed upon meaning of a word, usually found in the dictionary.

connotation
The secondary meaning of a word, often with a strong emotional, personal, and subjective component.

Connotative Meanings

Important to this discussion are the related concepts of denotation and connotation. **Denotation** involves the objective, conventional meanings you find in a dictionary for a word. **Connotation** involves meanings you won't always find in a dictionary for a word, or the ideas, images, and emotions people associate with a word. Although denotative meanings can be learned by reading a dictionary, connotations, which are largely determined by cultural usage, are learned over time from seeing and listening to examples. As an illustration of connotation, consider some of the various words used to describe a person who weighs more than average. The word *chubby* is appropriate when describing a baby or toddler, but it would prove hurtful when used to describe a teenager. The word *stocky* doesn't mean the same when used to describe a man as when it is used to describe a woman. And, although it would be okay for a physician to write on a chart that a patient was overweight, it wouldn't be appropriate to write "tubby."

Anxiety

As discussed in Chapter 3, anxiety significantly detracts from our ability to process the information to which we are exposed. Anxious speakers often are unable to focus on audience feedback as they speak or actively listen to an instructor's feedback when they finish speaking. Likewise, anxious audience members have difficulty listening actively.

Bad Listening Habits

Ralph Nichols, one of the seminal researchers on listening, found that poor listeners commonly shared a set of 10 bad listening habits.[14] According to Nichols, poor listeners tend to do the following:

1. Quickly decide that a subject is dull or uninteresting
2. Criticize the speaker's delivery rather than focus on content
3. Jump to conclusions and make a quick evaluation of speakers without hearing them out
4. Listen only for facts, thus missing the speaker's main ideas
5. Try to outline everything the speaker says rather than focusing on the important points
6. Fake attention when they are not really interested
7. Become easily distracted
8. Avoid difficult listening situations
9. Let emotional language interfere with listening to the speaker's message
10. Waste the differential between the rate of speaking (about 125 words a minute) and the rate of thinking (400 to 500 words a minute)

The audience member in the opening example of this chapter exhibited many of these bad habits. Deciding the speech topic was just more of the same old environmentalist rhetoric and becoming distracted to the point of sending a text message were just two of the manifestations of these bad habits. As teachers we've experienced these and many more bad listening practices from our students, who are then often puzzled by their low test scores or missed assignments. Obviously, the cure for these habits is to do just the opposite. You can assess your own listening habits by answering the questions in the box "How Well Do You Listen?" Later in this chapter we discuss a number of ways to improve your listening and overcome poor listening habits.

Self-Assessment

How Well Do You Listen?

When listening to a speaker, how often do you engage in the following listening behaviors? Circle the number on the scale that best describes your listening behaviors.

		Almost always				*Almost never*
1.	Dismiss the subject as uninteresting.	1	2	3	4	5
2.	Criticize the speaker's delivery.	1	2	3	4	5
3.	Make a snap judgment about the speech.	1	2	3	4	5
4.	Listen for facts rather than the main point of the speech.	1	2	3	4	5
5.	Write down virtually everything the speaker says	1	2	3	4	5
6.	Pretend to be paying attention when I'm not interested.	1	2	3	4	5
7.	Allow myself to be distracted.	1	2	3	4	5
8.	Avoid listening to difficult material.	1	2	3	4	5
9.	Let a speaker's words stir up my emotions.	1	2	3	4	5
10.	Daydream when a speaker speaks too slowly.	1	2	3	4	5

Add up your the points to see how your listening skills measure up.   Total _____

40–50 Excellent listening habits

30–39 Good listening habits, but could improve

20–29 Needs improvement in listening

10–19 Poor listening habits

Source: Based on Ralph G. Nichols, "Do We Know How to Listen? Practical Helps in a Modern Age," *Speech Teacher,* 10 (1961): 118–24.

Goals of Listening

The purpose or goal of a listener shapes the context in which listening occurs. It is one thing to listen to a stand-up comic and another to sit through a lecture on the theory of relativity. Just as speakers can have different general purposes, such as speaking to entertain, inform, or persuade, listeners can approach the public speaking transaction with different goals. The three listening goals most relevant to our purposes are (1) listening to understand, (2) listening to appreciate, and (3) critical listening (Table 5.1).

Listening to Understand

Understanding, in the truest sense of the word, is a multistep process. Further, there are different levels of understanding, depending on the goal of the listener. The first step in the process of understanding is to discriminate between differing auditory and visual stimuli.[15] As infants we first recognize parental voices, then sounds,

Type	Goal	Example
Listening to understand	To recognize meaning based on auditory and visual cues and to comprehend meaning	Listening to a lecture on Einstein's theory of relativity
Appreciative listening	To experience stimulation and enjoyment	Listening to a speech to entertain
Critical listening	To arrive at an informed judgment	Listening to candidates to determine how to vote

Table 5.1
Goals of Listening

words, and eventually the complex structures of language. Visual stimuli, such as facial expression, gesture, and movement, become part of meaning for us, as does touch. The careful listener is sensitive to both the verbal and the nonverbal nuances of messages. This is especially true for public speaking. Listeners in the audience need to look beyond just the words of a speaker's message. By the same token, speakers need to listen to the entire message received from the audience. This means they should listen not only for aural feedback but for feedback from other sources as well. These sources include the expressions on audience members' faces, their body orientation, and head movements such as nodding in agreement.

Once you have discriminated among various sounds and sights, the next step to understanding is making sense of the aural and visual stimuli received.[16] Successful listening to understand demands that the meaning you assign to a message closely approximates that of the source of the message. How well you understand depends on several factors. Chief among them are vocabulary, concentration, and memory.[17]

Vocabulary

Obviously, you cannot comprehend something for which you don't have meaning. Thus a limited vocabulary has the undesirable effect of limiting your ability to understand messages. In fact, failure to master the necessary vocabulary can be embarrassing or worse. For example, both authors of this text were high school debaters. One of us recalls a particularly embarrassing incident that resulted from not knowing the meaning of the word *superfluous*. Unaware that the other team's plan to remove all "superfluous United States tariffs" meant that they would remove only the unnecessary ones, the author's team produced several examples of tariffs that were essential to American industries. During cross-examination, an opposing team member asked the author, "Do you know what *superfluous* means?" Of course, the author did not know. When the opposition pointed out that every tariff the author's team had cited was, by definition, *not* superfluous, and that only superfluous tariffs would be removed, the debate was, for all practical purposes, lost. Needless to say, a dictionary became standard material for all future debates.

Concentration

A second important factor in listening to understand is concentration. As we know all too well, our minds are easily distracted from the task at hand. If you doubt that, think back to the last time you immediately forgot the name of someone to whom you had just been introduced.

There are two types of concentration: wide-band and pinpoint. Pinpoint concentration is most relevant to critical listening, whereas wide-band concentration is most central to listening to understand. **Pinpoint concentration** focuses on specific details. **Wide-band concentration** focuses on patterns rather than details. As a result, wide-band concentration assists you in listening for the tone of the speech or for its larger meaning in a particular context.

Both types of concentration, however, demand that you try to block out stimuli that compete with the message on which you are trying to focus. These competing stimuli range from the obvious, such as a garage band playing in the free-speech area outside your classroom, to the subtle, such as the gastrointestinal growls your stomach makes when you are hungry.

Memory

Closely related to concentration, memory is the third factor that influences listening to understand. Failure to remember often reflects the fact that you also failed to concentrate. Consider the example of forgetting the name of someone to whom you have just been introduced. Although this very common experience simply may be the result of "mental laziness," most often it is the product of the anxiety accompanying the situation. Both anxiety and preoccupation with feelings of anxiety have a devastating effect on our powers of concentration and memory. As you are being introduced to someone, you may be too busy thinking about how you are being perceived to concentrate on the person's name. It isn't that you forgot the name—it's that you didn't listen for and process the name in the first place.

Much of your day is spent in situations that require comprehensive listening. And nowhere is this more likely to be true than in your speech class. Here are some skills that will help you improve your listening to understand.[18]

> **pinpoint concentration**
> Listening that focuses on specific details rather than patterns in a message.

> **wide-band concentration**
> Listening that focuses on patterns rather than details.

Tips and Tactics

Improving Listening to Understand

- *Utilize the time difference between speech and thought effectively.* Most people speak at a rate of about 125 to 150 words per minute, but the human brain can process 400 to 500 spoken words per minute, although that is possible only with a special process known as "compressed speech." By using the time differential to think about what you are hearing, you can better interpret and understand the significance of what is said.
- *Listen for main ideas.* Don't get bogged down in insignificant detail. Rather, focus on understanding the main ideas and principles a speaker is discussing.
- *Listen for significant details.* Though not as important as main ideas, some details are fairly significant. Try to determine which details are illustrative of the main ideas and have significance for understanding what is being said.
- *Learn to draw valid inferences.* What does it all mean? Try to determine what conclusions you can draw from the speech.

> **appreciative listening**
> Listening that involves obtaining sensory stimulation or enjoyment from others.

Listening to Appreciate

Appreciative listening involves receiving enjoyment from others.[19] This could include listening to music, drama, poetry, or a speech to entertain. Though it might appear that such listening "just comes naturally," the fact is that you can enhance your pleasure by expanding your listening experiences, improving your understanding of what you are listening to, and developing your powers of concentration. Music appreciation classes, for example, help students learn what to listen for in different kinds of music.

This is also true of your speech class. Learning about the various types, styles, and structures of speeches should help you appreciate what a rarity a good speech is. Learning how important it is to construct and share a good speech, moreover, should reinforce your appreciation and give you a more finely tuned ear. Here are some skills that will help you improve your appreciative listening.[20]

Tips and Tactics

Improving Appreciative Listening

- *Use opportunities to gain experience with appreciative listening.* Listening appreciatively, as with all forms of listening, requires experience with different situations.

- *Be willing to listen appreciatively to a variety of writers, speakers, composers, and so on.* Even if you've developed preconceptions about a particular composer or type of music, for example, be willing to listen with an open mind. You may not appreciate Beethoven, and someone else may not appreciate the Deftones. Chances are that with a proper frame of mind you can learn what it is that makes them both appealing to large numbers of people.

- *Develop the ability to concentrate while listening appreciatively.* Many forms of appreciative listening depend on not letting your mind wander. Of course, the greater your experience with a variety of situations that involve listening, the more ability you will have to concentrate on the important aspects of the experience.

Critical Listening

Critical listening, which is an extension and refinement of the two types of listening just discussed, often requires skills similar to those required by listening to understand or to appreciate. There is a crucial difference, however: **Critical listening** is listening for the purpose of making reasoned judgments about speakers and the credibility of their messages. As we discuss in more detail in Chapter 14, when listeners are motivated to think critically and elaborately about what a speaker says, they are likely to reach conclusions with more staying power. They are more confident in what they believe and are less susceptible to having their views changed by subsequent speakers.

To be an effective critical listener, you need to know what constitutes a sound argument. A three-part model we have found useful for this purpose was proposed by philosopher Stephen Toulmin.[21] First, an arguer has a **claim,** or conclusion, that he or she wishes to establish. Second, there must be **grounds** or evidence to support the claim. Finally, there needs to be linkage between the grounds and the claim, which is provided by a **warrant.**

For example, let's go back to our hypothetical speech about SUVs. The speaker is making the *claim* that you should not buy an SUV. A claim alone, however, does not make an argument; there must be some evidence, or *grounds,* to support the claim. The speaker might point out that SUVs get lousy gas mileage. On the surface

critical listening
Listening for the purpose of making reasoned judgments about speakers and the credibility of their messages.

claim
A conclusion that persuasive speakers want their audience to reach as a result of their speech.

grounds
The evidence a speaker offers in support of a claim.

warrant
The connection between grounds and claim.

Figure 5.2
The Toulmin Model
of Argument

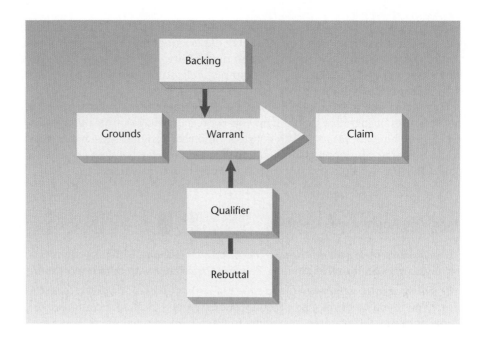

this might seem to be reason enough, but keep in mind that gas mileage per se is not the only thing a buyer evaluates. The buyer may be more concerned about performance, vehicle size, or safety than gas mileage. Thus there must be a *warrant,* or a reason, to value gas mileage over other considerations. In this case the *warrant* would be that gas mileage is the most important factor in choosing a vehicle.

Three additional features *may* be present in an argument. The speaker may provide **backing** to further support the warrant. Thus the speaker might point out that good gas mileage not only saves the consumer money but is also easier on the environment. There may also be an exception, or **rebuttal,** to the argument. For example, what if someone lives where it is necessary to drive off road or where four-wheel-drive is needed to cope with winter snows? The argument is not really so much that *no one* should buy an SUV but that *most* people don't really need one. Thus the argument needs to have a **qualifier** to indicate the level of certitude of the claim. For example, "it is likely" that you should not buy an SUV would qualify the speaker's claim. Visually, the Toulmin model can be depicted as in Figure 5.2. Figure 5.3 shows you how this analysis would look using our example of why one should not buy an SUV.

Critical listening and the companion process of critical thinking, then, frequently boil down to an analysis of grounds, warrants, and claims. In addition, it may sometimes involve looking at backing, rebuttals, and qualifiers. Ultimately, however, two questions must be answered: Is the reasoning valid, and is the evidence presented in support of the reasoning credible? All too often the answer to both questions is a loud "No."

To answer either question, you need to recognize what constitutes sound reasoning and credible evidence. A large body of skills facilitate critical listening and critical thinking, and the critical thinker must be on guard against arguments based on pseudoreasoning and fallacies.

Pseudoreasoning is an argument that appears sound at first glance but contains within it a flaw in reasoning that renders it unsound. A flaw in reasoning is often called a **fallacy,** defined by philosophers Brooke Noel Moore and Richard

backing
Support for a warrant.

rebuttal
An exception to or a refutation of an argument.

qualifier
An indication of the level of probability of a claim.

pseudoreasoning
An argument that appears sound at first glance but contains a fallacy of reasoning that renders it unsound.

fallacy
An argument in which the reasons advanced for a claim fail to warrant acceptance of that claim.

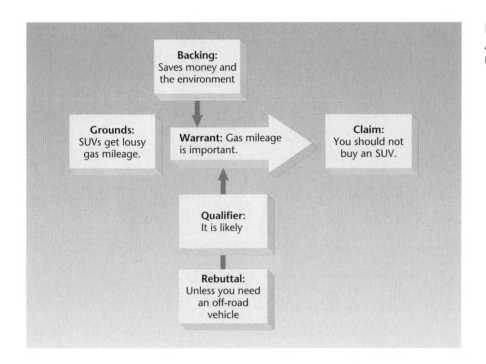

Figure 5.3
Analysis of an Argument
Using Toulmin's Model

Parker as "an argument in which the reasons advanced for a claim fail to warrant the acceptance of that claim."[22]

It is important to distinguish between intentional and unintentional fallacies. Certainly not everyone who makes an error in reasoning is intending to deceive. However, someone seeking to "pull the wool over an audience's eyes" may indeed use fallacies intentionally. Either way the consumer of communication—the audience—must remain vigilant to avoid being misled, whether by accident or design, by pseudoreasoning.

Common Fallacies

In Chapter 15 we provide a more detailed list of fallacies, but for now let's consider five of the more common fallacies. Regardless of how we classify them, all fallacies have the common feature that the argument presented fails to adequately support the claim being made. Be on the lookout for these types of reasoning errors.

Unsupported Assertion

The unsupported assertion is really the absence of any argument. An argument without grounds is no argument at all. Suppose someone says, "There's no way I am ever going to buy an SUV." "Why?" you ask. "I don't need a reason," is the reply. That may be an opinion, but it's not an argument.

Distorted Evidence

Less easily discovered than the total absence of evidence is distorted evidence, which occurs when significant omissions or changes in the grounds of an argument are used to alter its original intent. Suppose a speaker uses crash test data to claim that because SUVs weigh more than most vehicles they are safer in a crash.

During the California Recall, voters had the chance to use their critical listening skills while watching Arnold Schwarzenegger, Tom McClintock, and Peter Camejo in a debate moderated by Stan Statham.

This argument conveniently ignores the fact that SUVs are more prone to rollovers because of their high center of gravity, which means that they may not be safer. Beware of overly simplistic evidence. Most issues include shades of gray; they are not merely black and white.

Hasty Generalization

Reasoning that overgeneralizes from one or a few isolated cases is known as hasty generalization. For example, we've probably all heard of people who refuse to wear seat belts because they know of someone who wasn't able to get free from a car that had gone off a bridge and was under water. But the odds of being killed by being thrown clear of a car during an accident are much greater than the relatively isolated case of not being able to escape from a submerged vehicle. Examples need to be typical, not the exception that proves the rule.

Stereotyping

Assuming that what is true of a larger group is necessarily true of particular members of that group is stereotyping. This is the source of much prejudice, particularly against people of different cultures. One of the authors had a student from the Middle East give an entire speech dispelling stereotypes commonly held by many Americans about Muslims. As he informed the class, Muslims don't all have several wives, they don't all practice violence, and they don't all live in oil-rich nations. The assumption that all Muslims are the same is just as false as the view that all Christians or Jews are alike. The critical thinker and listener is on guard for such stereotypes.

False Analogy

A false analogy occurs when two things that are not really similar are compared as if they were essentially the same. For example, we recall a letter written to a newspaper by a reader angered with newly enacted laws requiring motorcyclists to wear helmets. This reader complained that the legislature had become another Saddam Hussein, acting like a dictator in passing a mandatory helmet law.

Of course, the differences in these two situations are dramatic. The legislature is an elected body. The law was passed based on safety concerns and is not unlike laws requiring motorists to wear seat belts. The key to the analogy is whether or not the legislature and Saddam are both dictators. In the case of Iraq, it took an invasion to remove the offending person, whereas the voters have an opportunity every two years to "throw the bums out."

This is not a comprehensive list of fallacies, but it does give you a sense of the kinds of reasoning mistakes to avoid if you are to be a truly critical thinker and listener. Detecting fallacies is one important step in the process of critical listening. As a constant recipient of messages designed to influence you to spend money, vote a certain way, or comply with another person's request, you need to evaluate each message for its logical validity. These fallacies are often used in political propaganda, advertising, and interpersonal compliance-gaining situations. To the extent that you comply with these messages despite their logical weaknesses, you are suspending your critical listening skills and allowing yourself to be manipulated. Knowing that critical listeners are on guard against pseudoreasoning should inspire you to build your speech with the best evidence and reasoning possible.

Here are some skills that will help you improve your critical listening.[23]

Tips and Tactics

Improving Critical Listening

- *Consider the credibility of the source.* How much confidence do you have in the goodwill, trustworthiness, and competence of the person to whom you are listening?

- *Recognize that the credibility of the source can influence you.* Although credibility is important and can be influential in and of itself, do not let another person's judgment automatically replace your own thinking. Even the most credible sources can be wrong.

- *Evaluate the validity of arguments.* Are the arguments presented reasonable? Don't be afraid to question the logic of a speaker if it seems weak.

- *Evaluate the evidence presented in support of arguments.* Is the evidence presented believable, from reliable sources, and documented for you?

- *Recognize fallacies of reasoning.* In Chapter 15 we discuss additional ways arguments that appear to be valid can be deceptive.

- *Identify emotional appeals.* Determine the type of emotions the speaker appeals to. Are these appeals ones with which you are proud to identify? Whereas appealing to legitimate human emotions is a necessary aspect of persuasion (as we see in Chapter 14), misguided appeals can be destructive. Use of appeals to hate, irrational fears, and prejudice should be rejected.

To improve his chances of being understood, our former student and San Francisco radio news reporter Bret Burkhart uses sound to convey visual as well as verbal information to his audience.

The critical perspective you bring to bear when listening to speakers and their messages is just as relevant to you and the message you ultimately share with others. Thus, learning to listen critically to others will help you become more objectively critical of yourself. This will assist you in both the preparation and the delivery of your own speeches because it will force you to apply a similar set of critical questions to yourself and your message.

Rules of the Road: Improving Your Overall Listening Skills

Whatever specific listening goal is pursued, there are some general rules of the road for listening. These tried and true techniques can help any listener do a better job. Many of these techniques will work in both public speaking and face-to-face interpersonal settings. Keep these rules in mind whatever your listening situation:

- *Block out distracting stimuli.* This includes avoiding distracting thoughts as well as external distractions such as looking out the window.
- *Suspend judgment.* Regardless of the type of listening, the same principle that applies to critical listening applies here—don't prejudge a speaker and don't rely on stereotypes. Keep an open mind.
- *Focus on the main points.* It's too easy to lose sight of the forest for the trees. Ask yourself what the speaker's main points are and resist the temptation to fix on minor details.
- *Listen for highlights and signposts.* These verbal cues will help you know what's most important to a speaker's message and when the speaker is moving on to a new main point.
- *Take effective notes.* As Nichols and Lewis point out, there are numerous ways to take notes.[24] Outlining is an obvious method, but there are less obvious ones as well. For example, you can record your notes in two columns, one for facts and the other for principles. Another useful technique is to listen for a while without taking notes and then write a brief paragraph summarizing what has been said. This technique allows you to alternate between intense listening and note-taking in three- or four-minute intervals.
- *Be sensitive to metacommunication.* The message a speaker conveys nonverbally about a message is called **metacommunication,** and it can often reveal much about a speaker's attitude and feelings. Checking what people say verbally against what they communicate nonverbally can bring to light subtleties in their messages. This is called **cross cue–checking.**

metacommunication
The message about the message, generally conveyed nonverbally.

cross cue–checking
Gauging what a person says verbally against the nonverbal behaviors that make up metacommunication.

- *Paraphrase what's been said.* Repeat what you think the other person has said in your own words. If the other agrees with your paraphrase, you both know the message has been received.
- *Ask questions.* Asking questions can help clarify a speaker's message and provide valuable feedback.

Listening to Provide Audience Feedback

One of the unique features about a public speaking class is that audience members are not just listening to speeches for their own benefit. Typically, they are also called on to provide feedback to speakers to assist them in improving their public speaking skills. Although an excessive focus on delivery skills is normally a bad listening habit, in a public speaking class, paying attention to the level of those skills in your classmates is often an integral part of the classroom experience. Not only may you be asked to provide written or oral feedback about other students' delivery, you may find things in your classmates' style that you will want to emulate in your own speeches.

A few guidelines for giving feedback and receiving it as well will help you improve your own performance. Much of what we say here harkens back to the basics of the speech process, which we explained in Chapter 2. Here are some things to look for in evaluating a speech. Your instructor may have specific additional requirements and may provide a standard form for speech evaluation.

Tips and Tactics

Listening to Evaluate Public Speaking

- What was the speaker's purpose? Did the speech successfully fulfill that purpose? Was the purpose appropriate to the audience and the situation?
- Did the speaker introduce and conclude the speech with impact?
- Did the speaker have a clear thesis for the speech?
- Did the speaker connect with the audience?
- Did the speaker organize the speech in a manner that was easy to follow? Were the main points previewed in the introduction and summarized in the conclusion?
- Did the speaker use good evidence to support claims? Were the sources of evidence disclosed and were they of high quality? Did the evidence justify the claims being made?
- Did the speaker use understandable and appropriate language? Were unfamiliar terms defined?
- Did the speaker deliver the speech effectively? Was it easy to hear the speaker's voice? Were the gestures and movement of the speaker effective or distracting?
- Overall, how effective was the speech in informing, persuading, or entertaining you as an audience member?

Speaking of . . .

Handling the Q&A

Frequently after a speech, you will be expected to take questions from the audience. You should not be fearful of this situation, as it is actually an opportunity to gain important feedback from your audience as well as to clarify points that may not have been completely understood. Successfully answering questions, even hostile ones, can add to your credibility as a speaker. The key is to regulate that feedback in a constructive manner. Some basic guidelines for handling the question-and-answer period following a speech are given below.[1]

- *Announce at the outset that you will take questions at the end of your speech.* Under no circumstances take questions during the speech, as it will cause you to lose control of the situation. When audience members know they will have the opportunity to ask questions at the end of the speech, they will be able to think about them as you speak.

- *Overprepare for your speech.* You need to know more than you cover in the speech if you are to take questions. If you expect a hostile audience, it is a good idea to anticipate their toughest questions and prepare answers in advance.

- *Restate questions if they cannot be heard by all.* If you are speaking with a microphone, someone asking a question from the audience probably cannot be heard. Restating the question not only allows everyone to hear what was asked, it also allows you time to think of an answer. If a question is wordy, hostile, or imprecise, try to rephrase it in a way that neutralizes some of the problems with the question.

- *Answer questions directly with facts to back up your answers.* This requires you to be fully prepared. However, if you don't know the answer, just say so. You can always promise to obtain the facts and get back to the questioner at a later date. It is better to admit you don't know an answer than to be proved wrong because you tried to bluff your way through an answer.

- *Take questions from different audience members.* Don't let yourself get into a debate or an argument with one audience member. Insist that everyone who has a question gets a chance to ask it before you return to a previous questioner. Choose questioners from different parts of the room as well so that everyone feels he or she will get a chance.

Retired professor and practicing journalist Richard Ek points to a questioner to regulate audience questions.

- *Be brief.* Answer questions as succinctly as possible and move on to the next question. Overly long answers bore the audience and frustrate others who want to ask questions.

- *Announce when you are near the end of the Q&A.* When you sense the audience growing restless, the questions have become repetitive, or you are near the end of your allotted time, simply announce that you can take only one or two more questions.

- *At the end of the Q&A, restate the focus of your speech and summarize its essential points.* This is your chance to get in the last word and remind the audience of the basic theme of your speech. Depending on the situation, you may want to make yourself available for informal discussion after the speech.

[1]Some of these guidelines are based on a pamphlet by Robert Haakensan, *How to Handle the Q&A* (Philadelphia: Smith Kline & French Laboratories, Department of Public Relations, n.d.).

As you provide feedback, keep in mind that your goal should be *constructive criticism*. If a speaker's delivery was ineffective, for example, don't just say the delivery was poor, give specific suggestions for how the delivery could be improved. Rather than saying, "I couldn't hear you," say something like "You should try to increase the volume of your voice so people in the back can hear you clearly." Rather than saying, "Your speech was totally disorganized," try something like "It would be easier to follow the speech if you previewed your main points at the beginning." If comments are to be provided orally, we always recommend that critics begin with a positive and avoid statements that could be embarrassing. Written comments should also be balanced between positive and those that suggest areas in need of improvement. However, one can often be more direct in writing because the comments are only seen by the speaker.

Of course, as a speaker, you need to know how to receive the feedback given by your classmates and instructor. Once a speech is over, you become a listener or a reader of written evaluations. The most important suggestion we can make for this role is to avoid the very traps that befall poor listeners. Recall Professor Nichol's list of bad listening habits. Avoid deciding that the feedback is uninteresting or biased. Hear out your critics, even if you disagree with their judgment. Focus on the main points; don't get distracted by nitpicking. Take notes on what is said. Be genuinely interested—after all the reason for taking the class is to improve your speaking skills. Don't let yourself get emotional or defensive; it will only make the situation worse. Ultimately, however, you have to be true to yourself. Take the comments as what they are—opinions, albeit educated ones. Use the feedback to improve your speaking, but don't allow yourself to become so obsessed with it that you become overly anxious about speaking. Keep in mind the techniques we discussed in Chapter 3 for dealing with public speaking anxiety. The same principles apply to the anxiety that occurs when we know we are going to be evaluated.

In addition to listening to feedback from classmates on your public speaking, you may have the opportunity to listen to audience members as they ask you questions. Once you leave the classroom, you will often be placed in situations where you need to take questions from the audience. The box "Handling the Q&A" provides some time-tested guidelines for effectively listening to and answering your audience's questions.

Summary

Listening is necessary to becoming a competent speaker and audience member. Keep the following principles in mind:

- Listening is the process of receiving, attending to, and assigning meaning to aural as well as visual and tactile stimuli.

- Active listening involves conscious and responsive participation.

- Active mindfulness involves conscious awareness of the transactions between speakers and listeners.

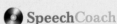

SpeechCoach

To evaluate your understanding of this chapter, see the Quizzes on your CD.

 www.mhhe.com
/brydon5

Visit the Online Learning Center for helpful study resources, including practice tests, key term crossword puzzles, and PowerWeb articles for research and review.

- Selective attention involves a conscious choice to focus on certain people and some messages.
- It is important to listen with *all* the senses.
- Comprehension is understanding what was said.
- Retention is storing what was said in memory.

You should avoid common misconceptions about listening, such as these:

- Listening is easy; it is not.
- Intelligence guarantees effective listening; it does not.
- There is no need to plan ahead; planning is essential.
- Reading skills correlate with listening skills. Such is not the case.

Obstacles to effective listening include the following:

- Physical conditions
- Cultural differences
- Personal problems
- Bias
- Connotative meanings
- Anxiety

Listening can have one of three goals:

- Understanding
- Appreciation
- Critical listening

Toulmin's model of argument assists critical listeners in identifying these key components of reasoning:

- Claims
- Grounds
- Warrants
- Backing
- Rebuttals
- Qualifiers

Critical listeners should guard against fallacies such as the following:

- Unsupported assertion
- Distorted evidence
- Hasty generalization
- Stereotyping
- False analogy

Techniques you can use to increase your overall listening skill include the following:

- Blocking out distracting stimuli
- Suspending judgment
- Focusing on main points
- Listening for highlights and signposts
- Taking effective notes
- Being sensitive to metacommunication
- Paraphrasing
- Questioning

Audience members should provide constructive feedback to speakers, and speakers should listen with an open mind to audience feedback.

Audience questions can provide useful feedback to a speaker who knows how to properly handle the Q&A.

Check Your Understanding: Exercises and Activities

For a review of key terms in this chapter, see the Key Terms Flashcards on your CD.

1. In a short paper or speech, describe an incident in which your message was misunderstood or you misunderstood another person's intended message. Were there any tip-offs that the speech transaction was not effective? How could the misunderstanding have been avoided?

2. Planning for upcoming listening situations is important. Consider one of your classes in which the instructor regularly lectures. In what ways can you prepare for listening to the next lecture? Are there any specific listening obstacles you need to overcome? After attending the lecture, see if your understanding was enhanced by your preparation for the class.

3. In a short paper, describe a situation you have experienced in which bias affected the listening process. Choose a situation in which you feel your meaning was distorted due to bias or a situation in which you feel your own biases handicapped you in the listening process.

4. Make a list of 10 words that have varying connotations to different people or in different situations. Be prepared to share your list with classmates in small groups or before the full class, depending on your instructor's directions.

5. Describe three times in a given day during which you engaged in critical listening. Be prepared to share your list with classmates in small groups or before the full class.

Notes

1. Andrew D. Wolvin and Carolyn Gwynn Coakley, *Listening,* 3rd ed. (Dubuque, Iowa: W. C. Brown, 1988), 12–13.
2. Lyman K. Steil, Larry Barker, and Kittie W. Watson, *Effective Listening* (New York: Random House, 1993), 12–13.
3. Anthony P. Carnevale, Leila J. Gainer, and Ann S. Meltzer, *Workplace Basics: The Skills Employers Want* (Washington, D.C.: American Society for Training and Development and U.S. Department of Labor, 1988), 12.
4. Wolvin and Coakley, *Listening,* 93.

5. Wolvin and Coakley, *Listening*, 115.
6. Melvin L. DeFleur, Patricia Kearney, and Timothy G. Plax, *Fundamentals of Human Communication* (Mountain View, Calif.: Mayfield, 1993), 112–13.
7. Gavin Edwards, *'Scuse Me While I Kiss This Guy and Other Misheard Lyrics* (New York: Simon & Schuster, 1995).
8. Gavin Edwards, *He's Got the Whole World in His Pants and More Misheard Lyrics* (New York: Simon & Schuster, 1996).
9. Robert Haakenson, *The Art of Listening* (Philadelphia: Smith Kline & French Laboratories, n.d.), 3.
10. DeFleur, Kearney, and Plax, *Fundamentals of Human Communication*, 113–17.
11. Edward T. Hall and Mildred Reed Hall, *Hidden Differences: Doing Business With the Japanese* (Garden City, N.Y.: Anchor Press/Doubleday, 1987), 7.
12. Hall and Hall, *Hidden Differences*, 10–11.
13. Tamar Lewin, "Sikh Owner of Gas Station Is Fatally Shot in Rampage" [from Lexis-Nexis, 24 September 2001] (*New York Times*, 17 September 2001, B16).
14. Ralph G. Nichols, "Do We Know How to Listen? Practical Helps in a Modern Age," *Speech Teacher*, 10 (1961), 118–24.
15. Wolvin and Coakley, *Listening*, 140.
16. Wolvin and Coakley, *Listening*, 188.
17. Wolvin and Coakley, *Listening*, 189–206.
18. Wolvin and Coakley, *Listening*, 207–25.
19. Wolvin and Coakley, *Listening*, 320.
20. Wolvin and Coakley, *Listening*, 330–33.
21. This was first developed by Stephen Toulmin, *The Uses of Argument* (London: Cambridge University Press, 1958). It has been revised by Toulmin, Richard Rieke, and Allan Janik, *An Introduction to Reasoning*, 2nd ed. (New York: Macmillan, 1984).
22. Brooke Noel Moore and Richard Parker, *Critical Thinking*, 5th ed. (Mountain View, Calif.: Mayfield, 1998), 476.
23. Wolvin and Coakley, *Listening*, 287–313.
24. Ralph G. Nichols and Thomas R. Lewis, *Listening and Speaking: A Guide to Effective Oral Communication* (Dubuque, Iowa: W. C. Brown, 1954), 41–53.

Effective public speakers must adapt their message to the situation they face, including sharing their platform with another speaker.

Chapter

6

Adapting to Your Audience

Objectives

After reading this chapter and reviewing the learning resources on your CD-ROM and at the Online Learning Center, you should be able to:

- Define and apply the concept of rhetorical situation.

- Identify short- and long-term goals for speaking to a particular audience.

- Determine whether your audience is voluntary or captive.

- Analyze the cultural, demographic, and individual diversity of your audience.

- Adapt to the cultural, demographic, and individual diversity of your audience.

- Gather information to learn about your audience.

- Confront and adapt to constraints associated with the rhetorical situation.

Key Concepts

attitude	growth needs
audience diversity	individual diversity
belief	long-term goals
captive audience	peripheral beliefs
central beliefs	primitive beliefs
constraint	rhetorical situation
cultural diversity	short-term goals
deficiency needs	socioeconomic status
demographic diversity	values
demographics	voluntary audience

> " I was not planning on speaking here tonight, but this is where my journey has taken me. . . . "
>
> –CAROLYN MCCARTHY, wife and mother of victims of the Long Island Railroad massacre, speaking to the 1996 Democratic National Convention.

Mary Fisher, who contracted the HIV virus from her husband, riveted the 1992 Republican Convention with her speech about AIDS.

If necessity is the mother of invention, then circumstance may be the father of public speaking. Consider two cases: Mary Fisher and Carolyn McCarthy. Their lives were dramatically altered by circumstances beyond their control, and both of them became powerful public voices in the process.

Mary Fisher appeared to have a life most people can only dream about. She was a rising star in the campaign machinery of the Republican Party, counted famous people among her friends, was married to a much admired artist, and was the mother of two adoring children. Even though her marriage ultimately failed, her success as a political adviser and as a mother continued to flourish. Then something terrible happened, threatening her very being. Her ex-husband was diagnosed with AIDS. Shortly thereafter, Mary tested positive for HIV, something she had never feared, given her monogamous relationship with her husband, and drug-free lifestyle.

Carolyn McCarthy's life was less glamorous than Mary Fisher's, but was still admirable. A registered nurse, wife, and mother, she was widowed by a deranged gunman who shot her husband and critically wounded her son on December 7, 1993. It was Carolyn's 50th birthday. What should have been a day of joy for Carolyn and the two people she loved most turned into one of inexplicable loss.

What happened next in the lives of these two remarkable people is what makes their stories worth telling. Instead of giving in to HIV and AIDS, Mary Fisher became a prominent AIDS activist as a result of the moving speech she was motivated to give at the 1992 Republican National Convention. You can read excerpts of her speech in the box "Mary Fisher Speaks Out on AIDS" and her full speech in Appendix B. To this day, she is one of the most sought after speakers in the world on the topic of AIDS.

Carolyn McCarthy, whose pleas to her congressman for tighter gun controls fell on deaf ears following her personal tragedy, also became an activist. In her case, however, she switched political parties, ran against the congressman who rebuffed her, and was elected in a huge upset. Like Mary Fisher, Carolyn also took advantage of an opportunity to address the national convention of her party, which established Carolyn as a national voice on the topic of gun control. You can read excerpts of her speech in the box "Carolyn McCarthy's Journey" and her full speech in Appendix B.

Neither Mary Fisher nor Carolyn McCarthy planned on becoming highly visible public speakers. Circumstances demanded that they take action. Although we hope you never have to face circumstances even remotely similar to Mary Fisher's

In Their Own Words

Mary Fisher Speaks Out on AIDS

The AIDS virus is not a political creature. It does not care whether you are Democratic or Republican; it does not ask whether you are black or white, male or female, gay or straight, young or old. Tonight, I represent an AIDS community whose members have been reluctantly drafted from every segment of American society.

Though I am white and a mother, I am one with a black infant struggling with tubes in a Philadelphia hospital.

Though I am female and contracted this disease in marriage and enjoy the warm support of my family, I am one with the lonely gay man sheltering a flickering candle from the cold wind of his family's rejection.

Source: Official Report of the Proceedings of the Thirty-Fifth Republican National Convention, August 19, 1992.

or Carolyn McCarthy's, the chances are good that you will one day find yourself speaking to an audience on a topic that you cannot possibly imagine today. The circumstance may be as ordinary as speaking out in favor or against a development project in your community or as compelling as speaking out on behalf of yourself and coworkers about the necessity of change in the management style at the company where you work. It's not a question of if, but when, the right circumstance will present itself.

This chapter is meant to help you prepare not only for these unforeseen circumstances in the future, but also for the one in which you find yourself right now: your speech class. In the pages that follow we focus on a variety of topics, all of which are related to the task of analyzing and adapting to your audience. These topics include the following:

- How public speeches emerge as a response to a rhetorical situation
- The importance of thinking about the purpose and goals of your speech relative to your audience
- How your purpose and goals are mediated by audience diversity
- How best to adapt your speech to diverse audiences
- The importance of identifying and adapting to your potential audience and to the situational constraints you may encounter
- How to gather information about your audience to help you analyze it

Carolyn McCarthy, a homemaker and nurse, never expected that one day her personal tragedy would lead her to address the 1996 Democratic National Convention about gun violence.

131

Carolyn McCarthy's Journey

December 7th, 1993—that was the day of the Long Island Railroad massacre. My life and the lives of many others changed forever. . . . On that day I started a journey, a journey against gun violence in this nation. Today I am here as a nurse, as a mother, as a person who isn't afraid to speak up on what is going on in this country. . . . The journey I began in 1993 wasn't one that I had planned. Getting involved in

politics wasn't anything I ever wanted to do. But this journey will make a difference when our neighborhoods pull together, when government listens to us again. When all of us, Democrats and Republicans, come together to solve our problems, not just fight about them.

Source: Reprinted by permission of the author.

The Rhetorical Situation

Before we turn to these very practical matters, however, we want to connect the past with the present. Thus we begin by sharing some of the history behind the art and science to connecting speakers with their audiences.

Although the specific term *rhetorical situation* wasn't coined until the late 1960s, its roots can be traced to ancient Greece and the fifth century BC. Then as now there was a need for public speaking skills because democracy requires that people talk about and debate public policy. Further, there were no lawyers, and people had to plead their own case in court. A group of teachers of rhetoric, known as *Sophists,* taught the skills of speaking for a fee. Plato opposed their approach to rhetoric as lacking in regard for the truth and proposed his own philosophy of rhetoric in two dialogues, the *Gorgias* and the *Phaedrus.* Plato believed that one should first discover the truth philosophically and then use rhetoric only in service to truth.

Plato's famous student Aristotle brought order and systematic focus to the study of the rhetorical situation. Aristotle wrote the *Rhetoric,* probably the most influential writing on the subject to this day. Aristotle defined rhetoric as the "faculty of observing in any given case the available means of persuasion."[1] He specified that rhetoric consisted of three modes of proof: *ethos,* the personal credibility of the speaker; *pathos,* putting the audience into a certain frame of mind; and *logos,* the proof or apparent proof provided by the actual words of the speech (*logos* being the Greek word for "word"). In many ways this classification foreshadows much of contemporary communication research with its emphasis on source credibility (*ethos*), audience analysis and reaction (*pathos*), and message construction (*logos*).

The study and practice of rhetoric was further refined by Roman rhetoricians such as Cicero and Quintilian, who developed the canons of rhetoric we discussed in Chapter 2: The classic laws of invention, organization, style, delivery, and memory.

After the Roman period, the study and practice of rhetoric went into a period of decline. As Europe plunged into the Middle Ages, the need for a complete rhetoric was diminished, and human affairs were largely governed by church dogma. Eventually, rhetoric came to be associated almost entirely with matters of style. It is also largely from this period that rhetoric came to be associated with empty words, signifying nothing, as the often heard expression, "that's just rhetoric," suggests.

With the coming of the Enlightenment, rhetoric was rediscovered. There is not sufficient space here to chronicle all the theorists who revived rhetoric. Particularly noteworthy, however, are the trio of Hugh Blair, George Campbell, and Richard Whately, who wrote in the late 18th and early 19th centuries. Blair concerned himself largely with style. Campbell was a proponent of a type of psychology emphasizing discrete mental faculties, returning rhetoric to a concern with the audience and pathos. Whately revived the concern with invention. His treatise on the *Elements of Rhetoric* gave a new importance to logic and reasoning in rhetoric.

By the early 20th century departments of speech began to emerge as discrete entities. Theorists again began writing about rhetoric and rhetorical theory. But one of the important features of the study of rhetoric in the 20th century was a return to its fifth century BC roots in ancient Greece.

Given this rich history, rhetorical scholar Lloyd Bitzer was following well-established tradition when he sought in 1968 to ground rhetoric in situational factors. He defined a **rhetorical situation** as "a natural context of persons, events, objects, relations, and an exigence [goal] which strongly invites utterance."[2] The elements of that situation include an exigence (goal), an audience, and a set of constraints that set the parameters for the rhetorical response.

Both Mary Fisher and Carolyn McCarthy are examples of people who responded to an exigence (goal) by facing audiences within their own political parties. However, because national political conventions are also telecast to the nation and the world, their real audiences were far larger. In a sense, they were speaking to people of all backgrounds, cultures, and ideologies. As we discuss your own speech situations, remember that your goals and the audiences you speak to are central to preparing just the right speech. And, as you will discover later in the chapter, there are also factors that will constrain or limit your choices—everything from how much time you have to speak to the legal limits of slander and libel. Let's begin, then, by looking at your goals as a speaker and the specific purpose you seek to fulfill in any given speech situation.

> **rhetorical situation**
> A natural context of persons, events, objects, relations, and an exigence (goal) which strongly invites utterance.

Goals and Specific Purpose

All too often beginning speakers get ahead of themselves in the planning process: for example, they start with the challenges an audience poses without first considering their own purpose in speaking and the goal they hope to achieve. If you have no clear goal to start with, no amount of audience analysis is going to help. We want you to be able to reasonably predict how your audience is likely to respond to your speech. This begins with deciding on your goal and then selecting a specific purpose that will make sense in light of the audience you know awaits you and the goal you hope to achieve.

You can have both **short-term goals** and **long-term goals.** For example, Mary Fisher sought in her speech to have her audience realize that AIDS is not a virus that only attacks gays, intravenous drug users, or the sexually promiscuous. She was a married professional, faithful to her spouse, and she contracted the virus from her husband. If audience members recognized that AIDS could infect anyone, not just a few groups, then she would fulfill her short-term goal. In the long term, of course, she desired more—an end to the epidemic and the stigma associated with it. But with one speech she had to choose an attainable goal. As with Carolyn McCarthy's campaign against gun violence, Fisher's long-term goals have yet to be realized, but progress has been made.

> **short-term goals**
> Those ends that we can reasonably expect to achieve in the near term.
>
> **long-term goals**
> Those ends that we can hope to achieve only over an extended period of time.

Your specific purpose, as discussed in Chapter 2, is the objective you hope to achieve in speaking to a particular audience on a particular occasion. Although your instructor will probably assign you a general purpose for each speech, such as to persuade, to inform, or to entertain, the specific purpose is up to you. The specific purpose should be chosen to fulfill a specific goal.

The Audience

Given the specific purpose and goals you have tentatively established for your speech, you now want to be able to predict whether they make sense in light of your audience. Analyzing your audience is an extension of the process we all go through when meeting and getting to know new people. It begins on a general level and then becomes increasingly specific. When we meet new people, we try to gauge the degree to which they are similar to us; for example, do they share our language and dialect? We then use this information as a basis for predictions about how to introduce ourselves and what topics of conversation and questions would be appropriate. As we get to know people better, we learn more about what makes them unique. We then use this new, more sophisticated knowledge to guide us in broaching more sensitive topics with them.

You do much the same thing with an audience. Instead of focusing on a single person, however, you have the more difficult task of focusing on many. What you discover about them helps you decide what to say and how to say it. You can never know all there is to know about even a small audience. Still, if you are systematic in your analysis, you can learn a tremendous amount about the increasingly diverse people you encounter. You can profitably use what you learn about such people to adapt your purpose, goal, and eventual message so that they welcome rather than reject your speech.

Any hope you have of achieving your speaking goals, however, depends on whether there is an audience "capable of being influenced by discourse and of being mediators of change."[3] Audience analysis begins by knowing who your audience is.

Audience Choice

In looking at your audience, ask yourself two basic questions:

- Do I get to choose my audience?
- Does my audience get to choose whether to listen to me?

In some situations you will be able to choose the audience for your speech. But in many cases, including your public speaking class, you will have no choice. Short of changing class sections, you will not be able to select another audience. Once you leave the classroom, however, you are likely to have some degree of choice about which audiences to address.

When you choose an audience, think about two important questions. First, what do they think of my goals? If an audience is likely to support your goals, then your task is quite different than if they are indifferent or dramatically opposed. Mary Fisher knew that many in her audience, although not opposed to fighting AIDS, were probably indifferent because they did not see a personal connection to the problem. Carolyn McCarthy knew that her audience belonged to a political party that was already supportive of her goal of greater gun control.

Second, ask if and how your audience can help you achieve your goals. We've heard speeches in a classroom that urged the approval of an international treaty to reduce global warming. This is a noble goal, but aside from writing a letter to public officials there is very little class members can do to help achieve this goal. On the other hand, college students can personally do their part to fight global warming: take public transportation, ride their bikes, and purchase cars with good gas mileage. The best public speakers not only ask whether their audience supports their goals but also how the audience members can realistically help them achieve those goals.

In addition to your choice of audiences, you need to consider the audience's ability to choose whether to hear you speak. Audiences can be broadly defined as voluntary or captive. A **voluntary audience** is one that chooses to hear a speaker. A **captive audience** is one that has no choice about hearing a speech. Whether audience members are present voluntarily can make a big difference in their response to a speech. For example, when controversial filmmaker Michael Moore came to our campus in the fall of 2003, a standing-room-only audience paid to see him. Although some audience members clearly came to heckle him, the vast majority was there to cheer him on. Compare this to the response of the captive audience who booed him when he used his Academy Award acceptance speech earlier in 2003 to denounce President Bush and the war in Iraq. Academy members and guests were not there to hear Michael Moore's political views but to celebrate their industry.

When speaking to your classmates, it is important to remember that they are in the room not as volunteers but because they are required to be there. We regularly discourage students from selecting topics that might be offensive or hurtful to their classmates. Pick topics on which your classmates can be influenced and have some power to act.

However you arrive at your audience–whether you choose them or they choose you–it is crucial that you learn as much as you can about them, beginning with an understanding of their diversity–culturally, demographically, and individually.

Audience Diversity

Audience analysis begins with recognition and acceptance of the fact that today's audience is more diverse than ever. **Audience diversity** represents the cultural, demographic, and individual characteristics that vary among audience members. According to an analysis of the most recent U.S. Census by *USA Today,* "The nation's diversity increased dramatically over the past decade. . . . There is nearly a 1 in 2 chance that two people selected at random are racially or ethnically different."[4] We see this increasing diversity daily in the classes we teach, and it is in these classes that our students present their speeches.

Recently, for example, one of us taught a public speaking class whose members resembled a small United Nations assembly. There were 15 men and 9 women, although statistically most classes at our university have more women than men. While the median age was about 20, one class member was almost 50, and another was in his 30s. Five students were from Japan. One was from Indonesia, and two others were from Malaysia. Another student was from the former Soviet Republic of Kyrgyzstan. One native-born American student was of Chinese origin, and another traced her ancestry to the Philippines. A number of students were hard-core

voluntary audience
Listeners that choose to hear a speaker.

captive audience
Listeners that have no choice about hearing a speech.

audience diversity
The cultural, demographic, and individual characteristics that vary among audience members.

There's a better than even chance that the student seated next to you comes from a different background than you do.

science majors, while others were pursuing music, public relations, and graphic design. Hobbies ranged from scuba diving and fishing to origami and batik. Although this class's diversity was more dramatic than most, we think it is a preview of a not too distant future.

Once you have recognized and accepted the fact that the people in your audience are not clones of each other, you need to learn about and adapt to their diversity. Three levels of audience diversity are depicted for you in Figure 6.1. We begin at the most general level, looking at the cultures to which members of your audience belong. Then we look at some differences in what are termed **demographics**—differences such as age, sex and gender, and ethnicity. Finally, we look at your audience members as individuals. The more you can learn about your audience at each level, the better you can predict their response to your speech.

demographics
Basic and vital data regarding any population.

Discovering Cultural Diversity

Culture is a learned system of beliefs, customs, and values with which people identify. Culture also is more a product of language than of geography. French-speaking Canadians, for example, think of themselves as more French than English, even though Canada has mainly English traditions. Barcelonians think of themselves as Catalonians rather than Spaniards because they speak a dialect that is distinct from the rest of their country. **Cultural diversity** refers mainly to differences among people in terms of beliefs, customs, and values—in a sense, their worldview.

cultural diversity
Differences among people in terms of beliefs, customs, and values—in a sense, their worldview.

Because culture is learned, what is appropriate in one culture may not be appropriate in another. The list of specific things that make one culture unique from another is inexhaustible. However, recognizing and responding to cultural diversity does not demand that you try to learn everything about a specific culture. To the contrary, discovering what is common but variable among cultures is the key to culturally responsive speaking.

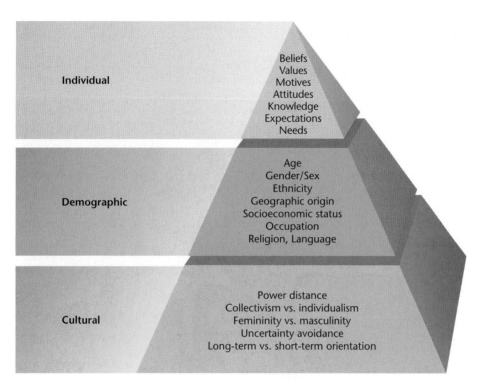

Figure 6.1
Levels of Diversity

Individual
Beliefs
Values
Motives
Attitudes
Knowledge
Expectations
Needs

Demographic
Age
Gender/Sex
Ethnicity
Geographic origin
Socioeconomic status
Occupation
Religion, Language

Cultural
Power distance
Collectivism vs. individualism
Femininity vs. masculinity
Uncertainty avoidance
Long-term vs. short-term orientation

Dutch communication scholar Geert Hofstede says that all cultures vary in terms of at least four dimensions: "power distance (from small to large), collectivism versus individualism, femininity versus masculinity, and uncertainty avoidance (from weak to strong)."[5] In addition, Hofstede notes that a fifth dimension has recently been discovered: long-term versus short-term orientation to life.[6] We think Hofstede's dimensions are a useful guide for analyzing an audience's cultural diversity.

Power Distance

Power distance is "the extent to which the less powerful members of institutions and organizations within a country expect and accept that power is distributed unequally."[7] All societies are unequal, some more than others. However, different societies handle inequality in different ways. For example, there are large power distances in countries in Latin America, Asia, and Africa and in some European countries such as Spain. On the other hand, countries such as the United States and Great Britain and some parts of Europe have smaller power distances. Sweden is an egalitarian country with a small power distance, whereas France has a large power distance.

Power-distance differences have important implications for you as a public speaker. Suppose you are a manager in an international organization announcing company downsizing. You could not assume that an audience from a small-power-distance culture, such as Sweden, would react in the same way to your speech as would one from a large-power-distance culture, such as Japan. Similarly, teachers are treated with deference in large-power-distance cultures, whereas they are treated as near equals in small-power-distance cultures. For example, a professor from a

Considering Diversity

Between Two Cultures: Tomoko Mukawa

Tomoko Mukawa was born in Japan and lived there until she was 15, when she first came to the United States as a high school exchange student. When she returned to the United States as a college student, Tomoko was struck by the differences in the way students and professors communicate in the two different cultures. Tomoko gives an example of differences between the two cultures:

> I wanted to keep my fluency in Japanese, so I took a class from a Japanese professor. Although the American students were allowed to call the professor by his American nickname, I was required to follow the Japanese tradition of always using his title and surname. He stressed that, as a Japanese student, I needed to preserve my cultural heritage.

Tomoko also noticed that the language in which she spoke made a difference in how she was treated. As an English tutor for Japanese students coming to the United States, Tomoko discovered that when she spoke English she was perceived as more assertive than when she spoke Japanese. "You are like a different person when you speak Japanese," she was told by one of her students.

These experiences illustrate the differences between a large-power-distance culture like Japan and a small-power-distance culture like the United States. In Japan, students would never be familiar with professors, and women are generally not assertive. Simply speaking in her native language changed the way Tomoko was perceived. Language and culture are closely intertwined, as her experience has shown.

Japanese university teaching in the United States might be surprised to be called by his or her first name, though such a practice is not uncommon at American universities. Conversely, a Japanese student studying in the United States might find it odd that professors expect students to treat them less formally than professors are treated in Japan. Interestingly, this respect is reciprocal. One of us was informed by a Japanese student that not only do students call their professors by last name as a sign of respect, but professors in Japan address students by their last names as well. For an example of how one Japanese student reacts to the culture of an American university, see the box "Between Two Cultures: Tomoko Mukawa."

Collectivism Versus Individualism

The second dimension common to all cultures is collectivism versus individualism. "Collectivism stands for a society in which people from birth onwards are integrated into strong, cohesive ingroups, which throughout people's lifetime continue to protect them in exchange for unquestioning loyalty."[8] In an individualistic society, on the other hand, "everyone is expected to look after himself or herself and his or her immediate family only."[9] Some cultures, notably Asian and Native American, believe the good of the many far outweighs the good of the few. In these collectivist cultures, people shun the individual spotlight. Singling out a member of a collectivist culture while you're giving a speech is likely to embarrass the person.

In cultures where so-called rugged individualism is admired and encouraged, the opposite is true. In the United States, for example, the dominant culture is very individualistic. We champion lone-wolf entrepreneurs who strike it rich, quarterbacks who stand alone in the pocket, and politicians who march to the beat of a different drummer. There is evidence to believe, in fact, that the United States is the most individualistic nation on Earth.[10]

Speaking to the GOP National Convention in 1992, Mary Fisher addressed an audience of people who probably assumed AIDS was not likely to affect them personally. At that point in time, many people thought of AIDS as a disease of gay men. As a straight woman, she was a living example that everyone was at risk. Mary Fisher stressed that AIDS "does not care whether you are Democratic or Republican; it does not ask whether you are black or white, male or female, gay or straight, young or old." She is saying to her highly individualistic audience—you too are at risk.

In speaking to a more collectivistic audience, one would emphasize the greater good rather than individual benefits. Carolyn McCarthy attempts to appeal to the collectivistic spirit of America when she says "this journey will make a difference when neighborhoods pull together, when government listens to us again. When all of us, Democrats and Republicans, come together to solve our problems, not just fight about them." Of course, Americans are not of one mind on gun control, and this more collectivistic approach has so far not achieved its goals. Gun control remains one of the most divisive issues in the United States, with those who value individual Second Amendment rights at odds with others who would restrict gun owners' rights for the greater good.

The highly individualistic orientation of Americans may be slightly changing given immigration patterns and birth rates. Census data show that more people from collectivist cultures such as Asia reside in the United States today than at any other time in history. American college students today find that people from collectivist cultures are an increasing part of their audience. To find out where you stand as an individual on this dimension, see the box "How Collectivistic or Individualistic Are You?"

Femininity Versus Masculinity

The third dimension of culture in Hofstede's scheme is femininity versus masculinity. Hofstede explains: "Femininity stands for a society in which social gender roles overlap: both men and women are supposed to be modest, tender, and concerned with the quality of life."[11] Masculinity, on the other hand, "stands for a society in which social gender roles are clearly distinct: men are supposed to be assertive, tough, and focused on material success."[12] The United States ranks relatively high on measures of masculinity, ranking 15th out of 53 countries. Despite traditionally being a highly masculine country, this is changing slowly, as evidenced by female CEOs at Xerox and at eBay. Nevertheless, the majority of CEOs in the United States continues to be male. The most feminine cultures are found in Scandinavia and tend not to assign one set of roles to men and another set of roles to women. In these cultures, the professional role a person assumes is a product of ability rather than biological sex. Thus, when imagining a physician or chief executive officer of a company, people don't automatically see a man. In imagining a nurse or secretary, they don't automatically see a woman.

The opposite is true for many other cultures. Some go to extremes in the degree to which one's sex decides one's role. Countries such as Austria, Venezuela, and

Self-Assessment

How Collectivistic or Individualistic Are You?

The purpose of this questionnaire is to help you assess your individualistic and collectivistic tendencies. Respond by indicating the degree to which the values reflected in each phrase are important to you: Opposed to My Values (answer 1), Not Important to Me (answer 2), Somewhat Important to Me (answer 3), Important to Me (answer 4), or Very Important to Me (answer 5).

_____ 1. Obtaining pleasure or sensuous gratification

_____ 2. Preserving the welfare of others

_____ 3. Being successful by demonstrating my individual competency

_____ 4. Restraining my behavior if it is going to harm others

_____ 5. Being independent in thought and action

_____ 6. Having safety and stability of people with whom I identify

_____ 7. Obtaining status and prestige

_____ 8. Having harmony in my relations with others

_____ 9. Having an exciting and challenging life

_____ 10. Accepting cultural and religious traditions

_____ 11. Being recognized for my individual work

_____ 12. Avoiding the violation of social norms

_____ 13. Leading a comfortable life

_____ 14. Living in a stable society

_____ 15. Being logical in my approach to work

_____ 16. Being polite to others

_____ 17. Being ambitious

_____ 18. Being self-controlled

_____ 19. Being able to choose what I do

_____ 20. Enhancing the welfare of others

To find your individualism score, add your responses to the _odd-numbered_ items. To find your collectivism score, add your responses to the _even-numbered_ items. Both scores will range from 10 to 50. The higher your scores, the more individualistic and/or collectivistic you are.

Source: William Gudykunst, _Bridging Differences,_ 2nd ed. Copyright © 1994 by Sage Publications. Reprinted by permission of Sage Publications, Inc.

Japan (which ranks highest on masculinity) have few women in positions of corporate or public authority. Women are assigned roles out of view and out of power. Thus an audience of Japanese men would be polite but predictably unreceptive to a woman speaking on a topic such as reengineering the Japanese corporation. By the same token, a Scandinavian audience would be wary of a male speaker suggesting women belong in the home.

This dimension can be a factor in a number of settings. For example, in masculine cultures, children in school tend to speak out and compete openly. Failure is viewed as a disaster and can even lead to suicide. Boys and girls tend to study different subjects. On the other hand, in feminine cultures, students tend to behave less competitively, failure is not viewed as a catastrophe, and boys and girls tend to study the same subjects. The more you know about which type of culture you are dealing with, the more effective speaker you will be. Even with an American audience, there are likely to be differences in masculinity and femininity based on cultural heritage, age, and progress in gender equity.

Uncertainty Avoidance

The fourth dimension Hofstede discusses is uncertainty avoidance, which is "the extent to which the members of a culture feel threatened by uncertain or unknown situations."[13] As a student you know all about uncertainty and the feelings of discomfort that can accompany it. Instructors who are vague about assignments, tests, due dates, and evaluation not only create uncertainty but also are the ones you probably try to avoid. Just as people vary in terms of the amount of uncertainty they can tolerate, so it is with whole cultures. People who live in "low-uncertainty-avoidance cultures" have considerable tolerance for the kind of ambiguity that can drive some people nuts.

Among societies that *avoid* uncertainty are Greece, Portugal, Guatemala, and Japan. Societies that tend to tolerate uncertainty include Singapore, Jamaica, Denmark, Sweden, Great Britain, India, Philippines, and the United States. If you think about it, if it were not for the tolerance of a certain amount of uncertainty, it is unlikely that new businesses would ever secure the funding of venture capitalists. The United States is by and large a nation of immigrants and their descendants, people who by coming to the "new world" were prepared to accept a very high level of uncertainty.

How is this important to you as a speaker? If you have an audience that can tolerate at least a moderate amount of uncertainty, you do not need to promise certainty. Highly probable outcomes may be sufficient to gain their support. Imagine during the dot-com boom of the late 1990s how entrepreneurs could have obtained funding if they had been forced to guarantee results. On the other hand, total uncertainty is likely to result in rejection of your ideas, particularly in those societies that do not tolerate such ambiguity. You should tailor your appeals to the likely level of uncertainty that your audience is willing to accept.

Long-Term Versus Short-Term Orientation

The final dimension Hofstede discusses is long-term versus short-term orientation to life. "Long-term orientation stands for the fostering of virtues oriented toward future rewards, in particular perseverance and thrift."[14] "Short-term orientation stands for the fostering of virtues related to the past and the present, in particular respect for tradition, preservation of 'face,' and fulfilling social obligations."[15]

Asian countries, such as China and Japan, tend to rank very high on the long-term dimension. In fact, this dimension is sometimes called Confucian because many of the values, on both sides of the dimension, are the same as the teachings of Confucius. The United States is in the lower third of countries, and Pakistan is at the bottom of the list, meaning both have a short-term orientation.

Those cultures with a long-term orientation to life tend to adapt long-standing traditions to modern situations, are willing to save and persevere to achieve long-term goals, are willing to subordinate themselves for a purpose, and are thrifty in their use of resources. Short-term-oriented societies respect traditions, are willing to overspend to maintain their lifestyle, and expect quick results. It is revealing that when President Bush and Congress wanted to stimulate the economy in the summer of 2001, they fashioned a $300 to $600 tax rebate, hoping that people would spend the money rather than save it for the future. In fact, many stores featured ads promising to stretch the rebate if people spent it at their business. Had Americans a longer-term orientation, the immediate tax rebates may have proved less appealing to the politicians promoting them.

Knowing whether your audience members share a short- or a long-term culture can significantly affect the content of your speech. Appeals to thrift and patience are likely to be effective in those societies with a long-term orientation, whereas appeals to instant gratification are more effective in societies that have a short-term view of the world. The current debate in the United States over the need to change the Social Security system to protect future generations reflects the results of years of a short-term orientation on the part of American society. That this issue is now being seriously debated suggests that both short- and long-term orientations are competing within the American culture.

Adapting to Cultural Diversity

All five of Hofstede's dimensions are important to analyzing cultural diversity. You shouldn't automatically give one greater credence than another. Rather, tailor your speech to fit with those dimensions that are most relevant to your topic. For example, a speech encouraging students to avoid accumulating credit card debt while in college is going to be better received by those with a long-term orientation than a short-term one.

Further, in a world where cultural diversity is the norm rather than the exception, you can count on audience membership that is not only culturally diverse but also variable with regard to such dimensions as femininity versus masculinity. Thus developing and delivering a speech that appeals to a majority of the cultures represented in your audience is tougher than ever. The wider the range of reasons you present for your position, therefore, the better your chances of success.

Demographic Diversity

After cultural diversity, the second major factor you will want to examine to better understand your audience is how people vary in terms of demographics, which are the basic and vital data regarding any population. Demographic factors include age, gender and sex, ethnicity, geographic origin, socioeconomic status, occupational role, religion, and language usage. **Demographic diversity** refers to the differences among people in terms of such factors. Many of these, such as age and ethnicity, are usually readily observable. Others, such as religion, occupation, and socioeconomic status, may be less obvious. We'll start with some of the easier ones to observe and move to the less obvious.

demographic diversity
Variations among people in terms of such attributes as socioeconomic background and level of education.

Age

You should know not only the median age of your audience but also their range of ages and how those ages compare to your own. The age demography of the United States is changing at an accelerated rate; so is the demography of the classroom. At one time, college classrooms consisted of a relatively homogeneous group of

18- to 22-year-olds. Today's classroom comprises a much more diverse mix of students. For example, college classes in a state university in the 21st century are likely to be of mixed ages. It's common for students to be as young as 17 or as old as 75. As a speaker, you need to take into account this demographic diversity in both preparation and delivery of your speech. You have to consider not only how 18- to 22-year-olds are likely to respond to your presentation, but also how continuing and reentry students are likely to respond. Likewise, you will also have to think through the response of students who may or may not be similar to you or other members of your audience. This makes it especially important that you compare your audience with yourself.

Some of the most effective speakers are similar but not too similar to their audience. Reentry students in their 40s can be somewhat intimidated by speaking to classes of 18- to 22-year-old classmates. Similarly, a 20-year-old asked to speak to a group of middle-aged people may feel uneasy. In situations where there is a big difference in age between speaker and audience, points of similarity can be stressed. For example, older students speaking to a younger audience can discuss their children, who might be the same age as the rest of the class. Similarly, younger persons facing an older audience can make reference to parents or grandparents in an effort to find a common thread linking them with the audience.

Gender and Biological Sex

Whether you agree that "men are from Mars and women are from Venus,"[16] you cannot deny that men and women often have difficulty communicating with each other. Gender's influence on how people perceive themselves and others is a subject receiving considerable attention. As scholars such as Julia Wood point out, gender is much more than your biological sex.[17] Gender is the blend of social and cultural characteristics associated with maleness or femaleness in a particular culture. Individuals learn gender roles—the expectations their cultures have of them as males or females—in the course of growing up.

As you look out at an audience, you can usually tell who is male and who is female by such outward signs as dress and hairstyle. But unless you have more specific information, you cannot tell who is gay and who is straight, or who is in a committed relationship and who is single. Much gender-related information is probably beyond your knowledge in most public speaking situations.

Some audiences will be predominately one gender or the other, and they may be the opposite of your own. Thus a male speaker facing a largely male audience is in a different situation than one facing a largely female or evenly mixed audience.

One of the first issues you will face is topic selection. For example, one of our students gave a speech about the dangers of breast enhancement surgery. She and the female members of the audience obviously had an interest in the topic. Why should the males care? She made a specific effort to include the men in her audience. She talked in terms of their girlfriends or wives, and made a strong plea to men to accept their mates as they are. Although this topic obviously had a greater direct relevance to the women in her audience, she was careful not to ignore her male audience members.

Ethnicity

Although closely related to culture, ethnicity is not the same thing. For example, in one of our classes recently, we had both a Japanese exchange student and a fifth-generation Japanese American. Both might appear outwardly to share the same ethnic background, but they identified with very different cultures. Anthropologists will tell you that all of us can trace our ethnic roots to other places on the globe. The ethnic origins of many of your classmates may be significant to their self-concept. These same classmates may be actively involved in maintaining and passing on the traditions that define their ethnicity. Thus, if you are ignorant of the ethnic diversity present on your campus, you may inadvertently violate or be insensitive to one or more of these traditions. For example, although born in the United States, one of our students was very proud of her Filipino heritage. Knowing that was important to predicting how she would respond to certain topics, for example, the crisis that was occurring at the time in the Philippines, where hostages had been taken by a rebel group.

It is also important to recognize that many Americans have multiple ethnic backgrounds. Tiger Woods, who is Asian, African American, Native American, and Caucasian, is one of the most prominent examples of this trend. According to the most recent U.S. Census, Woods is not alone. "About 2.4% of Americans, some 6.8 million people, reported themselves as belonging to more than one racial group."[18]

Geographic Origin

The varied makeup of today's audience is also reflected in the geographic origins of the audience members. One of our international students, when asked where she was born, said she was born in the USSR but lived in Kyrgyzstan without ever moving. Of course, when the Soviet Union fell, she became a citizen of a new country. Given that none of her classmates had ever heard of Kyrgyzstan, this student devoted her informative speech to telling us about her homeland.

Look around your campus. The chances are good that the population reflects national and regional demographic diversity. International student attendance at U.S. colleges and universities is at an all-time high. Faculties are becoming more international as well. To deny or ignore how this national diversity influences people's perceptions of each other, including how you are perceived as a public speaker, is foolish. The same can be said for the regional diversity reflected in your student body. Some campuses are near-mirror images of the region in which they exist. Others look more like international cities than like their regional environment.

A speaker can unknowingly offend audience members by using a reference that may be taken as a slight to their geographic home. When the rock group Lynyrd Skynyrd said "I hope Neil Young will remember a southern man don't need him around," they were getting back at Young for lyrics they thought disparaged people in the South. Simply put, some people can be genuinely put off by speakers they perceive to be unfairly stereotyping or making light of their geographic roots. And it's not just southerners, it's also New Yorkers, not-so-laid-back Californians, and a few South Dakotans who were not too happy with the Coen brothers' portrayal of their region in the film *Fargo*. Although you may regard a place as "the armpit of the universe," it's home to someone else who may well be an audience member.

socioeconomic status
Social grouping and economic class to which people belong.

Socioeconomic Status

The social grouping and economic class to which people belong is termed their **socioeconomic status.** Socioeconomic status is not always directly observable. Most universities want diversity of social and economic backgrounds of their students. Thus your speech class may include students who come from impoverished backgrounds as well as students from affluent families. Although you can sometimes make inferences regarding the social status of your audience, these are not always reliable. For example, one of us once suggested to his class that a proposed tuition increase might lead to fewer minority students attending California universities. An African American student objected, pointing out that one cannot assume that all African Americans are necessarily too poor to afford higher tuition.

Knowing the socioeconomic background of an audience is particularly important in speeches that are designed to persuade them to buy some product. For example, both of the authors earned degrees from the University of Southern California, which at the time had students drawn heavily from higher economic backgrounds. One of the authors recalls a speech encouraging classmates to spend their spring break on a cruise ship. Although the audience in this class was very responsive to this student's topic, imagine the irrelevance of the same speech at a commuter college where out of necessity students worked full time in addition to taking classes.

Occupation

Demographic diversity is also reflected by the kind of work people do. On a residential campus, occupational roles are generally expressed in terms of major. At many schools, however, students are already involved in an occupation and pursuing a degree for purposes of advancement or career change. This is especially true of urban and metropolitan schools in or near major cities. One cannot always assume from outward appearances what a person's occupation or former occupation might be. For example, we recall one female student, barely five feet tall, who revealed in one of her speeches that she had been a truck driver for several years. Obviously, her perspective on many issues was affected by that experience. To assume she was uninformed about basic auto mechanics, for example, would have been a clear mistake.

Occupations and coworkers influence how people see the world. Self-employed people, for example, probably see things differently than do people working in the public sector, at a large corporation, or in the home. Just as it is important for speakers to analyze age and social diversity, so it is important to respect the full range of occupations represented in audiences. As you get to know your classmates, you may be able to incorporate references to their majors or jobs when it fits your speech. For example, one student in our classes was a DJ. Other students often mentioned this when it fit with their speech topic, such as how to organize a special event. Audience members appreciate positive references to their occupations, and they can be offended by negative ones. For example, had a student made a derogatory remark about DJs, it could have alienated the audience member who earned his livelihood that way.

Religion

You need to consider religious diversity as a sensitive feature of your audience. At public colleges and universities, you can assume that almost every type of religious belief is represented. Even at universities like Notre Dame, which is affiliated with the Catholic Church, you will find diversity in the religious beliefs of groups of students. In some cases, a person's religion can be identified on the basis of apparel and appearance. Such cases include the Amish, Hasidic Jews, some Muslims, and Hindu Sikhs. Usually, religious affiliations will not be easily visible. You cannot tell a devout Catholic from an atheist by outward appearances. In one of our classes, several students were Muslims. One of the students spoke on common misconceptions about Islam. Moreover, he related his frustrations with American restaurants that did not disclose that some of their dishes contained pork, which he was forbidden to eat by his religious beliefs.

We want to point out, however, that religious beliefs do not always predict actual attitudes. For example, despite official opposition by many churches to using human embryos for stem cell research, a Harris poll of more than 1,000 Americans revealed that "slightly more than 60% of Catholics and half of born-again Christians surveyed agreed that scientists should be allowed to use stem cells in their medical research."[19]

Perhaps the most important advice we can give about religious beliefs is to be tolerant and respectful of those who do not share your own views. A speech class is a captive audience. A speech that attacks one set of religious beliefs or seeks to proselytize class members is not appropriate for most colleges and universities. Say, for example, that a student gave a speech accusing those who have abortions of committing murder. Imagine the effect on a student in a class who has herself had an abortion. You most likely won't know this sort of fact about your classmates; thus you should always assume that there may be audience members who will be deeply offended by religious topics. Although our Muslim student dealt with a religious topic, he did so in a nonjudgmental way. He did not attempt to challenge the religious beliefs of Christians and Jews in the class but rather sought to show that his beliefs were not what many Americans thought they were.

Language

Finally, audience members may differ in terms of how they use language in the reference group with which they most identify. Even people with a common native tongue often create a variation of their language that identifies them as a member of a specific reference group. Every generation of young people, for example, creates a shared vocabulary and syntax that distinguishes it from preceding generations. In the early 1950s college students referred to an object they liked as "real George." Generations that came later replaced *George* with *hip, cool, bitchin'*, and even *hella' bitchin'* in Northern California.

People of Mexican descent in the United States may refer to themselves as Mexican American, Chicano/Chicana, or Latino/Latina, depending on when they were born and where they were raised. And people of African descent may refer to themselves as Blacks or African Americans for similar reasons.

Language groups are not necessarily based on age or ethnicity, however. Special usage and vocabularies also can develop around an activity or interest. Surfers and sailboarders, snowboarders and skiers all have a vocabulary peculiar to their sport, as well as a way of using this vocabulary that is distinctive. The same can be said about computer hackers, photographers, serious backpackers, and white-water enthusiasts. What's more, these groups use their vocabulary not only to identify their own kind but also to differentiate themselves from others.

As the world becomes smaller and linguistic diversity grows even within the borders of the United States, it is important that speakers learn to adapt to their audience's linguistic background. According to the 2000 U.S. Census, 20 years ago only 1 in 10 Americans primarily spoke a language other than English, but today that number has reached 17.6 percent, nearly 1 in 5.[20] You may want to learn a few phrases in another language if you are speaking to an audience that doesn't share your primary language. Taking the time and making the commitment to learn another language signals to members of the language community that you are truly interested in them.

Individual Diversity

For most public speakers, the most difficult aspect of audience diversity is predicting how individual members of the audience will respond to them and their message. What are some of the specific things you should look for in analyzing the individuals who make up your audience? **Individual diversity** is deeply embedded in people's knowledge, beliefs, attitudes, values, motives, expectations, and needs. What makes people truly unique is their individual diversity, which cannot be determined on the basis of their culture or demography alone. When you know people as individuals rather than simply as members of a culture or group, you can make far more sensitive predictions about how they will respond to your speeches and to you. You can also use this knowledge to plan your speeches and decide whether your purpose and goal are realistic.

> **individual diversity**
> How individuals in an audience differ in terms of knowledge, beliefs, attitudes, values, motives, expectations, and needs.

One of the great advantages of most public speaking classes is that you will learn to know your audience members as individuals. As we pointed out in Chapter 5, in a class of 25 you will spend about 96 percent of your class speaking time listening to your classmates give their speeches. If you actively listen to them, you will learn a great deal about what they know and think about the world around them. You can use this information as you prepare your own speeches.

Although many of your public speaking situations after college may not allow you to hear all of your audience members speak, you can endeavor to learn as much about them as individuals as possible before you speak. Even in situations where you face an audience "cold," you may be able to make certain assumptions about their interests and belief systems beforehand. For example, if you are asked to speak to the Lion's Club, it is useful to know in advance that they are concerned about raising funds to combat blindness and that they sponsor a public speaking contest for high school students. Any clues you can obtain about the individuals to whom you will be speaking can be valuable in crafting an effective speech.

Knowledge

One of the first things you'll want to know about your audience is what they know—about you and your topic. This is particularly important in selecting a topic for an informative speech. You have probably had the experience of listening to a speaker who simply tells you what you already know. Chances are you were impatient and bored. You have also probably had the experience of listening to a speaker who was almost incomprehensible because he or she used vocabulary you had never heard before, or assumed you had prior knowledge you didn't have about the topic.

Learn as much as you can about your audience's knowledge. Chances are there may be a range of knowledge on the topic you have chosen. If the difference in audience knowledge levels is too varied, preparing your speech may be very difficult. You will find yourself boring some members while losing others. For example, a speech on the federal reserve board may be old hat to economics majors but leave humanities majors mystified. If possible, speak on topics about which audience members are likely to have similar levels of knowledge. If you must re-hash certain facts, at least try to put a new spin on them to keep the interest of well-informed audience members. In any event, you want to be sure you are the best-informed person in the room. It's embarrassing, to say the least, to be cor-rected on the facts by a member of your audience.

Beliefs

belief
An assertion about the properties or characteris-tics of an object.

We all hold certain beliefs about a wide variety of topics. A **belief** is "an assertion about the properties or characteristics of an object."[21] Some beliefs are relatively obvious and undeniable. For example, we all (presumably) share a belief that the earth is round and revolves around the sun. On the other hand, some beliefs are controversial—for instance, those concerning life after death, abortion, and evolu-tion. When you are dealing with matters on which people hold beliefs different from yours, you face a serious obstacle. You must either change their relevant be-liefs or convince them that such beliefs are not relevant and not necessarily in op-position to your own point of view.

Convincing her congressman, who had strong beliefs on the subject, to change his stand on gun control proved impossible for Carolyn McCarthy. So, rather than trying to move his position through speech, she used her newfound public voice to move him out of office. Simply put, all speakers must carefully choose their battles. That requires that you learn as soon as possible whether you have even the slight-est chance to engage your audience positively on your topic.

primitive beliefs
Those beliefs learned by direct contact with the object of belief and rein-forced by unanimous social consensus (also known as type A beliefs).

Social psychologist Milton Rokeach pointed out that some beliefs are more re-sistant to change than others.[22] **Primitive beliefs,** also known as type A beliefs, are learned by direct contact with the object of belief and reinforced by unani-mous social consensus. A primitive belief would be that "death is inevitable." Type B, or zero consensus, beliefs are based on direct experience but do not require social support. These beliefs are also very resistant to change. For example, "I like myself" is a type B belief; it is not reinforceable by social consensus. Together, type A and B beliefs are core beliefs, which are very resistant to change.

central beliefs
Beliefs based directly or indirectly on authority.

The next two types of beliefs are known as **central beliefs** and are still diffi-cult to change. Type C beliefs are authority beliefs. For example, beliefs in the truth of the Bible or Torah or Quran would be a type C belief. Type Ds are de-rived beliefs, based on authorities' beliefs. For example, Muslims who believe they should abstain from drinking alcohol and eating pork are said to hold de-rived beliefs. Changing a type D belief requires an understanding of the type C belief from which it is derived. Thus a speaker might point to scripture to try to change a believer's views on a religious matter, but such an argument would have no impact on an atheist or a practitioner of a different religion.

peripheral beliefs
The least central type of beliefs, the easiest to change.

The least central type of beliefs, type E, are called **peripheral beliefs.** For example, someone might like rap music, whereas another detests it. These are the most inconsequential of beliefs. Figure 6.2 illustrates the relationship among these levels of belief. Clearly, your chances of changing an audience member's core be-liefs are far less than changing central or peripheral beliefs.

How can you learn what people believe? One way is simply to ask. In a speech about cell phone safety, for example, one student asked for a show of hands on how many of her classmates owned cell phones and how many used them while driving. Politicians and pollsters are always asking the American public what it be-lieves about a variety of issues. Every year the Cooperative Institutional Research

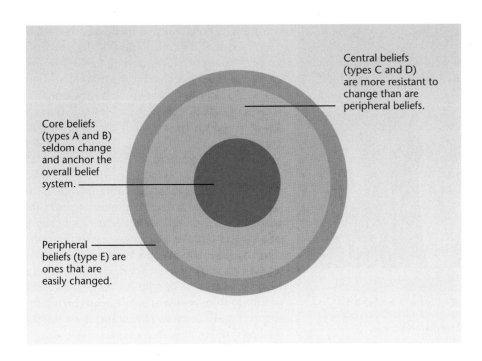

Figure 6.2
A Belief System

Central beliefs
(types C and D)
are more resistant to
change than are
peripheral beliefs.

Core beliefs
(types A and B)
seldom change
and anchor the
overall belief
system.

Peripheral
beliefs (type E) are
ones that are
easily changed.

Program at UCLA sponsors a national study of thousands of incoming first-year college students. You may learn from such sources, in a general way at least, what audience members are likely to believe. For example, among entering freshmen in 2000, the national survey showed that 34.2 percent believe that marijuana should be legalized, 31.2 percent oppose the death penalty, and 56 percent believe in legal marital status for same-sex couples.[23] You might use this information in one of your own speeches, knowing that the survey represents students at colleges throughout the United States.

Attitudes

An **attitude** is "a learned predisposition to respond in a consistently favorable or unfavorable manner with respect to a given object."[24] Attitudes are not simply beliefs but rather ways of responding, based in part on beliefs. Over the course of our lives, we develop innumerable attitudes on everything from our favorite brand of soft drink to globalization of world business. These attitudes affect how we respond to the messages we hear. Thus knowing your audience's attitudes toward your topic is crucial to your success as a speaker, as one speaker learned when she tried to challenge her classmates' aversion to eating a certain type of food–insects. Eating insects is rare in American culture, and most of her classmates groaned when they heard her topic. She attempted to convince her classmates that eating "bugs" actually could be healthy. Not everyone was convinced, but several of her classmates (and even the professor) ended up sampling her "mealybug chocolate chip cookies." While not dramatically changing her audience's attitudes, the speaker did induce at least some class members to soften their strong attitude against this type of food.

How do you learn your audience's attitudes? Sometimes they are fairly predictable. Most Americans don't eat bugs. On the other hand, without asking, it's not easy to know what your classmates think about the Kyoto Protocol on global

attitude
A learned predisposition to respond in a consistently favorable or unfavorable manner with respect to a given object.

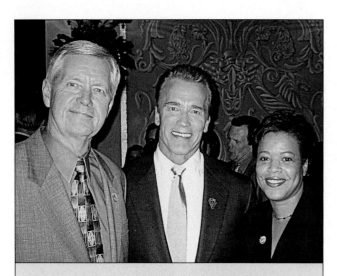

Although California Governor Arnold Schwarzenegger (pictured here with Stan and Roleeda Statham) is a nationally prominent Republican, his views on issues such as abortion and gay rights don't fit the Republican stereotype.

warming or how many of them are vegetarians. Never assume that all members of a particular group of people share the same attitudes: Not all Republicans think alike, any more than Democrats do. Nor do all members of a religion—whether Catholics, Protestants, Jews, Baptists, or Muslims—subscribe to exactly the same religious convictions.

It is entirely possible, in fact probable, that in a diverse audience, individuals will have conflicting and even contradictory attitudes. The more you know about the predominant or prevailing attitudes of the group, the better are your chances of a majority of the audience responding positively to what you say in your speech. When an audience is fairly evenly divided, you need to attempt to find some middle ground. Finding areas of common agreement while recognizing and respecting differences of opinion is essential to dealing with an audience of mixed attitudes.

Values

values
Our most enduring beliefs about right and wrong.

One scholar describes **values** as "more general than attitudes, . . . enduring beliefs that hold that some ways of behaving and some goals are preferable to others."[25] Underlying someone's opposition to animal testing in research, for example, is both a belief about how animals are treated in doing research and a value system that believes all life is important, not just human life.

Rokeach classifies values as either terminal (ends in themselves) or instrumental (those that help achieve the ends we seek as humans). [26] Examples of terminal values include a comfortable life, an exciting life, a sense of accomplishment, a world at peace, a world of beauty, equality, family security, freedom, and happiness. Instrumental values are guides to behavior, the means to achieve the ends specified in the terminal values. Examples of instrumental values include ambitiousness, broad-mindedness, capableness, cheerfulness, cleanliness, courage, forgiveness, helpfulness, and honesty.

Although one might not always agree with Rokeach's classification—for example, honesty can certainly be viewed as an end in itself—the basic notion is useful. Some values are desirable in and of themselves, whereas others are instruments for achieving higher, terminal values. For example, forgiveness and courage may be seen as means to achieving a world at peace.

Values, particularly terminal values, are difficult to change because they are learned at an early age and widely shared among people. Values such as fairness, justice, life, patriotism, and so on are not only fundamental but also are taught to us in our most formative years. In fact, our basic value system probably is pretty well determined at a very young age, as Robert Fulghum points out in his best-selling book, *All I Really Need to Know I Learned in Kindergarten.*[27]

Speakers are best advised to appeal to known values shared by their audience rather than try to convince their audience to adopt new values. Some speeches don't just appeal to existing values, they seek to re-inforce those values. A Fourth of July speech, a eulogy honoring a great hero, or an inspirational speech can be thought of as fulfilling a value-strengthening function. For the most part, speakers need to treat values as a given and build on them. For example, Martin Luther King Jr.'s "I Have a Dream" speech was not so much a call for new values as for Americans to live up to the values stated in the Declaration of Independence and the Bill of Rights.

Motives

Humans are motivated by a wide variety of desires, for example, popularity, financial security, love, peace, and so on. You should learn as much as you can about the likely motives of your audience relative to your topic. For example, a speaker at a graduation ceremony can assume that the audience is there to be inspired and to receive their diplomas. A lengthy speech on the Magna Carta would be inappropriate for this audience. On the other hand, a graduation speech focusing on the successes of graduates from the same school might be just what the audience wants.

On Independence Day, many Americans celebrate the values embodied in the Declaration of Independence at outdoor rallies and picnics.

One specific type of motive concerns why your audience members are attending your speech. In most classroom situations, the answer is simple: because they have to. In those situations, you have to work harder at holding the audience's interest and connecting to their needs than if they had come especially to hear you speak. In Chapter 9 we offer some suggestions that will help you connect with an audience and gain their attention. Even an audience member who has come to hear you needs to be held. It is easy to lose an audience and very difficult to recapture their attention, as any experienced speaker can testify.

Expectations

Closely tied to their motives for attending the speech are your audience's specific expectations. If audience members expect to be entertained, and you deliver a serious speech on the dangers of ozone depletion, you are unlikely to receive a favorable reception. Similarly, if most audience members expect a serious lesson on a topic not to be taken lightly, you owe it to them to meet this expectation. It is usually wise to match your speech as much to the audience members' expectations as is possible while still achieving your goals.

Generally, speeches contrary to a majority of audience members' expectations may backfire or, at the very least, be apathetically received. For example, we once attended a graduation ceremony where the speaker used the opportunity to preach his view on "political correctness." Families and friends were there to honor and celebrate the graduates' accomplishments, but they were instead treated to a

Figure 6.3
Maslow's Hierarchy
of Needs

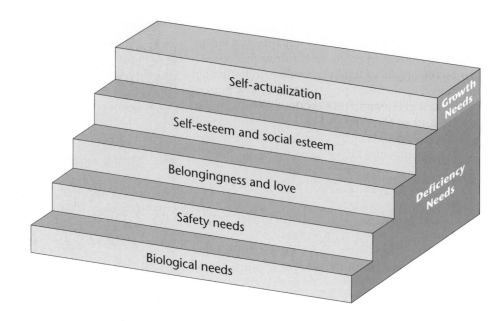

political statement. Whereas such an address might have been appropriate at a meeting of the faculty senate, it missed the mark for the assembled graduates and their guests. The fact that the audience prematurely applauded and shouted loudly at what they thought was the conclusion of the speech reinforced how inappropriate the speech was.

Needs

As we pointed out in Chapter 1, needs are physical and mental states that motivate us to behave in ways that lead to their satisfaction. Abraham Maslow wrote that we experience two sets of personal needs: deficiency needs and growth needs.[28] **Deficiency needs** are basic human needs. **Growth needs** are higher-order human needs. Maslow arranged these two sets of needs in the form of a hierarchy to show that our deficiency needs must be satisfied routinely before our growth needs become important to us.

As Figure 6.3 indicates, there are four sets of deficiency needs: (1) *biological needs,* such as food, water, and air; (2) *safety needs,* such as protection from physical harm; (3) *belongingness and love needs,* such as a child's need for the love of a parent; and (4) *self-esteem and social-esteem needs,* which involve believing in our self-worth and finding confirmation of that belief from others. Growth needs are not as straightforward as deficiency needs. They include self-actualization, knowledge and understanding, and aesthetic needs. Self-actualization is the most commonly discussed growth need. According to Maslow, *self-actualization* is the process of fully realizing one's potential. Self-actualized people not only understand themselves but also accept themselves for who they are and what they have achieved.

As you analyze your audience, consider how your speech can help them satisfy their likely needs. For example, many motivational speakers seek to help people satisfy their needs for self-actualization. On the other hand, someone selling home security equipment would appeal to safety needs.

Learning About Your Audience

The preceding discussion of audience diversity may seem overwhelming at first. After all, most of us have only a few friends who we could describe in terms of all of the attributes of cultural, demographic, and individual diversity. Fortunately, as a speaker, you do not need to know everything there is to know about your audience. Rather, focus your efforts on learning about those characteristics most relevant to your speech purpose. There are three basic ways to learn about audience members: observation, asking for information, and doing a survey.

Observation

The most direct way to learn about audience members is by careful observation. In your own public speaking class, you will observe your classmates on a daily basis and particularly when they are speaking. You will learn a lot about their cultural background, demographic characteristics, and even their beliefs, attitudes, and values. If you are speaking to an audience outside your classroom, try to observe them in advance of your speech. Many demographic characteristics should be readily observable: age, sex, ethnicity, and so on.

Ask Someone Familiar With the Audience

If you cannot observe the audience for yourself, talk to someone who knows them. In many cases you will be invited to speak by a member of the group. For example, the authors have spoken on numerous occasions to service groups in our community. One of us was recently asked to speak to a group that helps senior citizens deal with Medicare and other health insurance issues. Knowing that helped the speaker to choose examples that would be directly related to their mission. Having had a parent who spent time in a nursing home helped the speaker to relate to the audience's mission and understand their needs.

Survey Your Audience

In some cases you will have the opportunity to conduct a survey of your audience. This is one of the best ways to determine attitudes, values, beliefs, and knowledge levels, which are typically very hard to determine from mere observation. There is a danger of assuming that based on appearances your audience holds certain attitudes. A speaker may commit a major gaffe if he or she assumes attitudes based solely on culture or demographics.

Many professional speakers use survey data in designing their speeches. Your instructor may offer you the opportunity to survey your classmates prior to speaking. If so, avail yourself of the opportunity, but be sure to make the survey anonymous and brief. Too many questions will lead to no responses, and requiring respondents to identify themselves may inhibit candor. The box "Surveying Your Audience" provides an example of a survey by a student who plans to speak to the audience about cell phone safety. Notice that the questions focus on the use of cell phones while driving. In particular, this speaker wants to determine if the audience members think that by using hands-free headsets they are driving safely. If so, the speech will need to cite study results that claim that it's the distraction of a conversation more than the use of one hand that is the source of accidents.

Confronting Constraints

constraint
A limitation on choices in a speech situation.

We all face certain constraints on action. A **constraint** is a limitation on your choices. Among the common constraints you may face in giving your speech are the facts pertaining to the situation, legal constraints, ethical constraints, nature of the occasion, traditions, time, and resources. Let's examine each of these.

Facts Pertaining to the Situation

President John Adams observed that "facts are stubborn things."[29] Although some people seem oblivious to the facts governing their situation, sooner or later they must face reality. A speaker who hasn't done research is likely to be embarrassed by the lack of knowledge. As we noted earlier, part of preparing for a speech is to find out what it is that your audience knows, and make sure you know more. Furthermore, it is important to cite the sources from which you have learned your facts. Your audience will perceive you as a more knowledgeable speaker if they know you have solid sources for your facts.

Legal Constraints

We all must abide by certain legal constraints in our speaking. Libel and slander laws, for example, forbid certain types of speech. Other laws cover when and where groups may peaceably assemble. Some anti-abortion activists have been successfully prosecuted, for example, for blocking the entrances to abortion clinics. Although the First Amendment guarantees freedom of speech and assembly, these rights are not license to do what you please.

Some speakers, however, have effectively challenged and even broken laws for a purpose. Nelson Mandela was willing to spend much of his life in jail to bring

154

about the end of apartheid in South Africa. Ultimately, this self-sacrifice helped to sway world opinion against the White minority government of South Africa and led to Mandela's election as South Africa's president.

In your case, it is highly unlikely that you will choose to purposefully break the law to further the cause advanced in one of your speeches. Yet unless you check on the legal constraints relevant to your situation, you may accidentally break a law of which you are unaware. In our own experience, we've had students show up to class with everything from exotic beers to poisonous pets, both of which are illegal on our campus. We've learned, consequently, that it is necessary for us to check on the topics and plans of our students well before their time to actually speak. Check with your instructor before you unintentionally pit yourself against the law.

Legal constraints may also affect the range of topics and the positions you take on them. For example, we recently heard a speech on why sharing music files on the Internet through services such as Napster should be totally free of charge. Of course, at the time there had been a great deal of litigation on the issue, and the courts had ruled that such unfettered distribution of music on the Internet, without paying royalties to the artists, violated U.S. copyright laws. Thus the speech was about a topic on which the audience had no power to effect change.

Ethical Constraints

We discussed ethical considerations for public speaking in detail in Chapter 4. At this point, we simply want to remind you of the fact that as a speaker and as a listener you will face ethical constraints. Although something may technically be legal, that doesn't make it ethical.

Nature of the Occasion

What is the nature of the occasion prompting you to speak? You may recall that after the death of former President Ronald Reagan, his son Ron Reagan used the opportunity of his eulogy for his father to issue a thinly veiled attack against politicians such as President George W. Bush. The younger Reagan acknowledged that his father was a deeply religious man, but one who "never made the fatal mistake of so many politicians wearing his faith on his sleeve to gain political advantage. True, after he was shot and nearly killed early in his presidency, he came to believe that God had spared him in order that he might do well. But he accepted that as a responsibility, not a mandate. And there is a profound difference."[30] Some criticized the use of a solemn occasion such as this to raise a political issue; others applauded young Reagan's forthrightness at a time when the nation was watching.

You will most likely give speeches to classes during normal class times. Your audience is a captive one. Given that unavoidable fact, you must always decide whether your topic and presentation are appropriate to this context and occasion. One of our students made his classmates extremely uncomfortable by discussing his own first sexual experience. Such personal disclosure is inappropriate in a classroom setting. Similarly, vulgarity, profanity, and the like are obviously not suitable for the class. Even excessively casual slang is probably not appropriate for an academic environment. When you have a doubt as to the appropriateness of your speech for your class, it is always wise to check with your instructor.

Traditions

Many speeches are governed by tradition. Whereas this is not a major factor in most classroom speeches, it could be when you are called on to speak in situations outside the classroom. For example, many service clubs, such as Rotary or Lions, have a whole set of traditions that may seem puzzling to the outsider. For instance, there is a good deal of good-natured poking fun at certain members, "fines" are levied for infractions such as getting your name in the paper, and so forth. Major corporations, such as IBM and Apple, each have their own set of traditions. IBM is formal; Apple is much less so. In speaking to either group, therefore, you would want to reflect the degree of formality each expected in terms of dress, demeanor, and style of presentation.

Time

How much time do you have to give your speech? If you have been asked to speak for 5 minutes and you ramble on for an hour, the response will be predictably negative. On the other hand, imagine paying to hear an hour lecture by a major public figure and having the speech end in 10 minutes. You need to know and respect time limits, as well as match how much information you cover in your speech to your allotted time. For instance, it is generally better to cover a narrow topic thoroughly than to try to cover a wide range of points superficially.

Time is also a factor to consider in your preparation. If you have a week to prepare a speech, you probably don't have time to send for information from outside sources. If you have a month, you probably do. You also will need time for practice. Public speaking deserves the same degree of practice as shooting free throws, swinging a golf club, or learning a new exercise in gymnastics. Simply put, it cannot possibly be mastered without some degree of repetition. And this means committing time to practice as far in advance of the speech as possible. Relaxation techniques and other approaches to managing anxiety also require time to master.

Resources

Two questions are involved here. First, what resources do you have available to you? Resources include money, information sources, other people who might assist you, and the like. Second, what resources do you need to accomplish your speaking goal? If your resources match or exceed what you need, you are fine. If you lack the necessary resources, however, you must either redefine your goal or obtain more resources.

Suppose you are assigned to give a speech with at least three visual aids. How do you go about getting these? If you have enough money, you may be able to pay to have pictures enlarged to poster size or to have overhead transparencies prepared. If your classroom is equipped with a computer and projector, you may be able to use special software to present part of your speech. If not, what alternative resources do you have? If you have a friend who is an art major, perhaps he or she can help you make posters. Whatever your situation, you need to give careful consideration to the resources you have or will need to obtain to achieve your goal.

Summary

In this chapter, we have provided the tools to analyze your audience and adapt your speech goals, both long and short term, to the audience and the situation. Here, we recap the four major areas to consider.

Analyze your audience in terms of cultural variables:

- Power distance
- Collectivism versus individualism
- Femininity versus masculinity
- Uncertainty avoidance
- Long-term orientation versus short-term orientation

Analyze your audience in terms of demographic characteristics:

- Age
- Gender and biological sex
- Ethnicity
- Geographic origin
- Socioeconomic status
- Occupation
- Religion
- Language usage

Analyze your audience in terms of individual diversity, including their:

- Knowledge
- Beliefs
- Attitudes
- Values
- Motives
- Expectations
- Needs

Adapt your goals to the audience and the total rhetorical situation. Consider the following constraints:

- Facts
- Legal constraints
- Ethical constraints
- Nature of the occasion

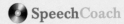

SpeechCoach

To evaluate your understanding of this chapter, see the Quizzes on your CD.

www.mhhe.com
/brydon5

Visit the Online Learning Center for helpful study resources, including practice tests, key term crossword puzzles, and PowerWeb articles for research and review.

- Traditions

- Time

- Resources

Check Your Understanding: Exercises and Activities

SpeechCoach

For a review of key terms in this chapter, see the Key Terms Flashcards on your CD.

1. Given the topic of alcohol abuse, how might you develop your speech presentation differently if your audience were made up of (a) high school students, (b) students your own age, (c) bar and tavern owners in your community, or (d) recovering alcoholics? In a short paper, explain how your approach and purpose would differ in each case.

2. Create a model of your belief system, including your core beliefs, authority beliefs, and representative derived beliefs, on one of the following topics: gun control, the importance of voting, abortion, civil rights. What does your belief system say about how susceptible you are to being influenced on the topic selected?

3. Interview a student from another country who is studying at your university. What most surprised him or her about American culture? What would Americans be most surprised to know about his or her culture? Write a short paper or give a short talk about what you have discovered.

4. Learn as much as you can about the cultural, demographic, and individual diversity of your classmates. Construct a short questionnaire that will guide you in preparing for an upcoming speech. After obtaining your instructor's approval, write a survey about your chosen topic. You might ask questions about what your audience already knows about the topic, their attitudes for or against your position, and their level of interest in the topic. Distribute the questionnaire to your classmates and collect their responses (anonymously, of course). Tabulate the results. For example, if your topic is banning the sale of handguns known as Saturday night specials, you might report that 60 percent of your classmates were familiar with the term, while 40 percent were not; that 50 percent agreed with a ban, 20 percent opposed one, and the remainder had no opinion; and that 30 percent felt gun violence was a major issue, while 70 percent did not. Based on these results, write a short paper on how you used this information to shape your speech. Also indicate how your plans for your speech may have changed based on the information from your survey.

Notes

1. Aristotle, *Rhetoric,* trans. W. Rhys Roberts (New York: Modern Library, 1954), 24.
2. Lloyd Bitzer, "The Rhetorical Situation," *Philosophy and Rhetoric* 1 (1968): 5. Bitzer further defines an exigence as "an imperfection marked by urgency; it is a defect, an obstacle, something waiting to be done, a thing which is other than it should be" (6). In this text we prefer to focus on the speaker's goal, which, strictly speaking, is to *overcome the exigence* present in the rhetorical situation.
3. Bitzer, "Rhetorical Situation," 8.
4. Haya El Nasser and Paul Overberg, "Index Charts Growth in Diversity Despite 23% Jump, Segregation Is Still Going on, Researchers Say" [Lexis-Nexis, 5 August 2001] (*USA Today,* 15 March 2001, 3A).
5. Geert Hofstede, *Cultures and Organizations: Software of the Mind* (London: McGraw-Hill, 1991), 14.
6. Hofstede, *Cultures and Organizations,* 14.
7. Hofstede, *Cultures and Organizations,* 262.
8. Hofstede, *Cultures and Organizations,* 260.
9. Hofstede, *Cultures and Organizations,* 261.

10. Hofstede, *Cultures and Organizations,* 53.

11. Hofstede, *Cultures and Organizations,* 261.

12. Hofstede, *Cultures and Organizations,* 262.

13. Hofstede, *Cultures and Organizations,* 263.

14. Hofstede, *Cultures and Organizations,* 261.

15. Hofstede, *Cultures and Organizations,* 262–63.

16. John Gray, *Men Are From Mars, Women Are From Venus: A Practical Guide for Improving Communication and Getting What You Want in Your Relationships* (New York: HarperCollins, 1992).

17. Julia T. Wood, *Gendered Lives* (Belmont, Calif.: Wadsworth, 1994).

18. Robert A. Rosenblatt, "Census Illustrates Diversity From Sea to Shining Sea; Population: Massive Surge of Immigration in '90s Makes Nearly One in Every Three U.S. Residents a Minority, Report Says. Trend Is Nationwide" [Lexis-Nexis, 5 August 2001] (*Los Angeles Times,* 13 March 2001, Part A; Part 1; Page 16).

19. Reuters News Service, "Six in Ten Americans Favor Stem Cell Research" [Yahoo News, http://dailynews.yahoo.com/h/nm/20010726/hl/stemcell_3.html, 26 July 2001].

20. David Westphal, "More Speak Spanish in U.S.," *Sacramento Bee,* 6 August 2001, A12.

21. Sarah Trenholm, *Persuasion and Social Influence* (Englewood Cliffs, N.J.: Prentice-Hall, 1989), 6.

22. Milton Rokeach, *Beliefs, Attitudes and Values* (San Francisco: Jossey-Bass, 1968), 6–21.

23. Cooperative Institutional Research Program, *The American Freshman: 2000 Executive Summary.* [http://www.gseis.ucla.edu/heri/00_exec_summary.htm, 24 July 2001] Los Angeles: Higher Education Research Institute, University of California at Los Angeles.

24. Martin Fishbein and Icek Ajzen, *Belief, Attitude, Intention, and Behavior: An Introduction to Theory and Research* (Reading, Mass.: Addison-Wesley, 1975), 6.

25. Trenholm, *Persuasion and Social Influence,* 11, based on Rokeach, *Beliefs, Attitudes and Values.*

26. Milton Rokeach, "Change and Stability in American Value Systems, 1968–1971," in *Understanding Human Values: Individual and Societal,* ed. Milton Rokeach (New York: Free Press, 1979), 129–53.

27. Robert Fulghum, *All I Really Need to Know I Learned in Kindergarten* (New York: Ivy Books, 1988).

28. Abraham H. Maslow, *Motivation and Personality,* 2nd ed. (New York: Harper & Row, 1970).

29. John Adams used this phrase in a summation to a jury. You can read a more complete text at http://www.law.umkc.edu/faculty/projects/ftrials/trialheroes/HEROSEARCH5.htm.

30. Ronald Prescott Reagan, "Remarks by [Ronald] Prescott Reagan," 10 June 2004 [Retrieved 10 June 2004 from http://www.ronaldreaganmemorial.com/remarks_by_Prescott_Reagan.asp].

Putting Theory
Into Practice

Sound research involves going beyond the Internet.

Researching Your Message

Objectives

After reading this chapter and reviewing the learning resources on your CD-ROM and at the Online Learning Center, you should be able to:

- Explain the benefits of focusing on the audience when you choose an appropriate topic, formulate a specific purpose, and research a speech.

- Conduct systematic library research to find support for a speech.

- Conduct a search of the Internet to find support for a speech.

- Conduct a meaningful interview with an expert on the topic of a speech.

- Prepare References or Works Cited for your speech.

- Record information in a usable form for your speech.

Key Concepts

abstract

Boolean operators

index

key word

online catalog

research

subject heading

> **❝** Genius is one percent inspiration and ninety-nine percent perspiration. **❞**
>
> –THOMAS EDISON

This chapter is about the hard work that is essential to transforming thought into public speech. We look at the process set into motion when your instructor first explains the nature of the speaking assignment you must complete. The specific topics we'll examine include focusing on the audience, topic, and specific purpose; finding support, including library resources, the Internet, and interviews; and finally, preparing References or Works Cited and recording information.

Focusing on the Audience, Topic, and Specific Purpose

As we discussed in Chapter 6, the situation we face as speakers includes our goals, the audience, and constraints. To successfully prepare a speech that fulfills our goals, we need to understand whether our audience favors, opposes, or is undecided about our goals. We need to understand the diversity of our audience, including cultural, demographic, and individual differences. Understanding our audience does not mean simply telling them what they want to hear; it means knowing whether our basic message is likely to fall on receptive ears or to be tuned out.

In addition to an audience's attitude toward our topic, we need to consider their level of knowledge about and interest in the topic. If they already know most of what we are going to say, they are likely to think our speech is a waste of time. On the other hand, if the audience members know nothing about our topic, they may not be able to understand the speech. So we need to meet our audience's level of knowledge—presenting them with something new and worthwhile, yet not going beyond what they can absorb in a short time. As we select topics, do research, and construct a speech, we should always keep our audience in mind. Focusing on the audience is the hallmark of the successful speaker.

As we discussed in Chapter 2, a good speech topic should be interesting to the speaker, interesting to the audience, appropriate to the situation, appropriate to the time available, manageable, and worthwhile. A thorough analysis of the situation should help meet these standards. Understanding the needs we share with the audience, the situation, the time available, and our resources should help to determine a topic the audience is likely to find involving.

The question for many students, though, is "Where do I find the ideas for a speech topic?" As we discussed in Chapter 2, you may begin with your own knowledge or turn to the popular media, the Internet, or a number of other sources.

In an introductory speech class, the general purpose of your speech–to inform, persuade, or entertain–probably will be assigned. What you will not be assigned is a specific purpose, which, as discussed in Chapter 2, is your goal or objective in speaking to a particular audience. If, for example, your general purpose is to inform, your specific purpose might be "to inform the audience on how to scuba dive."

Researching the Speech

Once we decide on a topic, we need to find materials to develop and support the speech. Keep in mind that the quality of our sources directly affects the quality of our insights within the speech. The process of gathering these supporting materials is called **research.** There are two basic steps to research. First there is the search, whereby we find the sources likely to contain information on our topic. Then there is the research, in which we examine these sources for materials we can use. Many people mistakenly rely on the first source they find on their topic, jotting down a few notes and then writing their speech. In other words, they skip to the research phase of the process before they have done a thorough search of information available on their topic. To avoid this mistake, which can lead to an incomplete and even deceptive speech, we look for as many sources as possible before deciding about the materials on which we'll most rely.

research
The process of gathering supporting materials for a speech.

There are innumerable sources from which to gather materials on a topic, including personal experience and knowledge, nonprint media, library resources, interviews, and the Internet. In this section we focus on three of these sources: the library, the Internet, and interviews with experts. This does not mean that you shouldn't use personal experience or other sources of information. However, to build a well-supported speech, authoritative sources, such as those discussed in the following section, are essential.

The Library

Most research for a public speaking class will involve a trip to the campus library. The library is the intellectual center of most universities and colleges–the repository of the history of ideas and thought. Although campus libraries vary in their extensiveness and degree of sophistication, the basic principles of a library search are the same. The library of the twenty-first century actually takes two forms. There is the traditional brick and mortar building, of course, but there is also an online presence. A good library needs both–and we need to be familiar with both to research our speeches.

The first step in using a library is familiarization. Most campus libraries feature in-person and online guided tours, handouts, and special seminars for groups interested in a particular area of research. Your instructor may have your class take a library tour or send you on a library scavenger hunt to familiarize you with the library. Whatever you do, though, don't wait until you are facing a deadline before familiarizing yourself with your library. If you didn't do it during your first few weeks on campus, make it a priority now.

We recommend the following four steps for library research.

Tips and Tactics

Four Steps of Library Research

1. Select key words.
2. Search the library catalog.
3. Search relevant indexes, abstracts, and other databases.
4. Consult reference sources.

Although each step isn't required every time for library research, it's useful to know about each step and how the steps are connected. Let's look at each step in detail.

Select Key Words

key word

A word in the abstract, title, subject heading, or text of an entry that can be used to search an electronic database.

subject heading

A standard word or phrase used by libraries to catalog books or other publications.

Key words are important words taken from the abstract, title, subject heading, or text of an entry and used to search an electronic database.[1] They are like the combination to a safe: If we have the right combination, we can easily open the door; without it, our chances of opening the door are slim. Thus, the most effective library search begins with searching key words on the topic of interest.

In addition to key words, **subject headings,** developed by the Library of Congress, are standardized throughout libraries across the country. These headings often lead to sources we might otherwise miss. For example, suppose we are interested in the topic of the "three strikes law." We searched our university library's catalog for books on the topic and found three. However, the detailed record for the books revealed that the Library of Congress uses the subject heading *mandatory sentence.* Searching for that term yielded 21 books–a sevenfold increase. Although we normally begin our search using key words and phrases that seem logical, we check the official subject headings and try them as well. These can multiply our results several times over.

Another hint for key word or subject searching is to use truncation and wildcard symbols. For example, in our university a star (*) is used for these purposes. Thus, to search for *sentence, sentences,* and *sentencing,* we would type *sentenc** in the search box. The search engine will find all records with any string of characters following *sentenc.* Similarly, to search for both *woman* and *women,* the key word *wom*n* would do the job. Be sure to ask what characters your library uses as wildcards as it varies from library to library and database to database.

Search the Library Catalog

online catalog

A computerized database of library holdings.

Boolean operators

Terms, such as *and, or,* and *not,* used to narrow or broaden a computerized search of two or more related terms.

Most libraries today use computerized online catalogs, accessible from off campus as well as in the library building. An **online catalog** is a computerized listing of library holdings. Library catalogs are searchable by key words for subject, author, and title. When beginning a search on a topic, it is unlikely that we will know specific authors or titles. Thus, the key words search is the most likely basis for a search.

When using an online catalog or similar database for a key word search, we use **Boolean operators.** These are terms, such as *and, or,* and *not,* used to narrow or broaden a computerized search of two or more related terms. Some data-

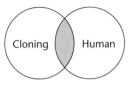
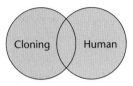
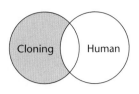

Cloning *AND* Human   Cloning *OR* Human   Cloning *NOT* Human

Figure 7.1
Boolean Operators
Help Narrow or Broaden
a Search

bases and library catalogs will *assume* the Boolean operator *and,* unless we supply another, while others will require us to type in *and* or +. For example, if we enter search terms *human cloning* and the database assumes the *and,* it will locate all sources that use both the word *human* and the word *cloning,* even if they are not used together. On the other hand, if the *and* is not assumed, the database may only locate sources where the phrase *human cloning* appears. Depending on our search needs, we need to determine which method is used in the library catalog. Check with a librarian at your school to learn whether you need to use Boolean operators, or experiment with different search combinations until you discover which way your library catalog operates. How Boolean operators can be used to broaden or narrow a search is shown in Figure 7.1.

Tips and Tactics

Expanding Your Search

- When we locate a book or other source that is interesting, we check to see what subject headings are used by the library to index the book in addition to the one used to find it. These subject headings can then provide new search terms to expand our search and locate additional sources on our topic.
- When we visit the stacks, we do a little browsing as we find the specific books we have noted. Because books are shelved by subject, it is not unusual to find a book closely related to our topic that we overlooked. This serendipitous search for information often turns up better sources than those we originally found.
- Follow the leads suggested by general books. The authors of books have done much of our work for us. A book's bibliography or footnotes lead to other sources. We read the more recent books first. In many ways, a researcher is like a detective looking for clues. A good general book on a topic is like a room full of clues. The author will have left fingerprints all over the place.

Search Relevant Indexes, Abstracts, and Databases

An **index** is a listing of sources of information, usually in newspapers, journals, and magazines that are not freely available via the open Internet, alphabetically by topic. An **abstract** is a summary of an article or a report. Every topic you can imagine is classified in one or more specialized indexes. A good library has hundreds or even thousands of indexes related to specialized fields. Some indexes list and abstract articles in journals. Today, more and more indexes are available in the form of online databases. For example, a partial list of databases available through our university library is provided in Table 7.1.

index
A listing of sources of information, usually in newspapers, journals, and magazines, alphabetically by topic.

abstract
A summary of an article or a report.

Table 7.1

Representative
List of Databases
at CSU, Chico

Academic Search	GROVEmusic
America: History and Life	Historical Abstracts
Anthropological Index Online	Lexis-Nexis Academic
Applied Science & Technology Index	Lexis-Nexis Congressional
Art Abstracts	Lexis-Nexis Government Periodicals Index
Biological Abstracts	BIOSIS	MEDLINE [NLM Gateway]
Biological & Agricultural Index	P.A.I.S. [Public Affairs Information Service]
Britannica Online	Philosopher's Index
Communication & Mass Media Complete	ProQuest Newstand
Contemporary Authors	PsycINFO
Country Watch	Religion Database
CQ Researcher	ScienceDirect
Encyclopaedia Britannica	SPORT DISCUS
Ethnic NewsWatch	Stat-USA
Factiva	Wiley InterScience
GROVEart	

You can probably guess from the titles what the subject matter is for most of these indexes. Whether your topic is art, science, religion, philosophy, or health and medicine, computerized databases can assist you in finding reliable information. Your library will undoubtedly differ from ours in the available indexes. However, the basic search principles will be the same regardless of the index used.

We will illustrate how to do a search using two popular databases. The first, Academic Search, is an excellent source for searching scholarly and professional journals in the social sciences, humanities, and physical sciences. This database contains information on everything from astronomy to religion, law, psychology, and current events. Not only are citations and abstracts of articles available, but Academic Search also allows us to access the full texts of many articles. To search, we simply follow easy on-screen directions to enter appropriate search terms. The same Boolean operators we would use in an online catalog search can be used with most computerized databases. When we enter our search, a list of citations will be produced, and we mark the ones that interest us for viewing. Depending on the library's facilities, we may be able to print, copy to a disk, or even e-mail the results of our search to ourselves.

To illustrate the power of Academic Search, in late 2004 we did a search for articles on human cloning. First we typed in the words *cloning and human,* which would retrieve any article in which both words appeared, even if they were not together. We got 3,050 hits, far too many to be useful. By limiting the search to the exact phrase *human cloning,* our search netted 1,219 citations, still more than we could use. Academic Search allows us to further refine our search, which we did by limiting it to only those articles that were peer reviewed or refereed. That means experts in the field had authenticated the article for publication. That narrowed our search to 374 sources, still more than we needed. Finally, we decided to limit our search to articles from the last six months, which reduced our results to a manageable 27 citations. Of these, 8 were available in full text, meaning we could actually print out a copy or e-mail them to ourselves without leaving our computer. Although databases such as Academic Search may initially seem to produce far too many results to be usable, a careful narrowing of the parameters of our search can lead to productive and easily accessible results. Although your library may not have this exact database, chances are it has a similar database that can access reliable published information on a wide variety of topics.

Of course, not every library has a physical or electronic copy of every journal listed in any given index or database. Thus you must compare the most promising articles from your search with your library's holding of journals. Some libraries provide listings of the journals they have. The online catalog may also list journals. You would look under the journal title, for example, to see if your library had a particular journal. Even if your library does not have it, you may be able to use interlibrary loan services to obtain a copy, if time permits. Also, some libraries subscribe to special services, which enable them to have copies of journals not held in their collections faxed to the library for a nominal charge.

Another powerful database is Lexis-Nexis, which is widely used in business, publishing, medicine, and law. The educational version is Lexis-Nexis Academic. You'll need to inquire at your library as to whether this database is available on your campus. If it is not, you may have access to a similar database, called ProQuest Newsstand. If your library has no database for searching newspapers and similar periodicals, you can go directly to the Web sites of most major newspapers, such as the *New York Times*. However, for articles more than a few days old, these databases normally charge a download fee. The advantage to Lexis-Nexis is that it includes virtually all major newspapers, magazines, scripts of televised public affairs programs, newswire reports (such as Reuters), medical, and legal sources. A database such as the one for the *New York Times* indexes only one paper. Lexis-Nexis is a full-text service. If we choose, it not only looks in titles for the words we search for but anywhere in the text. Thus, if we are looking for a report of a speech in which someone made a particularly memorable statement, we can use Lexis-Nexis to search for that specific phrase in any of the newspapers, magazines, or TV news reports that covered the speech. Unlike subject searches, when we do a search for a word in a text, we are going to get dozens to thousands of "hits" unless we carefully narrow our search.

We tried our search on human cloning on Lexis-Nexis, using the major newspaper database. Typing in the words *human and cloning,* we got the following message: "This search has been interrupted because it will return more than 1,000 documents." Even the exact phrase, *human cloning,* got the same response. So we narrowed our search by asking for only the last six months. That search yielded 441 citations, again far too many. Then we shifted to the medical and health journals database. Looking for the words *human and cloning* yielded five sources, while the phrase *human cloning* gave us two. These are some examples of how powerful databases can help us find high-quality information that is readily accessible in our library or even in full-text form that can be downloaded on a computer.

Consult Reference Sources

Frequently we need to find a very specific fact—for example, how much plastic was produced in the United States in a certain year. We could search a dozen articles and never find that number. But a good reference book, such as the *Statistical*

Abstract of the United States, puts that kind of information at our fingertips. For an on-line source of reliable government statistics, try the Web site http://www.fedstats.gov/, which bills itself as "the gateway to statistics from over 100 U.S. Federal agencies."[2] This site includes topics from A to Z, map statistics, links to various federal agencies, and even the ability to access the online version of the *Statistical Abstract of the United States.*

Perhaps we need a good quotation to begin or end our speech. Numerous books of quotations are available. Your library probably has books such as *Bartlett's Quotations* on its shelves. However, an easier way to find quotations is to go to Bartleby .com's Great Books Online at http://www.bartleby.com/, which includes more than 87,000 quotations. You can combine your search to include several sources at once, including the venerable *Bartlett's.* For the first edition of this book, we were interested in a quotation frequently used by the late Robert Kennedy that went something like, "Some men see things as they are and say, why; I dream things that never were and say, why not." We expended several hours of library research tracking down the original source. For this edition we used Bartleby.com, and in less than a minute we had found the original quotation. It is actually, "You see things; and you say 'Why?' But I dream things that never were; and I say 'Why not?'" The original source is George Bernard Shaw's play, *Back to Methuselah.* Ironically, although Kennedy used the quotation as a theme in his 1968 campaign for the presidency, the actual speaker of these words in Shaw's play is the serpent enticing Eve in the Garden of Eden.[3]

Numerous other reference books can be found in libraries, including encyclopedias, some of which are available online. Although the information in general encyclopedias is rather basic, a number of specialized encyclopedias are also available. Here's a representative list of encyclopedias provided by Kristin Johnson, an Instructional Librarian at our university:

- *Encyclopedia of Advertising*
- *Encyclopedia of Global Change*
- *Encyclopedia of the Human Brain*
- *Encyclopedia of Skin and Skin Disorders*
- *Encyclopedia of Death and Dying*
- *Encyclopedia of Criminology and Deviant Behavior*
- *Encyclopedia of Drugs, Alcohol & Addictive Behavior*
- *Encyclopedia of Interior Design*
- *Encyclopedia of North American Sports History*
- *Encyclopedia of Popular Culture*
- *Encyclopedia of Movie Special Effects*
- *Encyclopedia of Creativity*
- *Encyclopedia of Sleep and Dreaming*
- *Encyclopedia of Homosexuality*
- *Encyclopedia of Television*
- *Encyclopedia of World Terrorism*
- *The Film Encyclopedia*
- *International Encyclopedia of Sexuality*
- *Violence in America: An Encyclopedia*

There are countless other reference books to which you can turn in the effort to track down information. For example, almanacs and yearbooks, such as *The World Almanac and Book of Facts* and *Information Please Almanac,* are useful sources of statistics and facts. Digests of information, such as *Facts on File* and *Editorial Research Reports,* are useful sources for information on current issues. Biographies, such as the *Who's Who* series, help you find out about the qualifications of various sources. Atlases are valuable in learning about the world. By consulting an atlas, you can learn not only where a country is geographically but also important facts about it. Shortly after the attacks on the World Trade Center and the Pentagon, many Americans found themselves reaching for an atlas to find out exactly where Afghanistan was located.

The Internet

The first place most of our students look for information on their speech topics is the Internet. And why not? We go to the Internet ourselves for everything from the scores of our favorite sports team to research for scholarly articles. Many of the sources we consulted for this book were found on the Internet. There is nothing inherently wrong with using online sources for your speeches. It's not whether you find your sources online or on the shelf that matters. Rather, it's whether the sources are valid and reliable.

Unfortunately, the Internet is notoriously unreliable. For example, during the 2004 presidential campaign, a photo of Democratic nominee John Kerry sharing a stage with Jane Fonda to protest the war in Vietnam was widely distributed on the Internet. Because Fonda had actually gone to North Vietnam during the Vietnam War, many Americans regarded her as unpatriotic, and some called her Hanoi Jane. A picture of someone who wanted to be president on the same stage with Fonda would be damning. It turns out, however, that the photo was a fake as Ken Light, the photographer who shot the picture of Kerry alone at the podium, explained in an editorial in the *Washington Post:* "I found out somebody had pulled my Kerry picture off my agency's Web site, stuck Fonda at his side, and then used the massive, unedited reach of the Internet to distribute it all over the world."[4] As we were writing this book, we found the original photos and the faked composite posted on the Web (http://www.snopes.com/photos/politics/kerry2.asp). The faked photo looked very authentic until we saw the originals. If fake photos can be circulated worldwide via the Internet, imagine how much easier it is to circulate words that have been altered or even made up.

It is important to make a distinction between the *open Internet* and using the Internet to access otherwise credible sources. For example, when we accessed Lexis-Nexis to find the article about the faked photo, we used our library's Internet connection. Because Lexis-Nexis charges for its service, only faculty, students, and staff at our university are allowed this access. We could, of course, have dug through microfilmed copies of the *Washington Post* to find the same article. Either way, the credibility of the article is the same as that of the *Washington Post.* On the other hand, billions of Web pages have no gatekeepers determining the authenticity of the material they post. In this section, we discuss how to evaluate open Internet sources.

Most people who search the Web turn to the number one search engine, Google.[5] In December 2004 Google claimed to search more than 8 billion Web pages.[6] Although that makes it extremely powerful, it also makes it somewhat unreliable. Google refuses to disclose, for obvious reasons, the exact methods by which it ranks

"Why don't you Google it?" has become a common expression in our lives.

results. This can lead to some startling results. For example, we typed *martinlutherking* into the Google search engine on July 30, 2004. The number one hit was a Web site called Storm front (http://www.martin lutherking.org/), which is sponsored by a white supremacist organization. The likely reason it is the number one result on Google is that many librarians put this link on their own Web sites as an example of a bogus site, inadvertently causing it to rank very high in Google's results list.

In fairness, we should point out that Google normally returns highly useful results. When we typed *martin luther king* as separate words, rather than as one string of characters, we got much more reasonable results. The number one hit was the Martin Luther King Jr. papers project at Stanford University, a highly credible site (http://www.stanford.edu/group/King/). We have learned, however, to be critical of what we find and not to assume that a high ranking means the site is better than others. And some search engines (not Google) put Web sites that pay a fee at the top of their list. Google's sponsored links are clearly identified as such.

With more than 8 billion Web pages searched, another problem with Google is the vast number of sites that are found in most searches. Our *martin luther king* search revealed more than 2.7 million sites. The order of the results list may or may not reflect your actual interests. Selecting the right terms and properly limiting your search are very important to finding the best results with Google and other search engines.

It's also important to be familiar with "Google bombs." By manipulating various characteristics of a Web site, pranksters have been able to move the search results for particular phrases to the number one result in some comical ways. In July of 2004, for instance, if you typed *miserable failure* in the search box, you were directed to the biography of George W. Bush (http://www.whitehouse.gov/president/gwbbio .html). The number one search result for the phrase *weapons of mass destruction* was a hoax page claiming, "These weapons of mass destruction cannot be displayed" (http://www.coxar.pwp.blueyonder.co.uk/). Probably the most famous Google bomb was in 1999 when typing *more evil than satan* in Google's search box took you to Microsoft's home page. Today that phrase will lead you to several articles about Google bombing.[7]

Evaluating Internet Information

The trickiest part of doing Internet research is knowing how to tell reliable from unreliable sources. You can tell a lot from a Web site's URL. Once you've used a search engine such as Google to locate possible Web sites, look at the URL for clues as to whether it is a legitimate source.[8]

- **Is it a personal Web page?** You can usually tell from the URL because it will often include a person's name following a tilde (~) or percent sign (%).

Considering Diversity

Cultures on the Web

One of the great advantages of the Internet is that it is a global phenomenon. You can literally read newspapers from anywhere in the world. You can send e-mail to and receive it from people on the other side of the globe. In fact, Dr. Madeline Keaveney, a professor at our university, established an e-mail pen-pal program with students in Japan for her intercultural communication class. The possibilities of learning about other cultures and sharing information with people from these cultures is endless.

Although there are Web sites that deal with Native American, Latino, Asian, and African American cultures, any list of these sites would be incomplete and highly selective. Rather, we suggest that you do your own Internet surfing to learn about other cultures and then incorporate that information into your next speech. For starters, we suggest you try Yahoo!, which has numerous links dealing with society and culture (http://www.yahoo.com/Society_and_Culture/). For example, you can learn how different cultures deal with topics such as death and dying, disabilities, families, fashion, food and drink, gender, holidays, mythology and folklore, religion, sexuality, and weddings, just to name a few. So go ahead, reach out globally—from your own computer!

If the server is a commercial Internet service provider, such as geocities.com, aol.com, or angelfire.com, that is another hint it is a questionable source. For most speeches, personal Web pages should be avoided.

- **What is the type of domain?** Government sites are usually .gov, .mil, or .us. Educational sites are .edu. Nonprofit organizations are .org. The domains .com and .net are generally commercial. Look for the types of sites that are most appropriate for your speech topic. Government and educational sites are often the best place to begin for speeches on current events and issues.

- **Who is the Web page's sponsor?** For example, the Web site for this text (www.mhhe.com/brydon5) is published by McGraw-Hill Higher Education. One can assume this is a reliable source of information about our text and its supporting materials. Look for pages sponsored by reputable organizations that have a direct bearing on your speech topic.

Once you have decided a Web page is worth accessing, carefully evaluate what you find. Use this five-point test adapted from the California State University, Chico Meriam Library Instruction Program, called the CRAAP test, which stands for *Currency, Relevance, Authority, Accuracy,* and *Purpose*.[9] These questions are applicable to almost any source of information, but they include a number of specific tests for Internet-based sources.

Tips and Tactics

Evaluating Sources Using the CRAAP Test

Currency

- When was the information published or posted? Has the information been revised or updated? If this is not listed on the Web page, be suspicious. As Figure 7.2 illustrates, you may be able to find that information even if it's not listed by using the "Get Page Info" function in a Web browser such as Netscape. In the PC version of Microsoft's Internet Explorer, selecting *properties* from the *file* menu will often reveal when the Web page was last updated.

- Is the information current or out of date for your topic? If you are speaking about the French revolution, information from several years ago is probably

Figure 7.2

"Get Page Info" Screen
from a Web Page

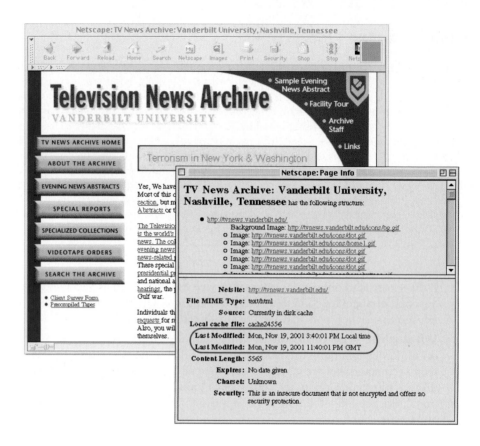

fine. But if you want to discuss the current situation in Iraq, information even
a few weeks old may be out of date.

* Are the links functional? One of the hints that a Web site is out of date is that
it contains dead links.

Relevance

* Does the information answer your question or need?

* Who is the intended audience? Is this information at a level appropriate to
your audience?

* Have you looked at a variety of sources before determining this is one you will
use? Is this the best source you can find to make your point?

* Would you be comfortable using this source for a research paper as well as a
speech?

Authority

* Who is the author/publisher/source/sponsor, and what are their credentials or
organizational affiliations? You can often find this out by clicking "about us" or
"contact us" on the Web page. The URL may also provide a clue.

* What are the author's qualifications to write on the topic?

* Is there contact information, such as a publisher or e-mail address?

- Does the URL reveal anything about the author or source: for example, is it .com, .edu, .gov, .org, or .net?

Accuracy

- Can you tell where the information comes from?
- Is the information supported by evidence such as footnotes, links to other sources, or verifiable sources?
- Has the information been reviewed or refereed by experts? A newspaper, for example, normally edits and checks sources before publishing a story; a personal Web site does not necessarily do so.
- Can you verify any of the information in another source or from personal knowledge?
- Are there spelling, grammar, or other typographical errors?

Purpose

- What is the purpose of the information: to inform, teach, sell, entertain, or persuade?
- Do the authors/sponsors make their intentions or purpose clear?
- Does the information seem unbiased, or is it merely opinion or propaganda? Does the language or tone seem unbiased and free of emotion?
- Are there obvious political, ideological, cultural, religious, institutional, or personal biases?

Interviews

We put off discussing interviews until now for a reason. It is tempting to go into an interview before researching the topic. In a sense, we expect the expert to write the speech. Although interviews with experts can offer useful information and may lead to other sources, they cannot substitute for doing our own research. Thus, an interview should be conducted only after going in person or online to the library and searching the Internet.

Finding potential interviewees on most topics is not difficult. On the topic of recycling, try to arrange an interview with the director of a local recycling center. Community leaders, including members of the city council, also may have information on topics such as recycling, traffic congestion, parking, and growth. At a university, most departments have experts on various topics. Often a call to the department asking if there is anyone familiar with your specific topic will elicit a name. In other cases, simply consult a department's course offerings. Someone who teaches a class on ecology, for example, most likely is an expert in that subject.

Another strategy is to contact organizations related to the topic and ask if someone there would be available to interview. For example, if we were researching the effects of secondhand smoke, the American Lung Association is a likely source of potential interviewees.

Sometimes we already know people who can help. We recall the case of one student who was speaking about a "miracle" weight-loss product. After calling the company's home office and getting the runaround, she contacted her local pharmacist. He informed her that the ingredients in the product were in no way capable of helping a person lose weight–in fact, they were potentially harmful. A brief interview with the pharmacist gave her information she would have had great difficulty finding on her own.

Once we have decided on a person to interview, we recommend the following basic guidelines for before, during, and after the interview. For additional advice, read the box "The Importance of Interviewing by Professor Rick Rigsby."

Before the Interview

- Contact the potential interviewee well in advance. Explain the reason for the meeting and how much time it will take. If the person agrees to be interviewed, ask for a convenient time and place for a meeting (usually at the interviewee's place of business). If possible, confirm the appointment in writing.
- Do some general reading on the topic. Read at least a book or two and some recent articles, or visit relevant Web sites. This will provide a basis for framing questions and focusing on those things that cannot easily be found elsewhere.
- Prepare specific questions in advance. Ask open-ended questions, which will allow the interviewee an opportunity to talk at some length. Of course, be prepared to deviate from the planned questions as answers suggest other avenues to follow.

During the Interview

- Show up on time, dressed professionally, and be ready to begin. Thank the person and explain how the interview will be used. Be sure to ask for permission to tape record the interview if this is desired. If an interview is by phone, there is a legal obligation to inform and gain consent from the other party to tape the conversation.
- Using previous research as a guide, begin with general questions, and then move to specific ones. Be sure to let the interviewee talk. Don't monopolize the conversation; doing so defeats the purpose of the interview.
- Ask the interviewee if he or she can suggest other sources of information–books, pamphlets, periodicals, or other experts. Often an expert will know of sources we never would have thought of ourselves. Sometimes the interviewee may even loan some relevant journals or other publications.
- Use the active listening skills discussed in Chapter 5, especially setting goals, blocking out distracting stimuli, suspending judgment, being sensitive to metacommunication, and using paraphrasing and questioning.
- Either tape record (with permission) or take complete notes during the interview. Ask follow-up questions to make sure to get the essential points on paper. Quotes from the interview used in a speech must be accurate.
- When time is about up, ask the interviewee if there is anything he or she can add to what has been said. Perhaps there is some area that has been completely overlooked.
- Thank the interviewee again for his or her time and exit graciously.

Speaking of . . .

The Importance of Interviewing by *Professor Rick Rigsby*

Dr. Enrique D. "Rick" Rigsby teaches speech communication at Texas A&M University in College Station, Texas. He also serves as a mentor for A&M athletes and is in great demand as a motivational speaker. Before becoming a teacher, he was a television news reporter for seven years. Not only did Rick use the interview as a principal technique in television reporting, he continues to conduct interviews as part of his research, as he explains below. We asked Rick to explain the importance of interviewing to students of public speaking.

To appreciate the role interviewing performs, one must understand that we humans tend to be storytelling animals. Everyone has a history filled with commendations, successes, and struggles. These stories are marked by significant dates and may include a supporting cast of characters. The stories develop in basements and ballparks, departments and dormitories. We experience life, record dramas, and share the stories when called upon. Thus, our stories contribute to newscasts, government reports, research projects, even speeches in communication classes!

For the college student preparing a speech, interviewing someone with expertise on the subject might produce insights other sources cannot generate. Make sure to avoid this one pitfall: Refrain from interviewing the person most available. Rather, carefully select the individual who will enhance your work. A simple question to ask yourself is "Will the interview I conduct enlighten the audience about the subject and increase my credibility as a speaker?"

I have used the medium of interviewing in both my collegiate and professional careers. When I was a speech communication major in college, interviewing individuals for speeches allowed me to use real-life adventure to help inform, persuade, or entertain my audience. As a television news reporter, I interviewed thousands of people in a variety of situations. Imagine talking to a person who has just won the lottery or thrown the winning touchdown pass! Getting the right interview can make the difference between a presentation that few hear or a speech that few will ever forget. I continue to use interviewing today. A large part of my job

as a college professor is to conduct research. My research focuses on volunteers who participated in the civil rights demonstrations of the sixties. An essential part of my research task is to interview those former protesters and document their stories.

If your future includes the preparation of a presentation, you would be well advised to consider the medium of interviewing as a way of obtaining information. Remember, we're a storytelling culture. But what good is a story if it's never told? You know, interviewing a subject as a part of your speech preparation could make the difference between a mediocre speech and a memorable oration. But don't take my word for it . . . go interview your speech prof!

After the Interview

- A follow-up thank-you letter is common courtesy.
- Transcribe the tape or notes while the interview is fresh in your mind. Notes that may have been clear at the moment will quickly fade from memory unless we flesh them out soon after the interview.
- Follow up on leads or other interviews suggested by the interviewee.

Interviews can not only provide a rich source of information but also add credibility to our speaking. The fact that a speaker takes the time to speak directly to an expert shows concern for the audience. Further, the audience's perception of a speaker's expertise is enhanced by virtue of the interview. Be sure to let the audience know why the interviewee is a credible source on the topic.

Using Your Research

Preparing References or Works Cited

Before beginning in-depth reading on a topic, we prepare a preliminary list of the sources we have found. For example, 20 sources on cloning might look like they will be relevant. Using either a computer word processor or small note cards (4 by 6 inches is a good size), list the following information about each source:

> For all sources: author(s), preferably by full name, if an author is listed
>
> For books: exact title and the following facts of publication: location, publisher, and date
>
> For periodicals: article title, periodical title, volume number, date, and pages
>
> For government documents: the agency issuing the document, as well as the document's full title, date, and publication information
>
> For electronic resources: author, title, publication information, the e-mail address, Web site, or path by which the material was located and the date you found it, which is very important as Web sites are constantly changing

We always leave space to add information to each citation as we read the source.

All of this information is needed for the formal speech outline. It is easier to prepare the outline if this information is handy rather than having to go back to find it later. In Appendix A we provide samples of how to correctly cite sources according to the systems developed by the American Psychological Association (APA) and the Modern Language Association (MLA).

Recording Information and Avoiding Plagiarism

As we gather materials, we find it is essential to carefully record the supporting materials for our speeches. In Chapter 8 we discuss the types of evidence you will want to record—facts, statistics, quotations from experts, and the like. Whether we write our information on 4 by 6 inch note cards, sheets of notebook paper, or on our computers, accuracy is essential. At the same time, it is important to record information in a way that ensures it will be honestly cited and represented in our speeches. We offer some suggestions to ensure that research information is properly recorded.

In this age of the Internet, the temptation is to simply cut and paste material from the Web pages that we find. This is simple and accurate, but there is one big downside. As discussed in Chapter 4, there is an increasing problem in society with the use of material written by others without proper attribution. *USA Today* recently dismissed a five-time Pulitzer Prize nominee, newspaper reporter Jack Kelley, when it was learned that he had plagiarized and fabricated numerous stories. As Blake Morrison of *USA Today* reports, there was "strong evidence Kelley fabricated substantial portions of at least eight major stories, lifted nearly two dozen quotes or other material from competing publications, lied in speeches he gave for the newspaper and conspired to mislead those investigating his work."[10] Numerous other highly publicized cases of plagiarism have damaged the careers not just of reporters but of many noted academics as well.

As professors, we've regrettably discovered numerous instances of plagiarism. In many cases, the culprit was a downloaded bit of text that the student failed to properly cite in a speech or paper. For example, when asked to write a personal brief essay about her chosen major, one student simply downloaded the description of Communication Studies from another university's Web site. Presumably she knew we would recognize the language from our own Web site, so she found a department elsewhere from which to crib her paper. The language didn't seem natural, so we did a simple Google search for some of the unusual phrases. The result was a clear case of plagiarism, which was reported to the university's authorities. Other students have cited the source in the References or Works Cited of their papers but not indicated which words were direct quotes and which were their own words. In this situation, it's often sloppy recording during the research phase that is at fault.

How can students avoid this type of accidental, yet potentially serious plagiarism? Here are some suggestions.

Tips and Tactics

How to Avoid Plagiarism

- Don't just automatically cut and paste from sources. Make notes in your own words about the main ideas.
- Keep printouts or photocopies. When doing the final draft of a speech or paper, be sure any direct quotes are indicated by quotation marks and cited in the body of the speech or paper, not just in the References or Works Cited.
- If a direct quotation is cut and pasted, use a different font to indicate it is a direct quote. For example, once we have cut and pasted the quotation, we change the font color to red or put it in italics.
- Err on the side of full disclosure. A close paraphrase that is not cited is considered plagiarism, even if it's not a direct quote. If there's any doubt, it doesn't hurt to cite the source, both in the speech outline or manuscript and orally. For example, we discussed Robert Kennedy's paraphrase of the George Bernard Shaw quotation earlier in this chapter. Even though he didn't use the exact words, he would always say something like, "As George Bernard Shaw was fond of saying . . ." Citing sources is not a sign of weakness; rather, research has shown it enhances a speaker's credibility.

Summary

The process of researching to support your speech is like the process of inventing a new product: You need both a source of inspiration and the willingness to engage in hard work.

 **Speech**Coach

To evaluate your understanding of this chapter, see the Quizzes on your CD.

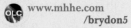
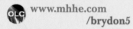
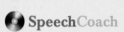
- Begin by analyzing the situation and focusing on your audience.

- Choose an appropriate topic.

- Formulate a specific purpose you wish to accomplish.

Possible sources of information for your speech include the following:

- Library resources, such as books, periodicals, and databases

- The Internet, but with particular attention to distinguishing authentic and reliable Web sites from questionable ones

- Interviews

Develop a recording system for both sources and data that avoids the danger of plagiarism and ensures accuracy.

Check Your Understanding: Exercises and Activities

1. Check your understanding of the American Psychological Association and Modern Language Association guidelines for source citations in Appendix A. Provide a correct source citation for each of the following hypothetical sources, using both APA and MLA guidelines:

   A book with one author named Jack Smith, titled College Life, published in New York by University Press in 2005. How would your citation change if Smith were the editor of the book? How would you list a second author, John Q. Doe? How would you list a third author, Mary A. Smith?

   An article titled Dorm Life in American Universities, by Peter Chu, published in the scholarly journal Universities and Colleges, volume 31, December 2005, pages 24–56.

   A chapter by Jose Sanchez titled The Nine Lives Myth, appearing on pages 99–109 in the book Cat Stories, edited by Morris T. Katt, published by Feline Press in San Francisco, California, in 2005.

   An article in Canine Magazine titled Snoopy and Me, by Charlie Brown, pages 56–57, on December 14, 2005, in volume 42. How would you list the article if no author were named?

2. *Worksheet for speech topic choice.* One way to select an appropriate speech topic is to begin with an inventory of your own interests and those of your listeners as revealed by their self-introductions in class. Under each of the following headings, list at least three things that are important to you and to your audience.

	My interests	Audience interests
Hobbies	_____	_____
	_____	_____
	_____	_____
School	_____	_____
	_____	_____
Work	_____	_____
	_____	_____
Goals	_____	_____
	_____	_____

Situational factors _____

Nature of assignment _____

Time available _____

List of three possible topics _____

_____

_____

3. How would you go about determining on what subject Arthur L. Schawlow and Charles H. Townes are experts? (Hint: They won Nobel Prizes for their discovery.)

4. Although the Internet is an invaluable source of information on almost any topic, it is also a notorious source of misinformation. As an exercise, try to locate the Web site of the Central Intelligence Agency (CIA). How many different Web sites did you find before locating the official page? How did you know when you were at the official site?

Notes

1. Adapted from Meriam Library, California State University, Chico, "Chico RIO: Research Instruction Online" [Retrieved from www.csuchico.edu/lins/chicorio/glossary.html, 12 November 2004].
2. See Fed Stats [http://www.fedstats.gov/].
3. Bartleby.com Great Books Online [http://www.bartleby.com/73/465.html, 27 July 2004].
4. Ken Light, "Fonda, Kerry, and Photo Fakery" [Retrieved from Lexis-Nexis Academic, 29 July 2004] (*Washington Post,* 28 February 2004).
5. Chris Gaither, "Google IPO Filing Leaves Out a Lot" [Retrieved from Lexis-Nexis Academic, 30 July 2004] (*Los Angeles Times,* 3 May 2004).
6. Google [http://www.google.com/, retrieved 30 July 2004].
7. "Google bomb" Wikipedia, 29 July 2004 [Retrieved from http://en.wikipedia.org/wiki/Google_bomb, 30 July 2004].
8. Based on UC Berkeley–Teaching Library Internet Workshops, "Evaluating Web Pages: Techniques to Apply & Questions to Ask," 27 July 2004 [Retrieved from http://www.lib.berkeley.edu/TeachingLib/Guides/Internet/Evaluate.html, 29 December 2004].
9. Adapted with permission from Meriam Library Instruction: Information Literacy, "Evaluating Information Resources: Applying the CRAAP Test," 9 October 2003 [Retrieved from http://www.csuchico.edu/lins/handouts/evalsites.html, 30 July 2004].
10. Blake Morrison, "Ex-USA Today Reporter Accused of Plagiarism," *Sacramento Bee,* 20 March 2004, A8.

Sometimes messages need visual, not just verbal support, especially when presenting statistics.

Chapter

8

Supporting Your Message

Objectives

After reading this chapter and reviewing the learning resources on your CD-ROM and at the Online Learning Center, you should be able to:

- Recognize the three basic types of claims: fact, value, and policy.

- Explain the role of evidence in grounding a speech.

- Support a speech with examples that are relevant, sufficient, typical, and without counterexamples.

- Support a speech with verifiable facts from reliable and unbiased sources that are consistent with other known facts.

- Support a speech with statistics from reliable, unbiased sources.

- Identify reliable polls based on fair questions, an adequate and representative sample, and a meaningful difference compared to the margin of error.

- Support a speech with reliable statistics, including percentages and averages.

- Support a speech with expert opinion, which is reliable and unbiased.

- Support a speech with clear and accurate explanations.

- Support a speech with vivid and accurate descriptions.

- Support a speech with narratives that have both probability and fidelity for your audience.

- Utilize valid warrants based on authority, generalization, comparison, cause, and sign to connect grounds to claims.

Key Concepts

authority warrant

causal warrant

comparison (analogy) warrant

expert opinion

fact

generalization warrant

narrative

narrative fidelity

narrative probability

primary sources

secondary sources

sign warrant

statistics

" Everyone is entitled to their own opinion, but not their own facts. **"**

–SEN. DANIEL PATRICK MOYNIHAN[1]

Figure 8.1
Grounds, Claims, and
Warrants Are Essential
to Any Reasoning.

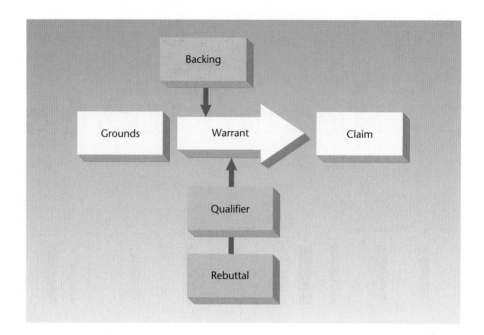

You've been to the library, interviewed an expert, and surfed the Web. You have
a speech topic and a lot of ideas. But how do you translate this into a speech? In
Chapter 5 we introduced Toulmin's model of reasoning. Figure 8.1 reproduces
that model to help refresh your memory. In this chapter, we are specifically concerned with three parts of the model: claims, grounds, and warrants. First, we discuss the kinds of claims a speaker can make in a speech. Then we discuss how to
find grounds—that is, evidence and supporting materials—to support the claims in
a speech. Finally, we discuss warrants, which are ways of relating grounds and
claims.

Claims

We make three basic types of claims when speaking: factual, value, and policy. A
factual claim states that something is true or false. Some facts are clear-cut: 2 plus 2
equals 4. Others aren't so easy to prove: Is Social Security in danger of bank-
ruptcy or not? The hallmark of factual claims is that they are theoretically verifiable. *Claims of value* make judgments about what is good or bad, right or wrong,
moral or immoral. Much of the debate over so-called wedge issues such as gay
marriage, stem cell research, and abortion concern value judgments. Finally,
claims of policy are statements about what a person should do. Most persuasive
speeches deal with either claims of value or policy or both. Most informative
speeches are primarily about claims of fact. As we look for grounds to support
our speeches, we need to carefully assess the types of claims we plan to make. We
also need to consider our audience. What facts do audience members already
know or believe? What additional facts do they need to know? Will they accept the
values implicit in our message? If we advocate policies, we need to base them on
facts and values that are established in our speech. Thus research and audience
analysis go hand in hand.

Grounds

To succeed as public speakers, we need to ground our claims in facts and opinions. For example, whether we are teaching someone how to swing a golf club or persuading them to share our views on stem cell research, we need to do more than just offer our own opinions. Audiences want us to provide evidence to support our claims. If a speaker says stem cell research could lead to a cure for diabetes, audience members are going to expect the speaker to tell them why and how. We can support a speech and answer the audience's desire for grounding in facts and reliable opinions using these methods:

- Examples
- Facts
- Statistics
- Opinion
- Explanations
- Descriptions
- Narratives

Examples

An example is a specific instance that represents some larger class. We might cite a recycling program in our hometown as an example of how curbside recycling can work. The test of an example is whether it is actually representative of the larger category. To test whether an example is representative, we need to ask the following questions:

- *What is the relevance of the example to the larger category?* If we are talking about products made from recycled material, then a cardboard box made from new materials, although it could be recycled by the consumer, is not relevant.

- *Are there enough instances to support the generalization?* A few years ago, a disposable-diaper manufacturer ran an ad campaign claiming that its diapers could be turned into compost. However, according to a *Consumer Reports* article, only about a dozen cities had the capability to compost disposable diapers.[2] Thus disposable diapers wouldn't be a good example of a recyclable product.

- *Is the example typical of the larger category?* We should avoid isolated and atypical examples. Just because some types of plastic can be recycled doesn't mean that *all* plastic is recyclable.

- *Are there counterexamples that disprove the generalization?* A counterexample is one example that contradicts the generalization. Whereas several examples can only suggest the truth of a generalization, even one example to the contrary can disprove it. If a speaker claims all American cars are unreliable, then pointing to just one car line–for example, the Saturn–as having been shown to be reliable disproves that generalization. If counterexamples exist, either the generalization is false or it needs to be reformulated to be less inclusive. Thus we might say, "Many American cars are unreliable," a generalization that one counterexample would not disprove.

Facts

A **fact** is something that is verifiable as true. It is a fact that there are 50 states in the United States. As former baseball great Yogi Berra might say, "You can look it up." On the other hand, the statement that Texas is the best state in which to live is not a fact, though it may be widely believed by Texans.

A fact, of course, is only as good as the source of that fact. To evaluate a fact, ask the following questions:

- *Does the fact come from a reliable source?* Encyclopedias, almanacs, authoritative books, and scholarly articles are usually reliable. On the other hand, if the "fact" comes from someone who has a clear bias about the topic, we should be suspicious. For example, many Internet sites claim to contain facts, such as the existence of extraterrestrials or that there are "black helicopters" waiting to take over control of the United States. Just because something is on the Internet, we shouldn't assume that it is true. Chapter 7 offered several tests for Internet sources.

- *Is the fact verifiable?* We should be suspicious of facts that are difficult to verify. For example, there are widely varying estimates of certain types of crime, such as rape. Part of the discrepancy is that many rapes go unreported. Thus the number of reported rapes is multiplied by some factor assumed to represent the number of unreported rapes for every reported rape. However, these numbers are impossible to verify for the very reason that the unreported rapes are, by definition, unverifiable. Although these estimates may be useful, they are not facts in the sense of being verifiable.

- *Is the fact the most recent available?* Until 2001, statistics about the federal budget projected a large annual surplus. Yet as this book is being written, these projected surpluses have been replaced by record deficits. A speech built around the existence of budget surpluses would clearly be out of date.

- *Is the fact consistent with other known facts?* Facts do not stand alone. We should be suspicious of alleged "facts" that seem to be inconsistent with other known facts. For example, many tobacco manufacturers once claimed that nicotine was not addictive. However, not only the surgeon general but anyone who has tried to give up smoking can tell you that such a "fact" is suspect. We should double-check sources for possible error and be particularly careful with **secondary sources,** which rely on another source rather than gathering the information firsthand. It is always better to look at **primary sources,** which are the original sources of information, because there may be honest mistakes in transferring information from one source to another. Finally, we should keep in mind what facts the audience already knows. If our facts are inconsistent with what the audience believes to be true, we first have to convince them that ours are more reliable if we are to have any success.

Statistics

Numerical summaries of data, such as percentages, ratios, and averages, that are classified in a meaningful way are known as **statistics.** These can be a rich source of information; yet they can also be confusing and misleading. For example, an American automobile manufacturer announced a survey showing that its cars were preferred overwhelmingly to foreign cars. However, it turns out that the company included only 200 people in its survey, none of whom even owned a foreign car.[3]

We are constantly bombarded by statistics that seem authoritative but are of dubious value. Some questions to ask about statistics are the following:

Using a visual aid such as the pie chart seen here helps your audience visualize statistics.

- *Is the source of the statistics reliable and unbiased?* The tip-off to the problem with the survey on foreign versus American cars is that it was sponsored by an American car company. Statistics found through general searches of commercial, individual, or organizational Internet sites are often particularly suspect. On the other hand, statistics found in official sources, such as www.fedstats.gov, are less likely to be biased, because this site collects official government statistics.

- *Is the statistic based on a poll?* Polls are statistically driven. A meaningful poll calls participants, not the other way around. Based on sophisticated sampling techniques and random selection, a national poll can predict a presidential election with about a four-percentage-point margin of error. But when our Internet provider, local television station, or newspaper conducts an "unscientific poll," in which people record their views, the results are meaningless. Only people who are interested in the topic will respond, and there is nothing to prevent someone from responding a hundred times. In short, such polls are worse than worthless because they undermine confidence in legitimate polls.

- *Were unbiased questions asked?* A poll asking whether disposable diapers should be banned was preceded by a statement that disposable diapers account for only 2 percent of trash in landfills. Not surprisingly, 84 percent of those polled felt disposable diapers should not be banned.[4]

- *Was the sample representative?* A representative sample is absolutely necessary for a statistic to be reliable and valid. A representative sample is one made up of people who possess the same attributes as the people in the population from which the sample is drawn. A speech class, for example, could be representative of the student body at a college. But unless the class was drawn randomly from the entire student body, we do not know for certain.

  There are many ways to obtain a representative sample, but the most common way is to randomly select people from the population in which we are interested: for example, college students between the ages of 18 and 25; all single mothers in the state; or members of a state bar association. Generally speaking, the larger the sample randomly drawn from a population, the more representative the sample.

  The complexities of statistical sampling are beyond the scope of this book. Even so, we want to emphasize that the value of any statistic depends on sampling. Thus, at a minimum, we should never accept a statistic at face value. We need to find information about the sample on which the statistic is based as well.

- *Are the differences in the poll greater than the margin of error?* Good polling results state the margin of error. Keep in mind that the margin of error increases as the sample gets smaller. Whereas the margin of error for a sample of 1,067 people is about 3 percent, for 150 people the margin of error is about 8 percent.[5] Suppose a poll has a margin of error of 4 percent. Thus, if a poll shows a political candidate ahead of her opponent by 51 to 49 percent, she could be ahead by as much as 55 to 45 percent, or behind by 47 to 53 percent–or any number in between. When only subgroups of a larger sample are considered, there are even more chances for error. For example, on the morning of November 2, 2004, supporters of Senator Kerry were ecstatic when early exit polls from key states such as Ohio and Florida indicated he was defeating President Bush. What they failed to realize was that voters who cast their votes early in the day were not representative of voters at large. In fact, the subgroup sampled in these early exit polls was 59 percent female, a group more likely to support Kerry than were men. When all the results were in, of course, Kerry was defeated in both states and Bush was reelected.[6]

- *What are the percentages based on?* "There's been a 10 percent increase in the rate of inflation!" Sounds pretty alarming, doesn't it? However, unless you know what the underlying rate of inflation is, this is a meaningless figure. Inflation rates are themselves a percentage. Say that inflation is running at 4 percent. That means what cost $100 last year now costs $104. A 10 percent increase in the rate of inflation means that it would cost $104.40–not too bad. On the other hand, a 10 percent rate of inflation means that what cost $100 a year ago now costs $110. Sound confusing? It is. The point is that we need to be sure we understand what percentages are based on before relying on them to prove a point.

- *What is meant by average?* One of the most frequently reported statistics is the average, or mean. Although easily computed, the average is often misleading because it is commonly distorted by numerical extremes. Consider a newspaper report that states the average salary for new college graduates is $40,000 a year. That doesn't mean a majority of college graduates are paid $40,000 a year. It simply means that when we add the salaries paid to all college graduates surveyed and divide that sum by the number of graduates in the sample, that's the mean (the arithmetic average). The number likely has been distorted by graduates in engineering, computer science, and information systems management, who, though few in number, start at salaries two to three times as much as their more numerous counterparts in the liberal arts and social sciences. The most telling statistic is always the *median,* which is the midpoint in a distribution of numbers. Knowing the median tells us that half of the numbers in the distribution are larger, and half are smaller. In Chapter 15, we discuss the mean and median in more detail.

This list of questions is not meant to discourage you from using statistics. They can be a powerful form of support. The key is to know what your statistics mean and how they were collected, and to avoid biased sources and questionable sampling techniques. Most important, you need to explain enough about the statistics to your audience so that they will have confidence in the claims you are using the statistics

Speaking of . . .

Statistics

Tests for using statistics

- Know the source—is it unbiased and reliable?
- Know what questions were asked—were they fair and unbiased?
- Know how the sample was chosen—is it representative?

- Consider the margin of error—do the differences exceed it?
- Know what percentages are based on—are they percentages of percentages?
- Know the kind of average used—was it the mean (average) or the median (midpoint)?

to support. In Chapter 12 we discuss the use of visual media, which are particularly helpful in explaining statistics to an audience.

Opinion

We all have opinions on all sorts of topics. One of the authors loved *Lost in Translation* and the other hated it. Some people love hip-hop, others can't stand it. The list of topics on which we all have opinions is endless. As a speaker, we want to share our opinions with our audience. If the speech is persuasive, we want them to come to share our opinion. However, unless a speaker is a recognized expert or authority on a topic, his or her opinion is unlikely to carry any weight with audience members. After all, why should a classmate give any more weight to your opinion than to his or her own?

Sometimes speakers have special qualifications that enable them to use their own opinions as support for their speech. For example, we recall a student whose mother had terrible complications from breast implant surgery. Her speech was short on quotes from experts but was still very powerful because she told the story of her mother's suffering in a convincing way. If we intend to use our own opinions as support in a speech, we need to be sure to explain to the audience why our opinions are worth considering.

More common than personal opinion in supporting a speech is **expert opinion**—a quotation from someone with special credentials in the subject matter. Quotations from experts, whether gathered from a personal interview or from written sources, can be a persuasive way of supporting your points. However, you need to ask three basic questions about expert opinion:

expert opinion
A quotation from someone with special credentials in the subject matter.

- *What is the source's expertise?* How do you know this person is an expert? Look at biographical sources (such as *Who's Who*) if you do not know who the person is. Look for marks of expertise, such as academic credentials, official positions, or references from other authorities. Finally, make sure your source is an expert in the subject matter of your speech. It is important to explain to your audience why the person you are quoting is an expert they should believe. For example, although the Dixie Chicks are great performers, their views on President Bush were largely ridiculed when the group expressed them at a concert.
- *Does the expert have a reputation for reliability?* How accurate have the expert's previous statements been? If someone has a record of either false or mistaken

statements in the past, it is misguided to rely on that person's statements today. For example, many questioned the reliability of U.S. intelligence-gathering agencies after they were embarrassed by the failure to find weapons of mass destruction in Iraq.

- *Is the source unbiased?* If a source has a vested interest in one side of a topic, his or her opinions are automatically suspect. Your audience needs to be assured that you are not relying on sources who have an axe to grind.

Explanations

An explanation is an account, an interpretation, or a meaning given to something. Detailed explanations may prove useful in a speech. But to be effective, explanations must meet two tests:

- *Is the explanation clear?* A complex or unclear explanation may only confuse your audience. One way to clarify an explanation is to use comparisons and contrasts. Thus someone might explain a nuclear power plant by comparing it to a teakettle whose source of heat is a nuclear reaction.

- *Is the explanation accurate?* An explanation that is clear is not necessarily complete or correct. Make sure the explanations provided are as complete and accurate as possible, given the limitations of the speech situation.

Descriptions

A description is a word picture of something. For example, you might describe a place you have visited or researched. Consider the following statement from a speech by one of our students, Chalsey Phariss: "Imagine a place where the rivers are flowing, the sun is shining, and the fun is unlimited, where there is never a dull moment, and the freedom of the outdoors will captivate your mind." This description leads into a speech about the "Lake of the Sky," Lake Tahoe.[7]

Descriptions should meet the following tests:

- *Is the description accurate?* Descriptions can be tested for accuracy by comparing them with the thing being described. Thus, for the Tahoe example, looking at pictures of the lake or actually visiting it would help to verify the description.

- *Is the description vivid?* To hold an audience's attention, we need to paint a word picture. Calling Lake Tahoe by its Indian name, "Lake of the Sky," is much more vivid than simply describing the blueness of the water. Photographs and other visual materials, which are discussed in Chapter 12, can sometimes supplement descriptions in a speech.

Narratives

narrative
An extended story that is fully developed, with characters, scene, action, and plot.

A **narrative** is an extended story that is fully developed, with characters, scene, action, and plot. Narratives sometimes provide an effective way of driving home a point to an audience. An effective narrative builds gradually from the beginning, through conflict, to a climax. The conflict is then resolved, and the ending of the story often ties back into the beginning.

Can you find words to accurately describe the beauty of Lake Tahoe?

Narratives can be more than a useful supporting tool for a speech; in some cultures narrative is an organizing principle of speaking. The storyteller in North and Central American cultures, for example, is revered. We were in the audience when actor-activist Edward James Olmos spoke at our university. His speech was largely a series of stories–about his career, his family, how people of different cultures can come to understand one another. Award-winning rhetorical scholar Walter Fisher has argued, in fact, that human beings are fundamentally storytellers. Fisher believes that reasoning is done in the form of narrative. Even if you don't accept Fisher's narrative paradigm, it is undoubtedly the case that a well-told story, real or fictional, can captivate an audience. Fisher claims that two basic tests apply to narrative reasoning:[8]

- *Does the narrative have probability?* **Narrative probability** is the internal coherence or believability of a narrative. Does a story make sense in and of itself? If you've seen the *Back to the Future* trilogy, you may have wondered how there could be two Doc Browns and two Marty McFlys and even two DeLorean time machines at the same time and place. Setting aside Doc's explanations of the space-time continuum, trying to sort out the paradoxes and inconsistencies of time travel is one sure way to a gigantic headache.

narrative probability
The internal coherence or believability of a narrative.

People were sharply divided in their views of the narrative fidelity of Michael Moore's *Fahrenheit 9/11*.

When using a narrative to support a speech, it needs to be clearly plausible to the audience for it to be believed.

- *Does the narrative have fidelity?* **Narrative fidelity** is the degree to which a narrative rings true to real-life experience. Even if a story makes sense internally, it may not make sense in terms of the real world. For example, there were sharply divided views on the narrative fidelity of Michael Moore's controversial film, *Fahrenheit 9/11.* Jonathan Foreman, a columnist for Rupert Murdock's *New York Post,* found Moore's film lacking fidelity to the facts. He writes that "if you take the lies, half-lies and distortions out of *Fahrenheit 9/11,* there isn't much of anything left."[9] In response to his critics, Moore posted a "line by line factual backup for *Fahrenheit 9/11*" on his Web site (http://www.michaelmoore.com/warroom/f911notes/). Although Moore's critics acknowledged his skill as a filmmaker, the controversy over the fidelity of his work continued right through election day 2004.

When we tell a story to an audience, we should let them know if it is true or hypothetical. But either type of story needs to ring true to the audience's own experience if it is to have impact. Although people may enjoy hypothetical stories for their entertainment value, they don't find these narratives real. For a speech to have impact, the narratives need to have probability and fidelity.

narrative fidelity
The degree to which a narrative rings true to real-life experience.

Warrants

Once we have provided grounds for a claim, we need to connect the grounds and the claim. Toulmin calls this link the warrant. A simple example will illustrate this point. I look out the window in the morning. It's an overcast, windy, gray day. I grab my umbrella before I head out the door. I've reasoned from *grounds* (clouds and wind) to the *claim* (I need my umbrella). What links the two? Clearly, my experience has taught me to believe the *warrant* that clouds and wind are a sign of impending rain (see Figure 8.2). We do not always have to state the obvious if we know our audience will mentally fill in the warrant. Thus, if I simply said that I grabbed my umbrella because it was cloudy, windy, and gray, everyone would know the reason. But on more complex issues, or where we don't know what warrants the audience might accept, it may be necessary to spell out this linkage.

In this section we describe five commonly used types of warrants. These are ways we can explicitly connect our grounds with the claims we make. To the extent that we are able to link our evidence with our claims, we are likely to be successful in

Figure 8.2
Supporting a Claim.
The claim "I should take an umbrella" is supported by appropriate grounds and a warrant.

convincing our audiences to accept what we say. The five most common types of warrants are these:

- Authority
- Generalization
- Comparison
- Causal
- Sign

Authority Warrants

When we rely on the opinions of experts to support our claims, we are using an authority warrant. An **authority warrant** asserts that the claim is to be believed because of the authority of the source. This is the reason it is important that we tell our audience why the people we quote are experts whose opinions matter. If a doctor tells us to lose weight, we are likely to trust her judgment and at least *try* to shed the unwanted pounds. If Oprah Winfry endorses a particular diet, however, that doesn't prove it will work for us. Unfortunately, celebrities often persuade people even though they don't have expertise in the area. In our speeches, we try to make sure the authorities we cite not only are credible to the audience but also are knowledgeable about the topic. When we cite our own opinion, we need to be particularly careful to explain to the audience why we have the authority to speak on the topic. Authority warrants are subject to tests of whether the authority is truly an expert, has accurate information, and is unbiased.

authority warrant
Reasoning in which the claim is believed because of the authority of the source.

Tips and Tactics

Using Authority Warrants

- Make sure the authority is an expert in the area being discussed.
- Make sure the authority is acting on reliable information.
- Use only unbiased authorities.

An example of reasoning from an authority warrant is shown in Figure 8.3. Based on the grounds (the doctor tells you that the best way to lose weight is to go on the South Beach diet) and the warrant (the doctor is an expert in treating obesity), you decide to accept the *claim* (and go on the South Beach diet).

To test the validity of this reasoning, we must know whether the doctor is an expert in the area of treating obesity, whether she has reliable information about

Figure 8.3
An Example of the Use of Authority to Support a Claim

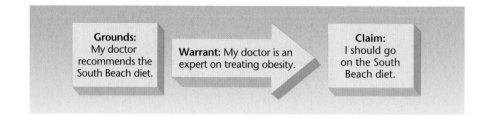

the state of your health and the effectiveness of the South Beach diet, and whether she is biased. If the doctor is a dermatologist, for example, there is no reason to believe she is competent to advise patients on what diet is best. Further, suppose the only information she has about the South Beach diet is what she's read in the popular press rather than in medical journals. And finally, suppose it turns out she gets a referral fee from the sponsors of the diet for sending them a customer. In such a case, that expert opinion would be unreliable on all three counts.

As speakers, we are wise to tell our audiences specifically why the experts we quote are reliable and that they have no axe to grind. Otherwise, a skeptical audience may reject our claims.

Generalization Warrants

generalization warrant
A statement that either establishes a general rule or principle or applies an established rule or principle to a specific case.

A **generalization warrant** is a statement that either establishes a general rule or principle or applies an established rule or principle to a specific case. Warrants involving generalizations are used in two ways. Some warrants take specific examples and use them to establish generalizations. Others take previously established generalizations and apply them to specific cases. Figure 8.4 illustrates the relationship between a generalization-establishing warrant and a generalization-applying warrant.

Establishing Generalizations

A warrant that establishes a generalization uses specific examples, statistics, narratives, and the like to reach general conclusions. Warrants establishing generalizations are subject to tests of relevance, quantity, typicality, precision, and negative example.

Tips and Tactics

Establishing a Generalization

- Are the specific instances relevant to the generalization?
- Are there enough specific instances to establish the claim?
- Are the specific instances typical of the larger population?
- Has overgeneralization from only a few instances been avoided?
- Are there no significant known negative examples?

Examples, statistics, and narratives are all good ways to establish a generalization. However, relying on isolated examples and narratives is risky. A blend of statistics

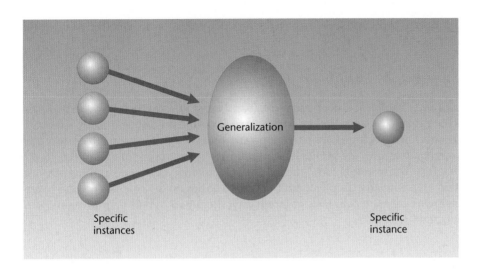

Figure 8.4

Relationship Between Generalization-Establishing and Generalization-Applying Warrants. Generalizations are established based on a number of specific instances. Once accepted, generalizations are then applied to further specific instances.

and examples is more effective in establishing a generalization than use of only a few examples or narratives. The story of Subway's spokesperson, Jared, who lost more than a hundred pounds on his all-sub sandwich diet, although compelling, hardly proves that eating at Subway will guarantee weight loss. Using his story along with other types of evidence—statistics, expert opinion, and descriptions of the low-fat, low-carb alternatives at Subway—would be a stronger way to establish the claim that eating at Subway is a good way to lose weight (assuming it really is).

Applying Generalizations

Once we know a generalization is true, we can apply it to a specific instance and reach some valid conclusions about that specific instance. For example, we know that anyone born in the United States or its territories is, by definition, a U.S. citizen. Thus, if Jane shows us her birth certificate and it says she was born in Alaska, we know she is a U.S. citizen. Warrants applying generalizations are subject to tests of support, applicability, and exceptions.

Tips and Tactics

Applying a Generalization to a Specific Instance

- The generalization needs to be well-supported and accepted by the audience.
- The generalization should apply to the case at hand.
- If there are exceptions to the generalization, make sure the specific case isn't one of the exceptions.

Even though all persons born in the United States and its territories are native-born citizens, there are exceptions—for example, someone who has renounced his or her citizenship. And, of course, just because a person isn't born in the United States doesn't mean that person is not a U.S. citizen. Children born of citizen parents are citizens even if they are born outside the United States. When applying generalizations in a speech, it is important to make sure the audience accepts the general rule being used and knows the instance being discussed clearly falls within that category.

Comparison (Analogy) Warrants

comparison (analogy) warrant
A statement that two cases that are similar in some known aspects are also similar in some unknown aspects.

Reasoning based on a **comparison (analogy) warrant** claims that two cases that are similar in some known respects are also similar in some unknown respects. We often use examples or narratives as points of comparison. In informative speaking, analogies are particularly useful for explaining complex subjects in simple terms. For example, one student drew an analogy between stripping the insulation off a wire and the effect multiple sclerosis has on the central nervous system. Analogies are subject to tests of familiarity, literalness versus figurativeness, similarity, and relevance.

Tips and Tactics

Using Comparisons or Analogies

- Make sure your audience is familiar with at least one part of the analogy.
- Use literal analogies for proof and figurative analogies for clarity and emphasis.
- Show that similarities outweigh the differences.
- The similarities, not the differences, should be most relevant.

Let's begin with whether or not the audience is familiar with one of the parts of the analogy. Suppose a speaker told you that a *euphonium* was like an *enthymeme*. What? Neither term is likely to be familiar, so the analogy is worthless (it is also wrong—but that's another story). We have to be sure our audience understands the point of comparison being made. There is a difference between literal and figurative analogies. A *literal analogy* claims that two different instances are really similar. For example, a lot of people compared September 11, 2001, to December 7, 1941 (the date on which Pearl Harbor was bombed). This is certainly a literal comparison—both were attacks on U.S. soil by foreign enemies (Hawaii was not yet a state, but it was a U.S. territory at the time of the attack). A *figurative analogy,* on the other hand, is a device of language used to enhance the effectiveness of a speech. A figurative analogy clearly seeks to establish some similarity between the two items being compared, but no one could reasonably argue that they are really alike. Saying September 11 was like being sucker-punched is not literally comparing two things that are the same. In the first instance, thousands died and the nation was plunged into war. In the second instance, about all that is hurt is the victim's pride. There's nothing wrong with figurative analogies—they can add a lot to a speech—but they don't constitute proof in the same way that literal ones can. There is no logical force to such arguments.

Next, in a good analogy or comparison, the similarities should outweigh the differences. If they do not, the analogy will not be very powerful. For example, when comparing September 11 and Pearl Harbor, there are clearly many similarities. However, unlike Pearl Harbor, our attackers did not identify themselves. Rather than being a state, we ultimately learned that our enemies were a shadowy network of terrorists scattered in many places. The tactics that worked to win World War II would not necessarily be the same as those needed in the War on Terror.

Finally, the similarities, rather than the differences, should be most relevant to the claim being made. In the comparison of 9/11 to Pearl Harbor, the difference in fighting terrorists as compared to a conventional army has made the War on Terror a long-term effort that will not end in a dramatic surrender ceremony as did World War II.

Causal Warrants

Reasoning based on a **causal warrant** claims that a cause will produce or has produced an effect. Reasoning from *cause to effect* involves predicting what will happen if some action is taken. For example, researchers have shown that over-exposure to the sun's radiation will *cause* skin cancers. Thus a doctor might tell patients who insist on getting a bronze tan every summer that they are increasing their chances of getting skin cancer. On the other hand, sometimes we reason from *effect to cause*. Looking for the reasons something happened involves effect to cause reasoning. When seeking a second term as president, George W. Bush often claimed the improved economy was caused by his tax cuts. He was claiming these effects were caused by his economic policy. Causal warrants are subject to tests of relatedness, other causes, and side effects.

causal warrant
A statement that a cause will produce or has produced an effect.

Tips and Tactics

Using Causal Warrants

- Show how the cause is related to the alleged effect.
- Rule out other causes of the effect.
- Consider "side effects" in addition to the desired effect.

We recall a student who wanted to convince her classmates to avoid getting a tattoo. One of the effects she claimed that could be caused by improper tattooing (with dirty needles) was hepatitis, a serious disease. She cited experts who cautioned against tattooing and pointed out that among the unintended side effects was the pain and expense of removing tattoos later in life. She even offered another way to cause the desired effect of a tattoo—namely, a technique called Mehndi, which creates body art that lasts only a few weeks.

Sign Warrants

Perhaps you've heard someone say, "It's going to rain. I can feel it in my bones." Or you've read a newspaper article stating that the economy is in a recovery because the latest "leading economic indicators" are pointing upward. These are examples of reasoning from sign. A **sign warrant** is reasoning in which the presence of an observed phenomenon is used to indicate the presence of an unobserved phenomenon. In sign reasoning, the warrant asserts that the grounds provide a reliable sign that the claim is true. Some signs are infallible; most are merely probable. The absence of brain waves is considered legally as an infallible sign of death. On the other hand, no one would claim that the rise or fall of stock prices is even close to an infallible sign of the state of the economy. Sign warrants are subject to tests of reliability and conflicting signs.

sign warrant
Reasoning in which the presence of an observed phenomenon is used to indicate the presence of an unobserved phenomenon.

Tips and Tactics

- Show that the signs are reliable indicators of the claim.
- Rule out conflicting signs.

A detective examines a crime scene for signs of forced entry, struggle, and the like. Anyone who is a fan of Sherlock Holmes will recall that he often made a case based on the most obscure signs. One small sign would point him to the guilty subject every time. Unfortunately, in real life such reliable signs are more difficult to find. In using sign reasoning, show how reliable such signs have been in the past. For example, in persuading students of the value of a college degree, we can point to evidence from countless surveys showing that having a college degree is associated with a higher lifetime income. It is important, however, to rule out conflicting signs for an audience. Some people question the correlation between college degrees and income by pointing out that those from affluent families are more likely to go to college in the first place. Thus the higher income later in life might be more a matter of greater family resources, not simply getting a college degree. Unless a sign is infallible, most sign reasoning at best indicates the probability that a claim is true.

Summary

SpeechCoach

To evaluate your understanding of this chapter, see the Quizzes on your CD.

 www.mhhe.com /brydon5

Visit the Online Learning Center for helpful study resources, including practice tests, key term crossword puzzles, and PowerWeb articles for research and review.

There are three basic types of claims:

- Claims of fact deal with statements that are verifiable.
- Claims of value deal with statements about right or wrong, good or bad, moral or immoral.
- Claims of policy state that something should be done.

Many types of grounds are effective in supporting speeches:

- Examples should be relevant, of sufficient quantity, and typical, and without counterexamples.
- Facts should be from a reliable source, verifiable, recent, and consistent with other known facts.
- Statistics should be from a reliable and unbiased source, based on fair questions, from a representative sample. Polls should report the sample size and margin of error. Know what percentages are based on and whether the mean or median is being cited.
- Expert opinion should come from a subject matter expert who is reliable and unbiased.

- Explanations should be clear and accurate.

- Descriptions should be accurate and vivid.

- Narratives should have probability (coherence) and fidelity for the audience.

Five basic types of warrants link grounds and claims:

- Authority warrants assert that the opinions of the experts quoted are reliable and valid to support the claim being made.

- Generalization warrants either establish a general rule based on specific instances or apply an accepted generalization to a specific instance.

- Comparison (analogy) warrants assert that two things are similar to each other and that what is true of the well known is also true of the less known.

- Causal warrants assert that either a cause will lead to an effect or a known effect was due to a cause.

- Sign warrants assert that a sign (such as clouds) is a reliable indicator of some other condition (such as impending rain).

Check Your Understanding: Exercises and Activities

1. A speaker arguing that we should buy American products presents the following example: "I purchased a Japanese car last year. Since I purchased it, I have had nothing but trouble. I think this proves that you should buy American!" Compare this example with the tests of examples discussed in this chapter. Which of the tests does it fail to meet?

2. How would you go about verifying the "fact" that the leading causes of death in the United States are heart disease, cancer, and infectious diseases? What sources would you consult? Are these in fact the three leading causes of death?

3. Obtain a recent poll (one that appears in an article in, for example, *USA Today* or *Newsweek*). Does the poll meet the tests of statistical evidence outlined in this chapter? How large was the sample, and what was the margin of error? Did differences in the poll exceed the margin of error? What, if anything, does the article on the poll not tell you that you need to know to properly interpret the statistics in the poll?

SpeechCoach

For a review of key terms in this chapter, see the Key Terms Flashcards on your CD.

Notes

1. FactCheck.org, 2004 [Retrieved 5 August 2004 from http://www.factcheck.org/].
2. "Selling Green," *Consumer Reports,* October 1991, 687–92.
3. Cynthia Crossen, "Lies, Damned Lies–and 'Scientific' Studies," *Sacramento Bee,* Forum, 24 November 1991, 1–2. (Reprinted from the *Wall Street Journal.*)
4. Crossen, "Lies, Damned Lies–and 'Scientific' Studies."
5. Robert S. Erikson and Kent L. Tedin, *American Public Opinion,* 6th ed. (New York: Longman, 2001), 29.
6. "Down to the Wire," *Newsweek,* 15 November 2004, 127.
7. Chalsey Phariss, "Lake Tahoe," speech delivered at California State University, Chico, 18 April 1998.
8. Walter R. Fisher, *Human Communication as Narration* (Columbia: University of South Carolina Press, 1987).
9. Jonathan Foreman, "Moore's the Pity" [Retrieved from http://www.nypost.com/postopinion/opedcolumnists/23542.htm, 3 August 2004] (*New York Post,* 23 June 2004).

MICROMEDIA

- Simplicity
- Flexibility
- Quality
- Productivity

Because organization is one of the most important ingredients in successful public speaking, overheads should reflect this fact.

Chapter 9

Organizing Messages

Objectives

After reading this chapter and reviewing the learning resources on your CD-ROM and at the Online Learning Center, you should be able to:

- Develop an organizational strategy geared to your audience and purpose.
- Refine the specific purpose of your speech.
- Develop a clear thesis statement for your speech.
- Organize the body of your speech.
- Appreciate organizational patterns from diverse cultures.
- Utilize appropriate signposts to indicate transitions from one point to the next in your speech.
- Construct an effective introduction and conclusion for your speech.
- Prepare a formal outline for a speech to your class.
- Prepare and utilize speaker's notes for a speech to your class.

Key Concepts

alphabetical pattern

categorical pattern

causal pattern

extended narrative

formal outline

Monroe's motivated-
sequence

problem–solution pattern

refutational pattern

rhetorical question

spatial pattern

speaker's notes

spiral pattern

star pattern

stock issues pattern

subpoint

supporting point

time pattern

wave pattern

> " Every discourse, like a living creature, should be so put together that it has its own body and lacks neither head nor feet, middle nor extremities, all composed in such a way that they suit both each other and the whole. "
>
> —PLATO

Well-organized presentations are easier for an audience to follow, as this teacher shows while talking to her class.

In everyday conversation, we often speak in a random and seemingly disorganized fashion. Particularly in interpersonal conversation, one idea will trigger another, which will trigger another, and so on. We all have had the experience of wondering how we ended up talking about the latest movie blockbuster when the conversation began with a question about the classes we are taking.

When engaged in casual conversation, we have no reason to worry about structuring our message. In fact, part of the fun of such conversations is that they are spontaneous and unpredictable. If we don't understand what someone has said, we can simply ask the person to explain what was meant. Feedback is immediate, verbal as well as nonverbal.

Unfortunately, as we move from engaging in conversation to speaking in public, such random and unpredictable speaking becomes a hindrance to effective communication. Rather than being fun, listening to the random thoughts of a disorganized speaker is frustrating. As listeners we desire structure. We want to know where speakers are going and when they get there. A stream-of-consciousness public speaker is usually an ineffective one.

Assume that we already have a general notion of what we want to communicate in a speech. But, as Plato implied in the quotation at the beginning of this chapter, simply knowing what we want to communicate is not enough. We need to know how to structure that information for maximum effect. There are some specific things we can do organizationally to help us achieve our goals. They include developing an organizational strategy geared to our audience, refining the specific purpose, focusing on the thesis statement, organizing the body of the speech, introducing the speech, concluding the speech, communicating organization through previews and signposts, and preparing the formal outline and speaker's notes.

Focusing on the Audience

Just as with the process of researching and supporting a speech discussed in the preceding chapters, the organization of a speech should be grounded in our analysis of the speech situation in general, and the audience specifically. For example, should we put our best foot forward, so to speak, or save our best for last? A lot depends on the audience and the speech purpose. Suppose we have an audience that is either disinterested or hostile. If we save our most compelling material until the end, we are likely to lose the audience long before we have a chance to enlighten them or influence their opinion. On the other hand, if our audience already is greatly interested in our topic, we may want to build to a climax so that our best material will be fresh in their minds at the conclusion of the speech. A careful analysis of the audience is also crucial to refining the specific purpose and formulating the thesis statement.

Refining the Specific Purpose

In Chapter 2 we defined specific purpose as a speaker's goal or objective in speaking to a particular audience. Although we will have a specific purpose in mind before we begin to construct our speech, we will need to refine the specific purpose in light of our research and our analysis of the audience. The specific purpose of a speech represents a compromise between our ideal goal and the constraints of the particular rhetorical situation. Let's suppose we know the audience is skeptical of our point of view. For example, we want our audience to stop using cell phones while driving but suspect that most audience members believe they can drive and talk at the same time. We might amend our purpose to convincing them to use hands-free devices when using the cell phone while driving.

Focusing on the Thesis Statement

Recall from Chapter 2 that a thesis statement focuses our audience's attention on the central point of the speech. Just as a photographer must clearly focus on the primary subject of a photo, a speaker must bring the principal thrust of the speech into clear focus for the audience. Our analysis of the audience may determine when and how to present our thesis statement.

Normally, the thesis statement comes early in the speech, right after the opening. It is frustrating to an audience not to know the central point of a speech early. However, there may be times when presenting the thesis statement early is not the best strategy. For example, in a persuasive speech, a hostile audience may tune us out as soon as they hear our position on a controversial issue. In that case, we may want to hold off stating our position until the end of the speech and instead begin with common ground. Again, audience-focused organization is a key to successful speech making.

Sometimes the thesis statement may be less specific than the specific purpose. For example, if we are dealing with a hostile audience, rather than saying, "I am speaking this afternoon to convince you that sex education needs to be part of the community's middle school curriculum," we might say, "Today's teens are becoming sexually active sooner than the generations ahead of them." We must be sensitive to our audience's attitudes, beliefs, and values in formulating a thesis statement that will both express the essence of the speech and allow the audience to give our views a fair hearing.

Once we know the specific purpose and have formulated the thesis statement, it is time to organize the body of the speech. Although you might think that the introduction should be written first, this is rarely the case. Until we have constructed the body of the speech, it is difficult to find an appropriate introduction. Also, in sifting through our ideas and research, we might find something that makes a perfect introduction.

Organizing the Body of the Speech

As Plato suggested, every speech needs parts that are "composed in such a way that they suit both each other and the whole." Thus, our speech needs not only a strong introduction and conclusion but also a well-organized body to support the thesis statement and achieve our purpose. Carefully thought-out main points, subpoints, and supporting points will provide that organization.

Main Points

As we discussed in Chapter 2, the key ideas that support the thesis statement of a speech are the *main points*. They should fully develop the thesis statement. As a result of understanding these points, our audience should be informed, persuaded, or entertained in accordance with our specific purpose. In developing our main points, we should keep five guidelines in mind. They are listed here and then described in more detail.

Tips and Tactics

Guidelines for Developing Main Points

- Limit the number of main points.
- Focus each main point on one main idea.
- Construct main points so that they are parallel in structure.
- State main points as simply as the subject will allow.
- Give all main points equal treatment.

Number

Every speech needs to be anchored around two or more main points. (If there is only one main point, then that is, in effect, the same as the thesis statement, and the subpoints are in fact the main points.) In our experience, more than five main points is too much for an audience to absorb. Three main points seems to be ideal. The audience (not to mention the speaker) usually can easily grasp three key ideas, especially if they are organized in a memorable way. As the number of points increases, each main idea tends to be devalued, and the chances of forgetting one or more ideas increases. Obviously, some topics do not fit into three neat pigeonholes. But if we end up with six, seven, or eight main points, our speech is likely to suffer. Either we are trying to cover too much, or we really have six to eight subpoints, which could be organized into fewer main points, each with two or three subpoints.

Focus

The main points should clearly relate to the thesis statement. They should fully develop the thesis statement without going beyond the focus of the speech. For example, if we are speaking about trends in contemporary music, our thesis statement might be "Pop music is more diverse than ever." This statement then could be divided into three main points:

  I. Pop music is international.
  II. Pop music is multicultural.
  III. Pop music is multitongued.

Imagine, however, that our speech excluded a major musical genre, for example, hip-hop. This would most likely leave our audience wondering why we left it out. On the other hand, suppose we decided to add another main point to the body, for example:

IV. Pop music is more profitable than ever.

Although this point is related to musical diversity, it is out of the bounds of the thesis statement.

We think of the thesis statement as limiting the territory covered by our speech. As we construct the body, we include only those items that directly support our thesis statement. At the same time, we do not allow our thesis statement to be incompletely supported. By the end of the speech, we should have fulfilled the promise of the thesis statement—no more, no less.

Each main point should focus on one main idea. For example, this main point is confusing:

  I. Today's pop music is international; the heart of the recording industry is in Los Angeles.

These ideas should be expressed in two separate main points.

  I. Today's pop music is international.
  II. Even so, the heart of the recording industry remains in Los Angeles.

Using two separate points does not mean they are unrelated. However, the two ideas are clearly different.

Parallel Structure

Main points form the essence of a speech, so they should be clear, concise, and memorable. One technique to help achieve this is to construct main points in parallel fashion. For example, which of the following versions of main points would work best for our pop music speech? Here is one version:

  I. Today's pop music comes from all over the world.
  II. Many cultures are represented in today's pop music.
  III. The language of pop music is no longer simply English.

Or consider this version:

  I. Pop music transcends national boundaries.
  II. Pop music transcends culture.
  III. Pop music transcends language.

Obviously, the second example is easier to remember. The repetition of the phrase "pop music transcends" in all three main points stresses the focus of this speech.

Simplicity Versus Complexity

A reader can reread anything that is complex or confusing. An audience has only one chance to process information. Main points phrased as complex sentences may lose an audience. Concise and simple language makes the structure of a speech clear. Compare the following two examples:

I. AIDS is transmitted through unprotected sexual relations, including homosexual and heterosexual encounters.
II. AIDS is transmitted when drug users, often desperate for their next fix, share dirty needles.
III. AIDS is transmitted by the exchange of blood, such as in a transfusion or between a mother and her unborn child.

I. AIDS is transmitted by unprotected sex.
II. AIDS is transmitted by sharing needles.
III. AIDS is transmitted by blood.

Which of the two do you think the audience will remember? Main points should be as simple as the subject will allow.

Balance

The main points of the speech should be in balance. For example, if one main point composes two thirds of the speech, audience members may become confused and wonder what they missed.

Subpoints

subpoint
An idea that supports a main point.

Subpoints are to main points what main points are to the thesis statement. A **subpoint** is an idea that supports a main point. Each main point should have at least two and no more than five subpoints. Consider, for example, our speech on diversity in pop music.

[main point]
[subpoint]

[subpoint]

I. Pop music transcends national boundaries.
   A. The pop music charts feature artists from not only the U.S. but Brazil, Canada, and France, to name a few.
   B. The most popular recording artist in the world is from Spain.
II. Pop music transcends cultures.
   A. African American and Caribbean cultures are well represented in today's pop music.
   B. Many Anglo musicians have adapted the music of their ancestral culture to the contemporary pop scene.
III. Pop music transcends language.
   A. Ricky Martin sings in Spanish about La Vida Loca.
   B. Lil' Kim, Pink, and Christina Aguilera sing in French about Lady Marmalade.

It makes no sense to have only one subpoint under a main point. For example:

I. Pop music transcends national boundaries.
  A. The pop music charts feature artists from not only the U.S. but Brazil, Canada and France, to name a few.

If a main point is not divisible into at least two subpoints, it probably isn't really a main point. Rather, it should be a subpoint under another main point. Like main points, subpoints should be parallel in structure, simply stated, and given equal treatment.

Supporting Points

Sometimes the subpoints within a speech require further support and subdivision. Thus, we might have supporting points for each subpoint. A **supporting point** is an idea that supports a subpoint. Returning to our example of pop music, the body of a speech might be organized as follows:

> **supporting point**
> An idea that supports a subpoint.

II. Pop music transcends cultures. *[main point]*
  A. African American and Caribbean cultures are well represented in today's pop music. *[subpoint]*
    1. Hip-hop music has obvious ties to African American culture. *[supporting point]*
    2. Reggae and SKA have obvious ties to Caribbean culture. *[supporting point]*
  B. Many Anglo musicians have adapted the music of their ancestral culture to the contemporary pop scene.
    1. Groups such as U2 and the Coors have been influenced by their Celtic roots.
    2. The lyrics of Sting are suggestive of traditional English ballads.

Each supporting point could be further subdivided, but such a detailed substructure probably would lose the audience. For a normal classroom speech, it is unlikely there will be time to develop points beyond this level.

If we must further subdivide a supporting point, we use lowercase letters in the outline as follows:

II. Pop music transcends cultures. *[main point]*
  A. African American and Caribbean cultures are well represented in today's pop music. *[subpoint]*
    1. Hip-hop music has obvious ties to African American culture. *[supporting point]*
      a. The rhythms are African American. *[further support]*
      b. The music fuses elements of rhythm and blues, soul, and rap. *[further support]*
    2. Reggae and SKA have obvious ties to Caribbean culture.
      a. Bob Marley continues to be popular.
      b. As does his son Ziggy.

Figure 9.1 illustrates the relationship among various levels of support in a speech.

Traditional Patterns of Organization

A number of different patterns can be used to organize the body of a speech. In Chapter 2, we introduced three of those patterns. We now will add seven traditional patterns of organization, for a total of ten: time, extended narrative, spatial, categorical, alphabetical, problem-solution, stock issues, refutational, causal, and

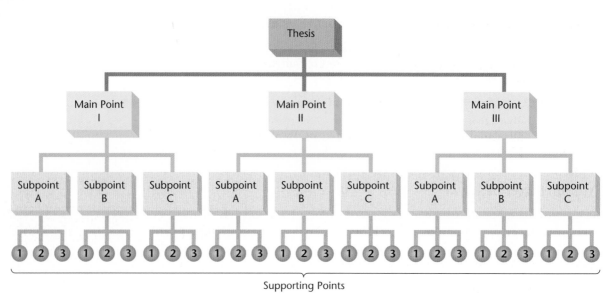

Figure 9.1
Relationship of Points in a Traditional Speech

Monroe's motivated-sequence. Later we introduce three organic patterns common in the diverse cultures of our contemporary society: wave, spiral, and star.

Time

time pattern
A pattern of organization based on chronology or a sequence of events.

Many topics, especially for informative speeches, lend themselves naturally to a temporal sequence. A **time pattern** is an organization based on chronology or a sequence of events. Topics of a historical nature are likely to follow a time sequence. Suppose we were speaking about the history of the U.S. space program, as did Tom Wolfe in his book *The Right Stuff.* We might divide the speech into the following main points:

   I. The race begins in the 1950s with the launch of *Sputnik.*
  II. The U.S.S.R. puts the first men into space in the 1960s.
 III. The United States sets the goal to land on the moon by the end of the 1960s.
 IV. Neil Armstrong is the first human to land on the moon in July 1969.

Topics that deal with a process, such as how-to speeches, can frequently be ordered by a time pattern as well. We might sequence a speech on learning to ski in these terms:

   I. Select the right equipment.
  II. Invest in lessons.
 III. Practice!

Extended Narrative

extended narrative
A pattern of organization in which the entire body of the speech is the telling of a story.

An **extended narrative** is a pattern of organization in which the entire body of the speech is the telling of a story. In Chapter 8, we introduced narrative as a form of support for a speech. As support, one main point of a speech might be a narrative, but the other main points might be in the form of statistics, expert opinions, facts, and the like. However, an extended narrative means the whole speech is one story. In this case we tell a story in sequence, with a climactic point near the end of the speech. This organizational pattern is often very useful in speeches to entertain. Thus, if we were to tell the story of a blind date, we might pattern our speech as follows:

I. I am asked to go out on a blind date.
II. I meet the date.
III. Disaster follows.

Sometimes a persuasive speech can also be built around an extended narrative of some incident that dramatizes the problem being addressed in the speech. An example of an extended narrative in a persuasive speech might be the following:

I. Jim had too much to drink at a fraternity party.
II. His frat brothers dared him to hop a moving freight train.
III. Jim attempted to jump onto the moving train.
IV. He lost his balance and fell under the train; both of his legs were severed.
V. Jim lived and has dedicated his life to fighting alcohol abuse.

Notice that a story needs not only a plot line but also characters, including a central character with whom the audience can identify. In this particular story, the speaker would seek to create a sympathetic portrayal of Jim, who becomes the protagonist. Of course, each point would be developed in detail, and the audience should be held in suspense as the story unfolds. The moral of the story should not have to be stated explicitly but should be apparent to the audience. This is one of those speeches in which stating the thesis at the beginning would actually undermine the effectiveness of the speech. By the end of the speech, however, no one would doubt the speaker's central idea.

Spatial

A **spatial pattern** is an organization based on physical space or geography. Some topics, usually informative, lend themselves to a spatial or geographic order. Suppose we want to discuss weather patterns in the United States. We might divide our topic geographically into east, south, north, and west. If we were trying to explain how a ship is constructed, we might do so in terms of fore, midship, and aft. Or if we were giving a tour of our hometown, our points might look something like this:

> **spatial pattern**
> A pattern of organization based on physical space or geography.

I. The east side is mostly residential.
II. The central part of town is the business district.
III. The west side is largely industrial.

Categorical

A **categorical pattern** is an organization based on natural divisions in the subject matter. Many topics, both informative and persuasive, naturally fall into categories. The federal government, for example, can be naturally divided into the legislative, executive, and judicial branches. The essential principle is that we divide our topic along its natural boundaries. Thus, a speech advocating solar energy might be organized as follows:

> **categorical pattern**
> A pattern of organization based on natural divisions in the subject matter.

I. Fossil fuels pollute the atmosphere.
II. Nuclear energy creates radioactive wastes.
III. Solar energy is nonpolluting.

TV meteorologists often use a spatial pattern to explain the weather.

When using this pattern, however, we need to be careful that we don't create false categories. Although it may be categorically convenient to cast people into some specific groups, for example, it also can be highly misleading or even offensive. Much social and ethnic prejudice is rooted in the stereotyping of people into arbitrary categories. All Muslims are not terrorists, for example, and all Christians are not peaceful, as the dispute in Northern Ireland sadly demonstrates.

Alphabetical

alphabetical pattern
Main points are in alphabetical order or spell out a common word.

A useful way to organize a speech is so that the main points are in an **alphabetical pattern** or so they spell out a common word. For example, dermatologists have developed what they call the A-B-C-D method of detecting skin cancer through self-examination.[1] These steps form a useful way of organizing a speech and help the audience remember what to look for. This pattern is particularly suited for informative speeches where the goal is for the audience to remember what they've learned. For example, here are the things we should look for in examining moles for skin cancer:

   I. Asymmetry–one half unlike the other half.
  II. Border irregularity–scalloped or poorly circumscribed border.
 III. Color varies from one area to another.
 IV. Diameter–larger than 6 mm (diameter of a pencil eraser).

Problem–Solution

problem–solution pattern
A pattern of organization that analyzes a problem in terms of (1) harm, (2) significance, and (3) cause, and proposes a solution that is (1) described, (2) feasible, and (3) advantageous.

Sometimes we speak to propose a solution to an ongoing problem. This is frequently the case when we speak persuasively. One way to approach this type of speech is to use the **problem–solution pattern,** a pattern of organization that analyzes a problem in terms of (1) harm, (2) significance, and (3) cause, and proposes a solution that is (1) described, (2) feasible, and (3) advantageous. A specific example of this pattern might be a speech about the need for better health care. In this case, we might organize the speech in the following way:

I. Millions of Americans are denied access to adequate health care.	*[problem]*
A. People suffer and die without this care.	*[harm]*
B. More than 40 million Americans lack basic health insurance.	*[significance]*
C. There is a gap between government-sponsored health care (Medicaid and Medicare) and private insurance.	*[cause]*
II. We need a program of national health insurance to fill the gap.	*[solution]*
A. All businesses will be taxed to provide national health insurance.	*[description]*
B. Similar programs exist in almost every other industrialized country in the world.	*[feasibility]*
C. No longer will people be denied access to medical care simply because they cannot pay.	*[advantages]*

The relationship between harm and significance is important. Harm has to do with the bad consequences of the problem—in this case, potential suffering and death. Significance has to do with the extent of the problem. If 100 people in a nation of 250 million were at risk of suffering or death because of an inadequate health care system, this would be unfortunate, but it would not be a significant problem relative to the population of the nation. If millions were at risk, then the problem would be significant.

We also need to recognize that there can be numerous different solutions to the same problem. Thus it is important to stress both the feasibility and the advantages of the solution we propose if we hope to have it adopted by our audience.

Stock Issues

Closely related to the problem–solution pattern is what is often called the **stock issues pattern,** which is well suited to persuasive speeches. This pattern is based on the model of deliberative debate, and it addresses four key questions: first, how serious is the problem; second, who is to blame; third, how it would be solved; and finally, whether the solution is worth the cost. These four stock issues are referred to as (1) ill, (2) blame, (3) cure, and (4) cost. For example, a speech about campus parking problems could have the following four main points:

> **stock issues pattern**
> A four-point pattern of organization that is based on (1) ill, (2) blame, (3) cure, and (4) cost.

I. The lack of parking is causing a serious problem on our campus.	*[ill]*
II. The problem exists because parking rules are not enforced, which allows many nonstudents to take up our parking spots.	*[blame]*
III. The problem can be cured by raising fines and increasing patrols.	*[cure]*
IV. The costs of the increased patrols will be paid for by higher fines.	*[cost]*

As with the problem–solution pattern, we need specific subpoints to show that the facts support the serious nature of the problem and that we have correctly identified the cause. The solution needs to be well thought out and explained. And we must be sure that the costs of our solution do not outweigh the benefits of solving the problem.

Refutational

Sometimes we are in a position to answer the arguments of another speaker, for example, in a debate. Alternatively, we may read or hear something with which we disagree. These types of persuasive speeches often call for the **refutational pattern** of organization, which involves the following steps:

> **refutational pattern**
> A pattern of organization that involves (1) stating the argument to be refuted, (2) stating the objection to the argument, (3) proving the objection to the argument, and (4) presenting the impact of the refutation.

I. State the argument we seek to refute.
II. State our objection to the argument.
III. Prove our objection to the argument.
IV. Present the impact of our refutation.

For example, if we wanted to refute a proposed national health insurance plan, we might proceed with the following points:

[States the argument you seek to refute.]

[States your objection to the argument.]

[Presents proof for your objection.]

[Presents the impact of your objection.]

I. The proponents of national health care say the government should control health care.
II. Government bureaucrats, not physicians or patients, will control medical choices.
III. People from Canada, which has national health insurance, often have to come to the United States for medical care they are denied by their government-run program.
IV. The quality of American health care will decline in a program run by government bureaucrats.

Causal

> **causal pattern**
> A pattern of organization that moves from cause to effect or from effect to cause.

The **causal pattern** is an organization that moves from cause to effect or from effect to cause. It is often useful in persuasive presentations and also can be used in some informative speeches. In cause-to-effect speeches, we are dealing with some known activity and showing our audience that it will produce certain effects. If these are desirable effects, we would be endorsing the activity. If they are undesirable, we would be suggesting that the audience avoid it. To illustrate this organizational pattern, suppose we wanted to convince our audience to quit smoking:

[Cause]

I. Cigarette smoke contains a number of harmful chemicals.
   A. Carbon monoxide reduces the body's ability to absorb oxygen.
   B. Nicotine is an addictive substance.
   C. Tar is made up of thousands of cancer-causing chemicals.

[Effect]

II. Cigarette smoking leads to significant health problems.
   A. Carbon monoxide has been linked to low-birth-weight babies.
   B. Nicotine makes quitting smoking difficult.
   C. Tar is the principal source of cancer-causing chemicals in tobacco.

On the other hand, if we wanted to convince our audience of the need to reduce the power of special interests in Washington, we might argue from various effects back to the cause:

[Effect]

I. The country is in economic trouble.
   A. Real wages are declining.
   B. Many industries are moving overseas.
   C. Our trade deficit is growing.

[Cause]

II. We have a system of government that is too tied to special interests.
   A. Lobbyists influence Congress to make bad economic decisions.
   B. Politicians are more interested in getting reelected than in solving problems.
   C. Only by breaking the power of special interests can we get our economy back on track.

Whether we move from cause to effect or from effect to cause, we need to provide proof of the causal links asserted in the speech. Simply because two things occur one after the other does not prove one caused the other. For example, just because a car breaks down doesn't mean the last person to drive it is responsible for the breakdown.

Monroe's Motivated-Sequence

A five-step organizational scheme developed by speech professor Alan Monroe, and thus termed **Monroe's motivated-sequence,** is another useful pattern.[2] These five steps overlap somewhat with the introduction and conclusion of a speech, as well as the body. They are as follows:

> **Monroe's motivated-sequence**
> A five-step organizational scheme, developed by speech professor Alan Monroe, including (1) attention, (2) need, (3) satisfaction, (4) visualization, and (5) action.

  I. *Attention:* Gain your audience's attention.   *[Introduction]*
 II. *Need:* Show the audience that a need exists that affects them.   *[Body]*
III. *Satisfaction:* Present the solution to the need.   *[Body]*
 IV. *Visualization:* Help the audience imagine how their need will be met in the   *[Body]*
      future.
  V. *Action:* State what actions must be taken to fulfill the need.   *[Conclusion]*

To see how this motivated sequence might work, consider a speech on national health insurance:

  I. *Attention:* A child dies when her parents can't afford to take her to the doctor.
 II. *Need:* You could become one of millions of uninsured Americans who face financial ruin if they become seriously ill.
III. *Satisfaction:* National health insurance would guarantee all Americans the right to health care, regardless of their income.
 IV. *Visualization:* The United States would join nations like Canada, where no one fears seeing a doctor because of the cost.
  V. *Action:* Write your senator and representative today, urging the passage of national health insurance.

Obviously, the motivated-sequence pattern is most directly suited to persuasive presentations. However, an informative presentation could use at least some of these steps, because informative speaking typically is the first step in a persuasive campaign. In an informative presentation, it is important to show the audience why they need to learn the information being presented and, of course, to satisfy that need. Helping an audience visualize how they will use the information is also valuable. And often the speaker will then want the audience to put what they have learned into action.

These 10 patterns of organization are primarily linear in nature and are well suited to audiences rooted in a Western European tradition. Other organizational patterns are rooted in other cultures. These organic patterns are increasingly relevant to today's audiences. We discuss three of these patterns: wave, spiral, and star.

Organic Patterns of Organization

Cheryl Jorgensen-Earp has suggested that women and some ethnic speakers use less linear, more organic patterns, such as the wave, the spiral, and the star.[3]

Figure 9.2
Wave Pattern
Martin Luther King Jr. used a wave pattern in his speech.

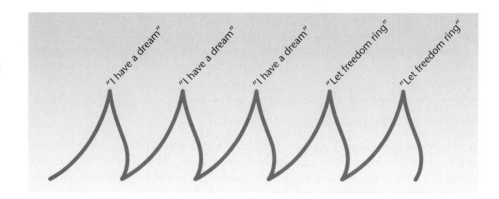

Wave

wave pattern
A pattern of organization in which the basic theme, often represented by a phrase, is repeated again and again, much like a wave cresting, receding, and then cresting again.

Many women and African Americans use the **wave pattern.** Much like a wave cresting, receding, and then cresting again, a speech following this pattern continually returns to the basic theme, repeating a phrase again and again throughout the speech. Perhaps the most familiar example is the "I Have a Dream" speech, by Dr. Martin Luther King Jr., which gets its title from the constant repetition of that phrase. In addition, King uses the theme "Let freedom ring" repeatedly as he brings the speech to its dramatic conclusion. Figure 9.2 illustrates the wave pattern of speaking.

Spiral

spiral pattern
A pattern of organization that employs repetition of points, with the points growing in intensity as the speech builds to its conclusion.

Another pattern suggested by Jorgensen-Earp is a **spiral pattern,** which repeats points, as does the wave, but each point grows in intensity as the speech builds to its pinnacle at the conclusion. For example, we recall a motivational speech by one of our former students, Rick Rigsby (who authored the box on interviewing in Chapter 7). He was speaking of how he learned about life from the death of his wife, Trina, from breast cancer when she was in her 30s. At one point she told him that it wasn't how long you lived but how you lived that mattered. As the speech progressed, Rick returned to this theme again and again, each time with more emotional intensity. At the end of his speech he asked the audience this question: "How are you living?" Thus he spiraled to a climax that had been foreshadowed throughout the speech. Figure 9.3 illustrates a spiral pattern of organization.

Star

star pattern
A pattern of organization in which all of the points are of equal importance and can be presented in any order to support the common theme.

A third organic pattern identified by Jorgensen-Earp is the **star pattern,** in which various points all grow from a central idea. Because all of the points of the star are of equal importance, a speaker can present the points in any order in support of the common theme that encircles the star and holds the speech together. When actor Edward James Olmos spoke at our university several years ago the speech seemed like a random list of stories and anecdotes to some in the audience. But a more careful analysis shows that each of his stories was really a point on a star, with a central message that "we are all one gang." Figure 9.4 illustrates the star pattern.

Figure 9.3
Spiral Pattern
Each point in a spiral pattern repeats the theme with greater intensity.

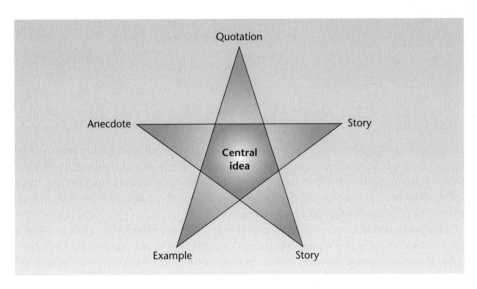

Figure 9.4
Star Pattern
In a star pattern all points grow from a central idea.

As a speaker, carefully consider both the audience's cultural background as it affects their organizational preferences and your own cultural affinity for certain patterns of organization. Although cultural diversity provides the opportunity to expand the ways in which speeches may be organized, it should not be used as an excuse for a lack of any coherent organizational pattern.

The box titled Organizational Patterns summarizes the patterns we have discussed and suggests which patterns work best for various speech purposes. Whatever pattern we choose, we want to be sure it is appropriate for our audience, topic, and purpose. Sticking with one pattern for all the main points of the speech helps to avoid audience confusion.

Speaking of . . .

Organizational Patterns

Any of the patterns we've discussed could be used to fulfill any speech purpose. However, certain patterns seem more suitable for one or two purposes than do others. This table highlights the patterns most likely to be useful for each speech purpose.

Pattern	Informative	Persuasive	Entertaining
Time	X		X
Extended narrative	X	X	X
Spatial	X		
Categorical	X	X	X
Alphabetical	X	X	X
Problem–solution		X	
Stock issues		X	
Refutational		X	
Causal	X	X	
Motivated-sequence		X	
Wave	X	X	X
Spiral	X	X	X
Star	X	X	X

Signposts

In addition to constructing the actual body of the speech, it is important to help our audience follow our organization. As Chapter 2 explained, *signposts* are transitional statements that bridge main points. They tell the audience where we have been and where we are going. Signposts help those who have become lost or inattentive to pick up the thread of a speech.

Signposts serve to verbally link our thoughts as we speak. It's always a good idea to let our audience know that there is a sequence to our message—"Let's consider three important issues"—and then to remind them where we are in that sequence—"Having covered the first issue, let's now look at the second."

For example, to add a point, we use words or phrases such as *furthermore, in addition to,* and *besides.* To emphasize something, phrases such as *above all, indeed,* and *most important* are useful. To emphasize time, we use words such as *then, afterward, eventually, next, immediately, meanwhile, previously, often, usually,* and *later.* Cause and effect can be suggested by the words *consequently, therefore,* and *thus.* To stress that we are using an example, we say, "for example" or "for instance." The progress from one point to another in our speech can be highlighted by terms such as *first, second, third,* or *furthermore.* Contrast can be indicated by use of *but, however, instead, nevertheless* and phrases such as *to the contrary, on the other hand,* and *in contrast.* The conclusion of a speech can be indicated by phrases such as *to sum up, for these reasons, in retrospect,* and *in conclusion.*[4]

Techniques for Signposting

- *Refer to preceding and upcoming ideas.* "Now that you know what computer viruses are, I'll discuss how to prevent their spread to your computer."
- *Enumerate key points.* "First, never assume that a program from a friend or computer bulletin board is virus free."
- *Give nonverbal reinforcement.* Changes in vocal inflection signal a change is coming. Movement can signal a signpost. Some speakers physically move from one place to another while speaking in order to emphasize that they are moving from one point to the next. Others hold up fingers to indicate number of points.
- *Use visual aids to reinforce signposts.* Moving to our next PowerPoint slide or putting up a new transparency clearly signals to the audience that we are moving on. It's also a way to help us remember the sequence of our speech.
- *Words can cue the audience that we are changing points: Next, another, number, moving on, finally, therefore,* and *in summary.*

It's also a good idea to let an audience know that the speech is close to the end by using transitional words and phrases such as *finally, in sum, in conclusion,* and *to close.* Far too many times we've watched audiences guess whether they're hearing the end of the speech; the sign of their uncertainty is premature clapping.

Introducing the Speech

After organizing the body of the speech, it is time to construct the introduction and conclusion. Recall from Chapter 2 that an introduction should do four things: open with impact, focus on the thesis statement, connect with the audience, and preview the rest of the speech. Let's look at each of these functions in turn.

Open With Impact

A speech should immediately grab the audience's attention. First impressions count. One way to control this impression is to open the speech with impact. The most common ways are a story; a quotation; a startling statement; a reference to the audience, the occasion, or a current event; appropriate humor; a personal experience; or a thought-provoking question.

Story

A brief story, real or hypothetical, is often a good way to begin. For example, one of our students began her speech by describing the strange behavior of a person who was staggering and incoherent, and who finally collapsed. The quick conclusion of most of her audience was that the person was drunk. Not only was this conclusion wrong, the truth startled the class. The person had diabetes and was suffering from insulin shock. Needless to say, the class became far more interested in hearing the speech about diabetes than if the speaker had simply begun, "Today I'm going to tell you about diabetes."

Quotation

As we pointed out in Chapter 7, there are numerous sources of quotations, including those online, usually organized by topic. If we are having trouble deciding how to begin a speech, we often look for a quotation that will captivate the audience and reinforce our main ideas.

Startling Statement

Humans are attracted naturally to surprising, startling, and unusual events. A surprising or startling statement will provoke the audience's undivided attention. For example, a student in our class began her speech by announcing that her sister had died of toxic shock syndrome. As you'd expect, her audience was startled and paid rapt attention to the speech that followed.

Reference to the Audience, Occasion, or Current Events

Professional speakers often tailor their speeches to a specific audience and situation, saying such things as "I'm so happy to be here at [fill in the blank] college" or "I join with you in praising your football team's come-from-behind victory last night."

Another possibility is to refer to a previous speaker. Consider an instance in one class when two students chose to speak on gun control, each taking the opposite side of the topic. The second speaker wisely incorporated a reference to the prior speech in her introduction. To ignore a speech on the same topic, particularly one at odds with your own speech, is likely to turn off an audience. Without attempting to refute the other speaker, she acknowledged those opposing views but also stated that she would present the other side of the issue.

Finally, current events may spark interest and controversy. We recall a student who spoke on binge drinking who began the speech by referring to the recent tragic death of a student on our campus.

Appropriate Humor

A classic *Far Side* cartoon shows Abraham Lincoln delivering the Gettysburg Address. His speech, however, begins with a joke, "And so the bartender says, 'Hey! That's not a duck!'" After a pause for laughter, Lincoln continues, "Fourscore and seven years ago . . . ."

Obviously, one would not begin a serious speech such as the Gettysburg Address with a joke. Humor, if not used properly, can backfire. It is best used on occasions when the audience will find it appropriate. An after-dinner speech, for example, is frequently an opportunity to employ humor.

However we use it, though, humor should be tied to the substance of our speech. Telling an irrelevant joke can detract from the main idea rather than enhance it. It can also make the speaker look foolish.

Finally, we need to be sensitive with regard to humor. Ethnic, sexist, and off-color jokes, for example, can get a speaker into justifiable trouble. For example, in the summer of 2004 comedian Whoopi Goldberg was widely criticized and lost her commercial endorsement contract with Slim-Fast for making sexually explicit jokes about President Bush at a fundraiser for Senator John Kerry. Kerry was also roundly criticized for not condemning her remarks on the spot. Speakers need to err on the side of caution when they treat sensitive subjects with humor.

Personal Experience

Often there is no other more compelling testimony on a topic than personal experience. Not only can a personal experience draw in the audience and get their attention, it also can serve to build speaker credibility. For example, the speaker on diabetes referred to earlier had a brother who was diabetic. However, she did not mention this fact until she had finished her speech. Had she begun with her own experiences with a diabetic brother, she would have enhanced her credibility for the remainder of the speech.

Thought-Provoking Question

Sometimes we can use a question to open a speech. A **rhetorical question** is one that the audience isn't expected to answer out loud. For example, one student began a speech on secondhand smoke this way: "How many of you have ever returned home smelling as though you were a stand-in for the Marlboro Man?"[5] The attention-getting language worked well. However, beginning with a question can be ineffective if the question is not thought provoking. For example, beginning a speech with "How many of you would like to learn to snow ski?" isn't likely to have much impact on an audience. Also, with rhetorical questions, audiences are sometimes unsure whether the question is meant to be answered out loud. On the other hand, we have seen speakers who effectively begin their speeches by asking audience members to respond to a series of questions with a show of hands. Questions, rhetorical or real, should be used only if they add impact to the opening of the speech.

> **rhetorical question**
> A question that the audience isn't expected to answer out loud.

Focus on the Thesis Statement

The central idea we want to convey to an audience should be captured by our thesis statement. Although we have developed a thesis statement before writing the body of the speech, now is a good time to reflect on its phrasing. Have we really focused on the essential theme of the speech? The thesis statement must be broad enough to incorporate all of our main points. At the same time, the thesis statement cannot be so broad that our speech seems to leave something out.

As noted earlier, there may be situations, such as with a hostile audience, when we should not explicitly state our thesis early in the speech. In the introduction in these situations, we indicate the general topic area of the speech, focusing on an area of common agreement, rather than the thesis. The thesis would then emerge toward the end of the speech, after the arguments in support have been explained.

Connect With the Audience

No speech should be constructed without asking, "What's in it for the audience? What needs or desires will be fulfilled by listening to my speech?" The introduction

THE WIZARD OF ID   **Brant parker and Johnny hart**

By permission of Johnny Hart and Creator's Syndicate, Inc.

is an opportunity to make the link between the speech topic and audience members. If we make this link in the introduction, we are much more likely to gain the audience's collective ear.

The introduction is another opportunity to build our credibility. We can stress our similarity to the audience. The student who spoke on toxic shock syndrome used her family's tragedy to stress that the same thing could happen to any woman. She not only made a connection with her classmates, she established her personal credibility by virtue of her experience and her subsequent research on the topic.

Although connecting with the audience is an important part of the introduction to a speech, the connection should not be made only once. In fact, throughout the speech we should draw a connection between our message and our audience whenever possible.

Preview the Speech

Although no one knows who first said, "Tell 'em what you're going to tell 'em; tell 'em; and then tell 'em what you told 'em," it is a saying with more than a grain of truth. As we noted in Chapter 2, a *preview* is a forecast of the main points of a speech. It simply tells audience members what they are going to hear. In many ways, it is a summary before the fact. By telling audience members what will follow, a preview helps them put our statements into a coherent frame of reference.

The way to preview a speech is rather simple: Cue the audience to the fact that we are previewing the main points of our speech, and then state the points in the same sequence they will be presented. A brief preview might be "In today's speech, I would like to share the definition, transmission, and prevention of computer viruses." Or we may want to enumerate our main points, saying, "Today, I want to first define computer viruses; second, explain how they are transmitted; and third, offer a way to prevent them from infecting your own computer."

It is not always necessary, however, to be so explicit. There are often subtler ways of previewing a speech. For example, "All computer owners need to know what computer viruses are, how they are transmitted, and how to detect and prevent them."

Ways to Open With Impact

Effective ways to open a speech with impact include:

- Story
- Quotation
- Startling statement
- Reference to the audience, occasion, or current events
- Appropriate humor
- Personal experience
- Thought-provoking question

Concluding the Speech

The conclusion of a speech should be brief and memorable. The last thing an audience wants to hear after "In conclusion . . ." is a 10-minute dissertation on some new aspect of the topic. When we say those magic words "in conclusion" or "to wrap up," we should be prepared to conclude. Avoid introducing points that were not covered in the body of the speech. If we have another main point to cover, then it belongs in the body of the speech, not the conclusion. There are, consequently, only two basic things to do in concluding a speech: summarize and close with impact.

Summarize

The summary tells the audience, very briefly, what we have told them in the speech. This is where clear, concisely developed main points pay off. Sometimes we may wish to explicitly number the main points in the summary. For example, "Remember, there are three types of bikes you'll see on campus. First, there are cruisers; second, there are mountain bikes; and third, there are touring bikes."

Close With Impact

The final words of a speech should be memorable. The close is our last chance to make an impression on the audience. As with the opening, it should be relevant to the main thesis of the speech. A few of the common techniques for closing are a short, memorable quotation, an anecdote or a brief story, a direct appeal to action, and a return to the opening theme. If we have delayed presenting our thesis statement for strategic reasons, it should be incorporated just prior to this point (right after the summary). If we stated the thesis earlier, it should be reiterated here.

Quotation

The same principles apply to a closing quotation as to an opening one. We want to capture the essence of our talk in a few words. If someone has said it better, then it is perfectly appropriate to quote that person. In the conclusion, first state the

Voter registration drives represent direct appeals to action, a technique we can use to close our speeches.

person quoted and then state the quotation. For example, it is less effective to say, "'I have a dream,' said Martin Luther King Jr.," than to say, "As Martin Luther King Jr. once stated, 'I have a dream.'"

Anecdote

The key in the closing is to be brief and to the point. A long, drawn-out story will undermine the effectiveness of the rest of the speech. A concluding anecdote should highlight our main focus, not detract from it. As with opening stories, such anecdotes can be real or hypothetical but should be clearly identified as such.

Direct Appeal to Action

Concluding with an appeal to action is typical of a persuasive speech and is an explicit part of the motivated sequence. It involves telling audience members specifically what they can do to fulfill their needs or solve a problem—for example, sign a petition, write to Congress, or change their own behavior. A direct appeal to the audience is often the most appropriate way to conclude a persuasive presentation.

Return to Opening

One of the most effective ways to close a speech is to return to where you began. Not only does this remind the audience of your introduction, it also gives your speech a sense of closure. It takes both you and your audience full circle. For example, the speech that began by describing a person suffering from insulin shock ended by telling the audience that they would now know how to recognize when someone was in insulin shock and would be able to get that person the help he or she needed. If you can find a way to tie your opening and closing together, you can intensify the impact of both.

Ways to Close With Impact

Effective ways to close a speech with impact include:

* Quotation
* Anecdote
* Direct appeal to action
* Return to opening

Preparing the Formal Outline

Once you have a rough structure of your speech, including the body, introduction, and conclusion, your instructor may recommend that you prepare a formal outline of the speech. A **formal outline** is a detailed outline used in speech preparation but not, in most cases, in the actual presentation. Usually, such an outline should be typed or prepared on a computer, depending on your instructor's requirements. Such outlines help you put your ideas down in a clear and organized fashion. If submitted in advance of a speech, it also allows instructors to give you feedback and make suggestions.

There are two basic types of outlines. *Phrase* or *key word outlines* are meaningful to the speaker but probably would not make a lot of sense to anyone else. For example, a speaker might prepare the following outline for her own use:

> Intro: Tell story
>   I. Rock music
>   II. Volume
>   III. Deafness
> Conclusion: Same story 10 years later

Because this outline probably would make sense only to the speaker, beginning speakers are frequently expected to prepare a *full-sentence outline*. In this type of outline, you include a full statement indicating what each main point and subpoint cover. All the parts of the speech are included, even signposts. Generally, a formal outline should include the following:

* The specific purpose, phrased as an infinitive phrase (to . . .), describing exactly what the speaker wants the speech to accomplish.
* Three sections–labeled introduction, body, and conclusion–each separately outlined and beginning with the Roman numeral "I."
* The introduction, including opening, focus on thesis statement, connection with the audience, and preview.
* The body, including main points, subpoints, supporting points, and further support, and, if your instructor requires them, signposts (in parentheses) between the main points.

SpeechCoach

To help you prepare your speech outline, see the Outline Tutor on your CD.

formal outline

A detailed outline used in speech preparation, but not, in most cases, in the actual presentation.

- The conclusion, including a summary and a close.
- "References" or "Works Cited" (depending on whether you use APA or MLA style). Specific quotations or facts drawn from a source should also be cited in the main outline. Of course, you should check with your instructor about the specific outlining requirements, if any, for your class. Some instructors prefer a different source citation system, for example, than the ones discussed in this text. Appendix A provides a Guide for Source Citation using APA and MLA formats.

Outlines typically use a standard outline notation, which indicates the levels of subordination of points:

I. Main point
  A. Subpoint
    1. Supporting point
      a. Further support

Any subdivision should include at least two matching points. Thus an "A" subpoint implies there should also be at least a "B." Supporting point "1" should be matched by at least a "2," and further support "a" should be followed by at least a "b."

Many instructors prefer that outlines be written in complete sentences, at least through the level of subpoints. This provides a clearer idea to your instructor of what you are going to say. Divide separate ideas into different sentences. If you outline using paragraph form, what you really have is an essay with outline notation scattered throughout. Thus, the following is not really in outline form:

I. The first men on the moon were Americans. Neil Armstrong stepped out first. He was followed by Buzz Aldrin. At the same time, Michael Collins orbited the moon.

This paragraph could be turned into the following outline:

I. The first men on the moon were Americans.
  A. Neil Armstrong stepped out first.
  B. He was followed by Buzz Aldrin.
  C. At the same time, Michael Collins orbited the moon.

Notice how each sentence is placed in a separate point. The more general statement is the main point, and the specific instances are subpoints.

Some aspects of an outline do not need to be in complete-sentence form. For example, a speaker who wants to list the components of a larger whole, such as ingredients or tools, could use an outline like this:

1. Cigarette smoke has three components:
  a. Carbon monoxide
  b. Nicotine
  c. Tar

You need to use judgment, therefore, when you are asked to write a complete-sentence outline. Use complete sentences for your main points and subpoints and anywhere the meaning would not be clear if not expressed in complete-sentence form. The box "Sample Speech Outline: Accident or Suicide: Driving Without a Seatbelt by Karen Shirk" follows the suggested format. Remember, however, to check with your instructor for specific requirements in your class.

SpeechCoach

To see this speech, go to segment 9.1 on your CD.

Preparing Speaker's Notes

The outline is a preparation tool. When presenting a speech, we use **speaker's notes,** which are brief notes with key words, usually written on cards (Figure 9.5). Final notes should be meaningful to us as speakers, but not necessarily to anyone else. However, we should rehearse until we don't need to look at the note cards frequently. It is especially important to know the introduction and conclusion very well. The best open or close to a speech can be undone by a speaker who reads it from cards rather than making direct eye contact with the audience.

Cards about 4 by 6 inches in size seem to work best. Larger cards are too obtrusive; smaller cards require us to strain to see our notes and to constantly be shuffling them. The following are some helpful hints for preparing note cards.

> **speaker's notes**
> Brief notes with key words, usually written on cards, used by a speaker when presenting a speech.

One of our students, Rachel Perahia, uses note cards that she has highlighted for quick reference.

In Their Own Words

Sample Speech Outline

Title of speech.

ACCIDENT OR SUICIDE: DRIVING WITHOUT A SEATBELT
by Karen Shirk

Karen Shirk

Specific purpose is to motivate audience to do what they know is right.

Specific Purpose: To persuade my audience to wear their seatbelts.

Introduction

Speaker begins with startling statements and visual aids of actual objects that survived a crash.

I. **Open With Impact:** This may be recognized as a piece of a brake light, but to me, it is a piece of brake light from my mother's car. This may be recognized as a CD-player face, but to me, it's the only thing left from an accident that happened earlier this year.
   A. Many times I have seen people getting in cars and driving away without a seatbelt on.
   B. This concerns me because I know how quickly a little drive can turn into a big accident.
   C. It doesn't matter if you are an expert driver, your safety is put into other people's hands, whether you're the passenger or the driver.

Thesis statement and connect with audience are clearly labeled.

II. **Focus on Thesis Statement:** It's important to take what little control you have on the road and utilize it.

III. **Connect With the Audience:** That's why it's so important to wear your seatbelt.

Preview of speech is provided.

IV. **Preview:** Today I will discuss the importance of seatbelts, the benefits of wearing a seatbelt, why some people still aren't wearing seatbelts, and some ways to remind you to strap on your seatbelt.

Body

Body of speech is labeled.

Main points begin with Roman numeral I.

I. **Main Point:** Putting on your seatbelt may be the most important part of driving.
   A. After all, a seatbelt is defined as "an arrangement of straps designated to hold a person steady in a seat" (*Merriam-Webster's,* 1993, p. 1054).

Direct quotations are indicated by quotation marks and source is cited in parentheses. Your instructor may prefer a different method of citing sources

   B. And, as Dr. Haddon says, "I would challenge those of you who do not use them to consider that . . . as persons sending something through the mail you would not ship things loose in an empty barrel to flop around with the barrel moving at high speed" (Haddon, 1968, p. 13).

Speaker includes note to self to turn on overhead projector.

   C. As an example, consider Barbie, who doesn't bother putting on her seatbelt (show overheads).
   D. Some important points to remember about seatbelts as listed online are:
      1. First, an adult can only hold back the weight of his body by the arms and legs at speeds of up to 7 kilometers per hour (*The seatbelt—a link with life,* 1998).
      2. Second, in a collision at 50 kilometers per hour, the force is the same as falling 10 meters.

Signposts are transitional statements between main points.

(**Signpost:** Now that you've been reminded of the importance of seatbelts, let's discuss how a seatbelt can benefit you.)

II. **Main Point:** A seatbelt can save you from serious or even fatal injury.
   A. First, if the vehicle you're in is rear-ended, a seatbelt will hold you from flying through the windshield.

B. Second, if your vehicle rolls or flips, the seatbelt will keep you from banging into the sides and roof of the car.

C. And third, it can keep you from getting a hefty fine from the highway patrol.

(**Signpost:** Now that we've discussed the benefits, let's try to analyze why some people still aren't wearing seatbelts.)

III. **Main Point:** There could be several reasons why some people still aren't wearing seatbelts, although none of them serves as a valid excuse.

A. One reason could be laziness.

B. Another reason could be forgetfulness.

C. One reason might be confidence.

D. Some people are afraid that a seatbelt will trap them in the event of an accident.

E. Finally, I've overheard someone say that wearing a seatbelt would wrinkle their clothes.

(**Signpost:** Basically, there's no excuse. But, instead of verbally abusing unsafe drivers, it's better to suggest a few solutions to remind yourself to strap on your seatbelt.)

IV. **Main Point:** These solutions are simple and don't require too much effort, considering the benefits involved.

A. Make putting on your seatbelt the first thing you do upon entering a vehicle.

B. Get into the habit of having it on.

C. Wear it no matter how far you're driving—no exceptions.

Conclusion

I. **Summarize:** Today I've discussed seatbelts and the safety they offer.

A. I've reinforced the importance of wearing a seatbelt.

B. I've listed some of the immediate benefits of wearing a seatbelt.

C. I've tried to explain some reasons why others may not wear a seatbelt.

D. And I've tried to offer some useful suggestions on how to increase your control on the road by wearing a seatbelt.

Conclusion begins with a summary of main points.

II. **Close With Impact:** It shouldn't be necessary to have to persuade you to wear a seatbelt.

A. But, as seen in the numerous fatalities each year in cases where someone wasn't wearing theirs, sometimes the message doesn't get through.

B. I hope I've reinforced that message enough so that you might think twice before driving unbuckled.

C. That way, if you're ever in an accident, your chances are much higher that you'll walk away unharmed.

Speech closes with impact. Ask yourself if it matches the impact with which the speech opened.

References

Haddon, W. (1968). The national highway safety program—18 months later. In J. O'Day (Ed.), *Driver behavior: Cause and effect.* Washington, DC: Insurance Institute for Highway Safety.

The seatbelt—a link with life. (1998). [Online]. Available: http://www.lycos.com/wguide/wire/wire_969214_2_0.html [1998, April 3].

Merriam-Webster's collegiate dictionary (10th ed.). (1993). Springfield, MA: Merriam-Webster.

Speaker lists references at end of speech with full bibliographic citation. We discuss American Psychological Association (APA) and Modern Language Association (MLA) methods of source citation in Appendix A. Your instructor may prefer a different method of citing sources. Whatever method is used, accurate source citation is important.

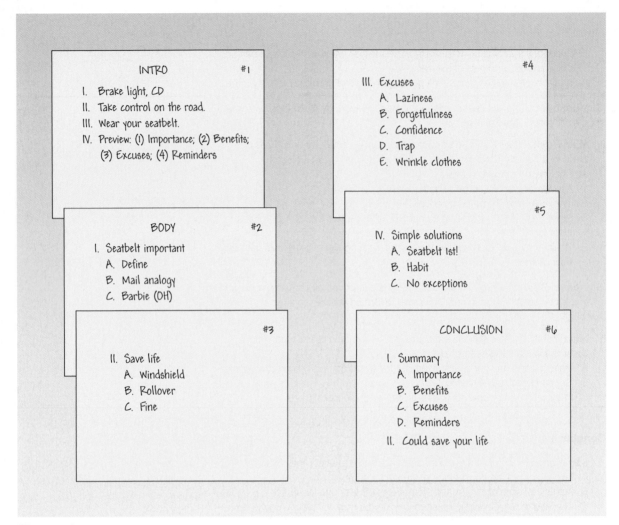

Figure 9.5
Speaker's Note Cards

Tips and Tactics

Tips for Preparing Note Cards

- *Use bright colors and large, bold lettering.* This will make the notes easier to see.
- *Use no more than five or six lines per note card.* If too much is crammed on one card, it will be confusing.
- *Put each part of a speech on a separate card.* For example, the introduction might go on one card, the body on another, and the conclusion on a third.
- *Number the cards.* It is easy to lose track of our place while speaking. One way to help prevent this from happening is to number each card.
- *Write on only one side of a card.* Writing on both sides compounds the chances of losing your place.

- *Highlight main ideas.* Just like highlighting key passages in books, highlight the points you wish to emphasize.
- *Use note cards to make comments to yourself.* It is perfectly appropriate, for example, to write prompts on note cards. For example, write "O.H." to remind yourself to show an overhead at that point in the speech.
- *Don't try to write out the speech word for word.* This only encourages reading the speech rather than presenting it in a conversational manner. The only exception to this rule would be exact quotations, facts, or statistics, which obviously need to be written out.

Speaker's notes contain all the same ideas as the complete outline, but the words are designed to cue us to what comes next. Only with practice can we speak from these notes and still be assured of covering all the ideas in the original outline. And this is the final point we wish to make: Successful speakers practice prior to an actual presentation. No matter how good our organization seems, it is only as good as our ability to deliver it. That takes practice. And practice doesn't mean running through the speech the night before or, even worse, the morning of the presentation. It means devoting significant amounts of time to practicing the speech until we have internalized its basic organization.

Summary

To effectively organize a speech:

- Focus on the audience when organizing the speech.
- Refine the specific purpose.
- Create a clear thesis statement.

Organize the body of the speech before tackling the introduction or conclusion. Remember that:

- Two to five focused main points should fully develop the thesis statement.
- Use parallel structure, simplicity, and balance.
- Develop main points by using subpoints, supporting points, and further support.

Organize the speech body in one of several patterns:

- Time
- Extended narrative
- Spatial

 **Speech**Coach

To evaluate your understanding of this chapter, see the Quizzes on your CD.

 www.mhhe.com /brydon5

Visit the Online Learning Center for helpful study resources, including practice tests, key term crossword puzzles, and PowerWeb articles for research and review.

- Categorical
- Alphabetical
- Problem–solution
- Stock issues
- Refutational
- Causal
- Motivated-sequence
- Wave
- Spiral
- Star

Use signposts as transitional statements to help the audience follow the organization of the speech.

The introduction to a speech should:

- Open with impact
- Focus on the thesis statement
- Connect with the audience
- Preview the body of the speech

Effective openings may include:

- A brief story
- A quotation
- A startling statement
- Reference to the audience
- The occasion, or a current event
- Appropriate humor
- A personal experience
- A thought-provoking question

The conclusion to a speech should:

- Summarize the main points of the speech
- Close with impact

Ways to close include:

- Quotation
- Brief anecdote

- Direct appeal to action
- Return to the opening theme

A formal outline is sometimes required of beginning speakers. Many instructors prefer students to use standard outline notation and write a complete-sentence outline.

Speaker's notes, usually placed on small cards, can be used when presenting the speech.

Check Your Understanding: Exercises and Activities

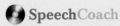 **Speech**Coach

For a review of key terms in this chapter, see the Key Terms Flashcards on your CD.

1. Consider the following speech introductions. Rewrite them to fit the "open, focus, and connect" model suggested in this chapter.

   Today, I'm going to talk to you about pit bulls. I got attacked last week by a pit bull, and I think they are really dangerous. Something's got to be done!

   Have any of you ever thought about going snowboarding? I really like to snowboard, and that's what my speech is going to be about.

   I think capital punishment is wrong. What if somebody who was innocent got killed? I'm going to persuade all of you that life without parole is a better way to go.

2. View a speech on your CD. Using the format described in this chapter, construct a complete-sentence outline of the speech. How closely did the speech seem to follow the steps indicated in the chapter? Was the speech easy to outline? If not, how could the speaker have made the organization clearer?

3. Analyze a print ad in a magazine or newspaper to see whether it uses a problem–solution, causal, or motivated-sequence. If so, explain how each step is fulfilled. If not, discuss how the ad might be modified to fit one of these organizational patterns.

4. On the following pages is an outline of a speech, followed by a list of points in scrambled order. Your task is to match the appropriate sentence from the scrambled list with the points in the outline. This may be done as an individual or a group exercise, depending on your instructor's preference.

Specific purpose: _____

Introduction

  I. Open with impact: _____

  II. Focus on the thesis statement: _____

  III. Connect with your audience: _____

  IV. Preview: _____

Body

  I. Main point: _____

    A. _____

    B. _____

    C. _____

(Signpost: _____)

  II. Main point: _____

    A. _____

    B. _____

    C. _____

(Signpost: _____)

  III. Main point: _____

    A. _____

    B. _____

    C. _____

Conclusion

  I. Summarize: _____

    A. _____

    B. _____

    C. _____

  II. Close with impact: _____

Scrambled list:

1. Use fresh bread, preferably whole grain.

2. Use a quality jelly or jam, made without artificial additives.

3. Use either plain or chunky peanut butter.

4. You must have the necessary ingredients.

5. Fold the wax paper neatly around the sandwich.

6. Place the sandwich in a paper bag.

7. Use a biodegradable wrapper, such as wax paper, rather than plastic wrap.

8. You need to package the sandwich to take to school.

9. Put the two slices together.

10. Spread the first slice with peanut butter.

11. Spread the other slice with jelly or jam.

12. You need to assemble the sandwich.

13. To inform the class how to make a peanut butter and jelly sandwich.

14. First make sure you have the necessary ingredients.

15. Finally, wrap the sandwich.

16. Second, assemble the sandwich.

17. Enjoy your lunch and go to a movie with the money you've saved.

18. You can save money and eat better.

19. Today you will learn how to make the perfect peanut butter and jelly sandwich.

20. Are you tired of spending $5 for a greasy hamburger and fries?

21. Making a peanut butter and jelly sandwich involves three basic steps: having the ingredients, assembling the sandwich, and packaging the sandwich.

22. After you have the ingredients, you need to make the sandwich.

23. Unless you are eating it immediately, the sandwich must be wrapped to stay fresh.

24. To review, there are three steps:

Notes

1. 2003 Skin Cancer Fact Sheet [Retrieved from http://www.aphis.usda.gov/mrpbs/safety_security/library/2003_skin_cancer_fact_sheet.pdf, 5 August 2004].
2. Alan Monroe, *Principles and Types of Speech* (New York: Scott, Foresman, 1935). See also the most recent edition: Bruce E. Gronbeck, Raymie E. McKerrow, Douglas Ehninger, and Alan H. Monroe, *Principles and Types of Speech Communication*, 12th ed. (New York: HarperCollins, 1994).
3. Cited in Clella Jaffe, *Public Speaking: A Cultural Perspective* (Belmont, Calif.: Wadsworth, 1995), 187–92. Based on a telephone interview by Jaffe with Jorgensen-Earp, as well as the latter's unpublished works.
4. Jay Silverman, Elaine Hughes, and Diana Roberts Wienbroer, *Rules of Thumb: A Guide for Writers* (New York: McGraw-Hill, 1990), 99.
5. Deidra Dukes, "The Right to Breathe," speech delivered at California State University, Chico, 1992.

Language is one of our most powerful tools for speaking. In response to a rash of hate signs posted in our community, students used graphic language and posters to communicate their feelings.

Language: Making Verbal Sense of the Message

Objectives

After reading this chapter and reviewing the learning resources on your CD-ROM and at the Online Learning Center, you should be able to:

- Construct examples that illustrate the relationship between language and thought.

- Describe the role language plays in relating to cultural, demographic, and individual diversity.

- Use rhetorical devices such as metaphor and simile to vary language intensity in your speeches.

- Use concrete language, as well as contrast and action, to reduce uncertainty on the part of your audience.

- Use verbal immediacy and transitional devices in your speeches.

- Avoid marginalizing and totalizing language, using inclusive language instead.

- Avoid sexist and stereotypic language.

Key Concepts

analogy

credibility-enhancing language

immediate language

inclusive language

language intensity

linguistic relativity hypothesis

marginalizing language

metaphor

receiver-centric

sexist language

simile

totalizing language

verbal qualifiers

" How can I tell what I think until I see what I say? "

–EDWARD MORGAN FORSTER[1]

Mary Shapiro and Thomas Donovan have always had a rocky relationship. Shapiro is the former chief of the Commodities Futures Trading Commission, the federal agency that polices the volatile commodities market. Donovan is the former president of the Chicago Board of Trade, which promotes the busiest commodities exchange in the United States. When Shapiro learned that Donovan had told his board members during a closed-door meeting that he wouldn't be "intimidated by some blond, 5-foot 2-inch little girl," their relationship took a turn for the worse.[2]

To suggest that Shapiro was displeased about the content of Donovan's speech would be an understatement. She quickly let the financial press know that she wouldn't be bullied by people "lobbing verbal grenades through the window."[3] For the record, Shapiro added that she was also 5-feet 5-inches tall and, at age 39, no longer a little girl.

This example points to a simple indisputable fact: Language, which is the rule-governed symbol system we use to verbally communicate, is not neutral. The words with which we choose to express ourselves and to describe others can elicit the full range of human emotions. This chapter is about language and its role in giving meaning and impact to our ideas. It is also about the power of words and how they affect the way we think about ourselves, our experiences, and the people with whom we come into contact.

On one level, our goal in this chapter is to assist you in appreciating the larger role language plays in our lives. On another level, our goal is to show you how you can use your appreciation of language to construct messages that will be appropriate to both your speech's purpose and the audience with whom you share it. We'll explore the relationship between words and the objects they are meant to represent, how language shapes our perceptions and beliefs, how language relates to audience diversity, and how you can use language to enhance how you and your speech are perceived by your audience.

Word Power

Stripped to the barest of essentials, words are symbolic substitutes for the things they represent. The word *chair* is not the actual thing, for example, but a symbolic representation of it. And the word *love* is not the emotion that prompts us to use it in conjunction with someone about whom we care deeply. Yet the power these "symbolic substitutes" have in shaping what we think or feel about persons, places, and things can be mind-boggling.

As a case in point, think about how the use of words shaped the thinking of both our nation's leaders and us about going to war in Iraq. What we now know, and didn't then, is that the CIA intelligence reports given to President Bush and his advisers were edited to cut words that qualified what could be concluded from them. Words such as "may" or "might" or "possibly" were removed from these reports, giving rise to the impression that the claims being made were certainties rather than possibilities. The fallout was predictable.

Some politicians said that this new information "proved" that the Bush administration had exaggerated the claim that Saddam Hussein was an imminent threat to our nation's security. Others said that the reasons for removing Hussein from power continued to outweigh the fact that some of the claims about his regime "unintentionally" may have been overstated. Regardless of what we may think, this example shows us that words matter. They not only can but frequently do shape

Last year, people skied on champagne powder, windblown pack, groomed, corn snow, cold smoke, frozen granular, firm, good crud, bottomless powder, sugar, machine tilled, crust, hero powder, buffed snow, man made, corduroy, ball bearings, velvet, cut up powder, spring snow, ballroom, and acre after acre of virgin powder.

[*Eskimos may have more words for snow, but we have more lifts.*]

THE ASPENS
SNOWMASS · BUTTERMILK
ASPEN MOUNTAIN

Aspen Central Reservations 1·800·262·7736 Snowmass Central Reservations 1·800·332·3245.
The Aspen Skiing Company Hotels: The Little Nell, The Snowmass Club 1·800·525·6200.

This ad uses words to describe snow conditions rich in imagery for skiers and snowboarders but meaningless for those not involved in these sports.

the world we see, including people and places we only know through what others say about them.

What is true of individual words is even more true of the language you speak. Whether you speak English, French, Spanish, or Russian makes a difference in how you experience and interpret the world. According to the **linguistic relativity hypothesis,** introduced more than 40 years ago by cultural anthropologist Benjamin Whorf, what we perceive is influenced by the language in which we think and speak. Different languages lead to different patterns of thought.[4]

Whorf formulated this hypothesis while studying the Native American language of the Hopi. He discovered there are no words in their language for the concept of incremental time: no seconds, no minutes, and no hours. Thus it would never occur to the Hopi that someone could be half an hour early or late for a visit, because they have no words for the concept.

Each language has certain concepts that cannot be easily expressed in other languages. The expression "something was lost in the translation" doesn't mean part of a statement was literally lost as it was translated from one language to another. It means an identical idea couldn't be found in the second language, so part of the statement's original meaning was diminished. In constructing a speech, the first

> **linguistic relativity hypothesis**
> The idea that what people perceive is influenced by the language in which they think and speak.

thing you'll want to do is choose words and sentences that you believe will lead people to perceive and think about your speech as you intend them to.

Language and Audience Diversity

Having seen that words and language color people's perception and experience, we can now examine the relationship between language and the three types of diversity (cultural, demographic, and individual) introduced in Chapter 6. Understanding the connections between language and diversity is crucial to effective speaking because today's audience is more diverse than ever.

Because we live in such a diverse world, the language we use to communicate is constantly evolving. Words and phrases that may have been acceptable yesterday may not be today or tomorrow. In addition, words and phrases that are acceptable in one situation may be taboo in another. Even though women movie critics may refer to a film as a "chick flick," for example, that doesn't mean it's okay to criticize a female in your class for a speech on a "chick topic." Lest you think otherwise, we're not talking here about the kind of politically correct language comedians and talk show hosts poke fun at. There's a difference between over-the-top phrases such as "vertically challenged" and those that unfairly stereotype individuals because of their ethnicity, gender, or sexual orientation.

When groups of people make it known that the language once used in reference to them is no longer acceptable, they are simply doing what people who have been disenfranchised have done throughout history. This is true, moreover, whether we are talking about Irish immigrants to this country in the 19th century or Italian immigrants in the 20th century.

receiver-centric
A person's assumption that the meaning he or she gives to a word or a phrase is its exclusive meaning.

Finally, some people tend to be **receiver-centric,** assuming that the only interpretation of a word or phrase is theirs. They either rule out or discount the possibility that speakers sometimes make innocent mistakes and say things they didn't know would alienate or offend audience members. Although ignorance is never an excuse for a speaker to use words or phrases that strike audience members in unintended ways, audience members have an obligation to at least consider the possibility that words and phrases may mean something other than the most common meaning they assign to them. Never forget that communication is a transaction in which speakers and audience members negotiate the meaning of their exchange.

Language and Cultural Diversity

The United States is a multiracial, multiethnic, multicultural nation. With the exception of Native Americans, 98 percent of the population can trace its ancestry to another country.

Recall from Chapter 6 that *cultural diversity* is multidimensional, including audience characteristics such as individualism/collectivism and masculinity/femininity. Knowing something about the dimensions of culture reflected in the audience is essential to choosing appropriate language for a speech.

One of the authors, for example, had the opportunity to attend an IBM recognition event where former NFL quarterback and Sunday Night football announcer Joe Theismann was one of the keynote speakers. Theismann's audience included many people from IBM operations in the Far East and Latin America, both of which are largely collectivistic in outlook. Although most North Americans in the audience responded positively to Theismann's speech, not everyone did. His remarks were perceived as egotistical and self-aggrandizing by people from such places as Japan, Taiwan, Singapore, Argentina, and Venezuela. As one person from Buenos Aires remarked, "You would have thought American football was an individual sport listening to him [Theismann]—that he won the Super Bowl single-handedly. Does he know a word other than I?"

All too often speakers choose language appropriate to their culture, but not necessarily to the cultures of their audience members. Like Theismann, they naively assume that what is good enough for their culture is good enough for everyone's. Of course, this kind of thinking is not only inaccurate, it is arrogant.

Even commonplace language choices, such as what name to call a person, can be influenced by culture. In many cultures, such as those that use the Spanish language, strangers are not addressed informally, and certainly not by their first names. A salesperson, for example, who addresses a potential client by his or her first name may, unintentionally, offend that person. The best advice is to ask people how they prefer to be addressed rather than automatically assuming that they want to be on a first-name basis.

Language and Demographic Diversity

You will recall from Chapter 6 that *demographic diversity* is reflected in the groups to which people belong and with which they identify. This includes such characteristics as nationality, race and ethnicity, gender, and religion. Demographic diversity also includes social and economic class, the region of the country that people call home, and the generation to which people belong.

Demographic diversity, although always an important consideration of a speaker's audience analysis, has become even more so. Today's college classroom is likely to be populated by people with a variety of different demographic backgrounds. Race and ethnicity, as cases in point, are often an important part of today's audience diversity.

How we refer to a specific racial or ethnic group can have a strong impact on the individual members of that group in our audience. For example, when Anglos speak to a gathering of English-speaking people of Mexican descent, they need to choose the appropriate language in referring to the audience. Scholars Mario Garcia and Rodolfo Alvarez suggest that people of Mexican descent in the United States constitute several rather than a single demographic group.[5] Two such reference groups are Mexican Americans and Chicanos/Chicanas. The Mexican American group comprises people who immigrated from Mexico to border states, such as California and Texas, following World War II. According to Garcia and Alvarez, people who consider themselves Mexican Americans are generally older and more conservative than those who identify themselves as Chicanos or Chicanas, who are generally younger and more militant.

Chicanos and Chicanas came of age in the 1960s and gained some attention in the 1970s. They perceived Mexican immigrants who wanted to assimilate with the predominant Anglo culture as sellouts. To distinguish themselves from the Mexican American group, Chicanos and Chicanas adopted specific patterns of behaving, including their own code words. The list of code words included *vendido* (sellout) and *socios* (the old boy network). Today, members of this demographic group sometimes refer to each other as *veteranos* (veterans). Thus, referring to Chicanos/Chicanas as Mexican Americans in a speech would be inappropriate. As speakers, we need to learn as much as possible about the language preferences of our audiences. Otherwise, we may inadvertently lose at least some of them.

Edward James Olmos's film *My Family, Mi Familia,* did an excellent job of showing how people who share the same culture use language differently depending on their generation.

The varied preferences of Spanish-speaking people apply to many other demographic groups as well. Some African Americans prefer being referred to as Black. And though they may be too polite to tell you so, the Chinese, Hmong, Japanese, Korean, Laotian, and Vietnamese prefer being referred to by their nationality rather than being categorized as Asian.

As speakers, we cannot afford to overlook the demography of our audience in choosing language. How we refer to people who identify themselves with specific demographic groups and the words we use in talking about the demographic groups themselves will influence not only how the content of our speech is received but audience perceptions of our credibility as well.

Language and Individual Diversity

Choosing appropriate language for a speech doesn't stop with a consideration of cultural and demographic diversity. We also must consider and evaluate *individual diversity,* which reflects such factors as personal views on the meaning of gender, sexual orientation, and religious beliefs. The fact that someone is Catholic, Jewish, Muslim, Hindu, or Protestant, for example, doesn't tell us much about the diversity of beliefs held by people who consider themselves members of one of these religious groups. Moreover, religious beliefs are only one element of the individual diversity of our audience. Consequently, before choosing the language with which to construct a speech, we will also have to explore other individual beliefs, attitudes, and values of the people in our audience.

As a case in point, think about an audience of people who describe themselves as Christians. Such people are extraordinarily diverse in what they believe individually. Some think the Bible is to be taken literally as the word of God; others believe the Bible should be interpreted metaphorically. Knowing this kind of information in advance is essential for speakers who want the language of their speech to be audience appropriate.

Remember, the words and sentences with which we construct the speech will influence the meaning of our speech in the minds of the audience members. We want to control this process as much as possible. Thus, doing our homework about the relationship between language and diversity as it reflects our speech transaction is a matter of common sense.

Using Language Effectively

Let's assume that we have thoroughly analyzed the speech situation, including how audience diversity should be reflected in our choice of words to construct our speech. We are now ready to begin writing the outline of our speech with language that will enhance our credibility with the audience and create a high degree of mutual understanding. There are a number of guidelines to follow in this process. The first rule concerns choosing language that makes every member of our audience feel included in our message. This is known as inclusive language, as opposed to marginalizing or totalizing language, concepts we will explain shortly. The second rule concerns choosing language that will enhance rather than undermine audience perceptions of our competence as a speaker.[6] The third rule concerns using language to its fullest potential to involve our audience in the speech. The fourth rule focuses on using language that will help us manage our speech, and help our audience understand what we want to communicate.

Use Inclusive and Immediate Language

The first rule in choosing the words of a speech is to use language that is inclusive. **Inclusive language** helps people believe that they not only have a stake in matters of societal importance but also have power in this regard. Inclusive language doesn't leave people out of the picture because of their gender, race, ethnicity, age, religion, sexual orientation, or ability. At the same time, however, it avoids defining people exclusively on the basis of such characteristics. Inclusive language is also **immediate;** it reduces rather than increases the distance that physically separates us and our audience from each other. Remember the example of Joe Theismann? His use of the personal pronoun "I" actually made him seem more distant from members of the audience. Inclusive language emphasizes the fact that a speaker and audience are a collective rather than two separate entities. For example, the late Barbara Jordan not only used immediate language in her distinguished political career, she also spoke eloquently about inclusive speech. Both facts are featured in her speech, "We, the People," printed in the box on page 242.

Remember the example with which we opened this chapter? Thomas Donovan, then president of the Chicago Board of Trade, referred to Mary Shapiro, former

inclusive language
Language that helps people believe that they not only have a stake in matters of societal importance but also have power in this regard.

immediate language
Language that reduces the psychological distance that separates speakers and audience members and stresses that speech is a transaction.

In Their Own Words

"We, the People" *by Barbara Jordan*

The late Congresswoman and scholar Barbara Jordan was one of the most impressive and eloquent speakers of the second half of the 20th century. Not only did she possess a powerful voice and impeccable diction, she used language in a way that few could match. Many compared her speeches to those of Winston Churchill and Franklin Roosevelt. Here is a brief excerpt of her statements during the debate on the impeachment of President Nixon in 1974:

We, the people. It is a very eloquent beginning. But when that document was completed on the 17th of September in 1787, I was not included in that "We, the people." I felt somehow for many years that George Washington and Alexander Hamilton just left me out by mistake. But through the process of amendment, interpretation and court decision I have finally been included in "We, the people."[1]

Two decades later, Jordan was asked to head the United States Commission on Immigration Reform. Testifying before the very congressional committee of which she was once a member, Jordan echoed her words from long ago:

I would be the last person to claim that our nation is perfect. But we have a kind of perfection in us because our founding principle is universal—that we are all created equal regardless of race, religion or national ancestry. When the Declaration of Independence was written, when the Constitution was adopted, when the Bill of Rights was added to it, they all applied almost exclusively to white men of Anglo-Saxon descent who owned property on the East Coast. They did not apply to me. I am female. I am black. But these self-evident principles apply to me now as they apply to everyone in this room.[2]

[1]"Barbara Jordan: A Passionate Voice," *Sacramento Bee,* 18 January 1996, A16.
[2]Jerelyn Eddings, "The Voice of Eloquent Thunder," *U.S. News and World Report,* 29 January 1996, 16.

---

marginalizing language

Language that diminishes people's importance and makes them appear to be less powerful, less significant, and less worthwhile than they are.

totalizing language

Language that defines people exclusively on the basis of a single attribute, such as race, ethnicity, biological sex, or ability.

chief of the Commodities Futures Trading Commission, as a "5-foot 2-inch little girl." Are his words an example of inclusive language? Of course not. His statement illustrates two types of language you'll want to avoid in constructing your speech: marginalizing and totalizing language.

Marginalizing language diminishes people's importance and makes them appear to be less powerful, less significant, and less worthwhile than they are. Marginalizing language also appeals to biases audience members may hold consciously or subconsciously. When Thomas Donovan called Mary Shapiro a little girl, for example, his language was more than sexist or politically incorrect. He was using language to make Mary Shapiro appear a powerless child incapable of directing powerful adults like himself.

Totalizing language defines people on the basis of a single attribute, such as race, ethnicity, biological sex, or ability. In a speech, the following statements would exemplify totalizing:

"The disabled in this audience . . ."

"As a woman, you've got to learn to assert yourself."

"As a victim of racism . . ."

"Because you are Latino . . ."

"This is really a guy book."

Each of these statements could be well-meaning and intended to demonstrate the speaker's sensitivity to people with disabilities, women, Latinos, and men. Yet what each statement does in reality is call attention to a single attribute among audience members and treat the attribute as if it were the only thing about audience members that truly counts. People are more than their disability, women and men are more than their biological sex, and people discriminated against by racists are more than simply victims. Speakers need to use language that acknowledges that people are complex individuals.

Tips and Tactics

Inclusive Language

1. Inclusive language avoids defining people on the basis of their gender, sexual orientation, disability, racial, ethnic, or religious identity. Inclusive language uses terms such as *humankind* rather than *mankind, athlete* rather than *woman athlete,* and *friend* rather than *Islamic friend.*

2. Inclusive language reflects the self-referents used by the members of a minority group; for example, *gay* or *lesbian* rather than *homosexuals* and *person with a disability* rather than *disabled person.*

3. Inclusive language is immediate. As you can read in Table 10.1, it's about *we* rather than *me* and *us* rather than *you and I.*

SpeechCoach

To hear more about these Tips and Tactics, go to Audio Tips and Tactics on your CD.

Use Credibility-Enhancing Language

In Chapter 4 we discussed credibility in terms of the relationship between ethical conduct and perceptions of the speaker's trustworthiness. Here we want to emphasize that credibility also depends on whether audience members perceive that

Less Immediate	More Immediate
I	
Me	We
You	Us
Them	
I think	Wouldn't you agree?
It's my opinion	How many of us believe . . . ?
I know	
Tell	Share
Show	Look at
Explain	
Talk from	Talk between

Table 10.1
How to Say It More Immediately

a speaker is a competent source of information. Does the speaker appear to know what he or she is talking about?

How speakers use language influences perceptions of competence in the eyes of audience members. For example, a number of researchers have documented that there is a difference between "powerful" and "powerless" speech.[7] Powerless speech is characterized by the use of language such as hedges (I *kind of* agree with you), qualifiers (I *could* be wrong), hesitations (uhs and ums), and tag questions (That's right, *isn't it?*). On the other hand, powerful speech is fluent and direct and avoids these types of phrases. Messages containing a significant amount of powerless language produce lower ratings of a speaker's competence and attractiveness, whereas powerful speech produces higher ratings on these dimensions.

Therefore, the second rule to follow in constructing the text of our speech is to use powerful, **credibility-enhancing language,** words that emphasize rather than undermine audience perceptions of our competence. Language that enhances perceptions of competence avoids verbal qualifiers.[8] **Verbal qualifiers** erode the impact of what we say in a speech.

Beginning speakers often use verbal qualifiers without thinking of them as such. They say, for example:

> "It's just my opinion, but . . ."
>
> "You'll probably disagree, but . . ."
>
> "This is my belief, but you may think otherwise."
>
> "I'm pretty sure, though I could be wrong in stating . . ."
>
> "Of course, your opinion counts at least as much as mine."

Credibility-enhancing language emphasizes the significance of what we say in a speech. Whether giving an informative, persuasive, or testimonial speech, we should be the expert on the subject or person. Not only does this require that we do our homework, it also requires that we choose language that illustrates the fact. Using language such as the following is one way of accomplishing this without appearing to be a "know-it-all" to the audience.

> "Ten years of research demonstrates that . . ."
>
> "For the past four summers, I've been involved with . . ."
>
> "Having lived all my life in the United States, . . ."
>
> "Scholars tell us . . ."

Each of these statements begins with a phrase that emphasizes the speaker's credibility. They imply that through either research or experience, the speaker knows his or her subject well. We should not exaggerate claims beyond what we know to be true, but we should take full credit for the facts as we know them. This is not to say that we should never qualify what we say. In persuasive speeches, especially, the evidence may demand that we temper the claims we make. It is unethical to make an absolute claim in a persuasive speech when the evidence fails to support or only partly supports the claim. This is another reason for conducting research on the topic prior to constructing a speech.

There are other ways to use language to increase the audience's perception of our competence. Some of the best are also the most obvious. They include using correct grammar, correct pronunciation, and correct usage of a word. Although we can get away with grammatically incorrect language in conversation, it usually sticks out like a sore thumb when speaking in public.

credibility-enhancing language
Words that emphasize rather than undermine audience perceptions of a speaker's competence.

verbal qualifiers
Words and phrases that erode the impact of what a speaker says in a speech.

Grammar

In an otherwise effective speech on educational reform, for example, President Bush asked his audience, " Is your children learning?" He meant to say, "Are your children learning?" Although this was but a single grammatical mistake, it became the most memorable part of the speech in terms of what was written and said about it afterwards.

Some of the most common grammatical mistakes we hear in our own students' speech are double negatives, incorrect subject-verb agreement, and inappropriate slang.

A double negative occurs when someone uses a negative to modify another negative. As in mathematics, a negative times a negative is actually a positive. Thus, "No one never works around here" really means that there is no person who "never works." That suggests people really do work—the opposite of what the speaker intended.

Incorrect subject-verb agreement occurs when a plural subject is matched with a singular verb or vice versa. Avoid such sentences as "We is going to the movies."

Finally, unless they are essential to the speech, certain expressions common in everyday conversation are inappropriate in a speech. Many speech teachers object in particular to the overuse of "you know," "you guys," and "like." It is irritating to hear, "You know, like, I really mean it, you guys."

This is far from a complete list of grammatical pitfalls for the speaker. And a speech is not as formal as written English. Although you are not supposed to end a sentence with a preposition, it is not uncommon to hear someone say, "I know what it's all about." The best advice we can give is that if you are in doubt about any grammatical issues, consult someone who is knowledgeable and ask his or her advice, or check a grammar handbook, such as Diana Hacker's *A Pocket Style Manual,* which you can order from Amazon.com.

Pronunciation

It is easy to mispronounce a word, especially when it is a word we do not routinely use or have heard others use incorrectly. For example, how do you pronounce the word *nuclear?* Many people, including those in positions of authority, pronounce it "nuk-u-lar." The correct pronunciation is "nuk-le-ur." How do you pronounce the word *vehicle?* Many people pronounce it "ve-hick-ul." The correct pronunciation is "ve-ik-ul." Mispronunciation of words may seem a picky point to you. Yet when speaking before an educated audience, mispronunciation is one of the surest ways to risk their perceiving you as incompetent.

Mispronunciation of words can lead to problems other than your competence being undermined. One of the most significant involves meaning. Frequently, for example, people say "assure" when they mean "ensure." Assuring your child that she is safe is not the same as ensuring the safety of your child. *Assure* and *ensure* mean two different things.

Usage

Incorrect usage of a word is the final credibility-detracting issue we want to caution you about. We hear many students who confuse the words *except* and *accept.* We also hear students use the terms *irregardless* and *orientated* when what they really mean is *regardless* and *oriented.* Again, this may strike you as picky on our part. But it's not. When we hear people use words inaccurately, it opens the door for us to question their credibility in areas other than language as well.

Tips and Tactics

Credibility-Enhancing Language

1. Avoid qualifiers such as *I'm pretty sure* or *I'm kind of certain.* Instead, assert yourself with statements such as *I'm convinced, I strongly believe,* or *I am of the firm belief.*

2. Avoid tag questions that make it seem as if you are uncertain. For example, instead of saying, "I think this is a problem but you may not," say, "This is a problem for all of us." Avoid saying, "I believe we have no other course, what do you think?" Instead, say, "Wouldn't you agree that we have no other choice?"

3. Don't be afraid to interject experience or training that gives you expertise or insight to your topic. Personal experience is a powerful form of evidence in the eyes of the audience. Share with your audience the fact that "I've now been rock climbing for over three years"; or "Proper nutrition is not only something I try to practice, it's a subject in which I've taken two courses"; or "This past year marked my tenth year of being smoke free."

4. Use familiar words. When we are not familiar with a word, we are more prone to mispronounce or misuse it. If the audience is unfamiliar with the word, they will fail to understand our meaning even when the word is used correctly. Our best advice is to stick to words that are familiar to both the audience and speaker.

5. Buy a dictionary so that when you do incorporate a word you do not routinely use in your speech, you can consult the dictionary to find out the word's denotative meaning and phonetically correct pronunciation. Watch out for words that sound alike but mean different things, such as *except* and *accept, access* and *assess,* or *ask* and *axe.* Also watch out for words that are spelled and pronounced alike but may have different meanings depending on usage (homonyms). For example, the word *quail* can be used in reference to a type of bird or in reference to cowering in terror.

Use Language to Its Fullest Potential

The third rule is to use language to its fullest potential in our speeches. There are many ways to do this. The ones we encourage involve the following:

- Using words and phrases that show and tell an audience something about a topic
- Using words and phrases that give the speech a rhythm that facilitates attention and listening
- Using words and phrases that vary in language intensity

Show and Tell

In the 1980s Professor Howard Gardiner introduced the idea that not all students learn the same way. He also pointed out that whether students learn what they are being taught depends on whether it is conveyed to them through a channel appropriate to their "preferred" style of learning.[9] What's true of students is also true of people in general, including those in your present and future audiences.

It's important to adapt the language in a speech to the preferred learning styles of the audience. One of the easiest ways to do this is to use language that creates images in the minds of people who need to visualize what they hear. For example, creative writing teachers coach their students to use language that evokes vivid images. We can do the same thing in our speeches by using metaphors, similes, and analogies.

Metaphor is one of the most powerful sources of expressive language. A metaphor is a figure of speech in which a word or phrase literally denoting one kind of object or idea is used in place of another to suggest a likeness or an analogy between them. It's one thing, for example, to say that a corporation is "polluting the environment." It's quite another to say that the same corporation is "raping virgin timberland." To say that "freedom is an open window" or that "music unshackles the mind and spirit" would be metaphorical. Metaphors provide an audience with a kind of linguistic break from the expected. Thus, just when audience members may be losing interest in a speech, a phrase or word can grab them by the lapels and help them "see" what we are trying to say.

Metaphors should fit the topic. For example, sports metaphors are often used in the popular media to describe political contests. Thus, a political candidate who does well in a debate "hits a home run," whereas a less successful candidate "strikes out." Sometimes a desperate politician is said to "throw a Hail Mary pass," while the favored candidate is said to "sit on a lead." Be careful, however, not to mix metaphors. It sounds odd to say, "He scored a touchdown while steering the ship of state through troubled waters." Metaphors can add spice and interest to a speech, but they must be used appropriately.

Simile is a form of figurative language that invites a direct comparison between two things that are quite different. A simile usually contains the word *like* or *as*. "Sharp as a tack," "tight as a snare drum," and "pointed as an ice pick" are examples of simile. Similes can also be used effectively to " show" the audience what we are attempting to communicate.

Similes differ from metaphors in that they explicitly state the comparison, whereas metaphors imply it. Similes are useful, therefore, in making a comparison very clear to the audience. For example, a speech on preventing sexually transmitted diseases might use a simile such as "Having unprotected sexual relations is like playing Russian roulette with a 357 Magnum." On a topic such as drunk driving, you might say, " Drunken drivers are like unguided missiles."

Analogies are extended metaphors or similes. Analogies can be effective in helping an audience imagine something you are trying to describe. In an informative speech on writing a basic software program, for example, one of our students used a cooking recipe to help students follow along. In another informative speech, we had a student describe fly-fishing for wild trout as analogous to chasing butterflies with a net.

Our use of metaphor, simile, and analogy in speeches is limited only by our imagination. What's more, we can get ideas for their effective use from listening to other speakers and from reading both fiction and nonfiction works.

metaphor
A figure of speech in which words and phrases that are primarily understood to mean one thing are used in place of another to suggest likeness or an analogy between them. Race car drivers, for example, may have to "wrestle with" a car that is difficult to control.

simile
Invites the listener to make a direct comparison between two things or objects that are quite different, such as "my roommate lives like a pig in slop" or is "dumb as a rock."

analogy
An extended metaphor or simile. Suggesting that the rebuilding of Iraq is much like rebuilding Germany and Japan after WW II is an analogy.

Rhythmic Speech

Rhythm is part of the natural order. We often hear people speak about the "rhythm of life" or the "rhythm of the season." Perhaps this is the reason we are so easily drawn to beating drums and chanting people. In any case, the best speakers know that a speech needs rhythm every bit as much as does the DJ at a dance club. To create rhythm, speakers commonly use alliteration, parallel structure, and repetition.

Alliteration is the repetition of the same initial sound in a series of words. Jesse Jackson is famous for using alliteration to make his speeches more expressive and memorable. Instead of saying, "People need to be given a purpose," for example, Jackson might say, "Empower people with pride, and purpose is sure to follow."

One of the most famous alliterations of American political history came from former Vice President Spiro Agnew, who called his opponents in the media "nattering nabobs of negativism." The power of alliteration comes from the way it sticks in audience members' minds. The danger is that if the alliteration seems forced, it may be memorable, but ineffective.

Parallel structure is the use of the same structure for each main point of the speech. It provides a way to help the audience remember key points, and at the same time it serves as a verbal cue that we are presenting a main point. For example, when John F. Kennedy ran for president, he used the phrases "I am not satisfied . . . we can do better" to highlight each of his major criticisms of the Republican administration.

In developing a speech outline, look for a consistent refrain or phrase that can serve as the touchstone for the structure of the speech. For example, a speech on gang violence might be built around several main points that each begin, "We can only stop gang violence if we all . . . ." The use of parallel structure helps audiences anticipate the points to come and remember them when the speech is over. However, be careful to use parallel structure that fits the speech. If not, it will seem forced and artificial.

Repetition is the use of the same words repeatedly in a speech to drive home a point. Unlike parallel structure, in which the same phrase is used only to build each main point, repetition uses a word or phrase repeatedly throughout the speech to emphasize the essential point that the speaker seeks to convey. If you recall the speech by Barbara Jordan in the box on page 242, you will note that the phrase "We, the people" is repeated three times in one short excerpt. The theme of that speech is clearly conveyed by that one phrase, taken from the U.S. Constitution.

Language Intensity

language intensity
The degree to which words and phrases deviate from neutral.

The degree to which words and phrases deviate from neutral affects **language intensity.** The intensity of words varies along a continuum ranging from relatively neutral to highly intense. For example, *savory and delicious* is more intense than *tastes good*. By the same token, the phrase *I find you attractive* is not nearly as intense as *I wanna' rock your world*. Intense language is much more likely to enlist the attention of the audience than neutral language. We can increase language intensity by using action words and humorous language. We can also increase intensity with metaphor and simile, which we have already discussed.

Action Words   Try to use words that are exciting and action oriented. For example, which do you find more involving, "The speech was well received" or "The speech was a knockout"? What about "He got mad" versus "He went ballistic"? Sports broadcasters are a good source of message-enhancing action words. Gary Gerould, who is pictured on the next page, "peppers" his radio broadcasts of the

Sacramento Kings basketball team with words such as "monster slam." He also uses metaphors with action words such as "Peja Stojakovic swatted that shot like it was a fly in the kitchen." Because the listener cannot see what's taking place on the arena floor, Gerould uses action words and action-loaded metaphors to help listeners picture what he sees.

Humor   In Chapter 9 we talked about using humor to open a speech. The guidelines for using humor we discussed there apply to this discussion as well. Humor should be appropriate and relevant to our topic or the occasion and mindful of the diversity in our audience. Having said that, we also want to emphasize what feminist Gertrude Stein is alleged to have said on her deathbed. When asked if it was hard to die, Stein said, "No . . . dying is easy. Comedy is hard."

Although humorous language can increase the intensity of a speech, not all speakers are well suited to using it. Some people really can't tell a joke. If you count yourself in this latter group, don't try being something you are not. On the other hand, if humor is customary to your communication style, use it to your advantage. Poke fun at yourself but not at your audience. Tell a joke you have successfully told before, if appropriate. And share humorous anecdotes you have shared before, assuming that they suit your speech purpose.

Contrast and Action   A final way to intensify language is to incorporate contrasting phrases and words that suggest action. In discussing the irrationality that often grips the minds of people when going to war, German philosopher Friedrich Nietzsche wrote, "How good . . . bad music and bad reasons sound when we march against the enemy."[10] Nietzsche's simple contrast between good and bad is much more effective in making war seem illogical than any extended discussion would have been. And this would have been especially true had Nietzsche delivered the line in a speech.

> As Gary Gerould told the authors, "As a sports broadcaster, being able to describe action as it unfolds in a quick, colorful manner is always the primary challenge."

Managing Language

The final rule for using language effectively involves using language that (1) assists us in managing our speech and (2) helps audience members understand the intended meaning of our message.

Define Terms

As discussed in Chapter 5, words have denotative and connotative meanings. If we look in the dictionary for the definition of a word, the first entry we will find is the most agreed-upon meaning for the word when the dictionary was published. This is also the denotative meaning of the word.

Connotative meanings for a word evolve over time. Usually, connotative meanings are given birth by groups of people bound by some collective purpose or activity. The word *nose* means the tip of the board to surfers, for example, but also may refer to the fragrance of a newly opened bottle of wine to the connoisseur.

Because words have both denotative and connotative meanings, we must be careful in our assumptions about shared meaning with an audience. We should never assume that the meaning we most commonly assign to a word will always be the same for our audience. When in doubt, then, it is in everyone's interest to define our terms in the course of our speeches.

Use Concrete Words and Phrases

Speakers do not always use language to enlighten an audience. Sometimes speakers intentionally use language to keep their audience in the dark. Political consultants will tell reporters that a candidate misspoke rather than said something stupid. Military spokespeople will tell an audience that collateral damage occurred rather than candidly admit innocent civilians were injured or killed. And the spokesperson for a company will announce to the general public that it is "right sizing" the workforce, when it would be more accurate to say 1,000 employees were losing their jobs.

We do ourselves and our audience a favor when we speak in concrete language. Concrete language consists of words and phrases that increase the chance of our audience interpreting the meaning of our message as intended. Put another way, concrete language is void of words and phrases so abstract that each person in our audience can walk away from the speech with a different interpretation of what was said.

The easiest way to make language concrete is to use words our audience recognizes and routinely uses; for example, *cat* instead of *feline, sneaky* rather than *surreptitious, book* rather than *tome,* and *abusive* rather than *vituperative language.* We can also make our language more concrete by providing our audience with details that will clarify our intended meaning. For example, instead of saying a person is tall or short, give the person's actual height. Rather than describing someone as a criminal, detail the nature of his or her crime or criminal record as well. And rather than arguing that someone is either conservative or liberal, provide the audience with detailed evidence that supports the claim.

Use Oral Language

The language in our speeches should look and sound more like the language of conversation than the language of written discourse. However, the language in our speeches needs to be a refined version of that used when conversing. We should strive to use language in our speeches that is grammatically sound and clearly enunciated. By the same token, we should feel free to use contractions more liberally in a speech, split all the infinitives we want, and end a thought with a preposition. Spoken thought and written sentences are similar but not identical. It's a good idea to read aloud and even record a speech. We can then listen critically to what we have said, and check to make sure that it sounds like we are conversing with rather than formally talking to our audience.

Keep It Simple

Less is often more in a speech. By that we mean simple words and simple sentences are usually better than polysyllabic words and compound, complex sentences. "Ask not what your country can do for you . . . but what you can do for your country," is much easier to hear and understand than the following:

> It's important that each of you gives some thought to the kinds of demands that you make on your government, and at the same time begin to think about the meaning of sacrifice, and what you possibly could do to help out your government and elected leaders.

Use Signposts

Still another technique to manage a speech is to make effective use of signposts, which we explained in Chapter 9. We've repeatedly emphasized how important it is to let our audience know where we are going with our speech. You know from your own experience in taking lecture notes that it's much easier to follow an instructor who uses verbal signposts that alert you to changes in direction or clearly link one thought to another. You need to do the same for the members of your audience.

Signposts are transitional words and phrases that tell our audience we are about to make or already have made a shift in direction. Signposts also serve to verbally link our thoughts as we speak. It's always a good idea to let the audience know that there is a sequence to our message—"Let's consider three important issues"—and then to remind the audience where we are in that sequence—"Having covered the first issue, let's now look at the second."

It's also a good idea to let the audience know that the speech is about to end by using transitional words and phrases such as *lastly, to summarize, to conclude,* and *in closing.* Audiences are likely to grow impatient if they think a speech will never end.

Use Visual, Kinesthetic, and Auditory Language

To repeat, not all people process information in the same way. Research shows that some people need to see a lesson, others need only to hear it, and still others need to become immersed in the subject matter. These three styles of learning are technically called visual, auditory, and kinesthetic. The obvious way for a speaker to deal with these three is to augment a speech with visual aids, speak audibly and clearly, or involve the audience in demonstrations or other hands-on experiences. Yet sometimes options one and three are impossible for a speaker.

To get around this fact, author and corporate trainer Loretta Malandro encourages her clients to connect metaphorically with the varied learning styles present in most audiences. Table 10.2 suggests a number of specific visual, auditory, and kinesthetic words that help the audience better process a speech.

Although we may not be able to literally show our audience members prejudice, we can connect with visual learners by

Table 10.2
Words Linked to Vision, Hearing, and Touch

VISUAL WORDS			
Focus	Graphic	Watch	Colorful
Bright	Illustrate	Vision	Glimpse
Show	Color	Brilliant	Look
Pretty	See	Evident	Sight
Envision	Picture	Sketch	Shining
Draw	Hazy	Oversight	Hidden
View	Peek	Clearly	Notice
Clear	Imagine	Perspective	

AUDITORY WORDS			
Listen	Ringing	Compliment	Pardon
Hear	Resonate	Loud	Sound
Discuss	Yell	Silent	Request
Declare	Told	Shout	Whispering
Implore	Call	Talk	Quiet
Acclaim	Assert	Noisy	Ask
Harmony	Profess	Orchestrate	
Petition	Noise	Address	

KINESTHETIC WORDS			
Feel	Terrified	Hunger	Contact
Pressure	Burdensome	Doubt	Nurture
Hurt	Firm	Shocking	Emotion
Get the point	Tense	Heavy	Graceful
Experience	Touchy	Touch	Sensual
Longing	Pushy	Concrete	Weighty problem
Wait	Shatter	Irritated	

Source: Excerpted from: *Twenty-First Century Selling.* © Dr. Loretta Malandro. Taught in her program "Speak With Impact," offered by Malandro Communication Inc., Scottsdale, Arizona.

- asking them to envision a world free of hate,
- drawing a picture of racism or sketching out an example for them, or
- making a hazy concept such as affirmative action crystal clear so that they can see the problem.

Although we may not be able to let them literally feel our thoughts, we can connect with audience members who need to experience some things by asking them to imagine

- what racism feels like,
- that a problem is a giant weight pressing down on them, or
- how oppressed people hunger for freedom.

And though we may not be able to literally produce the sound of abused children for our audience members, we can connect to auditory learners by asking them

- whether they hear what we are trying to say,
- to imagine what it's like to live in a world where they cannot speak out for themselves, or
- to imagine the mournful sound of children crying.

The point is simple. Not everyone in the audience will respond in a like manner to the words we speak. Thus, to maximize audience members' receptivity to what we say, we must make every effort to use expressive words that reflect their different styles of information processing.

Final Words of Caution

We conclude this chapter with a discussion of two issues that are not so much a matter of right and wrong but, rather, of rhetorical sensitivity. The use of language appropriate to your rhetorical situation is not just a matter of effectiveness; it is also one of being ethically sensitive to the detrimental effects stereotypic and biased language can have on people. We look at two specific types of problems caused by inappropriate language: first, the use of language that stereotypes people; second, the use of language that stereotypes people on the basis of their biological sex.

Avoid Stereotypes

Do you see anything wrong with the following references?

"John's a victim of cystic fibrosis."

"Don't forget that Susan's wheelchair bound!"

"It's okay, Lupe, there's plenty of disabled seating in the new auditorium."

"The Howards' baby is physically challenged."

According to the Disabled Student Services on our campus, each of these statements is constructed with inappropriate language. If you're surprised, then please know that so were we. We've heard terms like *victim of* and *physically challenged* used by people in all walks of life, including student speakers.

The fact that we think we know what constitutes appropriate language doesn't excuse us from researching the subject. Language is dynamic and in a continuous process of change. What's more, words such as *victim* or terms such as *wheelchair bound* once were acceptable. Today, however, people with disabilities are defining their own terms on their own grounds. Further, in doing so, those with disabilities have said they prefer the following descriptors to the first set we listed for you:

"John has cystic fibrosis."

"Don't forget that Susan's in a wheelchair."

"It's okay, Lupe; there's plenty of accessible seating in the new auditorium."

"The Howards' baby has a disability."

Thus, we want to remind you of the adage "It's better to remain silent and be thought a fool than to open your mouth and prove it." When in doubt about words

Considering Diversity

How Does Language Marginalize People?

A 53-year-old cabdriver is facing vehicular manslaughter charges in the hit-and-run accident that killed a Silicon Valley executive and critically injured his companion, a state trade official, police say.

Arthur Alan Smith of San Francisco, a driver for DeSoto Cab Co., was arrested at the Hall of Justice Thursday after a police inspector investigating the Friday night accident asked him to come in for additional questioning.

"We talked to him at the scene the night of the accident," Inspector Jeff Levin said. "He told us that another car hit the couple and threw them onto the hood of his cab. We have since been able to determine that was not what happened."

Calvin Threadgill II was killed instantly, and his companion, Tina Frank, was seriously injured when they were struck at about 9:30 p.m. last Friday as they crossed the Embarcadero near Mission Street.

Threadgill, 45, of Castro Valley, was recently appointed vice president of marketing for Zapit, a Silicon Valley environmental technology company.

Frank is the director of the Bay Area regional office of the California Trade and Commerce Agency. . . .

Investigators say the pair were walking in a marked crosswalk when they were struck.

Levin said a reconstruction of the accident by Sgt. James Hughes, evidence gathered by the police crime lab and new information from two eyewitnesses had led them to Smith.

Source: John D. O'Connor, "Cops Hold Cabbie in Hit-Run Death," *San Francisco Examiner,* 12 August 1994, A4. Reprinted by permission.

---

and their consequences, consult an authority. If that's not possible, then when in doubt about a word, leave it out.

Of course, it is not just people with disabilities who are stereotyped. People in different professions, of different ethnicities, and with different sexual orientations, to name just a few categories, are frequently the subject of stereotypic language. The speaker who is sensitive to language avoids such stereotypes. One particular type of stereotype deserves discussion in its own right, sexist language.

Avoid Sexist Language

sexist language
Language, such as *housewife* and *fireman,* that stereotypes gender roles.

Sexist language is language that stereotypes gender roles, for example, *housewife* and *fireman.* Why is sexist language a problem? It conveys, intentionally or not, a stereotype of certain roles and functions, based on sex. When the head of an academic department is referred to as a chair*man,* a member of the U.S. House of Representatives is called a Congress*man,* and a flight attendant on an airplane is known as a steward*ess,* it is clear which roles are held to be "male" and which ones "female." A sensitive public speaker needs to avoid sexist language.

One of the easiest ways to unintentionally convey sexism is to use singular pronouns in the masculine form. For years, speakers and writers excluded women from their examples involving a single person, saying such things as

"If a person is strong, he will stand up for himself."

"When someone believes something, he shouldn't be afraid to say so."

"An individual should keep his promise."

If we have no other choice in constructing examples to illustrate our speech, we can do one of two things with regard to singular pronouns. First, we can say "he or she" in conjunction with a singular verb. Second, we can use "she" in some cases and "he" in others. Yet both of these alternatives are awkward, and neither is likely to please everyone in our audience. Thus, we suggest a third alternative: Use plural nouns and pronouns when constructing examples to make the speech more vivid, involving, and inclusive. Instead of saying, "If a person is strong, he will stand up for himself," say, "Strong people stand up for themselves." Instead of saying, "When someone believes something, he shouldn't be afraid to say so," try, "When people believe something, they shouldn't be afraid to say so." And instead of saying, "An individual should keep his promise," simply say, "People should keep their promises."

Finally, be on the lookout for the subtle ways the news media can reinforce the use of sexist language and images in their reporting, as the article reprinted in the box "How Does Language Marginalize People?" illustrates.

What we read can subconsciously influence our views of men and women. Although both of the victims in the accident described held high positions in their work, the initial reference to the female describes her as the male executive's "companion" first and as a state trade official second. This may seem insignificant, and such examples are commonplace. But their impact over time adds up in terms of the impressions we form not just of women but also of many other groups of people who have been marginalized in the press. Don't just take our word for it; consider how you would react to the story if the first paragraph read as follows:

> A 53-year-old cabdriver is facing vehicular manslaughter charges in the hit-and-run accident that critically injured the Director of the Bay Area office of the California Trade and Commerce Agency and killed her companion, an employee with a Silicon Valley technology company.

Summary

Although words alone can't break our bones, words are powerful symbols and should be treated as such. In recognition of this fact, keep the following in mind as you construct your speeches:

- Language is symbolic and influences the process of perception.

- Language reflects the multiracial, multiethnic, multicultural audience of today.

- Effective language is inclusive rather than marginalizing or totalizing.

- Effective language enhances your audience's perception of your credibility.

- Effective language takes advantage of devices such as metaphor, simile, alliteration, parallel structure, and repetition.

- Effective language connects with the auditory, kinesthetic, and visual styles of processing information present in your audience.

- Effective language avoids unfair stereotypes and the use of words that perpetuate sexism.

SpeechCoach

To evaluate your understanding of this chapter, see the Quizzes on your CD.

www.mhhe.com /brydon5

Visit the Online Learning Center for helpful study resources, including practice tests, key term crossword puzzles, and PowerWeb articles for research and review.

Check Your Understanding: Exercises and Activities

SpeechCoach

For a review of key terms in this chapter, see the Key Terms Flashcards on your CD.

1. Rewrite the following paragraph using inclusive language:

   When a speaker begins his speech, the first thing he must do is thank the chairman of the group for the opportunity to speak to his group. As we know, the quality that separates man from the animals is the ability to speak. Regardless of his job, a man must know how to speak clearly. Similarly, a woman must know how to impart language skills to her children. Thus, every speaker is urged to use language to the best of his ability.

2. Write five transitional statements (signposts) without using the following words:

   first (second, third, etc.)

   therefore

   next

   finally

   in conclusion

3. Company X has an internal policies manual that is written in marginalizing language. As an employee of the company, you find the language disturbing and believe the language in the manual should be changed. Write a letter to the head of the documents division explaining why you believe such changes are necessary and why you believe the changes will enhance the image of the company. (Thanks to Dr. Madeline Keaveney for suggesting this exercise.)

4. Exclusive language is marginalizing and biased. Provide an inclusive-language alternative for each of the following, or state under what conditions the term might be appropriately used in a speech. [Adapted from Rosalie Maggio, *The Bias-Free Word Finder: A Dictionary of Nondiscriminatory Language* (Boston: Beacon Press, 1991).]

actress	meter maid
airline stewardess	mother
businessman	majorette
craftsmanship	Mrs. John Doe
doorman	old wives' tale
executrix	waitress
goddess	

Notes

1. W. H. Auden and L. Kronenberger, *The Viking Book of Aphorisms* (New York: Dorsett Press, 1981), 238.
2. "This Boss Is No Girl, She's Just Stunned," *Sacramento Bee,* 10 October 1995, C2.
3. "This Boss Is No Girl," C2.
4. Benjamin Lee Whorf, *Language, Thought, and Reality* (New York: Wiley, 1956).
5. Earl Shorris, *Latinos: A Biography of the People* (New York: Norton, 1992), 95–100.
6. Julia T. Wood, ed., *Gendered Relationships* (Mountain View, Calif.: Mayfield, 1996), 39–56.
7. See, for example: W. M. O'Barr, *Linguistic Evidence: Language, Power, and Strategy in the Courtroom* (New York: Academic Press, 1982); James J. Bradac and Anthony Mulac, "A Molecular View of Powerful and Powerless Speech Styles: Attributional Consequences of Specific Language Features and Communication Intentions," *Communication Monographs* 51 (1984): 307–319.
8. H. Giles and J. Wiemann, "Language, Social Comparison, and Power," in *Handbook of Communication Science,* ed. C. R. Berger and S. H. Chaffee (Newbury Park, Calif.: Sage, 1987).
9. Howard Gardner, *Intelligence Reframed: Multiple Intelligences for the 21st Century* (New York: Basic Books, 1999).
10. Auden and Kronenberger, *The Viking Book of Aphorisms,* 359.

How you say something can be as important as what you have to say.

Chapter

11

Delivery:
Engaging Your Audience

Objectives

After reading this chapter and reviewing the learning resources on your CD-ROM and at the Online Learning Center, you should be able to:

- Describe when manuscript, memorized, impromptu or extemporaneous methods of delivery are most appropriate to a speech.

- Define nonverbal behavior and distinguish between verbal and nonverbal behavior.

- Describe the relationship between delivery and the seven basic dimensions of the nonverbal system.

- Display nonverbal behaviors characteristic of effective delivery, including control of the speaking environment; proper attire; eye contact and expressive facial cues; vocal variation in pitch, range, rhythm, and tempo; clear and distinct vocal articulation; and gestures and movements that serve as emblems, illustrators, and regulators.

- Control distracting self-adaptive behaviors.

- Use time to enhance your credibility and communicate urgency, drama, humor, and the like during your speech.

- Explain the guidelines for developing a proactive, rather than reactive, delivery.

- Display nonverbal examples of complementing, contradicting, and repeating the message; substituting for a verbal cue; increasing the perception of immediacy; exciting the audience; and delivering a powerful speech.

Key Concepts

emblem

environment

illustrators

nonverbal behavior

proactive delivery

regulators

self-adapting behaviors

zone of interaction

“ What people do is frequently more important than what they say. ”

–EDWARD T. HALL, anthropologist[1]

SpeechCoach

To view examples of different styles of delivery, see segment 11.1 on your CD.

Elizabeth Dole broke with tradition during the 1996 Republican Convention in San Diego, California. Instead of addressing the assembly of delegates from the raised platform from which other speakers had spoken, she actually walked out on the convention floor and moved about the audience as she delivered her message. Dole did so even though Republican consultants had told her that such an approach wouldn't work in the context of a political convention.

Were they ever wrong! Dole's speech not only captivated the convention delegates but also favorably impressed network news anchors Dan Rather, Tom Brokaw, and Peter Jennings. Having seen nothing like it previously, these news anchors were effusive in their praise of Dole's performance.

This chapter focuses on the delivery of your speech. We want you to recognize from the beginning that there is no single method of effectively delivering your speeches. It depends on you and the style with which you are most comfortable, the occasion, and the context in which you find yourself. Perhaps you like to move in the manner of Elizabeth Dole, or stay firmly planted in close proximity to a lectern in the manner of former Secretary of State Colin Powell. Simply put, when it comes to delivery, you have options from which you can choose.

Given this framework, we first look at the four most common methods of delivery. Next we discuss how you can use your voice to enhance your delivery. Finally, we examine the functional role of nonverbal communication in the process of effectively delivering a speech.

Focusing Your Delivery on Your Audience

Never forget that public speaking is a transaction between the speaker and the audience. Just as the language we choose for our message should reflect the nature of our audience, so too should our delivery. As a result, we begin our discussion with some audience-related factors to consider while thinking about the delivery of a message. Specifically, we discuss choosing an appropriate method of delivery, adapting to diverse audiences, and adapting delivery to the speech occasion.

Choosing an Appropriate Method of Delivery

Recall from Chapter 2 that there is more than one way to deliver a speech. We discussed four different methods of delivery. As we review our analysis of our audience and rhetorical situation, one of our most important decisions will be choosing an appropriate method of speech delivery.

In your current class your instructor most likely has emphasized one of the following four methods. In another class or at work, however, you may choose to "try on" one of the others available to you. Your choice should complement your overall communication skills and reinforce your strengths as a public speaker. Realizing that none of these methods is foolproof, be sure to choose wisely.

Manuscript Delivery

Manuscript delivery involves writing out the speech completely and reading it to the audience. This method may be the best choice when an audience requires precise information. When speaking about highly technical matters before a group of engineers, for example, the precision with which we deliver the information

Speaking of . . .

"The Dole Stroll" *by Dr. Nichola D. Gutgold**

Former secretary of labor and transportation, former president of the American Red Cross, and now United States Senator Elizabeth Dole is one of the most polished and prepared public speakers in America. She made history and captivated the American public when, at the Republican National Convention, she abandoned the podium and walked among the delegates to speak on behalf of her husband's candidacy for president. Senator Dole explains why she chose to break with tradition:

Senator Elizabeth Dole and Dr. Nichola D. Gutgold.

> I was told by two experts that I could not walk around at the 1996 GOP convention successfully. . . . Walking down 12 steps in heels was something to think about twice before you do it! But I think when the audience saw me come down, they all got quiet. They hadn't seen this before. They all wondered "what is she doing?" And because of that, they were more attentive and cooperative as I walked around the audience. . . . That walking around really works well for me in other speeches as well. I like doing that, and I frequently use that style when I speak for the American Red Cross and I speak to victims and their families. I think that it is a very effective way for me to reach the audience. The audience seems to respond so much better when I move around and I am not behind the podium with bright lights glaring at me. I now feel that the podium is a barrier between the audience and me. What we found during the campaign was that a fascinating thing to do was to interview people—stop them and have them tell their story and then tell them what Bob Dole would do. . . . I found that the reason that I started moving from the podium is about three months before I left for my leave of absence from the

> Red Cross, when I was trying to get people to give money to the Red Cross, or blood or their time, if I could get close to them—if I could talk to them like it was a conversation, it worked much better.

Source: Elizabeth Dole, interview in Hershey, Pennsylvania, 7 April 1998.

*Dr. Gutgold is an assistant professor of speech communication at Penn State Berks-Lehigh Valley College and is writing a book about the public speaking of Elizabeth Dole.

may be extremely important. The same would be true for a plastic surgeon addressing a seminar on advances in rhinoplasty (nose job). Similarly, if we expect our words to be quoted by others, having a manuscript of our speech helps ensure accuracy.

Any time we use a manuscript, however, the dynamics of delivery are restricted. As we show later in this chapter, eye contact, movement, and gesture are important dimensions of nonverbal behavior that can enhance delivery. Tying ourselves to a manuscript interferes with each of these. Manuscript speaking also impedes spontaneity between the speaker and the audience because the manuscript restricts opportunities to survey and creatively respond to audience feedback. Further, a manuscript demands a lectern, which can stand as a barrier between a speaker and the audience. Finally, this method of delivery can sound stilted and artificial because the language of a written message generally is more formal than spoken language.

If a manuscript must be used, therefore, learn it well. Practice repeatedly so that you do not have to look down often. Mark up the manuscript with notes to

Informal situations such as this one invite a conversational delivery style.

yourself, and underline main ideas. Also, be sure pages are numbered so that they will not get out of order. Use a large typeface and double or even triple spacing. Manuscript speaking is far more difficult than most people realize. Success depends on practice and skill in converting words on a page into a living speech.

Memorized Delivery

A speaker using memorized delivery writes out the speech and commits it to memory before presenting it to the audience without the use of notes. Most audiences don't expect a memorized speech, unless they are watching a professional speaker who is highly paid, an actor delivering a soliloquy in a play, or a student competing in a speech tournament. In fact, in a typical speech class, an obviously memorized speech would probably strike most students and the instructor as odd. Although memorization allows the speaker to concentrate on eye contact, movement, and gesture, it does so at a price. You may forget parts of your speech, and it requires a greater investment of time than any other method.

When writing a speech to be memorized, keep the organization simple so that you will not confuse one point with another. A good rule of thumb is to memorize the speech in small chunks. Learn a paragraph, then move on to the next one, and so on. Practice reciting your speech from the beginning through as far as you have it memorized. The repetition of earlier parts will help fix them in your mind. Don't panic if you forget a part of the speech. Try to ad-lib for a bit, and often the next section will come to mind.

Even though professional speakers may memorize their speeches, they want to create the illusion that they are communicating spontaneously. As you can imagine, this is extremely difficult to do. Memorized delivery is not the best method for people in the beginning stages of their development as a public speaker.

Impromptu Delivery

There may be times when you have to give an impromptu delivery—a spontaneous, unrehearsed method of presenting a speech. Usually, these short speeches are given in response to someone who asks you to say a few words, make a toast, or respond to an inquiry. Although an audience is always appreciative of an eloquent impromptu speech, an organized and confidently spoken message is normally enough to fulfill any audience's expectations.

Impromptu speaking eliminates any impediments to using the full range of nonverbal behaviors available to speakers. This can be both good and bad, depending on the comfort level of the speaker. Speakers who are comfortable in an impromptu situation may benefit because their delivery will strike the audience as relaxed and genuine. Uncomfortable speakers, however, are likely to appear rigid, awkward, or distracted.

Impromptu speaking is not nearly as rare as you may think. In business meetings, people are frequently put on the spot and asked to speak on topics relevant to their responsibilities. Students, moreover, are frequently asked to make impromptu remarks. The lesson here is that you should always be prepared to speak on the spur of the moment. To help you in this regard, we offer the following tips. First, be proactive and anticipate situations where you might be asked to speak, for example, in class, at meetings, or social events such as a wedding, Bat Mitzvah, or memorial service. Second, realize that the key to effective impromptu speaking is organization. If you are asked to respond to a question, repeat the question to introduce your answer, specify the number of points you want to make, and try to conclude with a declarative statement. Third, approach your impromptu speech as if you were telling a story that has a beginning, middle, and end. Fourth, consider hitchhiking off the remarks of those who may have preceded you. For instance: "Julie's points are well taken, and I'd like to add to them by first seconding her belief that airport security should not be the responsibility of the airlines." Finally, don't be afraid to assert yourself when you have an informed opinion on the topic about which you've been asked to speak. Don't compound the nervousness you may feel as a result of having been put on the spot by telling yourself you have nothing worthwhile to say. Impromptu speaking is a skill. Like any other skill, it can be honed with experience and practice.

Extemporaneous Delivery

For most students who are still learning to give a speech, extemporaneous speaking remains their best choice of delivery method. Extemporaneous delivery combines careful preparation with spontaneous speaking. The speaker generally uses brief notes rather than a manuscript or an outline. Extemporaneous speaking enables us to maintain eye contact, move, gesture, and spontaneously adapt to audience feedback. We may choose not to use a lectern, depending on how extensive your notes are and how comfortable we are moving freely before the audience.

Today's audiences are more likely to expect and appreciate the extemporaneously delivered speech than other methods of delivery. Just as it allows the speaker to remain in contact with the audience, so does it allow the audience to remain

Table 11.1

Advantages and Disadvantages of Delivery Mode

Mode of Delivery	Advantages	Disadvantages
Manuscript	Accuracy Precision May be quoted	Loss of eye contact Written rather than oral style Easy to lose place
Memorized	Keeps eye contact with audience Freedom of movement	Easy to forget Appears "canned" Extensive preparation required Lack of spontaneity
Impromptu	Spontaneous Maintains eye contact with audience Adaptable to situation	Lack of time to prepare Can be anxiety arousing Can be embarrassing if speaker fails to anticipate possible questions
Extemporaneous	Combines preparation and spontaneity Can maintain eye contact Adaptable Allows for accuracy in wording where necessary	Excessive use of note cards can inhibit spontaneity Poor use of note cards can limit ability to gesture

connected to the speaker. Audiences not only can give feedback to someone speaking extemporaneously but also can assess the degree to which their feedback registers with the speaker.

This doesn't mean that extemporaneous speaking is without drawbacks. Note cards can restrict the range of gestures used when we refer to them, and they can also be distracting when waved about while we are speaking. Finally, we can get carried away with note cards, writing down so many of our thoughts that the note cards become almost a manuscript. (See Table 11.1 for a summary of the modes of delivery.)

Delivering Speeches to Diverse Audiences

Both the method and style of delivery should reflect the diversity of the audience. Throughout this chapter we offer numerous specific examples of cases in which a particular nonverbal behavior means one thing to one culture and something entirely different to another. For example, consider how three different audiences might respond to the same speech. As we speak, a North American audience returns our eye contact and nods in agreement with us. A British audience also returns our eye contact, but heads remain motionless. And a West African audience avoids making direct eye contact with us altogether. What should we make of their feedback in each situation? Before you decide, perhaps it would help to know this: When the British agree with a speaker, they sometimes blink rather than nod their head. Further, the more direct the eye contact of West Africans, the less they respect the person to whom it is directed. Knowing the typical patterns of nonverbal behavior in a given culture is essential if we are to accurately interpret the nonverbal behaviors of our audience members.

Another example of differences among culturally diverse audiences concerns voice. Almost from birth, the norm for the North American culture is "to speak up and let yourself be heard." What is normative here, however, may be loud in Japan or among the upper class in Great Britain. And much as we may want to be heard, we don't want to be perceived as loudmouths in these cultures.

In contrast to the norm in these two cultures, African American audiences sometimes are verbal participants in the speech transaction. When audience members agree with the speaker, they may let the speaker know with audible feedback. When they disagree, they may also let the speaker know. Rather than being a sign of disrespect to the speaker, this kind of audience participation is an outgrowth of a rich "call-and-response" tradition with roots in the African American church.

Adapting Delivery to the Speech Occasion

How we present our speech depends on the specific rhetorical situation we face and the kind of delivery our audience is likely to expect. A speech commemorating or honoring a person calls for a formal and dignified delivery. Other speech situations call for an energetic, dynamic delivery. A motivational speaker, for example, usually dispenses with the lectern and moves about the stage, perhaps even into the audience. A lively style is expected and rewarded. Then there are situations that call for a lighthearted, comic style of delivery. For example, "roasts" honoring someone are often punctuated with good-natured joking at the honoree's expense. Unlike a commemorative speech, a delivery at a roast should be informal and lively. The key is to understand what the audience expects in a given situation and match your delivery style to those expectations.

Discovering Your Personal Style

A class in public speaking shouldn't be looked on as an episode of *Extreme Make-Over*. All of us have a personal "style" of communicating that has been evolving over the course of our lives. Our goal is to assist you in developing and adapting your personal style to the demands of the public speaking transaction both now and in the future. This involves teasing out the elements of your personal style that can work for you when you speak, and modifying elements of your personal style that may be undermining your ability to truly shine.

Many styles of speaking can work to the advantage of a speaker. Some speakers are dramatic and have a flair for telling stories, revealing things about themselves with which the audience can identify. They have a high level of energy as is evidenced by their gestures and facial expressions. Other speakers are nearly deadpan but still highly effective. Build on the style of delivery that comes most naturally to you rather than trying to mimic a style unsuitable to you. To begin, let's focus on the discovery and development of your personal voice.

Your Voice

Before we talk about what makes voices as unique as fingerprints, we want to re-emphasize the fact that what you say and how you say it are not the same thing.

The spoken word has two dimensions. One dimension is content—the words themselves and the way they are configured to form sentences. The other dimension is vocalic—the sound that shapes the meaning the spoken word conveys to the audience. Consider the sentence "I love you." By changing the pitch, volume, and inflection of your voice as you utter the sentence, you can actually alter the meaning the sentence conveys to another person. It can be sensuous or sincere, for example, depending on the tone of voice with which it is spoken.

In a sense, words are like musical notes, and the voice is like an instrument. In the hands of a skilled musician, notes are not simply played but are shaped by the musician. Skilled guitarists playing the same notes can produce quite different sounds, depending on how they bend or agitate the strings with their fingertips. Skilled speakers do much the same thing with the pitch, tempo, and rhythm of their voices.

In the effort to help you gain better control of your voice, you need to know how sound is produced and how it can be manipulated. You also need to appreciate the role articulation plays in the process of shaping this sound so that it is meaningful to your audience. Finally, you need to accept the fact that you are better off speaking in your own voice than trying to imitate the voice of someone else.

Vocal Production

The production of sound in the voice is fairly straightforward. You take in air and expel the air through the trachea across your vocal cords, which are contained in the larynx (voice box), and then across your teeth, tongue, and lips. Variations in the amount of air expelled, the positioning of the vocal cords, or the placement of the teeth and tongue and position of the lips will result in variations in the sounds produced. Shallow breathing and the rapid expulsion of air across the vocal cords, for example, will produce a much different sound than breathing deeply and then slowly expelling the air. In the first case, your voice is likely to be described as feminine and in the second masculine, even though neither is necessarily true. The basic mechanical operation of the voice, however, is not as important to the topic at hand as are the characteristics of the voice. These include volume, pitch, range, rhythm, and tempo.

Volume

How loudly you project your voice is a consequence of both the amount of air you expel when speaking and the force with which you expel it. For example, try to speak loudly without first taking a fairly deep breath. Surprising, isn't it? Some examples of people capable of speaking with great volume are actor/talk show host Oprah Winfrey, broadcaster Rush Limbaugh, actor James Earl Jones (the person you hear saying "CNN"), and the entertainer/rocker Kid Rock. On the other hand, some examples of more soft-spoken public figures include Vice President Dick Cheney, actor Liv Tyler, and singer Sade.

You need not be loud to be heard. What's more, speaking in a consistently loud voice is likely to grate on the ears of your audience. You want to *project* your voice, not break eardrums with it. The key is to vary the volume of your voice depending on the impact you hope to have with your audience. Sometimes lowering the volume of your voice will draw your audience in, whereas a sudden increase in volume may startle your audience. As a public speaker, you need to have enough volume to be heard by your audience. But that can vary tremendously depending on the size of your audience, the room in which you are speaking, and the availability of a microphone. Seasoned speakers prepare differently depending on these factors. That is to say, they vary the volume with which they practice depending on where and with whom they will be speaking. You should do the same thing. Practice your speech as if you were delivering it in the classroom where you will speak, to an audience equivalent in size to your actual class. When you actually do speak to your class, moreover, look for feedback about volume in the faces and posture of audience members. If those in the back of the room are leaning forward or look puzzled, you may need to raise your volume. On the other hand, if people seated in the first row are leaning back in their seats, you may be speaking too loudly.

Pitch

The degree to which your voice is high or low is its pitch. A person who sings bass has a low pitch, whereas a person who sings soprano has a high pitch. The bass knob on your stereo lowers pitch, the treble knob raises it. The pitch of a bass fiddle is lower than that of a violin; the pitch of a ukulele is higher than the pitch of an acoustic guitar. Pitch is a key to vocal inflection, and effective speakers vary their pitch to shape the impact of their words. They may lower pitch to sound more serious or raise it to convey a sense of urgency. Control of pitch depends not only on their skill as a speaker but on the natural range of their voice as well.

Range

The extent of the pitch, from low to high, that lies within your vocal capacity is known as range. Just as a piano has a tremendous range in pitch, some speakers have a great vocal range. On the other hand, some speakers are like an electric bass guitar, which no matter how well played, does not have much range. As a speaker, you need to make the fullest use of your normal conversational vocal range. That means you first need to discover the bottom and top of your own vocal scale.

To get a sense of how pitch and range control the inflection in your voice, tape-record yourself. Recite the alphabet beginning in your normal voice. Then raise your pitch with each new letter until your voice cracks. Next do the same thing, but lower your voice as you recite. Play back the recording and note where your voice begins to break as you go up and then breaks as you go down. This will give you an audible idea about the limits of your vocal range, as well as at what pitches your voice sounds relaxed and natural. Then practice varying your pitch within this relaxed and natural range, using the tape recorder to further get in touch with your natural pitch and range.

Rhythm

Think of rhythm as the characteristic pattern of your volume, pitch, and range. Perhaps you have heard someone describe a speaker's voice as "singsong." This means the speaker's voice goes consistently up and then down in pitch, almost as if the person were talking to a small child.

Some speakers use predictable rhythm to great effect. Many Evangelical preachers have a decided rhythm in their sermons. The Reverend Jesse Jackson is an easy target for comedic impersonators because of the predictable rhythm with which he takes his audience up, and then pauses before taking them down. Jackson heightens this effect with his inflection and frequent use of alliteration, which we discussed in Chapter 10.

Tempo

The rate at which you produce sounds, or how quickly or slowly you speak, will influence how you are perceived. Tempo also tends to vary across and even within cultures. In the United States, for example, speech in the South is relatively slow in tempo, whereas in the East, tempo is accelerated. This is readily apparent if you compare the voices of actress Holly Hunter, who is from the South, and Marisa Tomei, from the East.

Because tempo varies, you have to use good judgment in terms of how quickly or slowly you speak. Doing either to the extreme can turn off your audience. An excessively rapid pace can be perceived as a sign of nervousness. An excessively slow pace may suggest a speaker is not well prepared. Researchers have found that moderate to fast rates of speaking tend to be associated with increased perceptions of a speaker's competence on the part of the audience.[2] Other researchers have noted a ceiling to that effect, however, meaning that too fast a rate of speaking can backfire.[3] In addition, when audiences perceive speech rates as similar to their own, they are more likely to find speakers socially attractive and to comply with their requests.[4] The best advice is to moderately vary your tempo. Not only will this accommodate the different preferences of individuals in your audience, it will also enhance the overall effect of your message.

Your tempo is also affected by pauses. Sometimes a brief moment of silence can convey much to an audience. Pausing just before delivering a crucial word or phrase helps grab the audience's attention. Pausing after you've made an important point gives it time to sink in. Used judiciously, pauses can be an effective rhetorical device. It is also better to pause a moment than to fill the air with "ums," "uhs," and "you knows," which are really vocalized pauses. The best way to control disfluencies such as these is to practice your speech until it is second nature.

Articulation

If you expect an audience to understand what you are saying, you need clear articulation, which refers to the distinctness with which you make individual sounds. You may have experienced the frustration of listening to someone who sounds mushy, failing to distinctly vocalize sounds. A common articulation problem comes from either running together differing sounds or dropping parts of a word: *goin'* instead of *going, wanna* instead of *want to,* or *whatcha doin'?* in place of *what are you doing?* A good way to test your articulation is to tape-record your speech and listen critically to yourself. If you find a consistent articulation problem or set of problems, you may want to find out if your college or university offers a course in voice and articulation. Sometimes drama or theatre department courses in voice for performers can be of assistance. Severe articulation problems are often best treated by a speech pathologist. But for most students in public speaking classes, exercising care, practicing, and slowing down are the keys to being understood by the audience.

In Chapter 10 we emphasized the importance of using words correctly. This is a good place to reemphasize the fact. As you practice articulating words, make sure that you are also pronouncing them correctly. "Nu-ku-lar" is still wrong, no matter how well you articulate it.

Mispronounced words tend to undermine audience perceptions of a speaker's credibility. This is true whether the mispronunciation involves a term unique to a profession or the name of a person or place. Medical terms such as hemangioma can tie up the tongue of even the most articulate speaker. So, too, can place names such as Mexico's Cacaxtla or the last name of the authors' mutual friend, Joe Olesiewicz.

For some words, the correct pronunciation is as close as a dictionary. For terms and names like those in our example, however, a dictionary may be no help at all, and the advice of an expert is required: a physician, an authority on Central America, or the actual person whose surname we will otherwise murder. The time for such consultation is well in advance of the day you are scheduled to speak. Until the correct pronunciation becomes a habit, you cannot be sure that you will be able to speak terms as they are intended to be spoken. That requires repetition and lots of practice using the terms in the body of your speech.

In the final analysis, judgments about the relationship between the qualities of your voice and the quality of your delivery will depend on the preceding characteristics operating in concert. Important as pitch or tempo may be on their own, it is their collective impact with range and rhythm that most counts.

Speaking in Your Own Voice

With these qualities of voice in mind, let's now turn to your voice specifically. Are you pleased with the way it sounds and complements your overall delivery? No matter how you answer this question, it is just as important for you to find your own voice as a speaker as it is for authors to find their own voice when they write. We mention this need to find your own voice with good reason. When public speaking students are advised to make better use of their voice in their delivery, all too often they take this to mean they must change their voice to some ideal. The ideal, moreover, is usually thought to be the voice of a television or radio personality.

We don't encourage you to imitate the vocal delivery of someone who hosts a game show, reads the news, or introduces music videos. Instead, we encourage you to experiment with your voice; for example, record your attempts to convey varying emotions in your voice, listen to yourself, and then repeat the process. This kind of exercise will let you hear what your vocal strengths and weaknesses are. In the process, be realistic but not unfairly harsh about how you think you sound. Chances are, what you think you hear is much different from what others hear.

Finally, recognize that important as it is, your voice is but a single component of your overall delivery. Not all good speakers have tremendous "pipes." For example, the *Today Show*'s Katie Couric and Matt Lauer are both engaging, but their voices would hardly be described as rich in timbre. Further, if you were to listen to a number of paid speakers, you would see that this is the case with them as well. All of us tend to underutilize the full potential of our voices. What ultimately counts, then, is whether we're willing to do the hard work necessary to rectify this fact.

Tips and Tactics

Improving Your Voice

Like it or not, people will make judgments about you based on the way you sound. Although we want you to be comfortable with your voice, the following tips may help you if you think something about your voice needs to be changed.

- *Relaxation:* More than one problem with voice can be solved by monitoring tension in your vocal apparatus. Nasality, shrillness, or screeching, and excessive rate of speech are often a consequence of tension/stress. The same relaxation techniques discussed in Chapter 3 can be used to alleviate the impact of tension/stress on your voice.
- *Vocal variation:* Tape-record yourself or have someone tape you when you speak. If you find as a result of monitoring your audiotape that greater vocal variation is needed, pick out someone whose vocal characteristics you admire and repeatedly listen to the person. Then try to model the vocal variation in which the person engages. Repeat this process while using a tape recorder.
- *Being heard:* Have a friend monitor your speaking volume. When you speak too softly, tell your friend to raise an index finger within your view. Use this signal to increase the volume of your voice. The goal is to be easily heard, even in the back of the room.

Nonverbal Characteristics of Delivery

nonverbal behavior
A wordless system of communication.

Nonverbal behavior is a wordless system of communicating. What makes a behavior nonverbal as opposed to verbal? Is it the absence of sound? That cannot be the case, because sign language is considered a form of verbal communication, with signs merely substituting for written or spoken language. Although scholars argue about the exact definition of nonverbal behavior, most agree that it is distinct from verbal behavior in at least three ways: It is continuous, uses multiple channels simultaneously, and is spontaneous. Among adults, nonverbal behavior also is considered to be more revealing about a person than it may actually be.

The Continuous Nature of Nonverbal Behavior

Verbal behavior, composed of words, is discrete. This means verbal behavior can be divided into distinct elements, as was the case when you first began to learn about nouns, verbs, and adjectives. These elements of composition are governed by complex rules, dictating how they should be combined in your speech to form phrases, clauses, and sentences. Each word has a denotative meaning that can be found in the dictionary. Words must be arranged in a precise manner to convey the intended meaning. For example, the words *I am happy* must be arranged in that order to convey the intended meaning. To say, "Am I happy" changes the statement to a question. To say, "Happy am I" seems odd to English speakers. When words with agreed-on meanings are used in a specified order, the meaning of the verbal behavior is apparent as in this example. This is not so with nonverbal behavior, which is continuous rather than divisible.[5]

Consider the expression of happiness as you speak. What the audience sees is a complex message that involves the entire face. The muscles of the face contract, affecting the eyebrows, the corners of the mouth, and the corners of the eyes. Unlike verbal behavior, these involuntary movements cannot be broken down into compositional elements. The eyes, for example, do not convey "I," while the eyebrows say "am" and the mouth represents "happy." You cannot rearrange the components to convey a different meaning, as you can with "I," "am," and "happy."

There are no highly defined rules of grammar to explain the meaning conveyed by these facial expressions. Only the total, continuous combination of these elements can constitute the nonverbal expression of happiness.

The Simultaneous Use of Multiple Channels

Returning to the example of expressing happiness, nonverbal behavior also involves the simultaneous use of multiple channels.[6] For example, try conveying an emotional expression, such as happiness, anger, sorrow, or bewilderment, through a single channel of communication, such as your mouth or eyes or hands. You'll soon see that it is difficult if not impossible. At the same time, you'll recognize that we use these multiple channels simultaneously rather than sequentially. When happy, we express the emotion all over our face, not with our eyes first, mouth second, eyebrows and forehead third and fourth.

The Spontaneous Nature of Nonverbal Behavior

As the preceding characteristics might lead you to believe, another distinguishing characteristic is that nonverbal behavior is spontaneous. With the possible exception of so-called Freudian slips, when people unintentionally say what they really mean, verbal behavior is planned behavior.[7] We consciously think about the words we speak and write, though we do so with such speed it may not occur to us.

Smiles, gestures, and body language occur at a subconscious level. This doesn't mean that people never plan or orchestrate gestures when they speak. Sometimes they do, and their nonverbal behavior is likely to look phony. Most of us learn to distinguish between authentic and phony nonverbal behaviors by the time we reach our teens. Unless nonverbal behavior is rehearsed to the point it becomes habit, planned gestures especially will be recognized as insincere. This is a major reason for people putting so much stock in the meaning they infer from nonverbal behavior.

What Nonverbal Behavior Reveals

Finally, adults tend to believe what they think nonverbal behavior reveals about people in general and speakers specifically. This is especially true when people perceive that a speaker's nonverbal behavior contradicts what the person says. In North American culture, for example, adults associate the truth with eye contact. In other cultures, however, direct eye contact is associated with disrespect if the speaker and listener have different levels of status.

A couple of points need to be made in this regard. Nonverbal behavior can be revealing about a person, but research tells us that we are far more confident in our conclusions about what it reveals than we should be. As an audience member, be cautious about inferring too much about a speaker on the basis of nonverbal behavior alone. As a speaker in this culture, though, you cannot afford to ignore the importance an audience will attach to your eye contact, posture, and manner of gesturing. This is particularly so with respect to audience perceptions of your credibility. Avoid innocent but consequential mistakes such as failing to look directly at audience members when you make claims you want them to believe.

Delivery and the Nonverbal Communication System

Recall that a system is a collection of interdependent and interrelated components. A change in one component will produce changes in them all. The nonverbal system has as its components several interdependent dimensions of behavior that profoundly affect the delivery of a speech. The specific dimensions we discuss in this section are the environment, appearance, the face and eyes, gestures and movement, posture, touch, and time. As a speaker intent on delivering a message effectively, you need to approach these dimensions systematically. Further, the verbal language with which you construct your speech should take into account what you've learned from your systematic assessment of the nonverbal dimensions.

The Environment

environment
The physical surroundings as you speak and the physical distance separating you from your audience.

For our purposes, **environment** refers to the physical surroundings as we speak and the physical distance separating us from our audience. Both surroundings and physical space have an undeniable impact not only on our delivery but also on how the speech is perceived by our audience.

The physical characteristics of the room in which we speak—for example, lighting, temperature, comfort, and aesthetics—will influence both us and the audience physically and psychologically.[8] A bright, aesthetically neutral room, which is neither sterile nor plushly decorated, and in which the temperature is 68 degrees, will have a much different overall impact on the speech transaction than a room that is dimly lit, richly furnished, and 75 degrees. Whereas in the first, both speaker and audience are likely to be alert and attentive, the second might prove so comfortable that neither the speaker nor the audience is sufficiently aroused for the transaction. Thus we would have to plan our delivery accordingly. Whereas a "normal" pattern of delivery probably would be appropriate in the first environment, we likely would need to put extra energy and enthusiasm into the delivery to succeed in the second.

A second environmental consideration is the physical layout of the room. We have been in situations where student presentations were hindered by pillars supporting the roof, by the width and length of the room, and by immovable objects such as tables. Sometimes we have no alternative but to do the best we can in such situations. As a result, we move more than we had planned as we speak, abandon visual aids that would prove impossible for our entire audience to see, or make gestures larger and more exaggerated than is customary.

At other times, however, we will have the opportunity to physically arrange the room in which we will speak. This may include the position of a lectern, elevation of a stage, and configuration of an audience. Given this opportunity, experienced speakers will arrange the environment in concert with their style of delivery. Speakers who have a traditional style of delivery may prefer a lectern, perhaps an overhead projector or keyboard immediately to their side, and an elevated stage from which to speak. Speakers who are much less formal in their style of delivery may want the room to be arranged so that they can move from side to side or even up and down its length.

Both the traditional and informal styles of delivery can be equally effective. However, the room layout consistent with the traditional style is more restrictive than

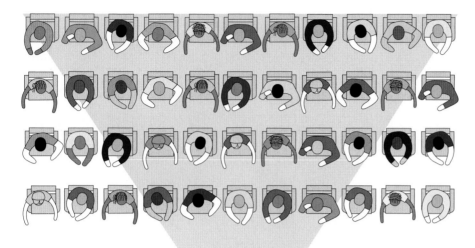

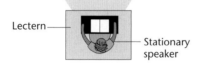

Lectern — Stationary speaker

Figure 11.1
Zone of Interaction in the Traditional Room Setting
Where people are seated in rows and the speaker is stationary, eye contact between speaker and audience is limited to the shaded area. The speaker must turn to make eye contact with those outside the shaded area.

its counterpart in two ways. The first way concerns the **zone of interaction,** the area in which speakers can easily make eye contact with audience members (Figure 11.1). The second way concerns the amount of space physically separating speakers from their audience.

The zone of interaction is limited to the range of your peripheral vision. The immediate zone of interaction between speakers and their audience diminishes as a room gets larger. To compensate for this fact, speakers have two choices. Either they can shift the zone of interaction by looking from side to side, or they can physically move from one point to another when they deliver their speeches. This latter choice is illustrated in Figure 11.2. Obviously, in a very large room the traditional style of delivery limits us to looking from side to side in the attempt to shift the zone of interaction. This means that we cannot help but ignore part of our audience part of the time.

The traditional style of delivery allows less flexibility in manipulating the physical distance separating speakers from their audiences. Whereas a speaker who moves about the room can reduce or increase distance physically as well as psychologically, a relatively stationary speaker is restricted to the latter. Thus, for those who prefer this style of delivery, eye contact becomes their primary agent for managing how immediate they are perceived to be by their audience, a point which we discuss shortly.

To summarize, the relationship of the speaking environment to delivery is a significant one. Not only does it influence our style of delivery, it also influences how we are perceived by our audience. Experienced public speakers try to plan the delivery of their speeches accordingly. When faced with a "tough room," for example, they know that the arousal level of their delivery will need to increase if they are to reach their audience. Inexperienced speakers, on the other hand, all too

zone of interaction
Area of audience in which speaker and audience members can make eye contact.

Figure 11.2
Shifting the Zone of Interaction With Movement
Changing positions can increase the perception of inclusiveness as well as add energy to your speech.

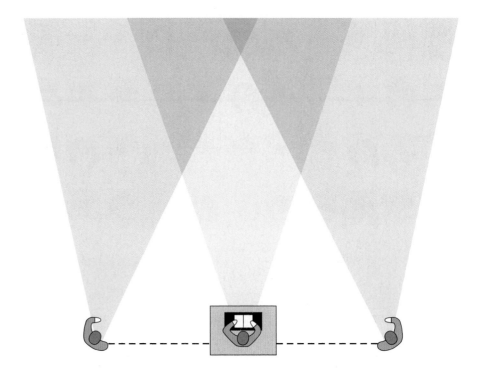

often play "victim" to their speaking environment. Instead of surveying and planning for the environment, they simply deliver their speech as if the environment were of no consequence to them. As a student of public speaking, you know what's good and bad about the layout of the classroom in which you must speak. Thus you, too, should plan your delivery accordingly. The box Seating Arrangements discusses another factor you should consider when planning your delivery.

Tips and Tactics

The Speaking Environment

- Check out the room in which you'll speak well in advance. Take note of the seating arrangement, availability of lectern, and availability of equipment necessary to any media you will be using.
- If permissible, consider changing the environment to better reflect your speech purpose and style of delivery.
- Rehearse planned movement, including how you will use any equipment necessary for your presentational media.
- If possible, try to set the room temperature to between 68 and 70 degrees. Check lighting at the same time.

Appearance

Appearance often has a disproportionately significant effect on audience perceptions of a speaker's message and delivery.[9] Speakers never get a second chance to make a first impression with an audience. First impressions are based largely on

Speaking of . . .

Seating Arrangements

Can the physical seating arrangement have an impact on both your speech and the manner in which it is perceived? A very dramatic one. As a result, you should think about your goals as a speaker and the physical layout of the room in which you speak. Traditional rows will focus attention exclusively on you. A horseshoe arrangement, however, allows audience members to make eye contact with each other. And speaking at the head of a conference table not only narrows the zone of interaction but also puts a physical barrier between you and your audience. Which of these arrangements do you think would most likely encourage audience feedback and participation? Why?

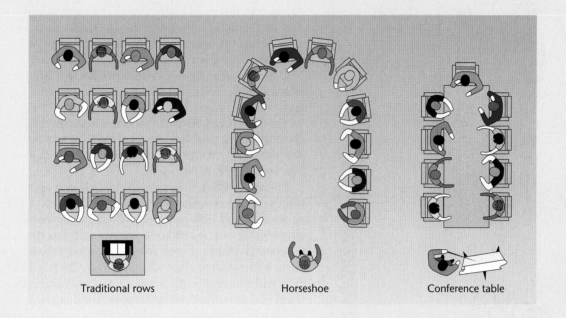

| Traditional rows | Horseshoe | Conference table |

appearance, including body type and height, skin and hair color, and clothing and accessories.

The significance of appearance to public speaking can be measured in at least two ways. The first involves audience members' first impressions. The second involves how people perceive themselves as a result of their appearance and the impact this perception has on their self-confidence and delivery.

According to communication expert Dale Leathers, "Our visible self functions to communicate a constellation of meanings which define who we are and what we are apt to become in the eyes of others."[10] These "others" are the people with whom we come into contact, including the members of our audiences.

Audience members use appearance initially to make judgments about a speaker's level of attractiveness. The consequences of this judgment are far-reaching for speakers. Research tells us that speakers perceived as attractive by audience members also are perceived as smart, successful, sociable, and self-confident. As a result, speakers who fall into this category enjoy an audience whose initial impression of them is favorable.

Yet appearance influences more than an audience's initial impression of a speaker. Appearance also can have a very real effect on a speaker's self-confidence.

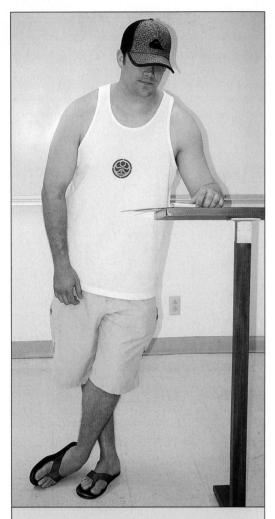

What does this speaker's dress and posture communicate about his attitude toward the assignment and the audience?

Research tells us that speakers who feel they appear attractive report greater self-confidence than those reporting otherwise.[11]

Although some facets of your appearance and their impact on audience perception are outside your control–for example, body type and height–you can easily control one facet: your dress. Simply said, your dress should be appropriate to the situation. Obvious as this advice may seem, it is frequently ignored by students in public speaking classes. All too often they show up to speak dressed as if they had thought little about the appropriateness of their attire. Their attitude, as reflected in their dress, seems to be saying, "It's just a speech class."

Consider an analogy. Good students know what the research suggests about the relationship between the appearance of a term paper and the mark it receives. Frequently, it's the difference between a minus or a plus in their grade. Good students, therefore, go to some length to make sure that their papers not only conform to the requirements but "look" impressive as well.

The same relationship may exist between appearance and the marks students receive on their speeches. Although an Armani suit may not turn a mediocre speech into an outstanding one, it certainly won't cause the speaker to lose points. Inappropriate attire or careless grooming will never add points to a speech; moreover, there is a chance they will unnecessarily detract from such things as the speaker's perceived competence. Although we do not recommend formal business attire for most classroom speeches, we urge you to consider a form of attire often called "business casual." For both men and women, business casual could include a polo shirt or sweater, slacks, and shoes you would normally wear in an office. Appropriate dress confers status on you and shows respect for your audience.

The Eyes

It is only a matter of time until technology makes it easy for all of us to actually see our online communication partner, but for now e-mail and Internet chat room users often use symbols such as those in Figure 11.3 to add emotion to their messages. Frustrated with their inability to convey their feelings along with their thoughts, these symbols and ones like them were developed to approximate what in conversation would be communicated through our eyes and face.

The eyes have been called the windows to the soul. Perhaps, then, it is only fitting that many people also believe eye contact is the single most important variable in delivering a speech. The eyes connect speaker and audience. The eyes also tell the speaker and the audience much about each other.

To repeat, in the North American culture, people use eye contact to make judgments about:

:-)	Smiley face	x-(	Mad	3:[	Pitbull
:)	Little kid	:-0	Talkative	:-#	Lips are sealed
:-t	Pouting	:-@	Screaming	=8-0	Yikes!
:*(	Crying softly	:-\	Undecided	=I:0}	Bill Clinton
>:)	Evil	=:-)	Punk	(_8(I)	Homer Simpson
:-*	Kiss	}:-x	Cat	:-C	Real unhappy
:-x	Big wet kiss	>:-1	Klingon	8(:-)	Mickey Mouse

Figure 11.3
Emotional Symbols
Emoticons are designed to communicate non-verbal expressions such as happiness and sadness. Source: www.netlingo.com

- Whether a person is competent
- Whether a person can be trusted
- Whether a person is approachable

Competence and trustworthiness are two key components of a speaker's credibility; that is, the degree to which a speaker is perceived as believable. Generally, the more a speaker makes eye contact with audience members, the more credible the speaker will be perceived. Because credible speakers are also likely to have more influence with an audience, it only makes good sense for the speaker to maintain as much eye contact as possible with an audience.

Eye contact also has the power to reduce physical distances psychologically. When we make and sustain friendly eye contact with people at a distance, it makes us feel "closer" to each other. It also helps to make people appear attractive and open to dialogue. As was the case with competence and trustworthiness, this is clearly to a speaker's benefit.

But there is yet another reason for maintaining eye contact with an audience. Eye contact is an important source of audience feedback. In North America, for example, an audience will use eye contact to let the speaker know the degree to which it is engaged. Speakers can then use this feedback to make decisions about whether they need to modify their speech to gain the audience's attention.

Having established its importance to delivery, let's talk about how you can optimize the positive effects of eye contact. First, recognize that you cannot fake eye contact! People know you are looking directly at them or looking only at the tops of their heads. Second, some eye contact is better than no eye contact at all. Ideally, however, eye contact works best when you look at individual members of the audience as you speak. This type of eye contact personalizes a public message. All too often, people think eye contact means looking at the audience members as a group, beginning with those in the center seats, and then turning to those seated to our right or left. To the contrary, effective eye contact means making every person in the room feel as if we were speaking only to him or her.

The Face

Eye contact works best when it is complemented with appropriate facial expressions. The face and eyes, for example, can communicate happiness, surprise, fear,

Can you identify the meaning of these different facial expressions?

anger, disgust, contempt, sadness, or interest. The face and eyes can also modify the intensity of any of these nonverbal expressions of emotion.[12]

Just as you can use metaphor to manipulate language intensity, you can use your face and eyes to intensify your delivery. In most cases, you intensify what you say in this manner with little or no conscious thought. As you grow angry, for example, the muscles in your face tense and your eyes narrow spontaneously. The purveyor of bad news can make things even worse by accentuating it with the face and eyes.

You can also use your face and eyes to neutralize the message you deliver. Based on an analysis of your situation, you may know that at least some members of the audience will disagree with your views. Suppose you are in a class situation that requires you to deliver a persuasive speech. If your topic is a truly controversial one, you can reasonably predict that not everyone in your audience will agree with everything you say. Although you may not be able to win them over, you also don't want to alienate them. As a result, you may want to use your face and eyes to neutralize some of the more contentious and evocative points you wish to make.

In a sense, what you give an audience in your face and eyes will determine what you can expect to get back from that audience. An intensely worded argument accompanied by the delivery of an equally intense message in the face and eyes invites the same from those who differ with you. On the other hand, using the face and eyes to neutralize the message improves your chance of a more favorable response from your audience. The city of Palo Alto, California, took this to an extreme when it considered a guideline that would have discouraged city council members from using facial expressions to show their disagreement, frustration, or disgust at meetings. The idea behind the guideline was that it would promote civility and defuse conflict among council members and between council members and constituents during public meetings. Good intentions, however, do not always make for good policy. The guideline was unworkable because it is nearly impossible to suppress nonverbal expressions of underlying feelings. In addition, the guideline violated council members' First Amendment rights.[13]

To close, keep in mind that what we have suggested here is based on North American norms. Remember that many cultures frown upon the sustained and focused eye contact that North Americans value. Members of many Asian cultures, for example, view such eye contact as rude and even hostile. Both speakers and audience members should keep this in mind. As a speaker, recognize that when international students appear uncomfortable or don't return your attempts to make eye contact, it may be the result of their culture. As an audience member, realize that your expectancies about eye contact may be at odds with the norms of the international student who is speaking.[14]

Using Your Eyes and Face

- Always face your audience when speaking; avoid turning your back to the audience unless absolutely necessary.
- Make eye contact with people before you begin. Maintain eye contact by meeting the gaze of individual audience members in all parts of the room.
- Avoid excessive eye contact with one person, for example, your instructor.
- Don't be afraid to be expressive with your face.

Gestures and Movement

You've heard the expression "different strokes for different folks." Nowhere is it more applicable than to the subject of gestures and movement relative to delivery. Although Ronald Reagan neither moved nor gestured very much when he spoke, he was a consummate public speaker. And though you practically have to nail Elizabeth Dole's feet to the floor to keep her from moving, she too is a public speaker of notable achievement. Thus, before we say a single word about how much or how little you should gesture or move as you speak, we want to say this: Your gestures and your movements as you grow as a public speaker should be a refined reflection of what you do naturally.

As is the case with the eyes and face, gestures and movements also can be used to intensify or lessen the emotional impact of verbal messages. Many gestures, for instance, serve as *affect displays;* that is, they visibly communicate feelings. Placing both hands near the heart at the same time you explain how important a subject is to you is an example. So, too, are clenched fists, open palms held face up, or lightly slapping the side of the face.

Given the preceding caveat, gesturing and moving can complement your delivery in several ways.[15] These include making your delivery more emblematic, making your delivery more illustrative, and regulating the speech transaction.

Emblems

The speeches of the best public speakers are usually rich in emblems. An **emblem** is a nonverbal behavior that can be directly translated into words and phrases and may replace them.[16] For example, Winston Churchill's "V" was an emblem for victory. Emblems must meet the following criteria:

emblem
A nonverbal symbol that can be substituted for a word

1. The emblem means something specific to the audience members.
2. The emblem is used intentionally by the speaker to stimulate meaning.
3. The emblem can be easily translated into a few words.

Gestures are defined by the culture in which they are learned. As a case in point, when Richard Nixon was Dwight Eisenhower's vice president, he incited an embarrassing protest while deplaning at a South American airport. He greeted the crowd with arms outstretched above his head, the thumb and first finger of each

Film and TV star Rob Lowe gives our students the thumbs up to emphasize his verbal message during a political rally on the authors' campus.

hand joined together in what North Americans take to mean "A-OK." In many South American countries, however, this nonverbal emblem was then synonymous with what we call "giving the finger" or "flipping someone off."

Illustrators

Nonverbal behaviors that accompany speech and "show" what is being talked about are called **illustrators.** Although a lot like emblems, they are more general and seldom translate into a few words. The most common way we nonverbally illustrate is with our hands. Verbal directions or descriptions beg for the use of our hands. Try giving someone directions or describing an object—say, a spiral staircase—without using your hands.

Regulators

Gestures called **regulators** influence the amount and type of feedback received from the audience. If you hold up your hand when asking audience members whether they've ever felt frustrated waiting in line, for example, you are much more likely to prompt them to raise their hands as well. If you are stationary throughout a speech, your audience will give you much different feedback than if you were to move and periodically change the zone of interaction. Using gestures and movement to regulate feedback requires planning and rehearsal. An unnatural or inappropriate gesture or specific movement may elicit a response from the audience that you don't expect.

Regulating audience feedback is particularly important when a speaker answers audience questions. Without regulation, such question-and-answer sessions can turn ugly.

illustrators
Nonverbal symbols used to visualize what is being spoken.

regulators
Nonverbal behaviors that influence the speech transaction.

Posture

This dimension is obviously related to movement, gestures, and your overall appearance. Posture is vital to your delivery and the manner in which it is received. People make all kinds of attributions about speakers on the basis of their posture, ranging from how confident a speaker is to how seriously the speaker takes the topic and the situation. At the least, consequently, you will want to guard against an audience making an incorrect attribution about you because you slouched, folded your arms across your chest, stood with one hand on your hip, or put your hands in your pockets.

Because the norms governing appropriate posture vary across cultures, there are no hard-and-fast rules for speakers to follow. Still, given what we know generally about the culture of the beginning public speaking class, there are some steps you can follow to achieve a good posture for delivering your speeches. Remember that the more you slouch and shrink posturally, the less powerful you are likely to be perceived. Remember as well that posture influences the mechanics of your voice. Standing with shoulders back stretches the diaphragm and opens the air passages. That's one reason opera singers invariably have good posture. It helps them use their voice to full effect.

Tips and Tactics

Guidelines for Posture While Delivering a Speech

- Find your center of balance. Usually this means standing with your feet apart at about shoulder width.
- Pull your shoulders back, sticking your chest out and holding your stomach in.
- Keep your chin up and off your chest.
- Initially let your arms rest at your sides with palms open, which will allow you to gesture easily as you speak.

Touch

Touch, which is by far the most intimate and reinforcing of the nonverbal dimensions, can affect your delivery in at least two ways.[17] The first involves **self-adapting behaviors,** which are distracting touching behaviors that speakers engage in unconsciously.

In arousing situations, people frequently touch their face, hair, or clothes without realizing it. Just as frequently they touch some convenient object. They may squeeze the arm of a chair, roll their fingers on a tabletop, trace the outside edge of a glass with a fingertip, or mistake the top of a lectern for a conga drum. They do these things unconsciously.

Because public speaking is arousing, it too can provoke these self-adaptive forms of touch. Further, they can needlessly detract from your delivery. Tugging at an earlobe, rubbing the outside of your upper arm, or jingling the change in your pocket won't help your delivery. Neither will pounding on the lectern with the palms of your hands or rocking it from side to side.

The second way touch can affect your delivery concerns other people. At some point it's likely that your presentations will involve other people. Corporate trainers spend much of their lives giving informative presentations that involve audience participation. The same can be said for sales managers, teachers, attorneys, and practitioners of public relations. Touch very often comes into play in these scenarios. Sometimes it's as simple but as important as shaking a person's hand. At other times it may involve guiding someone by the hand, patting someone on the back, or even giving a more demonstrative tactile sign of approval. At the same time, you must avoid touch that can be interpreted as inappropriate. For example, there have been several widely reported cases of schoolteachers accused of inappropriately touching students. Unwelcome touching can, in fact, be grounds for accusations of sexual harassment.

self-adapting behaviors
Nonverbal behaviors used to cope with nervousness; for example, self-touching or grasping sides of lectern with hands.

Time

The final nonverbal dimension to think about relative to delivery is time. As journalist Michael Ventura writes,

> Time is the medium in which we live. There is inner time—our personal sense of the rhythms of time experienced differently by each of us; and there is imposed time—the regimented time by which society organizes itself, the time of schedules and deadlines, time structured largely by work and commerce.[18]

First, time varies from one individual to the next. Research confirms what you no doubt long ago suspected. The internal body clock each of us has regulates not only when we sleep but also peak performance when we're awake. Some people perform best from early to midmorning, some during the middle of the day, and others late at night. What is true of performance in general, moreover, is true of public speaking specifically. During our time awake, there are periods when our speaking abilities peak, depending on our individual body clock. Most of us know from our own experience that we either are or are not very alert in the early morning or late afternoon. To the extent possible, attempt to schedule a speaking time when you know your mind and body will be alert.

Time affects your delivery in other ways as well. For example, the time limits you face as a speaker can have an impact on your delivery. As a result of attempting to cover too much material, for example, time limits may cause you to hurry your delivery. Conversely, if you find that you're about to finish your speech under the minimum time requirement of an assignment, you may slow down your delivery in an attempt to meet the time requirement.

The audience's perception of your delivery will also be affected by your "timing," a term frequently used in reference to actors and comics. Just as their timing of a joke or dramatic monologue can spell the difference between success and failure, so too can your timing. Rushing a punch line or dramatic anecdote, for instance, may negate its intended effect. Telling a story too slowly may do likewise.

Because the norms that govern the use of time vary across cultures, how quickly or how slowly you deliver your speech may be a consideration. Whereas a relatively speedy style of delivery may be well received in New York City, it may be received as evidence of the "little time" you have for an audience in parts of the South and Southwest. Conversely, a slow rate of speech, which some mistakenly confuse with the speed at which a person thinks, may prove irritating to audience members whose culture is fast paced.

Finally, whether you are "on time" or late, not only for a speech but just in general, affects your credibility in our North American culture. People who are on time are perceived as efficient and courteous, both of which affect perceptions of competence and trustworthiness. People who are routinely late give the impression they are disorganized and not especially considerate of the time needs of an audience. This is very true of both your classmates and your instructor.

Making the Most of Nonverbal Behavior in Delivery

The eight dimensions of nonverbal behavior we've been talking about perform a number of important functions in speech delivery.[19] As we've discussed, these dimensions interact to make speeches more emblematic and illustrative. They can also help regulate audience feedback and intensify or lessen the emotional impact of what you say during a speech. Other ways that nonverbal dimensions such as the face, eyes, and voice function to facilitate the delivery of your messages include complementing, contradicting, and repeating the message; substituting for a verbal cue; increasing the perception of immediacy; exciting the audience; and delivering a powerful speech. Consider how you might use these dimensions to maximize your nonverbal behavior in delivering your speech.

Complementing Your Message

A complementary nonverbal cue serves to reinforce what you verbally share with your audience. A genuine smile on your face as you thank your audience for the opportunity to speak, for example, carries more weight than either message standing on its own. There are many ways to complement the delivery of your message nonverbally. Changing the expression on your face, raising the pitch of your voice, or even breaking off eye contact are just a few of them.

Contradicting Your Message

Often, people contradict themselves nonverbally while communicating interpersonally. Forcing a smile and saying, "I had a great time" is a classic example. Although the smile may have covered up how they really felt, chances are it only served to contradict what they said but didn't mean. Usually people try to keep this from happening.

In the case of public speaking, however, you can use contradiction to enhance your delivery, for example, by rolling your eyes, shrugging your shoulders, or having a sarcastic expression. Certainly Shakespeare knew that contradiction could enhance delivery. He frequently wrote speeches for his characters that invited actors to contradict their verbal statements with nonverbal cues. For example, in Marc Antony's eulogy of Julius Caesar, the line "But Brutus was an honorable man" is usually delivered by an actor in a sarcastic voice that says exactly the opposite. Because it is an attention-getting device, this kind of antithesis in a speech can enhance the impact with which the verbal message is delivered.

Repeating Your Message

Repetition is one of the most common ways speakers manipulate their message nonverbally. It's also one of the easiest ways to do this. Raising three fingers as you say you have three points to make doesn't require the oratorical skill of a Colin Powell.

Repetition differs from complementing in a significant way. Whereas a complementary nonverbal cue reinforces the message, a repetitious one serves to make it redundant. The classic example is when *Star Trek*'s Mr. Spock makes the Vulcan V sign while saying, "Live long and prosper." Other examples include nodding your head up and down while communicating agreement and shaking your head from side to side when communicating disagreement.

Substituting for a Verbal Cue

Have you ever seen entertainers and politicians raise their hands and motion in the attempt to stop an audience's continued applause? They are using a nonverbal cue as a substitute for a verbal one. In many circumstances, such a nonverbal cue is both more appropriate and more effective than a verbal one. An icy stare shot in the direction of someone talking as you speak is likely to be less disruptive, for example, than politely asking the person to be quiet. Shrugging your shoulders, reaching out with open palms, and raising your eyebrows, moreover, may more clearly communicate your bewilderment than actually saying you're puzzled by something.

Increasing the Perception of Immediacy

Nonverbal behavior can also increase the perception of immediacy between you and your audience. Immediacy concerns how psychologically close or distant people perceive each other, as well as the degree to which they perceive each other as approachable.[20]

Generally, the perception of immediacy between people is desirable because people who are perceived as immediate are also perceived as friendly and approachable, stimulating, open to dialogue, and interpersonally warm.

Because public speaking normally takes place in a setting that arbitrarily puts physical distance between speakers and their audiences, speakers usually have to reduce this physical distance psychologically. You can do this in at least two ways. The first, which we discussed at length in Chapter 10, involves the use of immediate language. The second is to make your delivery more nonverbally immediate.

The easiest and most effective way to make the delivery more immediate is through nonverbal channels. Eye contact is the perfect medium. Even when people are separated by substantial physical distance, eye contact enables them to bridge this distance in a psychological sense. The best public speakers, for example, are often the ones who make you feel as if they are speaking to you, and only you, with their eyes as well as their voices.

Eye contact is not the only medium, however, through which you can achieve greater immediacy with your audience. Immediacy can also be achieved with facial expressions such as a smile, with a conversational rather than condescending tone of voice, and by standing beside the lectern instead of appearing to hide behind it.

Exciting the Audience

One way to gauge the effectiveness of a speech is by the degree to which it stimulates the audience. The best speakers make listeners think, provoke them to laugh, or motivate them to act. Generally, an audience's degree of excitement can be traced to the degree of excitement the audience senses in the speaker.

The level of excitement of public speakers is most noticeable in their delivery. This includes rate of speech, volume of speech, and vocal as well as facial expressions. Excited speakers, the research tells us, speak faster and louder than speakers unaroused by their topic or by the transaction between them and their audience. Excited speakers, the research also tells us, reveal more of themselves as they speak, through changes in facial expressions as well as changes in the pitch of their voice.

Does this mean that someone who simply is excited also is a good speaker? Of course not. Too much excitement can be as distracting as too little excitement can be boring. The idea, then, is to moderate your excitement for your topic or audience rather than to inappropriately exaggerate it with your delivery.

Delivering a Powerful Speech

When it comes to public speaking, the power of words depends mightily on the manner in which they are delivered. No doubt many speech writers have suffered as the power of the words they so carefully crafted was wiped out by the person delivering them. This shouldn't and needn't be the case. With care and practice, you can capitalize on the varying dimensions of nonverbal behavior to make the delivery of your speech powerful. Some of the ways you can do this are obvious; others are more subtle.

Posture is an obvious way you can control the power of delivery. Standing tall and self-assured, in and of itself, communicates power. When combined with movement away from the lectern, this is even more the case.

You can also enhance the power of your delivery with your eyes, with your voice, and through movement and gestures. In North America, at least, powerful speakers make eye contact, speak in a controlled and confident tone of voice, reduce the distance between themselves and their audience by moving closer to them, and gesture as a natural extension of their spoken message. In stark contrast, speakers whose delivery lacks power avoid eye contact, fail to speak up, and usually try to tie up their hands by sticking them in their pockets, gripping the side of the lectern, or hiding them behind their back.

Taking a Proactive Approach

Knowing something about the nature and functions of nonverbal behavior should assist you in making your speech delivery proactive rather than reactive. To engage in **proactive delivery** means that the speaker takes the initiative and anticipates and controls for as many variables as possible rather than merely reacting to them. Reactive delivery is like the boxer who only counterpunches. This wait-and-see attitude is rarely the mark of a championship boxer, and it can be disastrous for even the most seasoned public speaker. The guidelines that follow should assist you in making sure that your nonverbal behavior enhances, rather than detracts from, the delivery of your speech.

proactive delivery
Planned and rehearsed presentation.

Tips and Tactics

Guidelines for Proactive Speech Delivery

1. *Take control of your appearance.* Dressing appropriately is one of the easiest ways to enhance initial impressions of you as the medium of your message. Think about the possible effects of apparel, such as the baseball cap that seems to be attached to your scalp, the baggy shorts you prefer, or the saying on your favorite T-shirt.

2. *Use natural gestures.* Videotape your practice. Check on your gestures. Do they appear natural and complement your delivery, or do they appear forced and detract from your spoken message?

3. *Time your speech.* Do this more than once and on videotape if you can. Note your timing and the degree to which the rate at which you speak facilitates the mood you want to communicate to your audience. Also, remind yourself that your practice time probably will be longer than when you actually speak before your audience.

4. *Avoid self-adapting behaviors.* During practice, watch out for self-adapting behaviors such as playing with your hair, tugging on a finger, cracking knuckles, licking your lips, and hiding your hands. Self-adapters such as these will call attention to themselves and undermine perceptions of your power and self-confidence.

Summary

You have choices when making decisions about how to best deliver your speech. The bottom line, however, is that the method you decide on should reflect your preferred style of speaking, the environment in which you will speak, and the speech occasion.

- Effective delivery involves both what you say and how you say it.

- Effective delivery demands skill not only in articulating the words you use to express yourself but also in using your voice to shape the meaning of what you articulate.

- Nonverbal communication complements the verbal and vocal delivery of your speech. Unlike language, nonverbal communication is continuous, makes use of channels of communication simultaneously, and is spontaneous.

- Specific facets of the nonverbal communication system that influence delivery include the environment, the eyes and face, physical appearance, gestures and movement, posture, time, and touch.

- Gestures frequently take the form of emblems and illustrators, which regulate the speech transaction.

- Important functions of nonverbal communication in the delivery of speeches include complementing the verbal message, contradicting the verbal message, repeating/reinforcing the verbal message, substituting for a verbal cue, increasing immediacy, and increasing excitement and power in the verbal message.

Check Your Understanding: Exercises and Activities

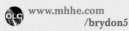

SpeechCoach

To evaluate your understanding of this chapter, see the Quizzes on your CD.

www.mhhe.com
/brydon5

Visit the Online Learning Center for helpful study resources, including practice tests, key term crossword puzzles, and PowerWeb articles for research and review.

SpeechCoach

For a review of key terms in this chapter, see the Key Terms Flashcards on your CD.

1. Observe a speaker outside of your class. Keep track of the number of times the speaker (a) changes the zone of interaction, (b) moves away from the lectern, and (c) gestures. On a scale of 1 to 10, with 10 being the high end, rate the speaker in each of these areas. Compare and discuss your observation and ratings with those of other students. See if a pattern emerges.

2. Differences in nonverbal norms, as well as differences in communication styles and patterns, are common across cultures. Choose two or three North American norms for nonverbal behavior—for example, eye contact, gesturing, and time. Interview a student or faculty member from a culture other than North American about how these communication behaviors differ in his or her culture. Write a short paper summarizing your findings.

3. Explain why sign language is a *verbal* behavior, whereas vocal variation in pitch, rate, tempo, and the like are *nonverbal* behaviors, even though sign language is not vocalized and vocal variation is.

4. Explain why nonverbal behavior is continuous, uses multiple channels simultaneously, and is spontaneous and how these characteristics distinguish it from the language of your speech.

5. Review the four guidelines for proactive delivery. Before your next speech, develop a plan to use at least three of these guidelines to improve your delivery skills in that speech.

6. Ask a classmate to apply Exercise 1 to your next speech. Talk with the classmate afterward about the relationship between his or her observations and the overall effectiveness of your delivery.

7. How would you describe your public speaking style? Is it a dramatic or understated style? Is it formal or informal? Ask some of your classmates to choose five adjectives they would use to describe your style of speaking. Compare their adjectives with five of your own. If you take advantage of this exercise, there is a good chance it will at least suggest a visual image of the style you communicate to others as you speak. You can then use this image to refine your style of speaking.

Notes

1. Edward T. Hall, *The Silent Language* (Greenwich, Conn.: Fawcett Publications, 1959), 15.
2. George B. Ray, "Vocally Cued Personality Prototypes: An Implicit Personality Theory Approach," *Communication Monographs* 53 (1986): 266–76.
3. Richard L. Street and Robert M. Brady, "Evaluative Responses to Communicators as a Function of Evaluative Domain, Listener Speech Rate, and Communication Context," *Communication Monographs* 49 (1982): 290–308.
4. David B. Buller and R. Kelly Aune, "The Effects of Speech Rate Similarity on Compliance: An Application of Communication Accommodation Theory," *Western Journal of Speech Communication* 56 (1992): 37–53.
5. J. Burgoon, D. W. Buller, and W. G. Woodhall, *Nonverbal Communication: The Unspoken Dialogue,* 2nd ed. (New York: Harper & Row, 1989). See also M. Knapp and J. A. Hall, *Nonverbal Communication in Human Interaction,* 3rd ed. (Fort Worth, Tex.: Harcourt, Brace, and Jovanovich, 1992).
6. L. A. Malandro, L. Barker, and D. A. Barker, *Nonverbal Communication,* 2nd ed. (New York: Random House, 1989).
7. V. P. Richmond and J. C. McCroskey, *Nonverbal Behavior in Interpersonal Relationships* (Englewood Cliffs, N.J.: Prentice-Hall, 1991).
8. R. Sommer, "Man's Proximate Environment," *Journal of Social Issues* 22 (1966): 60.
9. Ellen Berscheid and Elaine Walster, "Beauty and the Best," *Psychology Today* 5, no. 10 (1972): 42–46.
10. D. Leathers, *Successful Nonverbal Communication: Principles and Practices* (New York: Macmillan, 1986).
11. Malandro, Barker, and Barker, *Nonverbal Communication.*
12. P. Ekman and W. V. Friesen, *Unmasking the Face: A Guide to Recognizing Emotions from Facial Expression* (Englewood Cliffs, N.J.: Prentice-Hall, 1975). See also P. Ekman, W. V. Friesen, and S. Ancoli, "Facial Signs of Emotional Expression," *Journal of Personality and Social Psychology* 39 (1980): 1125–34.
13. Nicole C. Wong, "Palo Alto May Relent–It's OK to Frown." *Sacramento Bee,* 18 April 2003, A6.
14. P. Ekman, *Telling Lies* (New York: Norton, 1985). See also Bella M. DePaulo, Miron Zuckerman, and Robert Rosenthal, "Humans as Lie Detectors," *Journal of Communication* 30 (1980): 129–39; R. E. Kraut, "Verbal and Nonverbal Cues in the Perception of Lying," *Journal of Personality and Social Psychology* 36 (1978): 380–91.
15. Judee Burgoon, "Nonverbal Communication Research in the 1970s: An Overview," in *Communication Yearbook 4,* ed. D. Nimmo (New Brunswick, N.J.: Transaction Books, 1980), 179–97.
16. Joseph A. Devito, *The Communication Handbook: A Dictionary* (New York: Harper & Row, 1986), 105.
17. Stephen Thayer, "Close Encounters," *Psychology Today* 22, no. 3 (1988): 31–36. See also A. Montague, *Touching: The Significance of the Skin* (New York: Harper & Row, 1971).
18. Michael Ventura, "Trapped in a Time Machine With No Exits," *Sacramento Bee,* 26 February 1995, C1.
19. Burgoon, Buller, and Woodhall, *Nonverbal Communication: The Unspoken Dialogue;* E. T. Hall, "System for the Notation of Proxemic Behavior," *American Anthropologist* 65 (1963): 1003–26.
20. Malandro, Barker, and Barker, *Nonverbal Communication.*

As our student Shelly Lee demonstrates, media are meant to complement a presentation not substitute for it.

Chapter 12

Using Media in Your Speech

Objectives

After reading this chapter and reviewing the learning resources on your CD-ROM and at the Online Learning Center, you should be able to:

- Describe and explain how visual media can be used for cueing and signposting, illustrating, simplifying, and complementing the text and delivery of a speech.

- Describe content that is better depicted visually than described aurally.

- Describe presentational media, including objects, models, flip charts, audio and video recordings, CD-ROMs and DVDs, poster boards, overheads and computer-generated slides.

- Discuss the criteria for choosing the presentational medium best suited to your speech purpose.

- Discuss and appropriately follow rules for the construction and use of presentational media.

- List, explain, and avoid common mistakes speakers make when using presentational media including PowerPoint.

Key Concepts

audio media

bar chart

flip chart

flowchart

line graph

organizational chart

overhead transparency

pie chart

presentational media

visual media

" Is seeing believing? "

–ANONYMOUS

Computer-assisted presentations can still fall prey to human error. FOXTROT © 1988 Bill Amend. Reprinted with permission of Universal Press Syndicate. All rights reserved.

Murphy's Law states, "Anything that can go wrong will go wrong" (see box Murphy's Law Revisited). No one is immune from Murphy's Law, not even highly paid executives accustomed to making presentations in professional settings. Recently, for example, it has become routine for conferees in Silicon Valley to use Wi-Fi technology not only to take notes while they listen to a speaker but also to chat among themselves as the speech unfolds. What's more, at many meetings where this takes place, a large screen is prominently placed on the stage instantaneously projecting the content of these "chats."

Pity the executive from IBM at one of these conferences who suddenly found that his carefully planned PowerPoint slides on one screen were competing against instant and less than flattering feedback from his audience on an adjacent one. As he introduced a slide about IBM's "modular design componentisation," for instance, the following message appeared alongside from an anonymous audience member: "What is this dribble . . . what an incredible waste of 45 minutes."[1] And you thought you were having a bad day!

This chapter focuses on the effective use of presentational media, including the fact that the technology intended to help speakers can sometimes have an opposite effect. In our example, the electronic media on which the speaker had come to rely to visualize his remarks was also being used by audience members to hit him over the head with negative feedback. Although we cannot protect you completely from Murphy's Law or an unsympathetic audience when you use media in a speech, the information in this chapter will help you avoid many pitfalls.

We begin by explaining why presentational media can enhance a speech and show how these media can serve you and your purpose for speaking. We also discuss the types of presentational media from which you can choose and provide some tips to help you choose wisely. We suggest some simple rules of the road to follow as you develop your own presentational media and integrate them with the narrative of your speech. Finally, we discuss some common mistakes you'll want to avoid when you put presentational media into practice.

presentational media
Channels of communication that extend the five basic senses: touch, sight, sound, taste, and smell.

Effective Presentational Media

If you look up the word *medium,* you'll learn that it is a channel of communication. If you then look up the word *media,* you'll learn that it is the plural of medium and is defined as channels of communication. **Presentational media** are channels

Murphy's Law Revisited

There is no way to be completely prepared for the unexpected. The best defense is to anticipate problems and prepare alternatives. Here are a few of the things that you need to prepare for. (At one time or another, they have all happened to the authors of this book.)

Problem: The battery in your equipment (tape recorder, microphone, or whatever) is dead.

What to do: Test the equipment the morning of your speech and carry a spare battery.

Problem: There is no overhead projector, even though you reserved one.

What to do: Call to confirm your reservation on the morning of your speech. Physically check out the projector if possible.

Problem: The overhead projector's lightbulb is burned out.

What to do: Most overheads have a spare lightbulb. Make sure you know where it is beforehand.

Problem: The slide projector (film projector, VCR, etc.) does not work.

What to do: Again, check it out in advance if possible. If it unexpectedly fails, you will need to verbally describe what is on your slides. We recall one case where a person simply stood in front of a blank screen, pretended to show slides, and described them in elaborate detail as he went along ("As you can clearly see from this slide . . ."). It turned a frustrating situation into a humorous one.

Problem: Your visuals are out of order or upside down, or some are missing.

What to do: An ounce of prevention is worth a pound of cure. Check and double-check them before the speech. If you run into this problem, try not to get flustered. Make a joke while you look for the missing visual; if you can't find it, verbally describe the visual or skip a part of the speech.

Problem: The computer you are using for your PowerPoint presentation fails, or the projector does not work.

What to do: Be sure to prepare backup visuals. For example, we normally have overhead transparencies prepared that duplicate our PowerPoint presentations.

Problem: It takes a lot longer than you thought to demonstrate a process using your visuals.

What to do: First, always practice with your visuals so that you know how long it will take. Second, if you are demonstrating a multistep process, have various steps along the way already prepared.

Remember, nothing can happen to you that hasn't already happened to someone else. Most audiences are sympathetic to speakers who are obviously prepared and yet encounter technical difficulties beyond their control. At the same time, audiences have little sympathy when Murphy's Law strikes someone who is just winging it. And keep in mind, "Murphy was an optimist."

---

of communication that enhance the five natural senses—sight, sound, touch, taste, and smell—we use routinely to send and receive information. These tools also can be used to effectively supplement our natural means of communicating with voice and body. **Visual media,** which we emphasize in this chapter, involve both the speaker's and the audience's sense of sight to enhance the spoken message.

Examples of presentational media include objects, models, flip charts, audio and video recordings, CD-ROMs and DVDs, poster boards, overheads, and computer-generated slides projected onto a screen. These media vary in difficulty of use and construction as well as in technological sophistication. Using actual objects, such as a collection of different types of hats in a speech about sun protection, may require little special skill. In contrast, using PowerPoint slides effectively in a speech requires skill not only in constructing them but also in using the technology necessary to display them.

At their best, presentational media visually extend and amplify what we otherwise could only voice and gesture for our audience. Consider how a photograph of a malnourished child, for example, could visually extend and amplify a speech

visual media
The use of the sense of sight to communicate a message.

 **Speech**Coach

For an overview of the role of presentational media in public speaking, see segment 12.1 on your CD.

about saving children from famine in sub-Saharan Africa. Or consider how even something as simple as a pie chart might help us show the audience where and in what proportion the federal government spends our tax dollars.

Presentational media reinforce the effect of what we say and how we say it. They provide the audience with visual images that reinforce the examples we construct with words. And they inform our audience visually about concepts and processes we would be hard pressed to explain with only words and gestures.

The Functional Nature of Presentation Media

Regardless of type, presentational media should be treated as functional rather than decorative elements in the speech transaction. These functions include signposting and cueing, illustrating the spoken word, simplifying spoken examples, and complementing.

Signposting and Cueing

In our own experience we have found that our students appreciate a visual guide to our lectures. As a result, we use PowerPoint slides that (1) preview the topic and content of the lecture, (2) provide a brief outline students can follow as we talk about the points we want to make, and (3) visually illustrate examples that help us make our point and help our students better understand.

When we first talked about speech organization in Chapter 2, we introduced you to the concept of signposts. Then we were talking about verbal statements that

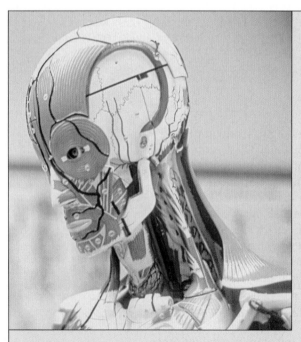
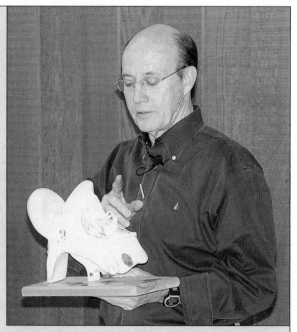

When the actual object cannot be used, models are an excellent way to illustrate your message, as our colleague Dr. Ray Bright shows.

let audience members know where the speaker is taking them, such as "Let's now turn to the second point I'd like to share." Here we are talking about using presentational media to achieve the same purpose.

Research shows that people find it easier to pay attention and remember when they are provided with a road map that visualizes what they are hearing and seeing. Providing an audience with a visual road map that contains signposts also helps speakers stick to their organization, pace the tempo of their speech, and free their hands from the note cards on which they normally rely. Thus even something as straightforward as a series of overhead transparencies with text can serve both our audience and us. At the very least, they help our audience follow us as the speech unfolds, and they can help us stay on task as well.

Illustrating the Spoken Word

Nonverbal gestures are often used to illustrate what we are trying to say (see Chapter 11). Presentational media serve a similar function. Further, when gestures cannot possibly convey enough detail in this regard, presentational media come to the rescue. A map, for example, shows what gestures may not be able even to suggest.

Different types of presentational media can be effective illustrations of the spoken message. Showing a model of the human body or the inner ear serves a speaker much better than words and gestures. The same is true when the actual object the speaker is explaining is available, as is the case with the speaker you see here holding his fencing mask.

Generally speaking, the more abstract or unfamiliar something is, the more it begs to be illustrated visually. If you plan to speak on a topic that involves subjects for which the audience has only a vague reference, and gestures alone will not suffice, illustrative media can make these subjects more concrete for the audience.

Simplifying Spoken Examples

In the course of speaking or listening to a speaker, you may encounter verbal examples that are so complex they demand to be illustrated visually. Certainly this is the case with many informative speeches. For example, it is next to impossible to adequately explain the structure of DNA, the process of nuclear fission, or global warming without visual illustrations. It's not that words cannot convey the complexity of these phenomena but that they are ill suited to the task. Why make it difficult for your audience by trying to verbally explain what can be readily understood in a diagram or a model?

Our student Evan Mironov uses an actual object to illustrate his passion for fencing.

This photo of a mariachi band was used to complement an informative speech on Mexican traditions.

Complementing

Finally, presentational media frequently serve more than a single purpose. For example, such media may illustrate what we say and also serve to visually complement the general topic about which we are speaking. One of our international students gave an informative speech on Mexican traditions. In addition to sharing verbal content about these traditions, she visually complemented her speech by wearing traditional folk dress. An Indonesian student did much the same when she wore a Batik skirt for her speech about the arts and crafts of her home country.

A student from Los Angeles created what amounted to a visual theme to complement his informative speech on hiking the Appalachian Trail. He created a large backdrop using a visible and colorful trail map dry-mounted on tag board along with several large colored photos similarly mounted. He also first displayed and then put on the actual backpack he used on his trek over the trail. As he talked about where he trekked, the things he saw, and the gear needed, he used each of these as both an illustration and as an overall complement to his speech.

Although presentational media may serve other functions, the ones described here will help you decide which function is most likely to serve your purpose. Keep this in mind as we turn to selecting the visual medium most appropriate to you and the purpose your speech is designed to serve.

Criteria for Selecting the Right Medium

Which is better? A poster board or an overhead transparency? A photograph of an object? Or the object itself? The answer, of course, is that it depends. It depends on your topic and purpose. It depends on the context in which you are speaking, including any constraints you will face as a result of the physical context in which you speak. It depends on the nature of the content you plan on sharing with your audience. And it depends on your skill in using specific types of presentational media.

Context

Recall from Chapter 6 that before we make any final decisions about a speech we must first account for the rhetorical situation we will face. In that discussion we introduced you to the concept of rhetorical constraints; that is, factors that might limit your choices as a speaker. Simply put, the context in which you speak may limit the presentational media from which you can choose. Not all classrooms feature the technology necessary to effectively use PowerPoint. Some may not even be suited to the use of an overhead projector because there are physical obstacles blocking the audience's line of sight. Thus your first consideration in the process of deciding on a presentational medium for your speech involves any constraints you face as a result of the physical context in which you'll speak.

Content

After thinking through the demands of the context, we can begin to focus on the relationship between the content of the speech and the presentational media from which we can choose. Some kinds of information are better suited to visual media than others. Ask yourself, "What is the best possible way to convey what I hope to communicate to my audience?" To answer this question, consider the following kinds of visual information, which are especially well suited to the contemporary presentational media at your disposal.

Diagrams and Illustrations

Sometimes a diagram or drawing will serve your purpose better than a photograph. Diagrams are a good way to represent the parts of an object. For example, a cutaway drawing of a firearm can be used to explain its functional parts, and the diagram—unlike a real gun—is neither illegal nor dangerous. Figure 12.1 illustrates an abstract concept, electrical feedback, through the use of a diagram.

Charts, Graphs, and Maps

Often a speech calls for a particular kind of visual representation of numbers and statistics. Information such as the range of starting salaries among recent college graduates with different majors or the median wage for different occupations are best explained and understood when given visual life. Charts and graphs are helpful in this regard. Three types of charts and graphs particularly useful for depicting statistical information are pie charts, line graphs, and bar charts.

pie chart
A graphic often used to show proportions of a known quantity.

Pie Charts. A **pie chart** is a circular chart that divides a whole into several parts, each represented by a slice of the circle proportional to its share of the whole.

Figure 12.1

Sometimes a diagram is worth a thousand words. The concept of electronic feedback is depicted here.

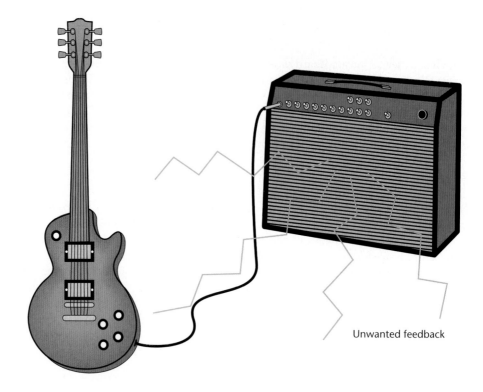

Unwanted feedback

Figure 12.2

Pie charts show the relative proportions of parts of a whole.

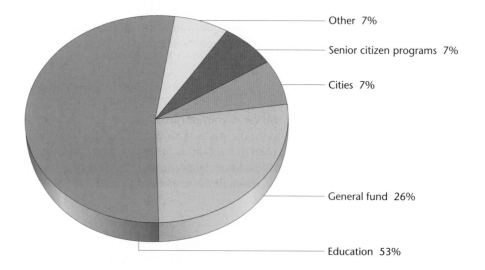

Percent Distribution of State Lottery Proceeds ($9 billion)

Other 7%

Senior citizen programs 7%

Cities 7%

General fund 26%

Education 53%

Figure 12.2 shows a typical pie chart, which represents the percentage distribution of state lottery proceeds in a specific year. The advantage of pie charts is that they simplify and dramatically illustrate the relative proportions of parts of a whole.

line graph

A graphic used to show points in time.

Line Graphs. Whereas pie charts are good for showing proportions, a **line graph** shows numerical data as a series of points connected by a line. Line graphs are

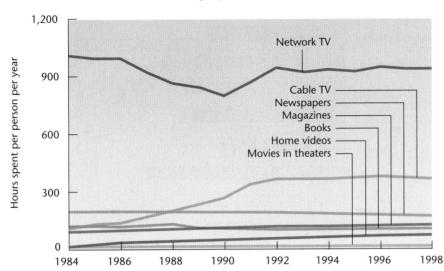

Figure 12.3
Line graphs show
changes over time.

convenient for showing changes over time; for example, Figure 12.3 shows changes in media use by consumers over a 15-year period. By using two or more lines with different colors, you can also show how two or more things compare across the same time period. Thus, if you want to compare spending on schools with spending on defense over the past 10 years, a line graph with two lines works well.

Bar Charts.　A **bar chart** uses filled-in vertical or horizontal bars to represent various quantities, as shown in Figure 12.4. By grouping two or more bars or by color-coding them, you can compare two or more categories. For example, the first bar chart in Figure 12.4 compares the participation of men and women in the 10 most popular sports in a given year. The other chart shows how per capita food consumption has changed over the period between 1970 and 1993. You can readily see that consumption of beef has declined while consumption of chicken and turkey has increased.

bar chart
A graphic used for comparing data side by side.

Organizational Charts.　The structure of an organization, including lines of authority, can be represented in an **organizational chart** like the one shown in Figure 12.5 onpage 299. Such charts are useful in business, industry, and governmental organizations. They might be given to new employees, and they are often part of an annual report to shareholders.

organizational chart
A graphic that illustrates hierarchical relationships.

Flowchart.　A **flowchart** uses boxes and arrows to represent the relationship of steps in a process. In other words, a flowchart shows how a process is carried out. For example, you might construct a flowchart like the one in Figure 12.6 on page 299 to illustrate the steps necessary in preparing a speech.

flowchart
A graphic designed to illustrate spatial relationships or the sequence of events in a process.

Text-Only Charts.　Sometimes a visual consists exclusively of text. For example, a speaker might copy the main points of a speech or the steps involved in a process onto an overhead transparency. Teachers commonly chart their lectures on overheads for students to follow. This textual material clues students to the major topics the teacher plans on covering.

Figure 12.4

Bar charts show various quantities. You can use them to compare two or more categories.

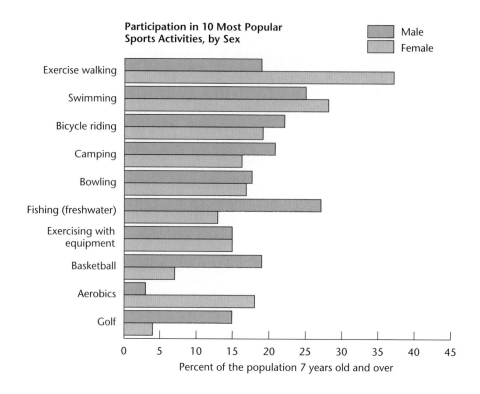

Participation in 10 Most Popular Sports Activities, by Sex

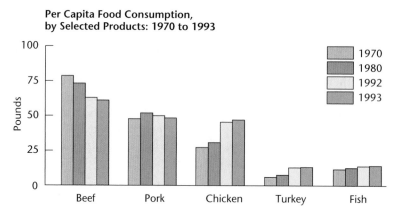

Per Capita Food Consumption, by Selected Products: 1970 to 1993

Maps. Whether a speaker is describing the spatial layout of an area, a dangerous intersection in town, or the disputed border between hostile nations, a map helps the audience orient themselves. Maps can also be used to describe a dynamic process such as a battle. At the site of the historic Civil War battle of Gettysburg, for example, numerous maps display various stages of the battle. One large-scale map uses embedded lights to show the daily progress of the battle.

Skill

Once we are confident about the content we plan on visualizing, we need to inventory our artistic and technical skills. What do we know about graphic design? And with which medium do we have the greatest familiarity? When it comes to

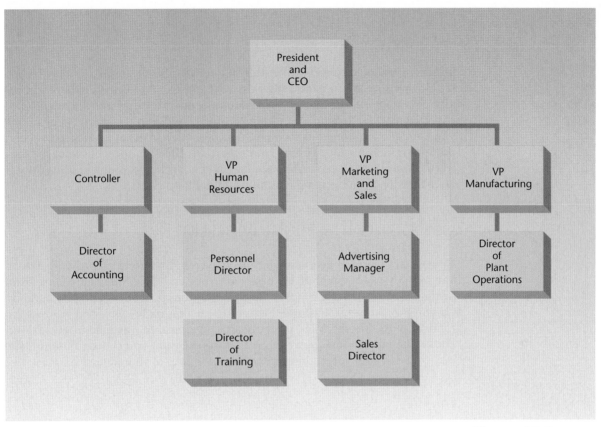

Figure 12.5
Organizational Chart

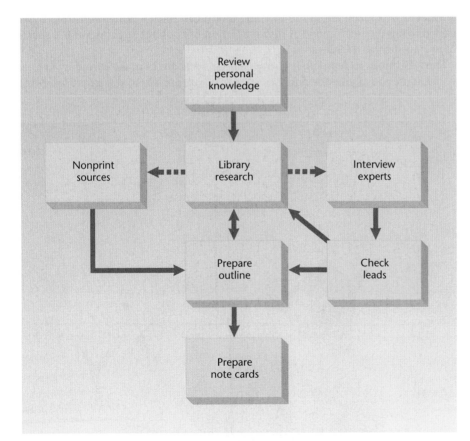

Figure 12.6
Flowchart Showing
Speech-Preparation
Steps

presentational media, we need to walk before we run. As a result, we may be better off choosing the simplest rather than the most sophisticated medium to visually complement our speech. For example, the fact that you have a ton of experience with a technology such as PowerPoint doesn't necessarily mean that you are skilled in using this medium to its best effect. We have watched students, professors, and businesspeople ruin otherwise effective speeches because they were "PowerPoint Crazy." Although they had no technical problem using Power-Point, they had trouble using it artfully and skillfully.

Choosing the Right Medium

Now we are ready to deliberate on the actual medium to use to visually extend and amplify what you hope to share with your audience. You can choose from media that are relatively simple to use such as objects, models, and photographs. Or you can choose from those that require increasing levels of skill such as flip charts, CD-ROMs or DVDs, poster boards, overhead transparencies, and Power-Point. The bottom line, however, is that the medium you choose should make both you and your speech more effective in the eyes of your audience.

Objects

In some cases, the object you are discussing in your speech is perfectly suited to your needs. A speech about the bagpipe might call for you to demonstrate by actually playing the instrument. A demonstration of cooking might require a special pot or pan such as a Chinese wok.

   The key things to remember about using objects are to make sure they are easily visible to your audience and that they are appropriate to the situation. Bring-

A speech on injury prevention can be greatly enhanced with the actual safety appliance, in this case a bicycle helmet.

ing a car inside your classroom for a speech about proper vehicle maintenance isn't possible, but you could use oil and air filters to emphasize the role both play in keeping a car on the road.

Before you bring any object into the classroom, be sure to get the approval of your instructor. The use of inappropriate objects can create problems. Every semester it seems that we have students who not only want to speak about firearms but bring one along as a visual aid. We also seem to have more than a few students who want to share their love of wine with students, including samples of their favorites. For obvious reasons, firearms are prohibited on our campus (except for those carried by campus police). So too is alcohol. Thus we insist that our students tell us in advance both their topic and any objects they plan on using in relationship to it.

Models

A three-dimensional model of an object may be used when it is impractical to use the actual object. One of our students spoke on the common American cockroach. Bringing live cockroaches to the classroom would have been disconcerting, to say the least. Instead, she cleverly constructed a large-scale model of a cockroach that she kept hidden in a box until just the right moment–when she revealed the topic of her speech. Not only was her speech informative and entertaining, it was also enhanced by her ability to explain her subject vividly using the model. Another student spoke on fly-fishing. Tying a fly with actual fish line would have been invisible to the audience, but the large-scale model he constructed out of coat hangers and yarn worked perfectly.

Flip Charts

There are two types of **flip charts;** one is basically text, and the other is for recording ideas as participants generate them. Although less common than they once were, flip charts are still used in business seminars. Typically, the speaker writes down what she wants to share ahead of time and reveals the information as her presentation progresses. To control the pace of delivery, the speaker may use blank sheets between points so the audience stays on the topic under consideration. Are flip charts a good medium for you and your purposes? They can be cumbersome, especially for those unaccustomed to using them. The pages can prove difficult to flip and require you to temporarily break off direct eye contact with your audience. They also require legible writing and minimum artistic skill if drawn on.

If you must use a flip chart to write or draw on, be sure the paper is thick enough that your writing or drawing will not bleed through to the next page. Better yet, prepare the flip chart well in advance of your speech, making sure you follow the guidelines stated here and in the rules of the road explained later in this chapter.

flip chart
Large tablet used to preview the outline of a presentation or to record information generated by an audience.

Photographs and Slides

Sometimes a picture is worth a thousand words. You may want to use personal photographs or those taken from another source to illustrate an example or as a complement to a point you make. To be effective, a photograph needs to be seen. In most cases this requires that a photograph be large enough to be seen by audience members in the back of the room.

For an actual photograph, enlarge and dry-mount it on poster board or foam core. Digital images need to be projected electronically. This usually is accomplished with a computer connected to an LCD projector or video monitor. If neither of these suggestions works for you, you can also enlarge a photograph and copy it onto an overhead transparency.

Slides are problematic. To be clearly seen, 35 mm slides require a special projector and screen. The main problem, however, is that slides must be shown in a darkened room, which impedes the audience's view of the speaker. It also makes the speaker secondary to the slide show, which is the opposite of what we want to happen.

If 35 mm slides are essential to your speech, we recommend that you import the slides to a computer or have them transferred to a CD-ROM. Then you can use a computer linked to an LCD projector or video monitor and show them without having to turn off the lights.

Audio

audio media
Aural channels you can use to augment your speech, such as a recording of a famous speaker.

Audio media such as a cassette tape or CD reproduce sounds you can incorporate in your speech. One of the laptop computers we use in our own classes includes Apple iTunes. This software allows us to add music as well as excerpts from speeches for our students to hear. We often talk about how Martin Luther King Jr. used repetition in his speeches to influence an audience. With the click of a mouse, iTunes allows students to actually listen to King's use of the technique.

The decision to use audio media in a speech rests on two factors. As is always the case, you must first conclude that it will make your speech better. We are fortunate enough to have at our fingertips both the software and the technology to use audio to improve our lectures. You may not. The second factor that goes into the decision to use audio is whether you can use it unobtrusively. Otherwise, it has as much chance to hurt as to help you.

Video

Another presentational medium is video, which can be imported from a tape, DVD, or mini-DV. Video is increasingly being used to augment speeches and presentations at corporate gatherings, at political conventions, in courtrooms, and in classrooms. Using video effectively in a speech requires both technological support and technological savvy. Video is not an option unless the context in which you are speaking is designed and equipped to easily show it. Further, unless you are knowledgeable in the use of the equipment or have support personnel who will supply you with video as needed, you should not even consider it.

All too frequently beginning speakers fail to consider the details of using video in a speech. Simply because they have access to a means of showing video (such as a playback device and monitor), beginning speakers decide to use it without first thinking about these issues:

- Cueing it ahead of time, including monitoring the sound level
- Lighting
- The distance between the means of showing it and its proximity to the audience

- The time it takes to introduce, show, and integrate the video with the remainder of the speech

Simply put, we do not recommend using video in a speech until giving speeches and using less demanding presentational media are second nature. We understand how easy it is to get excited about using a segment from a film or TV show to make a point, but it just isn't very practical in an introductory speech course.

Poster Boards, Overheads, and PowerPoint

Of the presentational media currently used by public speakers, poster boards, overheads, and PowerPoint are far and away the most common both in and out of the classroom. The latter two are also the most frequently misused. Because you are most likely to choose one of these three either now or in the future for a speech, let's look at them in more depth.

Poster Board

Poster board is one of the most common mediums used by students for their speeches. A well-drawn and lettered poster board can significantly enhance an audience's response to a speech. By the same token, poorly drawn or lettered poster boards detract from both the speaker's credibility and the content of the speech.

Poster boards are well suited to speakers who are just learning to complement their content and delivery with visual media. You can draw diagrams and charts on poster board, and you can use poster board to mount illustrations, photographs, and maps. No matter how you use poster boards, however, take care both in their construction and in how you display them as you deliver your speech.

Poster boards are commonly used for informative speeches, as this speaker demonstrates.

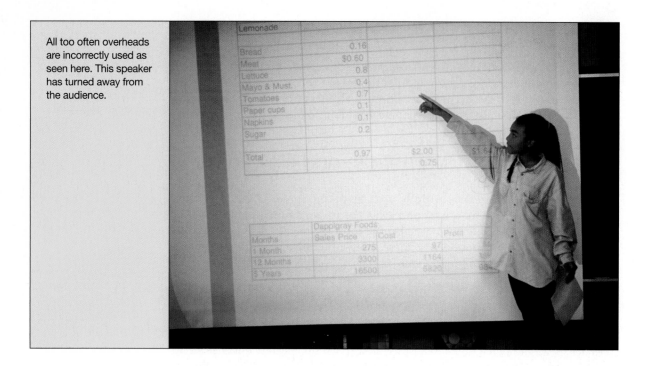

All too often overheads are incorrectly used as seen here. This speaker has turned away from the audience.

As is the case with any presentational medium, poster boards should add something to your speech that would otherwise be missing. Construct them in as professional a manner as possible. This doesn't mean that you have to hire a graphic artist, but it does mean taking advantage of these basic guidelines.

- Draw illustrations, diagrams, or charts with colored marking pens.
- Use rub-on letters and numerals for your text.
- Use colored poster board only if it contrasts markedly with the lettering you use.
- Choose very sturdy poster board, preferably with a foam core.

Flimsy posters have a tendency to curl up or fall over at the most inopportune times as you deliver your speech. Be sure to put your posters on an easel that is high enough to be visible to all of your audience. Finally, remember to cover your posters until you are ready to talk about them, revealing each one as you get to the point it reinforces. When you are done with a poster, either move to the next one or cover it up.

Overheads

overhead transparency
A visual depiction that can be projected.

In a sense, **overhead transparencies** simply are posters made of plastic and projected with a light source. As a result, overhead transparencies make the same set of demands on the user as poster boards. Overheads are a popular medium in business and classroom presentations. They have the advantage of low cost and ease of preparation, and they can be used without dimming the lights too much. Many classrooms and business conference rooms have overhead projectors, although you should always check in advance to make sure a projector is available and working. Also be sure to check out the equipment in advance because you may be unfamiliar with the operational features of a projector.

Speaking of . . .

PowerPoint Poisoning

Too much PowerPoint can be like too much of anything else—deadly, at least to your audience. Even in business the heads of some corporations are telling their subordinates to use this technology sparingly.[1] Here are some common pitfalls of PowerPoint use you'll want to avoid:

- **Too many slides.** We've seen PowerPoint presentations where almost every couple of sentences the speaker shifts to a new slide. Trying to keep up with what is being said and what is being shown is impossible.

- **Too much detail on slides.** Use key words, phrases, and visuals, not full sentences. We've seen speakers put virtually every word in their manuscript overhead. It left us wondering, what is the point of having a speaker?

- **Too much razzle-dazzle.** PowerPoint's special effects are "cool," but not necessarily helpful. If you

let them take over the show, you will be ignored as a speaker.

- **Too little focus on the speaker.** There have been times when normal delivery skills have been forgotten as a speaker focuses attention solely on the slides. No matter what visuals you use, ultimately it is you, the speaker, who is responsible for making your presentation engaging.

- **PowerPoint used when it shouldn't be.** Not *every* speech calls for a PowerPoint presentation. Imagine a wedding toast with PowerPoint. It just doesn't make sense. Make sure if you use PowerPoint that it really is necessary. If not, leave it out!

[1] Joe Downing and Cecile C. Garmon, "Teaching Students in the Basic Course How to Use Presentational Software," *Communication Education, 50* (2001): 218–29.

Overheads have many advantages, but not all speakers put them to good use. Instructors are notorious for writing illegibly on them or cramming them with so much information that they make your eyes blur. Speakers also can absent-mindedly block their audience's view of the projected overhead by standing over the projector or standing between the projector and the screen on which the image is displayed. Finally, a common mistake is for the speaker to either leave the projector on with no image to project, or to continue projecting a transparency with which the speaker is finished. Audience members are a little like the moth and the flame in this regard. They have a tough time taking their eyes off what is projected, even if it is simply a lighted but blank screen. Remember to always turn off the projector when it isn't in use. Be sure as well either to turn it off when you are between points or to keep upcoming points covered until you are ready to reveal them. What we said about poster boards is equally true of overheads: You'll need to practice care in both their construction and how you display them as you deliver your speech.

PowerPoint

Influential media critic Marshall McLuhan warned more than 30 years ago that new technologies sooner or later reveal their negative side and turn against you.[2] Although he didn't live long enough to see PowerPoint become the leading presentational tool for speakers in both the private and public sectors of the economy, he wouldn't be surprised that it also does more harm than good in the speeches of the unskilled and undisciplined user.

Information theorist Edward Tufte believes PowerPoint leads both its user and the audience to oversimplify the subject matter of an informative speech, especially. By encouraging speakers to reduce presentations to a bulleted list, for example, Tufte argues that speakers lose sight of the string that should tie together

SpeechCoach

For help in creating PowerPoint presentations, see the PowerPoint Tutorial on your CD.

PowerPoint can be an effective complement to your speech, but it should not replace the speech itself. This slide, for example, conveys too much information.

SpeechCoach

You can see Shelly Lee's speech and her use of PowerPoint on your CD. See segment 12.2.

for their audience the connections among these bulleted lists. In turn audience members form an inaccurate impression of the topic under consideration, including its larger ramifications for their lives.[3]

We do not disagree with Tufte's thesis, but we have seen another downside to this presentational tool. That is, the speaker not only seems to have a PowerPoint slide to accompany his or her every thought but the speaker also has taken advantage of nearly every feature the software offers. Rather than providing too little for an audience to digest, the speaker overindulges in the use of graphics, clip art, sound effects, and animation. Thus the technology gets in the way of the substance that needs to be communicated in the speech.

We are not opposed to the disciplined and creative use of this specific presentational medium. As we said earlier, we use it in our lectures. But we use it as support rather than as a substitute for our presence and the substance of our remarks. Put simply, unless we are selling the presentational medium we are using, it should make our speech and us more credible in the eyes of our audiences. Otherwise a class in public speaking becomes a class in the use of instructional media. The sample speech in the box Go Sun Smart illustrates how a PowerPoint presentation can enhance a speech.

Rules for the Road

Handed a script, filmmakers don't simply pick up a 35 mm camera and begin shooting. They start with a series of storyboards on which they begin to sketch out individual shots and scenes. Important as presentational media can be to a speech, it's even more important that we first learn to use a medium that will teach us easily learned principles of basic graphic design.[4] As a result, we encourage our own students to learn how to construct and use a well-put-together poster board before working with overheads or PowerPoint. What's good for poster boards, we point out to them, tends to be good for overheads and PowerPoint as well. With that in mind, remember these seven basic principles when creating everything from a flip chart to a PowerPoint slide: [5]

- Check out media prep services.
- Keep it simple.
- Make it visible.
- Lay it out sensibly.
- Use color.
- When in doubt . . . Leave it out.
- Plan ahead.

Check Out Media Prep Services

Our campus features a media prep center where students can get help in preparing professional looking media, including the diverse types we've discussed here. Students majoring in graphic design, instructional technology, and media arts staff the center and share their creative skills with students who need help preparing posters, overheads, PowerPoint presentations, and audio or video editing. We encourage our students to take advantage of this helpful and educational service.

If similar services are available on your campus, consider using them for your media needs. If not, look to local businesses that can help you produce professional looking media at minimal costs. Most of the people working in the design business, moreover, will give you valuable tips and provide you with examples of overheads and the like even if you do not use their services.

Keep It Simple

A common tendency is to put too much information on a single visual. We have seen people simply take a page from a magazine and copy it onto an overhead transparency. Some students try to save a few dollars by putting two or three ideas on one poster. These strategies undermine the effectiveness of visual media. In an age where we are constantly being bombarded by messages, *less is often more*. The best advice we can give you is to keep your visual media simple.

Tips and Tactics

Using Words and Numbers

- Limit yourself to one idea per visual medium.
- Use no more than six words per line.
- Use no more than six lines per visual medium.
- Use short, familiar words and round numbers.
- Keep charts and graphs simple enough to be sketched easily by your audience.

SpeechCoach
To hear more about these Tips and Tactics, go to Audio Tips and Tactics on your CD.

Make It Visible

If your audience can't see your visuals, instead of listening to you, they will be straining to see or asking a neighbor what's on the screen.

Tips and Tactics

Increasing Visibility

- Make your images at least 1 inch high for every 30 feet of viewing distance.
- Do not block your audience's view of the visual as you show it during the speech. Many PowerPoint projectors, for example, allow you to use a remote device to advance your slides so you can stand away from the projector.
- Make sure the visual can be seen by everyone in the audience. Use a tall easel with posters and photos and project PowerPoint slides or overheads high enough on the screen to be visible to everyone.

In Their Own Words

Sample Speech Outline

GO SUN SMART
by Shelly Lee

General purpose: To inform
Specific purpose: To inform the audience how to protect themselves from deadly skin cancer.

Introduction

I. **Open with impact:** How many of you can remember a sunburn so bad you could barely put your clothes on? How many of you have simply been burned while spending the day at the beach, tubing on the river, water skiing at the lake, or even skiing or riding your board on a fresh powder day at your favorite mountain?
   A. Did you know that there are over 1 million new cases of skin cancer each year in the United States, including over 51,000 cases of melanoma (Kalb, 2001)?
   B. Did you know that many of these cases can be directly linked to the cumulative effects of the sun?
   C. Did you know that there is no such thing as a safe tan, despite what the indoor tanning industry would like you to believe (Young and Walker, 1998)?
II. **Connect with audience:** Every one of you who raised your hand needs to know that those sunburns you got put you at increased risk for skin cancer. Further, even if you've never burned or you are dark skinned, the information I'll share in a moment is important to you as well.
III. **Thesis:** Skin cancer is not only the fastest growing form of cancer in the United States, it also is one of the easiest forms of cancer to prevent (American Cancer Society, 1996).
IV. **Preview:** As a result, I'd like to look at three important things we all need to know to reduce our risk for skin cancer. First, there are three basic forms of skin cancer. Second, skin cancer is all too often a by-product of too much fun in the sun. And third, you can reduce your risk for developing skin cancer by following some easy steps.

Body

I. There are three types of skin cancer: basal cell, squamous, and melanoma (Kalb, 2001).
   A. Basal cell is the most common and easily treated and is rarely life threatening.
   B. Squamous cell cancer is the next most common, and it too is easily treated and seldom fatal unless completely unattended.
   C. Melanoma, which is the form of skin cancer Maureen Reagan died from, is increasing at an alarming rate in the United States. It is deadly if not treated early in its growth.

(**Signpost:** So what causes skin cancer?)

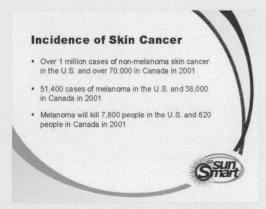

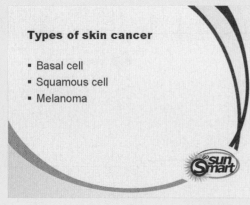

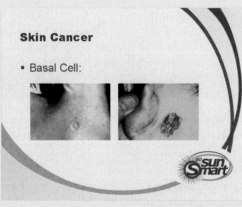

II. Much as we may like the sun, too much of this good thing is bad for us.
   A. The sun's rays contain ultraviolet radiation.
   B. Science has linked ultraviolet radiation from the sun with basal cell and squamous cell skin cancer (Kalb, 2001).
      1. Scientists at the National Cancer Institute also believe that ultraviolet radiation is linked to melanoma, although the relationship is not as clear (Kalb, 2001).
      2. Melanoma can show up anywhere on the skin and can develop in even dark-skinned people.
      3. For example, did you know that Bob Marley died from melanoma skin cancer?
   C. As few as three severe sunburns in childhood put you at increased risk for skin cancer.

(**Signpost:** Even though the incidence of skin cancer is increasing, you have considerable control over this risk.)

III. The American Cancer Society and the American Dermatological Association have developed some simple guidelines to follow: (American Cancer Society, 1996)
   A. Avoid the sun between 10 A.M. and 4 P.M. when possible.
   B. Always wear a sunscreen with sun protection factor of 15 or better, and wear sun-protective clothing such as a wide-brimmed hat, long-sleeved shirt, and long pants.
   C. Know the early warning signs of skin cancer, which are *A* for *asymmetry, B* for irregular *borders,* and *C* for irregular *color* on moles and freckles especially.
   D. Finally, give yourself a full body check every six months or have someone do it for you.

(**Signpost:** In conclusion)

Conclusion

I. **Summarize:** Remember these important facts:
   A. Skin cancer comes in three types: basal, squamous, and melanoma.
   B. Also, keep in mind that while we need the sun, a little sunning is actually a lot.
   C. Finally, be sun smart by practicing sun-safe behaviors such as those suggested by the ADA.
II. **Close with impact:** Skin cancer can kill. With a little common sense, however, it is easily prevented. Please be sun smart.

References

American Cancer Society (1996). *Cancer facts and figures.* Atlanta, GA: The American Cancer Society.

Kalb, C. (2001, August 20). Overexposed. *Newsweek,* 35–38.

Young, J. C. and Walker, R. (1998). Understanding students' indoor tanning beliefs and practices, *American Journal of Health Studies, 14,* 120–128.

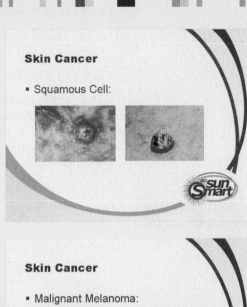

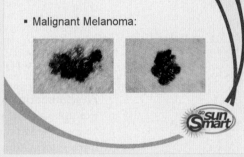

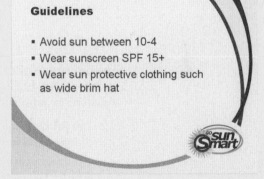

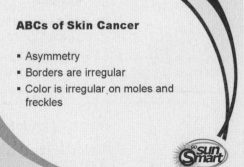

Lay It Out Sensibly

An organized, consistent, and uncluttered layout is necessary for an effective visual. One of the great advantages of visual media produced by computer programs, such as PowerPoint, is that the templates are designed for an effective layout depending on the speech purpose. That's also one of the reasons inexperienced speakers are tempted to use them before they should.

Tips and Tactics

Laying Out Information and Graphics

- Place images near the top of your visual to ensure maximum visibility.
- Accentuate key points with **bold type,** underlining, or a contrasting color
- Make sure text is horizontal, not vertical. Vertical writing is difficult to read.
- Leave generous margins, larger on top than bottom, and equal on the sides.
- Present information from left to right and from top to bottom. For example, a chart showing progression over time should have the oldest year on the left and the most recent year on the right, not vice versa. If the information is presented vertically, the oldest year should be at the top and the most recent on the bottom.

Use Color

The proper use of color helps your audience pay attention, comprehend, and remember your visuals. As you begin to consider color and its place in making your visuals more powerful, follow these guidelines.

- Use primary colors–red, blue, and yellow–which have been shown to create the strongest impact.
- Use contrasting but complementary colors so that your audience can see clearly. Yellow lettering on a white background, for example, is almost invisible.
- Use colored backgrounds as long as the color is not so dark that the message is hard to see. Colored backgrounds are more visually soothing.
- Don't use clashing or confusing colors. For example, don't use red to show profits and black to show losses.

When in Doubt . . . Leave It Out

This rule should come as no surprise given our previous remarks. As we've repeatedly said, you should only use presentational media when they truly add something to your speech. This is true of the content of a poster board, overhead, or PowerPoint slide. Always ask yourself whether a graphic or bit of text is absolutely necessary to achieve your speech purpose. If you have doubts, then the graphic or text can probably be left out.

Plan Ahead

As Murphy's Law reminds us, no plan is foolproof. Even so, only fools would try to integrate media with their speech without planning ahead. At a minimum, consider these recommendations, which we emphasize with our students.

Tips and Tactics

Using Presentational Media

Before your speech:

- Check the room and your equipment.
- Practice, if possible, with the same equipment in the same room where you will give your speech.
- Double-check your presentational media immediately before the speech. For example, make sure posters, overheads, or slides are in the proper order, right side up, and ready to go.
- Allow ample time for setup and takedown.

During the speech:

- Avoid distractions—cover or remove visuals and turn off projectors when not in use.
- Do not block the audience's view.
- Allow the audience enough time (at least 10 seconds) to process the information, then remove the visual.
- Talk to your audience, not to the visual.

Avoiding Common Mistakes

The rules of the road should help you avoid the most common mistakes we see in the presentational media of not just students but also many teachers and business professionals: overreliance on visual media, sometimes to the point of overkill; too much information crammed on a single hard-to-see visual; or the wrong type of presentational media to achieve the purpose

Overreliance on Visual Media

Once again, remember that presentational media, no matter how well constructed or technologically sophisticated, are no substitute for the skill of a speaker. Presentational media will not hide a speaker's lack of skill or lack of preparation. In fact, because the effective use of presentational media is a skill in itself, overreliance on presentational media is likely to call attention to, rather than disguise, any weaknesses in other areas.

Too Much Hard-to-See Information

Chances are you have attended a lecture where nearly every word the instructor utters appears on a series of overhead transparencies. Such a common mistake not only defeats the purpose of a transparency but also produces other unintended and undesirable consequences. First, the overhead causes eyestrain because the writing or print is difficult to see. Second, students are likely to bury their heads in their notebooks as they try to copy the overheads verbatim rather than focusing on their instructor. Thus students miss many of the nonverbal nuances of the instructor's remarks, which would aid their understanding. The same is true for a speaker who crams too much information onto a poster board, overhead, or PowerPoint slide.

Using the Wrong Type of Presentational Aid

The type of presentational medium you select should match the function it is meant to perform. Before you decide on a specific presentational medium, always ask yourself: "What is its purpose—what do I hope to gain from its use?" Next, ask yourself whether using the medium is absolutely necessary. All too often students choose and create a visual because it is required, without thinking through whether the visual both meets the requirement and adds something worthwhile to the speech's audience impact.

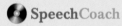

SpeechCoach

To evaluate your understanding of this chapter, see the Quizzes on your CD.

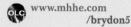

www.mhhe.com /brydon5

Visit the Online Learning Center for helpful study resources, including practice tests, key term crossword puzzles, and PowerWeb articles for research and review.

Summary

Properly used, presentational media can make the difference between a successful speech and a failure. Improperly used, they can undermine your purpose.

- Think of presentational media as extensions of your senses that can amplify your message.

- Use presentational media for signposting, cueing, illustrating the spoken word, simplifying the spoken word, and complementing.

- Choose presentational media carefully, using context, content, and skill as criteria to help you decide which will work best for your purpose.

- Match content with the appropriate medium; for example, use visual media such as pie charts and bar graphs to show statistical data.

- Consider all presentational media, but also be cautious about using presentational media that are overly technical or so dependent on technology that you have little room for error.

- Consider mastering the use of actual objects and models, if appropriate, before relying on media you will have to create on your own.

- Learn to walk before trying to run; poster boards may be a better beginning than overheads or PowerPoint.

- Follow the rules of the road. Keep presentational media simple, visible, easy to read, and colorful. Remember: When in doubt . . . leave it out.

- Give the audience at least 10 seconds to process presentational media.

- Be aware that presentational media may complement your speech, but they can never take your place or achieve your purpose and goals.

Check Your Understanding: Exercises and Activities

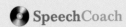

SpeechCoach

For a review of key terms in this chapter, see the Key Terms Flashcards on your CD.

1. Check on your campus or at local copy shops to find out where you can have the following made: black-on-clear overhead transparencies, color overhead transparencies, enlarged photographs.

2. Find out where on campus you can obtain an overhead projector, and find out who can answer questions about its operation. Learn how to turn it on and off, how to focus it, and what to do if the bulb burns out.

3. Find an example of a bar chart, a pie chart, a line graph, and a map in *USA Today* or your local newspaper, and describe whether each one would make a suitable visual for a speech. Evaluate them in terms of simplicity, size and visibility, layout, and color.

4. Contact the computer center at your college or university. What, if any, services are available to help you prepare computer graphics for your speeches? If you own or have access to a computer, go to a computer dealer or consult a software catalog and find at least three presentation graphics programs available for your computer.

5. Consider the following speech situations: an informative speech on the impressionist movement in art; an informative speech on a country you have visited; a persuasive speech about health insurance in the United States; a speech to entertain on the topic of traveling by train, plane, or automobile. What types of visual media would be most appropriate for each speech situation, and why?

Notes

1. "The New Networking," *The Economist,* 7 August 2004: 53.
2. Marshall McLuhan and Quentin Fiore, *The Medium Is the Massage* (New York: Bantam Books, 1967), 26–41.
3. John Schwartz, "Ideas & Trends; The Level of Discourse Continues to Slide" [Retrieved from LexisNexis Academic, 25 August 2004] (*New York Times,* 20 September 2003, 4:12).
4. Joe Downing and Cecile C. Garmon, "Teaching Students in the Basic Course How to Use Presentational Software," *Communication Education,* 50 (2001): 218–29.
5. Several of these suggestions are taken from Minnesota Western, *Visual Presentation Systems* (Oakland, Calif.: Minnesota Western, 1988–1989).

4

Contexts for Public Speaking

Jaime Escalante motivated his students to achieve through the power of *ganas*, the desire to succeed, as he taught them the skills necessary to succeed in mathematics.

Chapter 13

Informative Speaking

Objectives

After reading this chapter and reviewing the learning resources on your CD-ROM and at the Online Learning Center, you should be able to:

- Explain how to adapt your informative speech to audiences with diverse learning styles.

- Explain the relationship between informative speaking and learning.

- Prepare an informative speech that is audience involving, audience appropriate, audience accessible, and potentially life enhancing.

- Prepare informative speeches that explain, instruct, demonstrate, or describe processes, concepts, and skills.

- Illustrate how informative speaking can be used in your other classes, at work, and in your community.

Key Concepts

audience accessible

audience appropriate

audience involving

ganas

informative speaking

learning styles

> " Determination plus hard work plus concentration equals success, which equals *ganas*. "
>
> –JAIME ESCALANTE[1]

Jaime Escalante, whose picture you see in the opening photograph, is not simply a gifted teacher. He is a remarkable person. He immigrated to the United States from Bolivia in 1969, where he had taught mathematics and physics. He spoke not a single word of English. But Escalante had what he called **ganas**–that is, a desire to succeed regardless of the odds against it. Thus at age 30 he reentered school to work toward his teaching credential, even though it meant subjecting his out-of-shape body to a required course in P.E.

The rest of the story, of course, is probably well known to you. Escalante's life became the subject of the critically acclaimed film *Stand and Deliver.* In the movie, actor Edward James Olmos portrays Escalante, who took East Los Angeles barrio students who could barely do simple math and, in two years of intensive work, prepared them for the Advanced Placement Test in Calculus. His students were so successful that all 18 who attempted the test in 1982 passed, the most from any high school in Southern California. Each year more students passed; by 1987, 87 of his students passed the exam. Remember, these were students who were not expected to attend college, let alone receive college credit for calculus while still in high school. But as Escalante says, "Students will rise to the level of expectations." When students wanted to quit, Escalante would challenge them by saying, "Do you have the *ganas?* Do you have the desire?"[2]

Although there are many reasons Escalante was able to overcome odds others would have perceived as insurmountable, we think his success in life as well as in the classroom can be found in that word of his: *ganas.* Not only did Escalante have it when he needed it, but also his life is testimony to the fact that he has instilled it in many of his students. As a result, they too have succeeded.

In a sense, this chapter is about *ganas.* Like Jaime Escalante, the best informative speakers do more than simply pass on information to an audience. With their

French Open doubles and Wimbledon doubles champion and teaching professional Sandy Mayer instructs students using the principles of informative speaking.

words and actions, they create a desire in their audience to put the information to constructive use. In the case of Escalante, the desire involved a subject that many students prefer to avoid: mathematics. In yours, it may involve anything from how we treat our environment to the kind of foods we eat.

Informative speaking is the process by which an audience gains new information or a new perspective on old information from a speaker. Put another way, the goal of informative speaking is audience learning. An effective informative speaker needs to master several skills, which we will look at in this chapter. These skills include:

- Focusing on the audience and appealing to their various styles of learning
- Understanding the relationship between informative speaking and learning
- Making the message audience involving, audience appropriate, audience accessible, and potentially life enhancing
- Putting theory into practice in speeches that explain, instruct, demonstrate, or describe
- Understanding the differences and similarities among the forums in which you are likely to give informative presentations: namely, the classroom, the workplace, and the community

informative speaking
The process by which an audience gains new information or a new perspective on old information.

Focusing on the Audience: Adapting to Different Styles of Learning

Consider the following scenarios. In the first, a high school principal goes before the student body to explain the school board's decision to install metal detectors and surveillance cameras on campus. In the second, a doctor demonstrates to a group of nurses how to use a new skin test for food allergies. In the third, an offensive line coach teaches linemen a new offensive scheme they will use in their next football game. In the fourth, a driving instructor at a high-performance racing school explains the concept of heel-and-toe braking and shifting as a driver prepares to enter a turn on a road course. And in the fifth, a tennis pro explains how to improve your serve.

Each of these scenarios can be viewed as a speaking situation. Further, each involves a speaker publicly *informing* an audience. In each case, the speaker must focus on relating the information to the needs and goals of the audience members. Jaime Escalante had to first reach out to and connect with his students before he could really begin to teach them calculus. So, too, must every informative speaker reach out to and connect with his or her audience before presenting them with information.

Informative Speaking and Styles of Learning

One important consideration in focusing on the audience is recognizing that not everyone has the same style of learning. Not everybody thinks in a linear or "logical" fashion. Some people can simply read a book and absorb the information, whereas others need to hear and see to learn. Still others learn best by doing. Good public speakers recognize these differences and appeal to as many styles as possible. One list of diverse **learning styles** was developed by Barbara Solomon

learning styles
Differences in the way people think about and learn new information and skills.

and Richard Felder of North Carolina State University, who identify four different dimensions:[3]

- Active-reflective
- Sensing-intuitive
- Visual-verbal
- Sequential-global

The first dimension, *active-reflective,* is basically the difference between those who learn best by doing and those who learn best by thinking. As speakers, we need to realize that our audience will include both types of learners. If we incorporate activities, group discussions, and opportunities for questions, we can reach active learners who would otherwise be bored listening to us speak. At the same time, simply having learners do something, without any explanation of the principles underlying the activity, can be frustrating to reflective learners. Audience members can vary from one topic or occasion to another in terms of which style they prefer. Speakers need to appeal to both learning styles, even if they have reason to believe their audience is predominately of one type or the other.

The second dimension, *sensing-intuitive,* has to do with the differences between those who like to learn lots of specific facts and those who are more intuitive and like to focus on relationships. Sensors are more likely to listen to our speech if we can show the real-world application of what we are saying. At the same time, intuitors are likely to be unhappy with having to memorize lots of facts and details. Thus in our speeches we need a balance between factual content and general relationships. Recognize that people are not totally in one camp or the other, so a middle ground is probably most useful in most speeches.

With respect to the *visual-verbal* dimension, it probably comes as no surprise that some people are more likely to remember what they see and others what they hear. We strongly encourage the use of visual media in speeches where the content can be represented visually. The best way to ensure learning is to combine both visual and verbal methods, appealing to people from both camps and providing maximum reinforcement to all members of the audience.

The final dimension, *sequential-global,* is particularly relevant in deciding how to organize a speech. Sequential learners tend to learn best when information is presented in a linear fashion. When Jaime Escalante used a "step-by-step" method to teach calculus, that's exactly what he was doing. Global learners, on the other hand, often can't follow the step-by-step approach but will finally see the big picture and "get it" suddenly. Pick an organizational structure that meets the needs of sequential learners but is also useful to global learners. Repetition can be important in a speech to aid learners who may not get the point the first time. Also, summaries and restatement of the main points may be essential for such learners.

Most people are somewhere between the extremes of these learning styles. The crucial thing for us to remember as informative speakers is that not everyone learns the same way; we should provide as many different avenues for our audience to learn our material as we possibly can.

One speech we heard, for example, was about using acupressure to relieve stress. By instructing the class to press on certain points on their bodies, the speaker allowed the audience to use their sense of touch to understand what was being said. Other speakers appeal to the sense of taste. We frequently have international students speak about a food unique to their culture and bring samples for the audience to try. We have also seen student speakers involve their audiences in a group exercise to better appreciate the subject on which they are speaking. Specific examples include a speaker asking fellow students to model the simple yoga poses he first demonstrated, and a student who was blind talking in the dark for part of her speech, so that sighted students might better appreciate what she experienced when listening to a lecture.

Informative Speaking and Persuasion

As your own experience tells you, exposure to new information or a new perspective doesn't guarantee that you will learn it. No matter how convinced a teacher is of the importance of his or her subject matter, there is no guarantee students will share the teacher's conviction. So it is with informative speeches. Before we attempt to explain, describe, or demonstrate something to our audience, we must first connect with the self-interest of the audience. Then, and only then, will the audience be sufficiently motivated to listen to what we have to say.

Given this framework, you might ask, "How is informative speaking different from persuasive speaking?" There is no simple answer to this question. It is a matter of degree and purpose. The purpose of an informative speech is to provide people with knowledge from which they can potentially benefit. Suggesting to audience members that the information we are sharing can potentially benefit them, however, is not the same as trying to persuade them that they should change their attitudes, values, or behaviors toward the information. For example, informing people about the advantages of carrying a well-stocked emergency kit in their cars is not the same as trying to persuade them that the emergency kit you just happen to be selling for $29.95 is the *best* kit on the market.

Informative Speaking and Audience Analysis

In Chapter 6 we discussed how to analyze an audience in terms of cultural, demographic, and individual diversity. As we prepare our informative speeches, it is important to pay special attention to the results of such an analysis. For example, because the purpose of informative speaking is to increase audience knowledge, we need to know what our audience already knows about our topic. If they already know most of what we plan to say, then the speech will bore them. On the other hand, if they are clueless about the topic and we launch into a jargon-filled technical presentation, they will be lost.

Audience culture is equally important for informative speakers. For example, in the movie *Stand and Deliver,* one of the biggest challenges Jaime Escalante faced was the perception by Latino and Latina students that learning math would have no impact on their lives. Because he shared the culture, he makes a point in one scene of talking about how their ancestors, the Mayans, were more mathematically advanced than the Greeks or Romans, who lacked the concept of zero. Escalante says to his students, "you . . . have math in your blood." At another point he called "math the great equalizer" that would enable his students to succeed despite prejudice against them in society.

Age is another important factor to consider, particularly if it differs greatly from our own. Many older students have taken our classes, and sometimes they need reassurance that they can master the material. Similarly, as we continue to get older while our students for the most part remain 18–22 years old, we find that we must constantly remind ourselves that experiences we remember vividly may be only historical footnotes to our students. For example, the space shuttle *Challenger* exploded shortly after launch in 1986. Although that event is as vivid in our minds as if it had occurred yesterday, we have to remember that the students who read this book are unlikely to have even been born in 1986. On the other hand, they are likely to vividly remember the space shuttle *Columbia,* which disintegrated on re-entry in 2003. One example would be effective with an older audience, the other with a younger one.

We also need to carefully analyze our audience's beliefs, attitudes, and values for informative speeches as well as for persuasive speeches. For example, a biology major spoke to the class about how the theory of evolution should be taught in public schools. For most audiences, and certainly for students in his major, this was perceived as an informative presentation. However, some students in the class had strong religious convictions about creation, and they found the speech to be a persuasive, not informative, effort. Without knowing your audience's attitudes, values, and beliefs as they pertain to your topic, you may inadvertently be perceived as threatening cherished beliefs when all you are trying to do is impart information.

Message Keys of Effective Informative Speaking

What makes one speaker's presentation so informative and stimulating that we want to learn more about what we initially thought was a boring topic? And why does another speaker's presentation leave us cold from beginning to end? Is the reason (a) the speaker, (b) the topic, (c) the message, (d) our perceptions, or (e) all of the above? Because the public speaking transaction is an interdependent system, the answer, of course, is (e) all of the above.

However, if an informative speech is seen as personally or professionally relevant, it can be successful in spite of being delivered by a marginally skilled public speaker. The reverse is not always true; that is, we may not find an entertaining speaker personally or professionally informative.

Research over the past two decades suggests that the likelihood of an audience's perceiving information as relevant and conducive to learning depends significantly on the degree to which they find it involving, appropriate, accessible, and potentially life enhancing.[4]

Audience Involvement

audience involving
Informative topic and speech that succeeds in gaining the audience's attention.

Information is worthless unless people pay attention to it. Information needs to be **audience involving.** The history of the world is full of examples of great ideas, practices, and products that failed because no one paid much attention to them. One of the first things we'll want to ensure, then, is that our topic and speech get the audience involved.

Novelty is the quality of being new and stimulating. It can be useful in gaining an audience's interest. Just as plants are heliotropic, we human beings are stimulitropic. Whereas plants continuously orient themselves to the sun to activate the process of photosynthesis, we continually orient ourselves to new sources of stimulation.

Although novelty alone is not enough to sustain an informative speech, it certainly can make a speech more effective. Research has time and again documented the fact that the perception of novelty heightens selective exposure, selective attention, and selective retention of information. In other words, people are likely to seek out, pay attention to, and remember novel information. The most obvious way to get the benefit of novelty in an informative speech is to choose a topic that is novel for the audience. We are much more likely to captivate the audience members with the unfamiliar than with the mundane. Novelty, however, shouldn't be confused with the obscure. For example, whereas computer software for accountancy probably would be an obscure topic for most audiences, the fact that the software could save us money on our income taxes might be a novel topic.

Another way to use novelty to our advantage is in the construction of the message. Even though the rule of thumb is to structure a speech so that the audience can predict what comes next, this is not an unbending rule. Sometimes it is to our advantage to violate the expectancies of an audience. Writers, for example, sometimes begin with a story's end and then backtrack. Similarly, a skilled speaker could start a speech with what normally would be considered its conclusion and build backward. You may recall this is exactly what the storytelling speech by Montana Kellmer did in Chapter 2.

Finally, novelty in our delivery can work to our advantage when speaking informatively. Audiences, for instance, generally are accustomed to speakers who are relatively stationary. Movement may add needed novelty to our presentation. In addition, some of our suggestions about the nonverbal dynamics of delivery in Chapter 11 will help introduce novelty to a presentation.

Audience Appropriateness

Although novelty can increase the chances of an audience initially paying attention, the information we share also needs to be compatible with what audience members believe is appropriate to the occasion. If our topic immediately turns the audience off, the audience also will tune us out.

Early in this book we said that communication is perceptual and that the process of perception is selective. Basically, people perceive what they choose to perceive. **Audience appropriateness** is the audience's perception that a message is consistent with their belief systems–their attitudes, beliefs, values, and lifestyle. All too often, speakers fail to take appropriateness into account when choosing a topic and then constructing their informative speech.

audience appropriate
Informative topic and speech that takes into account the occasion and audience members' belief systems.

For example, we've heard several informative speeches on sexually transmitted illnesses (STIs) and their prevention. We've also had students approach us after class and tell us they were offended or made to feel uncomfortable as a consequence of (1) the information in some of these speeches, (2) their perception that these speeches promoted a lifestyle with which they disagreed, and (3) the use of visual aids they didn't perceive to be in good taste. To a large degree, we were surprised by these reactions to a topic we believe needs to be openly discussed. We don't feel that student speakers should altogether avoid sensitive topics such as this one. However, they do need to consider the question of compatibility so that they can soften or qualify the information to make it appropriate for the audience.

Consider how we might approach an informative speech on stem cell research for two different audiences. The first audience is composed of family members of people with diseases such as Alzheimer's, Parkinson's, and diabetes. The second is a religious group whose members believe that life begins at the moment of conception. The first group is likely to be hopeful that embryonic stem cell research can provide a cure for their loved ones. The second is likely to oppose any research

Demonstration speeches often involve live models as is the case at this hair show.

that could lead to the destruction of what they believe is human life. A speech virtually word for word the same would engender quite different reactions from these two groups. In approaching the second group, we need to make it clear that our intent is not to attack their deeply held religious beliefs. We might qualify the information in the speech with statements such as these:

> "I realize that for many people the whole issue of stem cell research raises ethical concerns, and I am mindful of these concerns."

> "Putting aside our religious views for the moment, let me describe what we know about the potential benefits of stem cell research."

> "Regardless of how you feel about this issue, I'd like you to put yourself in the shoes of someone who has just learned his or her young daughter has been diagnosed with juvenile diabetes and faces a lifetime of insulin shots, with potentially fatal complications."

The point is that information that is potentially incompatible with audience members' worldviews can be made appropriate if it is presented in a way that acknowledges the audience's point of view.

Audience Accessibility

audience accessible
Content the audience is able to understand, regardless of its complexity.

Simply put, audience members cannot benefit from information that they cannot grasp. An **accessible** informative speech is one that the audience readily understands. Suppose, for example, that you are a biology major and you want to inform an audience about mapping the human genome. Should you use words peculiar to your major? Should you use the same approach with an audience of beginning speech students as you would with a group of seniors in a biochemistry class? Of course not.

Research tells us that one of the quickest ways to turn off an audience is to unnecessarily complicate a topic. We don't have to avoid complex topics for our informative speeches. In fact, they are likely to be both novel for the audience and interesting for us to research. The goal is to make complex topics accessible and compelling.

Jaime Escalante's calculus classes in *Stand and Deliver* are models of the presentation of complex information. He broke the lessons into easy-to-digest bits, what he called "step by step." In fact, he would say to his students, "This is easy." It's not so much the complexity of the topic as the complexity of a speaker's explanation that makes a topic difficult for an audience to understand.

An excellent way to reduce the complexity of a speech is through analogies or comparisons. Explain a complex process, for example, by comparing it with a common process based on the same principle. In his speech on stem cell research to the Democratic National Convention, for example, Ron Reagan talked about such research providing us with a "personal biological repair kit."[5]

Visual media can also be helpful in reducing complexity. For example, we recall a speech about a complex carbon molecule in which the speaker used a Tinkertoy model to show what the molecule looked like. The speaker also used an analogy, calling the molecule a "soot ball," to help the audience visualize what it would be like.

Life Enhancement

When we introduced the tools you need to get started on your first speech, we talked about the importance of connecting with your audience. If they are to learn, audience members need to know explicitly why it is in their interest to listen to what you have to say.

When we connect with our audience, we are in effect saying, "My topic and message are potentially life enhancing." Life enhancement can take the form of a more informed view on some topic or an improved way of behaving. Don't think that just because you have a good idea, people will necessarily see the advantage in adopting it. History is replete with good ideas, the proverbial better mousetrap, that are collecting dust for want of the public's attention. Consider two examples from Everett M. Rogers's classic work, *The Diffusion of Innovations.*[6]

If you have studied the history of science, you may recall that the disease scurvy, caused by a deficiency of vitamin C, was a serious problem for sailors on long voyages. As early as 1601, it was found that sources of vitamin C effectively inhibited scurvy. Yet it took almost 200 years for the British Navy to put this finding to use on its ships, and almost 75 years more for sources of vitamin C to be made available on commercial ships.

The second example concerns the arrangement of the keyboard on typewriters and personal computers. If you have ever thought the keys were illogically arranged, you are not alone. A far better method of arrangement of keys has been available since 1932. The Dvorak method is more efficient than the system almost everybody uses and is more easily mastered. So why weren't you taught the Dvorak method in the beginning? Because the one you use was invented in 1873 and has been designed into almost all keyboards ever since. One of the reasons for staying with the less logical keyboard was that the metal keys of early typewriters stuck when the typist worked too quickly. Thus, the keyboard we use today on computers was originally invented to *slow down* typists on mechanical typewriters.

All too often speakers assume that audience members will recognize they have something to gain personally or professionally from a speech. What may be perfectly obvious to the speaker, however, may be just the opposite for the audience. Consider a case with which you already have some experience—college classes. Regardless of the subject matter of their classes, most college professors believe that the information they have to share is absolutely essential to every student's intellectual well-being. So secure are they in this belief, in fact, some seldom spend any time convincing students that there are "good reasons" for their being in the professor's class.

Occasionally, this oversight doesn't much matter—for example, when students are taking a course in their major. Students listen because they know they "have to learn" what is being taught, regardless of how well it's being taught. This is seldom the case, though, when they find themselves in a required course outside their major. "Why do I need a course in art history?" complains the computer science major, while the chemistry major asks, "Why do I need a class in public speaking?"

Just as teachers have an obligation to connect their course to the professional aspirations of students, speakers have the same kind of obligation to their audiences. It's not enough that their information is perceived as involving or appropriate by their audience. Their information—their speech—must also be readily perceived as enhancing audience members' lives.

The two sample informative speeches outlined in this chapter may, at first glance, seem to lack the attribute of life enhancement. A closer look, however, reveals that both speakers make the link to life enhancement. Kelsey Kinnard's speech on the skin disease epidermolysis bullosa was about more than this rare disease. Because Kelsey had personally worked with children who had the disease, she concluded her speech by saying, "I saw how a family deals with disabilities and how a disease can either be a burden or a blessing depending on your life outlook." That is a message all of us can appreciate—even those with the most debilitating fatal disease can have a positive outlook on life. Evan Mironov's presentation on fencing is presented in the hope that "if you ever see a match, you will understand what is occurring." As one of the oldest Olympic sports, it is likely to be watched by everyone in his audience at some time in their lives. Just as a class in art appreciation might help us when we visit a gallery, Evan hopes his speech will enhance his audience members' appreciation of this noble sport, even if none of the members is motivated to take up the sport of fencing.

Putting Theory Into Practice

Now that we have covered some of the principles related to conveying information to an audience, it's time to plan your own informative speech. This section offers some practical suggestions for how to give an informative speech. We discuss four ways to inform an audience: explanation, instruction, demonstration, and description. Informative speeches may employ more than one of these modes of informing. And the list is not exhaustive. Nevertheless, these four categories should be a useful way of thinking about how to translate the principles of informative speaking into an actual speech.

Speeches That Explain a Process

One of the primary functions you may wish to accomplish in an informative speech is to explain a process. Technically, a *process* is a continuous phenomenon without an obvious beginning or end. Examples of processes are plentiful in science and include photosynthesis, erosion, and osmosis. Because true processes are complex and often hidden from our ordinary senses, their explanation requires genuine creativity from a speaker. At a minimum, we must break down the process into increments that the audience can readily comprehend. If the process involves a specialized vocabulary, we also need to define terms for the audience. Because the process also may be invisible, we may have to create visuals that approximate the process.

The key to explaining a process is to find the right complement of language and visual media for your audience. This involves finding the best analogies, metaphors, and similes to start. You can then complement these elements of language with static visual media such as overheads or dynamic visual media such as a DVD or CD-ROM.

Speeches That Explain a Concept

Although not as difficult to explain as a process, a concept demands care on the part of the speaker who chooses to explain it. A *concept* is a symbolic abstraction that pulls together a class of objects that share common attributes. The word *ball,* for example, is also a concept that can be applied to baseballs, basketballs, footballs, golf balls, racketballs, squash balls, and volleyballs. Although different in size and purpose, these types of balls share at least one common attribute: They are round.

The key to explaining a concept is to describe the essential attributes that distinguish it from other concepts. How is a democracy different from a republic? The United States is a republic, yet most people refer to it as a democracy. A good informative speech would not only explain why this is the case but also point out the specific attributes that distinguish a republic from a democracy.

In selecting a topic for a speech that explains a process or a concept, keep in mind that the topic should be relevant to the audience, something they are capable of understanding, and something you can explain in the time allotted. Although the theory of relativity is highly relevant, explaining it in a 5- to 10-minute speech is a tall order.

The message attribute of accessibility is particularly important in speeches that explain. Recall that one way to reduce complexity for an audience is to use an analogy. Consider the use of analogy in this excerpt from a speech by Jonathan Studebaker explaining the progressive disease he has:

> Like I said, I'm a nice person. I'm cheerful, I'm energetic. Okay, so I have a disability. I was born with osteogenesis imperfecta, a disease which causes my bones to be fragile. Have you ever accidentally dropped a glass on the floor? What happens? It breaks. Well, my bones kinda break like glass, which is why I tell people, when you carry me, treat me like your best crystal.[7]

The use of a simple analogy of bones to glass helps the audience understand a disease most of us cannot even pronounce. For Jonathan's purposes, which are to introduce himself and explain his disability, that is the extent of the technical information his audience needs to know.

In Their Own Words

Sample Informative Speech Outline

EPIDERMOLYSIS BULLOSA
by Kelsey Kinnard

Kelsey Kinnard

Specific Purpose: To inform the audience about the skin condition epidermolysis bullosa.

Introduction

I. **Open With Impact:** What would you think if you heard the words: cruise. Bahamas, free? I thought it meant the chance of a lifetime.

II. **Thesis Statement:** Although to me these kids are just like any others, I want to share with you what I have learned about them and the skin condition they have called epidermolysis bullosa, or EB.

III. **Connect With audience:** These kids have taught me a lot about what you can get out of life and have also given me experience in the medical field. The way they deal with the conditions they are in and the different ways they must live their lives are so intriguing.

IV. **Preview:** Today I am going to tell you about EB, what causes it, what effects it has on a person and their family and what is being done to find a cure for it.

Body

I. **Main Point:** What is EB?
   A. The kids I know have dystrophic epidermolysis bullosa.
   B. Two of every 100,000 live births suffer from some type of EB, as stated on www.debra.org (2004).
   C. EB is caused by missing protein in the skin that connects dermis to epidermis.
   D. Friction of these layers causes blisters and scarring.
   E. Bandages are wrapped around the whole body to prevent blistering as R. Kinnard (personal communication, February 21, 2004) explained.

(**Signpost:** Now that I have explained to you what EB is, I'll tell you about how it affects the lives of those who have it.)

Is her specific purpose really complete? Isn't she also trying to make people appreciate how much they can learn from working with children with disabilities?

Notice how the speaker grabs audience attention with words like "cruise" and "free."

Does this statement really connect with the audience? Could she have done more to show the relevance of her topic—or would that have spoiled her conclusion?

Preview is simple and clear.

Should she explain Debra.org is the official Web site of Dystrophic Epidermolysis Bullosa Research Association?

The speaker accompanied descriptions with overhead transparencies. You can see these on your Speech Coach CD.

A second factor that is important in speeches that explain a process or a concept is to make it observable with visuals. They can make an abstract concept concrete and thus easier to understand.

During your college career, you will undoubtedly be called on to explain something to an audience, if not in your public speaking class, then in another setting.

II. **Main Point:** What are the effects of EB?
  A. Their nutrition is affected because of scarring and blisters in the esophagus as stated by Marinkovich (2002).
  B. They can suffer from deformities such as webbed toes, fingers and bent backs.
  C. Children suffering from EB can also be anemic, but there is a new process that gives them monthly doses of iron and blood transfusions. This gives them more energy and health explained R. Kinnard (personal communication, February 21, 2004).
  D. Skin cancer can also arise and become the cause of death.
  E. R. Kinnard (personal communication, February 21, 2004) stated that people with EB do not live to be very old, many children die of complications and mild cases still do not live past early twenties.

(**Signpost:** I have explained complications and effects of EB; now you may want to know what is being done to cure EB.)

III. **Main Point:** What is being done to lessen/cure EB?
  A. Bandage wrapping, salt water soaks and cleaning lessen the blistering and scars.
  B. R. Kinnard (personal communication, February 21, 2004) explained that "fake skin" is being developed to cover the skin that they do have so they do not need the bandages.
  C. Marinkovich (2002) explained that gene therapy/replacement is being researched at Stanford Medical Center.

Conclusion

I. **Summarize:** I have just told you about epidermolysis bullosa.
  A. You learned what EB is.
  B. I also told you about the effects of EB.
  C. And last, I talked about what is being done to treat and prevent EB.
II. **Close with impact:** So, while I was experiencing a cruise in the Bahamas, I was able to learn so much more than what a real sea turtle looks like. I saw how a family deals with disabilities and how a disease can either be a burden or a blessing depending on your life outlook.

References

Marinkovich, P. M. (2002). Epidermolysis Bullosa. *Emeaicine Online,* Retrieved February 23, 2004, from www.emedicine.com
What is the cause of dystrophic epidermolysis bullosa? (2003), Retrieved February 23, 2004, from www.debra.org/modules.php?op=modload&name=News&file=article&sid=18#19

Do these descriptions of the disease symptoms have strong emotional impact?

Notice how this bad news is coupled with the next main point, which is hopeful.

Kinnard is the speaker's mother and a nurse who deals with EB patients. Is this a credible source?

Use of term "fake skin" helps put this treatment in accessible language.

Is summary sufficient? Could it be more substantive rather than just listing the topics covered?

Does the point at the end help the audience see why the topic is important to everyone, not just those directly affected by EB?

Are References adequate or should she have consulted additional medical sources? Personal communication from R. Kinnard is listed only in the body of the speech as APA style requires.

Similarly, in the professional world, it is common for people to be called on to explain everything from a new product idea to why the last quarter's sales were so bad. Using the principle of accessibility can help you enhance your explanations. You can review the outline of this type of speech in the box Sample Informative Speech Outline: Epidermolysis Bullosa by Kelsey Kinnard.

 **Speech**Coach

To get a better handle on an informative speech explaining a concept, watch Kelsey Kinnard's speech on epidermolysis bullosa on segment 13.1 of your CD.

Speeches That Instruct

Informative speaking can also be used to instruct an audience. The key to instruction is to provide new information the audience can put to use, or a new perspective on old information. Modern educational theory emphasizes observable behavioral objectives; that is, after receiving instruction, students should be able to show that they have mastered the subject, either by answering questions or by engaging in some activity.

Involving the speech audience is important to speeches that provide instruction. Unless the information in a speech presents *new* information or a *fresh perspective* to our audience, all we have done is bore them with what they already know. For example, speeches on how to ride a bike or how to pack a suitcase are unlikely to provide anything new to an audience. However, even new topics can be perceived as irrelevant by large portions of an audience. For example, a speech on how to wax your skis is old news to experienced skiers but irrelevant to nonskiers in the class.

So, the key to speeches that instruct is to provide new yet relevant information to your audience, or at least a new perspective on such information. That means using the novelty of your topic to involve people while pointing out how learning the information can be life enhancing.

Speeches That Demonstrate How to Do Something

Speeches that demonstrate how to do something are closely related to those that provide instruction, but the speaker actually shows the audience how to do something. Further, a good demonstration allows the audience to try out what is being demonstrated, if not during the speech itself, then later on their own. A good example of a speech that demonstrates can be found on the Food Network's *Emeril Live*.

A demonstration speaker is demonstrating, he or she needs to provide audience members with enough information to do the activity on their own, or with information on where to obtain further instruction so that they can try out the activity. For example, although no one can master karate from just listening to a single speech, or even a series of speeches, a demonstration of karate moves can spur an audience member to seek out individual instruction in the martial arts. In fact, many martial arts studios make a practice of giving demonstrations in schools and at public events as a way of recruiting new students.

Topics for speeches that demonstrate need to be chosen with care. A complex, difficult task cannot be adequately demonstrated in a few minutes. There can even be the danger of making people think they know how to do something based on a speech when in fact they do not. Few of us could do CPR, for example, based on simply watching a speaker demonstrate the activity. We need the opportunity to try it out (perhaps on a life-size doll) before we can know whether we can do it. On the other hand, another lifesaving technique, the Heimlich maneuver, is often the subject of demonstration and can be learned in a reasonably short time.

The key to making a demonstration effective is careful planning. For example, if you have ever watched syndicated re-runs of the show *Home Improvement*, you know that Tim (The Tool Man) Taylor rarely has practiced what he is doing. If you plan to demonstrate a process in your speech, rehearse it carefully. Also, it is sometimes useful to prepare various steps of the process in advance. Watch any cooking show demonstration on TV. The onions are already chopped, the flour is already sifted and measured, and an example of the finished product is near at

Failure to properly prepare for a demonstration is the hallmark of Tim Allen's comedy on *Home Improvement*, but it can lead to disaster in an informative speech.

hand. We don't want the audience drifting off as we measure ingredients or sift the flour. Providing a written recipe in a handout or as a visual will save a lot of time and let the audience focus on watching the demonstration. In short, a demonstration requires extra preparation.

In addition, we should be sure that the demonstration is an accurate re-creation. If we misinform an audience, we have done more harm than good. Depending on what we are demonstrating, we might even be inviting injury to the audience members or someone else. We must make certain, therefore, that we can accurately demonstrate the process in the time allowed.

Finally, we should make sure the demonstration is visible to the audience. A demonstration speech on making sushi, or small origami paper figures, may initially seem like a good idea. Unless there is a way to magnify the demonstration so that all the audience can see what the speaker is doing, making sushi or origami figures isn't a very good idea. Fencing, on the other hand, is a dramatic and highly visible topic. (See the box Sample Informative Speech Outline: Fencing by Evan N. Mironov.)

SpeechCoach

To gain a clearer understanding of an informative speech demonstrating a speaker's topic, watch Evan Mironov's speech on fencing, segment 13.2 on your CD.

Speeches That Describe

Another function of informative speeches is description. Using visuals can enhance a descriptive speech. Not only can visuals be useful; you may also want to

In Their Own Words

Sample Informative Speech Outline

FENCING
by Evan N. Mironov

Specific Purpose: To describe fencing.

Introduction

I. **Open With Impact:** On-guard!, your opponent yells as he draws his sword.
   A. Take a deep breath and exhale slowly.
   B. He lunges wildly at you.
   C. The first point is good, as you watch your opponent's eyes fill with horror.
II. **Focus on Thesis Statement:** Fencing has evolved over time.
III. **Connect With the Audience:** Everyone has had dreams of damsels in distress and musketeers.
IV. **Preview:** Today I will tell you where fencing has come from and how it evolved into the different disciplines that are around today, as well as the modern equipment necessary to keep you safe. And finally the rules of the strip, so if you ever see a match, you will understand what is occurring.

Body

I. **Main Point:** Fencing has been around as early as 1190 B.C. (Lancaster University Fencing Club, 2000).
   A. The rapier was created in Italy and became the basis for modern fencing weapons (Fencing.net, 2000).
   B. Where did the rapier come from?
   C. How the rapier led to the foil.

(Signpost: This leads me to the three different styles of fencing that are practiced today.)

II. **Main Point:** The three disciplines of fencing are foil, epee, and saber (US Fencing Online, n.d.).
   A. Foil is the basic practice dueling weapon.
   B. Epee is more like a traditional dueling style because whole body is target area.
   C. Saber came from swords cavalry use.

---

provide a word picture of the subject. Consider the following description of a familiar character, Mickey Mouse, provided by student speaker Jennie Rees:

> They designed him using a circle for his head and oblong circles for his nose and snout. They also drew circles for his ears and drew them in such a way that they appeared to look the same any way Mickey turned his head. They gave him a pear-shaped body with pipe-stem legs, and stuffed them in big, oversized shoes, making him look like a little kid wearing his father's shoes.[8]

Can't you almost picture Mickey from that description? Visual language is key to effective description.

Examples of speech topics for each type of informative speech are offered in Table 13.1

(**Signpost:** Now that you know a little about the weapons, I'll talk about safety.)

III. **Main Point:** Since we no longer believe in hurting people, we use protection.
   A. The mask and its importance.
   B. The glove and how it protects the hand.
   C. The jacket and chest protector and what they prevent from happening.
   D. The knickers and what they protect.

(**Signpost:** You now know about the weapons, as well as the armor that a modern fencer must use; now I will tell you about the fencing strip and basic moves.)

IV. **Main Point:** The rules of fencing are difficult to fully comprehend.
   A. The fencing strip is 2 meters wide by 14 meters long.
   B. What is the concept of right of way.
   C. The basic movements.

Conclusion

Summarize: Recap each topic and say a little about it.
Close With Impact: I leave you with the ending of a bout, a salute.

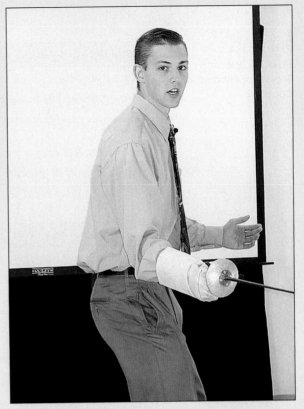

Evan N. Mironov

Could the speaker have provided more detail in his conclusion?

References are listed using APA style.

References

Fencing.net. (2000, May 22). *History of fencing—Where did it start?* Retrieved on October 7, 2001 from http://www.fencing.net/intro2.html

Lancaster University Fencing Club. (2000, August 6). *A brief history of fencing.* Retrieved on October 7, 2001 from http://www.lancs.ac.uk/socs/fencing/fenbri.htm

US Fencing Online. (n.d.) *What is fencing?* Retrieved on October 7, 2001 from http://www.usfencing.org/welcome/whatisfencing.asp

Tips and Tactics

Tips and Tactics for Informative Speaking

When putting an informative speech together, we need to do the following:

- Use words that appeal to the different learning styles of audience members.
- Use techniques that make the speech involving, appropriate, accessible, and potentially life enhancing.
- Establish whether the speech purpose is to explain a concept or a process, instruct, demonstrate, or describe.
- Maximize observability through the use of appropriate presentational media.

Table 13.1

Possible Speech Topics for Informative Speeches

Explaining a process such as . . .	Explaining a concept such as . . .
• Global warming • How hydrogen can power cars • How solar panels convert sunlight into electricity • How West Nile Virus is transmitted • How exposure to UV rays causes skin cancer	• Credit card fees and how they can accumulate • A type of art, for example, impressionism • The nature of a disease, for example, muscular dystrophy • Compound interest and how a small amount invested over time can grow • Musical harmony
Demonstrating how to . . .	**Describing . . .**
• Grow your own herbs • Fill out the EZ1040 income tax form • Fly fish • Give CPR • Prepare your favorite food • Properly protect yourself from injury while skiing	• A visit to Rio de Janeiro • The most unforgettable person you ever met • The weaknesses in airport security allowing hijackers to take over planes • The beauty of Yosemite National Park • The judging of an Olympic sport such as gymnastics

Informative Speaking Throughout the Life Span

Informative speaking is probably the form of public speaking you're most likely to be called on to do throughout your life. One of the chief reasons is that informative speaking is used in so many settings, including the classroom, the workplace, and the community.

Informative Speaking in the Classroom

Two time-honored traditions in the college classroom are the term paper and the oral report. Although most students have at least passing familiarity with the elements of a good term paper, many students don't make the connection between the elements of a good oral report and the process of informative speaking.

An oral report basically is an informative speech. Thus, by putting to use what you know about informative speaking, you will be able to give oral reports that are both substantively and stylistically more effective than those of your classmates.

Viewing the oral report as an opportunity to speak informatively has several advantages. First, it provides you with an organizational framework for constructing your report. Second, it reminds you that you have an audience for your report whose background and perceptual reality must be taken into account. Finally, it forces you to think about how relevant the information in your report is to both your instructor and student colleagues.

Informative Speaking in the Workplace

No matter what you plan on doing to make a living, the odds are great that you will need to make informative presentations. Although you won't necessarily have to speak to large numbers of people, you can reasonably expect to speak to your immediate coworkers, department, or supervisors. It is common in the workplace to make informative presentations before groups. For some presentations you will have to stand and speak; other presentations may be delivered from your seat.

Although the different situations require adjustments in your style of delivery, the substantive elements of your informative presentation are the same. You will still need to follow a cohesive organizational sequence, analyze your audience carefully, and consider the message attributes described earlier in this chapter.

Informative Speaking in the Community

You can reasonably expect to speak informatively with members of your community in at least one of two capacities: as a representative of your employer or as a concerned citizen. Private, as well as public, enterprises are justifiably concerned about their image within their local community. Opinion poll after opinion poll shows that the public is increasingly suspicious of the motives of private enterprise and increasingly dissatisfied with the performance of public agencies. It's not uncommon, therefore, for these organizations to make themselves available to service groups, such as Rotary International, the general public, or a citizens' group organized around a specific cause.

Some businesses have a person whose job is company spokesperson; large corporations may even have whole departments dedicated to public relations. Many organizations, however, have come to expect anyone in management to serve as an informative speaker to the community. In fact, private corporations, such as IBM, and public agencies, such as the police or fire department, may actually write such community service into their managers' job descriptions. Thus, just because you currently perceive your intended career as low profile, that doesn't necessarily make it so.

Finally, you may one day want or need to speak informatively as a private citizen. If you live in a community where cable television is available, your city council meetings probably are televised on your community access channel. If you tune in, you will see ordinary citizens making informative presentations at these meetings. Topics can range from the environmental impact of a new housing development to excessive noise from student housing. If you watch several of these presentations, you will probably conclude that very few of the speakers have much training in public speaking; people who do have training are easy to spot.

Your days as a public speaker will not be over once you've completed this class. Given what we've said here, in fact, you should now realize they are just beginning.

Summary

Informative speaking is the process by which an audience gains new information or a new perspective on old information from a speaker.

- Learning is frequently the goal of informative speaking.

- It's important therefore that the individual learning styles of audience members be reflected in the verbal and nonverbal content of informative speeches.

- Successful informative speeches are audience involving, audience appropriate, audience accessible, and potentially life enhancing.

- Informative speeches can be used to explain, instruct, demonstrate, or describe processes, concepts, and skills.

- Informative speeches are common in the classroom, the workplace, and the community.

Check Your Understanding: Exercises and Activities

1. Develop an outline for a one- to two-minute speech in which you inform an audience about a topic with which you are personally very familiar. Then show how you would adapt that speech to four different learning dimensions: active-reflective, sensing-intuitive, visual-verbal, and sequential-global.

2. Come up with at least two possible topics each for speeches that explain, instruct, demonstrate, and describe. Do some topics seem to fall naturally into one category? Are there other topics that might be used for more than one type of speech?

3. What is your preferred learning style? To find out, go to http://www.engr .ncsu.edu/learningstyles/ilsweb.html and take the "Index of Learning Styles Questionnaire" developed by Barbara A. Solomon and Richard A. Felder of North Carolina State.

Notes

1. Jay Mathews, *Escalante: The Best Teacher in America* (New York: Henry Holt, 1988), 191.
2. *Stand and Deliver,* director Tom Menendez, with Edward James Olmos, Lou Diamond Phillips, Rosana De Soto, and Andy Garcia, An American Playhouse Theatrical Film, A Menendez/Musca & Olmos Production, Warner Bros., 1988.
3. Barbara A. Solomon and Richard A. Felder, "Learning Styles and Strategies" [Retrieved from http://www.ncsu.edu/felder-public/ILSdir/styles.htm, 11 August 2004].
4. Michael D. Scott and Scott Elliot, "Innovation in the Classroom: Toward a Reconceptualization of Instructional Communication" (paper presented at the annual meeting of the International Communication Association, Dallas, Texas, 1983).
5. "Reagan Calls for Increased Stem Cell Research," *CNN.Com Inside Politics,* 28 July 2004 [Retrieved from http://www.cnn.com/2004/ALLPOLITICS/07/27/dems.reagan/, 11 August 2004].
6. Everett M. Rogers, *Diffusion of Innovations* (New York: Free Press, 1983).
7. Jonathan Studebaker, "Speech of Self-Introduction: Who Am I?" The full text appears in Chapter 2.
8. Jennie Rees, "Informative Speech: Mickey: A Changing Image," California State University, Chico, 1992.

When people think of persuasion, they often form an image of a politician running for office.

Persuasive Speaking

Objectives

After reading this chapter and reviewing the learning resources on your CD-ROM and at the Online Learning Center, you should be able to:

- Describe how your assessment of the audience and situation is important to persuasive speaking.

- Describe the four goals persuasive speeches are designed to achieve.

- Analyze the audience of a persuasive message in terms of cultural, demographic, and individual diversity.

- Define ethos, logos, and pathos.

- Achieve persuasiveness through the use of speaker credibility.

- Describe the process of elaborated thinking in relation to persuasion.

- Demonstrate how to use first-, second-, and third-order data as evidence in a persuasive speech.

- Explain the rationale for presenting a two-sided persuasive message, and construct a two-sided persuasive message.

- Demonstrate how certain types of persuasive appeals are linked to audience members' emotions and primitive beliefs.

Key Concepts

behavioral intention

elaboration likelihood model

ethos

first-, second-, and third-order data

inoculation

logos

pathos

persuasion

reinforcement

source credibility

❝ Character may almost be called the most effective means of persuasion. ❞

–ARISTOTLE[1]

Because of his high credibility with local youth, former San Francisco 49er and health club owner Jeff Stover is sought after to speak to children about the dangers of drug abuse.

If we asked you to form an image of a person giving a persuasive speech, who would come to mind? Many of us would imagine a politician running for elected office. And more often than not, that politician would be a prominent public figure we've seen only on television. Fortunately, political speech is not the most common form of persuasive speaking in which people routinely engage. Nor is it necessarily the best example of persuasive speaking for us to consider as a potential model for our own persuasive speeches, the subject of this chapter.

Persuasive speaking and the functions it serves are a part of everyday life. Examples of persuasive speaking are all around us even though we may not immediately recognize them as such. They include presentations designed to convince us to buy a time share at a resort property, pep talks delivered by the people who lead us at work or coach a team on which we play, and the monologues of entertainers whose running jokes night after night undermine the credibility of that public figure asking for your vote.

persuasion
The process by which a speaker influences what audience members think or do.

This chapter is about the art and science of **persuasion** and persuasive speaking. We draw examples from highly publicized speeches, such as those delivered by presidential candidates, but also from speeches we have witnessed firsthand to even know about. The topics covered in this chapter include the following:

- The process of persuasion as practiced in everyday life
- The primary functions and goals persuasive speaking serves in the effort to achieve our speech purpose
- The overriding significance of the audience's cultural, demographic, and individual makeup in determining the potential outcomes of a persuasive speech
- The likelihood of audience members thinking through the substance of a persuasive speech
- Practice in the art and science of persuasion to craft and deliver an effective persuasive speech

The Process of Persuasion

We introduced and described the role our beliefs, attitudes, and values play in the transaction between speakers and audiences in Chapter 6. We pointed out that these concepts vary in their intensity, and some are more easily changed than others. Persuasion seldom involves overnight changes in our beliefs, in our attitudes, or in our values. Persuasion is a gradual process. What's more, an initial persuasive speech typically is the first in a series of persuasive messages. The persuasive speech or speeches you develop both now and in the future should be crafted with this foundation in mind.

Persuasive speaking serves four primary functions or goals: reinforcement, inoculation, change, and action. Of the four, reinforcement and inoculation are the most common in everyday life.

Reinforcement involves giving people a reward for their beliefs, attitudes, values, and corresponding behaviors. Keynote speeches at national political conventions, for example, are usually designed to reinforce the common core of beliefs, attitudes, and values to which members of a political party subscribe. Party leaders know that party registration doesn't guarantee that people watching the convention on television will vote, much less vote the party line. Although people's political beliefs may lean in the direction of the platform of the party with which they are registered, these beliefs are often not deeply held. As a result, keynote persuasive speeches are targeted at getting party members at home to think about these beliefs favorably and to help them feel good about these beliefs in the process.

reinforcement
Rewards given to strengthen attitudes, beliefs, values, and behaviors.

Inoculation takes reinforcement a step further. The term *inoculation* was borrowed from medicine in the 1960s to describe a process where a person's belief system wasn't simply reinforced but was made resistant to persuasive messages attempting to change it.[2] Inoculation works best when people are asked to generate arguments that support their beliefs and to rehearse defending their beliefs from argumentative attacks they can reasonably anticipate. This approach isn't especially practical for speakers, so inoculation has to be adapted to be used in a persuasive speech.

inoculation
Techniques used to make people's belief systems resistant to counterpersuasion.

Assume for the moment that you are a parent who works in the health profession and you've been asked to speak to a group of children at your child's elementary school about "Saying No to Drugs." These children most likely have been exposed to many messages telling them that illegal substances are bad for their health, so it's not enough to simply reinforce the saying, "just say no to drugs." You need to help them resist persuasive messages they are likely to receive from their peers as they get older. Here is a strategy that could be effective in inoculating them against such peer pressure:

- Limit your persuasive speech to a single illegal substance in which there is no controversy about its dangers, for instance, methamphetamine.
- Tell the children that as they get older they are going to be pressured by other kids, including some who are popular, to "try speed." Give them realistic examples of the messages they are likely to receive in this regard. This technique is called *forewarning*.
- Give the children three simple but sound reasons (arguments) for turning down peers pressuring them to "try speed." This is a passive technique because *you* are supplying the reasons rather than having the children generate their own, which is an active technique.

Speaking of . . .

Does Drug Education Really Work?

Remember elementary school and the "just say no" campaign to discourage drug use? It is just one part of a massive drug education campaign, ranging from Drug Abuse Resistance and Education (DARE) to Red Ribbon Weeks, designed to inoculate youngsters against being persuaded to try drugs. Billions of taxpayer dollars are spent nationally on such programs, and the State of California alone spends about $400 million annually on drug education. To determine if the programs were worth the cost, the California Department of Education commissioned educational research consultants at the University of California at Berkeley to study the state's drug education programs. The results of the three-year study, completed in 1995, were so controversial that the Department of Education refused to release them. They were finally published two years later, in 1997, in the academic journal *Education Evaluation and Policy Analysis.* The results were shocking to drug educators. Only 15 percent of students found drug education persuasive. Nearly 70 percent of the 5,000 students surveyed were either neutral or even negative toward the programs.

According to the study's lead author, Joel Brown, "Not only are the programs ineffective, but for many youth they have an effect counter to what is intended." Among the comments from students about such programs, a typical one was "I don't think handing someone a ribbon saying 'Drug Free Is for Me' is going to make someone stop using drugs." In contrast, many students praised presentations by people suffering from AIDS as something that "really gets to you."

Brown's study has not been without its critics, however, including the California Department of Education, which rejected the findings as "significantly flawed." Nevertheless, the facts are that drug use among teens has risen in the past few years despite the expenditures of billions on drug education programs.

If you experienced drug education programs such as these during your elementary and secondary education, what did you think about their effectiveness? As attempts to inoculate youth against the temptation of drugs, were these efforts persuasive to you and your peers? If not, how could they have been made more persuasive?

Source: Peter Hecht, "School Anti-Drug Programs Bashed," *Sacramento Bee,* 19 March 1997, A1, A12.

- Finally, ask the children to recite back to you the reasons you've given them several times. Also have them write these reasons down on a sheet of paper. This oral and written rehearsal, as it is called, prepares the children to actually use the arguments you've given them when confronted by their peers.

Anti–drug use messages aimed at children are most effective when they give sound reasons not to use drugs rather than telling kids to "just say no." (See the box Does Drug Education Really Work?) Children can then use these "verbal antibodies" to defend their anti–drug use behavior when confronted with peer pressure to experiment with illegal substances.

The third goal of persuasive speaking is to *change* people. Generally speaking, persuasive speeches are most likely to first focus on people's attitudes or peripheral beliefs. The reason is straightforward: Attitudes and peripheral beliefs are more easily changed than primitive and core beliefs (see Chapter 6). They also are far easier to influence than our values, which are our most enduring beliefs.

The chances of changing attitudes and peripheral beliefs depend on the intensity with which they are held. Calling for the complete legalization of marijuana before a group of officers from the Drug Enforcement Agency, for example, doesn't make a lot of sense. On the other hand, such a call before a group of college students at least has a chance of persuading some of them, given the more favorable attitudes toward the use of marijuana uncovered by surveys of college students.

If we want to change the attitudes or peripheral beliefs of our audience, we first must determine whether the possibility for change even exists. During the 2004 presidential election cycle, for instance, polling data revealed that most people not

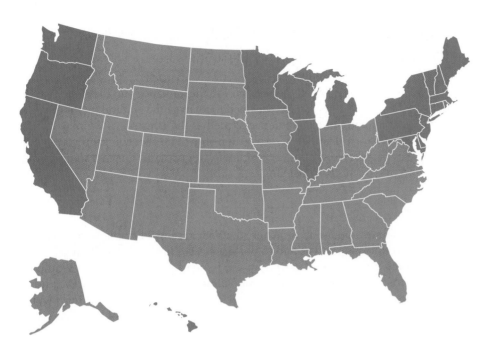

Figure 14.1
Results of the 2004
Presidential Election

only had made up their minds well in advance of voting but also were attitudinally entrenched–they were not about to change. As a result, the candidates and their parties spent most of their time trying to persuade the small percentage of voters whose attitudes about the candidates remained open to influence. Along the same lines, the candidates spent most of their time campaigning in states that were neither clearly "blue" nor clearly "red" (see Figure 14.1). Thus a small minority of states had a bigger hand in determining the outcome of the election than all the other states combined.

Difficult as it is to change beliefs, attitudes, and values, it is even more difficult to persuade people to *act* on the basis of what they believe, regard favorably or unfavorably, or value. As the saying goes, "you can lead a horse to water, but you can't make it drink." People are seldom moved to act as a result of a single persuasive speech.

If our goal is to persuade people to act, we need to first lay a foundation that will predispose them to do so. That takes time and repetition of the message. When it appears that people are responding to a single message, the persuasive speech is usually the most recent in a long line of speeches and related messages that have been building momentum for action. Consider the thousands upon thousands of public service messages designed to persuade people to put children in car safety seats, stop smoking, practice safe sex, and exercise their constitutional right to vote. Not only do these persuasive campaigns have a long history, they are also ongoing because some people refuse to act even when it is in their own self-interest to do so.

What this all boils down to is that the process of persuasion cannot begin until we've decided on the function or goal a speech is designed to serve. Do we want to reinforce or inoculate our audience? Do we want to change their attitudes or their peripheral beliefs? Or, most difficult of all, do we want our persuasive speech to move audience members to act?

Focusing on the Audience and Assessing the Situation

To determine our goal, we need to first focus on the audience and the rhetorical situation (see Chapter 6). Specifically, we need to analyze the cultural, demographic, and individual makeup of our audience as well as the constraints we may face as a result of the rhetorical situation. We'll then show you two common ways audiences process persuasive messages, and finally we provide some strategic guidelines for effective persuasive speaking.

Audience

The more we know about our audience, the better we will be able to predict how they are likely to respond to us and to our persuasive message. For example, if we are developing a persuasive speech on the issue of product safety, it would be helpful to know ahead of time whether our audience consists of product manufacturers or personal injury attorneys. In either case, we would construct our persuasive message on the basis of what we know about each demographic group. Learn as much as possible about the audience before you decide on your persuasive goal, much less decide on the content of your speech. One kind of audience analysis is presented in the box VALS Market Research and Persuasion.

Audience Attitudes Toward the Topic

In addition to a general analysis of your audience, in a persuasive situation you need to determine their specific attitudes toward your topic. For example, speaking to a group of your classmates about avoiding binge drinking, it's important to know whether they consider themselves to be heavy drinkers. If they do not acknowledge that there is a problem in their own behavior, they may agree with your speech but see no relationship to their own lives. Thus you may want to focus on defining binge drinking and showing them that their behavior may fit this category, something they previously would not have realized. On the other hand, if you are speaking to a group of acknowledged problem drinkers at a meeting of Alcoholics Anonymous, you would not need to convince them of the fact that they need to stay sober. Rather, you might focus on the importance of counseling other alcoholics to their own recovery.

Audience Attitudes Toward You

You also need to know how the audience perceives you as a speaker. For example, some speakers have a high degree of credibility because the audience perceives them to be trustworthy experts. Others are initially perceived to be similar to their audience members based on age and membership in the community. Research suggests that speakers who are perceived as credible or similar, or both, by their audiences have an easier time persuading listeners than do speakers who are either unknown or perceived to be dissimilar by their audiences.

behavioral intention
A person's subjective belief that he or she will engage in a specific behavior.

Behavioral Intentions Toward the Topic

Simply because people say they will do something doesn't necessarily mean they will carry through on the promise. A **behavioral intention** is a person's subjec-

Self-Assessment

VALS Market Research and Persuasion

One way to analyze an audience is in terms of the needs people experience. In Chapter 6 we pointed out that an audience whose primary motivation is survival is much different from one full of people focusing on the realization of their "true potential." As a result, skilled speakers take this into account in deciding on the purpose of their speech and the content of their messages.

Dissatisfied with the lack of research behind Maslow's hierarchy of needs, market researchers at SRIC-BI consulting (a spin-off of the Stanford Research Institute) developed an alternative we'd like you to consider as you develop your persuasive speeches. Instead of thinking of audience members in terms of needs, the consultants at SRIC-BI segment the audience into eight primary types:

- Innovators
- Thinkers
- Achievers
- Experiencers
- Believers
- Strivers
- Makers
- Survivors

Each type is qualitatively different in terms of motivations. For example, innovators are much more open to radically different ideas than are achievers, who are conservative of thought.

SRIC developed an online survey that not only will tell you your type but also will provide you with a profile of that type. We suggest you and your classmates visit the VALS site (http://www .sric-bi.com/VALS/presurvey.shtml) and take the survey. You can then talk about how to integrate what you have learned with your persuasive speaking plans.

tive belief that he or she will engage in a specific behavior.[3] The better we can predict our audience's initial intentions toward our topic, the better we can adapt our persuasive goal and message to them. Behavioral intentions sometimes can be inferred from a person's beliefs, values, and attitudes. As a result, it is essential that you canvass your audience to learn about their attitudes, beliefs, and values relative to their intentions, as well as your topic, and the direction in which you hope to persuade them.

Involvement in the Topic

According to one well-researched theory of persuasion, it's not enough to know whether a person is either for or against the position you plan on taking in a persuasive speech. Two people may hold roughly the same beliefs, attitudes, and values regarding a topic and yet be quite different in how easily they are influenced. Not everyone who signs a petition, for instance, volunteers to carry the petition door to door in the effort to get others to sign it. People who are actively involved with something like a petition drive in their local community are much more committed than people who simply sign the petition. Research demonstrates that the more involved people are with a topic, the more likely they are to interpret persuasive speeches that even mildly disagree with their own position as wildly discrepant from their own. This psychological distortion of a speaker's position is known as the *contrast effect*.

Highly involved people are also subject to the *assimilation effect* and may perceive messages reasonably close to their own as more similar than they actually are. This often happens when the speaker is perceived as a credible source with whom they generally agree on most issues. Thus highly involved people tend to polarize views: You are either with them or against them. Attempts to change their views even a little, moreover, are likely to be rejected out of hand.[4]

Related to the concept of involvement is the idea of latitudes of acceptance, rejection, and noncommitment. Highly involved persons normally have a very narrow latitude of acceptance of positions different from their own, and they have wide latitudes of rejection. Conversely, persons with low levels of involvement have large latitudes of noncommitment and small latitudes of rejection. These people are much more likely to listen to opposing views than their highly involved counterparts. In Figure 14.2, person A tends to have very little room for noncommitment and probably is highly involved in the topic. Person B, on the other hand, while holding the same most-preferred position as A, has a much greater latitude of noncommitment and is thus more open to different ideas on this topic. This is the group of people that politicians, marketers, and advertising professionals target. They recognize that they have little or no chance to gain the favor of people already involved and committed, but those less involved will not automatically reject their persuasion.

Often speakers need to make uninvolved audiences feel more involved in their topic. This is especially true if their goal is inoculation. By using real or even hypothetical examples, such as personal experiences, speakers can bring life to an abstract subject. Whatever the audience's initial level of involvement, successful persuaders need to make the topic come alive and seem directly relevant to their audience.

Rhetorical Constraints

In a sense we've been talking about rhetorical constraints imposed by the audience. Both our persuasive goals and the effectiveness of our persuasive speech will be constrained by the cultural, demographic, and individual attributes of our audience. Persuasion may be our goal, but persuasion isn't always possible.

Having said that, we want to discuss another constraint that seems to have escaped the attention of many powerful people in contemporary society: Persuasive speaking is bound by ethical constraints. Achieving your persuasive goals shouldn't come at the expense of your audience. Convincing Enron employees to hold onto company stock may have lined the pockets of Enron executives who sold their stock, but that doesn't make it right. The end you hope to achieve must reflect not only your interests but also those of your audience. Along the same lines, you need to think through the persuasive means you plan on using to achieve your goal. Noble ends do not justify ignoble means. As a case in point, we happen to believe that the remaining stands of giant sequoias should be protected from logging. We also would be happy to assist someone in preparing and delivering a speech that suggests reasonable means to achieve this end. This doesn't mean, however, that we would help someone who, as a part of his or her persuasive message, plans to advocate tree spiking (placing metal spikes in trees to keep them from being cut down). Such activity can lead to serious injury or even the death of loggers.

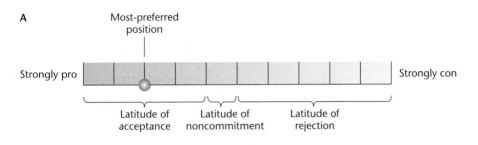

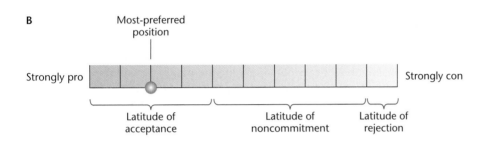

Figure 14.2
Latitudes of
Acceptance,
Rejection, and
Noncommitment

The point is that rhetorical constraints are not simply imposed by the attributes of the audience. They also are imposed by the ethical principles that have guided human conduct for more than 2,000 years.

Information Processing and Persuasive Messages: The Elaboration Likelihood Model

Before we introduce you to our guidelines for maximizing your persuasive speech's effect, we need to discuss one other audience-related matter. It involves the manner in which an audience processes the persuasive message we share. Aristotle used the Greek term **logos** in his discussion of the relationship between words in a message and the process of persuasion. Aristotle believed that logical proof in a speaker's message was a necessary condition for persuasion because audience members would think critically about the message. It would be nice to think that audience members are always objective and think critically about arguments and the evidence supporting them, but the modern reality is that they do not. To better understand this phenomenon, consider the thinking of two scholars on the subject, social psychologists Richard Petty and John Cacioppo.

In some persuasive transactions, the audience engages actively in thinking critically about a complex topic, whereas in others the audience responds almost without thinking. To explain this phenomenon, Petty and Cacioppo developed the **elaboration likelihood model** of persuasion.[5]

Consider, for example, a speech about doctor-assisted suicide. One possibility is that an audience is deeply concerned about the topic; perhaps members of the audience know someone who is terminally ill. They want a thorough and detailed discussion of the pros and cons of changing the laws to permit doctors to assist terminally ill patients in ending their lives. Another possibility is that audience members have no direct experience with the topic and simply prefer not to think about

logos
The proof a speaker offers to an audience through the words of his or her message.

elaboration likelihood model
A model of persuasion designed to explain why audience members will use an elaborated thinking process in some situations and not in others.

such difficult issues. Some ways of presenting the speech might invite the audience to engage in what Petty and Cacioppo call "central route processing," or elaboration. On the other hand, some messages on this topic might be designed to avoid elaborated thinking. Petty and Cacioppo call this "peripheral route processing."

The questions for a public speaker are (1) what factors are likely to lead an audience to engage in either central or peripheral message processing, and (2) which of these processes is most likely to lead to the achievement of the speaker's goals?

The second question is the easier to answer. In most situations, the speaker wants the audience to use the elaborated, or central, processing route. The reason is that if the argument presented by the speaker is accepted by audience members, they are more likely to undergo long-term attitude change. For example, if you are concerned that doctor-assisted suicide might lead to the patient's family members hastening their relative's death in order to collect on life insurance, you might want to cite examples from nations with such laws. Or you might want to discuss the moral issues involved in terminating a life, no matter how ill the patient. After all, one of the greatest minds of our time is Stephen Hawking, who suffers from ALS (Lou Gehrig's disease). In many cases, people with ALS would probably be considered prime candidates for doctor-assisted suicide by some of its advocates. On the other hand, if you are simply interested in a short-term goal, for example, getting voters to vote no on an upcoming initiative to allow doctor-assisted suicide in your state, you might simply want to say, "Killing is wrong, period. No ifs, ands, or buts about it. Vote no!"

To reiterate, then, the first question speakers should ask is "What factors in this situation will increase or decrease the likelihood of elaboration on the part of an audience member?" If audience members are motivated and able to understand a message, they are more likely to engage in elaborated thinking.

On the other hand, if they find a message irrelevant or are unwilling or unable to understand the message, they are more likely to follow the peripheral route. Some factors are beyond the speaker's control. For example, individual listeners differ in their "need for cognition," that is, their need to process information centrally.[6] There is not much a speaker can do to make people who don't like to think about messages do so. On the other hand, a speaker can take steps to make the topic relevant to the audience and to provide understandable and strong arguments that will be persuasive to those who are motivated to process the message centrally.

Let's walk through the elaboration likelihood model depicted in Figure 14.3 to further explain the process. On the far left we have the persuasive speech. Next we see the audience. There are two possibilities—that they are motivated and able to understand the message or that they are unmotivated or unwilling or unable to understand it. If the first condition applies, the process follows the boxes along the top of the model. It is likely that the audience will engage in central route processing. Two factors make this route more likely. First, if the message is perceived as *relevant,* the audience is more likely to pay attention. Second, the message needs to be *understandable.* An audience member may find a speech on nuclear terrorism relevant but be lost in the technical jargon and thus unable to process the message. Even when messages are understandable and relevant, there is no guarantee that the audience will accept them. If a message is perceived as incompatible with what audience members already know or believe in, it is likely to be rejected. For example, a speech on nuclear terrorism that misstated well-known facts or proposed violating basic civil liberties would likely be unacceptable to many audience members, even if they understood it and saw its relevance.

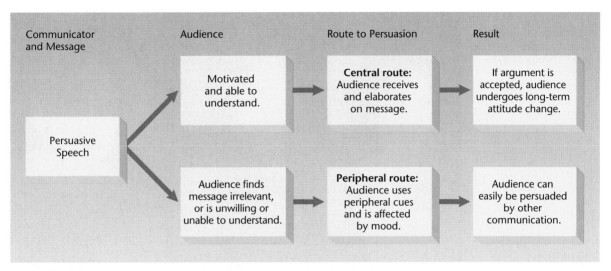

Figure 14.3
Two Routes to Persuasion in the Elaboration Likelihood Model

If an audience member engages in central route processing, then the quality of the message, in terms of evidence and reasoning, is the paramount basis for either accepting or rejecting the message. If the message is poorly constructed or presented, then even though the audience member engages in elaboration, the result may be contrary to the speaker's intent. Many times we have heard students speak on important, relevant, and significant topics only to discover that their research was shoddy and their reasoning flawed. Rather than being persuaded, we are in fact more likely to reject the message because we have thought critically about it. So, if you choose a message that is designed for central route processing, you must be sure to make a strong case for your position. If you do, the audience will be more likely to undergo long-term attitude change and be resistant to subsequent persuasion to the contrary.

The boxes along the bottom of the model in Figure 14.3 illustrate the peripheral route process. In this case, the audience either finds the message irrelevant or difficult to understand, or simply is uninterested in dealing with its complexities. Yet there is still the possibility of at least short-term persuasion taking place. Suppose you are having a busy day and suddenly the doorbell rings. At your door is a young girl in a soccer uniform with a box of chocolates for sale. It isn't likely you want to take the time to learn about the details of the local girl's soccer league. Perhaps you aren't a parent and never participated in sports yourself, so the message is largely irrelevant. Nevertheless, you might be hungry and the candy isn't very expensive. The girl is an appealing person, and she seems sincere. What the heck, you think, I'll take a box, no, make that two boxes. In this example, you haven't engaged in an elaborated process of critical thinking. Rather, you have just made a snap decision based on peripheral cues. The likelihood of being persuaded by the peripheral route usually depends on such things as your mood (hunger), emotional cues (such as the appealing salesperson), and perhaps the apparent credibility of the source (you know she's a member of the soccer league by the uniform). The problem with peripheral route processing is that it does not lead to stable attitude change. You might not be hungry the next time the girl comes by to sell the candy. But if, as a speaker, you are simply interested in a short-term persuasive

As members of MEChA these audience participants listen intently to Latina labor leader Delores Huerta.

effect, a peripheral route may be sufficient. And if your audience is uninterested or unwilling to engage in central route processing, it may be your only alternative. But beware: Persuasion that occurs as a result of the peripheral route is easily reversed. While this isn't a problem for the girl going door to door selling candy, imagine the effect on the tobacco education program if it turns out that most public service announcements on TV only stimulate peripheral route processing in youth. Do we really want a tobacco education program that doesn't involve long-term attitude change that is also resistant to subsequent change?

To summarize: Elaboration likelihood clearly suggests an active role on the part of the audience you hope to persuade. This active role includes (1) seeing your topic as relevant to their needs, (2) understanding and comprehending your message, and (3) centrally processing the nature and quality of the information you offer in terms of their preexisting knowledge and beliefs.

Persuasive Speaking in Practice

At this point we have covered the bases necessary to fully appreciate the complexity of the process of persuasion. Now we can turn our attention to some specific guidelines for developing a persuasive speech. These guidelines involve audience perceptions of you and your message and include credibility, similarity and attraction, and appearance.

Speaking With Credibility

We want you to think of yourself as the speaker as we begin our discussion of how to effectively present a persuasive message. Two thousand years' worth of theory and research suggest that whether an audience is likely to be persuaded by a

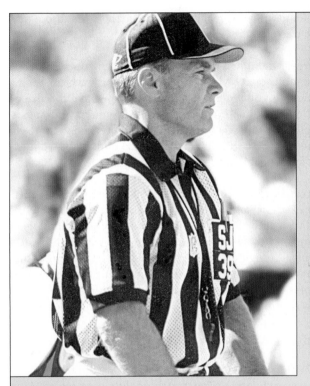 

When Don Carlson speaks to a group of recreation league coaches and referees, his credibility is based on his profession as an NFL referee.

speaker depends most on dimensions of perception. The first, and most important, involves the speaker's **ethos;** that is, the degree to which the audience perceives the speaker as credible. Aristotle believed that ethos is a personal attribute that is essential to a speaker's chances of persuading an audience. In fact, as the opening quotation in this chapter suggests, he viewed ethos as the most important aspect of a speaker's persuasiveness.

Modern communication researchers have substantiated Artistotle's thinking about the importance of ethos. Today's scholars use the term **source credibility,** which is the audience's perception of the believability of the speaker.[7] It is a quality your audience gives to you rather than one with which you are born. Thus a speaker might be truly competent in a particular subject matter, but if the audience does not know this, the speaker's expertise will not increase his or her credibility. Similarly, a speaker may be of good character, but if the audience does not believe it, the speaker will suffer low credibility.

Components of Credibility

Credibility is rooted in audience perceptions of believability. Researchers have shown that credibility consists of two primary components. Although researchers label these differently, the two perceptions that lead audiences to confer credibility on a speaker are competence and character.[8] Both are necessary to sustain the perception of ethos. To perceive you as credible, your audience must believe that

ethos
The degree to which an audience perceives a speaker as credible.

source credibility
The audience's perception of the believability of the speaker.

you are not only competent and knowledgeable about your topic but also a person of character who can be trusted.

Competence   If you are largely unknown to your audience, how your audience perceives you as a speaker in terms of knowledge, intelligence, and expertise on the topic of your speech is critical to your success. If you have special expertise or firsthand experience, by all means let your audience know. If you have done extensive research on your topic, this will help your audience appreciate your newly acquired competence on the subject. Use facts, statistics, and quotations from experts to help your audience know that you are well informed on the subject.

Character   Even an expert can lack credibility with an audience if he or she is perceived as untrustworthy. For example, attorneys frequently call on expert witnesses to bolster their cases. Scientists testify about DNA evidence, forensic pathologists testify to matters such as time and cause of death, and accident investigators testify about such things as driver negligence. The trouble with such experts is that they are usually paid handsomely for their testimony. This calls their character into question in the minds of many, including jurors. This can and often does undermine perceptions of their overall credibility.

Enhancing Audience Perceptions of Credibility

Speakers can enhance audience perceptions of their credibility at three times—before the speech; during the speech; and perhaps one you didn't expect, after the speech. Because it is a perception, credibility is dynamic and changeable. The fact that a speaker is perceived as credible going into a persuasive speech doesn't guarantee that he or she will still be perceived as credible afterward. Similarly, the speaker who begins with little credibility can build the perception in the process of speaking. One of your goals is to build and maintain your credibility as you speak. You want it to be at least as high—and preferably higher—when you conclude as it was when you began. This is one reason careful audience analysis is essential. You need to know how your audience perceives your credibility before you speak to determine whether you need to enhance it, and if so, how.

Credibility Before the Speech   Often, speakers' reputations precede them; in fact, reputation may be what prompts the audience to attend, especially when the speaker is famous, is an expert, or has new or unusual information about the topic. For example, the speech on our campus by actor Edward James Olmos was so well attended that there was standing room only. His fame as an actor and reputation as a powerful speaker and crusader against gang violence had ensured a degree of credibility with his audience before he spoke a single word.

Of course, most of us are not experts and may not even be known to our audience. One way to build credibility before we speak is to have someone introduce us to the audience. In Chapter 16 we discuss how to present a speech of introduction that will enhance an audience's perception of the speaker's credibility. If you are not introduced, you will have to establish your own credibility by what you say in your speech and how you say it.

Credibility During the Speech   Under most but not all conditions, the speaker's level of credibility at the outset of the speech is insufficient to sustain the audience's perception of believability. Credibility by way of reputation can be negated as a result of the speaker's appearance, message, and delivery. Audience members can quickly become disenchanted and may even turn against speakers whom they feel are just going through the motions or resting too much on their laurels.

On the other hand, even speakers with little initial credibility can build perceptions of competence and character during their speech. As a case in point, students in an introductory public speaking course may have little initial credibility with each other because they don't know each other and don't know each other's qualifications to speak on various topics. Practically speaking, then, these students begin to build their credibility with their first speeches. Their appearance, the care with which they have prepared their message, and their delivery can begin to establish their competence and character with their fellow students and instructor.

To make certain you are perceived as a credible speaker in a persuasive transaction, you need to provide your audience with proof of your credibility through the reasoning and evidence in your message. The reasoning and evidence you present in your persuasive speech should not only support the arguments you make but also support the audience's perception that you are competent and a person of high character. Also, if you have special expertise or credentials that are relevant to your topic, you'll want to share the fact with your audience.

Credibility After the Speech   Speakers whose persuasive message bolsters their credibility with an audience cannot rest on their laurels. Just as initial credibility can suffer from a poor speech, the credibility you establish during your speech can be negated as well. No one knows this better than New York Yankee slugger Jason Giambi. After denying publicly for months that he had used performance-enhancing drugs, he was forced to admit under oath to a federal grand jury that he had taken steroids and injected human growth hormone. His reputation was tarnished, and the scandal became a major embarrassment to professional baseball. Never lose sight of the fact that perceived credibility is dynamic. Once gained, credibility needs continued nourishment. The following list provides some reminders and tips for maintaining credibility.

Tips and Tactics

Speaker Credibility

- Ask yourself about the degree to which your audience already perceives you as credible. Also ask yourself whether your classroom behavior could have lowered your credibility in the eyes of the other students. For example, coming to class late and interrupting a speaker, not being ready to speak when it is your turn, or delivering speeches that are hastily put together tell other students about your competence and character. If this is the case, you'll need to work harder to establish your credibility.

- Dress appropriately for the occasion. Persuasion is serious business and should be approached seriously.

- Incorporate any special expertise or experience you have with your topic into the body of your speech. This information will enhance the audience's perception of your competence.

- Use evidence to support the claims you make. The facts and logical arguments you provide will help enhance your credibility.

- Engage your audience nonverbally, using the characteristics of effective delivery described in Chapter 11.
- Use powerful language (which research suggests is linked to persuasive effects), as described in Chapter 10.
- Use inclusive language, discussed in Chapter 10, to make certain all audience members believe they have a stake in the topic of your persuasive speech.

Similarity and Consequent Attraction

A second dimension of perception important to how an audience responds to you and your speech is similarity. As a rule of thumb, the more similar audience members perceive you to be to themselves, the more interpersonally attractive they will perceive you to be as well. The reason is not hard to understand. People are suspicious of those they feel are dissimilar to themselves. How can an outsider, they think, understand their needs or the needs of their local community?

Of course, appearance-based perceptions of similarity can disappear as soon as we open our mouths to talk or to express an opinion. Regional accents and dialects can interfere with appearance-based perceptions of similarity. So too can a person's vocabulary or use of slang. Before assuming that similarity exists, it's best to actually talk to the person. Even superficial conversations about hobbies and pastimes can be a source of information about another's culture, demography, and individual likes or dislikes. The box "How Similar or Dissimilar Are You and Your Audience?" will help you evaluate your audience before you speak.

Finally, although it is good to emphasize or take advantage of known similarities between the audience and the speaker, it's also crucial that the speaker establish expertise on the subject as slightly to moderately greater than that of most audience members. This doesn't mean saying something foolish such as, "I know more than you do." It means making yourself credible in the eyes of your audience.

Appearance

Perceptions of similarity are initially based on our appearance. The more we look like audience members themselves, the more similar the audience will perceive us to be in terms of background experience, attitudes, beliefs, and even values. Because students generally conform to the appearance norms practiced at their school, college students may look more similar than they actually are.

Obvious as this point may seem, some student speakers choose to ignore the simple fact that dress confers credibility. To repeat, you never get a second chance to make a favorable first impression. Thus you need to dress in a style that emphasizes your competence. Professional dress can lead to perceptions of not too much, not too little, but just the right amount of dissimilarity with your audience.

Constructing a Persuasive Message: Strategic Guidelines

Although you cannot always choose your audience and you cannot always ensure that they will have a favorable image of your credibility in the beginning of a persuasive transaction, you can control one element of the persuasive process–your message. We've come a long way in the past hundred years in terms of what we know about persuasive messages. And one of the chief things we've learned is that not all evidence is alike in the eyes of an audience. In this section we discuss types of evidence used in persuasive appeals and the importance of presenting a two-sided message.

Evidence and Persuasion

Assuming that your goal is long-term attitude change through central route processing, it is likely that you'll be seeking credible evidence to support your message. For many years social scientific research on the value of evidence in persuasion was thought to be conflicting and inconsistent. In 1988, however, communication scholar John Reinard published a thorough analysis of 50 years of research on the persuasive effects of evidence.[9] Unlike many previous researchers, Reinard did not rely solely on the conclusions of other studies; he went back to the original works and reinterpreted the data using comparable definitions. He found that the research was surprisingly consistent. Further, he found that evidence, under most conditions, did in fact enhance the likelihood of persuasive effects. As Reinard writes: "After fifty years of research on the persuasive effects of evidence, the claims for the persuasiveness of evidence emerge as quite strong."[10] Some of his most important findings follow.[11]

Testimonial assertions (the judgment and opinions of people other than the persuader) are most effective when the sources are identified and their qualifications explained to receivers. Mere "name-dropping" has not been found to be persuasive.

Reports (factual information that describes events as seen by either participants or observers) are persuasive, especially when they are believable, specific, and the receivers are intelligent. It is also important that the reporter's qualifications be explained for receivers.

Statistics, somewhat surprisingly, tend not to be very persuasive in the short term although results are better in the long term. To be most effective, statistics should be preceded by a specific example, which is then shown to be representative through the use of statistics. To be persuasive, it is also important to explain how statistics were gathered. Research has demonstrated that when examples and personal anecdotes conflict with statistics, people are more likely to be persuaded by the examples.

Source credibility—that is, the believability of the person delivering a persuasive message—has an important relationship to the persuasiveness of evidence. Using evidence tends to build a persuader's credibility. However, a source that is already highly credible is not likely to become more persuasive through the use of evidence in the short term (although long-term persuasiveness is enhanced). This is because of a *ceiling effect,* which means the persuader has already reached the maximum persuasive potential through his or her source credibility. With or without evidence, the persuader cannot become more persuasive.

Although the mode of presentation (video, tape, live, etc.) doesn't seem to make any difference, a poorly delivered presentation will not be persuasive no matter how good the evidence.

One very consistent research finding is that the most persuasive evidence comes from highly credible sources, found to be believable by receivers. The overall finding of the body of research is that high-quality evidence is more persuasive than low-quality evidence, especially for receivers who have a personal stake in the issue, who are trained in reasoning, who find the topic novel, who are not biased about the issue, and who have attended college.

Reinard's analysis supports the view that it is important to use credible, high-quality evidence in seeking to persuade others. Furthermore, he provides specific guidance as to the best evidence in specific situations. One of his most interesting findings is that statistics alone are not likely to be very persuasive. Persuaders need to bring the statistics to life by first presenting a vivid example. Statistics then serve to bolster the specific case rather than replace it.

Technically, there are three types of evidence. They are called first-, second-, and third-order data.[12] **First-order data** is evidence based on personal experience. When a person whose life was turned around by education speaks to a high school audience about staying in school, this is first-order data. It not only carries

first-order data
Evidence based on personal experience.

Considering Diversity

Culture and Persuasion

As a society, we value a reasoning process that is more likely to produce true than false beliefs, likely to produce a large number of truthful arguments and statements, and likely to do so with a fair amount of speed. Through our collective experience we learn that certain types of reasoning work well. We internalize these and use them as templates for evaluating communicators and their messages.

Some cultures value reasoning more than others. Western culture tends to value rational argument and view anything labeled fallacious with suspicion. As Rodney A. Reynolds and Michael Burgoon point out, "Logical explanations are typically rewarded and contradictions or absurdities punished as children develop."[1] Another culture, such as that of Japan, may place greater emphasis on tradition and appeal to authority than does the North American culture. Thus, operating in a system that values rationality requires a persuader to at least appeal to reason and evidence in order to be successful.[2]

[1]Rodney A. Reynolds and Michael Burgoon, "Belief Processing, Reasoning, and Evidence," in *Communication Yearbook 7,* ed. Robert N. Bostrom (Beverly Hills, Calif.: Sage, 1983), 88.
[2]John C. Reinard, *Foundations of Argument: Effective Communication for Critical Thinking* (Dubuque, Iowa: W. C. Brown, 1991), 171.

with it logical force but also helps enhance the credibility of the speaker. **Second-order data** is evidence based on expert testimony. When those who debate the research on global warming cite professors, public officials, and other experts on the subject, they are presenting the audience with second-order data. **Third-order data** is evidence based on facts and statistics. The number of teen pregnancies each year and the percentage of teenagers having unprotected sex are examples of third-order data.

Of course, the importance of evidence and reasoning can vary from culture to culture. As the box Culture and Persuasion points out, Western culture puts a premium on rationality.

> **second-order data**
> Evidence based on expert testimony.
>
> **third-order data**
> Evidence based on facts and statistics.

Tips and Tactics

Using Evidence

- If you want your audience to engage in central route processing, use credible evidence to support your position.
- Be sure to tell your audience who your sources are and what makes them qualified to speak on the topic.
- Statistics are most effective when preceded by specific vivid examples.
- Visuals help your audience to process statistics.
- If you are not perceived as highly credible by an audience, the use of high-quality evidence can enhance their perception of your credibility.
- Emphasize your personal experiences if they are relevant to your topic and persuasive purpose. Audiences relate to personal stories, so first-order data can be powerful evidence.
- When using second-order data, use experts with name recognition for your audience.
- Strive to balance first-, second-, and third-order data throughout your speech.
- Finally, use evidence your audience is likely to find memorable, particularly at the beginning and end of your speech.

The Importance of a Two-Sided Message

To be most effective, carefully order the arguments in your persuasive message and include an acknowledgment of the other side of the issue. Whereas the research once was not consistent in this regard, it now shows that a persuasive speech that is two-sided rather than one-sided will be more effective.[13]

A one-sided persuasive speech only offers evidence in support of your claim; a two-sided persuasive speech makes use of a brief statement of the other side of the issue and your response to it. Let's say, for example, that you want to persuade your audience to support the claim that the war on drugs is a failure. In a standard one-sided persuasive speech, you would only present evidence and appeals you believe will prove effective with your audience. In a two-sided speech, you would do all of this and more. After making the argument, you would indicate what the other side might have to say, as well as present your answer to those arguments. Of course, this does not mean you abandon your point of view. Rather, you acknowledge counterarguments to it. You would then go on in your speech to point out the weaknesses in the other side's point of view. You simply tell the audience that there are reasonable people who don't support your position and then give the audience an example of the kind of evidence these reasonable people have given for not supporting your side. You then refute this example with a further argument or show that in spite of their argument, your overall claim is more credible.

Not only is a two-sided message more persuasive than a one-sided message, but research suggests at least two other benefits from its use. First, a two-sided message enhances the audience's perceptions of the speaker's credibility. Second, it makes audience members more resistant to counterpersuasion because it gives them a rebuttal to common arguments associated with the opposing view.

Peripheral Cues to Persuasion

In spite of his emphasis on rationality, Aristotle recognized the role of emotions in the process of persuasion. He reasoned what modern researchers have demonstrated again and again: People are persuaded not simply by cold logic but also by emotional appeals. **Pathos** refers to the emotional states in an audience that a speaker can arouse and use to achieve persuasive goals.

pathos
The emotional states in an audience that a speaker can arouse and use to achieve persuasive goals.

Aristotle catalogued the many emotions a speaker can evoke in the attempt to persuade people. Specific emotions he mentions in his writings about persuasion include anger, fear, kindness, shame, pity, calmness, confidence, unkindness, friendship, enmity, shamelessness, and envy.[14] Sometimes the speaker may choose to appeal to the audience members' emotions or primitive beliefs. Because of social conditioning from the earliest years of childhood, people respond to some messages in specific, predictable ways. Whereas logical proofs are designed to induce elaborated thinking on the part of the audience, emotional appeals are designed to provoke audience members to respond without elaborated thought.

These methods are not inherently unethical, but they can be abused by unscrupulous persuaders. Emotional appeals do not necessarily lead to peripheral route processing, but many do. On the one hand, it is perfectly rational to be fearful of cancer and therefore to get regular checkups and eat a diet high in the proper nutrients. On the other hand, expensive early detection procedures on people with

Animal-rights groups often base their persuasive messages on strong appeals to their audience's emotions.

no reason to think they have the disease may be taking advantage of these fears. When emotional appeals are used to bypass central route processing, they become peripheral cues to persuasion. To illustrate the way appeals to the emotions operate, let's review one of the most researched: fear.

Motivating Through Fear

Common sense tells us that we sometimes do things as a result of fear; for example, we obey the law because we are afraid of the penalties we could suffer should we break it. Yet the research suggests that when it comes to persuasive speaking, fear has its limits. Whether your goal is to encourage the use of shoulder and lap belts while driving, demonstrate how flossing your teeth can prevent gum disease, or convince people everyone needs a gun for self-protection, the research is clear: Persuasive messages that arouse moderate levels of fear in audience members are more effective than those that generate high levels of fear. This fact is especially true, moreover, when the speaker gives audience members a set of clear-cut steps they can take to reduce the fear the speaker has aroused.[15]

As you can see in Figure 14.4, the relationship between fear and persuasive effects is like the relationship between speech anxiety and performance, explained

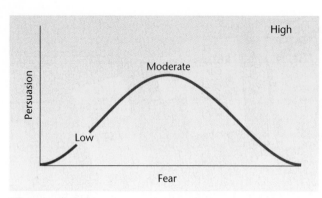

Figure 14.4

The Relationship Between Fear Appeals and Persuasion.
As the level of fear aroused in an audience begins to increase, so do persuasive effects. Too much fear, however, diminishes persuasive effects.

in Chapter 3. As the level of fear aroused in an audience begins to increase, so do persuasive effects. Too much fear, however, diminishes persuasive effects because it tends to elicit denial from audience members. In a sense, audience members respond to the high level of fear the speaker has aroused in them by thinking, "That could never happen to me." If employed in moderation, however, fear can be effective. Many public service campaigns use moderate levels of fear to encourage positive behaviors such as not smoking, practicing safe sex, and taking advantage of medications that control high blood pressure. The slogan "If not for yourself, then do it for the ones you love" is a good example. Produced by the American Heart Association, this persuasive message tells people with high blood pressure that they need to think about the feelings of the people they would leave behind if they failed to control their blood pressure. This message involves a mild but effective level of fear. Fear isn't an inherently unethical form of persuasion. Used moderately to achieve an ethical end, it is but one of the choices you have in deciding how to appeal to your audience.

Appealing to Primitive Beliefs

Appeals to emotions such as fear are frequently combined with appeals to primitive beliefs. Primitive beliefs are instilled from childhood. Research shows that the use of appeals that connect with primitive beliefs about reciprocity, liking, authority, social support, scarcity, and commitment is both widespread and effective in persuasive communication.[16]

Reciprocity

The saying "You scratch my back, and I'll scratch yours" illustrates reciprocity. A reciprocity-based appeal can work in one of two ways in a persuasive speech. Candidates for political office often promise to give something in return for a person's vote. They may promise to reciprocate by proposing legislation, supporting a specific bill, or voicing a concern of their constituency.

Another common way reciprocity is used in a persuasive speech is when the speaker calls on the audience to reciprocate. During homecoming week, as a case in point, the school president may appeal to alumni for financial support. The appeal is usually couched in terms of "giving something back to the institution that gave you so much."

Reciprocity appeals are effective because people are conditioned from an early age to return favors, gifts, and services. Reciprocity is a norm. Thus, when people receive a promise or are asked to return something received, the conditioned response is to reciprocate in kind.

Liking

Appeals to primitive beliefs about liking are commonly used in persuasive campaigns. Politicians, for instance, enlist stars from film and music to speak persuasively on their behalf. The assumption is that if a star is well liked, the feeling may be generalized to the candidate endorsed by the star. Liking is a staple of advertisers, who employ well-known people as spokespersons for a product. It's not that the celebrities are experts on the product, but they are well liked by the public. Thus, if well-liked figures Tiger Woods and LeBron James wear Nikes, the hope is that the public will also like the product.

Authority

Research shows that some people are predisposed to comply with the requests of individuals and institutions perceived as authoritative. Examples of these authoritative sources range from members of law enforcement and the clergy to federal agencies such as the military. Thus a speaker attempting to encourage a group of Catholics to voice their opposition to stem cell research might use the words of the pope as an appeal. Similarly, a politician speaking to veterans might rely on an endorsement received from a military hero to win the audience's vote in the election.

Social Support

An appeal based on social support is nothing more than an appeal based on numbers. There's a tendency among people to think that if enough folks say something is so, then it must be so. Thus product advertisers tout their product as "the number-one seller in its class" in an effort to convince consumers that their product must be the best. Research shows that when people are confronted with an appeal supported by large numbers, they are much more likely to be persuaded by the appeal—to jump on the bandwagon, so to speak. In a sense, they accept social support as a form of grounds for the argument.

Celebrities such as Tiger Woods are effective in promoting products because they are well liked by the public.

Scarcity

The appeal to scarcity is based on the law of supply and demand. It is a maxim in economics that when demand exceeds supply, the value of the commodity increases. Thus an appeal based on scarcity is also one based on relative value. As is the case with reciprocity, authority, and social support, people are conditioned to believe that something that is scarce is valuable enough to demand their attention. Persuasive speeches about the environment frequently use scarcity as the basis of appeal. For instance, the ecological benefit of the rain forests is made even more valuable when the speaker tells the audience that the world's rain forests are disappearing at an alarming rate.

Commitment

One of the most powerful methods of persuasion is the appeal to commitment. In the aftermath of September 11, 2001, millions of Americans made the commitment to donate blood. Even when the blood banks were overwhelmed with more donors than they could take, people were encouraged to pledge that they would come back at a later date when blood supplies needed replenishment. When people make even small commitments as a result of a persuasive message, the principle of psychological consistency comes into play. This principle tells us that we all feel pressure to keep our attitudes, beliefs, and values consistent with our commitments. If an appeal to commitment leads a person to write a letter, to volunteer to serve, or to sign a petition, it increases the chances that the person's attitudes, beliefs, and values will reflect the commitment. In some cases action may actually precede changes in attitude, reversing the normal order of persuasive goals.

To reiterate, the appeals you make in your persuasive message should reflect your goal and your audience. Not all audiences jump aboard the bandwagon after hearing an appeal based on social support. There are those who steadfastly refuse to get on a bandwagon, no matter how many other people have already done so. Choosing the right appeals to flesh out your persuasive message, therefore, is part science and part art.

Rules for the Road

Knowing what you now know, is there anything else you need to know to prepare your persuasive speech? We recommend three steps: (1) Adapt your goals to your audience, (2) organize your speech effectively, and (3) balance the means of persuasion.

Adapt Your Goals to Your Audience

Speeches to reinforce or inoculate an audience presume that your audience members are either already supportive of your point of view or uninformed about the topic. These are friendly or neutral audiences. In such cases, you can expect your views to receive a fair hearing. You will want to build a strong case, of course, but you need not fear that your audience will reject you and your message out of hand.

A speech to change attitudes, by definition, means your audience disagrees with you. This is termed a hostile audience. Although they may not be overtly hostile (booing and hissing), they are unlikely to be open to your point of view without a lot of work on your part. Such a speech requires you to begin with a common ground on which you and your audience can agree. After doing so, it is realistic only to try to move them slightly toward your position on the topic. One of our students, Mary Schoenthaler, faced exactly this kind of situation in her speech, which you can read in the box Sample Persuasive Speech: Tattoos v. Mehndi. Many of the students who listened to Mary's persuasive speech had one or more tattoos. Having already made the commitment to tattoo a part or parts of their bodies, Mary knew some of these students might denigrate her credibility or discount her evidence. At best, then, she hoped to gain the respect of these students while persuading the rest of her audience to seriously consider the risks to tattooing their skin.

SpeechCoach

To view this speech, go to segment 14.1 on your CD.

We think Mary did a masterful job. On one hand, she introduced information with which the students with tattoos could relate: for example, the pain most experience, and the considerable aftercare the process of tattooing requires. On the other hand, she also introduced a diverse body of evidence and types of appeals that suggested pain and aftercare are minor in comparison to the risks of infection and disease. She also discussed the fact that about half of the people who get tattoos eventually want them removed, which can cost up to $2,500.

Finally, Mary did something else for her audience. She gave them specific suggestions for reducing risk if some audience members still choose to be tattooed, and she gave them an alternative to tattooing for ornamenting their bodies. As previously mentioned, fear appeals work best when people are given specific remedies to reduce the fear. And that's exactly what Mary did for her audience members.

Mary's speech was designed to induce action among audience members. We think it also set the stage nicely for a subsequent speech or speeches with this persuasive goal in mind.

Speeches that seek to prompt people to act presume that your audience is prepared by prior messages to take action or that your topic is not inherently controversial. For example, prompting people to donate blood is not a topic that people are hostile to, though they may be fearful of doing so. Such a speech needs to focus on reducing irrational fears, such as the transmission of blood-borne diseases, which cannot occur for the donor. In the case of an audience already primed by previous messages, your main task is to motivate them to act. People have heard for years about the benefits of wearing seat belts, yet a significant number still fail to do so. Rehashing arguments they have already heard is of little use with such people. You need to tell them something new that will get them to act. A dramatic story, for example, about how your own life was saved by wearing a seat belt might be the key ingredient in such a speech.

Organize Your Persuasive Speech

In Chapter 9 we introduced a number of ways to organize a speech. Three organizational patterns described there are particularly suited to your persuasive speeches. The first is the problem–solution pattern, the second is called stock issues, and the third is Monroe's motivated-sequence pattern.

The problem–solution pattern of organization analyzes a problem in terms of harm, significance, and cause and proposes a solution that is described, feasible, and advantageous. Many persuasive topics are about problems we face individually or as a society. By beginning with a discussion of the problem, the speaker heightens the audience's interest but avoids turning off a hostile audience with a solution they might initially reject. A speech on trying juveniles as adults that begins with a discussion of the growing gang problem is far more likely to receive a hearing from a parent's group than a speech that begins by calling for locking up 14-year-olds as if they were 18.

The stock issues pattern uses *ill, blame, cure,* and *cost* to encourage people to make changes either in governmental policies or in their own lives. For example, a speech about cellular phones might identify an ill in terms of the greater risk of an auto accident when driving while using a cell phone. The blame might be due to the driver's divided attention, not just the use of one hand on the phone. Thus the cure wouldn't simply be hands-free phones but rather a law that banned use of phones while driving (such as was passed in New York). The costs of this proposal

In Their Own Words

Sample Persuasive Speech

TATTOOS V. MEHNDI
by Mary Schoenthaler

Mary Schoenthaler

Does the introduction capture your attention? Is the use of language effective?

Don't mind the burning smell. It reminds most people of chicken left in the oven too long. These are not the words of Julia Child discussing her latest recipe for frog legs flambé. They're the words of Bill Hatfield, a laser salesman, trying to reassure a patient as her dermatologist uses a laser to remove a tattoo. If you're thinking about getting a tattoo, think again, because a tattoo is not just another fashion accessory you can drop off at the Salvation Army store when you don't want it anymore. It's a subdermal deposit of ink that's with you forever—or at least until you have it burned off with a laser. If this class is any reflection of U.S. statistics, there are two or three people in this room with tattoos. You're not alone, there are at least another 10 million people in the United States with tattoos and about half of them— 5 million people—will someday want theirs gone. And though it might take you 30 minutes and $50 to get a tattoo, it may take you 10 months and $2,500 to remove it. Today, you'll learn about the rarely discussed risks and problems associated with tattoos, and then you'll discover other ways of expressing yourself that are less painful, and less permanent.

Notice how the speaker connects with her audience by personalizing her use of statistics.

Comparison of cost of getting a tattoo and cost of removal is startling.

Main points are previewed, including the promise of an alternative.

Now, tattoos might seem artistic, exotic, or even shocking on the surface, but they pose a number of problems because of the way that they're applied. First, tattoos are not for the squeamish, because tattoos are literally a pain. Why do they hurt? Because a tattoo machine is actually engraving your skin. According to Victoria Lautman's book, *The New Tattoo*, 1999, the tattoo machine is sort of a cross between a dentist's drill and a ballpoint pen. It's capable of holding up to a group of 15 needles that are dipped in ink and then move rapidly up and down, capable of pricking your skin at speeds of up to two to three thousand times per minute. You feel pain for a good reason; the needles are penetrating four layers of skin and depositing ink on the fifth. That's a lot of nerve stimulation. Now, as a tattoo is applied, you begin to bleed, so the tattooist has to keep wiping away blood and ink so he can see what he's doing.

Source cited. Vivid analogy of tattoo machine to dentist's drill and ballpoint pen.

How effective is her description of the process? Is it too vivid? Will some audience members become squeamish?

Now, just because you've gotten out of the tattooist's chair doesn't mean you're done. You still have a few things to think about. Because you've just had an invasive procedure, you now have a wound that you need to take care of. You've got to keep it clean and lubricated until healing is complete, about a week to 10 days, at which time the scab that has formed will fall off. You've got to stay out of the sun for two weeks to prevent sunburn or pigment changes. Swimming should also be avoided for the first couple of weeks so that the pigments don't leach out.

Is this information on aftercare merely informative, or is it added to further discourage tattooing?

Beyond the aftercare, though, are issues that are more serious that you can't see. Because the tattooing involves the use of needles and because it draws blood, you are at risk of being infected with hepatitis B or C. In fact, four states— Indiana, Massachusetts, Oklahoma, and South Carolina—ban tattooing because of previous outbreaks of hepatitis. You also cannot donate blood for a year after getting a tattoo for the same reason. Now, if blood banks are concerned about tattoos, you should be too.

How effective is the fear appeal used here? Does the banning of tattooing in some states and the blood bank policy add credibility to this argument?

Now, bacterial and viral infections happen because of dirty needles and contaminated inks. A tattooist should use an autoclave to sterilize all their equipment and anything that can't go into an autoclave should be wiped down with a disinfectant after each customer. Needles should come in sealed packages and be opened in front of you, and used needles should be disposed of properly in a medical sharps container. Ink should be poured off of a main bottle into individual disposable cups, and the tattooist should wear medical latex gloves and properly prep the area that is to be tattooed. But who is making sure this is happening? It's hard to figure out. The Food and Drug Administration only has jurisdiction over the needles and the inks, not over the procedures. And even here their policy is confusing. The tattoo inks are considered color additives, but no color additives have been approved for use in tattoos because the FDA doesn't know what the long-term effects of the inks are. State and local agencies are supposed to regulate tattoo establishments, but guidelines vary from county to county and from state to state. So, just because a tattoo parlor is open for business and hasn't been shut down by the health department doesn't mean that the proprietor is Mr. Clean. Simply put, if you want to get a tattoo, it's up to you to determine whether the establishment is reputable and clean.

Now, most people would counter, the majority of tattoo establishments are on the up and up and that chances for infection are practically nil. I would answer, perhaps, but consider the following. According to U.S. News & World Report, November 3, 1997, tattooing is the sixth fastest growing retail business in the United States, right behind Internet and paging services, bagel, computer, and cellular phone shops. Yet 27 states have absolutely no regulations at all to ensure proper hygiene in tattoo parlors. At the same time, 5 million people in the United States are infected with hepatitis B and C. So, when you couple a sporadically regulated booming business with a spreading communicable disease, the chances for contamination and infection increase.

Now, remember about half the people who get tattoos will someday want to get them removed. If you turn out to be one of them, there are a few things you should know. First, don't be fooled into thinking that a laser magically zaps away a tattoo. Just as erasing a pencil mark alters the appearance of a paper, so too does erasing the ink in your skin. Patients get only 85 to 90 percent clearance. Often there is permanent lightening of the skin or a shadow left behind. Another problem is paradoxical darkening. Light tattooing, such as beige, pink, or white, may turn black when treated by a laser. The Medical Letter on Drugs and Therapeutics, January 1997, states that no single laser can be used to treat all tattoos because different wavelengths of light are needed to treat different ink colors. Multiple sessions are required. It typically takes 6 to 10 sessions to remove a professional tattoo, but it sometimes requires up to 20. You're going to have to endure more pain, because when you have a tattoo removed, the laser is actually heating the tattoo pigments in your skin, causing it to break up into tiny particles that are expelled or absorbed by your body. Some people compare the feeling of the laser pulses to being splattered with hot bacon grease. It's also going to cost you. A small two-inch tattoo costs $1,500 to be removed. Larger ones are two-to-three thousand dollars or more. So, unlike a hangover, a tattoo will not disappear with a couple of aspirin the next morning. Even Axl Rose, a guy who knows a thing or two about tattoos, is quoted as saying, "Think before you ink."

What should you think about? Let's look at a few alternatives. For most people, a tattoo is an individual expression of identity that expresses some sort of personal, political, or artistic statement. And as humans, we all have a need to do this. Luckily, there are ways that are safer and less permanent than tattoos. Besides the obvious, temporary tattoos, wild clothes and hair, or makeup a la Marilyn Manson, Mehndi is perhaps the best alternative. If you've seen a Madonna video lately, you've seen Mehndi. Mehndi is the ancient art of drawing patterns onto the skin with an all-natural henna dye. With Mehndi you get body art that looks

(continued)

Notice that she gives those who choose tattoos advice on how to protect themselves from infection.

Why do you think she brings out that FDA lacks jurisdiction over the procedures? Are consumers not as safe as they might assume?

Source is cited to point out how rapidly the tattooing industry is growing.

Do these statistics convince you that the risk of hepatitis is a serious issue?

Does her second main point, that tattoos are difficult and costly to remove, strengthen her case against tattooing?

Again, she cites the source of her information on laser removal.

Does quoting Axl Rose help her adapt to members of the audience who are considering tattoos?

Effective use of fear appeal requires an alternative. She promises to provide one.

Is Mehndi a viable alternative to tattooing? How well does she make the case?

In Their Own Words

Sample Persuasive Speech (continued)

Notice that she again cites her source.

permanent but that can be reapplied or replaced when the original fades. According to Carine Fabious's book, Mehndi: The Art of Henna Body Painting, 1998, Mehndi has been practiced throughout Africa, India, and the Middle East for the last 5,000 years. Traces of henna have been found on the fingertips of mummies. It has been used for centuries in ceremonies to celebrate rites of passage. There are even references to Mehndi in the bible.

How does the description of the process of applying Mehndi compare with tattooing? Does she make it seem safer and easier?

The procedure goes something like this. After mixing henna powder with a variety of oils, lemon juice, and tea, tiny plastic bottles or cones are filled with a thick paste. Detailed drawings are then painted onto your skin—many of these inspired by ancient traditional patterns. The paste stays on for about 12 hours before cracking off, leaving you with a brown-orange stain that lasts about two to four weeks. In India it's traditional to have Mehndi applied to the hands, or brides are painted to celebrate their wedding day. In Morocco Mehndi is thought to ward off evil and to protect both mother and child through pregnancy and birth.

Notice she gives audience members local sources for Mehndi.

Now, since Mehndi is applied topically, there are no needles, no blood, and therefore no pain and no infection. Best of all, it's temporary, after about four weeks it's gone without lasers, dermabrasion, or surgery. You can even have it done right here in Chico. You can make an appointment with Juanita at Creative Solutions on Flume Street or you can buy a kit and learn how to do it yourself for about $25. They can be ordered through the campus bookstore; they can be purchased at Barnes and Noble or local beauty supply stores. Learning about Mehndi doesn't take much effort. Find a book or go online and peruse some Mehndi Web sites. So why make a commitment to a tattoo and be forced to deal with the consequences, when there is another, safer way to adorn yourself? I say, be different and go herbal; try Mehndi.

She does more than just summarize points; she advocates a specific alternative to tattooing.

Today, you've learned that a tattoo is more than just a decorative skin art; it's a painstaking process that poses real problems. The good news is that Mehndi is an excellent alternative. Because, ultimately, there's nothing wrong with wanting to adorn yourself, just understand that you can do it in a way that's not painful, that doesn't put you at risk for disease, and doesn't come with the possibility of regrets. Because at the end of the day or in five years you can always change your hair, switch your wardrobe or switch careers, but a tattoo is forever. And really, beauty is more than skin deep. Thank you.

Does her last line leave a strong impact, or could she have closed more effectively?

(Delivered April 24, 1999. Transcript prepared from videotape.)

---

might be higher law enforcement costs and some inconvenience to the drivers, but the lives saved would be well worth it.

The third pattern useful for persuasive speaking is Monroe's motivated-sequence, a five-step organizational scheme including attention, need, satisfaction, visualization, and action. Because the final step is action, this pattern is particularly well suited to speeches calling for your audience to act. As should all good speeches, this type begins by capturing the audience's attention. Like the problem–solution pattern, this speech focuses on a problem (called a need) before proposing its solution (satisfaction). But this pattern goes further by asking the audience to visualize the satisfaction of the need and then calling on them to act.

Regardless of the organizational pattern you choose, there are some principles of organization you should follow. First, always put your best arguments and support either early or late in the speech. Do not hide them in the middle. Over the years, research has shown that in some cases people best remember what they hear first, whereas in other cases, what comes last is most memorable. Either way, the middle of the speech is not the place for your best material.

Second, with hostile or indifferent audiences, it is particularly important to have some of your best material early in the speech. Otherwise, they will tune you out before you get to the critical points you want to make.

Balance the Means of Persuasion

Finally, although it might seem as if we have treated source credibility, evidence, and emotional appeals as separate means of persuasion, this is not really the case in practice. Your credibility will affect how your audience perceives the substance of your speech. If you have high credibility, the audience is more likely to accept your arguments. Similarly, if you have strong evidence and arguments in your speech, your credibility will grow in the audience's mind. And unless you touch the audience's emotions, it is unlikely that they will be motivated to act or believe in what they have heard. Mayor Giuliani was not only viewed as a credible figure as a result of his actions in the wake of September 11, 2001; he also used strong emotional appeals to get people back to some degree of normalcy and reasoning and evidence to calm people's fears of visiting New York City. In short, a good persuasive speech relies on using all the available means of persuasion for its success.

Summary

Four common functions/goals of a persuasive speech are to:

- Reinforce existing beliefs and attitudes
- Inoculate against counterpersuasion
- Change attitudes
- Prompt the audience to act

Focus on the audience and situation, including:

- The cultural, demographic, and individual diversity of the audience
- The audience's attitudes toward the topic
- Audience behavioral intentions toward the topic
- Audience involvement in the topic

Consider rhetorical constraints, including ethical considerations.

The elaboration likelihood model reflects two potential paths an audience can take in response to a persuasive message:

- Central route processing involves elaborated and critical thinking.
- Peripheral route processing relies on cues, such as emotional appeals.

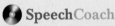 **Speech**Coach

To evaluate your understanding of this chapter, see the Quizzes on your CD.

 www.mhhe.com /brydon5

Visit the Online Learning Center for helpful study resources, including practice tests, key term crossword puzzles, and PowerWeb articles for research and review.

Credibility is composed of competence and character and can be enhanced before, during, and after a speech.

Audiences' perceptions of similarity of the speaker to themselves are helpful in enhancing a speaker's persuasiveness.

Evidence can greatly enhance a persuasive presentation. Three types of evidence are:

- First-order data: personal experience

- Second-order data: expert testimony

- Third-order data: facts and statistics

Two-sided messages are generally more effective than one-sided speeches:

- Two-sided messages confer greater credibility.

- Two-sided messages help inoculate an audience against counterpersuasion.

Peripheral cues include emotions such as fear and primitive beliefs about:

- Reciprocity

- Liking

- Authority

- Social support

- Scarcity

- Commitment

Persuasive patterns of organization include:

- Problem–solution

- Stock issues

- Monroe's motivated-sequence

Check Your Understanding: Exercises and Activities

For a review of key terms in this chapter, see the Key Terms Flashcards on your CD.

SpeechCoach

1. Suppose you are giving a speech on the topic of civil liberties versus national security. How would you change your persuasive message to achieve each of the four persuasive goals: reinforcement, inoculation, attitude change, and action? How would these goals differ depending on possible audiences for this topic and the constraints you would face in each situation?

2. On a topic of your choosing, construct examples of appeals based on the six primitive beliefs discussed in the chapter (reciprocity, liking, etc.).

3. Consider the following list of topics: (1) preventing AIDS, (2) preventing tooth decay, and (3) the importance of wearing seat belts. Construct a brief message based on a moderate-level "fear" appeal for each of these topics. At what level—low, moderate, or high—do you think your fear appeal would diminish the persuasive effects, causing audience members to reject your message? At what point do you think arguments based on fear about these topics would become unethical?

4. Follow up on the list of tips we gave for assessing and enhancing perceptions of your credibility. List the specific factors you believe make you credible about the topic of your persuasive speech. Then describe how you plan on using these specific factors so that they will sustain the perception of credibility as you deliver your speech.

5. Newspaper editorials constitute a persuasive message. To improve your ability in recognizing the types of appeals being used, select a recent column from a nationally syndicated writer such as George Will, William Safire, Molly Ivins, or Ellen Goodman. Mark what you consider to be appeals the columnist is using. Note whether these appeals are intended to affect your emotions or your primitive beliefs. Finally, label the emotion or belief that the appeal is targeted at arousing.

Notes

1. Aristotle, *Rhetoric,* trans. W. Rhys Roberts (New York: Modern Library, 1954), 25.
2. William J. McGuire, "Inducing Resistance to Persuasion: Some Contemporary Approaches," in *Advances in Experimental and Social Psychology,* ed. L. Berkowitz (New York: Academic Press, 1964), 191–229.
3. M. Fishbein and I. Ajzen, *Belief, Attitude, Intention, and Behavior* (Reading, Mass.: Addison-Wesley, 1975), 12–13.
4. M. Sherif and C. I. Hovland, *Social Judgment: Assimilation and Contrast Effects in Communication and Attitude Change* (New Haven: Yale University Press, 1961).
5. Richard E. Petty and John T. Cacioppo, *Communication and Persuasion: Central and Peripheral Routes to Attitude Changes* (New York: Springer-Verlag, 1986).
6. Irvin A. Horowitz and Kenneth S. Bordens, *Social Psychology* (Mountain View, Calif.: Mayfield, 1995), 287–88.
7. Sarah Trenholm, *Persuasion and Social Influence* (Englewood Cliffs, N.J.: Prentice-Hall, 1989).
8. Carl I. Hovland, Irving L. Janis, and Harold H. Kelly, *Communication and Persuasion* (New Haven: Yale University Press, 1953); James C. McCroskey, *An Introduction to Rhetorical Communication,* 5th ed. (Englewood Cliffs, N.J.: Prentice-Hall, 1986); David K. Berlo, James B. Lemert, and Robert J. Mertz, "Dimensions for Evaluating the Acceptability of Message Sources," *Public Opinion Quarterly,* 33 (Winter 1969–1970): 562–76; Kenneth E. Anderson, *Persuasion: Theory and Practice* (Boston: Allyn & Bacon, 1971). For a useful chart comparing various researchers' terms for these key components of credibility, see John R. Wenburg and William W. Wilmont, *The Personal Communication Process* (New York: Wiley, 1973), 145–47.
9. John C. Reinard, "The Empirical Study of the Persuasive Effects of Evidence: The Status After Fifty Years of Research," *Human Communication Research,* 15 (Fall 1988): 3–59.
10. Reinard, "The Empirical Study," 46.
11. This summary of findings is abstracted from Reinard's excellent book, *Foundations of Argument: Effective Communication for Critical Thinking* (Dubuque, Iowa: W. C. Brown, 1991), 125–27.
12. James C. McCroskey, *An Introduction to Rhetorical Communication,* 7th ed. (Needham Heights, Mass.: Allyn & Bacon, 1997).
13. Mike Allen, "Meta-Analysis Comparing the Persuasiveness of One-Sided and Two-Sided Messages," *Western Journal of Communication,* 55 (1991): 390–404.
14. Aristotle, *Rhetoric.*
15. Irving Janis, "Effects of Fear-Arousal on Attitude Change: Recent Developments in Theory and Experimental Research," in *Advances in Experimental and Social Psychology,* vol. 3, ed. L. Berkowitz (New York: Academic Press, 1967), 166–224.
16. Robert Cialdini, *Influence: Science and Practice,* 2nd ed. (New York: HarperCollins, 1988).

Does filmmaker Michael Moore's in-your-face style promote or hinder critical thinking?

Chapter 15

Thinking and Speaking Critically

Objectives

After reading this chapter and reviewing the learning resources on your CD-ROM and at the Online Learning Center, you should be able to:

- Explain the difference between argumentativeness and verbal aggressiveness.
- Evaluate arguments using the Toulmin model of reasoning.
- Differentiate among patterns of reasoning.
- Identify and refute common fallacies of argument.

Key Concepts

ad hominem	isolated examples
arguing in a circle (begging the question)	loaded language
	mistaking correlation for cause
argumentativeness	
critical thinking	misused statistics
distorted evidence	non sequitur
false analogy	post hoc, ergo propter hoc
false dilemma	red herring (smoke screen)
halo effect	slippery slope
hasty generalization	stereotyping
hyperbole	straw person
ignoring the issue	unsupported assertion
inference	verbal aggressiveness

> " It is better to debate a question without settling it
> than to settle a question without debating it. "
>
> –JOSEPH JOUBERT

What do you think? Is smoking marijuana any more harmful to your health than drinking alcohol? Does the recreational use of cocaine or ecstasy inevitably lead to a life of ruin? Should drug addicts be punished as criminals, or should they receive medical treatment for their addiction?

What do you believe about the war on drugs? Do you think it has reduced drug use in our country—for example, kept drugs out of the workplace or minimized their use among young people? Or do you think that the billions of dollars committed by government to the war on drugs could have been better spent elsewhere?

And what do you think about drug testing? Would you mind being routinely tested in order to keep your job? Or if you are an athlete, do you think collegiate associations should demand that football and volleyball players, or swimmers and divers, submit to drug testing before each competition?

These kinds of questions are not easily answered. Illegal drugs and their widespread use continue to be topics of heated discussions in the halls of Congress, during the meetings of school boards, and over the dinner table in many homes. What's more, they have even been the centerpieces of blockbuster films such as *Traffic*, which won four Academy Awards and was nominated for best picture, and *Blow*, which starred Penelope Cruz and Johnny Depp.

Recently, two of our students took opposite positions in their persuasive speeches. One took the position that mandatory drug testing in the workplace should be the law of the land. See excerpts in the box Sample Persuasive Message: Mandatory Drug Testing. The other emphatically declared that the war on drugs has been an abysmal failure. Excerpts of this speech are shown in the box Sample Persuasive Message: The War on Drugs. Both speeches made some good points; but more than that, each tested the audience's ability to think critically about a topic that is anything but black and white. You will find both speeches in their entirety on your CD. Decide for yourself who presents the stronger case.

This chapter continues the discussion that began in Chapter 5 with critical listening and was continued in Chapter 8 in the discussion of the use of grounds and warrants to support the claims we make. We continue to employ the Toulmin model of reasoning to help you further develop your ability to think critically, both as a speaker and a listener. As speakers, if we want our audience to experience an enduring attitude change or to inoculate them against counterpersuasion, the central route to persuasion is best (see Chapter 14). As listeners, we should always be critical of the claims speakers make when deciding whether to accept them. Whether we are speaking or listening to a message that seeks to persuade us, critical thinking is important.

SpeechCoach

To view Miranda Welsh's full speech, "Mandatory Drug Testing," see segment 15.1 on your CD.

SpeechCoach

To view David Sanders' full speech, "The War on Drugs," see segment 15.2 on your CD.

Critical Thinking and Public Speaking

Critical thinking is the process of making sound inferences based on accurate evidence and valid reasoning. Understanding how to think critically about arguments is the first step to constructing and communicating those arguments to an audience. As noted in Chapter 14, logical proof should be an ethical part of any persuasive message. To successfully persuade others of our side of a controversial issue, it is important to have well-constructed, sound arguments for our side. As the elaboration likelihood model introduced in the preceding chapter shows, we are more likely to induce a permanent change in attitude if we use sound evidence and reasoning.

critical thinking
The process of making sound inferences based on accurate evidence and valid reasoning.

BEWARE OF SPEAKERS BEARING GIFTS...

Pseudoreasoning and Fallacies

As pointed out in Chapter 5, we spend more of our time listening to others than actually speaking. Understanding critical thinking is essential to differentiating messages that are logical from those that are not. Frequently, something sounds good on first hearing but proves to be illogical. This is called pseudoreasoning. We also noted that a fallacy is "an argument in which the reasons advanced for a claim fail to warrant acceptance of that claim."[1] Thus one of the goals of this chapter is to identify fallacies that are a sign of pseudoreasoning. Even if we agree with the conclusion of a speaker, we ought to do so based on sound logic, not just because he or she sounds good. And as speakers, we should offer our audience good reasons, not pseudoreasoning.

Argumentativeness and Verbal Aggressiveness

When listeners detect fallacious reasoning, they are ethically obligated to bring it to light. Simply remaining silent allows the speaker to mislead those who are not well trained in critical thinking. However, there is an important distinction between being argumentative and being verbally aggressive. In his book *Arguing Constructively*, Dominic Infante makes the distinction between these two personality traits.[2] **Argumentativeness** is the trait of arguing for and against the *positions* taken on controversial claims. For example, an argumentative person might say, "Legalizing drugs could lead to more accidents on the job and on roads, endangering the lives

argumentativeness
The trait of arguing for and against the positions taken on controversial claims.

In Their Own Words

Sample Persuasive Message

MANDATORY DRUG TESTING
by Miranda Welsh

This is an excerpt from the speech by Miranda Welsh. The full speech can be found on your CD.

Why should we be concerned about drug use? Who other than the user is it affecting? There are some specific problems with student drug abusers. Often student drug abusers tend to drift from school, which is their number one job. They tend to drift from their family; they tend to get below average grades, and they tend not to be physically active. Or if they are, they often use their drugs to keep them that way.

There are also some specific problems with employee drug abusers. According to the drug testing website, employees who are on drugs are 3.6 times more likely than nonusers to injure themselves or others [in an] on-the-job accident. They are 5 times more likely than nonusers to file a workman's compensation claim, 2.5 times as likely as nonusers to have absences of 8 or more days; they are consistently tardy; they only work two-thirds as effectively as nonusers; and to the business, drug abusers increase insurance cost, increase employee theft and decrease productivity.

But, what about the drug problem in the United States as a whole? . . . According to the Department of Health and Human Services, American drug use is on the rise. It peaked in 1979 and has declined since but is back on the increase. If we don't start implementing drug testing now, we are allowing the problem in the United States to continue. . . .

There have been some unfortunate circumstances that have occurred due directly to drug use and could have been stopped by drug testing. In April of 1987, a bus driver drove his bus directly into a bridge in Virginia, killed one, injured thirty. Only after the accident was he drug tested positive for cocaine, valium and marijuana. In January of 1988, a pilot crashed his plane into rural Colorado. The crash was solely attributed to the pilot, which killed 30 people. Again, only after the accident was he drug tested positive for cocaine. And some years back, the federal railroad administration drug tested 759 of their railroad employees only after 125 different accidents had occurred. At that time 29 of their current employees drug tested positive for one or more illegal drugs. All of these stories are according to the Drug Testing book by David Newton.

Now, I wouldn't be much of a person if I stood up here and told you who the drug testing problem is harming and who we have to blame if I didn't give you a cure. Simply put, a cure for a large part of our nation's drug problem is drug testing. There are a few legal and constitutional ways to go about this, such as urinalysis, through other bodily fluids, by the human hair, and through a blood test. And, the government does see a need for a cure to the increasing drug

Miranda Welsh

problem. They have passed some laws that are still in effect today. For example, in 1981 President Reagan mandated that all military personnel be drug tested on a regular basis. In 1986 he extended that to all law enforcement, national security and public health and safety personnel. However, there is still more to be done. Not a single state in this nation mandates that all of their students and all of their employees be drug tested. It is apparent that something needs to be done. The CQ Researcher on American teens states that studies prove that drug testing deters drug use. So, my point is simple. Why not drug test all employees and all students?

What will drug testing specifically do for our nation? If we can identify all of the employees on drugs we will have caught three-fourths of the nation's illicit drug users. That means that 75% of our nation's drug users are employed. In the workplace drug testing will specifically reduce workplace accidents, increase productivity, support the goals of a drug-free nation, improve corporate morale, and reduce drug use in our society. And in schools, drug testing will specifically deter students from drug use. . . .

I would like to share with you some of my arguments to some common anti–drug testing viewpoints. Tests invade my right to privacy according to the 4th Amendment. Actually, if you read the 4th Amendment carefully, you would see that it only protects you from unreasonable searches done by the federal government . . . not by private organizations. People take [legal] drugs from prescriptions, and those can show up positive on tests. Yes, they can, but every employee application and every school application must ask about any prescriptions that you are currently taking. And before any drug test is administered, you must be questioned about your prescriptions. Some tests are wrong. Well some [in]accuracy is inevitable, but technology is working day by day to decrease that inaccuracy. Costs more than it helps. Actually, each urinalysis only costs one dollar per person per test and if that's done on a random basis in your school or your workplace, your name's only on the average going to be called up once every 2 years. You do the math. Why should we waste time on testing, there's work to be done. Not much work can be done if there isn't anybody alive to do it and that's what drug use does to our society. Any of the testing methods take 3 to 5 minutes. And if that's done on a random basis, your name's only going to be called out 3 to 5 minutes once every 2 years. 3 to 5 minutes is very worth it.

In Their Own Words

Sample Persuasive Message

THE WAR ON DRUGS
by David Sanders

This is an excerpt from the speech by David Sanders. The full speech can be found on your CD.

David Sanders

The war on drugs was founded during the Nixon presidency. Not of a need to cure a great social ill in America, but simply out of politics. Richard Miller in his book The Case for Legalizing Drugs *quotes Nixon's domestic policy chief, John Ehrlichman, as saying that "'Narcotics repression is a sexy political issue. Parents are worried about their kids using heroin, and parents are voters.' That is why the Nixon White House got involved."*

Now, every president since then has used the war on drugs to gain political mileage. . . . No president used the war on drugs more effectively than Ronald Reagan. In his book, Rhetoric in the War on Drugs, *William Elwood quotes Reagan's famous drug war speech. ". . . now we're in another war for our freedom, and it's time for all of us to pull together. . . . It's time, as Nancy said, for America to 'Just Say No' to drugs. When we all come together, united, striving for this cause, then those who are killing America and terrorizing it with slow but sure chemical destruction, will see that they are up against the mightiest force for the good that we know. They will have no dark alleyways to hide in."*

They didn't need them because they were hiding in the White House. Former Drug Enforcement Agent and author of the book The Big White Lie, *Michael Levine points out that the CIA and other federal agencies were deeply involved in the drug trade as part of the Iran-Contra scandal.*

Now our law enforcement and legal system are in equally precarious positions. Because of the nature of the politically motivated justice system it does not target all social groups equally. In her book, Power, Ideology, and the War on Drugs, *Christina Johns points out that "law enforcement tactics primarily target lower class individuals even within the drug using and trafficking communities." Another big legal problem is assets forfeiture. And this is really really important. Asset forfeiture is a program where if law enforcement individuals believe that you have gained some of your property by selling drugs and being involved in the drug trade, they can seize that property. They can take your house, your boat, your car, whatever it is that you've gained, they just seize it. They do not have to charge you with a crime, nor do they have to prove in any way that you actually gained it from selling drugs. If you want your property back and you feel you're innocent, you have to go to court and you have to prove that you are innocent. Big difference from our normal criminal laws. . . .*

Now with all that money flowing around, there are bound to be casualties in this war. So let's look at who the physical and emotional casualties are in the war on drugs. Now as in any war, it's not the generals on both sides that get killed and injured, but it's the soldiers and civilians in the field. In this particular war we can divide it into two groups—the good guys and the bad guys. Let's talk about the good guys. Unfortunately, hundreds of officers are killed and injured in the line of duty in the war on drugs every year. . . .

Now, unfortunately, the good guys are not always good. In the book America's Longest War: Rethinking Our Tragic Crusade Against Drugs, *Yale Law School Professor Steve Duke points out that "Only one time before in our history was corruption of law enforcement officials a more serious problem. And that was during our efforts to enforce alcohol prohibition. The corruption during prohibition may have been greater than it is now, but there are reasons to fear that it will eventually exceed that level if we continue on our present course."*

Now the bad guys. We pretty much all know who the bad guys are. But unfortunately hundreds and thousands of America's youth are being killed and injured on our streets every year. And it's not just the druggies or the dealers that are getting injured but it's innocent civilians who just happen to get in the way. Now society is the one that ultimately pays for this war. Not just the $75 billion [that is spent on the war] . . . , but another $70 billion is passed on to us as consumers every year by businesses to pay for things like insurance, the crime that's inflicted on them, and things like drug tests to make sure the person at Kmart who's serving you isn't a druggie. . . .

Who would lose if we stopped this war on drugs? The people who would lose are primarily the people that gain now. The prison system would have to build and staff about half the number of prisons that we're doing right now. And prisons is the biggest growth industry in America today. The other group that would lose, obviously, are the dealers. Drugs would be available from sources that were clean, safe, such as federal drug stores at a significantly reduced cost. In fact in the case of cocaine, the National Review points out it would be available at between 5,000 and 20,000 percent less cost.

Who would win? I think, we would all win if we were to end the war on drugs. The police and court systems would have been freed up to deal with the real problems that are effecting society and real crimes. We would have vast amounts of money to spend to get people off drugs and to keep them off drugs and to deal with other social problems that are in a way connected to this war, like AIDS.

375

Verbal aggression gets in the way of critical thinking.

verbal aggressiveness

The trait of attacking the self-concept of those with whom a person disagrees about controversial claims.

of innocent bystanders." **Verbal aggressiveness,** on the other hand, is the trait of attacking the *self-concept* of those with whom a person disagrees about controversial claims. A verbally aggressive person might say, "Only a drug-crazed maniac would favor legalizing drugs." Argumentativeness is not only socially beneficial, it is the only way to take the process of critical thinking into the public arena. Verbal aggressiveness, on the other hand, is a destructive and hostile trait that destroys personal relationships. Constructive argumentativeness is the best approach for the public speaker. Being able to disagree without being disagreeable fosters a positive communication transaction.

The authors have been witnesses to the possibility that people can disagree without being disagreeable. Mary Matalin, current adviser to Vice President Dick Cheney and former conservative talk show host, "debated" her husband, James Carville, who managed the 1992 presidential campaign of Bill Clinton and served as one of his chief defenders during the Lewinsky scandal. Despite their obvious political differences, they treated each other with good-humored respect. The audience, which was apparently deeply divided on partisan lines, nevertheless cheered both speakers and even gave them a standing ovation at the end of the evening. Learning to disagree about issues while respecting the other side's right to believe as they do, is the hallmark of civility in argument. You can be argumentative without being verbally aggressive.

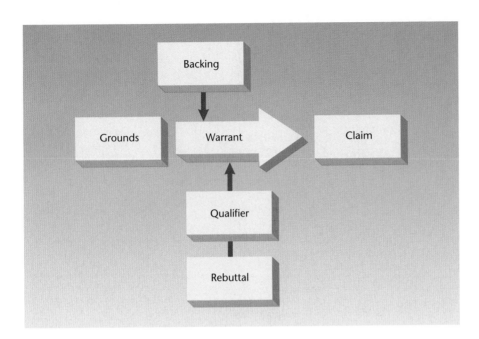

Figure 15.1
The Toulmin Model
of Argument

The Toulmin Model of Argument

The Toulmin model of argument, depicted in Figure 15.1, was introduced in Chapter 5 and further discussed in Chapter 8. All reasoning contains, at least implicitly, three things: *grounds,* to support the *claim* being made, and a *warrant* or linkage of the grounds and claim.[3] In Chapter 8 we introduced three types of claims (*fact, value,* and *policy*) and five types of warrants (*authority, generalization, comparison* or *analogy, causal,* and *sign*). Three other parts of the Toulmin model may be present but are not always needed. The *backing* provides support for a warrant that is either not accepted initially by an audience or that is challenged during the speech. A *rebuttal* is an exception or refutation to the argument. And a *qualifier* is an indicator of the degree of confidence we have in the claim we are making. Many of the fallacies we will discuss have to do with these three optional parts of the model. For example, claiming certainty for our reasoning, when there is actually only a chance that we are right, is fallacious. Ignoring legitimate rebuttals to our claims is also poor reasoning. Not backing up a disputable warrant is also a problem. Understanding the complete Toulmin model will help us construct better arguments as well as listen with a more critical ear to the arguments of others.

How does this model of argument apply in actual practice? Let's review the simple case we offered in Chapter 8. Suppose you glance out the window and the sky is filled with clouds. You think to yourself, "It's going to rain," and you grab your umbrella. Although you may not realize it, your reasoning can be analyzed as an argument using Toulmin's model. Figure 15.2 on the next page shows how this analysis would look. Based on the *grounds* of a cloudy sky, you reason using the *warrant,* cloudy skies are a sign of rain, which is based on the *backing* of your past experience, that there is a 75 percent chance (*qualifier*) of the truth of the *claim* that it is going to rain, unless (*rebuttal*) the clouds have a low moisture content.

Now that you understand this basic version of Toulmin's model, let's look at the relationships among claims, grounds, and warrants in more complicated

Figure 15.2

Analysis of an Argument Using Toulmin's Model

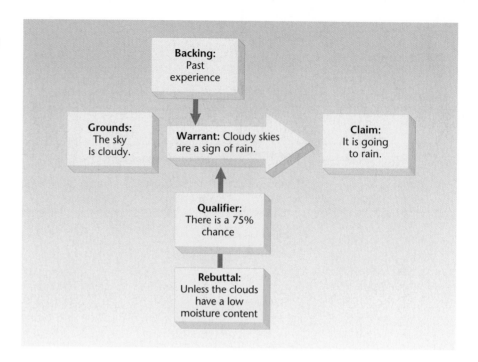

situations. As the speeches of our students illustrate, both sides of most controversies can cite evidence and reasoning to support their position.

In the spirit of constructive argumentation, therefore, we will consider how to test arguments for their soundness. We introduced 5 basic fallacies of reasoning in Chapter 5: unsupported assertion, distorted evidence, hasty generalization, stereotyping, and false analogy. In this chapter we add 15 to the list and illustrate how these fallacies fit into the Toulmin model.

Fallacies Associated With Grounds

All arguments are built on the grounds, or evidence, which the arguer points to in supporting the claim. If the grounds are either absent or defective, then the argument cannot be sound. In Chapter 8, we discussed various types of supporting material that might form the grounds of an argument, including examples, facts, statistics, expert opinion, explanations, descriptions, and narratives.

When you are examining the grounds of an argument, be sure that the examples are relevant, of sufficient quantity, and typical. Facts should come from a reliable source and be verifiable, recent, and consistent with other known facts. Statistics should be taken from a reliable and unbiased source, based on fair questions, and accurately collected. You should be told how the sample was selected to ensure that it was random and representative. Any differences should be greater than the margin of error, and the base of any percentages should be stated. Expert opinion depends on the source's expertise, reliability, and lack of bias. Explanations should be clear and accurate. Descriptions should be accurate and vivid. Narratives must have probability (coherence) and fidelity to the real world.

Grounds that fail one or more of these tests are likely to constitute a fallacy. In particular, there are four fallacies associated with grounds: unsupported assertion, distorted evidence, isolated examples, and misused statistics.

Unsupported Assertion

Unsupported assertions, the absence of any argument at all, can be found even in the best of speeches. For example, in making her argument for mandatory drug testing, Miranda Welsh answers the complaint that some tests are wrong by asserting that "technology is working day by day to decrease that inaccuracy." Where does she find the proof of that statement? No source is given and no specific technologies are mentioned. The claim is made with no grounds to support it. That is not to say that her statement isn't true. In fact, we suspect it probably is. But there is no evidence to support it in her speech.

Distorted Evidence

The **distorted evidence** fallacy occurs when the speaker leaves out or alters information to distort the true intent of the evidence. A good example of distorted evidence is found on the movie advertisement page of your local newspaper. Frequently, a movie will tout itself as "daring," "enthralling," or "thumbs up" when a reading of the full review will reveal that these words were used in a different context. Perhaps the reviewers really said, "This movie was a daring attempt that missed the mark. The only thing that was enthralling about this movie was the credits that signaled it was ending. In deciding whether to rate this movie thumbs up or down, it took only about 10 minutes to see that this was thumbs way down!"

Isolated Examples

Another problem with grounds lies in the use of **isolated examples,** nontypical or nonrepresentative examples, to prove a general claim. Recall that to reason from examples requires that the instances be representative of the larger class—in a word, typical. It is almost always possible to find an isolated example to illustrate just about any claim. For example, we often hear about cases of welfare abuse. One radio commentator recently told the story of a man who reported to the police that his food stamps had been stolen from his car—a Mercedes. Of course, most people on welfare don't drive a Mercedes. Yet the image of welfare recipients living it up at the taxpayers' expense has been a staple of popular mythology for decades. The reality is that most people on welfare are children living in poverty. Isolated examples do not prove that everyone on welfare is lazy or abusing the system.

Misused Statistics

Statistics are often very helpful in giving us a general picture of a topic, something not provided by examples. However, to be useful, grounds must meet the basic tests outlined in Chapter 8. Let's now look at four of the most frequent cases of **misused statistics.**

Poor Sampling

Statistics based on self-selected or nonrandom samples are worse than useless—they're misleading. For instance, many television stations and newspapers now have call-in polls whereby we can express our opinion on the issues of the day by dialing one of two numbers, each representing one side of the issue. Of course, there is no guarantee that the station's audience represents the public at large or that members of the audience will call in proportion to their number in the general population.

Lack of Significant Differences

Often the difference between two candidates in a preference poll is less than the poll's margin of error. Thus, if candidate A leads B by three points, but the poll has a five-point margin of error, there is no statistical significance to that difference, a fact often ignored by political pundits.

Misuse of "Average"

People frequently cite the "average," or mean, to support a claim. They say such things as, "The average salary for college graduates is X." The intent is for the audience to infer that most college graduates make the salary mentioned. However, the average (or mean) is only one of three numbers that can be used to describe a collection of numbers like the salaries paid to college graduates. The other two are the median and the mode. Further, the average is frequently misleading because it is so easily distorted by extreme numbers.

As an example, consider the differences between the mean, the median, and the mode of houses selling at a range of prices:

$250,000

$250,000

$300,000

$400,000

$2,000,000

Mean = $640,000

Median = $300,000

Mode = $250,000

The *mean* is simply the arithmetic average: Add all the selling prices, and divide the total by the number of houses sold. The *median* is the midpoint in a series of numbers. Half of the houses sold for more and half for less than the median. Finally, the *mode* is simply the most frequently occurring number or value. In most cases, the median is more accurate than the mean. Certainly that is the case here because the mean would lead you to believe that most houses in the area described are more expensive than they are in actuality. The single home selling for $2 million not only inflates the "average" but misleads your thinking in the process.

Misuse of Percentages

Percentages are meaningful only if you know the base on which they are computed. For example, suppose you are making $100,000 a year. You are told you must take a 10 percent pay cut because the company is in trouble. Reluctantly you agree. Now you are making only $90,000. The next year the company is doing better and says they will restore your pay by giving you a 10 percent increase. However, don't celebrate yet. The 10 percent is based on your current pay of $90,000, leading to a restored pay of only $99,000. Because the basis on which the percentage was figured changed, your 10 percent increase didn't really restore your pay cut. We need to be exceptionally careful in evaluating percentages to make sure apples are being compared to apples, not oranges. If you start out at a very low level, even large percentage increases may not be very large in real terms.

Fallacies Associated With Claims

Sometimes fallacies are not so much in how we get to the claim, but in the nature of the claims themselves. The two fallacies discussed here have to do with the relevance of claims and whether the claims are being used to, in essence, prove themselves. We need to guard against these fallacies both in our speeches and as listeners to the speeches of others.

Red Herring

Sometimes called a *smoke screen,* a **red herring** is an irrelevant claim introduced into a controversy to divert attention from the real controversy. Debates over public issues are well known for the use of red herrings to divert attention from the issues that concern most people. For example, suppose a speaker arguing for drug testing were to say, "The people who oppose drug testing are the same ones who were against fighting terrorism when America was attacked." Of course, drug testing and terrorism have nothing in common. Bringing up the discussion of terrorism would be an attempt to divert attention from the issue at hand. Fortunately, neither of our student speakers on the drug issue engaged in such spurious reasoning.

> **red herring (smoke screen)**
> An irrelevant issue introduced into a controversy to divert from the real controversy.

Arguing in a Circle

Another common fallacy is the use of a claim to prove its own truth. **Arguing in a circle,** sometimes called *begging the question,* occurs when the argument actually proves nothing because the claim to be proved is used as the grounds or warrant for the argument. For example, consider the door-to-door evangelist who insists that you must believe in his or her version of the Bible. Why? you ask. The person immediately opens a Bible and quotes you scripture to support the claim. Basically the argument looks something like this:

> **arguing in a circle (begging the question)**
> An argument that proves nothing because the claim to be proved is used as the grounds or warrant for the argument.

Claim: My version of the Bible is the truth.

Grounds: Quotation from scripture.

Warrant: My version of the Bible is the truth.

In other words, the claim is also the warrant.

Of course, such clear-cut expressions of question-begging are rare. But many arguments, when distilled to their essence, do in fact beg the question.

Fallacies Associated With Warrants and Backing

Toulmin calls the connection between the grounds and the claim the warrant. The warrant is the license that authorizes an arguer to move from grounds to a claim. Thus, if you were to argue, as in our earlier example, that it's going to rain because it is cloudy, the observation about clouds only proves it will rain given the warrant that clouds are a sign of rain. The process of moving from grounds, via a warrant, to a claim is called an **inference.**

inference
The process of moving from grounds, via a warrant, to a claim.

To his basic model of grounds-warrant-claim, recall that Toulmin adds backing, which is support for the warrant. In some cases a warrant is readily believed by an audience. In others, the warrant needs additional backing in the form of evidence before the audience will believe it is true. For example, suppose someone in the audience believes the Constitution prohibits mandatory drug testing by private companies. If the speaker said that it is permissible under the Constitution, she would have to present backing for the warrant, just as Miranda Welsh did when she said, "Actually, if you read the 4th Amendment carefully, you would see that it only protects you from unreasonable searches done by the federal government . . . not by private organizations." Backing is required, therefore, when a warrant either is not known to the audience or is contrary to what they already believe.

Different types of warrants provide different ways of moving from grounds to claim and are associated with different patterns of reasoning. In Chapter 8 we discussed the five most common types of warrants: authority, generalization, comparison, causal, and sign. In examining any argument, it is important to determine whether the warrant and its accompanying backing are sound. We look at each type of warrant and suggest some of the common fallacies peculiar to each type of argument.

Authority Warrants

When we use authority warrants, we are really saying that the reason the claim should be believed is because someone who is an expert says so. If our audience is not familiar with the source's qualifications, we need to provide backing for the warrant. For example, suppose I told you that Dr. John Doe said that the South Beach diet was the best way to lose weight. Why should you believe Dr. Doe? I would need more than just "Dr." preceding his name to back up my reasoning. Thus, as a listener, there are some important questions to ask about authority warrants.

Tips and Tactics

Evaluating Authority Warrants

- Is the authority an expert in the area under discussion?
- Has the speaker adequately backed the qualifications of the authority?
- Is the authority trustworthy and unbiased?
- Is the authority acting on reliable information?

Two common fallacies are associated with the misuse of authority warrants: halo effect and ad hominem.

halo effect
The assumption that just because you like or respect a person, whatever he or she says must be true.

Halo Effect

The **halo effect** fallacy is based on the presumption that because we like or respect certain people, we tend to believe them no matter what they say. This is commonly seen when movie stars and other celebrities endorse political causes. For example, although we enjoy Janine Garofalo's stand-up, that doesn't mean she's an expert on Iraq policy. Yet she is seen and heard discussing national security issues on cable TV and talk radio. We are not implying that her views are necessarily wrong. However, being a celebrity gives her no particular expertise or qualifications to discuss foreign policy. Her opinion is just that–an opinion–and deserves no more weight than the opinion of any other citizen.

Ad Hominem

In many ways, this is the reverse of the halo effect. **Ad hominem** means "against the person." This fallacy is based on the premise that just because the person who said it is not perceived as credible, he or she must be wrong. In many cases, this fallacy consists of simply substituting name-calling for reasoning. Numerous Web sites are devoted to trashing filmmaker Michael Moore. In fact, there's even a counterdocumentary called *Michael Moore Hates America.* Whether Michael Moore is a patriot or a traitor, his speeches, books, and films should be judged based on how well documented they are and whether their reasoning is sound, not on whether we like the author. As someone once said, even a broken clock is right twice a day. People we may dislike can be right as well as wrong. We deserve to give their views a hearing, and then reach a conclusion based on the facts. As we pointed out in Chapter 4, civility is a virtue that's becoming increasingly rare in our public discourse. Ad hominem arguments and name-calling only denigrate the public dialogue.

> **ad hominem**
> The claim that something must be false because the person who said it is not credible, regardless of the argument itself.

Generalization Warrants

As we pointed out in Chapter 8, a generalization warrant is a statement that either establishes a general rule or principle or applies an established rule or principle to a specific case.

Establishing Generalizations

A warrant that establishes a generalization uses specific instances, as represented in examples, statistics, narratives, and the like, to reach general conclusions. Consider Miranda Welsh's argument. She uses specific examples and statistics to support her generalization that drug use on the job can be dangerous. During her speech she cites specific examples of deaths due to drug use: "In April of 1987, a bus driver drove his bus directly into a bridge in Virginia, killed one, injured thirty. Only after the accident was he drug tested positive for cocaine, valium and marijuana. In January of 1988, a pilot crashed his plane into rural Colorado. The crash was solely attributed to the pilot, which killed 30 people." She also cites overall statistics on the higher costs to employers of employees who are drug abusers. Warrants establishing generalizations are subject to tests of relevance, quantity, typicality, precision, and negative example. These tests can be expressed in the questions listed in Tips and Tactics.

Tips and Tactics

Questions to Ask When Evaluating a Generalization

* Are the grounds relevant to the claim?
* Are there sufficient grounds to establish the claim?

- Are the grounds typical of the larger population?
- Is overgeneralization avoided?
- Are there significant negative examples?

Let's apply these tests to Miranda's generalization that mandatory drug testing is needed. Clearly her examples are relevant. Are there sufficient grounds to support the claim? She cites two specific cases of deaths from drug abusers, one of a bus driver and the other of a pilot. These examples are troubling, but are the grounds typical? Her argument is further bolstered by the statistics on the railroads. "And some years back, the federal railroad administration drug tested 759 of their railroad employees only after 125 different accidents had occurred. At that time 29 of their current employees drug tested positive for one or more illegal drugs." Still, her argument would be stronger if she had overall national statistics on the numbers of deaths from workplace-related drug use. Is overgeneralization avoided? She is calling for testing in all workplaces and schools. But, as David Sanders points out in his speech, there's a big difference between the grocery checker using drugs and a pilot or bus driver. At most, the examples of busses, planes, and trains justify drug testing when lives are at stake. Ask yourself if her examples are as applicable to other occupations as well. Finally, are there negative examples? Are there cases where using drugs might have saved lives? That's difficult to imagine, and even Sanders, in his speech against the drug war, admits using drugs is a bad idea. The complete argument might look like the model in Figure 15.3.

hasty generalization
An argument that occurs when there are too few instances to support a generalization or the instances are unrepresentative of the generalization.

Hasty Generalization   The most common fallacy associated with warrants that generalize from specific instances to a general conclusion is known as **hasty generalization.** This occurs when there are too few instances to support a generalization or the instances are unrepresentative of the generalization. The key here is to limit generalizations to the extent justified by the grounds. We live in a small college town. We often hear long-time citizens complain that college students are lazy, destructive, and irresponsible. These opinions are based on the misbehavior of a small fraction of the 16,000 students who attend our university. The tendency to generalize from a negative experience is a very human one and is part of our survival instinct. Our ancestors needed only one encounter with a saber-toothed tiger to know it was something to avoid. But this natural tendency to generalize from bad experiences can lead to very shoddy reasoning when those experiences are not really typical. This is also one of the reasons statisticians and quantitative researchers are so fond of the saying, "You can never generalize from a sample of one." Our individual experiences with the world may or may not be typical of others. Until the research is done, however, we cannot and should not be certain that they are.

Applying Generalizations

On the other hand, if we know a generalization is true, we can apply it to a specific instance and reach some valid conclusions about that specific instance. Warrants applying generalizations are subject to tests of applicability to all cases, exceptions, backing, and classification.

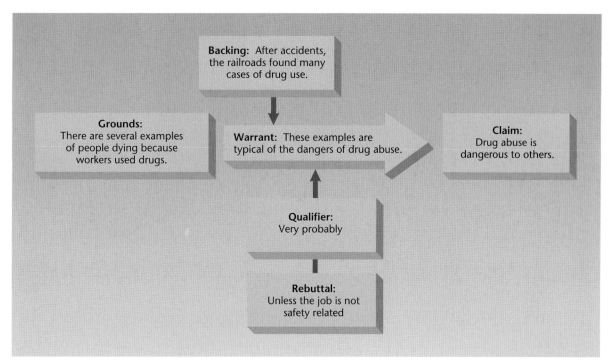

Figure 15.3
Argument Establishing a Generalization

Tips and Tactics

Questions to Ask When Evaluating Applications of a Generalization

• Does the generalization apply to all possible cases?
• Are there exceptions to the generalization? If so, does the specific case fall within one of the exceptions?
• Is the generalization well backed?
• Does the specific instance fall clearly within the category specified by the generalization?

Figure 15.4 on page 386 illustrates an argument that applies a generalization. In this case, we know that the generalization *warrant,* all native-born Americans are citizens, is true because of the *backing* found in the U.S. laws and Constitution. Given the *grounds* that John is a native-born American, we can be almost certain (*qualifier,*) that the *claim,* John is a U.S. citizen, is true. There is a possible *rebuttal,* however; the claim is true unless he has renounced his citizenship.

Stereotyping   The most common fallacy associated with warrants that apply established generalizations to specific instances is known as **stereotyping.** This fallacy assumes that what is considered to be true of a larger class is necessarily true of particular members of that class. We have known people with disabilities, for example, who are just as physically active as a person with no limitations. Jonathan

> **stereotyping**
> The assumption that what is considered to be true of a larger class is necessarily true of particular members of that class.

Figure 15.4
Argument Applying
a Generalization

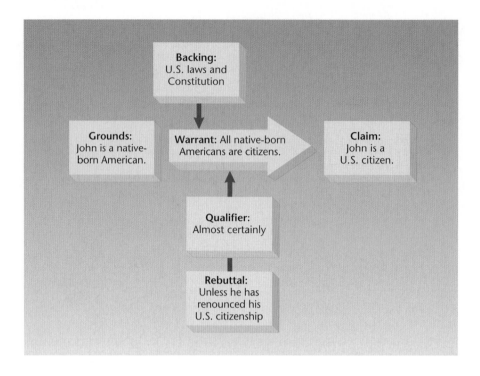

Studebaker, who you learned about in Chapter 2, spent most of his adult life speaking to school-aged children about the importance of not stereotyping people just because they have a disability. In dealing with generalizations, there is always a danger of stereotyping a whole group when there are notable exceptions to such generalizations.

False Dilemma   Another common fallacy associated with applying generalizations is the **false dilemma,** a generalization that implies there are only two choices when there are more than two. David Sanders suggests that either continuing the present war on drugs or ending it are our only choices. If we changed our tactics along the lines suggested by Miranda Welsh, would that present a viable third alternative? A true dilemma requires proof that there really are only two choices. Consider the following telephone call to a newspaper:

false dilemma

A generalization that implies there are only two choices when there are more than two.

> **They should fight child abuse**
> I'd like to talk to the pro-lifers about abortion. They want to stop abortion so bad and they take their time to do it. Why don't they take the same painstaking time to help fight children being killed by dads and moms when they get a very light sentence?[4]

Of course, someone can be both pro-life (or anti-abortion) and against children being killed by their parents. The key to a real dilemma is that there are in fact only two choices and that they are mutually exclusive. In this case, someone could support both of these values without contradiction, and thus no real dilemma exists.

Comparison (Analogy) Warrants

As we explained in Chapter 8, reasoning based on a comparison (analogy) warrant claims that two cases that are similar in some known respects are also similar in some unknown respects. These arguments are called comparisons or, more com-

Stereotypes about people with disabilities are generally wrong as these athletes show.

monly, analogies. The war on drugs is an analogy, but do the standards of a shooting war really apply to righting a social problem? Evaluate analogies by asking the following questions:

Tips and Tactics

Questions to Ask When Evaluating Comparisons or Analogies

- Are only literal analogies used for proof?
- Do the similarities outweigh the differences?
- Are the similarities more relevant than the differences to the claim being made?

False Analogy

The most common fallacy associated with comparison warrants is the **false analogy.** This occurs when two things that are not really comparable are compared as if they were essentially the same. For example, we recall a debate on our campus wherein a prominent administrator in a department other than communication claimed that we should abolish our campus requirement for a public speaking course. "After all," he stated, "our students have been talking since they were two." Although talking and delivering a public speech might seem like a fair comparison to the uninformed, presumably as you have learned in this class, there's a lot more to giving a speech than just being able to talk. Fortunately, those in charge of general education at our university quickly rejected the analogy.

> **false analogy**
> The comparison of two different things that are not really comparable.

Causal Warrants

As we pointed out in Chapter 8, reasoning based on a causal warrant claims that a cause will produce or has produced an effect. You can reason either from cause to effect or from effect to cause. Causal warrants are subject to tests of relatedness, other causes, other effects, and mistaking order in time for causality.

Tips and Tactics

Questions to Ask When Evaluating Causal Reasoning

- Is the cause related to the alleged effect?
- Are there other causes of the effect?
- Are there other effects from the same cause?
- Has time sequence been mistaken for cause (post hoc fallacy)?

Causal arguments can be successfully and persuasively made. For example, there is considerable scientific evidence to support the effects of tobacco on health, and few independent scientists dispute the harmfulness of the product. A speaker relying on such experts and scientific studies would be on solid ground. Often a speaker is best advised to make causal arguments when they can be buttressed by expert testimony and scientific studies, and clearly meet tests of relatedness, other causes and effects, and time sequence as outlined in this chapter.

Post Hoc

post hoc, ergo propter hoc

("after the fact, therefore because of the fact") The assumption that because one event preceded another, the first event must be the cause of the second event.

Warrants dealing with effect-to-cause reasoning frequently commit the fallacy of assuming that because one event preceded another, the first event must be the cause of the second event. Technically, this is known as the **post hoc, ergo propter hoc** fallacy ("after the fact, therefore because of the fact"). We recall a letter to the editor of our local newspaper heralding the end of a recent period of drought in California. As California natives, we realize that the state has historically gone through a boom and bust cycle with respect to rainfall. But this letter writer had a different explanation: The drought had ended because of the prayers of the people of the small town of Paradise, who had collectively gathered to pray for rain. The letter writer even referred to them as "God's chosen helpers." Far be it from us to denigrate anyone's faith, but clearly the drought was going to end some time (and it will return again). Just because this small community's prayers were followed by rain doesn't mean that's why the drought ended. Just because one event follows another doesn't prove they are cause and effect.

Slippery Slope

slippery slope

The assumption that just because one event occurs, it will automatically lead to a series of undesirable events even though there is no relationship between the action and the projected events.

Warrants that reason from cause to effect are susceptible to the **slippery slope** fallacy. This fallacy involves assuming that just because one event occurs, it will automatically lead to a series of undesirable events, like a row of dominoes falling down automatically once you knock over the first one. In common language, this fallacy is sometimes expressed, "If you give them an inch, they'll take a mile."

How many times have you heard someone argue that allowing physician-assisted suicide will lead to selective euthanasia, for example, killing the elderly and the severely disabled? Or perhaps you've been told that if you don't get a college degree, you will end up homeless and broke. The slippery slope fallacy occurs when you assume that a series of events will result from one action without there being a relationship between the action and the projected events. Nevertheless, it is not necessarily a slippery slope to argue that one action will follow another if the relationship can be clearly demonstrated. For example, it can be mathematically demonstrated that to continue to charge items on a credit card without paying any more than the minimum monthly payment will lead to deeper and deeper debt. And, of course, the judicial system relies heavily on the role of precedents in making decisions. Much of the debate surrounding the use of military tribunals to try suspected terrorists relied on the precedents set in the Civil War and World Wars I and II. So future effects are important, if they can be clearly shown by sound reasoning.

Sign Warrants

As we noted in Chapter 8, reasoning using a sign warrant infers the presence of an unobserved phenomenon from the presence of an observed one. Sign warrants are subject to tests of reliability and conflicting signs.

Tips and Tactics

Questions to Ask When Evaluating Sign Reasoning

- Are the signs reliable indicators of the claim?
- Are there conflicting signs?

Unfortunately, in real life, reliable signs are sometimes hard to find. In testing sign reasoning, ask how reliable such signs have been in the past. For example, economists often make predictions about the future of the economy based on figures for unemployment, housing starts, and so on. A careful examination of their track record in making such predictions will suggest just how much confidence you should have in their reasoning.

The second test is to look for conflicting signs. Whereas one economist may point to decreased unemployment as a sign of economic upturn, another may conclude that there are fewer unemployed because the economy is so bad many workers have given up seeking jobs.

Unless a sign is infallible, most sign reasoning at best indicates the probability that a claim is true.

Mistaking Correlation for Cause

The most common fallacy associated with sign reasoning is **mistaking correlation for cause.** A correlation simply means two things occur in conjunction with each other, without regard to their cause. How often have you heard someone claim that one event caused another just because they occurred in tandem? Historically, when the stock market was on the rise, so were women's hemlines. Although one may be a "sign" of the other, it is ludicrous to assume the stock market caused the hemlines to go up or vice versa. Just because one event signifies another does not mean they are causally related. For example, a recent news report noted that there is a higher-than-normal incidence of heart disease among bald men.

mistaking correlation for cause
The assumption that because one thing is the sign of another, they are causally related.

However, this does not prove that baldness causes heart disease or that wearing a toupee will reduce the risk of heart attack. Although the two factors are correlated, the most likely explanation is that common underlying factors cause both baldness and heart disease.

Fallacies Associated With Qualifiers

Toulmin believes that reasoners should qualify their claims. As we pointed out in Chapter 5, a qualifier is an indication of the level of probability of a claim. Some arguments are virtually certain to be true, whereas others have a much lower degree of certainty. Depending on the nature of the argument, a qualifier can make a big difference. For example, in a criminal trial, the claim that the defendant is guilty must be true "beyond a reasonable doubt," a phrase that acts as the qualifier of the argument for guilt. Thus a very high degree of certainty is required before a jury can convict someone of a criminal offense. On the other hand, in a civil case, the standard is "a preponderance of evidence." That is, if it is more likely than not that the defendant wronged the plaintiff, the judgment should go to the plaintiff. Because of the difference in the level of proof required, someone found not guilty in a criminal trial can still be sued in civil court.

So, too, in our reasoning, we need to know what level of proof our audience will expect. As with virtually every other aspect of public speaking, the success of our reasoning depends on careful analysis of the audience. As listeners, we should also be clear about what level of proof we need before accepting a claim. Many of the fallacies of reasoning associated with qualifiers are a result of overstating or distorting the degree of certainty with which the arguer has supported his or her claim. Two such common fallacies are the use of loaded language and hyperbole.

Loaded Language

loaded language
Language that has strong emotional connotations.

Language that has strong emotional connotations is termed **loaded language.** Depending on the specific characteristics of our audience, what we might consider neutral language may in fact carry strong emotional connotations. Recently our campus was the unfortunate site of racist graffiti painted on dorm walls. In addition, white supremacist groups placed hate literature on front doorsteps throughout the county. The language used was both offensive and crude. Such loaded language elicits one of two responses. Some people respond in kind–leading to an ever-escalating spiral of hate. Others speak out against hate language itself. Many in our community chose the latter course–holding a rally against hate speech. Avoid loaded language when preparing a speech, and when such language is used in the speech of others, avoid the temptation to simply engage in a shouting match. A reasoned and forceful call for civility is the best answer.

Of course, effective persuasion often requires vivid, intense, and expressive language, as we discussed in Chapter 10. There is a fine but important line between language that is necessarily vivid and language that is so "loaded" that it distorts the reasoning being presented. There is no hard-and-fast rule that can be applied here. Speakers and listeners need to exercise their judgment in evaluating the use of language.

This poster from a rally against hate speech in our community speaks for itself

Hyperbole

Hyperbole is an exaggeration of a claim. Rather than properly qualifying or limiting the impact of a statement, the person engaged in hyperbole exaggerates the claim in question. When boxer Mohammed Ali declared himself to be "the greatest," it may have been an effective way to build interest in his fights, but it was certainly an exaggeration of his prowess, especially since he didn't limit his claim to the boxing ring. Other examples of hyperbole include the use of such terms as "superstar," "greatest ever," and "mega-hit." It often seems as if it is not enough anymore to be a star, to be great, or to have a mere hit. Hyperbole ends up cheapening the currency of language, inflating claims and devaluing more moderate language.

hyperbole
An exaggeration of a claim.

Fallacies Associated With Rebuttals

The rebuttal to an argument is an exception to or refutation of an argument. It too can be flawed. Fallacies of rebuttal can occur when a speaker misanalyzes an opponent's argument or sidesteps the other side of the issue completely.

Straw Person

The **straw person** fallacy occurs when someone attempts to refute a claim by misstating the argument being refuted. Rather than refuting the real argument, the other side constructs a person of straw, which is easy to knock down.

Imagine a debate on gun control. One speaker proposes a five-day waiting period before purchasing a handgun at a gun show. The other speaker attacks the first person's position as seeking to take away the right to own a handgun. Of course the first speaker proposed no such thing. A waiting period to buy a handgun may or may not be a good idea, but to attempt to refute it by misstating the proposal is to attack a "straw person." We need to be sure that the rebuttal to an argument is

straw person
An argument made in refutation that misstates the argument being refuted. Rather than refuting the real argument, the other side constructs a person of straw, which is easy to knock down.

Speaking of . . .

Defects of Reasoning: The Fallacies

Fallacies Associated With Grounds

unsupported assertion: The absence of any argument at all.

distorted evidence: Significant omissions or changes in the grounds of an argument that alter its original intent.

isolated examples: Nontypical or nonrepresentative examples that are used to prove a general claim.

misused statistics: Statistics that involve errors such as poor sampling, lack of significant differences, misuse of average, or misuse of percentages.

Fallacies Associated With Claims

red herring (smoke screen): An irrelevant issue introduced into a controversy to divert attention from the real controversy.

arguing in a circle (begging the question): An argument that proves nothing because the claim to be proved is used as the grounds or warrant for the argument.

Fallacies Associated With Authority Warrants

halo effect: The assumption that just because you like or respect a person, whatever he or she says must be true.

ad hominem: The claim that something must be false because the person who said it is not credible, regardless of the argument itself.

Fallacies Associated With Generalization Warrants

hasty generalization: An argument that occurs when there are too few instances to support a generalization or the instances are unrepresentative of the generalization.

stereotyping: The assumption that what is considered to be true of a larger class is necessarily true of particular members of that class.

false dilemma: A generalization that implies there are only two choices when there are more than two.

Fallacy Associated With Comparison (Analogy) Warrants

false analogy: The comparison of two different things that are not really comparable.

Fallacies Associated With Causal Warrants

post hoc, ergo propter hoc ("after the fact, therefore because of the fact"): The assumption that because one event preceded another, the first event must be the cause of the second event.

slippery slope: The assumption that just because one event occurs, it will automatically lead to a series of undesirable events even though there is no relationship between the action and the projected events.

Fallacy Associated With Sign Warrants

mistaking correlation for cause: The assumption that because one thing is the sign of another, they are causally related.

Fallacies Associated With Qualifiers

loaded language: Language that has strong emotional connotations.

hyperbole: An exaggeration of a claim.

Fallacies Associated With Rebuttals

straw person: An argument made in refutation that misstates the argument being refuted. Rather than refuting the real argument, the other side constructs a person of straw, which is easy to knock down.

ignoring the issue: An argument made in refutation that ignores the claim made by the other side.

Additional Fallacy

non sequitur: An argument that does not follow from its premises.

---

actually refuting the argument that was presented, not some version that was concocted so that it would be easier to refute.

Ignoring the Issue

The fallacy of **ignoring the issue** occurs when the claim made by one side in an argument is ignored by the other. For example, imagine that you are speaking before a group about the effects of the depletion of the ozone layer on the environment. Skin cancer death rates will increase, you argue. We need to change over to safer refrigerants in our cars. Suppose someone attempts to rebut your argument by saying that environmental extremists have killed loggers by spiking trees. This rebuttal is simply not responsive to the argument you have posed. In short, the issue you have presented has been ignored, and the rebuttalist has shifted ground to another issue entirely.

The Non Sequitur: An Argument That Does Not Follow

Until now we've looked at each component of an argument as a separate source of fallacies. Of course, you also have to look at the argument as a whole. Even if the grounds are true, the warrant believable, and so on, if the argument doesn't hang together logically, it is still fallacious. Thus, the final fallacy of reasoning we examine is the non sequitur.

A **non sequitur** is an argument that does not follow from its premises. In Toulmin's terms, there is no logical connection between the claim and the grounds and warrant used to support the claim. Consider the example of a person who called in this opinion to a local newspaper:

> **No wonder welfare is so popular**
> I'd like to thank the person who dropped the two little black lab-mix puppies off at the golf course some time in the week of Jan. 28. What irresponsible person caused others to try to find homes for these dogs? It's amazing people don't take responsibility for their actions and cause other people to. No wonder everybody's on welfare.[5]

Aside from stereotyping people on welfare as irresponsible and hyperbolizing in claiming that "everybody's on welfare," this argument has absolutely no link between its grounds–the two dogs abandoned at the golf course–and its claim–that this irresponsibility is symptomatic of people on welfare.

We have discussed numerous fallacies in this chapter. To review them, see the box Defects of Reasoning: The Fallacies.

non sequitur
An argument that does not follow from its premises.

Summary

Reasoning and critical thinking are important both in constructing good arguments and in listening to the arguments of others.

Argumentativeness is the trait of arguing for and against the positions taken on controversial claims.

Verbal aggressiveness is the trait of attacking the self-concept of those with whom a person disagrees about controversial claims.

Grounds for an argument consist of evidence supporting a claim.

 SpeechCoach
To evaluate your understanding of this chapter, see the Quizzes on your CD.

 www.mhhe.com /brydon5
Visit the Online Learning Center for helpful study resources, including practice tests, key term crossword puzzles, and PowerWeb articles for research and review.

Fallacies associated with defective grounds are:

- Unsupported assertions
- Distorted evidence
- Iolated examples
- Misused statistics

Claims may contain the following fallacies:

- The red herring
- Arguing in a circle

Warrants link grounds and claims by means of:

- Authority
- Generalization
- Comparison
- Cause
- Sign

Backing is support for the warrant and is especially important in cases in which the audience is either unfamiliar with the warrant or unconvinced of its truth.

Fallacies associated with generalization warrants include:

- Hasty generalization
- Stereotyping
- False dilemmas

The fallacy associated with comparison warrants is:

- The false analogy

Fallacies associated with causation warrants are:

- Post hoc, ergo propter hoc
- Slippery slope

The fallacy associated with sign warrants is:

- Mistaking correlation for cause

Fallacies associated with authority warrants are:

- The halo effect
- Ad hominem

Qualifiers are an indication of the level of probability of the claim. Fallacies associated with qualifiers are:

- Loaded language
- Hyperbole

A rebuttal is an exception to or refutation of an argument. Fallacies associated with rebuttals are:

- Straw person
- Ignoring the issue

The non sequitur is a fallacy that occurs when an argument does not follow from its premises.

Check Your Understanding: Exercises and Activities

For a review of key terms in this chapter, see the Key Terms Flashcards on your CD.

1. Find a published argument, such as a letter to the editor, an advertisement, an editorial, or a political ad. Identify the claim being made and the grounds on which the claim is based. Is the warrant explicitly stated? If not, determine the implied warrant. What backing, if any, is offered for the warrant? Is the argument adequately qualified? Are there possible rebuttals to the argument?

2. Find an example of each of the following types of arguments in a publication: cause to effect, effect to cause, sign, comparison, establishing a generalization, applying a generalization, authority. Which of these arguments is the strongest, logically, and which is the weakest? Explain your answer in terms of the tests of reasoning outlined in this chapter.

3. Pick an advertisement from any print medium—for example, magazines, newspapers, or direct mail. In a brief paper, identify at least three fallacies used in the advertisement. Define each fallacy in your own words. Cite the specific example of each fallacy from the ad, and explain why the example meets the definition. Finally, highlight the fallacies on a copy of the ad and attach the copy to your paper.

4. Analyze the arguments for and against drug testing and the drug war as presented by Miranda Welsh and David Sanders in this chapter. Which argument is logically the stronger? Which contains more fallacies? Which do you find more persuasive?

Notes

1. Brooke Noel Moore and Richard Parker, *Critical Thinking,* 5th ed. (Mountain View, Calif.: Mayfield, 1998), 476.
2. Dominic A. Infante, *Arguing Constructively* (Prospect Heights, Ill.: Waveland Press, 1988).
3. Stephen Toulmin, Richard Rieke, and Allan Janik, *An Introduction to Reasoning,* 2nd ed. (New York: Macmillan, 1984).
4. "Tell It to the ER," *Chico Enterprise Record,* 13 March 1992, 2A. Reprinted by permission.
5. "Tell It to the ER," *Chico Enterprise Record,* 16 February 1992, 2A. Reprinted by permission.

This class is just the beginning of your public speaking career.

Chapter 16

Speaking Across the Life Span

Objectives

After reading this chapter and reviewing the learning resources on your CD-ROM and at the Online Learning Center, you should be able to:

- Make an effective impromptu presentation.
- Lead or participate in a small group and a panel discussion.
- Present a speech of introduction.
- Present or accept an award.
- Make a speech of commemoration.
- Make a speech to entertain.
- Be interviewed on television.

Key Concepts

agenda

eulogy

group

panel discussion

reframing

speech of acceptance

speech of commemoration

speech of introduction

speech of recognition

speech to entertain

> " You've been giving your attention to a turkey stuffed with sage;
> you are now about to consider a sage stuffed with turkey. "
>
> –WILLIAM MAXWELL EVARTS (1818–1901), American statesman,
> speaking after a Thanksgiving dinner[1]

When Russ Woody (pictured here on the set of *Murphy Brown*) left our university to seek his fame and fortune in Hollywood, little did he know he would one day get a call to speak at his alma mater's commencement.

When Russ Woody graduated from Chico State University and moved to Hollywood to become a television writer, the last thing he expected was to one day get a call from his alma mater and be asked to deliver the university commencement address to 10,000 people. Yet that's exactly what happened to the Emmy-award-winning producer of such hit shows as *Becker* and *Murphy Brown*. As you can imagine, few audiences are as tough to please as a graduating class anxious to be handed their diplomas and begin celebrating in earnest. In the nearly 30 years' worth of commencement speeches the authors have witnessed, we've seen more speakers alienate or lose their audience than succeed.

Russ, we're pleased to say, was not one of them. Drawing on his own experience as a student at Chico and as a Hollywood insider, Russ shared the "lessons" he had learned and wished to pass on. Not only could everyone in his audience relate to his lessons, but they were also funny and self-effacing. As a result, Russ's speech made this particular commencement better—not just longer.

Although we may never be called on to speak at our alma mater's commencement ceremony, we will be called on to speak at occasions both ordinary and special over our life span. Public speaking is an essential part of many of our culture's most important rituals. It is expected in celebration of life's most significant events, for example, birthdays, weddings, and anniversaries. And it is expected in solemn tribute even at life's end.

This final chapter focuses on the predictable circumstances in which we will be required to speak, both now and in the future. These situations include impromptu speaking, saying thank you when you've been singled out for recognition, introducing someone who is being honored or who is the principal speaker of the occasion, speaking to commemorate an occasion of celebration or solemnity, leading group discussions, or participating in a panel discussion. We begin by talking about reframing your perspective about speaking in situations both everyday and special.

Reframing: Speaking as Storytelling

The late Senator Robert F. Kennedy was fond of paraphrasing Irish playwright George Bernard Shaw by saying, "Some people see things as they are and say: why?

I dream things that never were and say: why not?"[2] This familiar quotation eloquently alludes to the importance of perspective in analyzing and responding to circumstance. This kind of behavior can be thought of in terms of **reframing**—revising our view of a situation or an event. Recall that the degree to which we are anxious about a speaking transaction depends on how we view it. As we said early in this book, looking at a speech as a performance is likely to make us more anxious than looking at a speech as a natural but refined extension of our everyday communication skills.

One effective way to reframe our point of view about the kind of speaking this chapter describes is to think of it as a form of storytelling. Although you probably gave few "speeches" prior to taking this class, chances are good that you told innumerable stories. Good stories share a similar organizational sequence with good speeches. An involving story hooks an audience with its introduction, builds to a climax either humorous or dramatic, and concludes with a memorable resolution to the climax.

Rhetorical scholar Walter R. Fisher argues that storytelling is not only an effective way to involve an audience but also an effective way to share a message.[3] As president, Ronald Reagan frequently conveyed the point he was attempting to make through storytelling. Many pundits in the media, moreover, attribute much of his reputation as an effective communicator to his ability to weave an involving and convincing story.[4]

Storytelling needn't be long-winded nor overly complicated. To the contrary, many of the best stories are short and to the point. Effective stories or narratives share two common elements, as we first discussed in Chapter 8: *probability* and *fidelity*.

> **reframing**
> Revising our view of a situation or an event, usually in a positive direction.

Probability

The property of storytelling termed probability is straightforward. Narrative probability is the internal coherence of the story. Coherence concerns the degree to which the structure of the story holds up in the eyes of an audience. Does the story make sense as told? Do the parts of the story hang together? Effective stories are logically consistent in structure, even if the content of the story requires that we suspend disbelief, as is the case with fairy tales and some science fiction. Did you know that Mark Twain, for example, was a gifted public speaker as well as writer? He could tell even the most improbable story in such a way that what he was suggesting seemed completely plausible. What's more, this was true whether he was talking about the exaggerated athleticism of a jumping frog in the gold fields of California or transporting a Connecticut man back into the time of King Arthur's court.

Fidelity

The second property of effective storytelling—fidelity—concerns truthfulness. We are predisposed to believe stories whose messages ring true with our own experience. Depending on the occasion, you probably share a lot in common with your audience, from being friends of the bride and groom at a wedding to sharing the sorrow of family members when giving a eulogy. You can draw on these commonalities to increase the narrative fidelity of your stories, whether they grow out of your individual experience or experiences with which most of your audience can relate.

Speaking of . . .

The Wedding Toast

In Chapter 3 we mentioned that approximately 40 percent of all adults report that their greatest fear is giving a public speech. Perhaps it is not too surprising to learn, then, that fully 97 percent of Americans fear presenting a wedding toast! The reasons offered by the people surveyed include but are not limited to (1) forgetting what to say, (2) being too emotional, (3) being boring, and (4) unintentionally saying something that is perceived as offensive. In response to this survey, Korbel Champagne Cellars, a California winery, established a hotline for people to call to learn tips about the do's and don'ts of wedding toasting. In its first three years of operation, the hotline received 22,000 calls.[1] It became so popular, in fact, that Korbel had to abandon it. The hotline was taking too much time away from more pressing business.

Here are some tips offered by the Korbel Wedding Toast Hotline for nervous toasters:

One of the most common speeches of tribute is the wedding toast.

1. Remember why you are being asked to give the toast.

2. Make sure your toast is something everyone can relate to.

3. Jokes, humor, and anecdotes are great ways to enliven a toast.

4. Try to know your material well enough so that you do not need your note cards.

5. Speak loudly enough so everyone can hear you.

6. Make your toast with your own personal style.

7. Remember, people will not be judging you as they might if you were giving a business presentation.

8. Toasts should be kept short and sweet.

9. When preparing your toast, sometimes it helps to look through old photographs or letters.

10. When delivering a wedding toast, make sure to stand and indicate the couple you are toasting.

1. *News from Korbel* [http://korbel.com/trade, 28 September 1998].
Source: Adapted from Korbel Wedding Toast Hotline Web site, http://korbel.com/trade.html#source.

It can be helpful to approach a speech task such as thanking people or making an introduction as a form of storytelling. Audiences relate well to recognition speeches and the like when they are told as a story. Remember, though, that to be effective our speech and the story it tells must meet the tests of probability and fidelity. This framework sets the stage for preparing to meet head-on the predictable situations in which you will be expected to speak both now and in the future. Because these situations vary tremendously in the degree to which you'll be able to prepare, let's look first at the type of speaking where you'll have little or no time to gather your thoughts and supporting material.

Impromptu Speeches: Speaking Without Advance Notice

There will be times in your life when you will be asked to speak without advance notice. Recall from Chapter 2 that such unrehearsed speeches are called impromptu. You may be asked to make an unanticipated toast or say a few words at a wedding, bar or bat mitzvah, or christening. Or you may be asked to defend or argue against the position of a colleague at work. Finally, you simply may be asked to explain yourself to a superior or agency to which you are accountable.

First Things First: Anticipate the Occasion

If you read Stephen J. Covey's book *The Seven Habits of Highly Effective People,* you'll learn that being unprepared isn't one of them.[5] Frankly, there are situations where the probability of your being asked to speak ranges from low to high. No one knows better than you the chances that you'll be asked to say a few words at a social occasion or in a professional setting. Forewarned is forearmed. Thus, if there is even the slightest chance you'll be asked to speak, you should prepare in advance. Does this mean that you should write out a speech? Not really. What we are talking about here is anticipating what you might be asked to say based on the context in which you'll find yourself. This will, at the very least, enable you to mentally and visually rehearse your response. Should you not be asked to speak as you'd anticipated, you'll only be better prepared for the next time one of these occasions to speak pops up.

Tips for Impromptu Speaking

If you were to participate in impromptu speaking at a collegiate speech tournament, this is what would typically happen. You would be handed a slip of paper with three topics on it. The topics might be general and abstract, such as the quotation we cited from Robert F. Kennedy, or an issue widely reported in the media. You would be given two minutes to prepare and five minutes to speak on the one topic you selected.

If this sounds frightening, then consider this: There may be times during your life when you don't even get two minutes to prepare, much less choose your topic from a choice of three. To assist you in adapting to such truly impromptu situations, we offer the following guidelines.

Get Organized

The thing that impresses people the most about people who speak effectively off-the-cuff is the appearance of organization. Whether we are responding to the query of a supervisor or speaking to an issue being debated at work, the first thing we want to do is get organized. One of the easiest and most effective patterns for organizing an impromptu speech is to (1) introduce the point(s) we want to make, (2) expand on the point(s) we make, and (3) conclude with a statement that summarizes the point(s) made. This harks back to the "tell 'em what you're going to tell 'em, tell 'em, and then tell 'em what you told 'em" sequence introduced in Chapter 9. Consider a classroom example, in which the instructor asks, "What's your take on the effects of rap lyrics on violence?" One student responds: "I have two points to make . . . about the effects of rap. First, the effects are exaggerated. Second, most people who think rap affects violence are clueless about modern music. So what I'm saying is they're making a mountain out of another molehill." Notice in this example that the first sentence not only previews the points being made but also restates in modified form the question asked. The two points are made and then summarized in the final sentence. Compare this response with another hypothetical but not atypical one from a student: "I don't know . . . I guess I disagree. It's just a bunch of people who are out of it coming down on alternative music. Get a life, you know?" This second response is both disorganized and equivocal, bringing us to our second guideline.

Take a Position

Few of us are favorably impressed with people who fail to take a stand, who equivocate even as they're trying to build a response to a query. When someone asks a speaker, "What's your opinion or your position?" we think the speaker is obligated to give it. On the other hand, if a speaker has not yet formulated a clear-cut opinion, an audience would much rather hear the person say "I'm ambivalent" or "I'll need more information than I've been given" than hem and haw in response to such a query.

Use Powerful Language

Powerful language goes hand in hand with the first two guidelines. Organization is key to appearing powerful. We expect powerful people not to equivocate, to take a stand even if it is clearly one of neutrality. For example, sometimes a person may say simply, "That is really none of my business. It is for the people directly affected to decide for themselves." Recall that powerful language avoids the use of unnecessary qualifiers and long questions. Powerful people say such things as "My opinion is firm" or "My experience leads me to the unequivocal belief. . . ." Powerful people do not say, "I could be wrong, but I think . . ." or "I believe it's okay, do you?" Impromptu speaking is tough enough without undermining your authority with powerless language.

Hitchhike

It's sometimes effective to begin an impromptu message with what others have already said on the matter. This hitchhiking technique shows that you have been actively listening. It also acknowledges the contributions of others, even when we disagree with what they've said. For example, "Bill's point that this situation demands caution is well taken, but I must respectfully disagree for a couple of reasons." We also might say, "Let me summarize what's been said thus far, and then I'll add my two cents worth." Again, this kind of bridge tells our audience we are tuned in *and* organized.

Use Stories and Anecdotes

If you know a story or an anecdote that contains a lesson that is both relevant and straightforward, by all means use it as a basis for your impromptu speech. History is full of examples of stories and anecdotes about the famous and notorious. Organizational culture, moreover, often gives rise to stories about people and events that can be used to make one or more points in an impromptu speech. Some stories and anecdotes are so general they can be applied to almost any point you choose to make. The real power of Aesop's fables, for instance, is that each contains multiple lessons you can apply to life. The same is true of many fairy tales and well-known children's stories such as *Goldilocks and the Three Bears* and *The Boy Who Cried Wolf.*

Invest in Reference Works

Impromptu speaking is a matter of when, not if. Thus, we recommend purchasing for your personal and permanent library at least two kinds of reference books in addition to a standard book of quotations such as *Bartlett's.* First, look for one composed of contemporary quotes from well-known and widely recognized people. At the same time, invest in a book of anecdotes compiled from the lives of the famous and notorious. Then find and commit to memory quotes and anecdotes that can be applied generally to topics and issues you may be asked to speak about. Although these tips are meant to help you most with impromptu speaking situations, they can be easily generalized to everyday situations where you know for certain that you will be speaking, and situations where there is a high probability that you will be speaking.

Speaking on Special Occasions

Speaking on special occasions is likely during the course of our lives. At such times our job is to emphasize the special nature of the occasion in thought, word, and deed. Most of the time we will be able to prepare and practice in advance of such situations. Other times we may be asked, in impromptu fashion, to "say a few words." The special occasions we can anticipate speaking at over the course of our lives include expressing thanks; introducing a speaker or an honored guest; speaking in recognition of a person, group, or organization; making a commemorative speech; and speaking to entertain people.

Speech of Acceptance

A **speech of acceptance** is a speech expressing thanks for an award or honor. In many cultures, calling attention to ourselves is considered to be in bad taste. Many of us have been taught this norm. Even so, there are times in our lives when we cannot help being the center of attention. One of them is when we are singled out publicly for some recognition or award. For some, this becomes a dilemma. On one hand, they know they need to accept the recognition or award in a fashion that recognizes and pays tribute to those responsible. On the other hand, they don't want to appear as if they expected the recognition or award and prepared their remarks well in advance of the event. All too often, therefore, they do not prepare or rehearse their response and end up appearing humble but tongue-tied. Believe us: Most audiences would prefer to hear someone accept recognition in a fashion that is both gracious and articulate. Being well-spoken does not mean that we are self-absorbed or glib. The thank-you also needn't be long.

A good speech of acceptance should serve four functions. First, it should either be brief or within the time constraints imposed by the situation, as is the case when we are one of several people being recognized. Second, it should be genuine and heartfelt. Audience members can typically tell by the speaker's nonverbal behavior whether expressions of gratitude are sincere. Third, it should reciprocate the

speech of acceptance
A speech expressing thanks for an award or honor.

recognition by praising the people or group who have singled us out. Fourth, it should engender liking. People like people who like them. It's well worth the effort to make audience members feel liked and attractive.

Speech of Introduction

speech of introduction

A speech that briefly sets the stage for an upcoming speaker.

A **speech of introduction** briefly sets the stage for an upcoming speaker. Speeches of introduction are designed to meet two objectives. The first is to enlist the audience's attention and interest. The second objective is to reinforce or induce audience perceptions of credibility. Perhaps the most unusual speech of introduction we have heard was in 1998 when James Carville and Mary Matalin, a married couple who represent the liberal and conservative ends of the political spectrum, debated each other at our university. They were supposed to be introduced by a graduate of our university, political consultant Ed Rollins. However, he was unable to attend. So Carville, in what appeared to be an impromptu speech, introduced his own wife and adversary for the evening, praising her as "my best friend, and the best wife any man could have."[6] His introduction set the stage for a spirited and entertaining debate between the oddest of couples in contemporary American politics.

Although we may never introduce our own opponent in a debate, it is likely that at some time we will be called on to introduce a speaker to an audience. Usually, the audience is favorably disposed toward the speaker or they wouldn't be there. However, sometimes a speaker is not well known and needs a buildup of credibility before the speech. In any case, a good way to look at a speech of introduction is to remember the three basic principles of introducing any speech: Open with impact, connect with the audience, and focus on the upcoming presentation.

Open With Impact

Our first task as an introducer is to build enthusiasm for the main speaker. A lukewarm or trite introduction is worse than none at all. Thus, look for a way to capture the audience's attention immediately. Sometimes humor, a brief anecdote, or a moving story will fill the bill.

Connect With the Audience

Why should the audience listen to the speaker? What's in it for them? Just as we must connect with the audience in our own speeches, the same is true in a speech of introduction. What special qualifications does the speaker have? Why is the topic of special concern to the audience? We need to answer these questions in terms the audience can relate to if we want them to be motivated to listen. Focus on the speaker's competence and character. Even if a speaker's credibility is established, we should reinforce the perception by mentioning one or two examples that clearly emphasize competence and character. If the speaker's credibility has yet to be established, mention at least one thing that addresses the speaker's competence on the topic and one that addresses the speaker's good character.

Focus on the Upcoming Presentation

Finally, it is the introducer's task to focus the audience's attention on the upcoming presentation. Make sure you know the speaker's topic, and coordinate your introduction with his or her speech. Nothing is worse than preparing an audience to hear a speech on one topic only to have the speaker announce that the topic has been changed. There are also some general guidelines that you should follow for a speech of introduction.

Tips and Tactics

Guidelines for a Speech of Introduction

- *Be brief.* The audience came to hear the speaker, not the introducer. A one- or two-minute introduction is sufficient for most speech situations. For a particularly lengthy or formal speech situation, the introduction might be longer, but in no case should it exceed about 10 percent of the speaker's time (six minutes out of an hour, for example).
- *Don't steal the speaker's thunder.* Although you want to prepare the audience for what is to come by focusing their attention on the topic, you should not discuss the substance of the speech topic. Again, the audience wants to hear the speaker's views on the topic, not yours. Your job is to create an appetite for the upcoming main course, not fill up the audience with hors d'oeuvres.
- *Be prepared: Work with the speaker in advance.* It is best to talk to the speaker or a representative about your role as introducer. Are there specific points to be stressed? Is there anything the speaker wants to avoid? Some speakers may even want to preview your introductory remarks or may provide written suggestions for you.

Speech of Recognition

The elements of a good speech of introduction also apply to speeches of recognition. A **speech of recognition** is a speech presenting an award or honor to an individual. In such speeches we need to open by discussing the importance of the occasion, the award being made, or the special contribution made by the honoree. We also need to provide examples or testimony from those who know the honoree to illustrate his or her merit. Also, we should consider couching our speech in the form of a story about the person.

Connecting with our audience is equally important. We can give them a personal glimpse, either from our own experience or from testimony of those who know the honoree. It is important for our audience to feel that the award is, in a sense, coming from them.

Unless the name of the honoree is known in advance, it should be saved until the end of the recognition speech. Not only will this build suspense, audience members will start to guess at the honoree with each new bit of information we provide. As we conclude, we focus on the honoree by name. Usually a recognition speech ends something like this, "And so it is my great pleasure to announce the winner of the lifetime achievement award, our own Taylor Smith!"

speech of recognition
A speech presenting an award or honor to an individual.

Speech of Commemoration

A **speech of commemoration** calls attention to the stature of the person or people being honored, or emphasizes the significance of an occasion. There are several

speech of commemoration
A speech that calls attention to the stature of the person or people being honored, or emphasizes the significance of an occasion.

Earl Spencer's moving eulogy for his sister, Diana, Princess of Wales, was seen throughout the world.

kinds of commemorative speeches. Some of these speeches focus on cause for celebration: for example, a national holiday or a 50th wedding anniversary. Remember, it is the occasion or people who have given cause for celebration that should be the focus of the speech.

Another type of speech of commemoration is one given to memorialize a specific person (Martin Luther King Jr.) or the people we associate with a special and solemn occasion (members of the armed forces on Memorial Day). Finally, a **eulogy** is a kind of commemorative speech about someone who has died that is usually given shortly after his or her death. For example, when Earl Spencer eulogized his sister, Diana, Princess of Wales, he spoke lovingly of her as "the very essence of compassion, of duty, of style, of beauty. All over the world she was a symbol of selfless humanity, a standard-bearer for the rights of the downtrodden, a very British girl who transcended nationality, someone with a natural nobility who was classless, who proved in the last year that she needed no royal title to continue to generate her particular brand of magic."[7]

In many ways, a speech of commemoration is like an extended recognition speech. With the obvious exception of a eulogy, the honoree may even be present and be asked to say a few words after the commemoration. Sometimes these speeches take a humorous form, such as a "roast." Although jokes and embarrassing incidents are recited, they are done in good fun and ultimately the honoree is praised for his or her accomplishments.

A speech of commemoration should, like any other speech, open with impact. Begin by calling attention to the stature of the person being honored or the occasion that necessitates the memorial.

As with any speech, it is important to connect with the audience. What ties the audience and the person, people, and occasion together? A eulogy often recounts the deceased's common ties to the audience. Family and friends are usually pres-

eulogy
A kind of commemorative speech about someone who has died that is usually given shortly after his or her death.

ent, and recounting memorable events from the life of the deceased helps everyone cope with their loss.

For the honoree, focus on the best that person has accomplished. For a retiree, it might be his or her accomplishments in the workforce. For a public figure, it might be what he or she stood for. For a fallen hero, the deeds and cause that cost a life are a source of meaning.

The substance of a speech of commemoration is usually less structured than that of other speeches. Nevertheless, there should be a theme or an essential point that you want to share with the audience. For example, many extraordinary events that have taken place in recent history have been commemorated by people known only to those in their own community or by public figures known throughout the world. Examples range from commemorative speeches in honor of the soldiers who landed on the beaches of Normandy to begin the liberation of France from Nazi Germany to the victims of the horrific attacks on September 11, 2001. Themes in these speeches include honor and sacrifice, love of family, and living life to its fullest, to name but a few. Such themes have universal meaning and can serve to tie together even the most loosely organized narrative in a speech.

Finally, a speech of commemoration should close with impact, leaving a lasting impression. A verse of scripture might provide just the right note to close a eulogy. But so too could the right anecdote, if it illustrated something meaningful about the life of the deceased.

Speeches to Entertain[8]

Sometimes known as after-dinner speaking because it's frequently given following a meal, a speech to entertain is more than just a string of jokes or a comedy monologue. A **speech to entertain** makes its point through the use of humor. Like all speeches, a speech to entertain should have a clear focus. Of course, many speeches contain humor as an element. What makes the speech to entertain different is that its primary purpose is to bring laughter to the audience, not to persuade or inform them, though that may occur along the way. A speech meant to entertain is ideally suited to the storytelling format of speaking. This type of speech is every bit as taxing as persuasive or informative speaking.

> **speech to entertain**
> A speech that makes its point through the use of humor.

Selecting a Topic

The first task is to select a topic. The best place to begin is with yourself. Have you had experiences that, at least looking back, were funny? A good topic needs to have the potential to develop into a full-blown speech, not just one or two good punch lines. It needs to be something your audience can relate to. Many of the funniest speeches are about the frustrations of everyday life. Avoid the temptation to adopt the latest routine from Chris Rock or Jon Stewart. Work from your own experiences and from experiences shared by those in your audience.

Consider your audience's expectations for the speech. You probably don't want to repeat stories you know your audience has heard before. If you are speaking to a group of lawyers, you probably can count on them having heard every lawyer joke known to humankind. Pick something that can connect you, assuming you are not a lawyer, to them. For example, there are few people today, including lawyers, who have not shared the frustrations of dealing with computers that seem to know just when to crash and make your life miserable.

You must, of course, be sensitive to an audience's diversity and state of mind in developing and delivering a speech to entertain. We live in an era in which a racial or ethnic joke that would have been accepted a few years ago can end a career or lead to the demise of a relationship. Remain mindful that what you say may find its way to an unintended audience too. Jokes of questionable taste about those not present may cause a minor firestorm, as Whoopi Goldberg has learned on more than one occasion.

In developing the content of your speech to entertain, brainstorming is a useful technique. Recall from Chapter 2 that brainstorming involves a group of people getting together and rapidly firing off ideas. Someone keeps a list. No criticism or evaluation of the ideas is permitted–that comes later. The key to brainstorming is to hitchhike one idea on another. The wilder and crazier the ideas, at this point, the better. You can always tone them down later.

Once you have a list of ideas, write each one on a card or slip of paper. The next step is to sort them out and organize them into a speech.

Organization

A speech to entertain should resemble any other good speech in organization: Open with impact, connect with your audience, and provide a clear focus in your introduction. It is very important to capture your audience's attention almost immediately. Unless you are already a highly skilled and entertaining speaker, this is not the time for a three-minute story leading to one punch line. So, try to get a laugh in the first sentence or two. Sometimes just an outrageous statement will do this.

Russ Woody began his commencement speech by stating:

> Look . . . I write sitcoms for a living, so don't expect much. Which means . . . basically, I'm gonna tell a few jokes. Hit a few well-worn platitudes. And try to sell you a Dodge minivan.

Russ's helpful hints for writing humor are summarized in the box Writing Humor.

Although it is important to focus the audience's attention on the topic of your speech, a preview of points is rare in a speech to entertain. Part of humor is surprise, and telegraphing your jokes in a preview will undermine the audience's surprise.

The body of the speech can be organized in a number of ways. A simple chronological or narrative form works well when telling a story or describing a series of events. A topical arrangement allows you to organize your speech around major topics.

In concluding a speech to entertain, you normally would not summarize your points. You would, however, want to close with impact or, as the old adage goes, "Leave 'em laughing."

Sources of Humor

What are some sources of humor? We hesitate to try to define what is funny. After all, everyone's sense of humor is different, and what is funny to one person will leave another completely stone-faced. Some people love Jon Stewart and hate Dennis Miller, others the reverse, and some people enjoy them both.

Nevertheless, a few traditional sources of humor deserve mention:

- *Exaggeration.* Exaggeration is a well-tested source of humor. Wits from Mark Twain to the present day have relied on exaggeration to make their point. Russ Woody used exaggeration to describe his own graduation experience:

Speaking of . . .

Writing Humor *by Russ Woody*

As a college student, Russ Woody excelled in an event called "Speech to Entertain." Not only was humor Russ's hobby, it became his profession. Russ began his writing career at MTM productions, where he wrote episodes for shows such as *Newhart, St. Elsewhere,* and *Hill Street Blues.* For two years he was a producer and writer for *Murphy Brown,* for which he received an Emmy in 1990. He received a Golden Globe as co-executive producer of *Cybill.* He has also served as a consulting producer for *Foxworthy* and was co-executive producer of *Becker.* We asked Russ to do the impossible: explain writing humor in 250 words or less. Here is the result.

Writing Humor?
by Russ Woody

Two-hundred fifty words on how to write humor? Gee, can't I just whack myself in the forehead with a ball peen hammer? Trying to explain humor is a little like trying to wrest a ripe banana from an immense and bitter gorilla. If not handled correctly, you can end up looking rather foolish.

With that in mind, "Hello, Mr. Gorilla . . ."

The fact of the matter is, humor is more difficult to write than drama. Because, while both humor and drama rely heavily on emotional content, humor is much more difficult to break down mechanically. Therefore it's more difficult to construct initially. It's relatively easy to figure out what makes a person sad or angry or uneasy or embarrassed or happy. Yet it is, for the most part, difficult to say why a person laughs.

So I guess the first thing you've got to do is figure out what type of humor appeals most to you. Monty Python, Andrew "Dice" Clay, The Naked Gun, *Murphy Brown,* Full House, Spy Magazine, Mad Magazine, Saturday Night Live.

Whichever it is, find it. Then—study it. Watch it, read it, take it apart, figure out how it's constructed, how it's set up, how it pays off—figure out the dynamics of humor. (Which will make it terribly unfunny when you do, but that's the perpetual hell comedy writers live in.)

For instance—one of my favorite jokes of all time is in one of the Pink Panther *movies where Peter Sellers goes into a hotel and approaches a man at the desk who has a dog sitting beside him. Sellers says, "Does your dog bite?" The guy says no. So Sellers reaches over to pat the little pooch, and it tries to rip his arm off. Sellers then looks to the guy and says, "I thought you said your dog didn't bite?" The guy says, "It's not my dog."*

I love that joke because every element of it is real, and nobody involved thinks it's funny. The man was quite correct in his literal interpretation of Sellers's question. Sellers is more than a little annoyed at the man for misunderstanding what seemed to be a logical and straightforward question. And the dog is just pissed off. In a more general sense, one person becomes a victim because the other is a stickler for precise wording. It is extreme focus on one character's part and vulnerability on the other character's part. In a way, it's like the movie The In-Laws, *with Peter Falk and Alan Arkin. Falk is intensely focused on his job with the government, which, in turn makes Arkin's life a living hell. (If you've seen the movie, you know what I'm talking about—if you haven't, go see it, because I'm coming up on two-fifty pretty fast here, so I can't get into it.)*

When you've taken enough jokes and stories apart, you may start to get an idea of how to construct your own. That's when it gets really tough. Just be sure you always remember the one, underlying key to writing humor—oops, outta time.

I will be brief . . . because I remember my own graduation . . . though not *too* clearly. We were over in Laxson Auditorium, and it was a comfy 105 degrees out . . . and just slightly less than double that in the auditorium.

Anyway, the man who gave the commencement speech talked for close to 15 hours. He said we were all sailing ships out on the ocean of life, and we were the beating hearts of an upwardly mobile nation, and we had a bunch of mountaintops to climb . . . And the only thing I *really* came away with, besides hathair, was something about a new technology in ventilation systems that was greatly improving the output of poultry in tested areas of Missouri.

- *Incongruity.* Something that doesn't fit in seems funny. Woody Allen once wore tennis shoes with a tuxedo (semiformal attire?). We frequently poke fun at politicians whose words and deeds don't match. When the state of California was sending out IOUs instead of checks, Jay Leno commented that the latest Southern California earthquake wasn't really an earthquake, just the governor bouncing more checks.

- *Attacking authority.* The attack on authority has been a staple of humor since anyone can remember. Will Rogers made fun of Congress, Jay Leno makes fun of politicians, and Chris Rock makes fun of everybody, himself included!

- *Puns.* Use at your own risk!

- *Sarcasm.* Used with care, sarcasm can be a good source of humor (particularly when directed against sources of authority). But be careful you don't create sympathy for your victim. Sarcasm that is too edgy or biting can seem mean-spirited and bitter rather than funny. David Spade gets away with sarcasm because we know he is trying to be funny rather than deliberately hurtful.

- *Irony.* Sometimes a powerful source of humor, irony can also make a serious point. The fact that Microsoft founder and billionaire Bill Gates had his presentation of Windows 98 marred by a computer failure was a source of material for late-night comedians for several days.

- *The rule of three.* Milton Berle once claimed that he could make an audience laugh at anything if he preceded it with two funny jokes. Try it. Once you have people laughing, they often will continue to laugh even at a line that isn't funny.

- *Self-deprecating humor.* Often the safest humor is that directed at yourself. Not only do you avoid alienating anyone, you show that you are a regular person. When Hall-of-Fame quarterback Terry Bradshaw spoke at a "speecha-thon" along with such luminaries as former president Gerald Ford, former congressman Jack Kemp, and former senator Bill Bradley, he wondered out loud why he was there. Gazing out at an audience of prominent business leaders, he admitted: "I made my living, unlike you, by putting my hands under another man's butt."[9]

- *Delivery.* Humor depends on direct contact and immediacy with your audience. Thus, use of a manuscript or conspicuous notes will destroy the spontaneity of the experience. Even if you have memorized your speech, however, it is important that it sound fresh and spontaneous.

  Use a lively and animated manner in presenting your speech. Timing in comedy is everything. Knowing when to pause, what word to punch, and the right tone of voice to use are not things you can learn from reading a book. Only by trying out your speech with friends and experimenting with different ways of delivering the same line can you tell what delivery is best.

Not everyone is comfortable with speaking to entertain. But done well and taste-fully, it can be an enjoyable experience for both the speaker and the audience.

Speaking and Leading in Small Groups

group
Three or more individuals who are aware of each other's presence, share a mutually interdependent purpose, engage in communication transactions with one another, and identify with the group.

Besides impromptu speaking, you will probably speak in numerous group discussions in both your educational and professional careers. A **group** consists of three or more individuals who are aware of each other's presence, share a mutually interdependent purpose, engage in communication transactions with one another, and identify with the group. As a leader of a group, you are also the chief spokesperson. As such, there are several important functions you will be asked to perform.

Although we cannot introduce you to all of these functions here, we want to alert you to those most relevant to the main topic and scope of this book.

Leadership Functions

As you attempt to lead a group, there are a number of functions that you need to perform yourself or delegate to someone in the group: These include but are not limited to developing an agenda, keeping the discussion on track, asking questions to promote discussion, summarizing and transitioning to other points, and setting the agenda for the next meeting.

Developing an Agenda

A group without an agenda is one that will likely flounder. The **agenda** defines the purpose and direction the group takes, the topics to be covered, and the goals to be achieved. A sound agenda is every bit as important to a group's success as sound organization is to a speech's success. For example, suppose you are dealing with the problem of crime on your campus. Each person in the group can be assigned to gather some information prior to the meeting. Then, you might meet with an agenda such as the following:

agenda
Something that defines the purpose and direction a group takes, the topics to be covered, and the goals to be achieved.

   I. What is the crime rate on our campus? What specific crimes occur and how often?
  II. What percentage of crime in our city is committed by college students? What types of crimes are committed against college students?
 III. What steps have been taken on campus to reduce crime?
 IV. How do our campus crime rates compare with national statistics?
  V. What conclusions can we draw? Is crime "under control" on our campus? Do we need to make changes to reduce crime?
 VI. Set agenda for next meeting.

Keeping the Discussion on Track

Although "off-topic" discussions can sometimes be productive, more often than not they are a diversion from the real issues at hand. Particularly disruptive are "ain't it awful" tangents, where everybody in the group shares their complaints—about the task, the boss, or whatever. These complaints may have their place, but they are unlikely to help the group get the job done. Most group members are reluctant to criticize their peers as being off the subject, and it is usually the leader who has to bring the group back on track. A tactful suggestion that "maybe we're straying from the topic" or a question that refocuses the group on the subject is usually enough to get things back on task. Even a little humorous reminder that the group has wandered can do wonders.

Asking Questions to Promote Discussion

There are many types of questions a designated leader (or any member, for that matter) can ask. Four of the most important types of questions are questions asking for information, those asking for interpretation, those asking for suggestions, and questions about procedure. A *question of information,* for example, might be to

Small group communication takes place in many unexpected situations, such as this scuba class.

ask, "What is the average crime rate for colleges our size?" Such a question requires a factually based response. A *question of interpretation* might be, "Do students really feel safe on our campus?" This question cannot be answered simply by reading off statistics. It calls for group members to form conclusions based on the information they've gathered, as well as to add their own subjective interpretation of the information. The third type of question, *asking for suggestions,* might be, "What can we do to reduce crime on this campus?" This question calls for ideas from group members aimed at solving a problem the group has identified. Finally, a *procedural question* might be asked of the group, "Do we want to brainstorm possible solutions?" This question asks the group if they want to follow a certain procedure. All four types of questions are important if a group is to achieve its goals.

Summarizing and Transitioning to Other Points

As we pointed out regarding your speeches, summaries and transitional devices such as signposts are highly functional. At some point it will become apparent that the group is moving in some direction. Although not everyone may agree on every point, as the leader you can try to summarize those points on which everyone agrees, thus defining which issues need further exploration. For example, you might say: "It seems that we all agree that there's a serious crime problem on our campus. Furthermore, it looks like assault and theft are the biggest problems. What we need to figure out is why these problems are getting worse and if there's anything we can do about them. Any ideas?"

Setting the Agenda for the Next Meeting

Assuming the group's task has not been completed, the next action is to agree on time and place and agenda items for the next meeting. Particularly important is making sure members know what their individual responsibilities are prior to the next meeting. One of the great advantages of groups is that tasks can be subdivided. But that works only if everyone does what is agreed upon.

Panel Discussions

A **panel discussion** is an extemporaneous group discussion held for the benefit of an audience. In a panel discussion, as in a speech, it is important that the group have a clear outline of the topics to be covered, and that members are adequately prepared. The advantage of a panel discussion is that it is a blend of preparation and spontaneity. Members should feel free to comment on one another's points, ask questions, and openly discuss points throughout the presentation.

> **panel discussion**
> An extemporaneous group discussion held for the benefit of an audience.

A panel discussion requires a leader to act as the *moderator* of the presentation. The moderator calls on members and keeps the discussion on track. Members who want to comment on another member's statement should wait to be recognized by the moderator. A panel discussion is more formal than a normal private group discussion.

Most panel discussions also provide an opportunity for audience members to ask questions. This can occur as the group moves through its outline or can be held as a *forum* period at the end of the panel presentation.

The outline for a panel discussion is similar to that of a speech; however, some modifications need to be made. Here is an example of a panel discussion outline on the topic of secondhand smoke:

   I. Introduction of topic and group members.
  II. Is secondhand tobacco smoke harmful?
 III. What is being done to limit exposure to secondhand smoke?
  IV. What is causing these efforts to fall short?
   V. Recommendations for new regulations on smoking in public places.

Ideally, each member should be able to offer comments on each of these topics, rather than having one member prepared on each topic. A panel discussion should be a true discussion, not a series of individual presentations.

Speaking on Television

Although you might not plan on being a television newscaster or celebrity, many people in ordinary life find themselves confronted with a television interview at some time or another. Business executives need to be able to handle a television interview, but so do supervisors and line personnel who may be on the scene of a breaking news event. Unless you expect to be on television and have been given a list of questions you will be asked in advance, speaking on TV is a lot like impromptu speaking. You want to appear organized, come across as firm rather than indecisive, and use powerful language. Speaking on TV also demands nonverbal immediacy behaviors, so you'll want to look back at Chapter 11 for a discussion of effective delivery tips.

Speaking of . . .

Chatting It Up on TV *by Paul Burnham Finney*

Many executives turn into TV regulars and routinely go out on cross-country tours to promote a new product or service. But few of the veterans take their camera assignments casually.

"Steal the show," says Mariana Field Hoppin, president of MFH Travel Marketing Ltd. and a longtime spokeswoman for Avis Europe. "When you walk into the studio, win over the camera crew and interviewer, and you've got them in the palm of your hands."

It's important to do that. "The public is taking the lazy way out—getting their information on the tube," as one corporate communications director puts it.

"Smart executives have to be prepared for surprises on the road," he goes on to say. When the Tylenol-tampering scare struck Johnson & Johnson, C.E.O. James E. Burke signed up for a crash course at the Executive Television Workshop [ETW] before facing the public.

Screen test: Among the tips ETW feeds its corporate students:

- Get a good fix on the questions you'll be asked by contacting the TV or radio station. (Ask around if the direct approach doesn't work.)

- Tell your story, or somebody else will—and not always correctly.

- Memorize the basic points you want to make, and keep them uppermost in your mind.

- Stick to solid colors in dress—no loud patterns allowed. And wear contacts rather than glasses, if possible.

- Women: don't show up in a short skirt that rides above the knees.

- Park yourself in the front third of the chair. You'll look more alert and interested that way.

- Glance at 3-by-5 card notes during commercials or station breaks—never when on camera.

- Say it all in 45 seconds when answering an interviewer. "Short, clear answers," as TV commentator David Brinkley advises.

- Use anecdotes and "sparklers" to brighten your delivery.

- Don't repeat a negative statement—it only lends credence to it.

Digestible bits: "We stress the importance of establishing a conversational tone," says Executive Television Workshop marketing director Carol Heimann. "Executives get very techy in the way they talk. A reporter is only a conduit to the public. Break your explanations into digestible bits. Try to act as though you're in a living room, chatting with someone."

Ultimately, the impression you leave with your audience counts more than your words. Some 90% of what they remember is your "voice" and "nonverbal communications," according to studies. In short, body language matters as much as your thoughts.

"One of your biggest assets," says Heimann, "is a smile. It can change a million opinions. You can disarm your audience. If you're relaxed, you'll relax the people who are watching."

Source: Article appeared first in *Newsweek*'s 1990 Special Ad Section, "Management Digest." Reprinted by permission.

One question that always arises when being interviewed on television is where to look. Do you look at the camera or at the interviewer or from one to the other? One suggestion comes from Dorothy Sarnoff, who provides communication training to corporate executives. She suggests: "Focus on the left eye of the interviewer, then the right eye—and back to the left. Not a windshield-wiper effect, but slowly so your own eyes don't look dead."[10] Some other suggestions for talking on television are included in the box Chatting It Up on TV by Paul Burnham Finney.

In conclusion, the best advice we can give is to be prepared and stick to your theme. Interviews are frequently videotaped and then edited for a sound bite. You want to make sure that regardless of what is left on the cutting-room floor your essential message reaches the viewers.

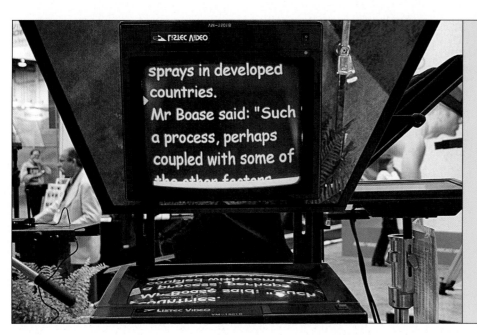

Speaking well from a Teleprompter requires practice.

Summary

Approach most special speaking occasions as storytelling. Good stories are:

- Organized
- Probable
- Have fidelity and ring true for the audience

Effective impromptu speeches should:

- Be clearly organized
- Take a stand
- Use powerful language

Other types of speeches that can benefit from storytelling include:

- Speeches of acceptance
- Speeches of introduction
- Speeches of recognition
- Speeches of commemoration, such as eulogies
- Speeches to entertain an audience

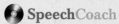

SpeechCoach

To evaluate your understanding of this chapter, see the Quizzes on your CD.

 www.mhhe.com /brydon5

Visit the Online Learning Center for helpful study resources, including practice tests, key term crossword puzzles, and PowerWeb articles for research and review.

Advice for speaking in and leading small groups:

- Develop an agenda
- Keep the discussion on track
- Ask questions to promote discussion
- Summarize and provide transitions to other points
- Set the agenda for the next meeting

Advice for participating in panel discussions:

- Select a moderator to lead the discussion
- Strike a balance between preparation and spontaneity
- Provide an opportunity to ask questions during a forum period after the discussion

Advice for TV interviews includes:

- Be well prepared
- Look at the interviewer, not the camera
- Dress appropriately
- Keep answers brief
- Use anecdotes and sparklers
- Appear relaxed

Check Your Understanding: Exercises and Activities

 **Speech**Coach

For a review of key terms in this chapter, see the Key Terms Flashcards on your CD.

1. Your best friend is getting married, and you will be asked to say a few words at the wedding. Prepare your toast. Do the same thing for a wedding anniversary, a baptism, and a bar or bat mitzvah.

2. Think of a special award for one of your classmates. Write a speech of recognition for presenting the award.

3. Track down several quotations and anecdotes that are general enough to be used as an opening or a closing for a speech of acceptance or a speech of recognition. Three sources to which you can turn are:

   Clifton Fadiman, ed., *The Little Brown Book of Anecdotes* (Boston: Little, Brown, 1985).

   Edmund Fuller, ed., *2,500 Anecdotes for All Occasions* (New York: Avenel Books, 1980).

   James B. Simpson, ed., *Simpson's Contemporary Quotations: The Most Notable Quotes Since 1950* (Boston: Houghton Mifflin, 1988).

4. A speech of nomination can either make or break the nominee's chances for being elected to office. Speeches of nomination are more common than you may think. Social clubs such as fraternities and sororities, business and professional associations such as the Soroptimists, Rotary, or local Bar are all examples. On a separate sheet of paper, list and explain what you think are the essential characteristics of a speech of nomination. Then see if you can find a published example of a speech of nomination that conforms to your criteria. Note conforming examples on a copy of the speech with a highlighter and share your analysis with classmates.

Notes

1. Edmund Fuller, ed., *2,500 Anecdotes for All Occasions* (New York: Avenel Books, 1980), 135.
2. Theodore H. White, *The Making of the President 1968* (New York: Atheneum, 1969), 171. Shaw's original lines appear in his play *Back to Methuselah,* Part I, Act I. The Serpent in the Garden of Eden says to Eve, "You see things; and you say 'Why?' But I dream things that never were; and I say 'Why not?'" See George Bernard Shaw, *The Complete Plays of Bernard Shaw* (London: Odhams Press Limited, 1934), 857.
3. Walter R. Fisher, *Human Communication as Narration* (Columbia: University of South Carolina Press, 1987).
4. Peggy Noonan, *What I Saw at the Revolution: A Political Life in the Reagan Era* (New York: Random House, 1990).
5. Stephen J. Covey, *The Seven Habits of Highly Effective People* (New York: Fireside Books/Simon & Schuster, 1989).
6. Kevin Jeys, "Irreconcilable Differences," *Chico News and Review,* 8 October 1998, 29.
7. "I Stand Before You . . . ," *Newsweek,* 15 September 1997, 24.
8. Adapted from Jack Perella and Steven R. Brydon, "Speaking to Entertain," in *Intercollegiate Forensics: A Participant's Handbook,* ed. T. C. Winebrenner, 42–46. © 1992 Northern California Forensics Association.
9. Sam Stanton, "Clinton Remains Topic A at Cal Expo Speechathon," *Sacramento Bee,* 10 October 1998, A23.
10. Article appeared first in *Newsweek*'s 1990 Special Ad Section, "Management Digest," Paul Burnham Finney, "The Business of Communicating," 16.

Appendix A
Guide to Source Citations

AMERICAN PSYCHOLOGICAL ASSOCIATION (APA) STYLE

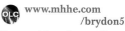

www.mhhe.com
/brydon5

For more information on citing sources in APA or MLA style, go to the Online Learning Center.

The following information is based on the *Publication Manual of the American Psychological Association,* Fifth Edition, 2001, and on their Web site, www.apastyle.org. Please note that there are several changes in APA style from the fourth edition. Hanging indents (not tabs) are to be used in the references list, titles should be *italicized* rather than <u>underlined,</u> and the citation of online sources has changed. It is important that you fully document the sources of information you use in preparing a speech outline. Cite the source in parentheses in the actual body of the outline by name and date. Include page numbers for quotations or specific facts, for example, (Jones, 2005, p. 1).

Include a list of "References" at the end of your outline. Always include the author, date, title, and facts of publication. Personal communications, such as letters, phone calls, e-mail, and interviews, are cited only in the text, not the reference list; for example, J. Q. Jones (personal communication, April 1, 2005). The format varies depending on the type of work referenced.

Here are some of the most common types of works you may use in a speech. Notice that APA style does not place quotation marks around the titles of articles or book chapters. Also, titles of books and articles are not capitalized, except for the first word, the first word following a colon, and proper names. Periodical titles are capitalized. Authors are listed by last name first, followed by first and sometimes middle initials.

Books

Single Author
Freeley, A. J. (1990). *Argumentation and debate: Critical thinking for reasoned decision making* (7th ed.). Belmont, CA: Wadsworth.

Multiple Authors
Germond, J. W., & Witcover, J. (1989). *Whose broad stripes and bright stars?* New York: Warner Books.

Corporate Author
American Psychological Association. (2001). *Publication manual of the American Psychological Association* (5th ed.). Washington, DC: Author.

Government Document
Department of Health and Human Services. (1989). *Smoking tobacco and health: A fact book.* (DHHS Publication No. CDC 87-8397). Washington, DC: U.S. Government Printing Office.

Chapter in a Book
Steeper, F. T. (1978). Public response to Gerald Ford's statements on Eastern Europe in the second debate. In G. F. Bishop, R. G. Meadow, & M. Jackson-Beeck (Eds.), *The presidential debates: Media, electoral, and policy perspectives* (pp. 81–101). New York: Praeger.

Periodicals

Weekly Magazine
Alter, J. (1988, September 26). The expectations game. *Newsweek, 112,* 16–18.

If the author is unknown, you would list the article as follows:

The expectations game. (1988, September 26). *Newsweek, 112,* 16–18.

Scholarly Journal Divided by Volume Numbers
Vancil, D. L., & Pendell, S. D. (1984). Winning presidential debates: An analysis of criteria influencing audience response. *Western Journal of Speech Communication, 48,* 63–74.

[This means the article was published in 1984, in volume 48, on pages 63–74.]

Newspaper

Rosentiel, T. H. (1988, October 14). Minus a Dukakis home run, Bush is called winner. *Los Angeles Times,* p. A25.

If the author is unknown, you would list the article as follows:

Minus a Dukakis home run, Bush is called winner. (1988, October 14). *Los Angeles Times,* p. A25.

Pamphlet (published by author)

American Diabetes Association. (1987). *Diabetes and you.* Alexandria, VA: Author.

Internet

As computer sources multiply, the citation format has been evolving. APA guidelines ask that you include the type of medium, the necessary electronic information to permit retrieval, and then the date you accessed the information. You should consult the APA Web site at www.apastyle.org for the most recent information on how to cite Internet resources. Here are examples based on the fifth edition of the APA *Publication Manual.*

Internet Articles Based on a Print Source Taken From a Library Subscription Database
Many databases provide assistance in how to cite sources. For example, if you click on the *help* link in the upper right corner of an EBSCOhost database citation, it will take you to a menu that includes a link to *styles of citation.* EBSCOhost provides examples for APA as well as numerous other citation styles.

Freeman, T., Sawyer, C. R., & Behnke, R. R. (1997). Behavioral inhibition and attribution of public speaking state anxiety. *Communication Education, 46,* 175–187. Retrieved September 3, 2004, from EBSCOhost Communication and Mass Media Complete database.

Article in an Internet-Only Journal
The date of retrieval and the URL are required in addition to normal publication information. Because a period can be confused with the dot (.) of a URL, there is no period at the end of the URL.

Guzley, R., Avanzino, S. and Bor, A. (2001, April). Simulated computer-mediated/
  video-interactive distance learning: A test of motivation, interaction satisfaction, delivery, learning & perceived effectiveness. *Journal of Commuter Mediated Communication,*
  6. Retrieved September 3, 2004, from http://www.ascusc.org/jcmc/vol6/issue3/
  guzley.html

Internet Document, No Author Identified

Begin with the title of the article, followed by the date of last update and retrieval statement. You can find the date of many Web pages, even if they are not
listed on the page itself, by going to the *file* menu and selecting *properties* in Internet Explorer (PC version) or going to the *view* menu and selecting *page info* in
Netscape.

Overcoming stagefright. (2004, June 10). Retrieved September 3, 2004, from http://www
  .anxietycoach.com/social1.htm

If no date is available, use (n.d.) in place of the date. The date of retrieval is still
required.

Overcoming stagefright. (n.d.). Retrieved September 3, 2004, from http://www.anxietycoach
  .com/social1.htm

All references are listed in alphabetical order by authors' last names, regardless of
type, at the end of the speech outline. Works listed by title, where the author is not
known, are placed alphabetically by title. For an example of a reference list using
APA style, see the outline in Chapter 9 on pages 226–227.

MODERN LANGUAGE ASSOCIATION (MLA) STYLE

This section is based on Joseph Gibaldi, T*he MLA Handbook for Writers of Research*
Papers, Sixth Edition, 2003. Also consult their Web site at www.mla.org/style_faq4.
Although there are numerous similarities between APA and MLA style, there are
also many differences. You may cite sources in parentheses in the actual body of
the outline, as you do with APA, but you use only the author's name and the page
number, not the date, for example, (Jones 1). Notice that in MLA style you do
not separate the name and the page number by a comma, nor do you use the letter "p." MLA also allows you to incorporate the name of the author in your text
and cite only the pages in parentheses. For example, John Jones tells us that "secondhand smoke is deadly" (1). Notice that the ending punctuation comes after the
page number in this example.

Include a list of "Works Cited" at the end of your outline. Always include the
author, title, facts of publication, and date. Personal communications are included
in the Works Cited list, unlike in APA style. For example, an interview would be
cited as follows: Jones, John Q. Personal interview. 1 Apr. 1992.

Here are some of the most common types of works you may use in a speech.
Notice that MLA style does place quotation marks around the titles of articles or
book chapters. Titles of books and periodicals may be underlined or *italicized,* although many instructors prefer underlining because it is easier to read. We have
used underlining in the examples that follow. Also, titles of books, articles, and
periodicals are capitalized. Authors are listed by last name first, followed by full
first names and sometimes middle initials. Finally, the date comes at or near the
end of the citation, not right after the author's name, as in APA style.

Appendix A   Guide to Source Citations

Books

Single Author

Freeley, Austin J. <u>Argumentation and Debate: Critical Thinking for Reasoned Decision Making</u>, 7th ed. Belmont, CA: Wadsworth, 1990.

Multiple Authors

Germond, Jack W., and Jules Witcover. <u>Whose Broad Stripes and Bright Stars?</u> New York: Warner Books, 1989.

Corporate Author

American Psychological Association. <u>Publication Manual of the American Psychological Association</u>, 5th ed. Washington, DC: American Psychological Association, 2001.

Government Document

United States. Dept. of Health and Human Services. <u>Smoking Tobacco and Health: A Fact Book</u>. Washington: GPO, 1989.

Chapter in a Book

Steeper, Frederick T. "Public Response to Gerald Ford's Statements on Eastern Europe in the Second Debate." <u>The Presidential Debates: Media, Electoral, and Policy Perspectives</u>. Ed. George F. Bishop, Robert G. Meadow, and Marilyn Jackson-Beeck. New York: Praeger, 1978. 81–101.

Periodicals

Weekly Magazine

Alter, Jonathan. "The Expectations Game." <u>Newsweek</u> 26 Sep. 1988: 16–18.

If the author is unknown, you would list the article as follows:

"The Expectations Game." <u>Newsweek</u> 26 Sept. 1988: 16–18.

Scholarly Journal Divided by Volume Numbers

Vancil, David L., and Susan D. Pendell. "Winning Presidential Debates: An Analysis of Criteria Influencing Audience Response." <u>Western Journal of Speech Communication</u> 48 (1984): 63–74.

[This means the article was published in 1984, in volume 48, on pages 63–74.]

Newspaper

Rosentiel, Tom H. "Minus a Dukakis Home Run, Bush Is Called Winner." <u>Los Angeles Times</u> 14 Oct. 1988: A25.

If the author is unknown, you would list the article as follows:

"Minus a Dukakis Home Run, Bush Is Called Winner." <u>Los Angeles Times</u> 14 Oct. 1988: A25.

Pamphlet (published by author)

American Diabetes Association. <u>Diabetes and You</u>. Alexandria, VA: ADA, 1987.

Internet

MLA has numerous differences from APA in citing Internet-based sources. Rather than a retrieval statement, the date of access is listed followed by the URL in angle brackets, for example: September 3, 2004 <http://www.urlname.com>. A period is placed after the last angle bracket, thus it cannot be confused with a dot (.) in a URL. The reader must infer that the date preceding the URL is the date of access. MLA requires that for printed documents, such as speech outlines, you turn off the autoformatting feature of your word processor. URLs are not underlined, they are enclosed in angle brackets. Here are some examples.

Internet Articles Based on a Print Source From a Library Subscription Database

Many databases provide assistance in how to cite sources. For example, if you click on the *help* link in the upper right corner of an EBSCOhost database citation, it will take you to a menu that includes a link to *styles of citation*. EBSCOhost provides examples for MLA as well as numerous other citation styles. In MLA both the name of the database (underlined) and the name of the subscribing library are required. Also, for the URL, if your database provides a persistent link to the article, use that as the URL. Otherwise use the URL of the service, such as <http://search.epnet.com>. In this example a persistent link is provided because it makes it easier for readers to find the article.

Freeman, Terri, Chris R. Sawyer, and Ralph R. Behnke. "Behavioral Inhibition and Attribution of Public Speaking State Anxiety." Communication Education, 46(1997),
   175–187. Mass Media Complete. EBSCOhost. Meriam Library, California State University, Chico, CA. 3 Sep. 2004 <http://search.epnet.com/direct.asp?AuthType=
   cookie,ip,url,uid&db=ufh&an=9708011184>.

Article in an Internet-Only Journal

Ruth Guzley, Susan Avanzino, and Aaron Bor. "Simulated Computer-Mediated/Video-
   Interactive Distance Learning: A Test of Motivation, Interaction Satisfaction, Delivery,
   Learning & Perceived Effectiveness." Journal of Commuter Mediated Communication,
   6 (2001, April). 3 Sep. 2004 <http://www.ascusc.org/jcmc/vol6/issue3/guzley.html>.

Internet Document, No Author Identified

Begin with the title of the article or the Web site, followed by the date the Web site was last updated. You can find the date of many Web pages, even if they are not listed on the page itself, by going to the *file* menu and selecting *properties* in Internet Explorer (PC version) or going to the *view* menu and selecting *page info* in Netscape. If there is a known date for the site, that date is listed first. If no date is known, then only the date of access is listed.

Overcoming Stagefright. 10 June 2004. 3 Sep. 2004 <http://www.anxietycoach.com/
   social1.htm>.

If there is no date for the article, only the date of retrieval is required.

Overcoming Stagefright. n. d. Sep. 2004 http://www.anxietycoach.com/social1.htm

As with APA, a complete list of sources—called "Works Cited"—in alphabetical order by author (if none, use title) should follow the text. If more than one work by the same author is included, replace the author's name with three hyphens (---) in all listings after the first.

Appendix B

Public Speeches

REMARKS BEFORE THE 1992 REPUBLICAN NATIONAL CONVENTION,

by Mary Fisher[1]

This speech was delivered by Mary Fisher at the 1992 Republican National Convention in Houston, Texas, on Wednesday, August 19. As founder of the Family AIDS Network and a person who is HIV-positive, Fisher addressed a convention that was largely socially conservative about issues such as AIDS. As you read this speech, attempt to answer these questions:

- How well did Mary Fisher adapt to the situation she faced as a speaker at the Republican National Convention?
- To what audience or audiences was this speech addressed?
- What do you see as Fisher's purpose or purposes in presenting this speech?
- How do you feel about the issue of AIDS after reading this speech? Have you changed your beliefs, attitudes, values, or behavioral intentions?

Thank you. Thank you.

Less than three months ago at Platform Hearings in Salt Lake City, I asked the Republican Party to lift the shroud of silence which has been draped over the issue of HIV and AIDS. I have come tonight to bring our silence to an end. I bear a message of challenge, not self-congratulation. I want your attention, not your applause.

I would never have asked to be HIV-positive, but I believe that in all things there is a purpose; and I stand before you and before this nation gladly. The reality of AIDS is brutally clear. Two hundred thousand Americans are dead or dying. A million more are affected. Worldwide, 40 million, 60 million, or 100 million infections will be counted in the coming few years. But despite science and research, White House meetings, and congressional hearings; despite good intentions and bold initiatives, campaign slogans, and hopeful promises, it is—despite it all—the epidemic which is winning tonight.

In the context of an election year, I ask you, here in this great hall, or listening in the quiet of your home, to recognize that the AIDS virus is not a political creature. It does not care whether you are Democratic or Republican; it does not ask whether you are black or white, male or female, gay or straight, young or old.

[1]This text is from the Official Report of the Proceedings of the Thirty-Fifth Republican National Convention, published by the Republican National Committee.

Tonight, I represent an AIDS community whose members have been reluctantly drafted from every segment of American society.

Though I am white and a mother, I am one with a black infant struggling with tubes in a Philadelphia hospital.

Though I am female and contracted this disease in marriage and enjoy the warm support of my family, I am one with the lonely gay man sheltering a flickering candle from the cold wind of his family's rejection.

This is not a distant threat. It is a present danger. The rate of infection is increasing fastest among women and children. Largely unknown a decade ago, AIDS is the third leading killer of young adult Americans today. But it won't be third for long, because unlike other diseases, this one travels. Adolescents don't give each other cancer or heart disease because they believe they are in love, but HIV is different; and we have helped it along. We have killed each other with our ignorance, our prejudice, and our silence.

We may take refuge in our stereotypes, but we cannot hide there long, because HIV asks only one thing of those it attacks. Are you human? And this is the right question. Are you human? Because people with HIV have not entered some alien state of being. They are human. They have not earned cruelty, and they do not deserve meanness. They don't benefit from being isolated or treated as outcasts. Each of them is exactly what God made—a person, not evil, deserving of our judgment; not victims, longing for our pity—people, ready for support and worthy of compassion. (Applause.)

My call to you, my Party, is to take a public stand, no less compassionate than that of the President and Mrs. Bush. They have embraced me and my family in memorable ways. In the place of judgment, they have shown affection. In difficult moments, they have raised our spirits. In the darkest hours, I have seen them reaching out not only to me, but also to my parents, armed with that stunning grief and special grace that comes only to parents who have themselves leaned too long over the bedside of a dying child.

With the president's leadership, much good has been done. Much of the good has gone unheralded, and as the president has insisted, much remains to be done. But we do the president's cause no good if we praise the American family but ignore a virus that destroys it. (Applause.)

We must be consistent if we are to be believed. We cannot love justice and ignore prejudice, love our children and fear to teach them. Whatever our role as parent or policymaker, we must act as eloquently as we speak—else we have no integrity.

My call to the nation is a plea for awareness. If you believe you are safe, you are in danger. Because I was not hemophiliac, I was not at risk. Because I was not gay, I was not at risk. Because I did not inject drugs, I was not at risk.

My father has devoted much of his lifetime to guarding against another holocaust. He is part of the generation who heard Pastor Nemoeller come out of the Nazi death camps to say, "They came after the Jews and I was not a Jew, so, I did not protest. They came after the trade unionists, and I was not a trade unionist, so, I did not protest. Then they came after the Roman Catholics, and I was not a Roman Catholic, so, I did not protest. Then they came after me, and there was no one left to protest." (Applause.)

The lesson history teaches is this: If you believe you are safe, you are at risk. If you do not see this killer stalking your children, look again. There is no family or community, no race or religion, no place left in America that is safe. Until we genuinely embrace this message, we are a nation at risk. Tonight, HIV marches resolutely to AIDS in more than a million American homes. Littering its pathway with the bodies of the young men, young women, young parents, and young children. One of those families is mine. If it is true that HIV inevitably turns to AIDS, then my children will inevitably turn to orphans.

My family has been a rock of support. My 84-year-old father, who has pursued the healing of nations, will not accept the premise that he cannot heal his daughter. My mother refuses to be broken. She still calls at midnight to tell wonderful jokes that make me laugh. Sisters and friends, and my brother Phillip, whose birthday is today, all have helped carry me over the hardest places. I am blessed, richly and deeply blessed, to have such a family. (Applause.)

But not all of you have been so blessed. You are HIV-positive, but dare not say it. You have lost loved ones, but you dare not whisper the word AIDS—you weep silently. You grieve alone. I have a message for you. It is not you who should feel shame. It is we, we who tolerate ignorance and practice prejudice, we who have taught you to fear. We must lift our shroud of silence, making it safe for you to reach out for compassion. It is our task to seek safety for our children, not in quiet denial but in effective action.

Some day our children will be grown. My son Max, now 4, will take the measure of his mother; my son Zachary, now 2, will sort through his memories. I may not be here to hear their judgments, but I know already what I hope they are. I want my children to know that their mother was not a victim. She was a messenger. I do not want them to think, as I once did, that courage is the absence of fear. I want them to know that courage is the strength to act wisely when we are most afraid. I want them to have the courage to step forward when called by their nation or their party and give leadership, no matter what the personal cost. I ask no more of you than I ask of myself or my children. To the millions of you who are grieving, who are frightened, who have suffered the ravages of AIDS firsthand—have courage and you will find support. To the millions who are strong, I issue the plea—set aside prejudice and politics to make room for compassion and sound policy. (Applause.)

To my children, I make this pledge: "I will not give in, Zachary, because I draw my courage from you. Your silly giggle gives me hope; your gentle prayers give me strength; and you, my child, give me reason to say to America, 'You are at risk.' And I will not rest, Max, until I have done all I can to make your world safe. I will seek a place where intimacy is not the prelude to suffering. I will not hurry to leave you, my children, but when I go, I pray that you will not suffer shame on my account." To all within the sound of my voice, I appeal: "Learn with me the lessons of history and of grace, so my children will not be afraid to say the word AIDS when I am gone. Then, their children and yours may not need to whisper it at all." God bless the children, God bless us all, and good night.

REMARKS BEFORE THE 1996 DEMOCRATIC NATIONAL CONVENTION,

by Carolyn McCarthy[2]

This speech was delivered by Carolyn McCarthy at the 1996 Democratic National Convention in Chicago. As the wife and mother of two victims of the Long Island train mas-

---

[2]Reprinted by permission of the author.

sacre, McCarthy had become a spokesperson for the victims of that crime and other violent crimes. When rebuffed by her Republican congressman, she registered as a Democrat and ran against him, defeating him and becoming a member of Congress herself. As you read this speech, ask yourself:

- How well did Carolyn McCarthy adapt to the situation she faced as a speaker at the Democratic National Convention?

- To what audience or audiences was this speech addressed?

- What do you see as McCarthy's purpose or purposes in presenting this speech?

- How do you feel about the issue of gun control after reading this speech? Have you changed your beliefs, attitudes, values, or behavioral intentions?

December 7th, 1993–that was the day of the Long Island Railroad massacre. My life and the lives of many others changed forever. A man with a semiautomatic weapon boarded the train that my husband and my son took to work every day. He killed 6 people and wounded 19. My husband, Dennis, was one of those killed. My son, Kevin, was left partially paralyzed. Kevin has had a courageous recovery. He's back at work. But he still spends many hours a day with rehabilitation. It's every mother's dream to be able to stand up on national TV and say she's proud of her son. Kevin, I'm very proud of you.

On that day I started a journey, a journey against gun violence in this nation. Today I am here as a nurse, as a mother, as a person who isn't afraid to speak up on what is going on in this country.

Gun violence adds millions of dollars in hospital costs every year, and threatens families with a mountain of bills, and so much pain. Until our government listens to ordinary people speaking out against gun violence instead of listening to special interest groups like the NRA leadership, we are not going to have safety in our streets!

I was not planning on speaking here tonight, but this is where my journey has taken me–to the Democratic Party, the party that believes in including ordinary citizens. That's why I'm here. I am here as a woman with common sense and determination, and I am going to make a difference.

I will fight to keep the assault weapons ban the law of the land. I–Yeah, I will. I will work for the day when President Clinton's Victims Rights Amendment is in the Constitution. And those of us who are concerned about gun violence will not tolerate being ignored, as I was by my congressman, who voted to repeal the assault weapons bill.

We have all been ignored by the Gingrich congress. They have not listened to us on education, on the environment, or on making our streets safe. We will not be ignored. We will make them listen.

The journey I began in 1993 wasn't one that I had planned. Getting involved in politics wasn't anything I ever wanted to do. But this journey will make a difference when our neighborhoods pull together, when government listens to us again. When all of us, Democrats and Republicans, come together to solve our problems, not just fight about them. We have a responsibility to our children to speak up about what we know is right and to do what is right. I ask you to join me and my son, Kevin, on that journey. Thank you so very much.

ADDRESS TO THE NATION, JANUARY 28, 1986
by President Ronald Reagan[3]

On January 28, 1986, the space shuttle *Challenger* exploded shortly after launch, killing all seven crew members, including the first teacher in space. Other than a ground accident during the Apollo program, which killed three astronauts, this was the first time America had lost astronauts, and the first time they had been lost in flight. Postponing his scheduled State of the Union Address, President Ronald Reagan addressed the nation. As you read this speech, try to answer the following questions:

- Is President Reagan effective at consoling a grieving nation?
- Does President Reagan affirm a commitment to continue space exploration?
- How effective are the language choices made by Reagan in his speech?
- How effective are the quotations used by Reagan?
- How effectively does he close his speech to the nation?

Ladies and gentlemen, I'd planned to speak to you tonight to report on the state of the Union, but the events of earlier today have led me to change those plans. Today is a day for mourning and remembering.

Nancy and I are pained to the core by the tragedy of the shuttle *Challenger.* We know we share this pain with all of the people of our country. This is truly a national loss.

Nineteen years ago, almost to the day, we lost three astronauts in a terrible accident on the ground. But we've never lost an astronaut in flight; we've never had a tragedy like this. And perhaps we've forgotten the courage it took for the crew of the shuttle; but they, the *Challenger* Seven, were aware of the dangers, but overcame them and did their jobs brilliantly. We mourn seven heroes: Michael Smith, Dick Scobee, Judith Resnik, Ronald McNair, Ellison Onizuka, Gregory Jarvis, and Christa McAuliffe. We mourn their loss as a nation together.

For the families of the seven, we cannot bear, as you do, the full impact of this tragedy. But we feel the loss, and we're thinking about you so very much. Your loved ones were daring and brave, and they had that special grace, that special spirit that says, "Give me a challenge and I'll meet it with joy." They had a hunger to explore the universe and discover its truths. They wished to serve, and they did. They served all of us.

We've grown used to wonders in this century. It's hard to dazzle us. But for 25 years the United States space program has been doing just that. We've grown used to the idea of space, and perhaps we forget that we've only just begun. We're still pioneers. They, the members of the *Challenger* crew, were pioneers.

And I want to say something to the schoolchildren of America who were watching the live coverage of the shuttle's takeoff. I know it is hard to understand, but sometimes painful things like this happen. It's all part of the process of exploration and discovery. It's all part of taking a chance and expanding man's horizons. The future doesn't belong to the fainthearted; it belongs to the brave. The *Challenger* crew was pulling us into the future, and we'll continue to follow them.

[3]Ronald Reagan, "Address to the Nation, January 28, 1986." *Weekly Compilation of Presidential Documents,* Vol. 22, No. 5, February 3, 1986, 104–5.

I've always had great faith in and respect for our space program, and what happened today does nothing to diminish it. We don't hide our space program. We don't keep secrets and cover things up. We do it all up front and in public. That's the way freedom is, and we wouldn't change it for a minute.

We'll continue our quest in space. There will be more shuttle flights and more shuttle crews and, yes, more volunteers, more civilians, more teachers in space. Nothing ends here; our hopes and our journeys continue.

I want to add that I wish I could talk to every man and woman who works for NASA or who worked on this mission and tell them: "Your dedication and professionalism have moved and impressed us for decades. And we know of your anguish. We share it."

There's a coincidence today. On this day 390 years ago, the great explorer Sir Francis Drake died aboard ship off the coast of Panama. In his lifetime the great frontiers were the oceans, and an historian later said, "He lived by the sea, died on it, and was buried in it." Well, today we can say of the *Challenger* crew: Their dedication was, like Drake's, complete.

The crew of the space shuttle *Challenger* honored us by the manner in which they lived their lives. We will never forget them, nor the last time we saw them, this morning, as they prepared for their journey and waved goodbye and "slipped the surly bonds of earth" to "touch the face of God."

REMARKS BY PRESIDENT GEORGE W. BUSH ON THE LOSS OF SPACE SHUTTLE *COLUMBIA*, FEBRUARY 1, 2003.[4]

Much like President Reagan seventeen years earlier, President George W. Bush also faced a grieving nation when the space shuttle *Columbia* disintegrated on reentry on February 1, 2003. Again, all seven crew members perished. Unlike *Challenger,* the destruction was not seen live on TV. However, Americans were no less troubled. As with Ronald Reagan's eulogy for the astronauts of the *Challenger,* read this speech with the following questions in mind:

- Is President Bush effective at consoling a grieving nation?
- Does President Bush affirm a commitment to continue space exploration?
- How effective are the language choices made by Bush in his speech?
- How effective is the quotation used by President Bush?
- How effectively does he close his speech to the nation?
- Which of the two eulogies do you find most powerful?

My fellow Americans, this day has brought terrible news and great sadness to our country. At 9:00 a.m. this morning, Mission Control in Houston lost contact with our Space Shuttle *Columbia*. A short time later, debris was seen falling from the skies above Texas. The *Columbia* is lost; there are no survivors.

On board was a crew of seven: Colonel Rick Husband; Lt. Colonel Michael Anderson; Commander Laurel Clark; Captain David Brown; Commander

[4]George W. Bush, "President Addresses Nation on Space Shuttle *Columbia* Tragedy, " *The White House,* February 1, 2003, <http://www.whitehouse.gov/news/releases/2003/02/20030201-2.html> (April 14, 2003).

William McCool; Dr. Kalpana Chawla; and Ilan Ramon, a Colonel in the Israeli Air Force. These men and women assumed great risk in the service to all humanity.

In an age when space flight has come to seem almost routine, it is easy to overlook the dangers of travel by rocket, and the difficulties of navigating the fierce outer atmosphere of the Earth. These astronauts knew the dangers, and they faced them willingly, knowing they had a high and noble purpose in life. Because of their courage and daring and idealism, we will miss them all the more.

All Americans today are thinking, as well, of the families of these men and women who have been given this sudden shock and grief. You're not alone. Our entire nation grieves with you. And those you loved will always have the respect and gratitude of this country.

The cause in which they died will continue. Mankind is led into the darkness beyond our world by the inspiration of discovery and the longing to understand. Our journey into space will go on.

In the skies today we saw destruction and tragedy. Yet farther than we can see there is comfort and hope. In the words of the prophet Isaiah, "Lift your eyes and look to the heavens. Who created all these? He who brings out the starry hosts one by one and calls them each by name. Because of His great power and mighty strength, not one of them is missing."

The same Creator who names the stars also knows the names of the seven souls we mourn today. The crew of the shuttle *Columbia* did not return safely to Earth; yet we can pray that all are safely home.

May God bless the grieving families, and may God continue to bless America.

Glossary

A

abstract A summary of an article or a report.

active listening Listening that involves conscious and responsive participation in the communication transaction.

active mindfulness The degree to which speakers and audiences are consciously aware of the transactions between them.

ad hominem The claim that something must be false because the person who said it is not credible, regardless of the argument itself.

agenda Something that defines the purpose and direction a group takes, the topics to be covered, and the goals to be achieved.

alphabetical pattern Main points are in alphabetical order or spell out a common word.

analogy An extended metaphor or simile. Suggesting that the rebuilding of Iraq is much like rebuilding Germany and Japan after WW II is an analogy.

appreciative listening Listening that involves obtaining sensory stimulation or enjoyment from others.

arguing in a circle (begging the question) An argument that proves nothing because the claim to be proved is used as the grounds or warrant for the argument.

argumentativeness The trait of arguing for and against the positions taken on controversial claims.

attitude A learned predisposition to respond in a consistently favorable or unfavorable manner with respect to a given object.

audience The individuals who listen to a public speech.

audience accessible Content the audience is able to understand, regardless of its complexity.

audience appropriate Informative topic and speech that takes into account the occasion and audience members' belief systems.

audience diversity The cultural, demographic, and individual characteristics that vary among audience members.

audience involving Informative topic and speech that succeeds in gaining the audience's attention.

audio media Aural channels you can use to augment your speech, such as a recording of a famous speaker.

authority warrant Reasoning in which the claim is believed because of the authority of the source.

B

backing Support for a warrant.

bar chart A graphic used for comparing data side by side.

behavioral intention A person's subjective belief that he or she will engage in a specific behavior.

belief An assertion about the properties or characteristics of an object.

Boolean operators Terms, such as *and, or,* and *not,* used to narrow or broaden a computerized search of two or more related terms.

brainstorming A creative process used for generating a large number of ideas.

C

canons of rhetoric The classical arts of invention, organization, style, memory, and delivery.

captive audience Listeners that have no choice about hearing a speech.

categorical imperative Immanuel Kant's ethical principle that we should act only in a way that we would will to be a universal law.

categorical pattern A pattern of organization based on natural divisions in the subject matter.

causal pattern A pattern of organization that moves from cause to effect or from effect to cause.

causal warrant A statement that a cause will produce or has produced an effect.

central beliefs Beliefs based directly or indirectly on authority.

channel The physical medium through which communication occurs.

claim A conclusion that persuasive speakers want their audience to reach as a result of their speech.

communication apprehension Fear about communicating interpersonally and in groups, not just in public.

comparison (analogy) warrant A statement that two cases that are similar in some known respects are also similar in some unknown respects.

comprehension The act of understanding what has been communicated.

connotation The secondary meaning of a word, often with a strong emotional, personal, and subjective component.

constraint A limitation on choices in a speech situation.

constructive self-talk The use of positive coping statements instead of negative self-talk.

content (of messages) The essential meaning of what a speaker wants to convey.

context Information that surrounds an event and contributes to the meaning of that event.

coping skills Mental and physical techniques used to control arousal and anxiety in the course of speaking in public.

credibility The degree to which an audience trusts and believes in a speaker.

credibility-enhancing language Words that emphasize rather than undermine audience perceptions of a speaker's competence.

critical listening Listening for the purpose of making reasoned judgments about speakers and the credibility of their messages.

critical thinking The process of making sound inferences based on accurate evidence and valid reasoning.

cross cue-checking Gauging what a person says verbally against the nonverbal behaviors that make up metacommunication.

cultural diversity Differences among people in terms of beliefs, customs, and values—in a sense, their worldview.

cultural relativism The notion that the criteria for ethical behavior in one culture should not necessarily be applied to other cultures.

culture A learned system of beliefs, customs, and values with which people identify.

D

decoding The process by which a code is translated back into ideas.

deficiency needs Basic human needs, which must be satisfied before higher-order needs can be met. They include needs for food, water, air, physical safety, belongingness and love, and self-esteem and social esteem.

demographic diversity Variations among people in terms of such attributes as socioeconomic background and level of education.

demographics Basic and vital data regarding any population.

denotation The generally agreed upon meaning of a word, usually found in the dictionary.

distorted evidence Significant omissions or changes in the grounds of an argument that alter its original intent.

E

elaboration likelihood model A model of persuasion designed to explain why audience members will use an elaborated thinking process in some situations and not in others.

emblem A nonverbal symbol that can be substituted for a word.

encoding The process by which ideas are translated into a code that can be understood by the receiver.

environment The physical surroundings as you speak and the physical distance separating you from your audience.

ethical relativism A philosophy based on the belief that there are no universal ethical principles.

ethics A system of principles of right and wrong that govern human conduct.

ethos The degree to which an audience perceives a speaker as credible.

eulogy A kind of commemorative speech about someone who has died that is usually given shortly after his or her death.

expert opinion A quotation from someone with special credentials in the subject matter.

extemporaneous delivery A mode of presentation that combines careful preparation with spontaneous speaking. The speaker generally uses brief notes rather than a full manuscript or an outline.

extended narrative A pattern of organization in which the entire body of the speech is the telling of a story.

F

fact Something that is verifiable as true.

fallacy An argument in which the reasons advanced for a claim fail to warrant acceptance of that claim.

false analogy The comparison of two different things that are not really comparable.

false dilemma A generalization that implies there are only two choices when there are more than two.

feedback Audience member responses, both verbal and nonverbal, to a speaker.

first-order data Evidence based on personal experience.

flip chart Large tablet used to preview the outline of a presentation or to record information generated by an audience.

flowchart A graphic designed to illustrate spatial relationships or the sequence of events in a process.

formal outline A detailed outline used in speech preparation, but not, in most cases, in the actual presentation.

G

ganas Spanish term that loosely translates as the desire to succeed.

general purpose The primary function of a speech. The three commonly agreed upon general purposes are to inform, to persuade, and to entertain.

generalization warrant A statement that either establishes a general rule or principle or applies an established rule or principle to a specific case.

good reasons Statements, based on moral principles, offered in support of propositions concerning what we should believe or how we should act.

goodwill The perception by the audience that a speaker cares about their needs and concerns.

grounds The evidence a speaker offers in support of a claim.

group Three or more individuals who are aware of each other's presence, share a mutually interdependent purpose, engage in communication transactions with one another, and identify with the group.

growth needs Higher-order human needs, which can be satisfied only after deficiency needs have been met. They include self-actualization (the process of fully realizing one's potential), knowledge and understanding, and aesthetic needs.

H

halo effect The assumption that just because you like or respect a person, whatever he or she says must be true.

hasty generalization An argument that occurs when there are too few instances to support a generalization or the instances are unrepresentative of the generalization.

hyperbole An exaggeration of a claim.

I

ignoring the issue When a claim made by one side in an argument is ignored by the other side.

illustrators Nonverbal symbols used to visualize what is being spoken.

immediate language Reduces the psychological distance that separates speakers and audience members and stresses that speech is a transaction.

impromptu delivery A spontaneous, unrehearsed mode of presenting a speech.

inclusive language Language that helps people believe that they not only have a stake in matters of societal importance but also have power in this regard.

index A listing of sources of information, usually in newspapers, journals, and magazines, alphabetically by topic.

individual diversity How individuals in an audience differ in terms of knowledge, beliefs, attitudes, values, motives, expectations, and needs.

inference The process of moving from grounds, via a warrant, to a claim.

informative speaking The process by which an audience gains new information or a new perspective on old information.

inoculation Techniques used to make people's belief systems resistant to counterpersuasion.

interdependence A relationship in which things have a reciprocal influence on each other.

invention The creative process by which the substance of a speech is generated.

isolated examples Nontypical or nonrepresentative examples that are used to prove a general claim.

K

key word A word in the abstract, title, subject heading, or text of an entry that can be used to search an electronic database.

L

language intensity The degree to which words and phrases deviate from neutral.

learning styles Differences in the way people think about and learn new information and skills.

line graph A graphic used to show points in time.

linguistic relativity hypothesis The idea that what people perceive is influenced by the language in which they think and speak.

listening The process of receiving, attending to, and assigning meaning to aural as well as visual and tactile stimuli.

loaded language Language that has strong emotional connotations.

logos The proof a speaker offers to an audience through the words of his or her message.

long-term goals Those ends that we can hope to achieve only over an extended period of time.

M

main points The key ideas that support the thesis statement of a speech.

manuscript delivery A mode of presentation that involves writing out a speech completely and reading it to the audience.

marginalizing language Language that diminishes people's importance and makes them appear to be less powerful, less significant, and less worthwhile than they are.

memorized delivery A mode of presentation in which a speech is written out and committed to memory before being presented to the audience without the use of notes.

message The meaning produced by communicators.

metacommunication The message about the message; generally conveyed nonverbally.

metaphor A figure of speech in which words and phrases that are primarily understood to mean one thing are used in place of another to suggest likeness or an analogy between them. Race car drivers, for example, may have to "wrestle with" a car that is difficult to control.

mistaking correlation for cause The assumption that because one thing is the sign of another, they are causally related.

misused statistics Statistics that involve errors such as poor sampling, lack of significant differences, misuse of average, or misuse of percentages.

Monroe's motivated-sequence A five-step organizational scheme, developed by speech professor Alan Monroe, including (1) attention, (2) need, (3) satisfaction, (4) visualization, and (5) action.

N

narrative An extended story that is fully developed, with characters, scene, action, and plot.

narrative fidelity The degree to which a narrative rings true to real-life experience.

narrative probability The internal coherence or believability of a narrative.

needs Physical and mental states that motivate us to behave in ways that lead to the need's satisfaction; for example, eating when we are hungry.

negative self-talk A self-defeating pattern of intrapersonal communication, including self-criticizing, self-pressuring, and catastrophizing statements.

non sequitur An argument that does not follow from its premises.

nonverbal behavior A wordless system of communication.

O

online catalog A computerized database of library holdings.

organizational chart A graphic that illustrates hierarchical relationships.

overhead transparency A visual depiction that can be projected.

P

panel discussion An extemporaneous group discussion held for the benefit of an audience.

pathos The emotional states in an audience that a speaker can arouse and use to achieve persuasive goals.

perception The process by which we give meaning to our experiences.

peripheral beliefs The least central type of beliefs, the easiest to change.

persuasion The process by which a speaker influences what audience members think or do.

physical arousal The physical changes that occur when a person is aroused, such as increased pulse, greater alertness, and more energy.

pie chart A graphic often used to show proportions of a known quantity.

pinpoint concentration Listening that focuses on specific details rather than patterns in a message.

plagiarism Stealing the ideas of others and presenting them as your own.

post hoc, ergo propter hoc ("after the fact, therefore because of the fact") The assumption that because one event preceded another, the first event must be the cause of the second event.

presentational media Channels of communication that extend the five basic senses: touch, sight, sound, taste, and smell.

preview A forecast of the main points of a speech.

primary sources Original sources of information.

primitive beliefs (also known as type A beliefs) Those beliefs learned by direct contact with the object of belief and reinforced by unanimous social consensus.

proactive delivery Planned and rehearsed presentation.

problem–solution pattern A pattern of organization that analyzes a problem in terms of (1) harm, (2) significance, and (3) cause, and proposes a solution that is (1) described, (2) feasible, and (3) advantageous.

pseudoreasoning An argument that appears sound at first glance but contains a fallacy of reasoning that renders it unsound.

Q

qualifier An indication of the level of probability of a claim.

R

rebuttal An exception to or a refutation of an argument.

receiver-centric A person's assumption that the meaning he or she gives to a word or a phrase is its exclusive meaning.

red herring (smoke screen) An irrelevant issue introduced into a controversy to divert from the real controversy.

reframing Revising our view of a situation or an event, usually in a positive direction.

refutational pattern A pattern of organization that involves (1) stating the argument to be refuted, (2) stating the objection to the argument, (3) proving the objection to the argument, and (4) presenting the impact of the refutation.

regulators Nonverbal behaviors that influence the speech transaction.

reinforcement Rewards given to strengthen attitudes, beliefs, values, and behaviors.

relational component (of messages) The combined impact of the verbal and nonverbal components of a message as it is conveyed.

research The process of gathering supporting materials for a speech.

retention The act of storing what was communicated in either short- or long-term memory.

rhetorical question A question that the audience isn't expected to answer out loud.

rhetorical situation A natural context of persons, events, objects, relations, and an exigence (goal) that strongly invites utterance.

S

secondary sources Information sources that rely on other (primary) sources rather than gathering information firsthand.

second-order data Evidence based on expert testimony.

selective attention Making a conscious choice to focus on some people and some messages, rather than others.

self-adapting behaviors Nonverbal behaviors used to cope with nervousness; for example, self-touching or grasping sides of lectern with hands.

self-talk (sometimes referred to as intrapersonal communication) Communicating silently with oneself.

sensory involvement A process that involves listening with all the senses, not simply the sense of hearing.

sexist language Language, such as *housewife* and *fireman,* that stereotypes gender roles.

short-term goals Those ends that we can reasonably expect to achieve in the near term.

sign warrant Reasoning in which the presence of an observed phenomenon is used to indicate the presence of an unobserved phenomenon.

signposts Transitional statements that bridge main points.

simile Invites the listener to make a direct comparison between two things or objects that are quite different, such as my roommate "lives like a pig in slop" or is "dumb as a rock."

situational ethics The philosophy that there are overriding ethical maxims, but that sometimes it is necessary to set them aside in particular situations to fulfill a higher law or principle.

slippery slope The assumption that just because one event occurs, it will automatically lead to a series of undesirable events even though there is no relationship between the action and the projected events.

socioeconomic status Social grouping and economic class to which people belong.

source credibility The audience's perception of the believability of the speaker.

spatial pattern A pattern of organization based on physical space or geography.

speaker's notes Brief notes with key words, usually written on cards, used by a speaker when presenting a speech.

specific purpose The goal or objective a speaker hopes to achieve in speaking to a particular audience.

speech anxiety The unpleasant thoughts and feelings aroused by the anticipation of a real or imagined speech in public.

speech of acceptance A speech expressing thanks for an award or honor.

speech of commemoration A speech that calls attention to the stature of the person or people being honored, or emphasizes the significance of an occasion.

speech of introduction A speech that briefly sets the stage for an upcoming speaker.

speech of recognition A speech presenting an award or honor to an individual.

speech to entertain A speech that makes its point through the use of humor.

spiral pattern A pattern of organization that employs repetition of points, with the points growing in intensity as the speech builds to its conclusion.

star pattern A pattern of organization in which all of the points are of equal importance and can be presented in any order to support the common theme.

statistics Numerical summaries of data, such as percentages, ratios, and averages, that are classified in a meaningful way. Age, height, and weight are not statistics, although they are commonly mistaken as such.

stereotyping The assumption that what is considered to be true of a larger class is necessarily true of particular members of that class.

stock issues pattern A four-point pattern of organization that is based on (1) ill, (2) blame, (3) cure, and (4) cost.

straw person An argument made in refutation that misstates the argument being refuted. Rather than refuting the real argument, the other side constructs a person of straw, which is easy to knock down.

subject heading A standard word or phrase used by libraries to catalog books or other publications.

subpoint An idea that supports a main point.

supporting point An idea that supports a subpoint.

symbol Something that stands for or suggests something else by reason of relationship or association.

system A collection of interdependent parts arranged so that a change in one produces corresponding changes in the remaining parts.

T

thesis statement A single declarative sentence that focuses the audience's attention on the central point of a speech.

third-order data Evidence based on facts and statistics.

time pattern A pattern of organization based on chronology or a sequence of events.

totalizing language Language that defines people exclusively on the basis of a single attribute, such as race, ethnicity, biological sex, or ability.

transaction An exchange of verbal and nonverbal messages between two or more people.

trustworthiness The perception by the audience that they can rely on a speaker's word.

U

universalism The philosophy that there are ethical standards that apply to all situations regardless of the individual, group, or culture.

unsupported assertion The absence of any argument at all.

utilitarianism The philosophy based on the principle that the aim of any action should be to provide the greatest amount of happiness for the greatest number of people.

V

values Our most enduring beliefs about right and wrong.

verbal aggressiveness The trait of attacking the self-concept of those with whom a person disagrees about controversial claims.

verbal qualifiers Words and phrases that erode the impact of what a speaker says in a speech.

visual imagery The process of mentally seeing (imagining) oneself confidently and successfully performing an action or a series of actions.

visual media The use of the sense of sight to communicate a message.

voluntary audience Listeners that choose to hear a speaker.

W

warrant The connection between grounds and claim.

wave pattern A pattern of organization in which the basic theme, often represented by a phrase, is repeated again and again, much like a wave cresting, receding, and then cresting again.

wide-band concentration Listening that focuses on patterns rather than details.

Z

zone of interaction Area of audience in which speaker and audience members can make eye contact.

Credits

Index